T0321751

Novel Practices and Trends in Grid and Cloud Computing

Pethuru Raj
Reliance Jio Infocomm Ltd. (RJIL), India

S. Koteeswaran
Vel Tech, India

A volume in the Advances in Computer and
Electrical Engineering (ACEE) Book Series

Published in the United States of America by
>   IGI Global
>   Engineering Science Reference (an imprint of IGI Global)
>   701 E. Chocolate Avenue
>   Hershey PA, USA 17033
>   Tel: 717-533-8845
>   Fax: 717-533-8661
>   E-mail: cust@igi-global.com
>   Web site: http://www.igi-global.com

Library of Congress Cataloging-in-Publication Data

Names: Raj, Pethuru, editor. | Koteeswaran, S., 1982- editor.
Title: Novel practices and trends in grid and cloud computing / Pethuru Raj
   and S. Koteeswaran, editors.
Description: Hershey, PA : Engineering Science Reference, [2019] | Includes
   bibliographical references.
Identifiers: LCCN 2019001908| ISBN 9781522590231 (h/c) | ISBN 9781522590248
   (s/c) | ISBN 9781522590255 (eISBN)
Subjects: LCSH: Cloud computing. | Computational grids (Computer systems)
Classification: LCC QA76.585 .N68 2019 | DDC 004.67/82--dc23 LC record available at https://lccn.loc.gov/2019001908

This book is published in the IGI Global book series Advances in Computer and Electrical Engineering (ACEE) (ISSN: 2327-039X; eISSN: 2327-0403)

British Cataloguing in Publication Data
A Cataloguing in Publication record for this book is available from the British Library.

The views expressed in this book are those of the authors, but not necessarily of the publisher.

For electronic access to this publication, please contact: eresources@igi-global.com.

Advances in Computer and Electrical Engineering (ACEE) Book Series

Srikanta Patnaik
SOA University, India

ISSN:2327-039X
EISSN:2327-0403

MISSION

The fields of computer engineering and electrical engineering encompass a broad range of interdisciplinary topics allowing for expansive research developments across multiple fields. Research in these areas continues to develop and become increasingly important as computer and electrical systems have become an integral part of everyday life.

The **Advances in Computer and Electrical Engineering (ACEE) Book Series** aims to publish research on diverse topics pertaining to computer engineering and electrical engineering. **ACEE** encourages scholarly discourse on the latest applications, tools, and methodologies being implemented in the field for the design and development of computer and electrical systems.

COVERAGE

- Sensor Technologies
- Computer Science
- Circuit Analysis
- Digital Electronics
- Analog Electronics
- Applied Electromagnetics
- Electrical Power Conversion
- VLSI Fabrication
- VLSI Design
- Power Electronics

IGI Global is currently accepting manuscripts for publication within this series. To submit a proposal for a volume in this series, please contact our Acquisition Editors at Acquisitions@igi-global.com or visit: http://www.igi-global.com/publish/.

Titles in this Series

For a list of additional titles in this series, please visit: www.igi-global.com/book-series

701 East Chocolate Avenue, Hershey, PA 17033, USA
Tel: 717-533-8845 x100 • Fax: 717-533-8661
E-Mail: cust@igi-global.com • www.igi-global.com

Table of Contents

Detailed Table of Contents

Pethuru Raj, Reliance Jio Infocomm Ltd. (RJIL), India
Jenn-Wei Lin, Fu Jen Catholic University, Taiwan

There are a number of noteworthy improvements and improvisations in the fields of information and communication technology (ICT) in the recent past. These continuous and consistent advancements have a direct and decisive impact on business offerings, operations, and outputs. Worldwide business enterprises, service providers, product vendors, government organizations, academic institutions, etc. are being sagaciously and strategically empowered through the distinct ICT capabilities. Especially, the role and responsibility of information technology (IT) is consistently on the rise for producing and sustaining next-generation business establishments. Precisely speaking, business acceleration and augmentation get fluently fulfilled through IT. Therefore, IT is being widely pronounced and presented as the best enabler of businesses. All kinds of business needs such as agility, affordability, adaptivity, customer propensity and delight, business productivity and expansion, etc. are being provided and performed through the growing list of innovations in the enigmatic IT domain. Cloud computing is the recent phenomenon in the IT domain bringing forth a number of crucial innovations, disruptions, and transformations for businesses and people. The cloud idea has permeated deeply and decisively and is being touted as the one-stop IT solution for all kinds of business needs. The cloud journey started a decade back and is steadily growing to bring in desired automation for businesses. This chapter is specially allocated for conveying the humble beginning, the sustained growth of the cloud idea, and the benefits for institutions, individuals, and innovators.

Lavanya S., Sri Krishna College of Engineering and Technology, India
Susila N., Sri Krishna College of Engineering and Technology, India
Venkatachalam K., Sri Krishna College of Engineering and Technology, India

In recent times, the cloud has become a leading technology demanding its functionality in every business. According to research firm IDC and Gartner study, nearly one-third of the worldwide enterprise application market will be SaaS-based by 2018, driving annual SaaS revenue to $50.8 billion, from $22.6 billion in 2013. Downtime is treated as the primary drawback which may affect great deals in businesses. The service unavailability leads to a major disruption affecting the business environment. Hence, utmost care should be taken to scale the availability of services. As cloud computing has plenty of uncertainty with respect to network bandwidth and resources accessibility, delegating the computing resources as services should be scheduled accordingly. This chapter proposes a study on cloud of clouds and its impact on a business enterprise. It is also decided to propose a suitable scheduling algorithm to the cloud of cloud environment so as to trim the downtime problem faced by the cloud computing environment.

Chapter 3

Suresh Annamalai, Nehru Institute of Engineering and Technology, India
Udendhran R., Bharathidasan University, India

In this chapter, the authors introduced cloudsim simulator and cloud computing role in online social networking. The communication incurred by other activities such as management jobs is negligible. Social relationships can be established for numerous reasons. For example, family members, colleagues, or classmates often have strong social interactions resulting in large communication load. Cloud computing as well as social network-based applications will become dominant in many aspects of life in the next few decades. The performance of such large-scale systems is characterized by system capacity in terms of number of users/clients, flexibility, scalability, and effective cost of operation, etc. Popular social networks have hundreds of millions of users and continue to grow.

Chapter 4

Suresh Annamalai, Nehru Institute of Engineering and Technology, India
Jotimani S., Nehru Institute of Engineering and Technology, India

Most of the people in India depend on the agriculture for their survival. Intelligent water grid control (IWGC) system is a trusted solution for resolving recent significant global water problems. The system will handle the dried geographical area in a smart way with internet of things and edge computing. Since the villages that are far from the rivers are not getting enough water, the smaller water saving areas like pool, lake, ponds can be filled with this smart water management system. In this chapter, the authors discussed the water problems faced by the farmers, dam authority, and by the government.

Chapter 5

Suresh Annamalai, Nehru Institute of Engineering and Technology, India
Udendhran R., Bharathidasan University, India
Vimal S., National Engineering College, India

This chapter covers important topics in development of efficient energy girds. Inefficient power generation, unbalanced consumption patterns that lead to underutilization of expensive infrastructure on the one hand, and severe overload on the other, as well as urgent issues of national and global concern such as power system security and climate change are all driving this evolution. As the smart grid concept matures, we'll see dramatic growth in green power production: small production devices such as wind turbines and solar panels or solar farms, which have fluctuating capacity outside of the control of grid operators. Small companies that specialize in producing power under just certain conditions will boom in forthcoming years. Energy is stored in the storage during low-cost periods, and the stored energy is used during high-cost periods to avoid the expensive draw from the grid. The authors evaluate the impact of large-scale energy storage adoption on grid electricity demand.

Chapter 6

Suresh Annamalai, Nehru Institute of Engineering and Technology, India
Udendhran R., Bharathidasan University, India
Vimal S., National Engineering College, India

The concept of predictive analysis plays complex information retrieval and categorization systems are needed to process queries, filter, and store, and organize huge amount of data, which are mainly composed of texts. As soon as datasets becomes large, most information combines with algorithms that might not perform well. Moreover, prediction is important in today's industrial purposes since that could reduce the issues of heavy asset loss towards the organization. The purpose of prediction is necessary in every field since it could help us to stop the cause of occurring the error before any vulnerable activities could happen. Predictive maintenance is a method that consumes the direct monitoring of mechanical condition of plant equipment to decide the actual mean time to malfunction for each preferred machine. The authors try to estimate the fault that could occur in the machines and decide the time that could cause a critical situation. This prediction should be done effectively, and for this purpose, they have stepped into the concept of machine learning.

Chapter 7

N. Malarvizhi, Vel Tech Rangarajan Dr. Sagunthala R&D Institute of Science and
Technology, India
J. Aswini, Meenakshi Academy of Higher Education and Research, India
E. A. Neeba, Rajagiri School of Engineering and Technology, India

Dynamic cloud computing technique enables resources to be assigned to different clients based on the current demand of each client turning the cloud to a limitless computational platform with limitless storage space which improves the performance of cloud services. To achieve best resource allocation in dynamic hosting frameworks, cloud service providers should provision resources intelligently to all clients. Cloud computing empowers consumers to access online resources using the internet, from anywhere at any time without considering the underlying hardware, technical management, and maintenance problems of the original resources. In this chapter, the authors present a detail study of various resource allocation and other scheduling challenges as well as cloud simulation frameworks tools like CloudSim and ICanCloud.

Chapter 8

Lucia Agnes Beena Thomas, St. Joseph's College, India

With the proliferation of new technologies such as augmented and virtual reality, autonomous cars, 5G networks, drones, and IOT with smart cities, consumers of cloud computing are becoming the producers of data. Large volume of data is being produced at the edge of the network. This scenario insists the need for efficient real-time processing and communication at the network edge. Cloud capabilities must be distributed across the network to form an edge cloud, which places computing resources where the traffic is at the edge of the network. Edge cloud along with 5G services could also glint the next generation of robotic manufacturing. The anticipated low latency requirement, battery life constraint, bandwidth cost saving, as well as data safety and privacy are also inscribed by edge cloud. A number of giants like Nokia, AT&T, and Microsoft have emerged in the market to support edge cloud. This chapter wraps the features of edge cloud, the driving industries that are providing solutions, the use cases, benefits, and the challenges of edge cloud.

Chapter 9

    Suresh Annamalai, Nehru Institute of Engineering and Technology, India
    Udendhran R., Bharathidasan University, India

This chapter presents techniques based on internet of things and cloud computing-driven waste management. The data of the World Bank says that the municipal solid waste generation by the year of 2025 will be 1.42 kg/capital per day in the urban residential areas, with the increase in cost of about $375.5 billion that has a major rise from an annual of $205.4 billion in the year 2012. Due to the high population with the extreme consumption of goods and services, this leads to a strong association among the income levels, quality of life, and waste generation. In the present situation, more than 50% of the total population is living in the cities. In the governance aspect, it is said that the cost of waste management will be highly expensive. This chapter deals with the effective waste management with the implementation of internet of things (IoT)-based cloud technology with the machine learning algorithm that could be highly intellectual in the management of waste.

Chapter 10

    Nirmalan R., Sri Vidya College of Engineering and Technology, India
    Gokulakrishnan K., Anna University Tirunelveli, India
    Jesu Vedha Nayahi J., Anna University Tirunelveli, India

Cloud computing is a modern exemplar to provide services through the internet. The development of cloud computing has eliminated the need of manpower, which is mainly used for the management of resources. During the cloud computing process, the term cloud balancing is a vital one. It deals with distribution of workloads and computing resources. The load balancing allows the company to balance the load according to the demands by the allocation of the resources to multiple servers or networks. The quality of service (QoS) metrics, including cost, response time, performance, throughput, and resource utilization are improved by means of load balancing. In this chapter, the authors study the literature on the load-balancing algorithms in heterogeneous cluster cloud environment with some of its classification. Additionally, they provide a review in each of these categories. Also, they provide discernment into the identification of open issues and guidance for future research work.

Chapter 11

Load balancing is one of the vital issues in cloud computing that needs to be achieved using proper techniques as it is directly related to higher resource utilization ratio and user satisfaction. By evenly distributing the dynamic local workload across all the nodes in the whole cloud, load balancing makes sure that no single node is overwhelmed, and some other nodes are kept idle. Hence, the technique helps to improve the overall performance resource utility of the system which will lead to high user satisfaction and resource utilization ratio. It also ensures the fair and effective distribution of each and every computing resource in the distributed system. Furthermore, the various load balancing techniques prevent the possible bottlenecks of the system created by the load imbalance. Maximization of the throughput, minimization of the response time, and avoidance of the overload are the other major advantages of the load balancing. Above all, by keeping resource consumption at the minimum, the load balancing techniques help to reduce costs.

Cloud computing is a service model in internet that provides virtualized resources to its clients. These types of servicing give a lot of benefits to the cloud users where they can pay as per their use. Even though they have benefits, they also face some problems like receiving computing resources, which is guaranteed on time. This time delay may affect the service time and the makespan. Thus, to reduce such problems, it is necessary to schedule the resources and then allocate it to using an optimized hypervisor. Here, the proposed method is used to do the above-mentioned problem. First, the available resources are clustered with respect to their characteristics. Then the resources are scheduled using this method. Finally, with respect to that of the clients request the resources, the resources are allocated. Here, the cost is the fitness of the allocation.

A remote mechanism-based new technology called wireless body area network (WBAN) is provided to observe and collect patient health record data with the aid of some wearable sensors. It provides privacy for healthcare professionals and an excellent degree of system security and also plays a major task in storing and ensuring the patient's records. A novel focus for preventing resources of wireless sensor network is implemented to bring a convenient plat form for the healthcare professionals. The adaptable energy efficient MAC protocol is presented in this chapter for the preservations of energy, and its result is discussed for the healthcare analysis.

Chapter 14

    M. Hemanth Chakravarthy, Vel Tech Rangarajan Dr. Sagunthala R&D Institute of Science and Technology, India

    E. Kannan, Vel Tech Rangarajan Dr. Sagunthala R&D Institute of Science and Technology, India

    M. J. Carmel Mary Belinda, Vel Tech Rangarajan Dr. Sagunthala R&D Institute of Science and Technology, India

Having understood the strategic significance of the flourishing cloud idea, enterprises across the globe are keenly strategizing and executing to embark on the cloud journey with all the clarity and confidence. There are product vendors bringing forth additional capabilities to easily and quickly setup and sustain competent cloud environments, which are being positioned as the one-stop IT solution for worldwide business organizations. The business domains such as governments, retail stores, healthcare providers, telecommunication service providers, supply chain and logistics, utilities, homeland security, etc. are keenly embracing the cloud idea to be ahead of their competitors in their operations, outputs, and offerings. However, there are some critical challenges and concerns being associated with the cloud paradigm. The widely quoted non-functional requirements (NFRs) and the quality of service (QoS) attributes such as security, performance, reliability, modifiability, and availability have to be fulfilled by cloud software, platform and infrastructures in order to boost the confidence level of business executives and institutions. There are mission-critical and emergency services, which are finding their residence in cloud environments (private, public, and hybrid). Their requirements are quite unique and hence researchers across the globe are striving hard and stretching further to bring forth innovative, disruptive, and transformation technology solutions to fulfill the various needs. This chapter proposes a cloud-based network architecture that contributes a consistent and ubiquitous internet connection. The mesh topology is recommended here to ensure that the connectivity is available all the time without any fail and slowdown. The security of data when it gets transmitted over channels, persisted in data stores, and used by applications, has to be ensured in order to boost the confidence of data owners and users. Hence, this chapter proposes a secure cloud-based heterogeneous network using a novel routing protocol.

Chapter 15

    R. Priyadarshini, Vel Tech Rangarajan Dr. Sagunthala R&D Institute of Science and Technology, India

    N. Malarvizhi, Vel Tech Rangarajan Dr. Sagunthala R&D Institute of Science and Technology, India

    E. A. Neeba, Rajagiri School of Engineering and Technology, India

Fog computing is a new paradigm believed to be an extension of cloud computing and services to the sting of the network. Similarly, like Cloud, Fog provides computing, data, storage, and various application services to the connected end-users. Fog computing uses one or a lot of combined end users or nearby end users edge devices to perform the configuration, communication, storage, control activity, and management functions over the infrastructure supported. This new paradigm solves the latency and information measure limitation issues encountered from the cloud computing. Primarily, the architecture of the fog computing is discussed and analyzed during this work and then indicates the connected potential security and trust problems. Then, however such problems are tackled within the existing literature is systematically reportable. Finally, the open challenges, analysis, trends, and future topics of security and trust in fog computing are mentioned.

Chapter 16

    B. Janet, National Institute of Technology, India
    Pethuru Raj, Reliance Jio Infocomm Ltd. (RJIL), India

We have been writing about the significant contributions of several proven and promising technologies in ensuring the desired success of smart cities. However, the selection of technologies for establishing intelligent cites has to be made after a careful consideration of multiple factors. There are several technologies coming and going without contributing anything substantial for the originally visualized and articulated needs, and hence, the choice plays a vital role in shaping up and strengthening our cities for future challenges and changes. Another noteworthy point is that instead of going for a single technology, it is prudent and pertinent to embrace a cluster of technologies to reach the desired state comfortably. Technology clusters are becoming prominent these days. Especially considering the growing complexity of smart cities (being touted as the system of systems), the need for a collection of competent technologies is being felt across not only the technology-cluster choice but also the appropriate usage of it also is pivotal in achieving the target in a risk-free and relaxed manner. Thus, any smart city strategy has to clearly illuminate resilient technologies and methodologies together towards accelerating and attaining the varied goals of smart cities in this vast and vivacious planet. In this chapter, the authors discuss the immense potential and promise of the newly coined paradigm of the internet of things (IoT) in making next-generation cities that sharply elevate the features, facilities, and functionalities of our crumbling and clogging cities.

Chapter 17

    E. A. Neeba, Rajagiri School of Engineering and Technology, India
    J. Aswini, Jawahar Engineering College, India
    R. Priyadarshini, Siddharth Institute of Science and Technology, India

Intelligent processing with smart devices and informative communications in everyday tasks brings an effective platform for the internet of things (IOT). Internet of things is seeking its own way to be the universal solution for all the real-life scenarios. Even though many theoretical studies pave the basic requirement for the internet of things, still the evidence-based learning (EBL) is lacking to deal with the application of the internet of things. As a contribution of this chapter, the basic requirements to study about internet of things with its deployment architecture for mostly enhanced applications are analyzed. This shows researchers how to initiate their research focus with the utilization of internet of things.

Chapter 18

In this chapter, the authors consider different categories of data, which are processed by the big data analytics tools. The challenges with respect to the big data processing are identified and a solution with the help of cloud computing is highlighted. Since the emergence of cloud computing is highly advocated because of its pay-per-use concept, the data processing tools can be effectively deployed within cloud computing and certainly reduce the investment cost. In addition, this chapter talks about the big data platforms, tools, and applications with data visualization concept. Finally, the applications of data analytics are discussed for future research.

Preface

The cloud adoption has been steadily growing across industry verticals. This is primarily due to the indisputable fact that here is a deeper and greater understanding of the cloud idea by worldwide businesses, government organizations, service providers (cloud and communication), system integrators (sis), independent software vendors (ISVs). Academic institutions and research labs through industry collaborations bring forth a variety of advancements in the cloud computing arena. Widely quoted limitations and issues of the cloud phenomenon are being meticulously addressed in order to boost the confidence of end-users, technical professionals and business executives to embrace this strategically sound technology. The digital transformation initiatives are being fully accomplished through this pioneering technological paradigm. Precisely speaking, cloud environments are being touted as the one-stop IT solution for all kinds of business requirements. The cloud journey is also on the right path. That is, there are a number of innovations and disruptions being brought in in this exotic and enigmatic discipline. This edited book is produced and prepared with the sole aim of expressing and exposing all the latest happenings in the cloud space. IT practitioners and academic professors have together contributed the book chapters.

Chapter 1 discusses the role and responsibility of information technology (IT) is consistently on the rise for producing and sustaining next-generation business establishments. Cloud computing is the recent phenomenon in the IT domain bringing forth a number of crucial innovations, disruptions and transformations for businesses and people. This chapter is specially allocated for conveying the humble beginning, the sustained growth of the cloud idea and the benefits for institutions, individuals and innovators.

Chapter 2 proposes a study on cloud of clouds and its impact on a business enterprise. It is also decided to propose a suitable scheduling algorithm to the cloud of cloud environment so as to trim the downtime problem faced by the cloud computing environment.

Chapter 3 introduced cloudsim simulator and cloud computing role in on-line social networking. The communication incurred by other activities such as management jobs is negligible. Social relationships can be established for numerous reasons.

Most of the people in India depend on the agriculture for their survival. Intelligent Water Grid Control (IWGC) system is a trusted solution for resolving recent significant global water problems. Chapter 4 discusses the water problems faced by the farmers, dam authority and by the government and will help the nation to achieve mission.

Chapter 5 covers important topics in development of efficient energy girds. Inefficient power generation, unbalanced consumption patterns that lead to underutilization of expensive infrastructure on the one hand, and severe overload on the other, as well as urgent issues of national and global concern such as power system security and climate change are all driving this evolution.

Chapter 6 presents the estimation of fault that could occur in the machines and decide the time that could cause a critical situation. This prediction should be done effectively and for this purpose we have stepped into the concept of machine learning.

Chapter 7 presents a detail study of various resource allocation and other scheduling challenges as well as Cloud Simulation Frameworks tools like CloudSim, ICanCloud in Cloud Computing.

With the Proliferation of new technologies such as augmented and virtual reality, autonomous cars, 5G networks, drones and IOT with smart cities, consumers of Cloud Computing are becoming the producers of Data. Chapter 8 wraps the features of Edge cloud, the driving industries that are providing solutions, the use cases, benefits and the challenges of Edge cloud.

Chapter 9 presents techniques based on Internet of things and cloud computing driven waste management. It also deals with the effective waste management with the implementation of Internet of Things (IoT) based Cloud technology with the Machine Learning algorithm that could be highly intellectual in the management of waste.

Chapter 10 studies the literature on the load-balancing algorithms in Heterogeneous Cluster Cloud environment with some of its classification. Additionally, it provides a review in each of these categories. Also, we provide discernment into the identification of open issues and guidance for future research work.

Chapter 11 helps to improve the overall performance resource utility of the system which will lead to high user satisfaction and resource utilization ratio. It also ensures the fair and effective distribution of each and every computing resource in the distributed system. Furthermore, the various load balancing techniques prevent the possible bottlenecks of the system created by the load imbalance is presented.

Chapter 12 discusses a proposed method in cloud computing which has two steps. First, the available resources in cloud are clustered with respect to their characteristics. Then the resources are scheduled using this method. Finally, with respect to that of the clients request the resources, the resources are allocated. Here the cost is the fitness of the allocation.

A remote mechanism based new technology called Wireless Body Area Network (WBAN) is provided to observe and collect patient's health record data with the aid of some wearable sensors. Chapter 13 provides privacy for health care professionals and excellent degree of system security and also plays a major task in storing and ensuring the patient's records. The Adaptable Energy Efficient MAC protocol is presented in this chapter for the preservations of energy and its result is discussed for the Health Care Analysis.

Chapter 14 presents the challenges and concerns being associated with the cloud paradigm. The widely quoted non-functional requirements (NFRs) and the quality of service (QoS) attributes such as security, performance, reliability, modifiability, and availability have to be fulfilled by cloud software, platform and infrastructures in order to boost the confidence level of business executives and institutions.

Chapter 15 discusses about Fog computing which is a new paradigm believed to be an extension of Cloud computing and services to the sting of the network. Similarly, like Cloud, Fog provides computing, data, storage, and various application services to the connected end-users. Fog computing uses one or a lot of combined end users or nearby end users edge devices to perform the configuration, communication, storage, control activity and management functions over the infrastructure supported.

Chapter 16 discusses about the immense potential and promise of the newly coined paradigm of the Internet of Things (IoT) in making next-generation cities that sharply elevate the features, facilities and functionalities of our crumbling and clogging cities.

Chapter 17 presents the basic requirements to study about Internet of Things with its deployment architecture for mostly enhanced applications are analyzed. Also this gives the hands to researchers how to initiate their research focus with the utilization of Internet of Things.

Finally, Chapter 18 considers different categories of data, which are processed by the big data analytics tools. The challenges with respect to the big data processing is identified and a solution with the help of cloud computing is highlighted.

Chapter 1
Delineating the Cloud Journey

Pethuru Raj
Reliance Jio Infocomm Ltd. (RJIL), India

Jenn-Wei Lin
Fu Jen Catholic University, Taiwan

ABSTRACT

There are a number of noteworthy improvements and improvisations in the fields of information and communication technology (ICT) in the recent past. These continuous and consistent advancements have a direct and decisive impact on business offerings, operations, and outputs. Worldwide business enterprises, service providers, product vendors, government organizations, academic institutions, etc. are being sagaciously and strategically empowered through the distinct ICT capabilities. Especially, the role and responsibility of information technology (IT) is consistently on the rise for producing and sustaining next-generation business establishments. Precisely speaking, business acceleration and augmentation get fluently fulfilled through IT. Therefore, IT is being widely pronounced and presented as the best enabler of businesses. All kinds of business needs such as agility, affordability, adaptivity, customer propensity and delight, business productivity and expansion, etc. are being provided and performed through the growing list of innovations in the enigmatic IT domain. Cloud computing is the recent phenomenon in the IT domain bringing forth a number of crucial innovations, disruptions, and transformations for businesses and people. The cloud idea has permeated deeply and decisively and is being touted as the one-stop IT solution for all kinds of business needs. The cloud journey started a decade back and is steadily growing to bring in desired automation for businesses. This chapter is specially allocated for conveying the humble beginning, the sustained growth of the cloud idea, and the benefits for institutions, individuals, and innovators.

INTRODUCTION

Definitely the cloud journey is on the fast track. The cloud idea got originated and started to thrive from the days of server virtualization. physical machines (bare metal (BM) servers) are being systematically virtualized in order to have multiple virtual /logical machines, which are provisioned dynamically and kept in ready state to deliver sufficient and on-demand coarse-grained resources (compute, storage and

DOI: 10.4018/978-1-5225-9023-1.ch001

network) for optimally running any software application. Accordingly, the fine-grained resources are typically memory and storage capacity, processing capability, input/output (I/O) power, etc. That is, a physical machine can be empowered to run multiple and heterogeneous applications through the aspect of virtualization, which is being termed as the finest abstraction mechanism.

Different operating systems (OSes) can be run on a single and same machine to accommodate disparate applications. Resultantly, the utilization of expensive compute machines is steadily going up. Further on, the much-anticipated IT agility, adaptivity and affordability through such virtualization mechanisms are also being realized with ease. It is not only partitioning of physical machines in any data center towards having hundreds of virtual machines in order to fulfil the IT requirements of business activities but also clubbing hundreds of such virtual/logical machines together programmatically brings forth a large-scale virtual environment for running high-performance computing (HPC) applications. Precisely speaking, the virtualization tenet is leading to the realization of cheaper supercomputing capability in an on-demand fashion. There are other crucial upgrades being brought in by the indomitable virtualization feature and we will write them too in this book in detail.

This chapter, specially prepared for telling all about the praiseworthy journey of the cloud idea, details and describes the nitty-gritty of next-generation cloud centers. The motivations, the key advantages, and the enabling tools and engines along with other relevant details are being neatly and nicely illustrated there. A software defined cloud environment (SDCE) is an additional abstraction layer that ultimately defines a complete data center. This software layer presents the resources of the data center as pools of virtual and physical resources to host and deliver software applications to their subscribers and users. A modern SDCE is extremely nimble and supple in order to artistically support the varying business requirements. SDCE is, therefore, a collection of virtualized IT resources (server machines, storage appliances, and networking solutions) that can be scaled up or down as required and can be deployed as needed in a number of distinct ways. There are three key components making up SDCEs

1. Software defined computing
2. Software-defined networking
3. Software defined storage

The trait of software enablement of different hardware systems has pervaded into other domains so that we hear and read about software-defined protection, etc. There are several useful resources produced by highly accomplished and acclaimed cloud evangelists, exponents and experts in the web on this key trend.

REFLECTING THE CLOUD JOURNEY

The prime objective of the hugely popular cloud paradigm is to realize highly organized and optimized IT environments for enabling business automation, acceleration, and augmentation. Most of the enterprise IT environments across the globe are bloated, closed, inflexible, static, complex, and expensive. The brewing business and IT challenges are therefore how to make IT elastic, extensible, programmable, dynamic, modular, and cost-effective. Especially with the worldwide businesses are cutting down their IT budgets gradually year after year, the enterprise IT team has left with no other option other than to embark on a meticulous and measured journey to accomplish more with less through a host of pioneering and promising technological solutions. Organizations are clearly coming to the conclusion that business operations can run without any hitch and hurdle with less IT resources through effective commoditization, consolidation, centralization, compartmentalization (virtualization and containerization), federation, and rationalization of various IT solutions (server machines, storage appliances, and networking components). Thus, IT automation and optimization processes are getting immense support from IT and business leaders.

IT operations also go through a variety of technologies-induced innovations and disruptions to bring in the desired rationalization and optimization. The IT infrastructure management is also being performed remotely and in an automated manner through the smart leverage of a host of automated IT operation, configuration, software deployment, monitoring, measurement, diagnosis (performance, security, etc.), and maintenance tools. The vision of DevOps and NoOps is steadily tending towards the reality. Next-generation data analytics platforms are going to contribute immeasurably in the days to come in decisively automating most of the manual IT operations. IT management and maintenance are a lot easier with prediction and prescription capabilities of IT data analytics tools. Resource failure is being proactively zeroed down through the employment of various analytical capabilities and the necessary countermeasures are being considered and performed proactively and promptly to ensure business continuity (BC). The application of analytics methods on all kinds of operational, log, performance, security, interaction, and transaction data emanating from every data center resource comes handy in ensuring the optimized service delivery in an automated manner. The optimal utilization of expensive IT resources is to be fully guaranteed with the number of advancements in various IT infrastructure management technologies and tools.

With the evolutionary and revolutionary traits of cloud computing, there is a major data center optimization and transformation. The acts of simplification and standardization for achieving IT industrialization are drawing a lot of attention these days. The various IT resources such as memory, disk storage, processing power, and I/O consumption are critically and cognitively monitored, measured and managed towards their utmost utilization. The pooling and sharing of IT solutions and services are being given the paramount importance towards the strategic IT optimization. Also having a dynamic pool of computing, storage and network resources enable IT service providers, as well as enterprise IT, teams to meet up any kind of spikes and emergencies in resource needs for their customers and users.

Even with all the unprecedented advancements in the cloud landscape, there are a plenty of futuristic and fulsome opportunities and possibilities for IT professors and professionals to take the cloud idea to its next level in its long journey. Therefore, the concept of software-defined cloud environments (SDCEs) is gaining a lot of accreditation these days. Product vendors, cloud service providers, system integrators and other principal stakeholders are so keen to have such advanced and acclaimed environments for their clients, customers, and consumers. The right and relevant technologies for the realization and sustenance of software-defined cloud environments are fast maturing and stabilizing and hence the days of SDCEs are not too far away. This chapter is specially crafted for expressing and exposing all the appropriate details regarding the eliciting and elaborating the architectural components of SDCEs.

That is, providing right-sized IT resources (compute, storage and networking) for all kinds of business software solutions is the need of the hour. Users increasingly expect their service providers' infrastructures to deliver these resources elastically in response to their changing needs. There is no cloud services infrastructure available today capable of simultaneously delivering scalability, flexibility and high operational efficiency. The methodical virtualization of every component of a cloud center ultimately leads to software-defined environments.

VISUALIZING THE FUTURE

1. **Automated Analytics through Cognitive Computing:** The above-mentioned transitions result in massive volumes of multi-structured data. We have been bombarded with a variety of solutions and services in order to realize a number of hitherto unknown analytical capabilities. The analytical platforms facilitate the extraction of actionable insights out of data heaps. There are big, fast, streaming and IoT data and there are batch, real-time and interactive processing methods. Herein we need to feed the system with the right and relevant data along with the programming logic on how to process the data and present the insights squeezed out. However, the future beckons for automated analytics in the sense that we just feed the data and the platform create viable and venerable patterns, models, and hypotheses in order to discover and disseminate knowledge. The unprecedented growth of cognitive computing is to bring the desired automation so that data gets converted into information and insights casually and cognitively.

2. **Cognitive Clouds**: The cloud journey is simply phenomenal. It started with server virtualization, and we are now moving towards software-defined cloud centers. The originally envisioned goal is to have highly optimized and organized ICT infrastructures and resources for hosting and delivering any kind of software applications. The ICT resource utilization is picking up fast with all the innovations and improvisations in the cloud field. The future belongs to real-time and cognitive analytics of every data emanating out of cloud environments. The log, security, performance and other operational, transactional and analytical data can be captured and subjected to a variety of investigations in order to establish dynamic capacity planning, adaptive task/workflow scheduling and load balancing, workload consolidation, and optimization, resource placement, etc. The machine and deep learning (ML/DL) algorithms are bound to come handy in predicting and prescribing the valid steps towards enhanced ICT utilization while fulfilling the functional as well as non-functional needs of business applications and IT services.

3. **No Servers, but Services**: The ICT infrastructure operations and management activities such as resource provisioning, load balancing, firewalling, software deployment, etc. are being activated and accelerated through a bevy of automation tools. The vision of NoOps is steadily seeing the reality. There is very less intervention, instruction, interpretation, and involvement of humans in operating and managing IT. People can focus on their core activities blissfully. On the other hand, we are heading towards the serverless architecture. The leading cloud service providers (CSPs) provide the serverless computing capabilities through the various offerings (IBM OpenWhisk, AWS Lambda, Microsoft Azure Functions and Google Cloud Functions). We are fiddling with bare metal (BM) servers, virtual machines (VMs) through hardware virtualization, and now containers through OS virtualization. The future is for virtual servers. That is, appropriate compute, storage and network resources get assigned automatically for event-driven applications in order to make way for serverless computing.

4. **Analytics and Applications at the Intercloud of Public, Private and Edge / Fog Clouds:** Clouds present an illusion of infinite resources and hence big, fast, streaming and IoT data analytics are being accomplished in on-premise as well as off-premise, online, and on-demand cloud centers. However, with the faster maturity and stability of device cluster/cloud formation mechanisms due to the faster spread of fog/edge devices in our personal and professional environments, real-time capture, processing, and action are being achieved these days. That is, the newer domain of edge

analytics directly enabled through edge device clouds for producing real-time insights and services is being widely accepted and accentuated.

5. **Secure Distributed Computing Through Blockchain:** It is a widely expressed concern that security is the main drawback of distributed computing. Similarly, the topmost concern of cloud computing is again the same security aspect. The blockchain technology, which is very popular in financial industries, is now being tweaked and leveraged for other industry segments. The blockchain is a sort of a public "ledger" of every transaction that has ever taken place. There is no centralized authority but it is a kind of peer-to-peer (P2P) network of distributed parties to arrive at a consensus and this consensus is entered into the ledger to be accessed by anyone at a later point in time. It is computationally infeasible for a single actor (or anything less than the majority consensus) to go back and modify history. Moving away from a single decision-maker to multiple decision-enablers towards the impenetrable and unbreakable security of any kind of transaction across a myriad of industry verticals is the game-changing breakthrough of the blockchain technology, which is immensely penetrative and participative. There are different viable and venerable use cases across industry segments being considered and empowered by the unlimited power of blockchain technology. There may be salivating convergence among multiple technology domains such as cloud environments, blockchains, artificial intelligence (AI), robotics, self-driving vehicles, cognitive analytics and insurance domains in the days ahead.

6. **Containerized Clouds:** With the surging popularity of containers as the most optimized, highly scalable and lightweight application runtime resource, the IT industry is speedily embracing the containerization paradigm in a big way in order to achieve the goal of "more with less". A number of IT operations are being smoothly automated through the adoption of the containerization paradigm. The IT agility is significantly achieved through this new trend and this directly enables enterprises to be nimble.

Especially with faster maturity and stability of the Docker platform, the containerization era has started to shine. Today, public and private cloud environments are being stuffed with a large number of containers. It is reported that Google data centers are leveraging billions of containers every week. For simplifying container lifecycle management along with container scheduling, the emergence of Kubernetes is being welcome. The key capabilities of the Kubernetes platform boost the confidence of cloud service providers and enterprises to have containerized clouds in order to run enterprise-scale and microservices-centric applications. The convergence of service meshes (Istio, Linkerd, etc.), container orchestration platform solutions, and containerization platforms along with other powerful products such as API gateways and management suites for microservices has energized business executives and IT experts to tend towards containerized clouds.

The tool ecosystem is steadily growing. Multi-container applications, which are process-aware, business-critical, service-oriented, cloud-hosted and composite, are being easily developed with the availability of competent tools. There are automated tools in plenty for monitoring and management of containerized cloud environments. Integrated dashboards to precisely take care of each and every participating and contributing containers. Data analytics through machine and deep learning algorithms comes handy in strengthening containers and their capabilities.

On concluding, the various technological evolutions and revolutions are remarkably enhancing the quality of human lives across the world. Carefully choosing and smartly leveraging the fully matured and stabilized technological solutions and services towards the much-anticipated and acclaimed digital transformation is the need of the hour towards the safe, smarter and sustainable planet.

The Major Building Blocks of Software-Defined Cloud Environments (SDCEs)

Software-defined infrastructures are the key ingredients of SDCEs. That is, an SDCE encompasses software-defined compute, storage, and networking components. The substantially matured server virtualization leads to the realization of software-defined compute machines. Highly intelligent hypervisors (alternatively recognized as virtual machine monitors (VMMs) act as the perfect software solution to take care of the creation, provisioning, de-provisioning, live-in migration, decommissioning of computing machines (virtual machines and bare metal servers), etc. Most of the servers across leading cloud centers are virtualized and it is clear that the server virtualization is reaching a state of stability. In a sense, the SDCE is simply the logical extension of server virtualization. The server virtualization dramatically maximizes the deployment of computing power. Similarly, the SDCE does the same for all of the resources needed to host an application, including storage, networking, and security.

In the past, provisioning a server machine to host an application took weeks of time. Today a VM can be provisioned in a few minutes. Even containers can be provisioned in a few seconds. That is the power of virtualization and containerization. This sort of speed and scale being made possible through virtualization platforms is being extended to other IT resources. That is, the whole cloud center is getting fully virtualized in order to tend towards the days of software-defined clouds.

In SDCEs, all IT resources are virtualized so they can be automatically configured and provisioned and made ready to install applications without any human intervention, involvement, and interpretation. Applications can be operational in minutes thereby the time to value has come down sharply. The IT cost gets reduced significantly. There are a number of noteworthy advancements in the field of server virtualization in the form of a host of automated tools, design and deployment patterns, easy-to-use templates, etc. The cloud paradigm became a famous and fantastic approach for data center transformation and optimization because of the unprecedented success of server virtualization. This riveting success has since then penetrated into other important ingredients of data centers.

IT resources are virtualized thereby are extremely elastic, remotely programmable, easily consumable, predictable, measurable, and manageable. With the comprehensive yet compact virtualization sweeping each and every component of data center, the goals of distributed deployment of various resources but centrally monitored, measured and managed is nearing the reality. Server virtualization has greatly improved data center operations, providing significant gains in performance, efficiency, and cost-effectiveness by enabling IT departments to consolidate and pool computing resources. Considering the strategic impacts of 100 percent virtualization, we would like to focus on network and storage virtualization methods in the sections to follow.

Network Functions Virtualization (NFV)

There are several network functions such as load balancing, firewalling, routing, switching, etc. in any IT environment. The idea is to bring forth the established virtualization capabilities into the networking arena so that we can have virtualized load balancing, firewalling, etc. The fast-emerging domain of network functions virtualization aims to transform the way that network operators and communication service providers architect and operate communication networks and their network services.

The today's IT environment is exceedingly dynamic with the steady incorporation of cloud technologies. New virtual machines can be spunup in minutes and can migrate between physical hosts. Application containers are also emerging fast in order to speed up application composition, packaging, and shipping across data centers. The network remains relatively static and painstakingly slow in the sense that it is an error-prone provisioning- process to provide network connectivity for applications. Data center networks have to facilitate the movement of applications between computing servers within data centers as well as across data centers. There is also a need for layer 2 VLAN extensions. In today's traditional LAN/WAN design, the extension of VLANs and their propagation within data centers is not an easy affair. Ensuring all redundant links, in addition to switches, are properly configured can be a time-consuming operation. This can introduce errors and risks. With the trends such as big data, bring your own devices (BYOD) and data and process-intensive videos, the IT infrastructures especially networks are under immense pressure.

Network virtualization provides a supple and nimble network environment and is being touted as the best-in-class solution approach for tackling all the above-mentioned trends in the IT landscape. Network Functions Virtualization (NFV) is getting a lot of attention these days and network service providers have teamed up well to convince their product vendors to move away from special-purpose equipment and appliances toward software-only solutions. These software solutions run on commodity servers, storages and network elements such as switches, routers, application delivery controllers (ADCs), etc. By embracing the NFV technology, communication and cloud service providers could bring down their capital as well as operational costs significantly. The power consumption goes down, the heat dissipation too goes down sharply, the cost of employing expert resources for administering and operating special equipment is bound to come down significantly, and time-to-market for conceiving and concretizing newer and premium services. Due to its software-driven approach, NFV also allows service providers to achieve a much higher degree of operational automation and to simplify operational processes such as capacity planning, job scheduling, workload consolidation, VM placement, etc.

In an NFV environment, the prominent operational processes such as service deployment, on-demand allocation of network resources such as bandwidth, failure detection, on-time recovery and software upgrades, can be easily programmed and executed in an automated fashion. This software-induced automation brings down the process time to minutes rather than weeks and months. There is no need for the operational team to personally and physically visit remote locations to install, configure, diagnose, and repair network solutions. Instead, all kinds of network components can be remotely monitored, measured, and managed.

In short, it is all about consolidating diverse network equipment types (firewall, switching, routing, application delivery controller (ADC), etc.) onto industry-standard x86 servers using virtualization. The immediate and strategic benefits include the operational agility, which could empower business agility, autonomy, and affordability.

Network virtualization helps worldwide enterprises achieve major advancements in simplicity, speed, and security by clinically automating and simplifying many of the data center operations and processes. NV also contributes immensely to reducing the network provisioning time from weeks to minutes. It helps to achieve higher operational productivity by automating a variety of manual processes. NV comes handy in placing and moving workloads across data centers. Finally, the network security gets a boost.

Software-Defined Networking (SDN): Software-defined networking is quite a recent concept that is to disaggregate the traditional vertically integrated networking stack in order to improve network flexibility and manageability. SDN represents a bevy of technologies that facilitate the data, control and management planes of the network to be loosely coupled to be distantly accessible through APIs, independently extensible and evolving. These APIs also facilitate the development of a rich new set of network applications and services from a wider range of sources, including independent developers, Value-Added Resellers (VARs), and user organizations themselves.

The brewing technology trends indicate that networks and network management are bound to change once for all. Today's data centers (DCs) extensively use physical switches and appliances that haven't yet been virtualized and are statically and slowly provisioned. Further on, the current environment mandate for significant and certified expertise in operating each vendor's equipment. The networking solutions also lack an API ecosystem towards facilitating remote discovery and activation. In short, the current situation clearly points out the absence of programmable networks. It is quite difficult to bring in the expected automation (resource provisioning, scaling, etc.) on the currently running inflexible, monolithic and closed network and connectivity solutions. The result is the underutilization of expensive network equipment. Also, the cost of employing highly educated and experienced network administrators is definitely on the higher side. Thus, besides bringing in a bevy of pragmatic yet frugal innovations in the networking arena, the expressed mandate is for substantially reducing the capital as well as the operational expenses being incurred by the traditional network architecture is clearly playing in the minds of technical professionals and business executives.

As the virtualization principle has been contributing immensely to server consolidation and optimization, the idea of network virtualization has picked up in the recent past. The virtualization aspect on the networking side takes a different route compared to the matured server virtualization. The extraction and centralization of network intelligence embedded inside all kinds of network appliances such as routers, switches, etc. into a centralized controller aesthetically bring in a number of strategic advantages for data centers. The policy-setting, configuration, and maneuvering activities are being activated through software libraries that are modular, service-oriented and centralized in a controller module and hence the new terminology "software-defined networking" (SDN) have blossomed and hugely popular. That is, instead of managing network assets separately using separate interfaces, they are controlled collectively through a comprehensive, easy-to-use and fine-grained interface. The application programming interface (API) approach has the intrinsic capability of putting a stimulating and sustainable foundation for all kinds of IT resources and assets to be easily discoverable, accessible, usable and composable. Simplistically speaking, the aspect of hardware infrastructure programming is seeing the reality and thereby the remote manipulations and machinations of various IT resources are gaining momentum.

The control plane manages switch and routing tables while the forwarding plane actually performs the Layer 2 and 3 filtering, forwarding and routing. In short, SDN decouples the system that makes decisions about where traffic is sent (the control plane) from the underlying system that forwards traffic to the selected destination (the data plane). This well-intended segregation leads to a variety of innovations and inventions. Therefore, standards-compliant SDN controllers provide a widely adopted API ecosystem, which can be used to centrally control multiple devices in different layers. Such an abstracted and centralized approach offers many strategically significant improvements over traditional networking approaches. For instance, it becomes possible to completely decouple the network's control plane and its data plane. The control plane runs in a cluster setup and can configure all kinds of data plane switches and routers to support business expectations as demanded. That means data flow is regulated at the network level in an efficient manner. Data can be sent where it is needed or blocked if it is deemed a security threat.

A detached and deft software implementation of the configuration and controlling aspects of network elements also means that the existing policies can be refurbished whereas newer policies can be created and inserted on demand to enable all the associated network devices to behave in a situation-aware manner. As we all know, policy establishment and enforcement are the proven mechanisms to bring in the required versatility and vitality in network operations. If a particular application's flow unexpectedly needs more bandwidth, SDN controller proactively recognizes the brewing requirement in real time and accordingly reroute the data flow in the correct network path. Precisely speaking, the physical constraints are getting decimated through the software-defined networking. If a security appliance needs to be inserted between two tiers, it is easily accomplished without altering anything at the infrastructure level. Another interesting factor is the most recent phenomenon of "bring your own device (BYOD)". All kinds of employees' own devices can be automatically configured, accordingly authorized and made ready to access the enterprise's network anywhere anytime.

The Key Motivations for SDN: In the IT world, there are several trends mandating the immediate recognition and sagacious adoption of SDN. Software defi4ned cloud environments (SDCEs) are being established in different cool locations across the globe to provide scores of orchestrated cloud services to worldwide businesses and individuals over the Internet on a subscription basis. Application and database servers besides integration middleware solutions are increasingly distributed whereas the governance and the management of distributed resources are being accomplished in a centralized manner to avail the much-needed single point of view (SPoV). Due to the hugeness of data centers, the data traffic therefore internally as well as externally is exploding these days. Flexible traffic management and ensuring "bandwidth on demand" are the principal requirements.

The consumerization of IT is another gripping trend. Enterprise users and executives are being increasingly assisted by a bevy of gadgets and gizmos such as smartphones, laptops, tablets, wearables etc. in their daily chores. As enunciated elsewhere, the "Bring Your Own Device (BYOD)" movement requires enterprise networks to inherently support policy-based adjustment, amenability, and amelioration to support users' devices dynamically. Big data analytics (BDA) has a telling effect on IT networks, especially on data storage and transmission. The proprietary nature of network solutions from worldwide product vendors also plays a sickening role in traditional networks and hence there is a clarion call for bringing in necessary advancements in the network architecture. Programmable networks are therefore the viable and venerable answer to bring in the desired flexibility and optimization in highly complicated and cumbersome corporate networks. The structural limitations of conventional networks are being overcome with network programming. The growing complexity of traditional networks leads to stasis. That is, adding or releasing devices and incorporating network-related policies are really turning out to be a tough affair at the current setup.

As per the leading market watchers, researchers and analysts, SDN marks the largest business opportunity in the networking industry since its inception. Recent reports estimate the business impact tied to SDN could be as high as $35 billion by 2018, which represents nearly 40 percent of the overall networking industry. The future of networking will rely more and more on software, which will accelerate the pace of innovation incredibly for networks as it has in the computing and storage domains (explained below). SDN has all within to transform today's static and sick networks into calculative, competent and cognitive platforms with the intrinsic intelligence to anticipate and allocate resources dynamically. SDN brings up the scale to support enormous data centers and the virtualization needed to support workloads-optimized, converged, orchestrated and highly automated cloud environments. With its many identified advantages and astonishing industry momentum, SDN is on the way to becoming the new norm and normal for not only for cloud but also corporate networks. With the next-generation hybrid and federated clouds, the role of SDN for fulfilling network function virtualization (NFV) is bound to shoot up.

In short, SDN is an emerging architecture that is agile, adaptive, cheaper and ideal for network-intensive and dynamic applications. This architecture decouples the network control and forwarding functions (routing) enabling the network control to become directly programmable and the underlying infrastructure to be abstracted for applications and network services, which can treat the network as a logical or virtual entity.

The Need of SDN for the Cloud: Due to a number of enterprise-wide benefits, the adoption rates of cloud paradigm have been growing. However, the networking aspect of cloud environments has typically not kept pace with the rest of the architecture. There came a number of enhancements such as network virtualization (NV), network function virtualization (NFV) and software-defined networking (SDN). SDN is definitely the comprehensive and futuristic paradigm. With the explosion of computing machines (both virtual machines as well as bare metal servers) in any cloud centers, the need for SDN is sharply felt across. Networks today are statically provisioned, with devices that are managed at a box-level scale and are under-utilized. SDN enables end-to-end based network equipment provisioning, reducing the network provisioning time from days to minutes, and distributing flows more evenly across the fabric allowing for better utilization.

The Distinct Benefits of Software-Defined Networking

The benefits of SDN are definitely diversified and gradually enlarging. SDN is being seen as a blessing for cloud service providers (CSPs), enterprise data centers, telecommunication service providers, etc. The primary SDN benefits are the following:

- **The Centralized Network Control and Programmability**: As we discussed above, the gist of the SDN paradigm is to separate the control function from the forwarding function. This separation resultantly facilitates the centralized management of the network switches without requiring physical access to the switches. The IT infrastructures deployments and management are therefore gaining the most benefits as SDN controller is capable of creating, migrating, and tearing down VMs without requiring manual network configurations. This feature maximizes the value of large-scale server virtualization.

- **Dynamic Network Segmentation**: VLANs provide an effective solution to logically group servers and virtual machines at the enterprise or branch network level. However, the 12-bit VLAN ID cannot accommodate more than 4096 virtual networks and this presents a problem for mega data centers such as public and private clouds. Reconfiguring VLANs is also a daunting task as multiple switches and routers have to be reconfigured whenever VMs are relocated. The SDN's support for centralized network management and network element programmability allows highly flexible VM grouping and VM migration.

- **High Visibility of VMs**: The virtual hypervisor switch and all the VMs running in a physical server use only one or two NICs to communicate with the physical network. These VMs are managed by server management tools and hence not visible to network management tools. This lacuna makes it difficult for network designers and administers to understand the VM movement. However, SDN-enabled hypervisor switches and VMs alleviate this visibility problem.
- **Capacity Utilization**: With centralized control and programmability, SDN easily facilitates VM migration across servers in the same rack or across clusters of servers in the same datacenter, or even with servers in geographically distributed data centers. This ultimately leads to automated and dynamic capacity planning that in turn significantly increments physical server utilization.
- **Network Capacity Optimization**: The classic tri-level design of data center networks consisting of core, aggregation, and access layer switches (North-South design), is facing scalability limits and poses inefficiencies for server-to-server (East-West) traffic. There are innovative solutions such as link aggregation, multi-chassis link aggregation, top-of-rack (ToR) switches and Layer 2 multipath protocols. These are able to fulfill load-balancing, resiliency and performance requirements of dense data centers. However, these are found to be complex and difficult to manage and maintain. The SDN paradigm enables the design and maintenance of network fabrics that span across multiple data centers.
- **Distributed Application Load Balancing**: With SDN, it is possible to have the load-balancing feature that chooses not only compute machines but also the network path. It is possible to have geographically distributed load-balancing capability.

OpenFlow is a kind of SDN protocol that specifies an API for programming the flow tables of a network switch. Traditionally, these flow tables could not be programmed remotely or by third parties. Network switches typically included a proprietary network operating system (NOS) and native programs which controlled the flow tables. With OpenFlow, the switch only manages flow tables. The OS and control programs get hosted and executed on a commodity server. This arrangement removes constraints on control software. That is, the control software can be programmed using any language and run on any operating system. Also, the control software can run on the virtual machine (VM) and bare metal (BM) server. With containerization sweeping the cloud space, we can expect the control software to be containerized.

With the embedded intelligence getting abstracted and extracted out of switches, the network switches are getting dumber, cheaper, and more capable. Precisely speaking, the OpenFlow enables the intelligence required to manage LANs and WANs to run in software while pushing the physical execution down to the switches. It is all about software-defined control and management of physical hardware. Further on, additional capabilities can be realized from hardware systems. That is, networks can perform faster, route data based on business needs, and enable Internet-scale application communication through SDN.

On summarizing, SDN is the definite game-changer for next-generation IT environments. SDN considerably eliminates network complexity in the midst of multiple and heterogeneous network elements. All kinds of network solutions are centrally configured and controlled to eliminate all kinds of dependencies-induced constrictions and to realize their full potential. Network capabilities are provisioned on demand at the optimal level to suit application requirements. In synchronization with other infrastructural models appropriately, the on-demand, instant-on, autonomic, and smart computing goals are easily delivered.

Accentuating Software-Defined Storage (SDS)

This is the big data era. Huge volumes of data are being generated, captured, cleansed, and crunched in order to extract actionable insights due to the realization that big data leads to big insights. Data is the new fuel for the world economy. IT has to be prepared accordingly and pressed into service in order to garner, transmit and stock multi-structured and massive data. Software-defined storage gives enterprises, organizations, and governments a viable and venerable mechanism to effectively address this explosive data growth.

We are slowly yet steadily getting into the virtual world with the faster realization of the goals allied with the concept of virtual IT. The ensuing world is leaning towards the vision of anytime anywhere access to information and services. This projected transformation needs a lot of perceivable and paradigm shifts. Traditional data centers were designed to support specific workloads and users. This has resulted in siloed and heterogeneous storage solutions that are difficult to manage, provision newer resources to serve dynamic needs, and finally to scale out. The existing setup acts as a barrier for business innovations and value. Untangling this goes a long way in facilitating instant access to information and services.

Undoubtedly storage has been a prominent infrastructural module in data centers. There are different storage types and solutions in the market. In the recent past, the unprecedented growth of data generation, collection, processing, and storage clearly indicates the importance of producing and provisioning of better and bigger storage systems and services. Storage management is another important topic not to be sidestepped. We often read about big, fast, and even extreme data. Due to an array of technology-inspired processes and systems, the data size, scope, structure, and speed are on the climb. For example, digitization is an overwhelming worldwide trend and trick gripping every facet of human life thereby the digital data is everywhere and continues to grow at a stunning pace. Statisticians say that every day, approximately 15 petabytes of new data is being generated worldwide and the total amount of digital data doubles approximately every two years. The indisputable fact is that machine-generated data is larger compared to man-generated data. The expectation is that correspondingly there have to be copious innovations in order to cost-effectively accommodate and manage big data.

As we all know, storage appliances are embedded with sophisticated software stacks. And there is storage management software to perform management tasks such as moving files and provisioning volumes. It is not just the abstraction of the embedded intelligence and the creation of a software module outside the storage appliances and arrays. The essence of SDS is to leverage the distributed computing techniques in designing and setting up storage appliances. That is, using commodity hardware and innovative storage optimization techniques for space and performance efficiencies, accessibility, manageability, etc. is being touted as the next-generation software-defined storage. This kind of advanced storage approach is inherently capable of tackling explosive data growth, bringing down storage costs through commodity hardware, leveraging already invested storage arrays, providing geographical data replication, etc. Further on, the SDS is famous for simplified and scalable storage management experience. A variety of data access protocols can be accommodated in the SDS environment. There are capital and operational cost savings with SDS and the experience of nimbler, supple, scalable and streamlined storage solutions is also accrued and availed.

Due to the distributed nature, the scale-out is inherently elastic in the sense that additional commodity nodes for storage can be obtained quickly if there is a fluctuation in data storage requirements. When the demand comes down, all the additionally provisioned storage systems can be brought into the storage pool in order to be ready to serve. This is a prime reason for the runaway success of the SDS concept.

The traditional storages primarily support the scale-up method, which is not in tune with the increasingly dynamic nature of IT environments.

Traditionally, storage administrators pre-allocate logical unit number (LUN) addresses of storage in shared storage hardware. This is for making any idle capacity to be available for virtual machine disks when virtual machines are created. Several different LUNs can be created and kept ready to accommodate varying performance and business requirements. With software-defined storage, virtual workloads are being decoupled from physical storage. Software-defined storage will pool all storage capacity into a data plane and assign storage by using a policy-based control plane that is informed with the performance characteristics of the underlying storage targets. The result is application-centric or virtual machine–centric control of pooled storage resources.

Software-defined storage (SDS) is a relatively new concept and its popularity is surging due to the abundant success attained in software-defined compute and networking areas. As explained above, SDS is a part and parcel of the vision behind the establishment and sustenance of software-defined cloud environments (SDCEs). With the virtualization concept penetrating and piercing through every tangible resource, the storage industry also gets inundated by that powerful trend. Software-defined storage is a kind of enterprise-class storage that uses a variety of commoditized and, therefore, cheap hardware with all the important storage and management functions being extricated and performed using an intelligent software controller. With such a clean separation, SDS delivers automated, policy-driven, and application-aware storage services through an orchestration of the underlining storage infrastructure. That is, we get a dynamic pool of virtual storage resources to be picked up dynamically and orchestrate them accordingly to be presented as an appropriate storage solution. Unutilized storage resources could be then incorporated into the pool for serving other requests. All kinds of constricting dependencies on storage solutions simply vanish with such storage virtualization. All storage modules are commoditized and hence the cost of storage is to go down with higher utilization. In a nutshell, storage virtualization enables storage scalability, replaceability, substitutability, and manageability.

An SDS solution remarkably increases the flexibility by enabling organizations to use non-proprietary standard hardware and, in many cases, leverage existing storage infrastructures as a part of their enterprise storage solution. Additionally, organizations can achieve massive scale with an SDS by adding heterogeneous hardware components as needed to increase capacity and improve performance in the solution. Automated, policy-driven management of SDS solutions helps drive cost and operational efficiencies. As an example, SDS manages important storage functions including information lifecycle management (ILM), disk caching, snapshots, replication, striping, and clustering. In a nutshell, these SDS capabilities enable you to put the right data in the right place, at the right time, with the right performance, and at the right cost automatically.

Unlike traditional storage systems such as SAN and NAS, SDS simplifies scale out with relatively inexpensive standard hardware, while continuing to manage storage as a single enterprise-class storage system. SDS typically refers to software that manages the capture, placement, protection, and retrieval of data. SDS is characterized by a separation of the storage hardware from the software that manages it. SDS is a key enabler modernizing traditional, monolithic, inflexible, costly and closed data centers toward software-defined data centers that are highly extensible, open, and cost-effective. The promise of SDS is that separating the software from the hardware enables enterprises to make storage hardware purchase, deployment, and operation independent from concerns about over or under-utilization or interoperability of storage resources.

Cloud-Based Big Data Storage: Object storage is the recent phenomenon. Object-based storage systems use containers/buckets to store data known as objects in a flat address space instead of the hierarchical, directory-based file systems that are common in the block and file-based storage systems. Non-structured and semi-structure data are encoded as objects and stored in containers. Typical data includes emails, pdf files, still and dynamic images, etc. Containers stores the associated metadata (date of creation, size, camera type, etc.) and the unique Object ID. The Object ID is stored in a database or application and is used to reference objects in one or more containers. The data in an object-based storage system is typically accessed using HTTP using a web browser or directly through an API like REST (representational state transfer). The flat address space in an object-based storage system enables simplicity and massive scalability. But the data in these systems can't be modified and every refresh gets stored as a new object. Object-based storage is predominantly used by cloud services providers (CSPs) to archive and backup their customers' data.

Analysts estimate that more than 2 million terabytes (or 2 Exabytes) of data are created every day. The range of applications that IT has to support today spans everything from social computing, big data analytics, mobile, enterprise and embedded applications, etc. All the data for all those applications has got to be made available to mobile and wearable devices and hence data storage acquires an indispensable status. As per the main findings of Cisco's global IP traffic forecast, in 2016, global IP traffic will reach 1.1 zettabytes per year or 91.3 exabytes (one billion gigabytes) per month, and by 2018, global IP traffic will reach 1.6 zettabytes per year or 131.9exabytes per month. IDC has predicted that cloud storage capacity will exceed 7 Exabytes in 2014, driven by strong demand for agile and capex-friendly deployment models. Furthermore, IDC had estimated that by 2015, big data workloads will be one of the fastest-growing contributors to storage in the cloud. In conjunction with these trends, meeting service-level agreements (SLAs) for the agreed performance is a top IT concern. As a result, enterprises will increasingly turn to flash-based SDS solutions to accelerate the performance significantly to meet up emerging storage needs.

The Key Characteristics of Software-Defined Storage (SDS)

SDS is characterized by several key architectural elements and capabilities that differentiate it from the traditional infrastructure.

- **Commodity Hardware**: With the extraction and centralization of all the intelligence embedded in storage and its associated systems in a specially crafted software layer, all kinds of storage solutions are bound to become cheap, dumb, off-the-shelf, and hence commoditized hardware elements. Not only the physical storage appliances but also all the interconnecting and intermediate fabric is to become commoditized. Such segregation goes a long way in centrally automating, activating, and adapting the full storage landscape.
- **Scale-Out Architecture**: Any SDS setup ought to have the capability of ensuring fluid, flexible and elastic configuration of storage resources through software. SDS facilitates the realization of storage as a dynamic pool of heterogeneous resources thereby the much-needed scale-out requirement can be easily met. The traditional architecture hinders the dynamic addition and release of storage resources due to the extreme dependency. For the software-defined cloud environments, storage scalability is essential to have a dynamic, highly optimized and virtual environment.

- **Resource Pooling**: The available storage resources are pooled into a unified logical entity that can be managed centrally. The control plane provides the fine-grained visibility and the control to all available resources in the system.
- **Abstraction**: Physical storage resources are increasingly virtualized and presented to the control plane, which can then configure and deliver them as tiered storage services.
- **Automation**: The storage layer brings in extensive automation that enables it to deliver one-click and policy-based provisioning of storage resources. Administrators and users request storage resources in terms of application need (capacity, performance, and reliability) rather than storage configurations such as RAID levels or physical location of drives. The system automatically configures and delivers storage as needed on the fly. It also monitors and reconfigures storage as required to continue to meet SLAs.
- **Programmability**: In addition to the inbuilt automation, the storage system offers fine-grained visibility and control of underlying resources via rich APIs that allows administrators and third-party applications to integrate the control plane across storage, network and compute layers to deliver workflow automation. The real power of SDS lies in the ability to integrate it with other layers of the infrastructure to build end-to-end application-focused automation.

The maturity of SDS is to quicken the process of setting up and sustaining software-defined environments for the tactic as well as the strategic benefits of cloud service providers as well as the consumers at large.

Software-Defined Cloud Environments vs Converged Infrastructure (CI): A converged infrastructure is typically a single box internally comprising all the right and relevant hardware (server machines, storage appliance, and network components) and software solutions. This is a being touted as a highly synchronized and optimized IT solution for faster application hosting and delivery. CI is an integrated approach towards data center optimization to substantially minimize the lingering compatibility issues between server, storage, and network components. This gains prominence because it is able to ultimately reduce the costs for cabling, cooling, power and floor space. CI, a renowned turnkey IT solution, also embeds the software modules for simplifying and streamlining all the management, automation and orchestration needs. In other words, CI is a kind of appliance specially crafted by a single vendor or by a combination of IT infrastructure vendors. For example, a server vendor establishes a kind of seamless linkage with storage and network product vendors to come out with new-generation CI solutions to speed up the process of IT infrastructure setup, activation, usage, and management.

Hyper-converged Infrastructure (HCI) is an extension of the proven CI approach for the highly visible cloud era. The CI vendor abstracts compute, networking, and storage resources from the physical hardware and bundles a virtualization software solution with their CI offerings. Hyper-converged vendors may also provide additional functionality for cloud bursting or disaster recovery and allow administrators to manage both physical and virtual infrastructures (on-premise or off-premise) in a federated manner with a single pane of glass. The CIs and HCIs

- Accelerate the time-to-market.
- Dramatically reduce downtime.
- Simplify IT and respond faster to business demands.
- Reduce your total cost of ownership

An SDCE expands this by providing abstraction, pooling, automation, and orchestration across product components from many vendors. This can leverage already running servers and other IT solutions resulting in higher return on investment.

Software-Defined Wide Area Networking (SD-WAN)

Application performance is very crucial for worldwide enterprises. There is a spurt in the number of applications being hosted in enterprise IT environments and applications are being relied upon for performing mission-critical functions. Networking plays a very vital role in shaping up the application performance. The public Internet is the mainstream communication technology and tool. MPLS is another popular but expensive networking solution for delivering highly reliable and faster connectivity for business automation.

The public Internet simply does not have the inherent wherewithal to support the global delivery of modern applications due to the unpredictable latency and congestion-based packet loss. The other prominent connectivity methods such as MPLS are not optimized for cloud service access. They are expensive and consume longer time to get deployed. As the cloud environments across the globe are being stuffed with SaaS applications to be delivered worldwide, the need for better alternatives surfaces and hence there is a surging popularity for SD-WAN that provides enterprise-grade connectivity and guarantees consistently fast performance for on-premises and SaaS-based applications, regardless of where they are located.

There are network providers and products such as Aryaka's Software-Defined Network Platform to ensure optimized, software-defined network connectivity and application acceleration to globally distributed enterprises. The key capabilities include the following.

- **SD-WAN Is a Kind of Global Private L2 Network:** This network is capable of bypassing the congested public Internet through a global private network (using an SDN/NFV framework) that delivers consistent latencies and negligible packet loss to provide predictable application performance to users.
- **TCP Optimization:** This software-defined network delivers end-to-end latency mitigation, packet loss mitigation, and enhanced congestion management that supercharges TCP applications for faster delivery.
- **Compression:** The SD-WAN solutions typically reduce the amount of data transferred across links using compression algorithms for higher throughput and faster application performance.
- **Deduplication:** This software solution eliminates the transmission of redundant data sent more than once over the network. This reduces bandwidth consumption up to 98% when transmitting data between locations and improves application performance.
- **SaaS Acceleration:** This specialized solution integrates cloud-hosted SaaS applications in a secure fashion. The attached application acceleration proxies in the SD-WAN solution could deliver up to 40x faster performance globally for cloud/SaaS applications.
- **Cloud Connectors:** There are multiple cloud service providers (CSPs) and the SD-WAN solution is stuffed with a number of connectors to facilitate private and dedicated connectivity to the leading public clouds such as IBM Bluemix, AWS, Azure and Google Clouds.

There are other features and functionalities being incorporated in the new-generation SD-WAN solutions in order to make the cloud idea more popular and pervasive.

The Key Benefits of Software-Defined Cloud Environments (SDCEs)

The new technologies have brought in highly discernible changes in how data centers are being operated to deliver both cloud-enabled and cloud-native applications as network services to worldwide subscribers. Here are a few important implications (business and technical) of SDCEs.

- **The consolidation and centralization** of commoditized, easy to use and maintain, and off-the-shelf server, storage, and network hardware solutions obviate the need for having highly specialized and expensive server, storage and networking components in IT environments. This cloud-inspired transition brings down the capital as well as operational costs sharply. The most important aspect is the introduction and incorporation of a variety of policy-aware automated tools in order to quickly provision, deploy, deliver and manage IT systems. There are other mechanisms such as templates, patterns, and domain-specific languages for automated IT setup and sustenance. Hardware components and application workloads are being provided with well-intended APIs in order to enable remote monitoring, measurement, and management of each of them. The APIs facilitate the system interoperability. The direct fallout here is that we can arrive at highly agile, adaptive, and affordable IT environments. The utilization of hardware resources and applications goes up significantly through sharing and automation. Multiple tenants and users can avail the IT facility comfortably for a cheaper price. The cloud technologies and their smart leverage ultimately ensure the system elasticity, availability, and security along with application scalability.
- **Faster Time to Value:** The notion of IT as a cost center is slowly disappearing and businesses across the globe have understood the strategic contributions of IT in ensuring the mandated business transformation. IT is being positioned as the most competitive differentiator for worldwide enterprises to be smartly steered in the right direction. However, there is an insistence for more with less as the IT budget is being consistently pruned every year. Thus enterprises started to embrace all kinds of proven and potential innovations and inventions in the IT space. That is, establishing data centers locally or acquiring the right and relevant IT capabilities from multiple cloud service providers (CSPs) are heavily simplified and accelerated. Further on, resource provisioning, application deployment, and service delivery are automated to a greater extent and hence it is easier and faster to realize the business value. In short, the IT agility being accrued through the cloud idea translates into business agility.
- **Affordable IT:** By expertly pooling and assigning resources, the SDCEs greatly maximize the utilization of the physical infrastructures. With enhanced utilization through automation and sharing, the cloud center brings down the IT costs remarkably while enhancing the business productivity. The operational costs come down due to tools-supported IT automation, augmentation, and acceleration.
- **Eliminating Vendor Lock-In:** Today's data center features an amazing array of custom hardware for storage and networking requirements such as routers, switches, firewall appliances, VPN concentrators, application delivery controllers (ADCs), storage controllers, intrusion detection

and prevention components. With the storage and network virtualization, the above functions are performed by software running on commodity x86 servers. Instead of being locked into the vendor's hardware, IT managers can buy commodity servers in quantity and use them for running the network and storage controlling software. With this transition, the perpetual vendor lock-in issue gets simply solved and surmounted. The modifying source code is quite easy and fast, policies can be established and enforced, software-based activation and acceleration of IT network and storage solutions are found to be simple, supple and smart, etc.

- **Less Human Intervention and Interpretation:** SDCEs are commoditized and compartmentalized through abstraction, virtualization, and containerization mechanisms. As accentuated above, there are infrastructure management platforms, integration, and orchestration engines, integrated brokerage services, configuration, deployment and delivery systems, service integration and management solutions, etc. in order to bring in deeper and decisive automation. That is, hitherto manually performed tasks are getting automated through toolsets. This enablement sharply lessens the workloads of the system, storage, and service administrators. All kinds of routine, redundant and repetitive tasks are getting automated on a priority basis. The IT experts, therefore, can focus on their technical expertise to come up with a series of innovations and inventions that subsequently facilitate heightened business resiliency and robustness.

- **Hosting a Range of Applications:** All kinds of operational, transactional, and analytical workloads can be run on SDCEs, which is emerging as the comprehensive yet compact and cognitive IT infrastructure to ensure business operations at the top speed, scale, and sagacity. Business continuity, backup and archival, data and disaster recovery, high availability, and fault tolerance are the other critical requirements that can be easily fulfilled by SDCEs. As we expectantly move into the era of big data, real-time analytics, mobility, cognitive computing, social networking, webscale systems, the Internet of Things (IoT), artificial intelligence, deep learning, etc., the SDCEs are bound to play a very stellar and sparkling role in the days ahead.

- **Distributed Deployment and Centralized Management:** IT resources and business applications are being extremely distributed these days by giving considerations for cost, location, performance, risk, etc. However, a 360-degree view through a single pane of glass is required in order to have a firm and fine grip on each of the assets and applications. The centralized monitoring, measurement, and management is the most sought-after feature for any SDCE. The highly synchronized and unified management of various data center resources is getting fulfilled through SDCE capabilities.

- **Streamlined Resource Provisioning and Software Deployment:** There are orchestration tools for systematic and swift provisioning of servers, storages, and network components. As each resource is blessed with RESTful or other APIs, the resource provisioning and management become simpler. Policies are the other important ingredient in SDCEs in order to have intelligent operations. As we all know, there are several configuration management tools and in the recent past, with the culture of DevOps spreads widens overwhelmingly, there are automated software deployment solutions. Primarily orchestration platforms are for infrastructure, middleware, and database installation whereas software deployment tools take care of application installation.

- **Containerized Platforms and Workloads:** With the unprecedented acceptance of Docker-enabled containerization and with the growing Docker ecosystem, there is a wave of containerization across the data centers and their operations. Packaged, home-grown, customized, and off-the-shelf business applications are being containerized, IT platforms, database systems, and middleware are getting containerized through the open source Docker platform and IT infrastructures are increasingly presented as a dynamic pool of containers. Thus, SDCEs are the most appropriate one for containerized workloads and infrastructures.
- **Adaptive Networks:** As inscribed above, an SDCE comprises network virtualization that in turn guarantees network function virtualization (NFC) and software-defined networking (SDN). Network bandwidth resource can be provisioned and provided on demand as per the application requirement. Managing networking solutions such as switches and routers remains a challenging assignment for data center operators. In an SDC, all network hardware in the data center is responsive to a centralized controlling authority, which automates network provisioning based on defined policies and rules. A dynamic pool of network resources comes handy in fulfilling any varying network requirements.
- **Software-Defined Security:** Cloud security has been a challenge for cloud center professionals. Hosting mission-critical applications and storing customer, confidential, and corporate information on cloud environments are still a risky affair. Software-defined security is emerging as the viable and venerable proposition for ensuring unbreakable and impenetrable security for IT assets, business workloads and data sources. Policy-based management, the crux of software-defined security, is able to ensure the much-required compliance with security policies and principles. SDCE is innately stuffed with software-defined security capabilities.
- **Green Computing:** SDCEs enhance resource utilization through workload consolidation and optimization, VM placement, workflow scheduling, dynamic capacity planning, and management. Energy-awareness is being insisted as the most vital parameter for SDCEs. When the electricity consumption goes down, the heat dissipation too goes down remarkably thereby the goal of green and lean computing gets fulfilled. This results in environment sustainability through reduced release of harmful greenhouse gasses.

In summary, applications that once ran on static, monolithic and dedicated servers are today hosted in software-defined, policy-aware, consolidated, virtualized, automated and shared IT environments that can be scaled and shaped to meet brewing demands dynamically. Resource allocation requests that took days and weeks to fulfill now can be accomplished in hours or even in minutes. Virtualization and containerization have empowered data center operations, enabling enterprises to deploy commoditized and compartmentalized servers, storages and network solutions that can be readily pooled and allocated to fast-shifting application demand.

On concluding, an SDCE delivers two prominent outcomes. Firstly, it enables businesses to shift their time, treasure and talent towards innovation and growth by encapsulating agility, adaptivity, and efficiency into IT offerings and operations.

CONCLUSION

The aspect of IT optimization is continuously getting rapt and apt attention from technology leaders and luminaries across the globe. A number of generic, as well as specific improvisations, are being brought in to make IT aware and adaptive. The cloud paradigm is being touted as the game-changer in empowering and elevating IT to the desired heights. There have been notable achievements in making IT being the core and cost-effective enabler of both personal as well as professional activities. There are definite improvements in business automation, acceleration, and augmentation. Still, there are opportunities and possibilities waiting for IT to move up further.

The pioneering virtualization technology is being taken to every kind of infrastructures such as networking and storage to complete the IT ecosystem. The abstraction and decoupling techniques are lavishly utilized here in order to bring in the necessary malleability, extensibility, and serviceability. That is, all the configuration and operational functionalities hitherto embedded inside hardware components are now neatly identified, extracted and centralized and implemented as a separate software controller. That is, the embedded intelligence is being developed now as a self-contained entity so that hardware components could be commoditized. Thus, the software-defined computing, networking, and storage disciplines have become the hot topic for discussion and dissertation. The journey of data centers (DCs) to software-defined cloud environments (SDCEs) is being pursued with vigor and rigor. In this chapter, we have primarily focused on the industry mechanism for capturing and collecting requirements details from clients.

Chapter 2
Impact of Cloud of Clouds in Enterprises Applications

Lavanya S.
Sri Krishna College of Engineering and Technology, India

Susila N.
Sri Krishna College of Engineering and Technology, India

Venkatachalam K.
Sri Krishna College of Engineering and Technology, India

ABSTRACT

In recent times, the cloud has become a leading technology demanding its functionality in every business. According to research firm IDC and Gartner study, nearly one-third of the worldwide enterprise application market will be SaaS-based by 2018, driving annual SaaS revenue to $50.8 billion, from $22.6 billion in 2013. Downtime is treated as the primary drawback which may affect great deals in businesses. The service unavailability leads to a major disruption affecting the business environment. Hence, utmost care should be taken to scale the availability of services. As cloud computing has plenty of uncertainty with respect to network bandwidth and resources accessibility, delegating the computing resources as services should be scheduled accordingly. This chapter proposes a study on cloud of clouds and its impact on a business enterprise. It is also decided to propose a suitable scheduling algorithm to the cloud of cloud environment so as to trim the downtime problem faced by the cloud computing environment.

INTRODUCTION

In today's digital world, being technology driven, cloud computing plays vital role in E-commerce, etc. Task scheduling is the primary concern to achieve high performance in distributed systems such as cloud computing, grid computing, utility computing and peer to peer computing. There are several researchers concentrated on improving the task of resource scheduling to enhance output of cloud computing. Almost all the researchers enhanced the cost, waiting time, make span, resource utilization, execution time, and round trip time. Load balancing on cloud computing has attracted many researchers. cloud

DOI: 10.4018/978-1-5225-9023-1.ch002

opens up challenging issues in terms of downtime of the cloud providers that an enterprise interact with and to deliver its service to business environment.

RELATED WORK

There are two ways of computing namely heterogeneous distributed computing systems and homogenous distributed computing systems approaches are used in design of distributed systems. In addition to server heterogeneity, depending on the basic applications, outstanding burden spreading over numerous cloud clients may require tremendously unique measure of resources (CPU, memory and capacity). The heterogeneity of the two servers and remaining burden requests noteworthy specialized difficulties on resource assignment, decreasing down time and numerous sensitive issues. This paper represents thorough investigation to propose solution provable advantages that cross over any barrier between resource request and downtime decrease models.

In recent year, the new buzz word called "downtime" has become more popular in the world of business. The downtime is the biggest challenge of cloud migration followed by staying within budget, performance disruption, data loss, and security requirements.

According to recent studies, downtime costs businesses an average of $7,900 per minute, or more than $450,000 per hour, and costs all businesses in North America $700 billion every year. Data loss, meanwhile, is estimated to cost US businesses $18.2 billion per year, and enterprises around the world $1.7 trillion per year. The cloud leads a long way in reducing downtime and keeping companies online in which application downtime is costing enterprises across the globe an estimated $16 million (approximately £12.9 million) annually.

Enterprise Strategy Group (ESG) research indicated that 46% of organisations say that, in 2016, they have a "problematic shortage" of cyber security skills. Based on these figures, incident detection and responses to cloud-based cyber threats would undoubtedly be a problem for those organisations, as they have inadequate staff available to manage any cyber security risks that may arise.

The risk that every organization meets is a big challenge when encountered downtime. So why is "downtime" meant to be prioritized and important to any organization?

- **Downtime reduces productivity**. Every hour down is an hour you cannot help a client.
- **Downtime has the potential for lost data**. IT system crashes can cause data loss.
- **Downtime affects overall IT efficiency**. If one of your systems goes down, generally everything is affected
- **Downtime can result in lost productivity, lost sales, and lost customers**. It can be especially expensive and disruptive if the asset or service is relied upon by many employees or customers, such as a CRM, PoS system, or e-commerce system. Data loss can be expensive and disruptive, too, depending on what type of data is involved. Data that can be expensive to lose includes:
  - Internal documentation (training manuals, policies and procedures, etc.)
  - Sales and marketing documents
  - Financial records
  - Customer records
  - IT settings files
  - IT logs

- Product designs/blueprints
- Internally-developed code

Consequences of data loss include wasting all the time and effort that went into the creation of the data, investing more time and effort in recreating the data, productivity loss as a result of employees not having all of the data necessary to do their jobs, upset and/or lost customers due to the delays or inconveniences caused by the data loss, and lawsuits, fines, and/or criminal prosecution for the loss of sensitive data such as financial records, customers' personal information, and healthcare patient records.

So how can businesses reap the benefits of the cloud while minimizing the risk of downtime?. There are numerous ways to find out and to minimize downtime and create a more productive business environment.

1. Capitalize in the right solutions
2. Engage a proactive managed service provider
3. Have a disaster recovery and backup strategy
4. Appropriate redundancy
5. Better IT systems
6. Server Failovers
7. Security
8. Reliability
9. Mobility
10. Fast, Flexible Environment
11. Ensure ongoing monitoring
12. Load Balancing and Resource Scheduling

Capitalize in the Right Solutions

The best way is to choose the right solution for your organization as a smart decision in prior that will minimize downtime in the long run.

Engage a Managed Services Provider That Is Proactive

A Managed Services Provider (MSP) who proactively monitors your systems will minimize downtime. MSPs charges any user to have a flat monthly fee in which it runs IT systems smoothly and limiting problems unlike traditional ad hoc IT providers where you pay by the hour. This seems to be highly great because you can pass on all your IT responsibilities to them since they are charging a flat fee. It minimizes problems in IT and increase IT efficiency for the smooth running of business.

Have a Disaster Recovery and Backup Strategy

The next best way to minimize downtime is to make a plan for disaster recovery and backup solution. For instance, an organization's IT facility gets impacted, they must have a necessary plan for how to access their own data. A best sort of service named as "disaster recovery as a service (DRaaS)" used by the businesses to have an advantage of being able to access their backups from anywhere, even if their primary facility has been affected. As capacity grows, they have the potential to leverage various cloud models depending on the use case.

When recovery is necessary, stored data can be restored to either virtual or physical machines. The limited bandwidth can extend recovery times especially when recovering a large amount of data and applications. Hence, many businesses are complementing cloud backups with an on-site storage appliance, which allows data to be recovered within hours or even minutes. These recovered data would require either accessing an alternate backup stored at an off-site location or waiting until the business regains access to the facility, assuming it's still intact.

A research towards hybrid approach to disaster recovery reduces the overall risk of downtime with the right support. The key for client is to know upfront what level of support the vendor can provide and plan accordingly.

- Do we have any solution that can recover data in the event of a system failure?
- How to deal with backups of your data?
- How are you doing that?

These are the main questions one should ask IT firm to make sure that the systems are in place to manage and handle these unforeseeable circumstances. There are two main services available to make sure about the appropriate Disaster Recovery namely Recovery Point Objective (RPO) and Recovery Time Objective (RTO).

Importance of Having Disaster Recovery Plans

It is the responsibility of any Business Continuity department to provide them with a source of income. The loss of customer data or other events that could impact on their online presence could affect these income flows greatly. There are several crucial factors needs to be considered to make effective DR includes

- **Maximum Tolerable Downtime (MTD):** This is the amount of downtime a business can cope with before the impact of the downtime will be sustained and more long term
- **Recovery Time Objective (RTO):** The RTO is the amount of time in which a business should be able to restore its systems to a point that will allow it to carry out the impacted operations, even if this is in a limited function
- **Recovery Point Objective (RPO):** This is the point to which a business can cope with data loss; as every business has their own backup routines with some having constant synchronization in place and others with daily, weekly and month backups, data loss could occur when a DS solution has to be implemented to its full effect.

Recovery Speed is also plays one of the best role in cloud. Always cloud businesses need access their data with a low-latency network and need fast data recovery which is an exciting part in online. Seriously, we're talking milliseconds standing between you and your data. These latency speeds become important in the event of a disaster as you fight to get your business back online before serious loss of time and revenue. The cloud makes it easy to define Recovery Time Objectives (RTO), giving you more control over downtime

Know the Ins and Outs

Keep a record of logging activities, dependencies and mission critical controls in your cloud contingency plan. If you're not aware of what is running in the cloud, you may have a hard time putting things back together in case of server outage, or taking your operations to another data center if your data is stored in multiple locations and one of the data centers go down. If your company is heavily dependent on the cloud for mission-critical data and key services, you need to create a road map containing core operations and the order of downtime recovery. In some cases, minimizing downtime and continuing functions may not need the entire data to be recovered during a cloud outage. However, knowing what to recover, and in the right order, will always be critical to save effort and time in case of an outage.

Evaluate the Risks

The task of performing risks analysis is to evaluate the risks of your organization in the event of a server outage. In such case, have key aspects that need to be addressed as given below Determine the operational assets of your organization. What are the chances that your business might suffer a downtime? How will an outage impact your organization's bottom line? What plans do you have in place to bring down or predict the downtime?

REDUNDANCY

- What do you have in place if suddenly your servers crash?
- What about if your internet goes down?
- Do you have a backup connection?

To answer the above, we need redundancy plans to ensure that if something does go down. Redundancy describes computer or network system components that are installed to ensure that there is at least one extra unit of each important aspect of your IT than is necessary for your IT to function normally (i.e., In simple words, have a backup of secondary resources in case they primary resource fail). Some examples of redundancies include:

1. Backing up your data
2. Purchasing spare hardware (including PCs, keyboards, mice, monitors, routers, switches, servers, and storage devices), and either keeping them close at hand so you can quickly replace failed hardware with them, or integrating them into a fault-tolerant architecture so that IT workloads are automatically transferred to them after the other hardware fails
3. Signing up for and maintaining Internet access with two or more Internet service providers (ISPs) at the same time
4. Signing up for electrical power from two or more different power companies at the same time
5. Purchasing, installing, and maintaining uninterruptible power supplies (UPSs) and diesel backup generators

These redundancies ensure that even if an important component of your IT fails, you will be able quickly to replace it with an identical component, minimizing your downtime; or your IT will be able to switch over to the backup component immediately and automatically, which will prevent downtime altogether.

Better IT Systems Will Minimize Downtime

Encountering downtime because of slow IT systems is also a major challenge in the production environment. It affects the whole team's productivity. Hence, make sure that you are intact with IT firm about the right solutions to minimize downtime and to value your staff's productivity. Can you afford to be down more than three hours every month? How much wills that cost your organization in productivity. So, Choose a best IT systems to improve productivity and to minimize downtime

How Server Failovers Remove Downtime

Modern data and application servers are virtualized systems that reside on a virtualized enterprise server. The physical servers may be in one or many locations, but their physical location has little relevance to the failover system that ensures uptime. The three main providers of virtualization software are VMware, OpenStack and Microsoft.

Each has failover features that allow the simultaneous synchronizing of data and applications from one virtual server to another. The decision to switch from one active system to an exact mirror takes place when network-monitoring tools identify a possible issue with your IT. Network monitors and indicators can identify a problem before your systems go down and this enables your failover device to kick-in and prevent downtime.

Many be spoke IT solutions include failover systems as a feature or benefit because they are essential for mission-critical services. Your data solutions provider should be able to demonstrate how they use instant failover systems to ensure your data availability.

Security

Your company's data is very important to your business and needs to be protected at all times. Despite the fact that you do not own or control the systems storing your data, you are actually in better hands, security wise, within the cloud. The cloud offers controlled access, strong perimeters, and surveillance systems to ensure the safety of your data. As such, businesses might require a managed firewall service that can keep their network secure while freeing up their staff to focus on day-to-day responsibilities. Different organizations will require different levels of support, but one advantage of a cloud-based firewall service is that it is scalable and can be changed to meet ever-increasing demand and usage, both now and into the future.

Regardless of whether cyber security is managed in-house or outsourced, it should feature advanced security capabilities such as intrusion detection and prevention, and a safe tunnel for remote employee access. On top of this, you get top cyber security expertise that ensures thorough and frequent audits, to continually make the security system stronger. With the prevalence of cyber attacks on the rise, it is no longer wise to have only one copy of your data, let alone to keep that copy on premises. The cloud works to ensure the security of your business critical data, even in the event of a cyber-attack.

Reliability

When selecting a cloud service provider, it is important to make sure they are reliable and have employed redundant solutions to ensure high availability. If your provider's main system goes down, it should have the following safety nets in place: automatic failover, servers, backup storage, security systems, and some sort of redundancy of power (i.e a generator). These safety nets increase SLA percentages, which lower the chances of the cloud provider, and ultimately you, experiencing downtime. For this reason, service providers are fighting to add an extra 9 to the end of their SLA percent (99.99999%), just to stay competitive.

Mobility

The cloud gives you the ability to access your data from anywhere in the world, at any time. This mobile benefit is enabling many global businesses to stay connected from around the world. It also allows employees to work remotely if needed. Additionally, by hosting your data in a cloud environment, as opposed to building your own infrastructure, your business is not confined to the office. If you outgrow your current building, or want to move to another location, the headache is significantly reduced.

Fast, Flexible Environment

The cloud offers users a dynamic environment to perform tests and work on development, as well as offers solutions for backup and disaster recovery. With the flexibility of the cloud, businesses have many options when deploying a cloud environment, including the ability to scale environments up or down to suit data needs. With the capacity for growth and the numerous possibilities for provsioning, the cloud helps businesses stay online by reducing the time it takes to deploy new environments. During a time when outages can mean huge financial loss for businesses, the cloud offers a competitive advantage by ensuring maximum uptime. For companies looking for high availability at an affordable price, the cloud is a great option, as it does not require extensive investment in infrastructure.

Ensure Ongoing Monitoring

Even if a business has invested in top-of-the-line cybersecurity solutions and backed up data to multiple targets, the organisation still risks downtime if the entire environment isn't properly monitored. To assess whether or not a business has the resources required for adequate oversight of the environment, it should consider the following questions:

Is there any period of time when the environment is unmonitored (e.g. during shift changes or holidays)?

Do any on-site IT personnel lack the skills required to manage software settings, remediate failures, and so on?

When considering past downtime events or security threats, were the systems always brought online or the threats mitigated within the required time frame?

The greater the number of yes responses, the greater the risk of downtime. Some businesses might indeed have the resources required for ongoing monitoring. For those that don't, it is worth considering outsourcing cyber security monitoring and DRaaS. Vendors offering these services should provide service level agreements (SLAs), 24/7/365 support and the services of qualified engineers.

Cloud computing offers the potential for greater business agility, but unless a business has the right support, it is all but guaranteed to experience downtime.

Load Balancing Also Reduces Downtime

Server crashes become a common issue in cloud environment and it is manageable now by using load balancing. You can now stop your servers from grinding to a halt by spreading the demand for compute and storage I/O over multiple servers. Recent days, your business' busiest times are manageable by load balancing that activates when your business needs to call on more processing power. This is possible, only because of availability of the excess processing power from other virtual machine instances in cloud. It's easy to spin up extra virtual machines in minutes or even scale up the processor cores to existing setup when your applications demand is more with the help of load balancing technology. Disposing of the extra compute is just as easy and gives you the opportunity to spend only what you need and limit hardware redundancy.

The survey behind all the researchers is to ensure effective utilization of each resource in a cloud. Out of many researches done, load balancing and resource scheduling plays a major role in reducing "downtime". Hence, the following algorithms ensure minimum downtime and make the business environment to hold strong business continuity.

SURVEY ON SCHEDULING ALGORITHMS IN CLOUD COMPUTING

Harshil Mehta (2017) et al, use Hidden Markov Model (HMM) model to resource monitoring and resource will be classified based on less, average and heavily loaded categories available. Based on availability appropriate scheduling algorithm will be selected on demand. For the better utilization of resources, resources classifier has been developed and classified.

Cloud resources such as virtualized and physical resources along with CPU, memeory and storage resources are managed and aggregated by data center. The scheduler analysis these resources and determine to which VM task to be assigned and assigns every task. Gobalakrishnan (2018) et al, proposed mean grey wolf optimization algorithm to schedule the task in cloud environment to optimize execution time and energy consumption. The proposed mean GWO algorithm has been evaluated using CloudSim toolkit for standard workload. It outperforms than other existing algorithm.

Many existing works limit their discussion to allocation of resource from either single data center or single type server such as CPU, memory, storage and bandwidth etc. Wei Wang (2015) et al, proposed multi-resource allocation mechanisms Dominant Resource Fairness called (DRFH). Multi-resource allocation constructed from large number of heterogeneous servers, represting different configuration space of resources such as processing, memory and storage. Proposed method analyzes DRFH and show that it retains almost. all desirable properties that DRF provides in the single-server Scenario. Best-Fit heuristic that implements DRFH in a real-world system. Our large-scale simulations Driven by Google cluster traces show that, compared to the traditional single-resource abstraction such as a slot scheduler, DRFH achieves significant improvements in resource utilization, leading to much shorter job completion times.

The main objective of this research paper is discussed how to achieve effective load balance, how to schedule the resources and how to improve resource utility in cloud computing. prabhjot kaur et ai (2015) discussed how to achieve load balance, how to schedule the resources and how to improve resource utility in cloud computing. Workload can be considered in terms of CPU load, Network load, delay and amount of memory used. Most common load balancing algorithms are Active monitoring, Throttled load balancer and Round Robin Algorithm. Proposed algorithm achieves both green computing and overload avoidance for system with multi resource constraint.

The existing deadline-constraint Map Reduce scheduling schemes do no not consider the following two problems: various node performance and dynamic task execution time. Chien-Hung (2018) et al, used the Bipartite Graph modeling to propose the new MapReduce scheduler called BGMRS. The proposed BGMRS can obtain the optimal solution of deadline constraint scheduling problem by transforming the problem into well known graph problem. BGMRS problem can be optimally solved by Integer Linear Programming [ILP]. BGMRS supports heterogeneous cloud computing environment and also it can minimize the number of jobs with the deadline violation. Finally both simulation and testbed experiments are performed to demonstrate the effectiveness of BGMRS in the deadline-constraint scheduling.

Resources in cloud environment are constraint. Hence it is not easy to deploy different applications with unpredictable limits and functionalities in heterogeneous cloud environment. Phani Praveen (2018) et al, have proposed two phases such as allocation of resources and scheduling of task. Effective resource allocation is proposed using social group optimization algorithm and scheduling of task using shortest job first scheduling algorithm for minimizing the makespan time and maximizing throughput. Experimental results are compared with first-in, first-out and genetic algorithm based shortest job scheduling. Proposed method gives improved performance of the system in provisions of makespan time and throughput.

Sanjaya (2015) et al, proposed allocation aware task scheduling algorithm for multi cloud environment. it minimized overall execution time. the experimental results has been compared with two multicloud task scheduling algorithms such as RR and CLS. Proposed algorithm results show superiority over existing algorithms in terms of makespan and average cloud utilization

Task scheduling problems are a typical NP-hard problem. Dynamic task scheduling algorithms are ant colony optimization (ACO), is appropriate for clouds. ACO can be used to solve many NP hard problems as traveling salesman problem graph coloring problem vehicle Routing and scheduling problems. Qiang Guo et al (2013) proposed a Multi-objective Optimization Algorithm for Cloud Computing Task Scheduling Based on Improved Ant Colony Algorithm (MO-ACO) to find the optimal resource allocation for each task in the dynamic cloud System which minimizes the makespan and costs of tasks on the entire system, and balance the entire system load. Then, this scheduling strategy was simulated using the Cloudsim toolkit package. Experimental results compared to Ant Colony Optimization (ACO) and Min-Min showed the MO-ACO algorithm satisfies expectation.

SURVEY ON LOAD BALANCING ALGORITHMS IN CLOUD COMPUTING

Load balancing is a vital piece of distributed computing condition which guarantees that all device or processors perform same measure of work in equivalent measure of time. Distinctive models and algorithm for load adjusting in cloud computing has been created with the mean to make cloud assets open to the end clients effortlessly and comfort. Sidra Aslam (2015) et al,discussed about different organized and complete outline of load balancing algorithms. Number of work have been done to balance the load so as to enhance execution time and maintain a strategic distance from over usage of resources. Different load balancing algorithms have been examined including round robin (RR), Min-Min, Max-Min and so forth. Load balancing algorithms are partitioned in two fundamental classifications, to be specific static and dynamic. There are various load balancing algorithms are available in cloud computing namely round robin (RR), Min-Min, Max-Min, Ant settlement, Carton, Honey bee were discussed. The imperative of this paper is examination of various algorithms and considering the attributes like reasonableness, throughput, blame resistance, overhead, execution, and reaction time and resource use to show better performance. The research issue needs to be addressed is to utilize the crossover way to deal with better execution and ensure secure environment.

Reena Panwar (2016) et al, proposed a dynamic load balancing algorithms for the distribution of whole approaching solicitation among the virtual machines viably. The execution time is minimized by utilizing CloudAnlyst test system which is dependent on different parameter like data processing time and response time. The proposed algorithm simulated and exhibition has appropriated load consistently among server.

Enhancing response time for user request on cloud is a basic issue to battle bottlenecks. As for as the cloud computing concern, transfer speed of to/from cloud service providers is a bottleneck. Nguyen (2018) et al, proposed Throttled Modified Algorithm (TMA) for improving response time of VMs on cloud computing to improve the performance of end users. TMA effectively manages the load and out-performed than round robin and Throttled Algorithms

One of the real difficulties faced in cloud is proficient dispersion of resources for serving a great many client request in less time. Distribution of workloads across multiple computing resources known as Load balancing which are used in cloud in order to serve the demand from customer in profitable way. Sukhpal (2016) et al,proposed balance load on cloud based on arrangement of resource, according to speed of virtual machines and dispensing resources to their processing requirements. The proposed method has attempted to balance the load by orchestrating the virtual machines based on their handling force and organizing the cloudlets as indicated by their Length.

Zhang (2017) et al, proposed a load balancing system for cloud platform that utilizes threshold window strategy and advanced AR prediction model to diminish the movement of VMs. Investigations demonstrate that this technique can successfully accomplish load balancing, advance the usage of the physical machines, and take care of the frequent migration issue caused by high instantaneous peak values essentially.

CONCLUSION

The survey has led to the few findings on how to ensure high availability and business continuity using different measures. To pour salt on the wound, down applications can mean losing users and customers. These days, users seem more likely to quickly switch to a competitor's app instead of waiting out an outage. This means a single, unplanned application failure could not only cost your organization tens of thousands of dollars per minute, but also the loss of future potential sales or revenues. Customer loyalty shifts quickly. 1) MINMAX scheduling algorithm outperform then all other algorithm with respect given task. 2) The Execution time, throughput, make span, memory utilization were used as performance metrics in the existing systems. 3) This paper presents a new proposal that the best way to reduce the potential

Table 1. Survey on various scheduling algorithms

S.No	Name of Technique	Objective	Parameters Used	Standard Scheduling	Outcome
1	Efficient Resource Scheduling in Cloud Computing	For better utilization of Resource, Resource classifier is developed based upon the usage pattern Different algorithm can be classified for different scenarios	Execution Time	FCFS, MCT, MINMIN, MAXMIN, RR, DATA AWARE	In the proposed model MINMAX outperform then all other algorithm with respect given task.
2	Task scheduling in heterogeneous cloud environment using mean grey wolf optimization algorithm	Optimize the execution time and energy consumption by proposed method	Execution Time, Energy Consumption(KWH)	Genetic Algorithm (GA), Particle Swarm Optimization (PSO), Grey Wolf Optimization (GWO)	Proposed mean-GWO are Better in comparison with PSO and standard GWO.
3	Multi-Resource Fair Allocation in Heterogeneous Cloud Computing Systems	Proposed method analyzes DRFH and show that it retains almost all desirable properties that DRF provides in the single-server Scenario. DRFH achieves significant improvements in resource utilization, leading to much shorter job completion times.	CPU Utilization, Memory Utilization, Job Size, Execution Time	Dominant Resource Fairness (DRF), Dominant Resource Fairness heterogeneous (DRFH)	DRFH achieves significant improvements in resource utilization, Leading too much shorter job completion times.
4	Energy Efficient Resource Allocation for Heterogeneous Cloud Workloads	a)heterogeneous workload and its implication on data center's energy efficiency b) solving the problem of VM resource scheduling to cloud applications.		Common load balancing algorithms are 1)Active monitoring, 2)Throttled load balancer and 3)Round Robin Algorithm	Proposed algorithm achieves both green computing and overload avoidance for system with multi resource constraint.
5	MapReduce Scheduling for Deadline-Constrained Jobs in Heterogeneous Cloud Computing Systems	The proposed BGMRS can obtain the optimal solution of deadline constraint scheduling problem by transforming the problem into well known graph problem. BGMRS problem can be optimally solved by Integer Linear Programming [ILP]	Proposed Scheduling Algorithm, Consider Four Metrics Such As Job Elapsed Time Deadline Over Job Ratio Overtime Ratio Algorithm Computational Time	used the Bipartite Graph modeling to propose the new Map Reduce scheduler called BGMRS	The proposed BGMRS can obtain the optimal solution of deadline constraint scheduling problem
6	Effective Allocation of Resources and Task Scheduling in Cloud Environment using Social Group Optimization	Effective resource allocation is proposed using social group optimization algorithm and scheduling of task using shortest job first scheduling algorithm for minimizing the makespan time and maximizing throughput	Makespan Time And Throughput.	Resource allocation is proposed using social group optimization algorithm and scheduling of task using shortest job first scheduling algorithm	Experimental results are compared with first-in, first-out and genetic algorithm based Shortest-job-first scheduling. The proposed method gives improved performance of system in provisions of makespan and throughput.
7	Allocation Aware Task Scheduling for Heterogeneous Multi Cloud systems	Allocation aware task scheduling (ATS) algorithm for heterogeneous multi cloud systems. It reduces overall completion time. i.e. makespan time is minimized	Make Span	Allocation aware task scheduling algorithm for heterogeneous multicloud systems	The proposed allocation aware task scheduling for heterogeneous multicloud systems outperforms both the algorithms in terms of makespan and average cloud utilization.

impact of a problem is to ensure good and strong IT resources with proper cloud technologies which have been discussed above and keep maintaining applications at peak performance. Application performance management (APM) enables you to proactively monitor business applications to continuously deliver optimal availability and performance. Organizations that incorporate robust APM already have an edge when it comes to application availability. Hence, a new approach hybrid methodology where inbuilt load balancing, cyber security and APM will enhance business continuity with negligible downtime.

REFERENCES

Aslam & Shah. (2015). Load Balancing Algorithms in Cloud Computing A Survey of Modern Techniques. In *National Software Engineering Conference (NSEC 2015)*. IEEE Xplore.

Chen, C.-H. (2018). MapReduce Scheduling for Deadline-Constrained Jobs in Heterogeneous Cloud Computing Systems. *IEEE Transaction on Cloud Computing*.

Guo, Q. (2013). Task Scheduling Based on Ant Colony Optimization in Cloud Environment. *8th International Conference on Computer Engineering and Systems (ICCES)*.

Kaur & Kaur. (2015). Energy Efficient Resource Allocation for Heterogeneous Cloud Workloads. In *2nd International Conference on Computing for Sustainable Global Development (INDIA COM)*. IEEE Xplore.

Mehta, Prasad., & Bhavsar. (2017). Efficient Resource Scheduling in Cloud Computing. *International Journal of Advanced Research in Computer Science, 18*.

Natesan & Chokkalingam. (2018). *Task scheduling in heterogeneous cloud environment using mean grey wolf optimization algorithm.* The Korean Institute of Communications and Information Sciences (KICS), publishing services by Elsevier.

Panda, Gupta, & Prasanta.(2015). Allocation Aware Task Scheduling for Heterogeneous Multi Cloud Systems. *2nd International Symposium on Big Data and Cloud Computing Procedia Computer Science*, 50.

Panwar & Mallick. (2016). Load Balancing in Cloud Computing Using Dynamic Load Management Algorithm. In *International Conference on Green Computing and Internet of Things (ICGCIoT)*. IEEE Xplore.

Phi, Tin, Nguyen, & Hung. (2018). Proposed Load Balancing Algorithm to Reduce response time and processing time on cloud computing. *International Journal of Computer Networks and Communications, 10*.

Praveen, P., Rao, K. T., & Janakiramaiah, B. (2018). Effective Allocation of Resources and Task Scheduling in Cloud Environment using Social Group Optimization. *Arabian Journal for Science and Engineering, 43*(8), 4265–4272. doi:10.100713369-017-2926-z

Sidana & Tiwari. (2017). NBST Algorithm: A load balancing algorithm in Cloud computing. In *International Conference on Computing, Communication and Automation (ICCCA2016)*. IEEE Xplore.

Singh, S., & Chana, I. (2016). A Survey on Resource Scheduling in Cloud Computing Issues and Challenges. *Journal of Grid Computing, 14*(2), 217–264. doi:10.100710723-015-9359-2

Wang, W., Liang, B., & Li, B. (2015). Multi-Resource Fair Allocation in Heterogeneous Cloud Computing Systems. *IEEE Transactions on Parallel and Distributed Systems*, *26*(10), 2822–2835. doi:10.1109/TPDS.2014.2362139

Zhang, Liu, & Chen.(2017). An Advanced Load Balancing Strategy for cloud Environment. *17th International Conference on Parallel and Distributed Computing, Applications and Technologies.*

Chapter 3
Role of Cloud Computing in On–Line Social Networking and In–Depth Analysis of Cloud–Sim Simulator

Suresh Annamalai
Nehru Institute of Engineering and Technology, India

Udendhran R.
Bharathidasan University, India

ABSTRACT

In this chapter, the authors introduced cloudsim simulator and cloud computing role in online social networking. The communication incurred by other activities such as management jobs is negligible. Social relationships can be established for numerous reasons. For example, family members, colleagues, or classmates often have strong social interactions resulting in large communication load. Cloud computing as well as social network-based applications will become dominant in many aspects of life in the next few decades. The performance of such large-scale systems is characterized by system capacity in terms of number of users/clients, flexibility, scalability, and effective cost of operation, etc. Popular social networks have hundreds of millions of users and continue to grow.

A BRIEF INTRODUCTION TO ON-LINE SOCIAL NETWORKING

For the purpose of proper understanding in this chapter, an on-line social network application is defined as a system in which communication load is generated mostly by the interactions or social relationships among users or clients. There is no single server or even cluster (a group of servers) can handle such large amount of data. These social networking applications are served by datacenters which consist of hundreds of thousands or even more than one million networked servers in total. The goals of resource allocation problems are to decide how resources are allocated to deliver specific services or to process computation requirements of clients/users. Specifically, solving resource allocation problems is to as-

DOI: 10.4018/978-1-5225-9023-1.ch003

sign clients/users to servers in order to minimize operational costs or maximize resource utilization. The dependencies among clients/servers might incur inter-server communications, which increases the operational costs. The total operational costs are comprised of some components such as energy consumption, network bandwidth, load balancing, etc. Therefore, the resource allocation problems are often formulated as multi-objective optimization problems.

Among many technical challenges, resource allocation becomes one of the most important factors determining the viability of systems. Good resource allocation schemes help increase the availability and scalability of the systems as well as reducing operational costs significantly as shown in figure 1. With the number of users of social networking applications increasing quickly during last few years, the data generated has grown dramatically accordingly. Schoolmates and/or transitive friends often interact infrequently, thus result in weak connection. In general, a social network can be represented as a weighted graph of vertices and edges representing users and their social relationships respectively. The weights of edges represent frequencies of interactions among users. Depending on the interests of analysis, edges of social network graphs can be undirected (symmetric) or directed (asymmetric). Some people are talkative, continually posting updated news or information with their friends; others might just enjoy receiving news from friends. Understanding the behaviours of users as well as types of information in each social network might help reveal the network structure and the growth model which support the designing of systems to operate efficiently.

The weights of edges represent frequencies of interactions among users. Depending on the interests of analysis, edges of social network graphs can be undirected (symmetric) or directed (asymmetric). Some people are talkative, continually posting updated news or information with their friends; others might just enjoy receiving news from friends. Understanding the behaviours of users as well as types of information in each social network might help reveal the network structure and the growth model which support the designing of systems to operate efficiently as shown in figure 2.

Figure 1. Service layers of cloud computing

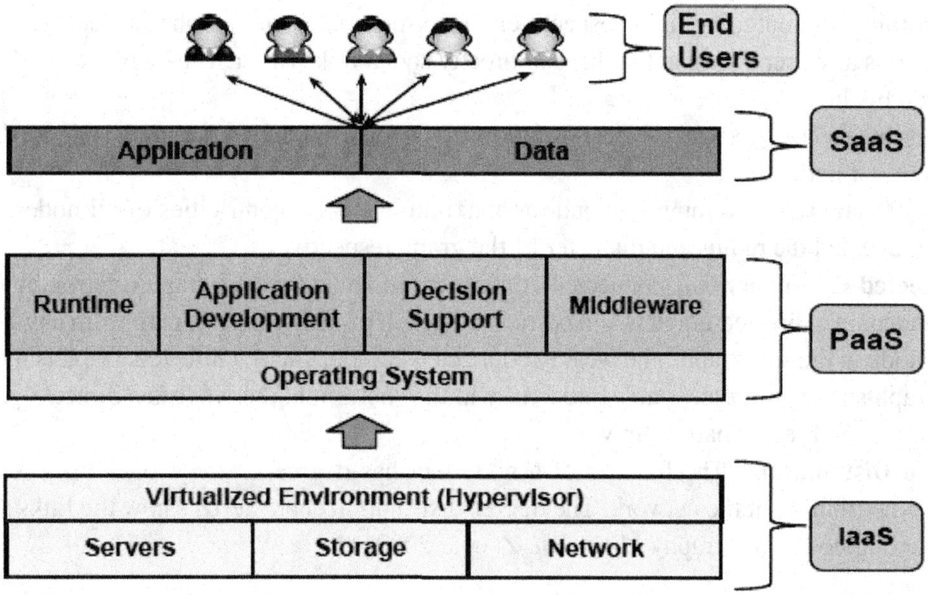

Figure 2. Social aware cloud computing/Storage

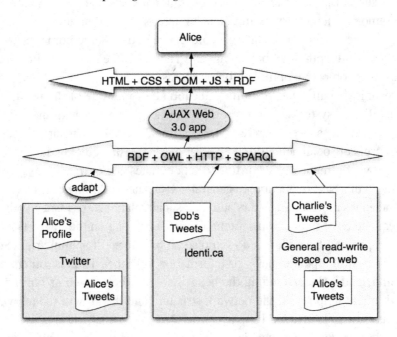

SOCIAL NETWORK ANALYSIS

There are various methods to characterize and analyze social networks. This section discusses some metrics which are often used in social network analysis. First, let G(V, E) be the graph representing a considered social network, where V and E are the set of vertices (users) and edges (social links) respectively.

- **Degree:** The degree of a node u is defined as the number of social links that u has.
- For asymmetric social graphs (direct network), we define in-degree and out-degree as the numbers of incoming and outgoing links respectively. In symmetric social graphs, we define a neighbour of user u is any user or friend that have a directly social link with u. The degree of node u is often denoted by du.
- **Eccentricity:** The maximal shortest path between node u and any other node is defined as the eccentricity of node u.
- **Radius/Diameter:** The minimum and the maximum of all eccentricities of all nodes in the network are called the radius and diameter of the graph respectively.
- **Connected Component:** A connected component in an undirected graph or strongly connected component in a directed graph is a maximal sub-graph in which exists a path from any node to any other node in the sub-graph. The weakly connected component of a directed graph is the maximal sub-graph such that for any pair of node u, v in the sub-graph, there exists a directed path from u to v and an undirected path from v to u.
- **Degree Distribution:** The fraction of a node that has degree k, denoted as P(k), is called the degree distribution of the network. The degree distribution characterizes how the links are distributed among nodes in a graph (Al-Qudah, Z. et al 2009).

- **Betweenness Centrality:** Let $\sigma(u, v)$ be the number of shortest paths between node u and v, and $\sigma e(u, v)$ be the number of shortest paths between u and v that includes e. The betweenness centrality of an edge e, denoted by B(e), is computed as

$$B(e) = \sum \sigma e(u, v)$$

Network Models

- **Random:** In random graphs, links are added randomly to a static set of nodes. A typical characteristic of random graphs is the very short average path lengths between two nodes. Typical random graphs are the Poisson random graph or the Bernoulli graph which has poisson degree distribution and the generalized random graph which has arbitrary degree distribution(Calheiros, R et al 2011).
- **Power-Law:** Power-law networks are a class of of random networks that have the degree distributions being proportional to $k-\beta$, for large k and $\beta > 1$. Many real-world applications exhibit power-law networks including online social networks and Internet applications.
- **Scale-Free:** Scale-free networks are a subclass of the power-law networks in which high degree nodes connect to other high degree nodes with high probability.
- **Small-World:** Small-world networks are networks that have small diameters and high clustering co-efficient. For example, collaboration networks and general social networks have the properties of small-world networks.

Network growth models refer to the dynamic changes or the evolution of social networks. They are based on models of the preferential attachment, also known as cumulative advantage, that characterizes the process of adding new edges to a graph. Specifically, the node degree decides the probability distribution of new links added to the network (Calheiros, R. N et al 2009). In other words, cumulative advantage represents the likelihood a new edge attached to a node is proportional to the degree of the node.

- **Price's Model:** In Price's model, an old node gets new edges proportional to the number of existing edges. Let pk be the fraction of nodes with degree k in the graph, i.e., $\sum |V| = 1$. Nodes are added to the graph continuously. Let m be the mean out-degree of a node and assume that m is constant.

$$\sum k(k + 1) \, pk = m + 1$$

- **Barabasi-Albert's Model:** ´Unlike Price's model which considers directed graphs, the Barabasi-Albert model considers undirected graphs. A new edge connects to any node with degree k with the probability of

$$\sum k \, kpk = 2m$$

GRAPH PARTITIONING PROBLEM

The resource allocation problem can be seen as the distribution of clients/users to available servers in order to achieve specific objectives. In other words, the resource allocation problem can be viewed as an instance of a graph partitioning problem. Specifically, the clients/users and their dependencies can be denoted as vertices and edges of a graph respectively (Chase, J. S et al 2001) . The dependency is often communication demanded among users and the corresponding graphs are un-weighted. The goal of graph partitioning problems is to partition the vertices into sub-groups, i.e., clusters, such that the total weights among clusters are balanced. The k-way graph partitioning problem is defined formally as follows: Given a weighted graph $G = (V, E)$ with $w(e)$ and $w(v)$ denoting the weight of edge $e \in E$ and the weight of vertex $v \in V$, respectively. The problem is to partition V into k subsets, V1,V2, ..., Vk such that $Vi \cap Vj = 0 / \forall i = j$ and $w(Vi) \approx w(k\ V)$.

The general k-way graph partitioning problem has been shown to be NP-complete. In other words, there is currently no known polynomial time algorithm to obtain the exact optimal solution, and it is likely to remain so. Therefore, a large part of the literature on the k-way partitioning problem has been focused on developing heuristic algorithms and determining special conditions for which exact solutions can be obtained. Notably, the k-way partitioning problem has been widely studied in VLSI applications, high performance scientific applications, and in finding shortest paths, etc. That said, almost all of these heuristic algorithms can be classified into a number of approaches, ranging from local search methods, e.g., Kerninghan-Lin algorithm (KL), the Fiducial-Matthew algorithm (FM) to simulated annealing (SA) and genetic algorithms (GA) ; from large-step Markov chain, to spectral methods, graph combinatoric and multi level schemes. The local search methods by Kerninghan-Lin (KL) algorithm B.W.Kerninghan and S.Lin proposed a heuristic algorithm for partitioning edge-weighted graphs such that the total cost on all edges cut is minimized and the size of partitions is maintained (Devi, C., et al 2016) .

Multilevel graph partitioning was first introduced in (Doyle, B., & Lopes, C. V. (2005) and was officially formulated as a graph partitioning method. The main idea of the multi-level graph partitioning methods is recursively creating smaller graphs by merging or contracting nodes based on edge weights.

The smaller graphs are called coarser graphs and reflect the same structure of the original graph. The final coarsen graph, small in size, will be partitioned by highly accurate but expensive algorithms. The merging/contracting in each partition of the coarsen graphs are then undone. Finally, the local search or other refinement methods are employed to refine the quality of the partitions. Multi-level graph partitioning methods can be summarized by Figure 3.

Cloud computing is a new paradigm in which computing is offered as services rather than physical products. Computing services are provided by third-party service providers which offer consumers affordable and flexible computing services via shared resources. Cloud providers offer different layers/levels of services to consumers over many types of application domains.

The SPI service model, depicted in Figure 4, is commonly used to classify cloud services.

- **Software as a Service:** This type of service represents software applications which are provided by cloud service providers via APIs to promote use of applications .
- **Platform as a Service:** This type of service represents software platforms which are offered to customers so that they can develop their own software services that run on the cloud.

Figure 3. Multi level graph partitioning

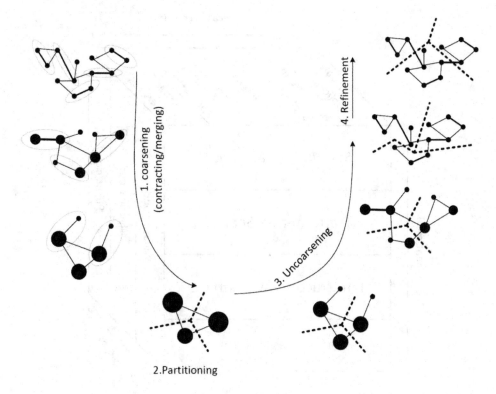

- **Infrastructure as a Service:** This is the lowest level of cloud services. These kind of services offer highly scaled and elastic computing environments that are used to develop and run software applications. For instance, virtualized servers (or virtual machines), storage, and databases are classified into this type of cloud services (Duggan, J., Cetintemel, U., Papaemmanouil, O. & Upfal, E. (2011)).
- **Network as a Service:** This type of service offers virtualized network services and often uses the OpenFlow protocol (Jena, S. R., & Ahmad, Z. (2013)).

TYPES OF CLOUD COMPUTING

Cloud services are commonly classified into three categories:

- **Public Cloud:** The cloud computing service offered to the general public over the Internet. Services are often provided on demand or on pay-as-you-go basic via a pool of shared resources (Issawi, S. F., Halees, A. A., & Radi, M. (2015)).
- **Private Cloud:** The infrastructure deployed within the corporate network, protected by firewall security system and serving corporate applications only.
- **Hybrid Cloud:** This type of cloud service is composed of two or more cloud infrastructures, i.e., private cloud and public cloud. The core applications are often deployed to private cloud for high

Figure 4. Taxonomies of service models

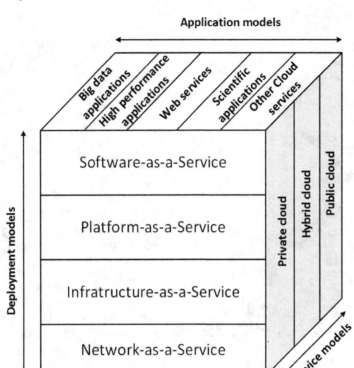

security; meanwhile the non-confidential data and applications are deployed to public cloud to save cost (LaCurts, K. L. (2014,).

Attributes of Cloud Computing

Cloud computing are usually characterized by the following attributes:

- **Multi-Tenancy:** Resources such as CPUs, storage, network, etc. are managed as a pool to provide to users simultaneously. Multiple users might use the same resource based on their demands (Mahmood, Z. (2011)).
- **Massive scalability:** Cloud datacenters have the ability to massively scale resources such as CPU, storage, memory, network bandwidth in order to serve a tremendous number of customers from individual users to enterprises (A. Suresh, et al 2017).
- **Elasticity:** Resources are provided to customers dynamically based on the demand at a specific moment. This enables users to increase or decrease the amount of resources for their applications as needed. This feature enables cloud providers to allocate resources to users efficiently. Resources freed from one user's applications can be allocated to another user's applications (almost) immediately.
- **Self-Provisioning:** Resources are provisioned by the end users in order to setup or start their services and applications.

- **On-Demand (Pay-As-You-Go):** The financial cost charged to users based on the actual amount of resources consumed by their applications. This feature helps users reduce cost dramatically compared to maintaining their own computing infrastructure.

VIRTUALIZATION IN CLOUD SIMULATOR

Virtualization is the abstraction of computing resources such as CPU, storage, memory, network, etc. from applications and users which make shared resource available and accessible to any authorized users and applications. Specifically, virtualization creates simulated virtual machines for guest softwares to run on as if physical servers. The guest softwares can be applications, databases, services, or even operating systems (Suresh, A. & Varatharajan, R. 2018).Hypervisor technique is often employed to create and manage virtual machines such that physical resources are allocated or adjusted dynamically as well as allow many virtual machines to be hosted by on the same physical server. Server consolidation is a technique for reducing operating costs of computer resources in virtualization as shown in figure 5.

These costs can be financial costs of servers, power consumption of servers, datacenter cooling systems and labour costs (R. Udendhran. 2017). It is inefficient if there are underutilized servers that have more space and consume more resources than needed by their workload. Server consolidation is to combine the workload, e.g., virtual machines, of different servers and assign them to the common set of target servers. Server consolidation is enabled by the ability to migrate virtual machines from one server to another.

However, virtual machine migration also takes some costs such as CPU, memory, network bandwidth and even service downtime. The problem of server consolidation including virtual machine placement and migration is still attractive to be investigated.

Figure 5. Virtualization

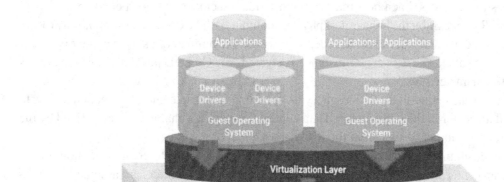

IN-DEPTH EXAMINATION OF CLOUDSIM SIMULATOR

In this chapter, we introduce the operation of the cloud simulator. The sample data center for this chapter will be simulated and the initial result of the simulation will be printed at the end of the chapter. The simulation envisaged in this study utilizes CloudSim simulation tool, a generalized framework that allows a controllable environment for the simulation and modelling of application performance (Cloud Computing and Distributed Systems (Clouds) Laboratory)[19]. The use of CloudSim simulator in this study is justified because the simulator allows developers to focus on the design issues specific to a particular system, without concerns over the cloud-based infrastructure and services as shown in figure 6. According to Calheiros et al., the CloudSim toolkit can perform both system and behavior modelling of cloud components like virtual machines, data centers, and policies for resource provisioning. In particular, simulation of the cloud computing environments can provide insights into the performance of cloud components. The main advantages of cloud simulations are, improved flexibility in application configurations, ease of use and enhanced customization, as well as the cost savings achieved by reusing the models created during the design phase. CloudSim provides a robust tool for simulating datacenters because the toolkit provides the basic classes for defining datacenters. A data center refers to a remote facility comprising of a set of networked servers that an organization uses for the data processing and or storage to meet the organization's IT needs. The term 'datacenter' describes the facility's physical and the virtual infrastructure. CloudSim supports data center modelling and simulation because datacenters behave like Infrastructure as a Service (IaaS) provider; that is, the datacenter accepts VMs requests from brokers and generates the VMs in hosts. The following steps were used to simulate the data center in CloudSim:

Step 1: Initial step for data center simulation: The initial step in CloudSim for data center simulation is to create a data center called Cloud Information Service (CIS). CIS is a registry of all the data center resources that are available on the cloud. Each resource contains a data center and each data center contains one or multiple hosts. A cloud host describes a network of servers dedicated to providing hosting services. Each host must contain virtual machines (VMs),specialized software programs or OSs that exhibit the behavior of physical computers. The CloudSim simulation process requires three fundamental parameters in order to initialize: the number of users, calendar instance, and the traceflag value. The data center instance is created via "CreateDataCenter", which creates the datacenter characteristics.

Step 2: Registering a date center in the CIS registry: After creating a data center, the second step is to register the data center in the CIS registry. Data centers have unique characteristics defined by the hardware configuration of hosts within the data center.

Step 3: Creating and submitting each task to a data center: The third step is to create and submit each task to the data center Broker which keeps a list of cloudlet(s). Data centers are assigned to a broker, which directly interacts with data center and cloudlet(s). Essentially, the Broker conceals the VM management including the VM creation and the submission of cloudlets. It also implements policies for VM selection for running cloudlets and datacenter selection for executing submitted VMs. No sub initializations were done at the Data center broker instance stage.

Step 4: Allocation of policies and importing cloudlets: The fourth step is the allocation of policies
  ○ The datacenter uses the VM allocation policy to allocate machine
  ○ The hosts uses VM scheduling policy

      ○   Cloudlet Scheduler policy involved processing of cloudlets on the VMs

      ○   This is the stage where cloudlets can be imported to the simulator from a .swf file, however in this chapter hypothetical cloudlets will used to achieve this goal.

Step 5: Defining characteristics of VMs and resource allocation algorithm: The fifth step of the policy simulation is to define the characteristics of VMs and define the algorithm which will be used for the resource allocation. In this step we define whether each VM will be Time or Space Shared. The following parameters of VMs will be defined in this step disk size, memory ram, VM mips, VM bandwidth and number of CPU for each virtual machine.

Step 6: Start of the simulation and requesting results: The sixth step is to start the simulation, request the results as a list and then stop the simulation, this can be done by the following three command lines:

```
CloudSim.startSimulation();
List<Cloudlet> Finalresults = dcb.getCloudletReceivedList();
CloudSim.stopSimulation();
```

Step 7: Printing results of the simulation: The seventh step is to print the result of the simulation.

Figure 6 demonstrates the procedures and operations behind the workload balancing. All resources are registered in Cloud Information Service and then sent to the broker. All cloudlets will be registered in the broker directly.

CloudSim Programming and Implementation

This section entails a description of the main steps of java code implementations required for datacenter simulation. In the present study, the following data center model was simulated in the CloudSim.

```
************** Length of Instruction from the (Task and Workloads) Section
**************
Cloudlet Length 5000000
# of Task CPU: 1
Input file size: 100000
Output file size: 300000
************* Each Host ***************************
Memory RAM: 32 GB
Bandwidth: 8 Mbps
Storage (SSD/HDD): 2000 GB
************* Each VM (Virtual Machine) *************
Disk Disk: 20 GB
Memory RAM: 1 Gb
VM MIPS: 1000
VM Bandwidth: 1 Mbps
# of VM CPU: 1
```

Figure 6. CloudSim datacenter 1 diagram

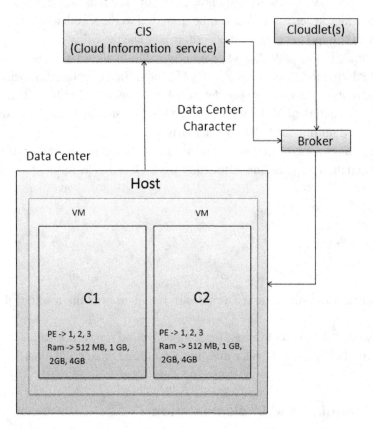

Figure 7. Data center 1 specifications table

Each Hosts

CPU	Quad cores (Each core has 1000 mips)
Memory RAM	32 GB of memory
Storage	50 GB of storage (50000)
Bandwidth	8 mbps (2000 kbits/s)

Number of Data center brokers: 1

20 Cloudlets (task and workloads)

Length of Instruction	5000000 length of instruction
Input file size	100000 kb input file size
Output file size	300000 kb output file size
CPU core	1

5 Virtual machines

Storage	20 GB
Memory	1 GB RAM
Virtual CPU	1 (each with 1000 mips CPU speeds)
Cloudlets Scheduler	Timeshared

The first step is the CloudSim initialization process, a stage that involves initialize the simulation toolkit for the experiments. In this step a loudSim was initialized using the CloudSim.init() method. The initialization approach entails defining the number of users based on the num-user parameter, determining the simulation start time defined by the calendar parameter, and using the trace_ flag parameter to track the simulation events. That it, the initialization method takes in the number of cloud users in integer value and an instance of calendar and a Boolean value as shown in figure 7.

CONCLUSION

Generally, we can classify entities in distributed systems as resource consumers such as clients/users, and resource providers such as servers and networking devices. Resources are organized and managed in datacenters as a shared pool of resources. Users access resources from their devices such as workstations, smart phones, tablets, etc., via access networks connecting to datacenters via the internet. This chapter explained the fundamental requirement for Cloud simulation and the sample data center was simulated and the result of the sample simulation was included at the end of the chapter.

REFERENCES

Al-Qudah, Z., Alzoubi, H. A., Allman, M., Rabinovich, M., & Liberatore, V. (2009). Efficient application placement in a dynamic hosting platform. *'09 Proceedings of the 18th ACM International Conference on World Wide Web*, 281-290. 10.1145/1526709.1526748

Calheiros, R. N., Ranjan, R., Beloglazov, A., De Rose, C. A., & Buyya, R. (2011). CloudSim: A toolkit for modeling and simulation of cloud computing environments and evaluation of resource provisioning algorithms. *Software, Practice & Experience, 41*(1), 23–50. doi:10.1002pe.995

Calheiros, R. N., Ranjan, R., De Rose, C. A. F., & Buyya, R. (2009). *CloudSim: A novel framework for modeling and simulation of cloud computing infrastructure and services*. Technical Report GRIDS-TR-2009-1, Grid Computing and Distributed Systems Laboratory.

Chase, J. S., Anderson, D. C., Thakar, P. N., Vahdat, A. M., & Doyle, R. P. (2001, October). Managing energy and server resources in hosting centers. *Operating Systems Review, 35*(5), 103–116. doi:10.1145/502059.502045

Devi, C., & Uthariaraj, R. (2016). *Load balancing in cloud computing environment using improved weighted Round Robin Algorithm for non-preemptive dependent tasks*. Hindawi Publishing Corporation. doi:10.1155/2016/3896065

Doyle, B., & Lopes, C. V. (2005). Survey of technologies for Web application development. *ACM Journal, 2*(3), 1–43.

Duggan, J., Cetintemel, U., Papaemmanouil, O., & Upfal, E. (2011). Performance prediction for concurrent database workloads. *SIGMOD '11, 978*(1), 337-348. 10.1145/1989323.1989359

Issawi, S. F., Halees, A. A., & Radi, M. (2015). An efficient adaptive load-balancing algorithm for cloud computing under bursty workloads. Engineering, Technology, &. *Applied Scientific Research*, 5(3), 795–800.

Jena, S. R., & Ahmad, Z. (2013). Response time minimization of different load balancing algorithms in cloud computing environment. *International Journal of Computers and Applications*, 69(17), 22–27.

LaCurts, K. L. (2014, June). *Application workload prediction and placement in cloud computing systems* (Unpublished doctoral dissertation). Massachusetts Institute of Technology, Cambridge, MA.

Lee, R., & Jeng, B. (2011). Load-balancing tactics in cloud. *Proceedings of the International Conference on Cyber-Enabled Distributed Computing and Knowledge CyberC Discovery*, 447-454.

Mahmood, Z. (2011). Cloud computing: characteristics and deployment approaches. *11th IEEE International Conference on Computer and Information Technology*, 121-126. 10.1109/CIT.2011.75

Suresh, A. & Varatharajan, R. (2018). Recognition of pivotal instances from uneven set boundary during classification. *Multimed Tools Appl.*

Udendhran, R. (2017). A hybrid approach to enhance data security in cloud storage. *Proceeding ICC '17 Proceedings of the Second International Conference on Internet of things, Data and Cloud Computing.* 10.1145/3018896.3025138

Chapter 4
An Intelligent Water Grid Control Using Cloud Computing

Suresh Annamalai
Nehru Institute of Engineering and Technology, India

Jotimani S.
Nehru Institute of Engineering and Technology, India

ABSTRACT

Most of the people in India depend on the agriculture for their survival. Intelligent water grid control (IWGC) system is a trusted solution for resolving recent significant global water problems. The system will handle the dried geographical area in a smart way with internet of things and edge computing. Since the villages that are far from the rivers are not getting enough water, the smaller water saving areas like pool, lake, ponds can be filled with this smart water management system. In this chapter, the authors discussed the water problems faced by the farmers, dam authority, and by the government.

INTRODUCTION

In recent scenario, flooding in India is most natural disaster resulting in a loss of human beings animal as well as many goods. The flooding happens due to improper water redirection planning among all states since we have a individual plan across the states, while one state unaware of water distribution plan of other states and the sudden opening of one dam leads to many loses in some other areas. The existing manual detection of dam water level prediction and lack of knowledge about the other small reservoirs other than the dams are not filled when the dam water directly goes to river or sea. And the overflow of river water causes the damages to the peoples and the livelihoods of nearby areas due to overflow. The water is being wasted in wide amount of range instead of increasing the ground water level (Carlos Oberdan Rolim et al 2010). The Intelligent Water Grid Control involves in monitoring, measuring, and deciding to distribution of water from the flooded area to the dried geographical region. The usage of wireless communication, observation and all electrical devices are integrated through IoT. With the observation of the amount of water being filled in the dam, the amount of moistures in the soil, the

DOI: 10.4018/978-1-5225-9023-1.ch004

level of rain fall in the region are being collected from various sensors allowing continuous automatic measurement and recording in the particular time interval.

The collected data's will be saved in the cloud and are available at any region at any time. The most dried areas will be identified and the water can be easily opened from the connected dam and to the valleys which connects the smallest water saving areas. Although we have much smart agriculture in terms of weeding, bird and animal scaring, smart irrigation techniques, in the current scenario, the biggest challenge is the lack of rain in some areas while flooding in another area. Conservative centralized water flow networks are typically based on unidirectional flow. The construction of distribution elements and the transportation of water from a single source to the entire rural/urban area are not only economically infeasible but are also prone to distributed to the same flooded area. The manual monitoring of water management includes lack of knowledge about the other regional areas and the tremendous water is being wasted and diverse into the sea water without the proper water management. There is a need to incorporate these two variant environment changes. During the thousands of years we are following the manual operators for opening and maintains the water level in dams and reservoirs which requires the human resources to be present all the time and the manual error may occurs due to lack of integrity and accuracy. Hence we are suggesting the recent developing technologies to identify the most possible rain falling areas and the dams and the small reservoirs and redirecting the water flow across the nation by the centralized manner. This is the way of avoiding the flooding in one region while some other areas are drained (Aras Can Onal, 2010).

CLOUD COMPUTING

In a current scenario, with the digitalized world, the amount of data being searched stored back at the storage location is widely increasing in a rapid manner. The storage location may be at a private area as a private server or as a shared storage space or may be in a public area space. Day by day the computer architecture is emerging in a world. The heterogeneous resource data may be utilized by the different architecture. To compatible with this rapid changing environment the cloud technology offers the storage location with the different types of service as a cost effective as shown in figure 1.

The cloud computing and the Internet Of Things are the very most hard core technologies used in a recent computing environments (Wojciech Moczulski 2016).

A large organizations, companies and institutions are collecting large amount of data and continuously facing the big challenges while processing those data (2015).

Carlos Oberdan Rolim says, the data collection process which requires a more number of labor work to collecting, processing and analyzing the information, typically slow and error prone.

A real time data accessibility will be prevented by the latency because of this type of data processing. Hence we need of sensors which are to be attached everywhere, where we want to collect the data that are interconnected to exchange and optimizing the data. The use of cloud computing and the wireless sensors makes the data available to be processed and can be easily distributed throughout the world (Saha, D. and Mukherjee, A. (2003)).

Cloud computing also includes grid computing, virtualization and utility computing. The cloud computing is also same as the grid computing. The main goal of the grid computing is to reduce the resource needs as it coordinates all the resources together to satisfy the needs of the requirements. The virtualization is also the better method for utilization of resources and for provisioning of dynamic resources. The

Figure 1. Typical processing of data storage using cloud

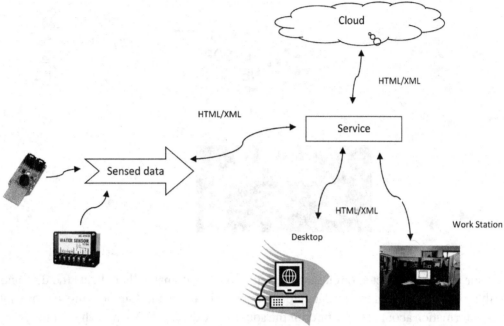

cloud computing is the realization of the utility computing that includes on demand resource. Although it provides the all other computing methodologies characteristics to provide the unique benefits, there are the issues arises during processing in cloud (Fan TongKe, 2015). The security of the data is the most thinkable issue. This is because of the remote accessing of server which is sited too far from the client.

INTERNET OF THINGS WITH CLOUD SERVICE

Internet of Things- as the name says, it is all about the integrated networking of all the smallest things together to be communicated widely as an interconnected networking. All the mechanical, digital and electronic devices connected together via a common circuit board. This connection can transfer million amounts of data over the networks without the manual help of human being or computer as shown in figure 2. By simply saying it is an automated one (Buyya et al 2008).

The IoT is an intelligent technology by sensing identifying and analyzing data from the heterogeneous environment (Mei Fangquan et al 2009).

The Cloud computing, ubiquitous networks and the intelligent sensing networks are combined together and called as internet of things. The ubiquitous computing networks which consists of Wireless LAN, LTE, WiMax, 3G, RFID and NFC etc., The wired communication and optical cable wires also included(Cao Qinglin, 2010).

To provide the great support system we are proposing the wireless sensor model. It facilitate the information collection from the sensor to the database through the cloud. There are two reason, first it is very much useful for the automated data gathering. Second, need for reliable data even in case of natural disasters(Yang Guang, 2015).

Figure 2. Integration of cloud, ubiquitous and intelligent system

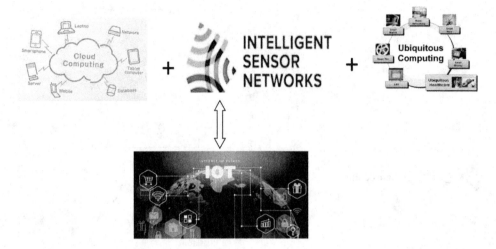

The sensor that are connected through this circuit boards automatically collects the data and to the cloud for the storage as well as for the data processing. For example the soil moisture sensor which collects all the information about the moistures of the soil and the data to the farmer whether the crops needs the irrigation or not. Instead of informing to the farmer directly it can be forwarded to the automated system or analysis of data, and the decision may be initiated from the result of the data analysis(Tian Yu et al 2014).

Prior Art

Nikhil Kedia entitled "Water Quality Monitoring for Rural Areas - A Sensor Cloud Based Economical Project." Published in 2015 1st International Conference on Next Generation Computing technologies (NGCT - 2015) Dehradun, India. This paper highlights the entire water quality monitoring methods, sensors, embedded design, and information dissipation procedure, role of government, network operator and villagers in ensuring proper information dissipation. It also explores the Sensor Cloud domain. While automatically improving the water quality is not feasible at this point, efficient use of technology and economic practices can help improve water quality and awareness among people(Panachakel J T et al 2016).

Wojciech Moczulski entitled "a methodology of leakage detection and location in water distribution networks – the case study", published in Conference Paper September 2016. He indicated detecting and localizing leakages in water distribution networks. Two approaches are presented: based on a hydraulic model of the network, and based on approximate models and fuzzy classifiers. Moreover, a case study concerning applications of the methodology to a real network in Rybnik, Poland is presented. A pilot version of the system has been running since 2013 and shows quite satisfactory efficiency (Gavalas D et al 2016).

WATER FLOW DETECTION USING SENSOR

To monitor and regulate the levels of flow-water with the specified area we need level sensors. This also used to monitor some solid like powdered substances. Level sensors are widely used in industrial. Vehicles use liquid level sensors to monitor a variety of liquids, including fuel, oil and rarely also specialist fluids such as power steering fluid. They can also be found in industrial storage tanks, for slurries, and in household appliances such as coffee machines. Basic level sensors can be used to identify the point at which a liquid falls below a minimum or rises above a maximum level. Many sensors can detail the specific amount of liquid in a container relative to the minimum/maximum levels, to provide a continuous measurement of volume (Gabrielli L et al 2014). The sensor nodes are placed as a wireless networks in order to collect data and encoding and transmitting the data over the cloud. Normally there will be broker system; it collects the data from the sensor and forward to the proper storage space which is hosted on the cloud. The sensor module collects the data from the hardware that is attached along with the sensor device.

Types of Sensor for Water Flow Detection

To find the point level of any liquid we have a 'n' number of variety of liquid sensors. The magnetic float which rise and fall with the level of liquid container is used in some type of sensors. When it reaches the certain level the reed magnetic switch will be activated. To detect the minimum and maximum level of the liquid the switches at the top and bottom of the container is used. The magnet is protected from the turbulence or from the interference with the liquid; a protective shield is fixed with the sensors as shown in figure 3.

Conductive Sensors

Apart from the above sensor we have a conductive sensor top measure the liquid level. This conductive sensor can be used only with the liquids that conduct electricity. It needs a low voltage and a source of power and two electrodes will be placed inside a container. When the certain level is reached by the conductive liquid, it conducts with the electrode and the switch will be activated.

Figure 3. Water flow Sensor

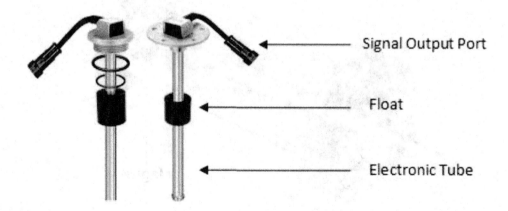

Signal Output Port

Float

Electronic Tube

The conductive sensor's conductivity is dependent on temperature, hence it is recommended to use the temperature remunerated instrument or it should be regulated at the same temperature when the solution is measured. Electrode conductivity will increase when the temperature is increased.

For the hazardous liquid the pneumatic sensors is used, since the sensor alone itself cannot conduct with the water like liquids as shown in figure 4. The level air between the pneumatic sensor and the liquid is detected by the sensor. After this, it is used to calculate the liquid amount to fill the remaining portion of the container. This is very cost effective sensors.

The displacement is measured by the pneumatic sensors which is also used to measure the proximity of the objects that are very close to it.

Magnetostrictive Sensor

For the continuous measurement of liquids the magneto-strictive sensors are widely used. This sensors are look like a magnetic float sensors in design, but the level of magnetic is measured by the magnetostrictive wires, it will be react only when its magnetic field is interrupted by the magnet presence as shown in figure 5.

Our focus is on various data collection, distributing and processing over the data. The current solutions are on the manual monitoring and human based processing. This leads to an obstacle in real time data accessing and delays the decision making and monitoring and results in flooding. Here we argue that the cloud technology which provides the desirable features for automation of data and addressing the solution for the emergency situations by analysis. The solution is to provide a two way in social as well as in modern scientific fields. As in social we offer a low cost solution to improve the needs in terms of agriculture and human needs for water. To the scientific fields the sensors are integrated together to provide service of data collection, distribution and analysis normally and as well as in case of emergency.

The high level requirements for the solution:

1. *Implement the methods to collect, process and distribute Dam water essential data*, from dam and river to remote ease of access.

Figure 4. Pneumatic sensor

Magnet

Figure 5. Magnetostrictive sensor

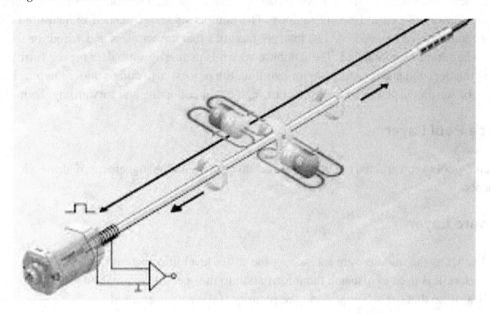

2. It must be *open, flexible and extensible*; that is, it must support diverse equipments in diverse numbers that can be added to system on *ad hoc* basis.
3. It must be *secure*; that is, the system must guarantee the integrity and confidentiality of dam water data.
4. It must be *manageable*; that is, it must provide control over the innumerable of computing devices connected to the environment.
5. It must be *reliable*; that is it must guarantee system availability despite of natural disaster issues.
6. It must be *scalable*, to support the deployment in large water environments and the integration of different water sources.
7. It must be *optimized* for computing resources; that is, the application must run in inexpensive, low-profile computing devices.

CONSTRUCTION OF SMART WATER DISTRIBUTION BASED ON CLOUD COMPUTING

The cloud computing technology associated with the IoT for the smart agriculture management which is included as the prior most part of the smart dam water distribution. The architecture of smart water distribution which consists of the four important layers those are:

Physical Layer

The physical layer which consists of all types of physical requirements as well as the hardware requirements that is included in our smart water distribution over the nation.

The physical layer includes all the physical servers that are needed to store the information collected from all the sensors placed indifferent regions. The number of server needed is measured as per the number of regions to be considered. The internet facilities that are wireless and wired for the communication to the server also included. The database which is primarily store data for the further analysis for making the decision and the software for handling the process also comes under the physical layers. The variety of sensors is placed in 'n' number of regions for collecting and forwarding the information.

Resource Pool Layer

The resource pool is constructed to be regarded as integration and management of above physical layer requirements.

Middleware Layer

The cloud is act as the middle ware for storing the water level information that are collected from the different region. It is used to dispatch the information to the specific automation tool for the activation and inactivation so that the efficiency and the security if the data is ensured.

Construction Layer

The cloud computing capacity is to be encapsulated to the web services for management and also for service registration, visiting and constructing the work flow

Smart Water Control Architecture

This control Structure which consists of two level of servers

1. Central database server
2. Resource Control Server

The central Database server consists of three level of information

1. The information that are collected from the overall dam across the nation
2. The information of the small water storage areas like pool and the pond
3. The flooding information that may possible from the rain forecasting

The resource Control server consists of three level of authority to make decision

1. List of Dams that water level that may leads to full and in the stage of overflow
2. Re-directional Information for the river flow
3. Flooding alert in case of emergency for the people safety

Figure 6. Architecture of smart water control

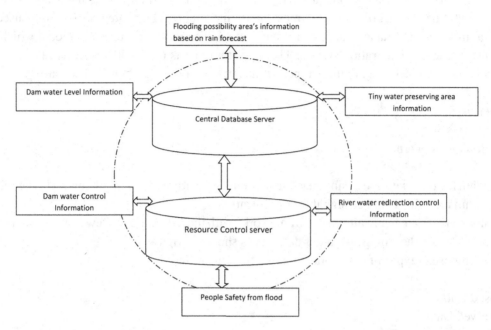

The central database server which collects the information from the various source will send the data to the software which can analyze and predict the needed information. The analyzed data will be passed over to the resource control server to make the decision of redirection of river and the decision to expelling the dam water as a centralized decision as shown in figure 6.

COLLECTIVE DATA PROCESSING

The unstructured data that are collected from the various sensors has to be analyzed and concluded for the better decision making. The data that are collected from sensors are called as unstructured data. Theses tremendous data cannot be processed with the regular data warehouse which is simply based on the relational database management system. And these tremendous data also be updated within the time slot frequently, and also need to remove all the duplicate data being collected within the specified time slot. Hence the traditional way is not enough to handle, the new emerging technique of big data has to be utilized in our paper.

These big data analytic methods process the data and send those data to the central database server. The big data which uses the hadoop data lake as the primary and prior most repositories for the incoming data is being collected from the sensors. In this method the data can be analyzed directly in the hadoop data lake. When the data is ready from the hadoop, it should be send to the software for analysis. This tool may include data mining concepts, predictive analytic i.e. the behavior of the system can be predicted from the data analysis. It also includes machine learning which analysis the big amount of data.

If there is any lack of data analytics it will leads to data hazards. The big data analytics uses the new generation technologies to support huge amount of data and this needs huge space. Typically big data and cloud is clustered among network attached with storage space.

For effective usage of applications of microcontroller, high speed networks, the frames integrating the big data with the internet of things are most emerging solution. This integration will be used in environmental monitoring, financial applications and so on. The weather clustering model which is also implemented using this integration system. The algorithm that is used with these types of IoT are the machine learning based. There are three types of machine learning algorithms. They are

1. Supervised,
2. Unsupervised,
3. Reinforcement learning

For the labeled data the supervising machine learning algorithms can e implemented. The reinforcement algorithm have the feedback signal for optimization.

Even though there are many number of frameworks with the IoT, there are few issues associated with these frameworks are the storage of larger datasets as shown in figure 7.

The two important types of data collection, via the sensor nodes.

1. Sensed Data
2. Observed Data
3. Failure observation Data

Figure 7. Structure of data collectivity

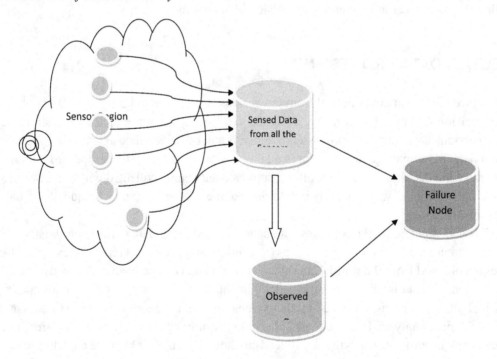

The observed data is being extracted from the sensed data by the sensor placed among the several regions. The sensed data is collected from the millions of sensors placed with the distance gap. The failure observation data is the data reported by the neighbourhood sensor about the failure status of the nearby sensor and intimates the need of replacement. This is the foremost important for the reliable data collection.

All the sensor nodes are interconnected with the ADC to each other and it is connected with the microcontroller. The microcontroller consists of the power source, transceiver and the external memory. Each sensor is capable of gathering information from the circumstances and distribute the information to all other nodes via the communication channel. The microcontroller is the heart of the network and controls all other devices and equipments connected with it. The microcontroller is used with the sensor nodes. Since it is very cost effective, it is widely used. But for the wide band wireless connection the microcontrollers are liable to more power consumption. In these cases the digital signal processor is strongly recommended. All the transceivers are working in idle mode, it leads to lowest power consumption.

CONCLUSION

Internet of Things with Cloud computing for remote sensing and data gathering and analysis is the powerful method for extracting and processing data. This smart water distribution is build upon the prescribed technology will help to avoid flooding in one region while the dryness in other region. Large amount of data is handled by the big data processing which will give the reliable data.

REFERENCES

Buyya, R., Yeo, C. S., & Venugopal, S. (2008). Market-Oriented Cloud Computing: Vision, Hype, and Reality for Delivering IT Services as Computing Utilities. *High Performance Computing and Communications, 2008. HPCC '08. 10th IEEE International Conference.*

Cao, Q. (2010). Present research on IOT. *Software Guide, 59,* 6–7.

Gabrielli, L., Pizzichini, M., & Spinsante, S. (2014). Smart water grids for smart cities: A sustainable prototype demonstrator. *Proceedings of the 2014 European Conference on Networks and Communications (EuCNC),* 1–5. 10.1109/EuCNC.2014.6882685

Gavalas, D., Venetis, I. E., & Konstantopoulos, C. (2016). Energy-efficient multiple itinerary planning for mobile agents-based data aggregation in WSNs. *Telecommunication Systems,* 1–15.

Guang, Guining, Jing, Zhaohui, & He. (2011). Security threats and measures for the Internet of Things. *Qinghua Daxue Xuebao/Journal of Tsinghua University, 51*(10), 1335-1340.

Kedia. (2015). *Water Quality Monitoring for Rural Areas - A Sensor Cloud Based Economical Project.* 1st International Conference on Next Generation Computing Technologies (NGCT - 2015), Dehradun, India.

Mei, F. (2009). Smart planet and sensing china—analysis on development of IOT. *Agricultural Network Information, 12,* 5–7.

Panachakel, J. T., & Finitha, K. C. (2016). Energy Efficient Compression of Shock Data Using Compressed Sensing. Intelligent Systems Technologies and Applications, 273-281.

Rolim, Koch, Westphall, Werner, Fracalossi, & Salvador. (2010). *A Cloud Computing Solution for Patient's Data Collection in Health Care Institutions*. IEEE Xplore.

Saha, D., & Mukherjee, A. (2003). Pervasive computing: A paradigm for the 21st century. *IEEE Perspectives, 36*(3), 25–31.

Yu, Jiang, & Yang. (2014). Foundation and development strategy for wise water affair management. *China Water Resources, 2014*(20), 14-17.

Chapter 5
An Intelligent Grid Network Based on Cloud Computing Infrastructures

Suresh Annamalai
Nehru Institute of Engineering and Technology, India

Udendhran R.
Bharathidasan University, India

Vimal S.
National Engineering College, India

ABSTRACT

This chapter covers important topics in development of efficient energy girds. Inefficient power generation, unbalanced consumption patterns that lead to underutilization of expensive infrastructure on the one hand, and severe overload on the other, as well as urgent issues of national and global concern such as power system security and climate change are all driving this evolution. As the smart grid concept matures, we'll see dramatic growth in green power production: small production devices such as wind turbines and solar panels or solar farms, which have fluctuating capacity outside of the control of grid operators. Small companies that specialize in producing power under just certain conditions will boom in forthcoming years. Energy is stored in the storage during low-cost periods, and the stored energy is used during high-cost periods to avoid the expensive draw from the grid. The authors evaluate the impact of large-scale energy storage adoption on grid electricity demand.

SMART GRID ON CLOUD COMPUTING INFRASTRUCTURES

Cloud computing is of interest to the power community for several business reasons. Some parallel the green energy considerations that have stimulated such dramatic change in the power industry: cloud computing is a remarkably efficient and green way to achieve its capabilities (Ali and K. A. Smith, 2016). Others reflect pricing: cloud computing turns out to be quite inexpensive in dollar terms, relative

DOI: 10.4018/978-1-5225-9023-1.ch005

to older models of computing. And still others are stories of robustness: by geographically replicating services, companies like Google and Microsoft are achieving fraction of a second responsiveness for clients worldwide, even when failures or regional power outages occur. Cloud systems can be managed cheaply and in highly automated ways, and protected against attack more easily than traditional systems. Finally, cloud computing offers astonishing capacity and elasticity: a modern cloud computing system is often hosted on a few data centers any one of which might have more computing and storage and networking capacity than all of the world's supercomputing centers added together, and can often turn on a dime, redeploying services to accommodate instantaneous load shifts. We shall enumerate some of the issues in the debate about using the cloud for building the smart grid.

The Cloud Computing Scalability Advantage

The cloud and its transformation of the computing industry have resulted in the displacement of previous key industry players like Intel, IBM, and Microsoft by new players like Google, Facebook, and Amazon. Technology these new-age companies created is becoming irreversibly dominant for any form of computing involving scalability: a term that can mean direct contact with large numbers of sensors, actuators or customers, but can also refer to the ability of a technical solution to run on large numbers of lightweight, inexpensive servers within a data center. Earlier generations of approaches were often abandoned precisely because they scaled poorly. And this has critical implications for the smart grid community, because it implies that to the extent that we launch a smart grid development effort in the near term, and to the extent that the grid includes components that will be operated at large scale, those elements will be built on the same platforms that are supporting the Facebooks and Amazons of today's computing world (Davidson. 2015).

Cloud Cost Advantage

The Smart Grid needs a national-scale, pervasive network that connects every electricity producer in the market, from coal and nuclear plants to hydroelectric, solar, and wind farms, and small independent producers, with every electricity consumer, from industrial manufacturing plants to residences, and to every device plugged into the wall. This network should enable the interconnected devices to exchange status information and control power generation and consumption. The scale of such an undertaking is mind boggling(P. Budde, 2015). Yet, the key enabler, in the form of the network itself, already exists. Indeed, the Internet already allows household refrigerators to communicate with supermarkets and transact purchases. It won't be difficult to build applications ("apps") that inform the washing machine of the right time to run its load, based on power pricing information from the appropriate generators. Whatever their weaknesses, the public Internet and cloud offer such a strong cost advantage that the power community cannot realistically ignore them in favor of building a private, dedicated network for the smart grid(European Technology Platform, 2015).

Migrating High Performance Computing (HPC) to the Energy Grid

We noted that SCADA systems are instances of "high performance computing" applications. It therefore makes sense to ask how the cloud will impact HPC. Prior to the 1990s, HPC revolved around special computing hardware with unique processing capabilities. These devices were simply too expensive, and around 1990 gave way to massive parallelism. The shift represented a big step backward for some kinds of users, because these new systems were inferior to the ones they replaced for some kinds of computation. Yet like it or not, the economics of the marketplace tore down the old model and installed the new one, and HPC users were forced to migrate. Today, even parallel HPC systems face a similar situation(G. M. Shafiullah et al 2016).

HIGH ASSURANCE APPLICATIONS BY CLOUD COMPUTING

The cloud was not designed for high-assurance applications, and therefore poses several challenges for hosting a critical infrastructure service like the smart grid. One complicating factor is that many of the cost-savings aspects of the cloud reflect forms of sharing: multiple companies (even competitors) often share the same data center, so as to keep the servers more evenly loaded and to amortize costs. Multiple applications invariably run in a single data center. Thus, whereas the power community has always owned and operated its own proprietary technologies, successful exploitation of the cloud will force the industry to learn to share. This is worrying, because there have been episodes in which unscrupulous competition within the power industry has manifested itself through corporate espionage, attempts to manipulate power pricing, etc. (ENRON being only the most widely known example). Thus, for a shared computing infrastructure to succeed, it will need to have ironclad barriers preventing concurrent users from seeing one-another's data and network traffic. The network, indeed, would be a shared resource even if grid operators were to run private, dedicated data centers. The problem here is that while one might imagine creating some form of separate Internet specifically for power industry use, the costs of doing so appear to be prohibitive. Meanwhile, the existing Internet has universal reach and is highly cost-effective. Clearly, just as the cloud has inadequacies today, the existing Internet raises concerns because of its own deficiencies. But rather than assuming that these rule out the use of the Internet for smart grid applications

SMART GRID FEATURES

Self-Healing

The security and stability calculation and development of emergency plans of current power grids are still off-line analysis; thus, the results are comparatively conservative. However, smart grid has better self-management and self-healing ability. With real-time monitoring, problems can be automatically detected and responded to. With the incorporation of micro grids affected areas can be isolated from the main networks limiting disruption.

If an overhead power line has an error, there is inevitable power loss. In the case of urban/city networks that for the most part is fed using underground cables, networks can be designed (through the use of interconnected topologies) such that failure of one part of the network will result in no loss of supply to end users.

Usually, self-healing has 3 steps:

Step 1: Using AMI, the utility company collects real-time usage data.

Step 2: It analyses the data to identify a potential power failure during a high-demand period.

Step 3: The utility redistributes power across its service area and send radio signal to turn on or off smart application.

With self-healing function the power grid can maintain its stable operation, estimate weak stage, and deal with emergency problem

Combination of Devices and Energies

Considering the climate changes over decades, it is important to bring out a technology that uses renewable sources. The Electric Power Research Institute (EPRI) calculates that a national smart grid could reduce annual GHG emissions by 60-211 million metric tons of carbon dioxide equivalent.

Key Characteristics of a Micro Grid

- Connecting to the traditional grid is optional.
- Resiliency, reliability, and sustainability are the core responsibilities.
- Backup for all system loads, not just the critical loads.
- Modern technology is needed to optimize energy production and usage.

Although Internet enabled smart appliances and proposed techniques for programmatic appliance control in the literature are beginning to employ intelligence to achieve energy efficiency goals and cut electricity bills, most of them have limited scope and work in isolation to each other. In this thesis, we devise techniques for controlling home appliances collectively, to regulate home's consumption profile. Also, as opposed to some of the prior work, we do not assume that the appliance duty cycles are predictable and hence we devise online energy optimization techniques. In general, we employ several computing techniques including machine learning, optimizations, online algorithms lto enable global energy optimizations across several appliances in a building, and across thousands of homes in a grid, while ensuring the aggregate grid-wide consumption profile becomes more sustainable.

Asset management is becoming more important in asset concentrated industries. This is because industries have become extremely spirited and restricted markets. In order to increase the business performance, profit margins have become very low that causes business to explore with their new innovative performance (M. Weedall, 2016). Two main aspects are been considered in the asset management: 1) Business performance and 2) Asset technical necessity. Though, this falls in the same category they disagree with each other. For instance, economic prerequisite should be done only at the minimum cost for the maintenance of the asset management. But cutting the cost of expenses could affect the quality of the asset's performance and thus this could have a fall in the revenue of the business profit and thus occurs in the fall of the business. Hence, there should be a balance between both the financial and the performance of the equipment (Technical report by US depart of Energy, 2015). This is popularly said to be "optimization". In this chapter we are going to deal with the production line asset management of a transformer. Transformers are the most important component in the field of electrical engineering which could have a long life and said to be a cost intensive component. These transformers constitute an electrical supply network. When we take a power plant transformer play a major role either in the transformation line as well as for the input power supply (Ergon Energy, Queensland). The asset management decision making for power transformer as follows.

- To obtain the level of maintenance of a transformer that is to be carried out in its whole life time
- Obtaining the inspection that is to be carried out in a power production line. The time line is the very important factor for how frequently the inspections must be carried out in a production line stating the pipe work, dissolved gas oil sampling, external factors like corrosion etc.
- Obtaining the transformers that is to be sending for the service and the type of services that is to be carried out in a transformer.
- Transformers must be invigorated. It is necessary to obtain the timeline to renovate a power production line.

A NOVEL APPROACH FOR SMARTER ENERGY GRID

Modern buildings are heavy power consumers, hence making buildings efficient and shaping their electricity demands can help in making the electric and energy grid more sustainable as shown in figure 1. For instance, smart buildings may use motion sensors to track occupants and opportunistically disconnect loads in empty rooms. Flattening demand implies reducing the difference between the peaks and troughs in a home's electricity usage, thereby creating better usage pattern that lessens the deviation from the average usage. As appliances begin to allow remote actuation at finer granularities, advanced techniques for controlling power will be possible. Given current standards for remote actuation, connecting loads to external programmable switches and outlets using home automation protocols, such as X10 or Insteon, is enough in many cases to provide programmatic load actuation in today's appliances. We currently use Insteon-enabled outlets and switches in our home deployment and tested the gateway receives information from multiple potential sources, including real-time electricity prices and demand-response signals from the grid, generation data from on-site renewable, and consumption data from each household load. The gateway's data sources inform its load scheduling policy. This policy determines which loads to power and when by issuing actuation commands to loads. While we focus on the problem of scheduling background loads to attend demand without affecting occupants, our home gateway can implement scheduling policies with other objectives, such as ensuring home power demands are always less than supply when using intermittent on-site renewable.

Loss Estimation

In order to evaluate the loss that is caused due to the transformer, the life time of the transformer is estimated by the commercial and the industrial owners. There is a necessity of the transformers which should be maintained annually, and it should be regularly monitored. In comparison, if the transformer is getting replaced before its lifetime due to the failure that is caused due to the overloading, then the expected loss could higher that estimated when compared. The power production grid could be affected by many factors. It could be either the insulation fact that greatly reduces the life of the transformer. It could the poor quality of the oil or the moisture content in a transformer or it could be overloading factor. This could be caused due to the extreme heat of the transformer, which affects greatly in the insulation property. According to the nameplate reading, transformers are designed to operate in a maximum life of 20 years. Transformers that are loaded higher than the nameplate reading have a life of less than 20 years and the transformers that are loaded lower than the nameplate reading have life more than 20 years.

The customer of the transformer should have a special contract with the manufacturer else, the service time for replacing the transformer could be extended. Therefore, utilizing the transformer to a maximum extend without any risk is extremely important as shown in figure 2. It has become critical to study the lifetime models of the transformers, since 30 percentages of the transformer failures is caused due to the ageing. Heavy investments for the transformer were made in the year of 1960-1970 that made the population of the transformer till 30 years. IEEE survey says that the ageing was caused in the transformer after the 25th year. Therefore, large transformers end their life at the 25th year and the replacement of the transformers couldn't be done all at once. This becomes tedious and hence there occurs some cause of loss and this should be estimated and tried to be avoided at a maximum extent(M. Weedall. 2016).

Ageing is the most important factor in an electrical plant that causes a greater concern and challenges in the industry. Rather than this Dissolve Gas Analysis (DGA), insulation etc, also plays a vital role in the field of electrical plant. The consumption of the electrical energy is increasing day by day due to the rapid growth of commercial and industrial sectors around the world especially in the urban areas. Due to this, the business is also affected now-a-days. The foremost concept of the business is to utilize the asset to the maximum extent. In industries, in order to provide a feasible operation of the system and to utilize the asset properly, regular maintenance and monitoring of the equipment is very important. Any perceivable or non-perceivable one that can be owned or controlled by anyone, which brings out a profit to an organization is considered as an asset. An asset is considered to the ownership of a value that could be converted to cash. An asset is an important factor for the profit of an organization by the

Figure 1. Important components in smart energy grid

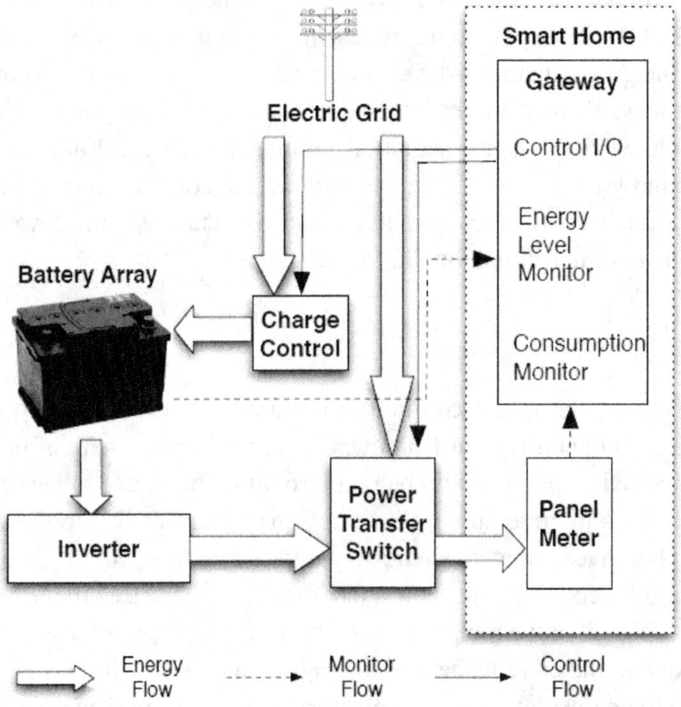

products generated by the company. The asset of the power production industry could be transformer, wire, other electrical factors etc. Given the constraints above, we frame smart charge linear optimization problem as follows. The objective is to minimize a home's electricity bill using a battery array with a usable capacity (after accounting for its DOD) of C kWh. We divide each day into T discrete intervals of length l from 1 to T. We then denote the power charged to the battery during interval i as s_i, the power discharged from the battery as d_i, and the power consumed from the grid as p_i. We combine both the battery array and inverter efficiency into a single efficiency parameter e. Finally, we specify the cost per kWh over the ith interval as c_i, and the amount billed as m_i. Formally, our objective is to minimize P_T $i=1 m_i$ each day, given the following constraints.

1. **Monopolization:** This is said to have an overview regarding the whole business and analysing the entire network of the plant.
2. **Decision Key:** This is estimating the key decision excluding the other factors of decision.
3. **Decision Making:** This is nothing but implementing the policy. This will focus extremely on developing a strategy.
4. **Business Network:** The entire business must be taken into consideration rather than taking a network.
5. **Profit Making:** Business point of view is making a profit from the estimated asset and this should be primarily a focus that should be a long-time profit. The maximization of the short-term profit for maximum years by saving the unrequited spending amount, could lead an accountability of the long-term profit.
6. **Maximum Level for Service:** The safety is the foremost consideration including the environment safety and performance for the best delivery of the product should be maintained.
7. **Risk Management:** The 100 per cent efficiency couldn't be guaranteed. But the maximum acceptable level should be maintained that could save a company or an industry from any risk factors.

BUSINESS KPI

A business case or a process is to meet the requirement of client by collecting the related and structured activity inside the industry or a plant, which promote a service or a product. Key Performance Indicators (KPI) is said to be followed by many data driven organization that motivates them in their efficiency. It is defined as the "measures that helps to monitor a company's performance by the manager and spot out the changes that could be done in order to increase the efficiency". The processes are designed in reducing the spending cost but increase in the efficiency of the product or produce the profit from the increased efficiency. This could add value to the business case. Objective, source, performance criteria and the action plan are the key roles to be performed to make a KPI meaningful. The foremost endeavour of a business is, "utilization of the assets to a maximum extend. The business clutches the assets regularly, which led to the production of higher revenue. However, the condition could get worsen due to this. At the plant or in industries, regular monitoring and control should be maintained, in order to utilize and sustain the asset properly. The investment in this monitoring and management will prolong the life of the asset. Hence, a balancing act should be maintained that utilizes the asset at a maximum and lowering the cost to the minimum, so that the business could be enhanced.

CASE STUDY ON IOT SMART ENERGY MANAGEMENT STRATEGY

- **Industry Name:** SA Power Networks
- **Strategy Plan:** Asset Management Plan 3.2.01 Substation Transformers 2014 to 2025

SA Power Networks is a sole industry in South Australia that delivers the electricity from the high voltage transmission network connection points, which is operated by ElectraNet. The power lines have the network of about 87,500 kilo meters. They have business customers of about 830,000 in South Australia. The Strategy of the Asset Management is: "to revamp the capital investment through targeted substitution of assets, depending on assessment of asset condition and risk, and also seeks to provide sustainable life-cycle management of assets through the use of condition monitoring and life assessment techniques." For the successful implementation of the substation power transformer asset management plan, it is necessary to create, develop and implement the planned stages. Through this SA Power Network industry meets the standard of the industry and give and optimum satisfaction for the stack holders and the handling customers. Management of the substation power transformers in managing the asset is the industry's focus until the end of the life cycle of the transformers. If any issues are to be found in the previous stage, then the stage is necessarily corrected in the next proceeding stages. Through this feedback, the feasibility and reliability of the life cycle plan of the substation transformers could be increased which thereby increases the efficiency of the power distribution networks.

BUDGET PLAN

Substation Power transformers transfer the transmitted voltage in the form of the distribution voltage, which is situated at the mass electricity supply substations. About 696 substations are found in that station, which is under the service condition. The average unit replacement cost could be at the estimated level of about $260,000 to $1,640,000 that is found to be greater than the estimated cost. The asset management plan in this industry is carried out by regular monitoring and maintaining the condition and performance of the transformer that will extend the life term of the asset life and this will surely help us in achieving the long-term replacement plan.

SA Power Network provides certain key aspects that satisfies the risk management principles, provides the customers satisfaction, transport most favourable returns to the shareholders, provide environmentally friendly surroundings which provides the safety situation for the people around as well as the employees. According to the history of the SA Power Networks, the transformers used here are highly reliable with the low service failure rate. The situation that arises to the service failure is due to the supply disruption to the maximum number of customers, up to 20,000 and shattering failure that is caused due to the explosion of the transformer or due to the oil fire or due to the issues that are caused by the atmosphere. The replacement of the transformers could take about 5 to 20 days, although the enough spare parts are easily available in the industry. With the help of the utilization of the Insurance spare unit that is held at the industry store the failed transformers could be easily replaced. The unit to be replaced enters the Insurance spare store as a spare part. About 12 months' time will be required for purchasing, manufacturing and delivering a novel unit. For the last five years there have been a maximum number of failures in the power production line. With the adequate monitoring of the transformer condition, the failure of the transformer could be avoided. The risk and the cost of failure that is caused by the transformers could be avoided due to this continuous management plan. From the period of year 2014 till 2025, a total of 135 substation power transformers are programmed to be replaced.

The estimated expenses are generally in line with the average annual expenditure over the last 5 years, ±$0.78million or $13 per cent. The greater part of the expenses, around 83%, recounts the non-estimated replacement due to certain faults and failures over the past 5 years.

IMPROVEMENTS IN BUDGET PLAN

The replacement of the substation transformers and the expenses plan is available in the Risk management framework of the SA Power Network industry depending on the asset past information and general guidelines. The industry tries to maintain the records of the asset management plan that helps them to continue their development process in the following manner:

1. Asset situation as well as imperfections that includes the category condition ratings/scores
2. Asset mistake as well as malfunction that includes aspects that causes the mistake/malfunction
3. Estimated amount that they spend due to the replacement which includes labour as well as the material cost.

CURRENT MAINTENANCE STRATEGY

The detailed explanation of the asset management plan that is carried out at SA Power Network industry is mention in the figure. The plan of the substation power transformers in the power distribution process ensures that the transformer is getting operated in a safe, secure and an environmentally friendly condition. The plan between the year 2014 and 2025 is stated ensuring a dividend profit for the shareholders of the SA Power Network. A new management plan is currently activating at the SA Power Networks that is mentioned by the Condition Monitoring and Life Assessment (CM&LA) Methodology in the asset management approach. The Condition Monitoring and Life Assessment at the present scenario replace the current carried situation plan in the asset management as shown in figure 2. This method provides an approach that is highly reliable, economically safe in using the asset in the power substation transformer.

RISK MANAGEMENT AND IMPROVEMENTS

The term Risk management means any systematic method that logically identifies, analyse, assess, treat, and monitor the risk associates' factor in an event or an activity. This will enable the industry or the plant to minimize the loss factor and maximize the opportunity. The processes of the risk management are as follows:

1. Categorize the activity or a situation that necessarily causes the risk event
2. Analyse the type of risk that has happened in the scenario. Potential consequence that causes the risk to occur and their level of magnitude is estimated.
3. Priority of the risk is estimated and determination the management priority.

Figure 2. Asset management plan that is currently carried out at SA power networks

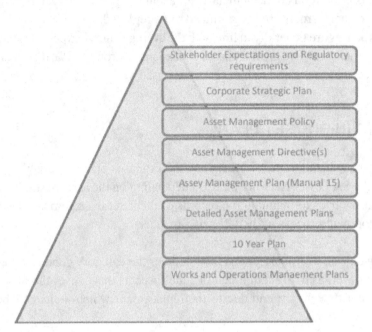

4. Control procedures are taken to neglect the risk factors.
5. Monitoring and reviewing the risk management system is necessarily carried out.

Risk assessment and management is used in the decision-making process by the SA Power Networks, in order to estimate the capital and expenditure of the network during their maintenance and transformer operation. Probably the transformer failure is caused due to the following reasons:

- **Mechanical Failure:** This occurs normally due to the component failure of the distribution network.
- **Insulation Failure:** This happens due to the poor oil quality which is used as an insulation factor. This could also be caused by the short- circuit of the transformer. In order to maintain the quality of the gas in the insulation oil Dissolved Gas Analysis (DGA) test is carried out which is explained later in this chapter.
- **Thermal Failure:** Caused due to the problems caused by the cooling circuit or due to the large resistance associations or overloading.

Dissolved Gas Analysis (DGA)

Performance which is carried out by DGA in the insulating oil with the oil sampling analysis test is used as an evaluation of the transformer health. Any malfunction that happens inside a transformer and its required equipment could generate some gases inside it. Therefore, the identification of these gases and the information obtained from that could be very useful for some maintenance and prevention. There are many methods to estimate these gases but the Dissolved Gas Analysis (DGA) is said to be the most efficient. In order to measure the concentration of the dissolved gases, there are two process carried out:

1) Sampling the oil obtained 2) Testing the samples. This DGA analysis should be carried out at least a year and the details should be compared with the previous analysis data. There are several standards such as ASTM D3613, ASTM D3612, and ANSI/IEEE C57.104, respectively to evaluate the result.

The main causes of the formation of the gases are due to the electrical strife and thermal putrefaction. At some point, each transformer could produce gases in usual working temperature. The transformer insulation process is done through several mineral oils which is said to be the composition of several hydrocarbons. The decomposition process in these hydrocarbons is said to be tedious due to the thermal and the electrical fault. The basic reaction occurs due to the breakage of C-H bonds and C-C bonds. Hence, we could get the fragments of hydrocarbon and some hydrogen atoms. This leftover mingles with each other and leads to the formation of gases such as hydrogen (H_2), methane (CH_4), acetylene (C_2H_2), ethylene (C_2H_4), and ethane (C_2H_6). Moreover, due to the cellulose insulation, thermal decomposition or electrical problem generates methane (CH_4), hydrogen (H_2), carbon monoxide (CO), and carbon dioxide (CO_2). These gases are the key gases and their property is said to be combustible (here the exceptional gas is CO_2 which is non-combustible).

This key gas depends highly on their temperature which is based on their volume of material at that circumstantial temperature. The small volume at high temperature could produce the same quantity of gases as produced by the huge volume at restrained temperature. This is mainly caused because on volume. For this reason, the gases which are formed due to the transformer's insulating oil is used for the evaluation process by comparing with the history of these transformers in order to find out any faults that could happen potentially or thermally.

Later the appropriate samples are examined and evaluated, the foremost step of the DGA analysis is to find the concentration levels of each key gas's samples. This could be expressed in parts per million (ppm). It is endorsed that the concentration of the key gases changes in time and therefore the rate of change of the concentration is calculated. Fundamentally, the probable fault in the transformer could be indicated by the sharp rise in the value of key gas concentration. Therefore, it could be said that the result of the DGA analysis gives a sharp rise in the value of the concentration level of the gases. If the normal value limit is surmounted, then supplementary analysis of the sample should be taken and once again we must confirm where the key gas concentration level is accumulating. When the level reaches the action level point then the transformer should be considered, and that transformer should be removed. Therefore, care must be taken while taking this sample analysis test. This test involves in the calculation of the key gas ratio and then correlating it with certain limit range as shown in table 1.

Table 1. The description of the gas with their limit range and their fault type

Gas Description	Normal Limit(<)	Actual Limit(>)	Potential fault type
H_2(Hydrogen)	150	1000	Corona, Arcing
CH_4(Methane)	25	80	Sparking
C_2H_2(Acetylene)	15	70	Arcing
C_2H_4(Ethylene)	20	150	Severe Overheating
C_2H_6(Ethane)	10	35	Local Overheating
CO(Carbon Monoxide)	500	1000	Severe Overheating
CO_2(Carbon dioxide)	10000	15000	Severe Overheating
TDCG(TotalCombustibles)	720	4630	

The Gas Description with their respective key gas concentration is given in table 1. When the value exceeds the normal limit then the sample frequency should be increased with the consideration given to planned outage in near term for the further evaluation. When the value exceeds the Action limits then the transformer should be removed immediately from the service (A. Zahedi, 2015).

FMEA PROCESS BASED ON PRIORITY

The Failure Modes and Effects Analysis (FMEA) is an analysis technique that helps in reducing the risk factors as shown in figure 3. This is a very effective way that increases the reliability of the transformer that is widely used in the power grid system. FMEA technique was proposed in the field of the power system, in order to increase the efficiency of the power system and enhance the economy at a period of one year. In other words, this can be stated as an important analysis that is carried out to determine and assess the risk factors with the help of potential failure modes. This technique is a quality-based analysis technique that lists the failure modes, reason for the failure, consequences caused due to the failure and the actions, which are carried out due to the failures. Risk priority numbers (RPN) is calculated by assigning a value for each risk causing factor that could lead to failure and severity of the transformer which is given by a formula:

RPN = (Severity) * (Occurrence) * (Detection)   (1)

Consequently, this also gives the priority to the action that is to be carried out in order to avoid the failure. Higher the value of the RPN, higher is the case of the failure actions that could occur. The focus of the SA Power Networks depends on the following criteria:

- **Failure:** When a functionality is terminated then that case is mentioned as a failure.
- **Mode of Failure:** Behaviour of an item that causes failure.
- **Mechanism or Cause of a Failure:** This represents the cause or the situation that initiates the failure situation which is stated by a term known as "Possible failure causes".
- **Effects of Failure:** Status of an item or a process after the failure has occurred in that process.
- **Severity:** It refers to the level of the system affected by the failure. If the severity is said to be in a peak level, then it means that the system causes a huge damage which is to be considered.
- **Occurrence:** This refers to the number of occurrences that describes the situation to occur. This is not referred in time but is expressed in terms of the root causes for the situation.
- **Detection:** This is termed as identifying the root cause before the failure beings to occur.

Based on this situation or scenario, an algorithm is represented in figure. For each case, we can able to identify the risk causing factor at an early stage and we can try to reduce or eliminate the cause. Two control methods are associated with the cause:

1. **Prevention Control:** This is proposed to reduce the cause and consequences of fault at an early stage before the failure could occur.
2. **Detection and Identification Control:** This control is proposed to identify the failure of the process before the problem reaches the end user or the customer.

As soon as all the possible Risk priority numbers is identified, focus should be given to the one that increases the priority of the RPN. In this situation, an asset manager should detect the situation and identify the entire problem that causes the failure. An asset manager is responsible for assigning the task to the appropriate person and solves all the issues. At once the risk reduction factor is carried out and the RPN rating will be changed automatically. Hence, the modified RPN is estimated and intended by the envisaged brutality, happenings and exposure levels.

Smarter Decision Making for Grid Station Using IoT

The Asset manager must choose on a consolidation of various activities that imitate plant stacking and stretch levels, support plans, and substitution timetabling. These things are for the most part forbid additionally depend upon the framework necessities of the gear. It is conceivable that one course to resource cultivation includes changing the working environment of the thing to expand life or reduce prompt disappointment probability. These things are by and large forbidding additionally depend upon the framework necessities of the gear. It is conceivable that one course to resource cultivation includes changing the working environment of the thing to amplify life or decrease quick disappointment probability as shown in figure 4.

The described system architecture has been realised by using the JADE platform and employed to perform several simulation implementing variations of the management policy as well as different configurations in terms of involved network elements. In order to improve the realism of the simulation, a few sets of environmental historical data have been used for smart grid transformers.

Figure 3. Algorithm of FMEA process

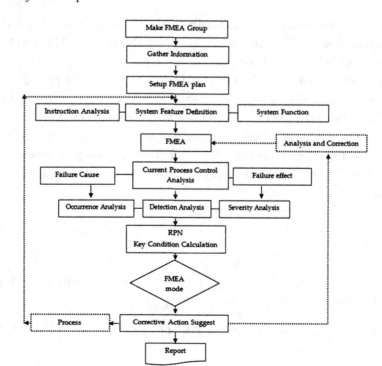

Figure 4. The decision made by an asset manager based on the following consideration

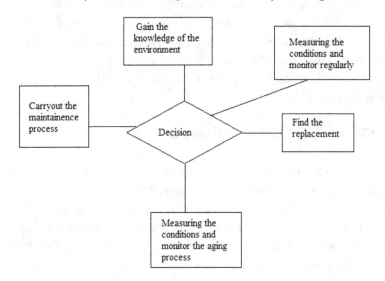

Loads data used to feed the simulator have been collected by real data coming from historical sets of an industrial area and a prevalently residential area. In order to test the behaviour of the system indifferent conditions, the available sets have been randomly mixed so that meteorological conditions and load values substantially differ from day to day.

CONCLUSION AND FUTURE WORK

The difference between a transmission and the distribution of the power is described as well as the asset management technique followed in this differential system is also discussed in this chapter. Asset manager has the right to decide and he/she is responsible for implementing the action plan that deals with the maintenance timetabling, substitute scheduling and level of stress in that plant and they are mutually dependent1) on the system necessities of the equipment. This chapter also dealt with the implementation of FMEA analysis procedure, in order to avoid the risk factor that is caused in the power transmission industry with the calculation of RPN priority estimation. The result obtained by this procedure is much satisfied, which leads to the development of FMEA for future purposes. When the data is evaluated by FMEA, ranking should be made with the help of RPN to determine the case of the irregularity of working mechanism.

REFERENCES

Ali, S., & Smith, K. A. (2016). On Learning Algorithm Selection for Classification. *Journal on Applied Soft Computing*, 6(2), 119–138. doi:10.1016/j.asoc.2004.12.002

Budde. (2015). *Smart Grid Australia Provided the Vision for the Smart Grid/Smart City Project*. Smart Grid Australia.

Davidson, M. (2015). *Smart Grid Australia: An Overview. Technical Report*. Wessex Consult.

Grid Intelligent Grid. (n.d.). Technical Report. Retrieved from http://www.igrid.net.au/

Shafiullah, Oo, Jarvis, Ali, & Wolfs. (2016). Prospects of Renewable Energy—A Feasibility Study in the Australian Context. *Journal of Renewable Energy, 39*(1).

The Smart Grid: An Introduction. (2018). Technical report by US Department of Energy.

Townsville Solar City. (n.d.). *Ergon Energy, Queensland*. Retrieved from http://www.townsvillesolarcity.com.au/Home/tabid/36/Default.aspx

Weedall. (2016). *BPA Smart Grid Overview*. Energy and Communications, Washington House Technology.

Zahedi, A. (2011). Developing a System Model for Future SmartGrid. *Proceedings in 2011 IEEE PES Innovative SmartGrid Technologies Conference*, 1-5.

Chapter 6
Cloud–Based Predictive Maintenance and Machine Monitoring for Intelligent Manufacturing for Automobile Industry

Suresh Annamalai
Nehru Institute of Engineering and Technology, India

Udendhran R.
Bharathidasan University, India

Vimal S.
National Engineering College, India

ABSTRACT

The concept of predictive analysis plays complex information retrieval and categorization systems are needed to process queries, filter, and store, and organize huge amount of data, which are mainly composed of texts. As soon as datasets becomes large, most information combines with algorithms that might not perform well. Moreover, prediction is important in today's industrial purposes since that could reduce the issues of heavy asset loss towards the organization. The purpose of prediction is necessary in every field since it could help us to stop the cause of occurring the error before any vulnerable activities could happen. Predictive maintenance is a method that consumes the direct monitoring of mechanical condition of plant equipment to decide the actual mean time to malfunction for each preferred machine. The authors try to estimate the fault that could occur in the machines and decide the time that could cause a critical situation. This prediction should be done effectively, and for this purpose, they have stepped into the concept of machine learning.

DOI: 10.4018/978-1-5225-9023-1.ch006

A BRIEF INTRODUCTION TO INTELLIGENT MANUFACTURING

In this modern era new technologies, innovation and developments are increasing day by day that leads to mass production of voluminous data. This huge volume of data seems to be more informative, which leads to the production and enhancement of the manufacturing process in various industries. This could save the asset of a production industry. The main role of prediction is best suitable in the field of health monitoring that helps in continuously monitoring the health of the patient without the need of a caretaker near them. Motivated by the quality of life and less expensive healthcare systems, a change in existing healthcare system should be focused to a home centred setting including dealing with illness to preserving wellness. Innovative user-centred preventive healthcare model can be regarded as a promising solution for this transformation. It doesn't substitute traditional healthcare, but rather directed towards this technology. The technology used in the pervasive healthcare could be considered from two aspects: i) as pervasive computing tools for healthcare, and ii) as enabling it anywhere, anytime and to anyone. It has progressed on biomedical engineering (BE), medical informatics (MI), and pervasive computing. Biomedical engineering is the integration of both engineering and medical science that helps in the improvement of the Equipment used in the hospitals. Medical informatics comprises of huge amount of medical resources to enhance storage, retrieval, and employ these resources (Bond, J. (2015)). The advancement has been done to monitor the health of the patients and provide the details to the caretakers, who are near by the remote areas. This could be done in a real-time with the help of the internet access. Due to the condition of monitoring the patient at a real-time, the caretaker can provide the suggestions regarding their essential signs of their body situation through a video conference.

Another key aspect of predictive maintenance deals with the condition monitoring or condition-based maintenance. Condition based monitoring deals with the analysis of the machine or anything without interrupting its regular work. Moreover, monitoring the condition of equipment is like decision making strategy, which could avoid any types of faults or failures that happens at the near future to that equipment and its components. This is like the Prognostic and Health Monitoring (PHM) that is mentioned above. Prognostic is nothing but analysing the upcoming situation that could occur for the patient. Similarly, for the machines it could be stated as Remaining Useful Life (RUL). The latest advancement of computerized control, information techniques and communication networks have made potential accumulating mass amount of operation and process's conditions data to be harvested in making an automated Fault Detection and Diagnosis (FDD) and increasing more resourceful approaches for intelligent defensive maintenance behaviour, also termed as predictive maintenance.

According to the estimation about 20 to 30 percent of the periodically monitored Equipment for predictive maintenance have been affected from its production and quality that must be examined regularly. In fact, monitoring the Equipment in a weekly or monthly manner does not prove to be enough for detecting certain abnormalities in the machines (Boschrexroth.com. (2017)). If we change the Equipment from periodical to continuous monitoring, then it could lead to lower the cost of expenditure for the machines considerably. This could save the expenditure from on-line monitoring systems on PC and accelerometer. Artificial Neural Network (ANN) could be used effectively in this type of evaluation for detecting the abnormal patterns of the sensor validation and for trend evaluation.

APPLICATION OF PREDICTIVE MAINTENANCE

Predictive maintenance is a method, which consumes the direct monitoring of mechanical condition of plant Equipment to decide the actual mean time to malfunction for each preferred machine (Buntz, B. (2016)). Based on the mechanical construction of the equipment we could able to estimate the fault that could occur in the machines and decide the time that could cause a critical situation. With the help of predictive maintenance, we could able to detect the equipment that could seriously be affected before the happenings of the situation. The information could be generated before any hazardous situation could occur in the equipment. For this estimation, one of the most popularly used equipment is vibration signature analysis. With the help of this analysis we could able to predict the mechanical condition of the machines. But there is a condition that this analysis method alone could not be used for the estimation of the mechanical failure, which does not include the oil lubricating condition, displacement of axis and many other parameters. There is another method called failure modes that could estimate the components and the magnitude obtained by the method could detect the fault evolution and machine operating conditions.

In general, Prediction is something that finds pattern in the huge quantity of data. The best statistical model had to be chosen in order to gain the right insight of data from our disposed information (Cisco (2015)). The hidden pattern disclosed by a process could make us to find the prediction. This is what is termed as predictive analysis. In a production or manufacturing environment, we encounter with the concern of optimizing the process, appointing the job-shop, decoding or arranging, organizing the cell, controlling the quality, labour work maintenance, planning the required material, activity resource planning during inclined situation, supply-chain management and future-worth examination of cost inference, but the acquaintance of data-mining tools that could decrease the general nightmares in these areas is not extensively obtainable. Not only in the manufacturing industries but also this could be best suitable for the retail industries, where they must know the wish list of the customers that they are going to purchase at the month in the particular period of time based on the fashion, weather etc. The best formula for this is 1) collect data 2) clean data (remove the unwanted data from the list) 3) identify patterns (it is necessary to group the data making a similarity list from the insights) and finally 4) Make predictions (foresight).

In relevant forms predictive modelling, decision analysis and optimization, deal outlining and prognostic hunt and explore. Predictive analytics can be functional to an assortment of industry approaches and plays a key role in search marketing and commendation engines that is shown in the figure 1.

Predictive modelling and analysis could be the utmost importance factor in every business organizations that leads to noteworthy development in their quality and function and plays a major role in the decisions they take that could improve their asset value. In present scenario we could consider the Amazon and EBay which depends on the online ad network like Face book and Google. Each and every organization could find a statistical analysis of their data and could analyse their environment well at certain limits like present clients, turnover activities, follow the supplies and so on. The maximum profit could be yield by the predictive maintenance thus identifying the best course of plan and work accordingly (Christensen, C.M., Raynor, M.E. and McDonald, R., 2015). Despite the achievement stories of integrated predictive analytics by practitioner's large touchable and considerable payback to organization, information systems researchers as well comprise the significance and meaning of predictive analytics when discussing the future trends and evolution of decision support systems. Certain points are to be considered while following the rules.

Figure 1. Manufacturing industry quality and analysis

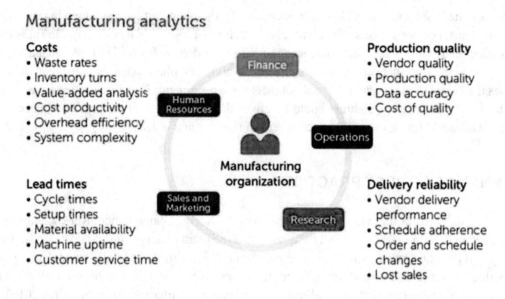

ANN IN INTELLIGENT MANUFACTURING

The machines are trained in certain manner of detecting the fault and at the first defect indication itself the fault should be noted since the similar signal pattern and various fault mechanism could lead a machine to show evidence of analogous vibrational symptoms. But with the help the inherent capacity of the generalization of ANN will be very useful in handling the situation. Expert systems are particularly useful where the knowledge of an expert is unambiguously available. ANN could "take out" the knowledge with the accessible information although the operator is not available. For the alarm system and diagnosing the fault the best integrated system that could be used with the neural network is the expert system. Connectionist expert systems along with the ANN in its knowledge bases could provide maximum reimbursement in terms of velocity, toughness and knowledge attainment. It could be either object-oriented language or procedural language or functional language. Huge amount of calculations could be carried out with the python of python very easily. The companies who involved in this predictive maintenance could achieve practical. In every manufacturing company it is necessary to collect the data regarding the quality of the product, machine safety, personnel fulfilment as well as the recording level. These data could be collected with the help of product and quality manager, professionals and the operators who oversee each and every particular task. Through these data we could obtain the efficiency of a machine (Columbus, L. (2017)), circumvent injuries, avoiding the unwanted products to pass through the process and the companies should have these details to face the audit. These details are collected normally in a pen and chapter method where later it could be digitalized. There is a common thinking that the collection of these relevant data could help to improve the quality of the company, but the real factor is different. The problem arises with the quantity of data that could be useful as well as useless. The reality is it does not matter about the quantity of data but the right data and better analysis. The collected data should be meaningful and brief. Bringing the Statistical Process Control (SPC) method in the place of accurate data will necessarily help us in a proactive control process and avert the quality of manufacture malfunction before they appear.

Knowledge regarding the prediction of suitable opportunity:

In this case the best opportunity should be identified by the plant, which could help in improving the company. For instance, let's take a client who comes to buy a product of a company. He finds a defect in that product and informs the plant manager regarding the defect. Immediately the manager should necessarily act if the information given by the client is valid. The plant manager comes into action and determines the defect of the product that did not meet the requirement. It could take certain expenditure to cure this defect, but that expenditure could be given as a profit to the company. Within certain time period the plant could run at the top that could reduce the cost and defects.

MAINTENANCE OF BEST PRACTICES

It is necessary to adjust in the wide range of enterprise by having maintenance over the entire project not to their own plant. In a company both the quality and the plant manager should take decision wisely. For example, if the plant manager tries to cut down the cost of $ 1 million dollars by neglecting the raw materials that hold minimum good to a product then there could be sustainable cost reduction to the profit which could exceed more than a million dollar in that particular year (Gilchrist, A., 2016). So, it is necessary to take the decisions wisely not quickly.

Manufacturers give their concentration more on the quality of the product. They also need to ensure that there is an optimal functioning around the whole manufacturing plant, updated, efficiency of the workers, appropriate measurements, and the finest creation potential. With predictive analytics, it's doable to not only get better the quality of manufacture, increase equipment return on investment (ROI) and overall equipment effectiveness (OEE), and look forward to the needs across the plant and enterprise, but also improve the brand's status, leave behind the competition and make sure the safety of the customer. Hence, mainly focusing on the predictive analysis benefits, it is necessary to find the possible routes that how it could be used within the organization in order to save the industry.

They have certain advantages that are as follows:

1. **Minimization of Downtime Cost:** When the machine has malfunction and the time required to make its functionality to normal condition is known as downtime. This could be totally minimized with the predictive analysis since it could predict the abnormal condition of the machine at a very early stage.
2. **Minimize the Production Loss:** The major advantage of predictive analysis is that it could necessarily indicate us at which part the replacement has to be done rather than indicating us the maintenance around the whole machine (Haight, J. and Park, H. (2015)).
3. **Reduction of Man Work:** Since prediction analysis with the procedure of ANN helps us in detecting the defect found in the part of the machine, it could reduce the effort of the man power. Hence the labour cost could be reduced abruptly.
4. **Revenue Maximization:** Normally increase in the machine production could lead to the huge revenue to the industries. The maintenance could help us in monitoring the unusual shut downs and helps in analysing the smoother operation of the machines.
5. **Improve Employee's Maintenance:** Predictive maintenance will permit more liberated time for labours maintenance by determining the accurate mend job desirable and subordinate extent of job.

Analytics is associated to the usage of large amount of data that could be either quantitative or statistically analysed, either descriptive or analytical models and either fact-based management to drive judgement and append assessment" (IBM Internet of Things (Software Group). (2016)). There are many variations among these analytical models and these variations could lead to the categorization of the following: descriptive, prescriptive and predictive. The descriptive analytics is something that is purely based on reporting the interested phenomenon. With the help of this analysis we could able to gather, collect, organize, tabulate and depict the data but it does not provide the user with any sort of information regarding how the event occurred or regarding the happenings that could occur soon which could be a drawback.

The prescriptive analytics on the other hand, is related to making certain predictions regarding the Equipment that it could happen soon (ITU, 2017). To make this understanding very clear and precise, predictive analysis is analysing the near future happenings events and it may cause bad then it must be stopped at once. A shorter form of this analysis is described in the table given below. Certain suggestions were done by (Jeschke, S., Brecher, C., Song, H. and Rawat, D. (2017)) that include experimentation design and optimization. These experimental designs explain the causes why a happening happens by making experiments where independent variables are manipulated, exterior values are proscribed and hence the results are being completed that concludes with activities that the decision producer should follow. These have produced a report regarding the intelligence based predictive modelling that is shown in the figure 2 given below.

INDUSTRY 4.0

The most recent industrial revolution has enabled a cross-linking between people, objects and software systems for the first time ever. This cross-linking ability is giving rise to broad spectrum of opportuni-

Figure 2. Predictive analysis with the degree of intelligence

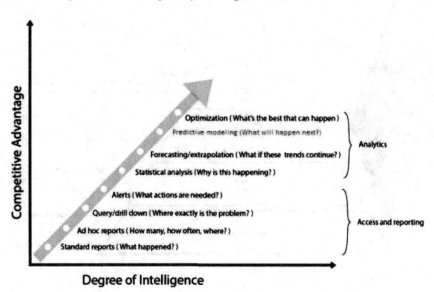

ties to increase productivity, quality, efficiency and flexibility of manufacturing processes (Jones, J. (2017)). In simple words, Industry 4.0 is supposed to firstly bridge the industrial production with the information technology and then with the help of advanced data analytics achieve the above-mentioned opportunities. When it comes to the structure of Industry 4.0, it is often described as a four-layer one, where the base and the crucial part is the Internet of Things (Lee, J., Bagheri, B. and Kao, H. (2015)) .

Following this shown in the figure 3 and 4, given above structure, Industry 4.0 will merge the physical actions with the digital world, where the outcome will be a more advanced manufacturing process leading to the creation of smarter factories. (Lewis, D. (2016)). If built correctly, these Cyber Physical Systems, will enable the smart factories to disrupt the manufacturing industry, lead to faster production processes and a safer environment for the workers. According to, Lee, Bagheri and Kao, (2015) the Industry 4.0 factories will differ from exiting one in many ways. Among other attributes they will possess self-awareness, self-predictiveness, self-configurability and self-organizing. This will allow a thorough knowledge and understanding of the monitored factory.

Figure 3. Industry 4.0 main layers

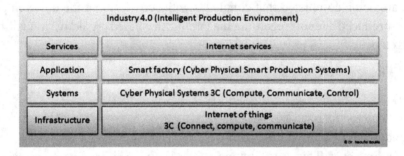

Figure 4. Smart assets

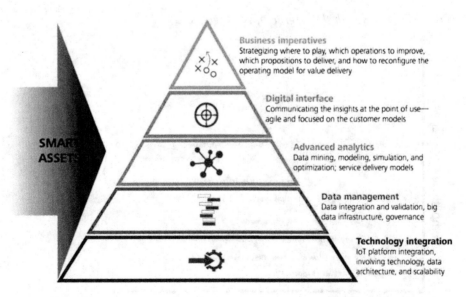

In a chapter by Jones, J. (2017) it is argued that the data privacy challenges created by IoT are not largely different than those created by the existing digital technologies, but that it must be addressed differently. IoT is connecting the physical with the digital operations, where the data is controlling the physical parts of the system (pumps, lightning, ventilation, production line, etc.), indicating that a security breach could cause damage to both digital data and the physical production. For example, back in 2005, an internet worm infection stopped 13 Daimler Chrysler manufacturing plants for almost an hour, causing a total halt of production (Cisco, 2015). Existing labour skills and knowledge are an additional problem that adopters might encounter. Having the most efficient IoT systems would not be enough if there are no employees who understand it, can monitor it and are able to develop it further. In the future, we might see a decline of traditional jobs and instead, there will be an increasing demand for skillful labour, that can program and design new digital systems shown in the figure 5, given below.

With time the IoT will become a building block of every industry, which will cause a shift to a pull-based economy, where the production will be driven by a real-time demand and products that are tailor-made according to the individual consumer. This flexibility in production is currently unimaginable, but the IoT based production will allow for much higher level of agility and adjust ability that will ultimately shift the manufacturing industry from product-oriented to customer-oriented.

CASE STUDY

This case study is regarding the Highlanders Company that had made an investigation with the management team, in order to replace the Toyota vehicles from the courier services and replace with the best-selling automobile that could increase the efficiency and decrease the cost.

How Ford Ventured Into New Zealand Automobile as an Alternative for Toyota

This was started by setting a goal that drive more qualified customers to Ford NZ in order to maximize visitors of this website, which could convert into inquiries. Ford New Zealand (Ford NZ) and J. Walter Thompson (JWT NZ) analysed the significance of intensifying their online viewers by transferring them into customers. They constructed brand preference and drive deliberation that converts more site

Figure 5. IoT in manufacturing

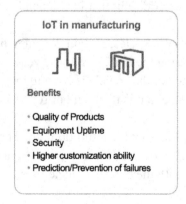

viewers as customers. In order to make this idea possible they banged the Google Display Network. For the suitable customers they started to deliver the appealing digital impact. About seventy five percent of the clients were involved in their web search, sites, videos and other sources to view their new model car. Though this method they started to guess the information regarding their brand which the customers got attracted and the reports were framed that gather the positive and negative impact of the upcoming model. Although this method banged the eyes of the customer view, they again started to get the clients attention by establishing the idea of JWT NZ. The agency made collaboration that demonstrated banners and attached them with customized content that targeted in engaging the consumers across various websites during their acquisition journey. At past they followed the plan of "set-and-forget" where it came to be called later as "test-and-refine" approach.

Next Ford started a method of "in-market" audiences that targeted the customers who were to purchase the new vehicles. Through the In-market strategy they reached the customers by the data they have, who were enthusiastically glancing to formulate an acquisition. With these approaches they started to reach many customers and, they bought the viewers of Google audience as clients. At last, they used GDN's marketing tool that bought the previously viewed customer of the site again to view their site newly. They used a customized message setting that made numerous visitors of that site to visit again.

Chris Masterson the head of the Ford group says that, "It's critical to use the right data to drive your marketing strategy. We learned that there is a unique data insight about our audience at each stage of the purchase journey. Acting on those right insights opened the door for us to truly deliver the right message at the right moment to the right potential customer". This is how Ford strengthens their business strategy. The top vehicle that makes a best service includes Ford Ranger, Holden Colorado, Mitsubishi Triton, Kia Sportage, Mazda CX-5, Nissan Navara.

Commercial Vehicle Movements in New Zealand

In our study we have taken the light weight commercial vehicles (LMCV) that could travel well in the urban areas. These are designed under certain criteria that are as follows:

- Cars that contains traditional insignia (this indicates the person who is the owner/ operator of the vehicle)
- Vans, less weight trucks and utility that takes about 3.5 times larger gross laden weight (typically we consider the light commercial vehicles to have only a sole rear tyre but here we can include dual rear tyre also).
- Two-axle large trucks more than 3.5 tones gross laden weight that is independent of a trailer.

Though the study has more significance in the LMCV vehicles, certain consideration was made in the vehicle that makes the commercial purpose by entering the corridor. These vehicles were analysed based on the goods and service related and analysed whether the vehicle is coming into the city or going out of the city. Certain consideration regarding the vehicle that is made in our report includes:

- The vehicle should carry the good or provide services or it should do both. The purpose of the vehicle should satisfy the business meets, picking up of goods from certain organizations, attend the expectation of the employer and finally deals with the confidential actions.

- This involves LMCV, HCV (high commercial vehicles) and other type of vehicles such as personal cars, taxi, in fact it also deals with the non-motorized vehicles such as bicycle or walk
- The term "incoming" means that somebody arrives from different site to the organization or business beneath surveillance and "outgoing" means that somebody from the pragmatic business or organization is moving to various site.

The New Zealand Qualifications Authority (NZQA) is the New Zealand government top body that plays a major role in offering their control during the assessments and qualification. This educational act came in the year of 1989. The National Certificate in Motor Industry (Automotive Electrical and Mechanical Engineering) Level 6 with filaments in Electrical as well as Electronics, Light Vehicle, Motorcycle, Outdoor Power Equipment, and Trailer Boat Systems identifies the skills and acquaintance necessary for people in responsibilities within the automotive electrical and mechanical division of the motor industry, which engage common vehicle or tool repair and service work at an initial level to transitional level.

The execution of fleet management is very important that could create efficiency in the utilization of the fuel. According to the New Zealand, the term heavy vehicle means the trucks or lorry or vehicles that weight more than 3.5 tons. This is defined as a heavy weight group of vehicles. This could be managed by an individual company although it has a single owner operator within the circle. These vehicles are created for the specific purposes and the driver who drives these vehicles should be well equipped with specified skills. The vehicles are extremely costly. For operating the fleet, the company must come forward to show their interest. For example, the company can increase the amount of production by increasing the profit by efficiently utilizing the vehicle.

New Zealand has also defined the light fleet vehicles evidently. They provide vehicles to companies like taxi, courier, provide vehicles to employees, government and public sectors. The fleet ensure in following the "safety driving policy" among the employees. They could also vary at certain circumstances. The country tends to reduce the circumstances by reducing the consumption of fuel using certain factors like slow driving, using the vehicles for a long distance, regularly monitoring the fuel tank etc. Due to this the country not only provide a safe and secure environment but also it raises the profit and the business economy of the industry by increasing it' productivity. In this chapter we have presented certain specification of the commonly used vehicles in New Zealand and made a study based on their cost, which is presented in a spreadsheet

IoT Based Fleet Management

Fleet management is very necessary that falls under the hands of a transport operator who select a vehicle by considering the fuel management, safety for the transportation and select a driver who could manage the task efficiently. The operator is responsible for managing other factors too that could enhance the fuel-efficiency, safety and cost. The factor of saving fuel is very important since this could have impacts on the following factors:

- This could increase the fleet profit by lowering its operating cost and increasing its demand and productivity
- Enhances the economy of the country by reducing the imports, which does not affect the employment

- The energy security of the country could increase since the country need not depend on the fuel from other countries
- Highly saves the environment by decreasing the emission of carbon dioxide. This could have an impact in the reduction of toxic gases that could save the people health.

This factor forms a strong bond between the safety and the efficiency. Certain steps are required to bring these factors into activity: 1) managing speed 2) predicting the situation at a prior stage 3) reduction in rash driving 4) regularly monitoring the type pressures 5) maintaining the vehicle and avoiding the vehicle usage for a minimum distance. The increase in the vehicle driving could contaminate the road and affect the brake system of the vehicle.

IoT Smart Way of Transport (Fleet Logistics Energy and Environmental Tracking)

Smart way of transport is also the similar way of achieving the sustainability of vehicle like fuel efficiency. Smart Way Transport recognizes the operators of the transport system and shippers who help them in improving their environmental facilities by certain measures. Those operators should involve in cost savings and fuel efficiency to improve the business strategy once in three years. They are required to measure their performance using the Smart Way Fleet Logistics Energy and Environmental Tracking (FLEET) system and sign the Smart Way partnership agreement. Once they receive this recognition, they can receive their logo and display it in their systems. Shippers are the major user of the transport facility and they must spend 50% of their goods with the smart way transport operators. This quantity is monitored by the FLEET. By their own facility they must agree in the reduction of the emission. The most significant concept of this system is to increase the popularity of Smart way transport to the public by helping them in reducing the environmental factors.

Transport Supply Within a Corridor

Transportation is a major part of function in the courier deliver. There are numerous factors that involves in providing the transport facility within the corridor based on the time, logistics etc., that are as follows:

- Organizations mixture and its density within the corridor
- Service prospect based on the customer's point of view
- The standards followed by the operators of the transport service
- Volume of the traffic
- Competitors among the suppliers. This could create a sustainable solution by providing the best services with lowering the cost of the transport.

SPARE PARTS FOR TRANSPORT VEHICLES INTEGRATED WITH IOT

Chassis Design

The chassis design is the main objective that is to be considered while designing a vehicle. This design requires the use of certain software such as CAD and other simulation software such as CATIA V5 R19 and ANSYS 15.0. The chassis design must be considered based on the level 7 consideration of NZQA. During this measure it is necessary to consider base of the wheel, width of the track and other vehicle measurements that are listed below:

- Track Width (Front)
- Track width (Back)
- Overall Weight (without tyres)
- Overall length (with tyres)
- Overall width
- Distance from back to back wheel axle
- Distance from front to front wheel axle
- Tube thickness

The wire frame of the chassis model of a car is shown in the figure 6 and 7.

Backup

Again, coming back, the environmental issue is the major role that is to be considered while making chassis. Carbon fibre composite material that is used while manufacturing the chassis utilizes Petroleum based resin material. This material may not be a biodegradable and it could also be hazardous to the environment. Due to this material, it can affect the human health of the employers who work there during the time of manufacturing. Hence maximum steps should be taken to avoid the petroleum-based

Figure 6. Wire frame of a chassis model

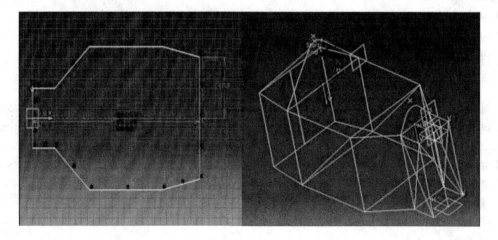

Figure 7. Final design of the chassis model

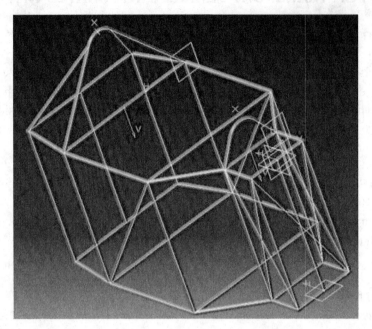

resin and replace it by sustainable and secure resin materials like bio based green resins that serves best to the environment.

TYPES OF SMART VEHICLES ITS RANKING

Light Vehicle Fleet

The term 'light vehicle fleet' comprises of five types of companies that includes certain safe driving policies for the employees that are as follows:

- Taxi companies
- Car or light vehicle rental companies
- Courier companies
- Companies, which supply vehicle for the employees
- Government and public agency vehicles

Certain light weight vehicle with their fuel types is listed in the table given below. There are about 20 vehicles in the below table and these values are taken from the registration database. Other than these fuel certain light vehicles use compressed gas, electricity and liquid petroleum that are not considered in our chapter. It is to be notes that the amount of diesel as well as petrol fleets in the category of fleet size does not match the number of fleets of that size of vehicle. This is because large fleet vehicles could use both type of fuels. This states that the fleet of 400 vehicles could contains 250 petrol-based vehicles and the remaining 150 diesel-based vehicles.

Table 1. Light vehicles with the petrol and diesel fuel type with varying fleet size

Vehicle fleet size	Light vehicles	Petrol vehicles	Diesel vehicles
21-50	1540	1077	476
51-100	527	330	164
101-200	242	159	54
201-400	89	53	18
400+	45	28	7

Transit Vans

In the business era the model of Mark 7 or 6 is most adapted that offers both the front and the rear wheel drive. The transit vehicles are the most versatile one since this comes in a most flexible style and range that gives more comfort. Certain points to remember while choosing a transit van that requires a test driving and inspection, which are as follows:

1. Careful inspection should be done on the tyres by checking whether there are any cracks, bulges and any patchy wear on the treads. When these are found then it means that the tyres are not properly aligned.
2. Load area should be checked properly. During the time of loading and unloading, ply lined vans could suffer denting and scraping that is to be considered
3. There should not be any rust found on the wheel arches, sills and door slide. Make sure that the door handles work in a proper condition and radio work is also checked.
4. A test drive is carried out that ensure the smooth drive of the van and no noise should be produced while catching the break. A solid feel should be produced while driving.
5. It is necessary to check the seat belts that should properly fit with the passenger. Ensure their presence and check whether they work well.
6. The electronic parts should be checked such as lights, sensors, which forms a major problem. Check the brake light, front and back light and make sure whether the indicator works well during their indication.

CONCLUSION AND FUTURE WORK

All these improvements that Industry 4.0 and IoT will bring are still, in most cases, a prediction. It is still early to be able to statistically test the productivity and efficiency improvements as the digital transformation is yet to fully unroll. However, there are predictions and estimations which argue that the IoT is a profitable investment as the benefits it brings will lead to a better resource efficiency, shorter time to market, close to zero waste, shorter production times and a higher labour productivity (Jeschke et al., 2017). The main aim of this chapter is to be to investigate the development and applications of

"Predictive Maintenance" concept in industrial machines. In addition to the survey, different machine learning approaches and their applicability in predictive maintenance applications are successfully explained and compared. In this comparison we have estimated the accuracy, precision and specificity. Finally, a detailed analysis was made between these approaches to determine the best method to be used to overcome some of the current industrial predictive maintenance challenges.

REFERENCES

Bond, J. (2015). *How the Internet of Things is Transforming Manufacturing Today - Supply Chain 24/7*. Available at: http://www.supplychain247.com/article/how_the_internet_of_things_is_transforming_manufacturing_today

Boschrexroth.com. (2017). *Industry 4.0: Smart Manufacturing - Bosch Rexroth AG*. Available at: https://www.boschrexroth.com/en/xc/trends-and-topics/industry-4-0/internet-ofthings/internet-of-things-1#

Buntz, B. (2016). *The 20 Most Important IoT Firms according to You*. Available at: http://www.ioti.com/iot-trends-and-analysis/20-most-important-iot-firmsaccording-you

Christensen, C. M., Raynor, M. E., & McDonald, R. (2015). Disruptive innovation. *Harvard Business Review*, *93*(12), 44–53. PMID:17183796

Cisco. (2015). *The IoT threat environment*. Available at: http://theinternetofthings.report/Resources/Whitepapers/4c7c4eca-6167-45c3-aac8bff6031cadc9_IoT%20Threat%20Environment.pdf

Columbus, L. (2017). How IoT, big data analytics and cloud continue to be high priorities for developers. *Cloud Tech News*. Available at: https://www.cloudcomputingnews.net/news/2016/jun/27/internet-of-things-machine-learning-robotics-are-high-prioritiesfor-developers-in-2016/

Davis, R. (2015). *Industry 4.0: Digitalisation for productivity and growth*. European Parliamentary Research Service.

Deakin, S., Sausman, C., Sones, B., & Twigg, C. (2015). *The Internet of Things: Shaping Our Future*. Cambridge, UK: Cambridge Public Policy.

Gilchrist, A. 2016. Industrial Internet of Things. In Industry 4.0 (pp. 153-160). Apress.

Haight, J., & Park, H. (2015). *IoT Analytics in Practice*. Available at: https://www.sas.com/content/dam/SAS/en_us/doc/research2/iot-analytics-in-practice107941.pdf

IBM Internet of Things (Software Group). (2016). *Journey to Industry 4.0 and beyond with Cognitive Manufacturing*. Available at: https://www.slideshare.net/IBMIoT/journey-toindustry-40-and-beyond-with-cognitivemanufacturing?cm_mc_uid=11464795721414860817594&cm_mc_sid_50200000=1498031505&cm_mc_sid_52640000=1498031505

ITU. (2017). *ICT Facts and Figures, s.l.* International Telecommunication Union.

Jeschke, S., Brecher, C., Song, H., & Rawat, D. (2017). *Industrial Internet of Things* (1st ed.). Cham: Springer International Publishing. doi:10.1007/978-3-319-42559-7

Jones, J. (2017). How the Internet of Things is Driving Sustainability Strategy. *Conscious Connection Magazine*. Available at: https://www.consciousconnectionmagazine.com/2017/02/internet-of-things-sustainabilitystrategy/

Lee, J., Bagheri, B., & Kao, H. (2015). A Cyber-Physical Systems architecture for Industry 4.0-based manufacturing systems. *Manufacturing Letters*, *3*, 18–23. doi:10.1016/j.mfglet.2014.12.001

Lewis, D. (2016). Will the internet of things sacrifice or save the environment? *The Guardian*. Available at: https://www.theguardian.com/sustainable-business/2016/dec/12/willthe-internet-of-things-sacrifice-or-save-the-environment

Chapter 7
Resource–Aware Allocation and Load–Balancing Algorithms for Cloud Computing

N. Malarvizhi
Vel Tech Rangarajan Dr. Sagunthala R&D Institute of Science and Technology, India

J. Aswini
Meenakshi Academy of Higher Education and Research, India

E. A. Neeba
Rajagiri School of Engineering and Technology, India

ABSTRACT

Dynamic cloud computing technique enables resources to be assigned to different clients based on the current demand of each client turning the cloud to a limitless computational platform with limitless storage space which improves the performance of cloud services. To achieve best resource allocation in dynamic hosting frameworks, cloud service providers should provision resources intelligently to all clients. Cloud computing empowers consumers to access online resources using the internet, from anywhere at any time without considering the underlying hardware, technical management, and maintenance problems of the original resources. In this chapter, the authors present a detail study of various resource allocation and other scheduling challenges as well as cloud simulation frameworks tools like CloudSim and ICanCloud.

INTRODUCTION

Cloud computing services play a major role in today's computing. Leading information technology companies like Amazon's AWS, HP, Microsoft, and Google deploy large data centers with extensive hardware network for effective service delivery to cloud clients. Cloud service providers require proper resource management and provisioning to allow clients to access cloud services from the internet. In recent years, cloud service providers have shifted towards dynamic resource management to enable shar-

DOI: 10.4018/978-1-5225-9023-1.ch007

ing of cloud computing resources between different users. This intelligent resource balancing is known as workload balancing in a cloud service model. Cloud service environments have adapted different provisioning strategies to improve their service level.

Some Important Research Questions

With these goals in mind, the following research questions will help the researcher to explore the most efficient intelligent load balancing algorithm for dynamic internet hosting.

1. Under what conditions the prediction of Cicada cannot be reliable to predict the amount of workload in a dynamic internet hosting platform?
2. Under what conditions CloudSim cannot generate a reliable workload simulation?

Cloud computing services play a major role in today's computing. Leading information technology companies like Amazon's AWS, HP, Microsoft, and Google deploy large data centers with extensive hardware network for effective service delivery to cloud clients. Cloud service providers require proper resource management and provisioning to allow clients to access cloud services from the internet. In recent years, cloud service providers have shifted towards dynamic resource management to enable sharing of cloud computing resources between different users. Dynamic cloud computing technique enables resources to be assigned to different clients based on the current demand of each client turning the cloud to a limitless computational platform with limitless storage space which improves the performance of cloud services. To achieve best resource allocation in dynamic hosting frameworks, cloud service providers should provision resources intelligently to all clients. This intelligent resource balancing is known as workload balancing in a cloud service. Cloud service environments have adapted different provisioning strategies to improve their service level. Today cloud computing enables companies to delivery different computing services such as storages, software, and databases to their clients over the Internet. This resource sharing technique enables organizations to focus on their main objectives rather than on computer infrastructure and maintenance. There are two resource management models, static and dynamic. Initially, cloud computing services were introduced as static computing services where a specific amount of resources was assigned to specific organizations however over the time with the rapid growth of computing needs for many organizations and business, dynamic cloud computing was introduced. Dynamic cloud computing allowed cloud service providers to share and assign resources based on the demand for a specific workload. The dynamic resource management model enabled limitless computational platform with unlimited storage which improves the performance of cloud computing. For instance, in a static computing, any outrages can generate downtime, wherein dynamic computing, if any outages occur the computing job can be automatically shifted to another location.

INTRODUCTION TO CLOUD SERVICE AND CLOUD DEPLOYMENT

There are three types of Cloud computing service model as shown in figure 1:

- Software As A Service (SaaS)
- Platform As A Service (PaaS)

Figure 1. Generic 3-Layer model of cloud computing

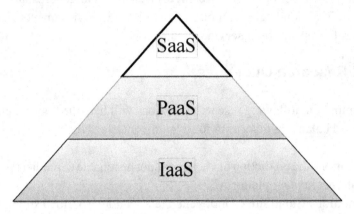

- Infrastructure As A Service (IaaS)

Software As A Service is the top layer of cloud computing services where software applications mainly standard software is offered as a cloud service to the users. An outstanding example of a SaaS service is Google Docs. Google docs offer a free fully functional word processor, the spreadsheet application, and presentation creator software enabling users to collaborate with each other from different locations. If users need to develop their own application on the cloud, they must use Platform As A Service (PaaS). This platform provides a cloud service environment in which developers can use appropriate APIs to make an application such as Facebook, which can be run and shared in anywhere in the world with any platforms without the risk of software pirating.

Infrastructure as a Service segment of cloud services provide developing tools with limitless storage and computing powers to developers and ordinary users. For example, Google drive and Apple iCloud offer cloud storage service for all people including ordinary users and developers. Allowing them to develop, run, and store different applications in cloud environments. For example, Amazon EC2 and Windows Azure are typical. Cloud deployment model can be categorized into 5 types:

1. Private clouds
2. Public clouds
3. Community
4. Hybrid
5. Hybrid with Cloud bursting application

A cloud-computing environment is called a private cloud when the provider and consumer are associated with each other, however, in public clouds, there are no associations between the provider and the customer as shown in figure 2. The customer rents machines from the provider either by the hour or by a different function of time. Hybrid computing is a mixture of public and private computing models and a community cloud is computing infrastructure shared between different organizations.

In public cloud computing, workload balancing is needed for both provider and consumer. In public cloud computing, providers must utilize their resources so that their consumers can have the assurance of receiving sufficient amount of resources. In public cloud computing, workload balancing is needed for both provider and consumer.

Figure 2. Cloud Computing Framework

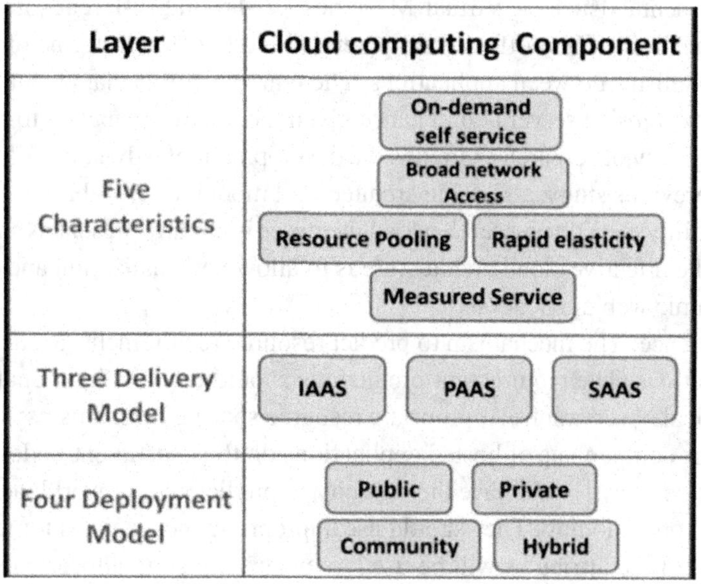

Layer	Cloud computing Component
Five Characteristics	On-demand self service Broad network Access Resource Pooling Rapid elasticity Measured Service
Three Delivery Model	IAAS PAAS SAAS
Four Deployment Model	Public Private Community Hybrid

DIFFERENCE BETWEEN DYNAMIC AND STATIC RESOURCE ALLOCATION OF CLOUD SERVICES

In Cloud computing, the goal of resource allocation is to maximize the possible number of requests that can be processed to reduce application completion time. Dynamic environments can easily create a scarcity of resources in the system, creating a need to find efficient methods of resource allocation. This chapter will examine the solutions to these problems. To achieve a reliable workload balancing, there is a need to ensure that hosted applications can handle an unpredictable spike in workload. Dynamic resources must operate at an optimal level even when experiencing significantly higher request rates. This means that it needs to be able to shift resources to where they are needed when they are needed.

Dynamic Cloud Provisioning

VM machines allow emulation of a different computer system based on the specification and computer architectures of a physical computer. VM machines and virtual process machines first were introduced in the 1960s by IBM. Initially, virtual machines were created to run multiple operating systems, by allowing time-sharing between multiple sing-tasking operating systems. There are different kinds of virtual machines, each designed with different functions.

System Virtual Machines (full virtualizations VMS), is designed to provide a substitute for a real machine allowing them to execute entire operating systems.

Process virtual machines can execute computer programs in a platform independent environment. Today majority of cloud service providers use the full virtualizations VMs to provide cloud services such as web hosting services. There are also different kind of VM software, the most popular ones are VirtualBox, Parallels, and VMware. One example of the dynamic cloud provider is GoDaddy which is a web hosting service provider which also uses dynamic provisioning for their cloud services. Building and operating dynamic cloud services require a deep study of cloud resource management and understand its fundamentals such as Virtual Machines (VMs) and different job scheduling policies. Dynamic Virtual Machines (VMs) offers great potential and benefits in terms of supporting efficient communication mechanisms between applications. The main benefit is that Dynamic Virtual Machines (VMs) do not require extensive server maintenance given the inherent capacity to respond to additional workload. A growing body of research examines the development of a dynamic VM resource allocation cloud services. In a previous study, a scalable architectural model for Web-based applications to ensure availability and reliability even during sudden load increases is already present as shown in figure 3. The overarching idea in the effective cloud architecture is to allow personalization and distributed updating of data through dynamic web applications.

Requirement Inference: The mechanism to predict resource requirements accurately based on workload needs of applications. The requirement predictions should rely on either analytical framework of application or empirical observations Appropriate resource sharing mechanisms: They should have the mechanism to support components of hosted applications on the constituent nodes.

Workload prediction: they should have the capacity to predict system workloads.

Dynamic capacity provisioning: They should use appropriate mechanisms for resource allocation to the hosted platforms. These attributes will be used to evaluate hosting allocation strategies to find the most efficient load-balancing alternative for dynamic hosting platforms.

PREDICTIVE LOAD BALANCING ALGORITHMS FOR CLOUD

Many researchers have been conducted to explore the predictive load balancing for the cloud while introducing many different algorithms. One load balancing method introduced in (Alexandre, D., Tomasik, J., Cohen, J., & Dufoulon, F. (2017)) is to use Predictive Load Balancing Algorithm in both burst and non-burst periods to maintain service quality and minimize energy consumption of cloud network. (Alexandre,

Figure 3. Scalable distributed architecture for web applications

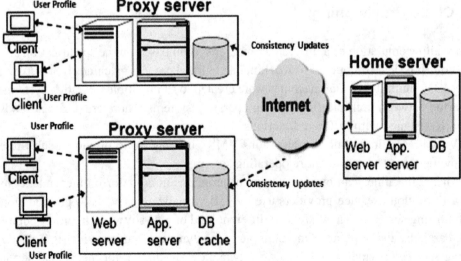

D., Tomasik, J., Cohen, J., & Dufoulon, F. (2017)) also, suggest the use of Right Scale Algorithm (RSA) for consolidating Virtual Machines (VM) into physical machines. Both algorithms use mathematical equations for load balancing and management of cloud resource, however, the research paper does not provide any simulation or real scenario to prove the efficiency of the algorithms. The prediction simply predicts the burst time and it caps the cloud resources in burst time for better management and the algorithm uses the QoS parameters to add or remove virtual machines in order to meet the QoS goal. Another predictive load balancing research based on ensemble forecasting (Matthias Sommer, Michael Klink, 2016) uses a reactive overload detection method to predict any overloads. Reactive overload detection uses different CPU parameters such as static threshold (ST) value and when CPU utilization exceeds the static threshold value by 80% or 90% then it will detect it as an overload. This approach also uses various computation intensive statistical calculations to compare CPU utilization values to historical data. After detecting an overload, the chapter suggests the use of CloudSim for forecasting CPU utilization in a theoretical level. The CloudSim simulation proposed in this chapter is only in theoretical level and this chapter does not provide any clear simulation results to prove its method and suggest further study in order to improve the load balancing results. Another load prediction study for energy-aware scheduling suggests training predictors for predicting a load without mentioning any accurate tool for prediction.

The literature review of predictive load balancing algorithms for cloud indicates that all previous literature has used statistical calculations for the prediction that predicts overloads that have already begun to happen. All the previous methods need high computational and centralized approaches that need to be configured and trained for overloads. For load balancing all previous literature have used mathematical equations which needs high computation power for load balancing and management of cloud resource without offering any simulation or real scenario to prove the efficiency of the introduced algorithms. This chapter tends to introduce a new accurate and reliable and less computational approach for cloud load prediction which can accurately predict cloud load. This chapter will also investigate all cloud simulation frameworks, in order to find the most accurate simulation platforms.

Next section reviews the different literature on cloud simulations frameworks in order to choose the most accurate cloud simulation framework to generate accurate simulation results.

DIFFERENT CLOUD SIMULATION FRAMEWORKS

The main step in analysing a cloud provisioning is to simulate a Cloud computing model, where simulation enables provisioning of a Cloud computing model. To evaluate the performance of a workload model, the simulation software must be able to simulate application models, resources, and policies (Fei, L., Scherson, I.D., & Fuentes, J. (2017)).

CloudSim Simulation Framework

CloudSim is one of the most popular and well know open-source cloud simulator. CloudSim can simulate large-scale data centres by virtualizing server hosts. CloudSim is capable of provisioning host resources to virtual machines. CloudSim can also model and simulate energy-aware computational resources and dynamic provisioning of simulation elements. In CloudSim simulation can be stopped or resumed at any time. CloudSim can simulate a cloud computing workload efficiently with a set of applications as shown in figure 4. CloudSim offers support for system modelling of Cloud systems but also it enables users to simulate system component behaviour for resource provisioning such as simulation of virtual machines (VMs). CloudSim can support a single cloud as well as inter-networked clouds, which consists of integrated clouds. CloudSim allows researchers to investigate Cloud resource provisioning and power consumption of data centres.

ICanCloud Simulation Platform

ICanCloud is another cloud simulation platform, which is capable of framing and simulating many cloud computing systems as shown in figure 5. The main functionality of iCanCloud is to analyse and predict the trade-offs between performance and cost of different applications. iCanCloud can simulate multiple applications in different hardware while considering information about cost. iCanCloud can model and simulate many different computing architectures with different cloud brokering policies such as customized VMs with different single-core and multi-core systems.

GreenCloud Simulation Platform

GreenCloud simulator is another cloud simulator which focuses on energy power consumption and cost of the physical components of a cloud computing network as shown in figure 6. With GreenCloud simulator, the workload of cloud computing scenarios and of all its infrastructural elements of a data centre can be simulated in order to calculate the total cost of energy consumption.

Figure 4. Screen-shot CloudSim set-up with NetBeans

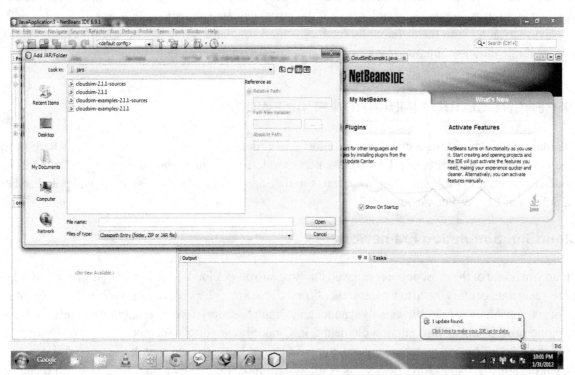

Figure 5. ICanCloud Simulation set-up

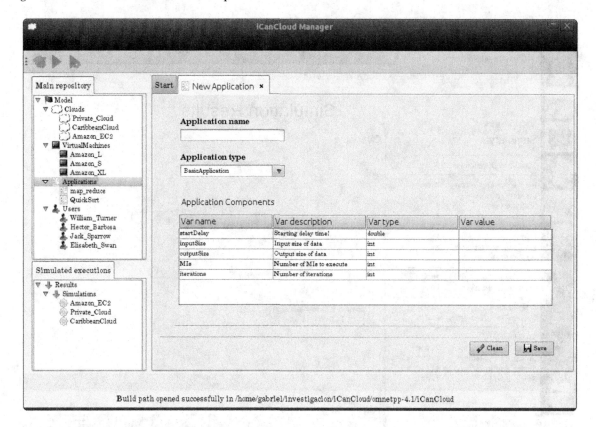

CloudSched Simulation Platform

CloudSched is also another simulation platform which can model and simulate large Cloud computing environments such as VMs, data centres, and physical machines. CloudSched can also use different resource scheduling policies and algorithms to simulate a network infrastructure. An extensive study (Wenhong, 2015) on the most popular open-source cloud simulators such as ICanCloud, GreenCloud, CloudSched, and CloudSim has proven that the most efficient cloud simulator for computationally intensive tasks, data interchanges between data centres and internal network communications is CloudSim.

Workload Balancing Algorithms

The main goal of load balancing is to achieve the minimum process execution wait time with minimum amount of computational resources. In a perfect load balancing, which has a zero execution wait time, all processes are handled simultaneously and there are no wait-times for processing information. Many algorithms were introduced to address workload prediction and workload balancing, the most popular algorithm for workload balancing are Round Robin, Random Algorithm and least loaded algorithm. The following literature below explains the most concept behind the popular workload balancing algorithms.

Figure 6. Screen-shot of GreenCloud simulation

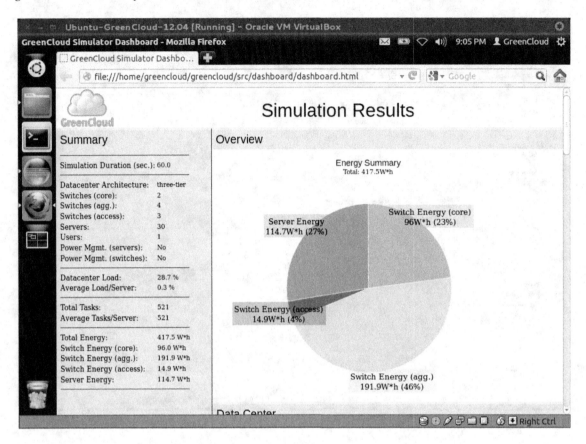

Round Robin Algorithm

Round-Robin (RR) is scheduling technique that achieves load balancing by assigning equal time quanta to cyclic tasks and processes (Issawi, S. F., Halees, A. A., & Radi, M. (2015)). In RR, the algorithm divides time quanta are into equal slices and assigns with the specific time interval as shown in figure 7. The time scheduling principle describes the scheduling of the time slides when using the algorithm such that all the nodes are assigned with a quantum and with an operation. All resources are treated as time slices. While RR provides an efficient mechanism for load balancing in terms of meeting peak user demands and providing high quality services, this approach presents significant challenges in bursty workloads (Issawi, Halees, & Radi, 2015). Bursty workload refers to uneven pattern of data transmission, a common problem in large systems such as web-based applications. The problem with bursty workload is that it can degrade system performance and lead to system unavailability. Burstiness is a major problem in the context of cloud computing given the increasing number of cloud users. Static algorithms such as RR have inherent limitations given that they depend on prior knowledge without considering current state of a node. This means that the algorithm can degrade system performance. The limitations of RR algorithms in environments characterized by bursty workloads indicate the need for enhanced algorithms. The Round Robin (RR) algorithm has two major advantages. Firstly, the algorithm is easy to implement. Secondly, it requires a simple scheduler. Thirdly, the RR algorithm is useful for a small and static system.

However, the RR algorithm has its limitations in the context cloud environments. For example, the RR model does not take into consideration the current load on the VMs such as the processing capacity and size of tasks being scheduled (LaCurts, K. L. (2014)). Moreover, the static and centralized nature of RR algorithm makes it unsuitable for cloud environments.

Random Algorithm: Random Algorithm connects cloud-lets and servers randomly by assigning random numbers to each server as shown in figure 8. Unlike Round Robin algorithm, Random algorithm can handle large number of requests and evenly distribute the workload to each node. Similar to Round Robin algorithm, another advantage of Random algorithm is that it is sufficient for machines with similar Ram and CPU specs. Random algorithm is the most efficient algorithm for peak time traffic and when Cicada cannot detect a reliable prediction, random algorithm can distribute the workload evenly between different VMs.

In a previous study, Issawi et al. (2015) proposed a novel load-balancing algorithm, Adaptive Algorithm, which can adapt to variations in the request by combining RR algorithm and Random algorithm. The strategic objective of the proposed algorithm is to use RR policy in high workload and deploy the Random policy in low workload. The system comprises a burst detector, which detects workload state. The Random policy activates when the system detects normal burst with a fuzzier supplying candidate list of balanced virtual machines in the data-centre. If the workload state is burst, the fuzzier uses the supplied list of VMs to allocate workload. Simulation experiments using CloudAnalyst showed that the new algorithm decreases the response and processing time (Issawi et al., 2015). These findings suggest the feasibility of using Adaptive Algorithm to achieve improved performance in cloud systems characterized by bursty workloads. Another problem in cloud computing environments which needs to be addressed is the scheduling of non-preemptive tasks. According to Nema, R., & Edwin, S. T. (2016), load balancing of non-preemptive tasks on VMs is a vital task-scheduling feature in cloud environments.

Figure 7. Round robin algorithm

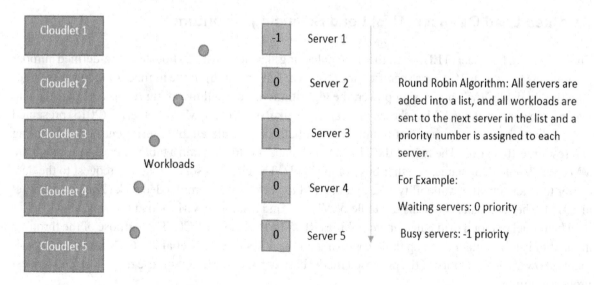

Figure 8. Random algorithm

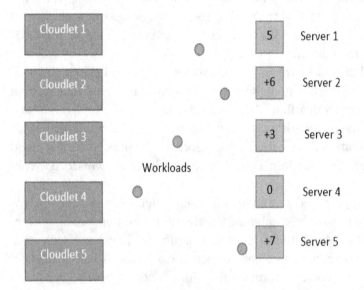

The objective is to ensure that share load among the VMs for optimal resource utilization and lower the task completion time. Nema, R., & Edwin, S. T. (2016) proposed an improved weighted RR algorithm that takes into account the capabilities of all the VMs. To achieve this, an effective resource scheduling system integrates a static scheduler algorithm that focuses on the initial placement of tasks and a dynamic scheduler that focuses on the load in the configured VMs. The load balancer in the proposed algorithm distributes the load evenly across the VMs. Further experiments to evaluate the performance of the algorithm demonstrated its suitability in both homogeneous and heterogeneous tasks, but with improved performance compared to other RR algorithms.

Throttled Load Balancer (TLB) Load Balancing Algorithm

Throttled Load Balancer (TLB) is another load balancing algorithm which allocates a pre-defined number of cloudlets to a single VM for a specific time (Nema & Edwin, 2016). If the number of requests is larger than the available VM's processing power, the algorithms allocate all incoming requests in a queue and wait for the next available VM as shown in figure 9. Wolke, A., Bichler, M., & Setzer, T. (2015) presented a Throttled-scheduling system that maintains load balancing while enabling efficient task scheduling and resource allocation. The role of the TLB's load balancer is to maintain a table of the entire candidate VMs and denote their status, whether busy or available. The client or server makes a request to the data center to determine the availability of a suitable VM to perform a recommended task (Wenhong Tian et al 2015). The load balancer scans the table of VMs to find a suitable VM to load the data.

The model of cloud load balancing combines RR, Throttled, and ESCE. The purpose of the throttled algorithm is to maintain the map table capturing all the VMs (Zhou, X et al 2016). Simulation experiments showed the feasibility of the proposed model based on metrics like response time, cost, and request processing time.

Figure 9. Throttled algorithm

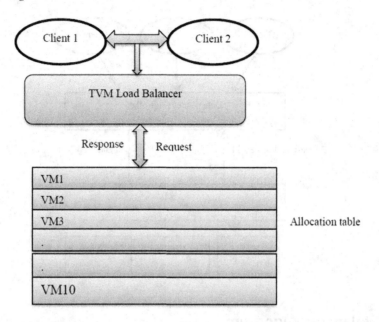

Active Monitoring Load Balancer (AMLB) Algorithm

Active Monitoring Load Balancer (AMLB) algorithm stores all information related to each VM such as the number of requests and their specific location as shown in figure 10. When a VM is activated, it is assigned with a VM id and the data controller maintains ids of all VMs and sends the new location of each VM to AMLB. This algorithm comprises four main components: clients, Data Center Controller, the AMLB, and the VMs. In order to allocate new VMs, the controller should receive new requests from the clients. The AMLB parses the index table of candidate VMs to find the least loaded and returns the VM ID to the controller.

The Central Load Balancing Decision Model (CLBDM) Algorithm

The Central Load Balancing Decision Model (CLBDM) is an algorithm, which combines the Round Robin Algorithm and session switching of the application layer. CLBDM is the improved version of Round Robin Algorithm and threshold time is added to the algorithm. In this new approach the difference between the client and the node in the cloud is calculated and if this round is greater than the threshold time then the connection between the client and node will be disconnected and that specific task will be moved. Round Robin will be used to determine the new node for this task. That is, CLBDM uses RR but it relies on the measurement of the execution time of tasks in a cloud resource calculated as the duration of connections between server and client.

Figure 10. Active monitoring load balancing

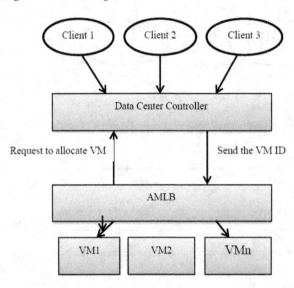

Min-Min Load Balancing Algorithm

The existing load balancing algorithm for cloud computing differ in several ways. The Min-Min Load Balancing algorithm provides remarkable performance regarding task scheduling as it assigns tasks to resources starting with the tasks that require the minimum execution time. The Max-Max Load Balancing algorithm is similar to the Min-Min algorithm in that it calculates the execution completion time of tasks. It performs well in a static environment. According to Mathur, Larji, and Goyal (2017), Min-Min algorithms are efficient when the resources require less execution time, but the Max-Min algorithm works better when handling tasks with higher time requirements. RR is a static algorithm that does not use task prioritization. The algorithm is unaware of the running time of processes. The Genetic Load Balancing algorithm provides better performance compared to RR as it has vast search space. The Game Theory algorithm works best in public clouds, but it lacks the capacity to predict the arrival of tasks.

LOAD BALANCING ALGORITHMS IN LARGE-SCALE CLOUD COMPUTING SERVICE PROVIDERS

The conventional load balancing algorithms feature severe limitations and drawbacks in cloud environments. In order to address these challenges, researchers have proposed prediction algorithms using genetic algorithms and genetic programming (Zhou et al., 2016). These algorithms aim to simplify task scheduling in cloud platforms characterized by a large volume of users. In particular, Zhou, X et al (2016) presented a novel adaptive algorithm to improve on the original adaptive algorithm (AGA). The proposed scheme meets the requirements for inter-nodes load balancing. Simulations to compare the performance of the proposed scheme and the AGA demonstrated the effectiveness and validity of the proposed method in cloud computing. The GA method has advantages related to limited parameter setting and ability to initialize from possible solutions. However, the application of GA comes with drawbacks

Table 1. Comparison of load balancing algorithm

Algorithm	Category	Parameters	Processing Power	Response Time	Advantages	Disadvantages
Round Robin	Static	Waiting time	Optimal power allocation	381.05 ms (average) No task prioritization	Reduced response time	Poor resource utilization
Max-Min	Static	Waiting time	Uses Minimum Execution Time (MET)	Uses Minimum Execution Time (MET)	Executes tasks with MCT	Starvation
Min-min	Static	Waiting time	Uses Minimum Execution Time (MET)	Uses Minimum Execution Time (MET)	Good performance for multiple small tasks	Starvation

such as the paucity of fast convergence towards optimal values given that crossover and mutation exist as random events (Wahab, Mexiani, & Atyabi, 2015).

Zhou et al (2016) proposed a method for predicting cloud storage based on a technique called analytic hierarchy process (AHPGD) and hybrid hierarchical genetic algorithm (HHGA). The AHPGD evaluates the load state of server nodes while the role of the HHGA is to train the algorithm to optimize a radial basis function neural network (RBFNN). The centralized load-balancing algorithm consists of three steps: centring nodes to predict the load of service nodes per periodic time (T), calculation of polling weight value for back-end service nodes, and central node allocation using the polling weight value after receiving request tasks. While GA provides capabilities for dynamic load balancing, the main limitation is that they are centralized.

The use of SI algorithms is expected to ameliorate some of the challenges associated with the GA. Hashem, Nashaat, Rizk (2017) proposed a load balancing algorithm based on the Honey Been Behaviour. The proposed method is based on the natural foraging behaviour of honey bees. That is, in hives, foraging bees give information to other bees about the location of food sources they visit. The allocated tasks update other tasks about the status of VM in the same way bees find food sources. The main goal of the proposed scheme is to distribute workload in a manner to optimize the utilization of cloud resources. The researchers evaluated the performance of the proposed method by simulating on CloudSim (Hashem et al.,2017). In addition, the authors compared the performance of the novel HB technique with the performance of two conventional algorithms: the RR algorithm and the Modified Throttle algorithm. The simulation results showed that the HB method achieves up to 50% increase in the response time compared to other algorithms, with balance a cloud. These algorithms cannot prevent any over-loads, they can simply react to a current overload scenario. In this chapter, the most reliable workload prediction and cloud simulation method will be used to introduce a rule-based algorithm for a predictive workload balancing. This chapter explores the resource management in the IaaS level and will work based on the prediction of incoming workload rather than load-balancing of current overloads.

Load Prediction Based on Incoming Network Traffic

There is a relationship between network traffic and processing load of a cloud. Cloud computing computers receive and forward packets via physical interfaces, typically Layer 2 technologies like the Ethernet. These technologies, or so-called network links, have their characteristics defined in terms of parameters such as bandwidth. Therefore, the amount of network traffic determines the required capacity of the network links due to the nexus between bandwidth and packet forwarding rate. The relationship between the network traffic and processing workload in any region of a network is often expressed using Little's Law, which is derived from queuing systems theory. The Little's Law states that the average number of items in a queue system is a product of the average rate at which the items arrive and the average time that an item spends in the system. The Little's Law expresses the ratio of the mean traffic demand to the mean number of users in a network segment.

IMPACT OF THE RESOURCE ALLOCATION IN CLOUD COMPUTING

Finding the most efficient resource allocation strategy depends on resolving the major challenges in dynamic server provisioning. The resolution of these problems will have an impact on the ability of businesses to allocate their resources effectively and to provide an efficient load-balancing alternative for the more cost-effective delivery of hosting services. Three challenges hinder the deployment of dynamic server provisioning policies. The resolution of these challenges is the key to reaching the goals of this chapter. The challenges include:

- Uncertainty in workload predictions
- Challenges in simulating network resources and load.
- Challenges of intelligent load balancing in dynamic Internet Hosting Platforms.

A Study Into Load Predictor: Cicada Toolkit

Previously, LaCurts (2014) presented Cicada, which is an end-to-end toolkit software that can predict an applications workload and model the application's workload based on prediction. Cicada can minimize the application completion time when a Cloud provider uses it; it will guarantee specific network performance. To minimize the completion time of applications and load balancing, Cicada minimizes the completion time in load balancing by enabling efficient variation in the underlying network based on the concept of the fastest path (Katrina, L., Mogul, J.C., Balakrishnan, H., & Turner, Y. (2014)).

A Study Into Cloud Simulator: CloudSim Framework

CloudSim is framework that can be used to simulate and model a cloud computing infrastructure services very efficiently, this is one of the platforms that will be explored in relation to the research questions. Timeline analysis and model building are the two most frequently used methods for predicting concurrent database workloads. CloudSim has proven to improve QoS requirement of applications by

the fluctuation of resource and service demand patterns and CloudSim is a framework that has proven to be a valuable tool in the simulation of cloud environments and the evaluation of resource allocation methods/algorithms. CloudSim extensible simulation toolkit was introduced to simulate a workload efficiently and to model Cloud computing systems and applications. CloudSim not only offers support for system modeling of Cloud systems but also it enables users to simulate system component behaviour for resource provisioning such as simulation of virtual machines (VMs). CloudSim supports a single cloud as well as inter-networked clouds, which consists of integrated clouds. CloudSim allows researchers to investigate Cloud resource provisioning and power consumption of data centres. CloudSim has proven to improve QoS requirement of applications by fluctuation of resource and service demand patterns and CloudSim is a framework that has proven to be a valuable tool in the simulation of cloud environments and the evaluation of resource allocation methods/algorithms.

CONCLUSION AND FUTURE WORK

Bursty workload refers to uneven pattern of data transmission, a common problem in large systems such as web-based applications. The problem with bursty workload is that it can degrade system performance and lead to system unavailability. Burstiness is a major problem in the context of cloud computing given the increasing number of cloud users. Static algorithms such as RR have inherent limitations given that they depend on prior knowledge without considering current state of a node. This means that the algorithm can degrade system performance. The limitations of RR algorithms in environments characterized by bursty workloads indicate the need for enhanced algorithms. To prevent any overloads or any over-provisioning in a dynamic cloud environment, one must find a reliable method of workload prediction and a reliable framework for simulating a cloud environment. This chapter reviews previous literatures to presents a reliable prediction This research explores the effectiveness of different cloud simulators and different prediction tools to predict a workload of a cloud efficiently. This chapter will explore the cloud service simulation problems and resource management algorithms.

REFERENCES

Alexandre, D., Tomasik, J., Cohen, J., & Dufoulon, F. (2017). Load prediction for energy-aware scheduling for Cloud computing platforms. *IEEE 37th International Conference on Distributed Computing System.*

Fei, L., Scherson, I. D., & Fuentes, J. (2017). *Dynamic Creation of Virtual Machines in Cloud Computing Systems.* Las Vegas, NV: IEEE.

Gamal, M., Rizk, R., Mahdi, H., & Elhady, B. (2017). Bio-inspired load balancing algorithm in cloud computing. *Proceedings of the International Conference on Advanced Intelligent Systems and Informatics*, 579-589.

Hashem, W., & Nashaat, H., & Rizk. (2017). Honey bee based load balancing in cloud computing. *Transactions on Internet and Information Systems (Seoul)*, *11*(12).

Issawi, S. F., Halees, A. A., & Radi, M. (2015). An efficient adaptive load-balancing algorithm for cloud computing under bursty workloads. *Engineering, Technology, &. Applied Scientific Research*, *5*(3), 795–800.

Katrina, L., Mogul, J.C., Balakrishnan, H., & Turner, Y. (2014). *Cicada: Predictive Guarantees for Cloud Network Bandwidth*. Cambridge, MA: MIT.

LaCurts, K. L. (2014). *Application workload prediction and placement in cloud computing systems* (Unpublished doctoral dissertation). Massachusetts Institute of Technology, Cambridge, MA.

Mathur, S., Larji, A. A., & Goyal, A. (2017). Static load balancing using SA Max-Min algorithm. *International Journal for Research in Applied Science and Engineering Technology*, *5*(4), 1886–1893.

Matthias, S., Klink, M., Tomforde, S., & Hahner, J. (2016). *Predictive Load Balancing in Cloud Computing Environments based on Ensemble Forecasting* (4th ed.; Vol. 11). Augsburg: *IEEE*.

Nema, R., & Edwin, S. T. (2016). A new efficient virtual machine load balancing algorithm for a cloud computing environment. *International Journal of Latest Research in Engineering and Technology*, *2*(2), 69–75.

Sheng, Q. Z., Qiao, X., Vasilakos, A. V., Szabo, C., Bourne, S., & Xu, X. (2014). Web services composition: A decade's overview. *Information Sciences*, *280*, 218–238. doi:10.1016/j.ins.2014.04.054

Tian, W., Xu, M., Chen, A., Li, G., Wang, X., & Chen, Y. (2015). Open-source simulators for Cloud computing: Comparative study and challenging issues. *Simulation Modelling Practice and Theory*, *58*, 239–254. doi:10.1016/j.simpat.2015.06.002

Wahab, M. N., Mexiani, S. N., & Atyabi, A. (2015). A comprehensive review of swarm optimization algorithms. *PLoS One*, *10*(5), 1–36. doi:10.1371/journal.pone.0122827 PMID:25992655

Wolke, A., Bichler, M., & Setzer, T. (2015). *Planning vs. dynamic control: Resource allocation in corporate clouds*. Academic Press.

Zhou, X., Lin, F., Yang, L., Nie, J., Tan, Q., Zeng, W., & Zhang, N. (2016). Load balancing method of cloud storage based on analytical hierarchy process and hybrid hierarchical genetic algorithm. *SpringerPlus*, *5*(1), 1–23. doi:10.118640064-016-3619-x PMID:26759740

Chapter 8
Edge Cloud:
The Future Technology for Internet of Things

Lucia Agnes Beena Thomas
St. Joseph's College, India

ABSTRACT

With the proliferation of new technologies such as augmented and virtual reality, autonomous cars, 5G networks, drones, and IOT with smart cities, consumers of cloud computing are becoming the producers of data. Large volume of data is being produced at the edge of the network. This scenario insists the need for efficient real-time processing and communication at the network edge. Cloud capabilities must be distributed across the network to form an edge cloud, which places computing resources where the traffic is at the edge of the network. Edge cloud along with 5G services could also glint the next generation of robotic manufacturing. The anticipated low latency requirement, battery life constraint, bandwidth cost saving, as well as data safety and privacy are also inscribed by edge cloud. A number of giants like Nokia, AT&T, and Microsoft have emerged in the market to support edge cloud. This chapter wraps the features of edge cloud, the driving industries that are providing solutions, the use cases, benefits, and the challenges of edge cloud.

INTRODUCTION

With the rapid development of internet, provisioning of computing resources as a utility came into existence in the name of Cloud Computing. Cloud services influenced both the individual as well as the business by its cost-efficiency and scalability through centralized architecture. Since 1999, the tremendous growth of different internet connected devices give rise to a new technology called Internet of Things (IoT). Initially, IoT was applied to supply chain management and now it is adapted to health care, transport and smart home environment (Peng et al., 2018). IoT applications involve the machine to machine (M2M) interaction without the human intervention. These real time applications handle large amount of data that has to be analyzed critically for patterns, trends which help in better hold on problem assessment and decisions. This promising technology introduced new challenges.

DOI: 10.4018/978-1-5225-9023-1.ch008

The Cisco Global Cloud Index estimated that nearly 850 ZB will be generated by all people, machines, and things by 2021 (as cited in Cisco Global Cloud Index, 2018). Cloud services are to be leveraged to handle this huge data. Businesses in the utilities, oil & gas, insurance, manufacturing, transportation, infrastructure and retail sectors can reap the benefits of IoT by making more informed decisions, aided by the stream of interactional and transactional data at their disposal (as cited in happiestminds, 2018). These industrial IoT applications need high speed internet connectivity and rapid data analysis which facilitate in decisions made by autonomous or semiautonomous systems and actuators. The traditional network find it difficult to face the challenge of sending bulk data from a remote place to cloud for processing and to deliver a quick decision in a short time span to the appropriate device. Also the cost of data transfer through the satellite communication is elevated. Gartner the world's leading research and advisory company's October 2018 blog, reports that currently around 10% of enterprise-generated data is created and processed outside a traditional centralized data center or cloud. By 2022, Gartner predicts this figure will reach 75% (as cited in gartner, 2018). These challenges can be tackled by Edge Computing. For instance, in medical internet of things, wireless diabetes devices such as blood glucose monitors, continuous glucose monitors, insulin pens, insulin pumps, and closed-loop systems are used. The Cloud data centers are unable to store and analyze the data generated by these devices. The processing has to be pushed out to the edge (IoT device) of the network where the data is being generated. This give rise to a new paradigm called Edge computing. Edge computing architecture can relieve the Cloud from processing an outsized data but to store vital information. The data generated by the medical IoT devices can be processed by the device themselves nearby the patient, and transmit information machine-to-machine or machine-to-human in milliseconds or seconds (Klonoff & David, 2017). The increase in the use of IoT devices, swift data transmission speed, the necessity for faster processing and reduced latency in response time drive the Edge computing.

EDGE COMPUTING AT A GLANCE

Modern industries need innovations in products, services, and trade model. The technologies like IoT, Cloud help the industries in digital transformation in every aspect of its operations in an efficient way. For a smart IoT application, that offer real time services require heterogeneous connections, data optimization techniques and security. The term IoT was first articulated by Kevin Ashton at Procter & Gamble (P&G) in 1999 (Ashton, 2009). Days are gone where the data is created and processed by Human being with computers. Today any electronic device that is capable of accessing an internet becomes a data producer. Starting from the wearable device in the health care, tablets, game controllers and smart phones referred as edge devices, use the Cloud data centers, increase the communication between the user and the Cloud. But the Cloud applications could not satisfy its users by rapid response. This elevates the need for the processing at the edge of the network. Only the optimized data are sent to the Cloud rather than forwarding the raw data produced from the edge devices.

To promote the processing at the edge, various initiatives were taken by industries and few consortiums were formed. In 2012, Cisco (Bonomi et al., 2012) introduced a new platform named Fog Computing to meet the challenges faced by the Cloud with respect to the IoT applications. They proposed Fog (close to the Ground) computing with the connotation computing close to the edge devices. Fog computing, the data gets processed in a fog node or in an IoT gateway at the local area network level and the device or thing level (as cited in i-Scoop, 2018). Nokia Solutions and Networks designed an innovative network technology Mobile Edge Computing(MEC) through Liquid applications in 2013, at the base-station level. The application developers used the real-time network data to create innovative services, such as connecting mobile subscribers with local points-of-interest, businesses and events (as cited in Nokia Solutions and Networks, 2013). In 2014, Edge Computing Consortium (ECC) (as cited in iotaustralia, 2017) formed by six industries such as Huawei Technologies Co., Ltd., Shenyang Institute of Automation of the Chinese Academy of Sciences, China Academy of Information and Communications Technology (CAICT), Intel Corporation, ARM Holdings, and iSoftStone Information Technology (Group) Co., Ltd with the motive of promoting the development of the edge computing industry. The ECC's White Paper released at the 2016 Edge Computing Industrial Summit, during the ECC's launch ceremony, emphasis on the ECC's future development.

Different edge computing solutions for IoT are being proposed. The emerging solutions are Cloudlet, Mobile Edge Computing, Fog Computing and Edge Cloud. Figure 1 illustrates the edge computing paradigm. Based on the IoT applications, the data can be processed at the device or at the gateway level. For the applications that are sensitive to latency can apply Cloudlet or Edge cloud solutions. Mobile Edge Computing (Hu et al., 2015) unlocks services to consumers and enterprise customers as well as to adjacent industries that are engrossed in mission-critical applications over the mobile network. It facilitates a new value chain, fresh business opportunities and a countless applications across multiple sectors. Fog computing is useful for new paradigms in medical data analysis and remote health monitoring, where there is a requirement for immediate analysis of data (Klonoff & David, 2017).

Figure 1. Edge computing paradigm

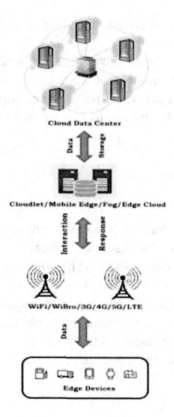

The edge cloud places compute capabilities at the edge of the network, to decrease latency and to optimize the use of network resources. Edge cloud resources serve new applications, such as virtual reality, augmented reality and autonomous driving. This chapter opens up the opportunities, benefits and challenges of Edge Cloud.

VISION OF EDGE CLOUD

The current industries demand, efficient computing to be performed in smaller devices using less expensive and powerful processors. Small data analytics has to be performed at the device level for the improved machine intelligence (as cited in ge, n.d). Edge cloud moves analytics and custom business logic to devices so that the organization can focus on business insights instead of data management. The IoT device can detect the anomaly and respond to emergencies as quickly as possible (as cited in Microsoft, 2018). In the same way data cleaning and aggregation can be performed locally to avoid terabytes of raw data being transferred to cloud. Thus reducing the bandwidth cost and only important insights can be forwarded to cloud. Irrespective of the applications, whether it is health care, economic models, business processes, Media and Broadcasters, Software and Device Manufacturers, Retail and Ecommerce, Gaming, warning of events or failures must be identified and resolved. The energy and cost are to be optimized and the future opportunities have to be forecasted. Here the edge cloud come into the picture to Monitor or analyze and perform the necessary actions. The role of Edge Cloud is depicted in Figure 2. The inspiration behind the Edge Cloud is to place the resources such as computing power, storage and network devices in the environs of the end users which serve the real time applications. For example,

1. The traffic monitoring and navigation system can report traffic data for route maintenance of a specific region in a smart city.
2. The content & data filtering and aggregation can be performed at edge before sending it to cloud to reduce the data volume being transferred to Cloud.
3. In time sensitive applications like augmented reality and health monitoring systems, faster responses can be produced using edge nodes, thereby user experience for time-sensitive applications can be improved (Bilal et al., 2018).

Definition

Edge computing is an emerging field. Various definitions were given by different researchers. Nokia (as cited in Nokia,2018), Fastly (as cited in Fastly, 2018a), Apigee (as cited in apigee, n.d), Infradata (as cited in infradata, 2018), Ciena (as cited in ciena, 2018) and Limelight (as cited in limelight, 2018) the current leading edge cloud platform expresses *Edge Computing* as *Edge Cloud*. In this chapter, Edge cloud and Edge computing are used interchangeably. Santhosh Rao of Gartner (as cited in gartner, 2018) said that Organizations that have embarked on a digital business journey have realized that a more decentralized approach is required to address digital business infrastructure requirements. This perspective of Rao is reflected in the following *definition of edge computing*:

Figure 2. Role of edge computing paradigm

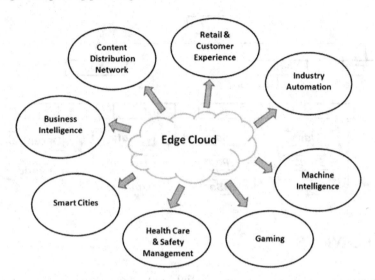

Edge computing is a set of solutions that facilitate data processing at or near the source of data generation. For example, in the context of the Internet of Things (IoT), the sources of data generation are usually things with sensors or embedded devices. Edge computing serves as the decentralized extension of the campus networks, cellular networks, data center networks or the cloud.

In the perspective of IoT, Edge Cloud can gather the available computing power near the edge devices and form micro data centers where local computing needs are fulfilled. With this idea, is highlighted in the definition of edge cloud by ECC (as cited in iotaustralia, 2017) in 2014.

Edge computing is performed on an open platform at the network edge near "things" or data sources, integrating network, computing, storage, and application core capabilities, and providing edge intelligent services. Edge computing meets the key requirements of agile connection, real-time services, data optimization, smart application, security, and privacy protection.

An Edge Cloud is used to decentralize processing power to the edges (clients/devices) of your networks (as cited in infradata, 2018). The data processing power of devices in the distributed systems reduce the burden of the cloud. The data is processed and analyzed at edges and then forwarded to the cloud. Thus, the influence of cloud and edge are fused to form Edge Cloud. For example, the connected cares are able to analyze data themselves instead of using a server's processing power. In Edge Cloud, the goal is to get higher performance and lower cost. For which location becomes a critical issue. Techniques such as Geo-analytics are used to place Edge Cloud Data Centers near the clusters of end-users or devices. Thus achieving Fast, reliable and secure edge cloud services for time-sensitive applications. Edge Cloud will not replace cloud rather it extend Cloud to the edges of the real time applications.

Figure 3. Taxonomy of edge cloud services

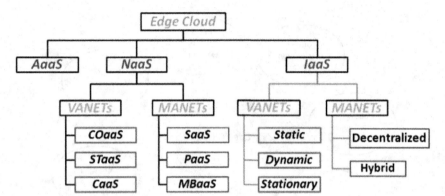

EDGE CLOUD SERVICES

Edge Cloud will have a greater impact in the ICT field in this decade. It can also influence the human life in all perspectives. Unlike Cloud Computing, edge cloud drives the intelligence, processing power and communication capabilities of an edge gateway or appliance directly into devices (as cited in ge, 2018), which stress on some specific needs like latency reduction, effective bandwidth, fast response time, less storage, near to the ground network congestion and low energy consumption. Based on these characteristics the Edge Cloud offers various services are depicted in Figure 3. The major services are Application as a Service (AaaS), Network as a Service (NaaS) and Infrastructure as a Service (IaaS) (El-Sayed et al., 2018).

Different types of wireless networks like mobile ad-hoc networks (MANETs), vehicular ad-hoc networks (VANETs), the Internet of Things (IoT) and intelligent transport systems (ITSs) are currently being used by the user. Edge Cloud can incorporate these networks to mitigate network-related and computational problems at the edges. Sayed et. al. discussed the taxonomy shown in Figure 3 with this perspective.

Application as a Service (AaaS)

This service helps the users for better interaction in real-time applications thus offering better Quality of Experience (QoE).

Network as Service (NaaS)

In many time-critical applications, the integration of VANETs and MANETs with Edge Cloud is crucial. This assimilation yields energy efficiency and avoids congestion in the transportation network. Thus, the services offered in NaaS, depend on the type of the network being used by the User. In VANETs, Computing as a Service (COaaS), Storage as a Service (STaaS) and Cooperation as a Service (CaaS) are feasible. Software as a Service (SaaS), Platform as a Service (PaaS) and Mobile backend as a Service (MBaaS) are viable under MANETs. STaaS Service is for small business applications that store cached data during transient time. Huge data storage is not possible and only temporary data can be used. Cooperation as a Service (CaaS)/ Collaborative edge can combine geographically distributed data by creating virtualized data views for the users, to reduce operational cost and to improve profitability (shi et al., 2016).

Infrastructure as a Service (IaaS)

VANETs are able to provide all three (Static, Dynamic & Stationary) services. In case of MANETs, dynamic IaaS is offered via decentralized, Stationary IaaS by means of Hybrid approach. But static IaaS is not applicable for Edge Cloud.

The various Edge Cloud Services are listed in Table 1.

EDGE CLOUD REFERENCE MODEL

The key technologies like Big Data, machine learning, and deep learning are used in applications such as speech recognition, image recognition, and user profiling, and they progressed in terms of algorithms, models, and architectures. Engineering sectors such as manufacturing, power, healthcare, agriculture and transportation have begun to adapt these technologies, which has created new requirements and challenges. This epoch will be an industry intelligence era. It requires four important key industry transformations. They are:

- Integrated collaboration of the physical world and the digital world
- Renovation from vague experience-based decision-making to scientific decision-making based on digitalization and modeling
- Conversion from process separation to full-process collaboration
- Transformation from independent innovation of enterprises to multiparty open innovation in an industry environment.

Over the past decade, the computing, storage and network domains grew exponentially in terms of technical and economic viability. With the influence of these domains, Edge Cloud enables the industry needs by means of Smart gateways, Smart systems, Smart services and Smart assets. Hence, the Edge cloud development service framework must closely collaborate with the deployment and operation service framework to support efficient development, automatic deployment, and centralized operation of solutions. The ECC (as cited in ecconsortium, 2017) discussed that Edge Cloud must provide a "CROSS" value i.e. Mass and Heterogeneous Connection, Real-Time Services, Data Optimization, Smart Applications, Security and Privacy Protection. Based on the above concepts, the ECC proposed a Edge Computing Reference Architecture 2.0 shown in Figure 4. The different layers in Edge computing reference architecture 2.0 are Smart Service, Service Fabric, Connectivity and Computing Fabric(CCF) and Edge Computing Node (ECN).

Table 1. Edge cloud services

Type of Service	Edge Cloud Provider	Description
COaaS	Azure IoT Edge (as cited in Microsoft, 2018)	• Allow to deploy complex Artificial Intelligence activities like event processing, machine learning and image recognition using the Azure IoT edge.
	Predix Edge (GE Digital) (as cited in ge, 2018)	• It is an IIoT computing platform positioned at the intersection of industrial control systems and the enterprise. • The user can Collect data from assets and Information & communication Technology (IT) / Operational Technology(OT) sources, apply local machine learning analytics, Execute container-based applications, Securely and reliably forward data to Predix Cloud. • It has a secured stack with embedded OS and easily configurable and manageable edge devices and workloads
	Limelight Edge (as cited in limelight, 2018)	• Provides Flexible compute options where user can either rent compute resources as with cloud-based models or they can use their own hardware as with co-location models. • Organizations can easily focus building their business rather than building out a network by using the benefits of a private, high performance Limelight Edge Cloud
	Nebula (Ryden et al., 2014)	• This lightweight architecture enables the distributed data intensive computing services by optimizing location-aware data, computation placement, replication, and recovery.
	Nokia & Intel (as cited in Nokia Solutions and Networks, 2013, 2018)	• Helps in driving the implementation of Cloud RAN and Multi-access Edge Computing (MEC) using the distributing computing capacity in the network.
SaaS	Ciena (as cited in ciena, 2018)	• Blue Planet software of Ciena enables AI-enabled analytics for real-time resource sharing environments. • Orchestrates services and virtualization functions that facilitate the enhancement for real time applications.
NaaS	Infradata (as cited in infradata, 2018)	• Provides advanced container networking, security, and service chaining to users by extending their network capabilities. • The user can deploy, manage, and monetise new low-latency services such as IoT and connected cars closer to their end users. • It also provides an important foundation for 5G network.
	Fastly Edge Cloud platform (as cited in Wikipedia, 2014)	• Offers a content delivery network, Internet security services, load balancing, and video & streaming services.
PaaS	Apigee Edge (as cited in apigee, n.d)	• platform for developing and managing API proxies. • Provides value-added features like security, rate limiting, quotas, analytics, and more.
	Azure IoT Edge (as cited in Microsoft, 2018)	• offers services both for Linux and Windows • supports Java, .NET Core 2.0, Node.js, C, and Python • The developers can code in a known language and use existing business logic without writing it from scratch.

Smart Services

This layer is based on the model-driven unified service framework. The development service framework yields smart coordination between service development and deployment and deployment & operation service framework. These frameworks enable reliable software development interfaces and automatic deployment and operations.

Figure 4. Edge computing reference architecture 2.0

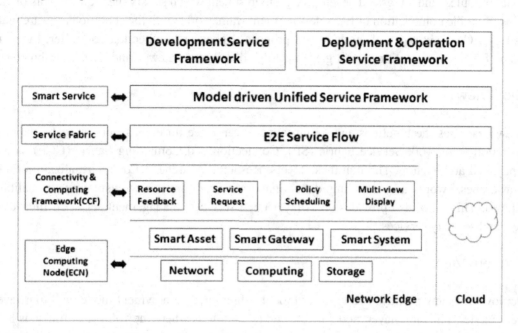

Service Fabric

This orchestration defines the Edge to Edge (E2E) service flow through the service fabric (SF) to realize service agility.

Connectivity and Computing Fabric (CCF)

The CCF enables a simplified architecture. The CCF also enables automatic and visualized deployment and operations of the OT & IT infrastructure, supporting coordination between edge computing resource services and service needs of industries.

Edge Computing Node (ECN)

ECNs support real-time processing, response & deliver, integrated hardware and software security with a variety of heterogeneous connections.

This Edge Computing Reference Architecture 2.0 is framed based on the Guide lines given by international standards defined by ISO/IEC/IEEE 42010:2011. Edge Computing Reference Architecture 2.0 can be explained using the following views:

Concept View

The Concept view provides ICT resources such as networks, computing, and storage, and can be logically abstracted as Edge Computing Nodes (ECNs). This architecture defines four types of ECN development frameworks for different application scenarios of ECNs. Each framework comprises of an operating system, functional modules, and integrated development environment which satisfy the requirements of various scenarios. Suitable combination of ECN development frameworks with the specific hardware platform required by ECNs, six types of products are proposed. They are Embedded controller, Independent controller, Terminal perception, Smart gateway, Edge distributed gateway and Edge distributed server.

Function View

This view describes the functions and design concepts in three different layers, namely, deployment and operation framework Service Fabric (SF), Connection and Computing Fabric (CCF), and ECN based physical architecture. Through these layers, Resource awareness, Edge Virtualization Function (EVF) awareness, workload scheduling, data collaboration and multi-view display functionalities can be achieved. This view also provides cross-layer open services, management services, lifecycle data services, and security services.

Deployment View

The Deployment view portrays two types of models, three-layer deployment model and four-layer deployment model. The three-layer model is relevant to situations where the volume of traffic is low and services are deployed in one or more scattered areas in decentralized manner. The areas such as smart street lamps, smart elevators, and smart environmental protection can adopt this model. In case of the four-layer model, the services are deployed centrally and the traffic volume is high. Smart video analysis, distributed grid, and smart manufacturing are some of the sites where the four-layer model can be deployed.

CHARACTERISTICS AND BENEFITS

When the goal is on the spot analysis of data followed by instantaneous generation of a rules-based command (Klonoff & David, 2017), Edge computing could potentially be preferable to fog computing due to fewer potential failure points. Each sensor or device in the network would be independently programmed to decide the type of information that should be stored locally and the data that need to be sent to the cloud for further use. The following characteristics of Edge Cloud have made it possible (El-Sayed et al., 2018).

- **Low Latency:** Aids in time critical events occur in Healthcare applications
- **Very Low Bandwidth Utilization:** Support multiple devices to access the edge at the same time.
- **Low Response Time:** Improves the data analytics and there by the overall performance of real-time applications.
- **Less Storage:** Less storage allows only the needed data is to be kept in the edge and other data are pushed to the cloud.
- **Very Low Service Overhead:** The decentralized processing and distributed computing lessen the service overhead.
- **Low Energy Consumption:** The low bandwidth usage ensures the low energy consumption.
- **Low Network Congestion:** By using backhaul links, and distributed computing the network traffic is alleviated.

- **High Scalability:** By increasing virtualization, the scalability is improved.
- **High Quality of Service (QoS) and Quality of Experience (QoE):** By minimizing the data transfer distance the QoS and QoE are enhanced.

Edge computing saves time and money by streamlining IoT communication, reducing system and network architecture complexity, and decreasing the number of potential failure points in an IoT application. Reducing system architecture complexity is key to the success of IIoT applications.

CHALLENGES AHEAD

Edge Cloud Computational Offloading

It is reported that during a period of one minute, YouTube users upload 43,33,560 videos, Amazon ships 1,111 packages, Twitter users share 4,73,400 photos, Instagram users post 49, 380 new photos, and Vine users share 8333 videos (as cited in domo, n.d). Usually, when a video or photo is uploaded, it is subjected to lossy compression to reduce the media size. Uploading the high resolution photos and videos from user devices need lots of bandwidth and it degrades the Edge performance in the poor internet connectivity areas. Similar concerns arise in live health monitoring applications, or smart city applications where live streams of data from surveillance cameras and other sensors needs to be uploaded to cloud (Bilal et al., 2018). Owing to the flooding of data, big data mining / Hierarchical data mining techniques (Peng et al., 2018) can be applied at the edge devices, to lessen the burden on the fronthaul / backhaul while transmitting large volume of data to the Cloud. But the characteristics of Edge like less storage and quick response time compel for advanced data mining algorithms that are to be proposed.

Empowered Distributed System

The massive rise of personal computing devices introduces human-centered applications that reduce the boundaries between man and machine. For example, in the applications like crowd sensing, humen are introduced in the data-analysis loop. This brings in the challenge of designing an innovative socially-informed architecture where the information provided by the users must be hold in a secure way (Lopez, 2015). In healthcare applications, users act as a sensor and become an important source of data, which can be applied in learning algorithms and visualization tools. The Edge Cloud architecture must apply adaptive distributed systems to analysis the user behaviors depending on their location or context. It will also handle the interaction with other humans through their available connected devices. This poses serious challenges to the distributed systems. Edge cloud is based on a decentralized model that interconnects heterogeneous cloud resources controlled by a variety of entities. A fresh combination of overlay technologies with cloud resources may create another challenge.

Resource Management

Resource management is a key challenge in time critical and real-time systems. Edge cloud has to dynamically allocate resources for delay sensitive tasks. Hence priority-aware computation is required in Edge cloud (Bilal et al., 2018). As Edge cloud is an emerging arena, simple architectures are proposed for resource management. Based on the number of users and their demands, provisioning of the resources is to be made by the edge node. The Edge cloud has to choose an appropriate edge node depending on certain parameters. They are node's capacity and the proximity of the node from the user and the communication & computation resources among competing users. These parameters must also focus in energy conservation and quality of service. This state of affairs necessitates novel optimizing algorithms to address efficient resource management.

Energy Efficiency

Generally, the end devices and IoT nodes involved in the Edge Cloud are constrained by computing capabilities, battery life, and heat dissipation. Energy consuming application running in the user devices are to be offloaded to the Edge Cloud for energy consumption (Mahmud et al., 2018). While concentrating on energy consumption, the computation delay due to offload has to be tolerated. The factors that influence the energy consumptions are (i) end user device accessing the service (ii) energy consumed by internal network, storage, and servers (iii) the volume of traffic exchanged between the user and cloud (iv) the computational complexity of the task to be performed and (v) factors such as the number of users sharing a computer source (Bilal et al., 2018). However, energy can be saved by employing intelligent client-side caching techniques, and optimizing the synchronization frequency of contents between Edge Cloud and IoT devices. The optimization algorithms that minimize the additional energy wastage and Green edge cloud architecture can be applied to address this key issue.

Security and Privacy

The enabling technologies of Edge Cloud, namely, wireless networks, distributed systems, IoT and virtualization platform enforce the security and privacy issues. These technologies must provide secure communication during integration and interoperation of the devices. As the IoT devices are lightweight, Edge cloud must provide a middleware to secure data that is send out to the internet or Cloud. Also most of the end users are not aware of privacy and security issues. So an automatic mechanism ensuring security and privacy of the user data must be imposed (Bilal et al., 2018). Generally, end to end encryption is followed in Edge Cloud. For more secure communication, re-encryption, quality based encryption or attribute based encryption can also be exploited. The Edge Cloud has to identify the malicious nodes and trusted nodes while data is transmitted between nodes. Secure routing, redundant routing and trusted topologies (Lopez, 2015) are utilized to maintain integrity. Sensitive data protection is ensured by applying fragmentation of information with encryption joined with decentralized overlay technologies. Another solution for privacy protection is that the owner of the data must be given full control over the data that is used by the service providers (shi et al., 2016). Security in Edge Cloud not only comprise of data security, it also includes device security, network security and application security.

Data Abstraction

The IoT devices connected to the Edge Cloud generated huge amount of data. Handling the huge data by the devices or transmitting the raw data directly to the Cloud is the challenging process. Hence, Data abstraction (preprocessing, filtering and restructuring the raw data) (Bilal et al., 2018) can be performed at the Edge. There are a number of challenges in this process. First, the data collected from different devices are in diverse format. The privacy and security concerns may affect the applications accessing the raw data. Consequently increases the complexity level of entire data abstraction. Secondly, too much of data filtering may not provide useful knowledge, at the same time, less filtering challenge for storage. Thirdly, data collected from low precision sensor, hazard environment and unreliable connections may produce unreliable data (shi et al., 2016).

Fault Tolerance and Quality of Service

Another significant confront is QoS and Fault tolerance. The Edge Cloud is primarily utilized by the real time applications. So, automatic fault recovery may improve the QoS of the Edge Cloud. Therefore, in peak hours efficient task partitioning and scheduling mechanism are to be employed (Bilal et al., 2018). In Collaborative edge, the user data has to be cached in multiple edge nodes for better service. This amplifies the traffic among the participating nodes. Thus, best possible data placement, replication guidelines are to be designed to reduce the traffic and for better QoS.

EDGE COMPUTING PARADIGMS

Different architectures have been proposed to appreciate edge computing platforms. Currently there are four paradigms in Edge computing that serve the IoT applications. They are Cloudlet (Peng et al., 2018), Mobile Edge Computing (MEC)(Hu et al., 2015), Fog Computing (Dastjerdi et al., 2016) and Edge Cloud (Chang et al., 2014). Based on the applications and the service request of the users, any one of the four models can be used by the edge computing ecosystem.

Cloudlet

The term Cloudlet is coined by a team at Carnegie Mellon University (CMU). A cloudlet is a trusted, resource-rich computer or cluster of computers that are well-connected to the internet and available for use by nearby mobile devices (Peng et al., 2018). The cloudlets provide powerful computing resources to mobile devices that are needed by the resource-intensive and interactive mobile applications. The mobile devices involved in the edge computing can access the cloudlet for computing resources through wireless local area network. The three layers in this architecture are mobile device layer, cloudlet layer and the cloud layer. Cloudlets are more responsive and dynamic in its provisioning as it is the needed for any mobile devices. The mobile devices have to discover, select, and associate with the appropriate cloudlet among multiple candidates before it starts provisioning. To support user mobility from one location to another, Virtual Machine(VM) handoff technology are to be used for offloading the services from one cloudlet to the another cloudlet.

The edge devices communicate to the cloudlet for the service. The customized VM called VM overlay is received from the devices. The cloudlet has to convert the basic VM to custom VM to satisfy the user request. The process of using VM overlays to provisioning cloudlets is called VM synthesis. This procedure (Peng et al., 2018) is explained in Figure 5. The mobile devices at the edge send the VM overlay. The cloudlet decompresses the overlay, applies it to the base VM to derive the launched VM, and then creates a VM instance from it. The mobile device performs the offload operations at this instance. At the end of the session, the instance is destroyed, but the launched VM image can be retained

Figure 5. Dynamic VM synthesis

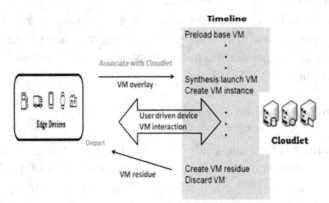

in a persistent cache for future sessions. To retain some training data for future offload sessions, the cloudlet generates a VM residue that can be sent back to the mobile device and incorporated into its overlay. This is a potential technique for enabling user mobility with low end-to-end latency application. The Cloudlets support and enables many exciting mobile applications that are both compute-intensive and latency-sensitive (Satyanarayanan et al., 2015a). In wearable cognitive assistance, to improve the end-to-end latency and real-time interaction Cloudlet is implemented (Ha et al., 2014). Cloudlets act as a cloud during its unavailability due to failure or cyber attacks to improve the reliability (Satyanarayanan et al., 2013, 2015b). Remote access of desktop window-based applications is also feasible with Cloudlets.

Mobile Edge Computing (MEC)

The ETSI Industry Specification Group (ISG) on Mobile Edge Computing (MEC) launched in December 2014, is a new emerging technology designed to push resources closer to the radio access networks in 4G and 5G (Hu et al., 2015). The "Mobile Edge Computing" is renamed as "Multi-Access Edge Computing" in 2017 by the ETSI MEC industry group to reflect the significance of MEC. The Mobile Edge Computing is characterized by low latency, proximity, high bandwidth, and real-time insight into radio network information and location awareness (Hu et al., 2015). MEC offer services to consumers and enterprise customers in delivering their mission-critical applications at a location considered to be a rewarding point over the mobile network (Beck et al., 2014) . MEC is used in Video acceleration, augmented reality, connected vehicles, IoT analytics, enterprise services, network performance and utilization optimization, retail, and eHealth.

MEC servers are deployed next to base stations: they are co-hosted with base stations and are directly linked to them. MEC servers are equipped with commodity hardware, i.e. usual server CPUs, memory, and communication interfaces. In 2014, Nokia Networks introduced a very first real-world MEC platform Radio Applications Cloud Servers (RACS) represent real manifestation of MEC servers shown in Figure 6 (Beck et al., 2014). MEC servers are co-hosted with base stations and are directly linked to them. MEC servers are equipped with server CPUs, memory, and communication interfaces. Cloud technology and virtualization enable the application deployment. RACS also have a VM hypervisor for the deployment of VM images running MEC applications. VMs and RACS platform communicate with each other by means of a message bus. VMs send heartbeat messages to the RACS system as a self-monitoring service.

Figure 6. RACs architecture

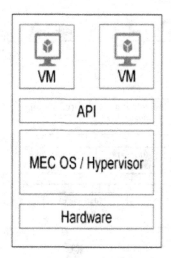

If heartbeat messages are not sent by the VM, the hypervisor will reboot the VM, ensuring that the VM is automatically reinitialized after some applications crashed. To secure the VMs from malicious offenders, before deployment VMs have to be signed and it is verified by the operator. VMs communicate mobile devices with a specific destination address or port number. Based on the application type, additional header information is included to HTTP requests consisting of network-specific information, which is not accessible to ASP services in traditional cellular networks. The forwarding and filtering rulesets for traffic routed through MEC servers are defined by Mobile network operators. Based on both privacy concerns and application providers' demands, these rulesets specify which data are sent to which type of application. In accordance with the subscriptions, mobile traffic is routed through the VMs. Some of the applications of MEC include content scaling, edge content delivery, augmentation, aggregation, local connectivity and offloading (Beck et al., 2014).

Fog Computing

Fog computing as a distributed computing paradigm that fundamentally extends the services provided by the cloud to the edge of the network (Dastjerdi et al., 2016). Bonomi et. al. define Fog Computing as a highly virtualized platform that provides compute, storage, and networking services between end devices and traditional Cloud Computing Data Centers, typically, but not exclusively located at the edge of network (Bonomi et al., 2012). The characteristics of Fog computing are scaling computing resources, support for user mobility, communication protocols, interface heterogeneity, cloud integration, and distributed data analytics to addresses requirements of low latency applications that are geographically distributed. The application of Fog computing is preferred when reduction in network traffic, low latency requirement and scalability are the users' concern. At the same time, it is also more suitable for IoT tasks and queries processing. The Fog architecture (Dastjerdi et al, 2016) is shown in Figure 7.

The data from the sensors and actuators in a heterogeneous network is managed by efficient Software defined network. Edge and cloud resources communicate using machine-to-machine standards such as MQTT (formerly MQ Telemetry Transport) and the Constrained Application Protocol. The tasks from different users are prioritized by resource management layer in multitenant applications. The monitor-

Figure 7. Fog architecture

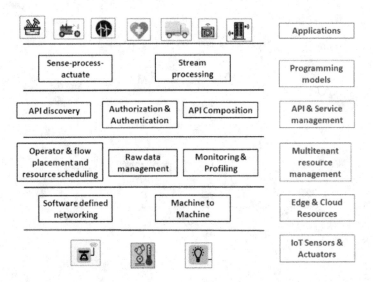

ing component in the resource management layer tracks the state of the fog resources and chooses the best resource for the incoming task. In the API service management layer, APIs needed for the complex functionalities are decided dynamically. Applications running on the fog devices obtain insights from the stream data of the devices and the action to be taken are translated & sent to the actuators. This process is performed with the help of the sense-process-actuate and stream processing programming model in the fog architecture. Fog computing is more suitable for Healthcare and activity tracking, Smart utility services, Augmented reality, cognitive systems, and gaming.

Edge Cloud

A compute or storage node attached to the edge network and associated to the data center cloud is called Edge node. Edge Zone is formed by grouping together the Edge nodes in the same edge network. The Edge Cloud (Chang et al., 2014) is the association of the data center nodes along with all the edge zones. The Edge Cloud operator can extend the traditional cloud's IaaS capabilities to install applications in the Edge cloud with the pre-existing cloud functionalities. The Edge Cloud architecture (Chang et al., 2014) is shown in Figure 8.

The Edge Cloud services are offered through Edge Apps for mobile devices and smart IoT devices. An Edge app is a package of IaaS images designed to initiate and work together in agreement with data centers and edge nodes. It consists of two types of compute instances. One type of compute instances run in the data center and other type in the edge zone of the edge owner. There are different form of IaaS images in each type of compute instance, which can be replicated. In virtual networks, there are two types. They are App-Private network and Edge-Local network. The App-Private network is instantiated to interconnect all instances of each Edge App at the launch. The Edge-Local network establishes the communication of the Edge App with end users and resources in the edge network. Chang (2014) discussed two Edge apps, 3D indoor Localization Application and Video Surveillance Application.

Figure 8. Edge cloud architecture

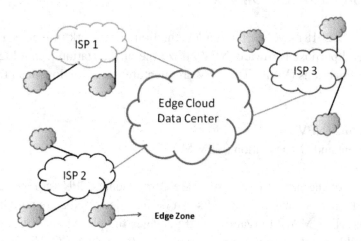

ENABLING TECHNOLOGIES OF EDGE CLOUD

Edge Cloud is realized with the existing as well as emerging technologies. They are Virtualization, Network Function Virtualization (NFV), Software Defined Networking (SDN), Network Slicing and Computation offloading (Taleb et al., 2017a, Premsankar et al., 2018). These technologies play a key role in the development of edge computing platforms.

Virtualization

Virtualization is a key technology for Cloud computing. Using virtualization multiple independent software instances can run on a single physical server. All these instances access the underlying physical resources without interfering with other instances (isolation) running on the same server. The software abstraction layer called hypervisor, the intermediate between the VMs and physical hardware directs the VMs to use the underlying CPU, storage and network resources. On top of the host server OS, the VM runs its own guest operating system. This technique is best suited for mult-tenancy but the presence of hypervisor invites non-negligible overhead. To overcome this overhead, Container-based virtualization has been proposed as a light-weight alternative.

In case of Container-based virtualization, the virtualized instances use the underlying host OS, instead of using their own guest OS. To guarantee isolation between containers, modifications are made to the OS. The container-based virtualization reduces instance start time and hence results in better performance. To support mobility, an important characteristic for the Edge Cloud, migration techniques are applied. Moving computing resources from one physical server to the other is called migration. The migration technique helps in energy consumption also. Live migration is a practice that reduces the time during which a virtual instance is not accessible as it is being moved from one server to another, which is vital in case of IoT applications. The virtualization forms the basis for Network Function Virtualization and Software Defined Networking.

Network Function Virtualization

NFV (Premsankar et al., 2018) involves the implementation of network functions as software modules that can run on general purpose hardware. NFV utilize the virtualization technologies and establishes Virtualized Network Functions (VNF). The NFV architecture has three domains (Taleb et al., 2017a):

1. VNF
2. NFV Infrastructure (NFVI)
3. NFV Management and Orchestration (NFV MANO)

NFVI is a package of the hardware and software components (CPU, storage, virtualization layer) that offer the network environment where VNFs can be installed. VNFs are software implementation of network functions. NFV MANO organizes and manages the physical and virtual resources of the NFVI and is responsible for the lifecycle management of VNFs. In MEC, VNFs enable the mobility, scalability and migration. With this technique, no dedicated hardware is needed. Hence, it is suited for efficient delivery of mobile applications and services. Portability, Network slicing, Federation support and on-demand access of pooled resources are other benefits of employing NFV in Edge Cloud.

Software Defined Networking

SDN is a technology that supports network programmability and multi-tenancy for fast deployment of innovative services at the edge of the network. By utilizing common APIs, SDNs have a logical centralized control which separates data plane from control plane and offer virtual network instances, by abstracting the underlying network infrastructure. By linking VNFs and MEC services, SDN offer a dynamic service provisioning. This satisfies the performance demand of the users at the edge by exploiting the network infrastructure. Using the concept of re-routing or changing the codec scheme of wireless microwave links, SDN overcome the routing challenges connected with IP address translation, large volume of control signaling, tunneling overhead and dynamic resource management. SDN converts the proprietary firmware-based network switches and routers forming a simple data plane, which can be controlled at the opening and outlet points of the network.

Network Slicing

Network slicing (NS) is dividing one network into multiple instances, each architected and optimized for a specific requirement of specific application or service (Taleb et al., 2017a). The network hypervisor in NS allocates the shared resources such as bandwidth, network functions, storage and access to big data or RAN analytics necessary for the tenant. The resource isolation and customization support the operation of Mobile Edge computing. It is utilized by the Personalized Mobile Telecom (Taleb et al., 2017b) and grabbing the attention of Mobile Network Alliance (NGMN), Third Generation Partnership Project (3GPP), and International Telecommunication Union — Telecommunication Standardization Sector (ITU-T). The potential benefits of NS fetch fully personalized and scalable end-to-end mobile connection service and easy, efficient access to advanced mobile services.

Computation Offloading

Computation offloading (Taleb et al., 2017) is a process where a resource constrained mobile device offloads a computation-intensive task to a resource-sufficient cloud environment. Computation offloading is carried out to save energy, battery lifetime or in case where the end device is unable to process a computation-heavy application. The computation offloading methods used by the mobile cloud computing environment are Cyber foraging (Balan et al. 2002) and CloneCloud (Chun et al., 2011). In video services, the compute-intensive encoding part can be offloaded. In the same way, in M2M, wearables and other IoT devices, splitting the compute-intensive application and offloading only the data-intensive part to the edge can be performed. In mobile gaming, by offloading the rendering part from mobile devices, gaming becomes more interactive with quick responses.

EDGE CLOUD ENVIRONMENT

Apigee Edge

Apigee Edge is a platform for developing and managing API proxies. The app developers who need backend services are the primary consumers (as cited in apigee, n.d). A company that want to expose services that provide product pricing and availability information, sales and ordering services, order tracking services, and any other services required by client apps can adopt Apigee Edge. Apigee Edge is built on Java. It enables a secure access to the services with a well-defned API that is consistent across all services, regardless of service implementation. A consistent API provides the following benefits:

- Makes it easy for app developers to consume company services.
- Provision to change the backend service implementation without affecting the public API.
- Provides additional features like analytics, monetization and developer portal that are built into Edge.

The Apigee Edge forms a layer between the client apps and backend service provider. To consume the backend services, the app developers, access an API proxy created on Edge. Thus the Edge handle the security and authorization tasks required to protect the services, as well as to analyze, monitor and monetize those services.

Limelight Networks' Edge Cloud Services

Limelight Networks' edge cloud services (as cited in limelight, 2018) offer networking solutions that allow organizations to concentrate on scaling their businesses instead of extending the underlying infrastructure. The services provided by Limelight are

- **Private managed network backbone:** Limelight's private network is one of the world's largest network that allows data to bypass the public internet and travel at high speed across the globe securely and reliably. Limelight's components ensure industry leading performance consistently, throughput the world.
- **Connections to all the last-mile providers:** Limelight provides businesses with one-hop connectivity to more than 900 global ISPs by leveraging over greater than 80 Points of Presence(PoPs). Irrespective of the users' connectivity (fixed broadband, wireless, or even emerging 5G connections) Limelight brings computing as close as possible to reduce latency.
- **Data centers at the edge:** Compute services offered by Limelight allows the customers to either rent compute resources in Limelight's data centers or deploy their own hardware. In addition to managing all aspects of data center operations for customers, Limelight ensures fulfillment of regional data autonomy regulations.

Nokia AirFrame Open Edge Infrastructure

In April 2018, Nokia has launched the industry's first Edge Cloud data center solution "Nokia AriFrame" (as cited in Nokia, 2018) to meet the diverse low latency data processing demands of Cloud RAN and advanced applications for consumers and industries. The Nokia AirFrame open edge cloud infrastructure is designed to deliver a layered network architecture that optimizes performance and operator costs for 5G era, the next generation wireless technology. This open edge infrastructure offers

- A Cloud data center solution, based on x86, designed to support edge cloud deployments.
- An edge server with the dimension 133.5 x 444 x 430mm (HWD), can be installed at existing base station sites.
- The hardware acceleration capabilities for 4G and 5G functions and applications are also offered by the AirFrame open edge server combined with Nokia ReefShark. It includes Cloud RAN and artificial intelligence (AI).
- The edge cloud with low latency along with AirFrame supports the acceleration of key machine learning and AI workloads.
- Nokia's real-time Open platform for NFV (OPNFV) which is compatible with cloud infrastructure software delivers high-performance demands of operators and applications in an edge environment.

Fastly

In 2017, Fastly edge cloud platform (as cited in Fastly, 2018b) delivers three new services Web Application Firewall (WAF), Image Optimizer and Load Balancer.

- **Web Application Firewall:** Fastly's web application firewall protects customers' applications from malicious attacks. It also protects against injection attacks, cross site scripting and HTTP protocol violations. WAF is continuously updated to address ongoing threats using multiple rulesets. Rules can be configured in real time via Fastly's API, and can run in active blocking mode or passive logging mode only

- **Image Optimizer:** The Fastly Image Optimizer, manipulates and delivers real-time images to on-line users irrespective of their geographic location. It images dispensed by the optimizer are pixel-perfect, bandwidth-efficient and device-specific images. The Fastly's network, avoids manual optimization by adopting the offloading optimization logic at the edge and offers pre-processed images across varying devices, browsers and resolutions.
- **Load Balancer:** Today, Service providers have to plan ahead to deliver consistently exceptional, scalable experiences. Hence they use multiple active data centers, a multi-cloud strategy or a combination of both. Fastly's cloud-based Load Balancer optimizes traffic distribution across a powerful network for scalability and high availability.

StreetSmart Edge

StreetSmart Edge (as cited in StreetSmart, 2012) is "Inspired Trading, By Design." The platform focuses on the trader's workflow. It provides a robust trading experience in a user friendly way. With the StreetSmart customer can keep track of their gains and losses, and monitor their balances real-time. Additionally, there is a provision to access streaming quotes and real-time charting. User can specify Market Limit, Stop Limit, Trailing Stop and Trailing Stop Limit orders. It also allows the user to add a bracket to the primary order or filled order and option orders, depending on the option approval level.

Chart pattern recognition in StreetSmart Edge with a third party program from Recognia, support user in decision making by automating pattern recognition of more than 60 chart patterns, indicators and standard oscillators. Users can set up custom screens and email alerts, and monitor realtime technical analysis.

Azure IoT Edge

Azure IoT Edge (as cited in Microsoft, 2018) shifts cloud analytics and custom business logic to IoT devices. It helps the user to configure their IoT software and deploy it to devices using standard containers and monitor it all from the cloud. Azure IoT Edge is made up of three components:

- Azure services, 3rd party services, or customer own code are executed in IoT Edge modules using container technique. They are installed in IoT Edge devices and executed locally on those devices.
- The modules deployed in each IoT device is managed by the IoT Edge runtime environment.
- Remote monitoring and management of IoT Edge devices is performed by a cloud-based interface.

SUMMARY

Due to the innovation of various gadgets, more and more IoT devices are used in the area of public safety, transport, and healthcare. With the aim of providing better solution, new technologies, standards and policies are being proposed by leading industries. IoT applications generate large volume of data and they need rapid response. Owing to the characteristics such as less storage, short battery life, the IoT devices are not suited for storing and processing the huge data produced at the edge. The conventional cloud computing is unable to face the challenge. The enabling technologies like virtualization, software defined networks, computational offloading realized the existence of Edge Cloud Computing. Thus allowing the computational process to happen at the proximity of the edge and reduce the workload of the Cloud. Based on the requirement of the IoT applications, the edge computing technologies like, Cloudlet, Fog, Mobile Edge Computing and Edge Cloud can be adopted. The vision and services provided by Edge computing are elaborated in this chapter. The benefits of implementing edge cloud and the challenges faced are enlightened. The solutions like Limelight Network's Edge Cloud, Apigee Edge, Nokia AirFrame Open edge infrastructure and Azure IoT Edge magnetize the IoT applications as well as open new research challenges.

REFERENCES

Ai, Y., Peng, M., & Zhang, K. (2018). Edge computing technologies for Internet of Things: A primer. *Digital Communications and Networks*, *4*(2), 77–86. doi:10.1016/j.dcan.2017.07.001

Ashton, K. (2009). That 'Internet of Things' thing: In the real world, things matter more than ideas. *RFID Journal*. Retrieved from http://www.rfidjournal.com/articles/view?4986

Balan, R., Flinn, J., Satyanarayanan, M., Sinnamohideen, S., & Hen-I., Y. (2002). The case for cyber foraging. *Proceedings of the 10th workshop on ACM SIGOPS European workshop*, 87-92. 10.1145/1133373.1133390

Beck, M. T., Werner, M., Feld, S., & Schimper, S. (2014). Mobile edge computing: A taxonomy. *Proc. of the Sixth International Conference on Advances in Future Internet*, 48-55.

Bilal, K., Khalid, O., Erbad, A., & Khan, S. U. (2018). Potentials, trends, and prospects in edge technologies: Fog, cloudlet, mobile edge, and micro data centers. *Computer Networks*, *130*, 94–120. doi:10.1016/j.comnet.2017.10.002

Bonomi, F., Milito, R., Zhu, J., & Addepalli, S. (2012). *Fog Computing and its Role in the Internet of Things*. MCC Work. Mob. Cloud Comput.

Chang, H., Hari, A., Mukherjee, S., & Lakshman, T. V. (2014). Bringing the cloud to the edge. *Computer Communications Workshops (INFOCOM WKSHPS), 2014 IEEE Conference*, 346-351.

Chun, B.-G., Ihm, S., Maniatis, P., Naik, M., & Patti, A. (2011). Clonecloud: elastic execution between mobile device and cloud. *Proceedings of the sixth conference on Computer systems*, 301-314. 10.1145/1966445.1966473

Ciena. (2018). Retrieved from https://www.ciena.com/insights/what-is/What-is-Edge-Cloud.html

Cisco G. C. I. Forecast and Methodology 2016–2021. (2018). Retrieved from https://www.cisco.com/c/en/us/solutions/collateral/service-provider/global-cloud-index-gci/white-paper-c11-738085.html

Dastjerdi, Gupta, Calheiros, Ghosh, & Buyya. (2016). Fog computing: Principles, architectures, and applications. *Internet of Things*, 61-75.

Dastjerdi, A. V., & Buyya, R. (2016). Fog computing: Helping the Internet of Things realize its potential. *IEEE Computer Society*, *49*(8), 112–116. doi:10.1109/MC.2016.245

Data never sleeps 6.0. (2018). Retrieved from https://www.domo.com/assets/downloads/18_domo_data-never-sleeps-6+verticals.pdf

Edge A. (2018). Retrieved from https://docs.apigee.com/api-platform/get-started/what-apigee-edge#make-avail-web

EdgeC. R. A. 2.0. (2017). Retrieved from http://en.ecconsortium.net/Uploads/file/20180328/1522232376480704.pdf

Edge Computing Driving New Outcomes from Intelligent Industrial Machines. (2018). Retrieved from https://www.ge.com/digital/sites/default/files/download_assets/Edge-Computing-Driving-New-Outcomes.pdf

Edge computing and IoT 2018 – when intelligence moves to the edge. (2018). Retrieved from https://www.i-scoop.eu/internet-of-things-guide/edge-computing-iot

Edge computing consortium. (2017). Retrieved from https://www.iotaustralia.org.au/wp-content/uploads/2017/01/White-Paper-of-Edge-Computing-Consortium.pdf

El-Sayed, H., Sankar, S., Prasad, M., Puthal, D., Gupta, A., Mohanty, M., & Lin, C.-T. (2018). Edge of things: The big picture on the integration of edge, IoT and the cloud in a distributed computing environment. *IEEE Access: Practical Innovations, Open Solutions, 6*, 1706–1717. doi:10.1109/ACCESS.2017.2780087

Fastly. (2018). Retrieved from https://www.fastly.com/press/press-releases/fastly-builds-content-delivery-network-heritage-unveils-edge-cloud-platform

Fastly. (2018a). Retrieved from https://www.fastly.com/edge-cloud-platform

Fastly. (2018b). Retrieved from https://en.wikipedia.org/wiki/Fastly

Ha, K., Chen, Z., Hu, W., Richter, W., Pillai, P., & Satyanarayanan, M. (2014). Towards wearable cognitive assistance. *Proceedings of the 12th annual international conference on Mobile systems, applications, and services*, 68-81.

Hu, Y. C., Patel, M., Sabella, D., Sprecher, N., & Young, V. (2015). Mobile edge computing—A key technology towards 5G. *ETSI White Paper, 11*, 1-16.

Infradata. (2018). Retrieved from https://www.infradata.com/resources/what-is-edge-cloud

Klonoff, D. C. (2017). Fog computing and edge computing architectures for processing data from diabetes devices connected to the medical Internet of things. *Journal of Diabetes Science and Technology, 11*(4), 647–652. doi:10.1177/1932296817717007 PMID:28745086

Limelight. (2018). Retrieved from https://www.limelight.com/resources/data-sheet/edge-analytics

Lopez, G., Pedro, A. M., Epema, D., Datta, A., Higashino, T., Iamnitchi, A., ... Riviere, E. (2015). Edge-centric computing: Vision and challenges. *Computer Communication Review, 45*(5), 37–42. doi:10.1145/2831347.2831354

Mahmud, R., Kotagiri, R., & Buyya, R. (2018). Fog computing: A taxonomy, survey and future directions. In *Internet of everything*. Springer.

Microsoft Azure IoT Reference Architecture. (2018). Retrieved from http://download.microsoft.com/download/A/4/D/A4DAD253-BC21-41D3-B9D9-87D2AE6F0719/Microsoft_Azure_IoT_Reference_Architecture.pdf

Nokia. (2018). *The edge cloud: an agile foundation to support advanced new services.* Nokia White paper. Retrieved from https://onestore.nokia.com/asset/202184

Nokia launches industry-first Edge Cloud data center solution for the 5G era, supporting industry automation and consumer applications. (2018). Retrieved from https://www.nokia.com/about-us/news/releases/2018/04/25/nokia-launches-industry-first-edge-cloud-data-center-solution-for-the-5g-era-supporting-industry-automation-and-consumer-applications

Nokia Solutions and Networks, Increasing Mobile Operators' Value Proposition with Edge Computing. (2013). Retrieved from http://nsn.com/portfolio/liquid-net/intelligent-broadband-management/liquid-applications

Predix Edge – GE Digital. (2018). Retrieved from https://www.ge.com/digital/asset/predix-edge-ge-digital

Premsankar, G., Di Francesco, M., & Taleb, T. (2018). Edge computing for the Internet of Things: A case study. *IEEE Internet of Things Journal, 5*(2), 1275–1284. doi:10.1109/JIOT.2018.2805263

Ryden, M., Oh, K., Chandra, A., & Weissman, J. (2014). Nebula: Distributed edge cloud for data-intensive computing. *IEEE 2014 International Conference on "In Collaboration Technologies and Systems (CTS)",* 491-492.

Satyanarayanan, M. (2017). The emergence of edge computing. *Computers & Society, 50*(1), 30–39. doi:10.1109/MC.2017.9

Satyanarayanan, M., Lewis, G., Morris, E., Simanta, S., Boleng, J., & Ha, K. (2013). The role of cloudlets in hostile environments. *IEEE Pervasive Computing, 12*(4), 40–49. doi:10.1109/MPRV.2013.77

Satyanarayanan, M., Schuster, R., Ebling, M., Fettweis, G., Flinck, H., Joshi, K., & Sabnani, K. (2015a). An open ecosystem for mobile-cloud convergence. *IEEE Communications Magazine, 53*(3), 63–70. doi:10.1109/MCOM.2015.7060484

Satyanarayanan, M., Simoens, P., Xiao, Y., Pillai, P., Chen, Z., Ha, K., ... Amos, B. (2015b). Edge analytics in the internet of things. *IEEE Pervasive Computing, 2*(2), 24–31. doi:10.1109/MPRV.2015.32

Shi, W., Cao, J., Zhang, Q., Li, Y., & Xu, L. (2016). Edge computing: Vision and challenges. *IEEE Internet of Things Journal, 3*(5), 637–646. doi:10.1109/JIOT.2016.2579198

StreetSmart. (2018). Retrieved from http://help.streetsmart.schwab.com/edge/printablemanuals/Edge-Manual.pdf

Taleb, T., Mada, B., Corici, M.-I., Nakao, A., & Flinck, H. (2017b). PERMIT: Network slicing for personalized 5G mobile telecommunications. *IEEE Communications Magazine, 55*(5), 88–93. doi:10.1109/MCOM.2017.1600947

Taleb, T., Samdanis, K., Mada, B., Flinck, H., Dutta, S., & Sabella, D. (2017a). On multi-access edge computing: A survey of the emerging 5G network edge cloud architecture and orchestration. *IEEE Communications Surveys and Tutorials*, *19*(3), 1657–1681. doi:10.1109/COMST.2017.2705720

The lifeline for a data driven world. (2018). Retrieved from https://www.happiestminds.com/Insights/internet-of-things

What Edge Computing Means for Infrastructure and Operations Leaders. (2018). Retrieved from https://www.gartner.com/smarterwithgartner/what-edge-computing-means-for-infrastructure-and-operations-leaders

Chapter 9

An Efficient Framework Based on Cloud Computing Integrated With Internet of Things Technology for Intelligent Waste Management

Suresh Annamalai
Nehru Institute of Engineering and Technology, India

Udendhran R.
Bharathidasan University, India

ABSTRACT

This chapter presents techniques based on internet of things and cloud computing-driven waste management. The data of the World Bank says that the municipal solid waste generation by the year of 2025 will be 1.42 kg/capital per day in the urban residential areas, with the increase in cost of about $375.5 billion that has a major rise from an annual of $205.4 billion in the year 2012. Due to the high population with the extreme consumption of goods and services, this leads to a strong association among the income levels, quality of life, and waste generation. In the present situation, more than 50% of the total population is living in the cities. In the governance aspect, it is said that the cost of waste management will be highly expensive. This chapter deals with the effective waste management with the implementation of internet of things (IoT)-based cloud technology with the machine learning algorithm that could be highly intellectual in the management of waste.

DOI: 10.4018/978-1-5225-9023-1.ch009

A BRIEF INTRODUCTION INTO WASTE MANAGEMENT

Communications between the devices are meaningful to common users in a sense that it helps them simplify various day-to-day tasks (Akash k t, 2017). Some of the common example could be fire alarms, door locking system, automatic switching of lights etc. These examples come under simple IoT based application. There are major impacts that could be done by IoT when dealing with the higher end technologies. IoT involves in sensing, actuating, collecting, processing and storing of data (Anguelovski, I. (2016)). Thus, smart city will have these impacts that could be handled for several applications such as citizen observatory, traffic management, energy management and use of smart grids to flood detection and prediction systems (Alexandra Klimova, 2016).

The payments done at a small scale could be extremely difficult due to their massive overhead (Furlong, C, 2016). Bitcoin, that was introduced at the year of 2009 makes the financial transactions much easier that purely displaces the intermediaries in terms of security and transaction overhead cost by the blockchain technology. Although bitcoin has both a positive and negative side, the blockchain technology works well finding its impact in both the financial and non-financial systems (Ajuntament de Barcelona. 2016). This is an automatic system where the changes must be made by voting the members (Martí, I. 2016). DAO has an ability to interact with other DAO or various smart contracts. This could evolve a new business model with the broad scope of implementation. With the approach of DAO, one can imagine government bodies and various companies running on top of the blockchain (Christopher Krauss, 2017) as shown in figure 1.

There is a huge impact in sustainability with the generation and the management of waste (Medvedev A, 2015). Based in the time and situation, the sustainability has several dimensions. Due to the improper disposal of waste, there is a chance of occurrence of greenhouse gases (Navghane S S, 2016). These gases are dangerous that could lead to direct or indirect impact on the human health. With the proper waste management, we can promote the concept of recycling and reusing. Moreover, the waste could be effectively converted into energy that increases the quality of life. This has been implemented in Sweden that had made a revolution by promoting recycling of rubbish from other countries.

Flat-rate based pricing system has been adapted by many waste management systems at the present, in order to compensate with the waste management services. There is another system known as weight-

Figure 1. Current waste generation per capita by region

Region	Waste Generation Per Capita (kg/capita/day)		
	Lower Boundary	Upper Boundary	Average
AFR	0.09	3.0	0.65
EAP	0.44	4.3	0.95
ECA	0.29	2.1	1.1
LAC	0.11	5.5	1.1
MENA	0.16	5.7	1.1
OECD	1.10	3.7	2.2
SAR	0.12	5.1	0.45

rate based waste management system that charges the amount based on the amount of waste produced (Soto, R. 2016). This could be a motivation for promoting less quantity of waste. This system is currently deployed in South Korea, which results in 33% of less waste production shown in the figure 2.

WASTE MANAGEMENT USE CASE

In this scenario, the people should involve together for producing their waste management DAO in their community. As stated earlier, weight-rate based system functions by charging an amount of money based on the waste produced. Blockchain technology rather reduces the overhead financial transaction that was crucial for the minimum financial transactions. This could help the developed countries with their minimal payment that was an issue and helps the developing countries with their effective payment infrastructure. The social and the economic problem have been outlined by the Department of Computer Science, Stanford University due to the micropayment structure.

The two major technologies that were found to be the top of Gartner's Hype Cycle was the IoT and block-chain technology. Several tools were being evolved with the concept of IoT technologies. Although these technologies are under rapid development, there is a lack of maturity among these technologies. Commercial waste management involves dealing with the collection of wastes, gather them and recycle the waste materials or parch them when they couldn't be recycled. In order to motivate the people, the pricing-based system was introduced to promote less waste. Certain limitation falls with the waste collection trucks (that could overlap with the other waste collecting vehicle on that route) as well as the data generation. The level sensors promoted with the IoT technology could determine the level of waste produced based on which the users will be charged. This could also help in changing the trucks when the trash is filled. The pervasive nature of IoT, has its own advantages. Alternatively, the associated

Figure 2. DAO enables formation of different kinds of organization on top of blockchain

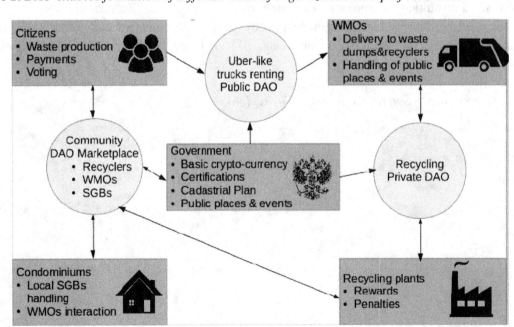

privacy concerns can direct to disinclination of adoption of such system, thus minimizing its usability. By promoting highly available, secure and public network, the blockchain promotes an ideal solution for the security and privacy purposes, thus promoting payment progress too. These two technologies have a greater impact to the economy and the environment of the society.

PRIOR ART

In developed countries, people spend their maximum cost in disposing the waste since the garbage has been collected in the larger trucks and it is carried to the recycle plants or landfill sites. This is not the case in developing countries since they spend maximum cost in the production of waste and spends less in their disposal. European Union estimated a report in the year of 2014, which says that more that 2503 million tonnes of waste has been generated on that particular year by the households and certain economic activities. Nearly 36 percent of this waste has been recycled, 47 percent has been burnt up, 10.2 percent has been land filled and the remaining has been used for the generation of energy. Asian countries are exactly opposite to this since they dump the waste without being used.

From the previous data produced it could be noticed that there was a major correlation among the income level and the quantity of waste generated. In order to get rid of this problem huge amount of money is being invested with high budget every year. But this solution is temporary. Unless people analyse the problem regarding the huge consumption, there will be no solution to this problem permanently. The data is not reliable too, regarding the amount of waste disposed based on which they will be charged. This reliability test was conducted in Sweden. Only a fraction of data from the entire dataset is being utilized due to the deficient in the quality control shown in the figure 3.

To deal with this problem various solution has been determined with the use of IoT devices. But in a resource constrained environment these solutions couldn't be used with the IoT protocols. MQTT or CoAP could be used effectively in a constrained environment that leads to the rise in the energy efficiency.

Cryptocurrencies do not involve with any third-part interruption that leads to the minimum overhead transactions. With the DAO organization, there will be a bypass among the requirements of the third-party or government with the lawful regulation and asset security. Smart contractors are designed initially to behave before executing and the codes could not be changed once it is employed into the block-chain network. Initially, DAO organization also needs investment unlike other organizations.

DISPOSE WASTE EMPLOYING TAG

According to common users these terms seems to be too technical and difficult to remember. For this TAG could be a useful source. When a user needs to dispose waste using TAG, he requires two main things: 1) A Telegram App and 2) an Ethereum account. From the Ethereum Wallet we could download and create an Ethereum account. Minting is an alternative source to an Ethereum account for crypto - currency. The entire facility of the DAO could be found in the TAG that runs with the common currency activated by a central bank. People who use the TAG services must transfer some funds to the central bank to activate his account shown in the figure 4 and 5.

Figure 3. Waste Management

Activity	Low Income	Middle Income	High Income
Source Reduction	No organized programs, but reuse and low per capita waste generation rates are common.	Some discussion of source reduction, but rarely incorporated into an organized program.	Organized education programs emphasize the three 'R's' – reduce, reuse, and recycle. More producer responsibility & focus on product design.
Collection	Sporadic and inefficient. Service is limited to high visibility areas, the wealthy, and businesses willing to pay. High fraction of inerts and compostables impact collection—overall collection below 50%.	Improved service and increased collection from residential areas. Larger vehicle fleet and more mechanization. Collection rate varies between 50 to 80%. Transfer stations are slowly incorporated into the SWM system.	Collection rate greater than 90%. Compactor trucks and highly mechanized vehicles and transfer stations are common. Waste volume a key consideration. Aging collection workers often a consideration in system design.
Recycling	Although most recycling is through the informal sector and waste picking, recycling rates tend to be high both for local markets and for international markets and imports of materials for recycling, including hazardous goods such as e-waste and ship-breaking. Recycling markets are unregulated and include a number of 'middlemen'. Large price fluctuations.	Informal sector still involved; some high technology sorting and processing facilities. Recycling rates are still relatively high. Materials are often imported for recycling. Recycling markets are somewhat more regulated. Material prices fluctuate considerably.	Recyclable material collection services and high technology sorting and processing facilities are common and regulated. Increasing attention towards long-term markets. Overall recycling rates higher than low and middle income. Informal recycling still exists (e.g. aluminum can collection.) Extended product responsibility common.
Composting	Rarely undertaken formally even though the waste stream has a high percentage of organic material. Markets for, and awareness of, compost lacking.	Large composting plants are often unsuccessful due to contamination and operating costs (little waste separation); some small-scale composting projects at the community/neighborhood level are more sustainable. Composting eligible for CDM projects but is not widespread. Increasing use of anaerobic digestion.	Becoming more popular at both backyard and large-scale facilities. Waste stream has a smaller portion of compostables than low- and middle-income countries. More source segregation makes composting easier. Anaerobic digestion increasing in popularity. Odor control critical.
Incineration	Not common, and generally not successful because of high capital, technical, and operation costs, high moisture content in the waste, and high percentage of inerts.	Some incinerators are used, but experiencing financial and operational difficulties. Air pollution control equipment is not advanced and often by-passed. Little or no stack emissions monitoring. Governments include incineration as a possible waste disposal option but costs prohibitive. Facilities often driven by subsidies from OECD countries on behalf of equipment suppliers.	Prevalent in areas with high land costs and low availability of land (e.g., islands). Most incinerators have some form of environmental controls and some type of energy recovery system. Governments regulate and monitor emissions. About three (or more) times the cost of landfilling per tonne.
Landfilling/ Dumping	Low-technology sites usually open dumping of wastes. High polluting to nearby aquifers, water bodies, settlements. Often receive medical waste. Waste regularly burned. Significant health impacts on local residents and workers.	Some controlled and sanitary landfills with some environmental controls. Open dumping is still common. CDM projects for landfill gas are more common.	Sanitary landfills with a combination of liners, leak detection, leachate collection systems, and gas collection and treatment systems. Often problematic to open new landfills due to concerns of neighboring residents. Post closure use of sites increasingly important, e.g. golf courses and parks.

IoT Protocols in MQTT

To monitor the wastage disposal in the region, MQTT have been used due to their increased bandwidth and power economic protocol. The devices are connected to the expensive satellite link. It is publish/subscribe based protocol, where a node / device needs to provide some data, pushes the data to a broker that broadcasts the obtained data to all subscribing devices. TCP/IP protocol stack is been utilized. The key features are as follows: 1) asynchronicity 2) open standard 3) multiplexing multiple subscribers through a single channel. Necessary Quality of Service (QoS) is also provided based on the message delivery service provided. MQTT has three main components namely Subscriber, Broker and Publisher. The connected is entirely based on the TCP.

1. **MQTT Broker:** It serves as a bridge between the message sender and the receivers. It makes enough provisions to end the process by collecting the messages and checking the particular message topic from the rightful receivers. The messages will be stacked if the channel from the receiver side is not in function. For implementing the MQTT, Mosquitto Broker is been used widely.

Figure 4. Waste generation

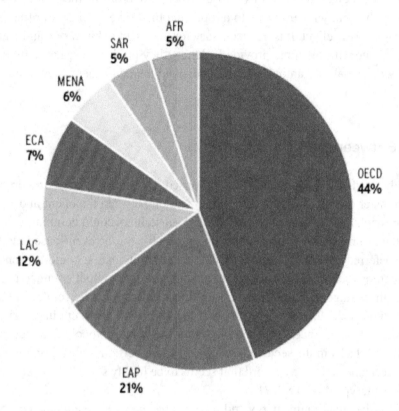

Figure 5. Components of MQTT

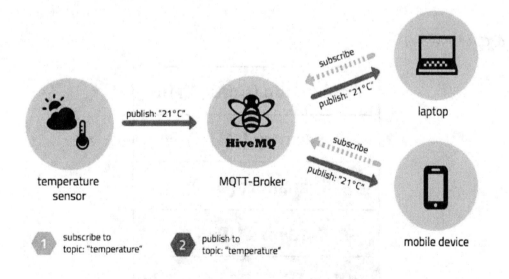

2. **Subscriber:** This device functions by subscribing to the kind of message. The message that is received by each client will subscribe to a topic and the broker will deliver the matching topic of all the messages to the client. It is not necessary for the client to know one and another, rather they only communicate with the topic provided. Hence, they produce a scalable function where there won't be any dependability among the producers and the consumers shown in the figure 6 given below.

Comparison Between MQTT and CoAP

Selection should be made for implementing our proposed system that is more important. CoAP is best suitable for the transfer of state due to their communication between the client and server. MQTT is a many to many protocols where various publishers and subscribers could communicate with each other with the help of the central broker that could be highly suitable for the event-based models. The state of SGB could be transferred by TAG using a protocol, the communication could be done with the server based on the happenings such as opening the lids, closing etc. Throughput obtained in the MQTT could be better when high wastage disposal areas are used. Since TAG can be implemented in community setting to metropolitan scale, high wastage disposal scenario should be kept in priority. TLS/SSL support is not possible in CoAP, since it runs on the top of the UDP protocol. The security agent used by it is DTSL. DTSL still lacks in the security feature and cause certain issues. For connecting the client, MQTT uses the username and the password that seems to be highly secure. To ensure privacy, the TCP connection may be encrypted with SSL/TLS.

CoAP does not utilize maximum energy and seems to be energy efficient when compared to MQTT. For connection of TCP with handshaking signals, no energy will be utilized by CoAP. Considering all these factors, MQTT will be the best choice for TAG.

Figure 6. CoAP Protocol

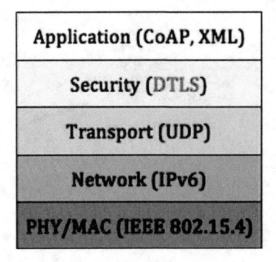

BLOCKCHAIN DRIVEN WASTE MANAGEMENT

Bitcoin and its essential technology i.e. blockchain were introduced to the world. Bitcoin has been the most thriving implementation of blockchain. Blockchain is said to be the distributed database system that interacts with several nodes, which will maintain all the records and transaction in a chronologically secured manner. With this system we do not need the interaction of intermediate systems, which will transfer the data in a secure manner thus lowering the costs. The data once transferred cannot be reversed thus preventing from fraudulent. They are decentralized in nature, where the occurrence of failure is minimum, which is one of the major advantages. If a node has certain problem due to some reason (DDOS attack, node failure etc.), then there are several other nodes that supports the network continuation thereby maintaining the state.

Based on the values of each transaction, Miners will decide the transactions that is to be included and excluded that could increase their benefits. To sort out the computational error, nodes play a major role in the blockchain network to mine a block. In order to mine a block, the problem should be solved by the first network. This will get the highest authority. Proof of Work or PoW algorithm has been used to solve the computational error. Several type of implementation will be used by the PoW algorithm. Bitcoin uses Hash-cash variation of PoW.

ENERGY USAGE WHICH INFLUENCES ENVIRONMENT

The quantity of the energy that we use in our daily lives depends on the types of devices that utilize the amount of energy as well as depending on the climate and the weather condition. The devices that we use for transport vehicles have been increased rapidly. In United States, the use of air conditioner has been increasing from the year of 1980. The household plugs in numerous electronic and other appliances that have been comparatively increased than before. Before the usage of refrigerators and other equipment used for cooking has been in common. At the present scenario, usage of dishwasher, washing machine, dryers, and ovens has been used commonly with the use of televisions and computers (Oh, Chang-Se 2015). Moreover, this technique tends to increase their mode of innovation that motivates the usage of the gaming system and other rechargeable electronic devices that becomes a part of integration for our modern lifestyle. This result in the increase in the energy usage and the top three primary types of energy that powers the transport vehicles in a community are as follows:

Natural Gas

This is commonly found deep under the earth, which is colorless, tasteless and odorless in nature. The main substance of the natural gas is methane that could be denoted as CH_4. Natural gas also consists of hydrocarbon gas liquids and non-hydrocarbon gas. The natural gases could be used as a fuel. Coal-bed methane is said to be a natural gas substance that could be found in the coal. U.S. and other few countries produce the natural gas from the shale and various types of rocks that consists of natural gases within the pores of the rock. This formation of rocks gets fractured by the water forces or either chemical down a well and releases the natural gases.

The amount of natural gas utilized by the U.S. was found to be 27.49 trillion cubic feet (Tcf) by the year 2016. This account 29% of usage is done by the natural gases. The total consumption done by various sectors with the natural gas in the year 2016 is listed as follows:

- Electric power—9.987 Tcf—36%
- Industrial—9.31 Tcf—34%
- Residential—4.35 Tcf—16%
- Commercial—3.11 Tcf—11%
- Transportation—0.74 Tcf—3%

Natural gas has been ultimately used to produce electricity, but some commercial sectors use the resource for heating the building and for other purposes. The utmost resource to produce electricity is mainly done by natural gas. Over 27% of electricity has been produced mainly by burning natural gas in the United Stated in the year 2016.

Nuclear Energy

Commercially nuclear power production has been in use from the year 1950. At present, there are about 99 nuclear reactors with 61 plants over 30 states of U.S. Although some of the reactor core has been shut down, the power produced in the year of 2017 seems to be same as in the year of 2013. The commercially operating nuclear reactor of U.S is located at the east of Mississippi river. The largest reactor core that operates in the United States produces an electricity of about 1400 MW. Each nuclear power plant (above 32) has at least two nuclear reactors. The main source of the nuclear particle is Uranium. They utilize more capacity than other plants that have been shown in the figure 7.

ENVIRONMENTAL IMPACT AND NUCLEAR WASTE

Several impacts could be caused due to the non-renewable sources of energy that we commercially use, which are as follows:

- Over the past, tiny animals and sea plants died on the sea or land is found to be buried under the earth that decays for several years. They were buried deeper and deeper which could be forced by the reaction of temperature and pressure that could change them into oil and gas. At present, we dig the layers of sand, silt, and rock for determining the natural gases.
- The cost of the heating oil price seems to be very large. Crude oil accounts for 55% average price of gallons during the winter and 29% per gallon accounts for the cost of refining the oil and the remaining percent fall under the category for the distribution, marketing and profits. This increases the rate of the heating oil. Households who use heating oil should buy them before winter and store it for the future purposes.
- Like the other natural gases and fossils, the nuclear reactor does not show any impact to produce carbon dioxide. Moreover, the equipment that are used for the mining of the uranium seems to pollute since this equipment could be operated by the means of burning the fossil fuels that seems to associate with the electricity the nuclear plant produces.

Figure 7. Electricity generation at the year of 2016 using nuclear energy

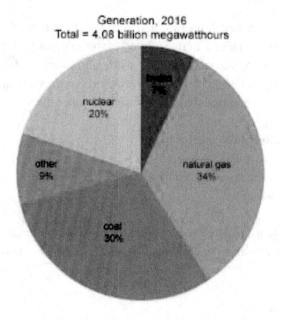

Generation, 2016
Total = 4.08 billion megawatthours

Disposal of Nuclear Waste

A major threat to the environment occurs due to the emission from the radioactive waste from the uranium mill tailings, reactor fuel and the remaining nuclear waste. This could remain radioactive and can cause several threats. Hence the handling of these nuclear wastes is ultimately very important. Handling necessarily deals with the proper transportation, disposal and storage of nuclear materials. In the United States, the U.S. Nuclear Regulatory Commission (NRC) handles the operation of Nuclear power plants.

The waste from the nuclear plant is been classified under 2 categories namely: 1) low-level waste and high-level waste. The radioactivity from these wastes could be in the range of low background level that could be in the uranium mill tailings to the higher background, which could be seen in the reactor fuels. The term radioactive decay means that the nuclear waste decreases with the increase in time. As the year passes, the radioactivity of the substance could reduce. Radioactive half-life means, the time requires for the radioactive substance to reduce half of its original level. In order to reduce the potential of the radiation, the nuclear waste should be properly stored at the temporary period. Uranium mill tailing releases a radioactive element called radon which is in a gaseous state at the time of their decay. They are often placed near their processing facility, from the place they occur. They are enclosed properly with the seal bearings that could be in the form of clay so that this could avoid radiation from entering the atmosphere. These barriers are covered by large rocks or other materials and buried deep into the soil that could prevent erosion. Low radiating waste could be the protective clothes, tools and other small disposal that could contain only a minimum amount of radiation. These are subjected to special regulations that could prevent them from contacting the atmosphere (Oh, Chang-Se et al 2015).

Local Air and Water Quality

The United States promotes a greater impact in their safety and the risk of the contamination of water, land, and air is considered very low due to their diverse, superfluous barriers and their various safety requirements. The contamination due to the nuclear waste and burning of natural gases could raise an abundant pollution into the air and water. But the government fixes certain norms for running the power production plant. They enhance their local quality of air and water by

- Maintaining the operation of the reactor plant
- Effectively utilizing the available resources
- Maintaining and testing the regular activity
- Proper disposal of the waste

Moreover, the reactor plant utilizes the containment vessels for the disposal of waste so that the vessel could promote enough strength to withstand the extreme weather conditions and earthquakes or other natural calamities.

RENEWABLE ENERGY RESOURCES AND THEIR IMPACTS

According to U.S. Energy Information Agency, 16.9% of energy resources occur from the hydro-electric power, solar, biomass, wind and geothermal resources. The most important thing to be noted is that these resources are said to be renewable resources. Among these, the solar and the wind energy is the popularly used one. The emission of carbon dioxide is greatly reduced using these resources. The benefits and their impacts are many that are as follows:

- Reduction in global warming
- Enhancement of public health
- Lowers the energy price
- Inexhaustible energy
- Promotes better employment and other economic benefits.

Figure 8 clearly shows the petrol produced from the renewable resources.

It could be difficult for the whole community to adapt to the new methods. This could lay on the expenditure, location and various other factors.

Cost Expenses of the Alternative Resources

It is known that the renewable energy is said to be costly when compared to the fossils and nuclear power. Moreover, there are some additional conventional improvements that must be done for the renewable energy technologies. Levelized energy costs (LEC) is the more common term used by the economist that says regarding the ratio of the total cost of the construction of the equipment to the expected annual electricity generated. The LEC cost of the U.S. has been compared with the alternative fuels at the year 2017 and it has been mentioned in the figure 9.

Figure 8. Power generated by the various resources

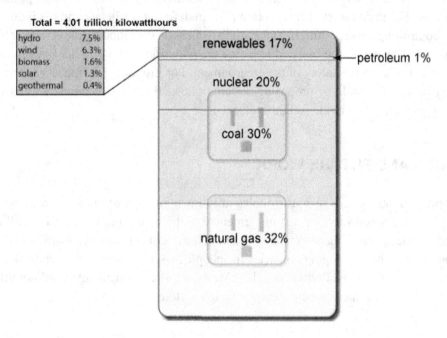

Figure 9. U.S. cost comparison of various sources of energy

Power Plant Type	Cost $/kW-hr
Coal	$0.11-0.12
Natural Gas	$0.053-0.11
Nuclear	$0.096
Wind	$0.044-0.20
Solar PV	$0.058
Solar Thermal	$0.184
Geothermal	$0.05
Biomass	$0.098
Hydro	$0.064

The purpose of vehicle selection is important to lessen noise pollution and other pollution emitted from the vehicles. The main target of this section aims in defining the heavy and the light vehicles best optimized for controlling noise pollution. This mainly focuses on the reducing the efforts of the managers by increasing the efficiency of the fuel and reducing the pollution of the vehicle. By achieving this, the company should also target the safety of the environment. For instance, the impacts of the government in any country plays a vital role by proposing certain policies that could reduce the carbon deposition and efficient steps were taken in the freight sector.

CONCLUSION AND FUTURE WORK

Many developing countries have serious troubles in following this waste management system (Chesa, M.J. 2016). Many IoT based services was implemented in the waste management but still they rely on the third-party services due to the financial problem ad payment services (Cousins, J.J. 2016). Due to the high population in the developing countries the people lack in having their own bank account with the online payment services (El Periódico.2016). Moreover, the government could not afford enough funds to raise an advanced management Equipment and system.

REFERENCES

Ajuntament de Barcelona. (2016). *Statistical yearbook of Barcelona 2016.* Retrieved from www.bcn. cat/estadistica/angles/dades/anuari/index.htm

Anguelovski, I. (2016). From toxic sites to parks as (green) LULUs? New challenges of inequity, privilege, gentrification, and exclusion for urban environmental justice. *CPL Bibliography, 31*(1), 23-36.

Chesa, M. J. (2016). *Stormwaer management in Barcelona. Evolving approaches.* Paper presented at the Baltic Flows Conference, Barcelona, Spain.

Cousins, J. J. (2016). Volume control: Stormwater and the politics of urban metabolism. *Geoforum.* doi:10.1016/j.geoforum.2016.09.02021016

Furlong, C., Gan, K., & De Silva, S. (2016). Governance of integrated urban water management in Melbourne, Australia. *Utilities Policy, 43*, 48–58. doi:10.1016/j.jup.2016.04.008

Klimova, A., Rondeau, E., Andersson, K., Porras, J., Rybin, A., & Zaslavsky, A. (2016). An international master's program in green ict as a contribution to sustainable development. *Journal of Cleaner Production, 135*, 223–239. doi:10.1016/j.jclepro.2016.06.032

Krauss, Do, & Huck. (2017). Deep neural networks, gradientboosted trees, random forests: Statistical arbitrage on the S&P 500. *European Journal of Operational Research.*

Medvedev, A., Fedchenkov, P., Zaslavsky, A., Anagnostopoulos, T., & Khoruzhnikov, S. (2015). Waste management as an IoT-enabled service in smart cities. In *Conference on Smart Spaces.* Springer International Publishing.

Monika, K. A., Rao, N., Prapulla, S. B., & Shobha, G. (2016). *Smart Dustbin-An Efficient Garbage Monitoring System. International Journal of Engineering Science and Computing, 6,* 7113–7116.

Moss, T. (2016). Conserving water and preserving infrastructures between dictatorship and democracy in Berlin. *Water Alternatives, 9*(2), 250–271.

Navghane, S. S., Killedar, M. S., & Rohokale, D. V. (2016). *IoT Based Smart Garbage and Waste Collection Bin. International Journal of Advanced Research in Electronics and Communication Engineering, 5,* 1576–1578.

El Periódico. (2016, November 17). *Barcelona beberá agua reciclada en la depuradora de El Prat.* Author.

Chapter 10
Load Balancing in Heterogeneous Cluster Cloud Computing

Nirmalan R.
Sri Vidya College of Engineering and Technology, India

Gokulakrishnan K.
Anna University Tirunelveli, India

Jesu Vedha Nayahi J.
Anna University Tirunelveli, India

ABSTRACT

Cloud computing is a modern exemplar to provide services through the internet. The development of cloud computing has eliminated the need of manpower, which is mainly used for the management of resources. During the cloud computing process, the term cloud balancing is a vital one. It deals with distribution of workloads and computing resources. The load balancing allows the company to balance the load according to the demands by the allocation of the resources to multiple servers or networks. The quality of service (QoS) metrics, including cost, response time, performance, throughput, and resource utilization are improved by means of load balancing. In this chapter, the authors study the literature on the load-balancing algorithms in heterogeneous cluster cloud environment with some of its classification. Additionally, they provide a review in each of these categories. Also, they provide discernment into the identification of open issues and guidance for future research work.

INTRODUCTION

Cloud computing generally refers to providing delivery of hosted services through internet. It can be used like electricity in our day to day life rather than building and maintaining a computer infrastructures. It has more benefits which make it attractive for the end users. Due to the self-provisioning of the cloud computing, the customers can utilize it for several applications. The development of cloud computing

DOI: 10.4018/978-1-5225-9023-1.ch010

has eliminated the need of manpower which is mainly used for the management of resources. It provides better elasticity so that the companies can increase the load whenever they want and decrease it whenever the demand decreases. This eliminates the huge investment for the company for development of infrastructure. The end users can pay according to their workloads and resources used by them which would be a greater benefit for the end-users.

The workload resilience in the cloud computing often implements their redundant resources which ensures that the resilient storage keeps the end user workloads running even in the multiple countries. It also provides migration flexibility which enables the organization to move their workloads to several platforms to save cost or to adopt new services.

In the present scenario, the companies are growing regarding their end-user requirements which require the need for more databases to be stored. As the flow of data in the company increases the need for multiple servers increases since a single server cannot handle enormous data at a single time. Clustering in the cloud data helps in lining any number of servers, and it can act as a single server which could handle several servers. It can provide continuous operation even if any one of the servers fails. It needs some special computers and different versions of operating systems for synchronization of data. It also demands the needs of advanced networking adaptors which could be applied to the movement of data at higher speed. The parameters considered during the clustering processes are energy efficiency and location. The energy consumed by both the parameters are very high. The optimized energy consumption is the foremost principle considered by different clustering algorithms. The location awareness can be carried out either by using global positioning systems or by estimating the strength of the returned signal. Several algorithms are developed during the clustering process which eliminates the need for precious locations or even the location of the subsequent servers.

In the case of homogeneous cloud computing the whole software stack from the remote cloud provider goes through various several management layers which finally reaches the end-user through one vendor. While considering the heterogeneous cloud, it combines the components provided by different vendors either at different levels or in the same levels.

The clustering of nodes can be done using algorithms like Fuzzy K-Means, Streaming K-Means, Spectral clustering, Dirichlet clustering. Fuzzy K- means algorithms use only one data point to form a single cluster. If a single point belongs to multiple clusters, it creates an overlapping cluster. Fuzzy K-Means algorithms are unsuitable if the volume of data is too high which has to be stored in the main memory as it's batch processing mechanism repeats over all the data points. It is also very sensitive to the noises present in the data. In the case of Streaming, K-Means algorithms solve by operating in two steps. On the first step, a set of weighted data points are created for further processing. In the second step, the outliers are removed.

The spectral clustering algorithm is used for solving hard and non-convex clustering problems. The cluster points use eigenvectors of the matrix to derive their data. Dirichlet clustering algorithms use the Fuzzy K-Means and K-Means algorithms model clusters as spheres. Initially, K-means assumes a commonly fixed variance and it does not model the distribution of the data points. For the efficient usage of the Spectral clustering algorithm, a normal data distribution can be done by the usage of K-Means and Fuzzy K-Means algorithms. If the distribution of data is different, the efficiency of the K-means algorithm will be very less and the final output will not be good. Dirichlet clustering can be effective in the case of modeling different data effectively. It fits into a dataset according to the model, and it tunes its parameters which adjusts it to a model parameter which correctly fits the data. It can be applied to the problems dealing with the hierarchical-clustering problem.

During the cloud computing process, the term cloud balancing is a vital one. It deals with workload distribution and resources needed for computing. The LB allows the organization to adjust the load according the demands of the allocation of the resources to multiple servers or networks. The load sharing in the cloud involves the traffic distribution and their demands that reside over the internet. Cloud load balancing helps the enterprises to perform at a lower cost. The cloud load balancing technology provides a health check during the cloud applications. To eliminate the noisy neighbors and poor performance the cloud load balancing uses virtual local area networks which group's nodes in different locations and it communicate as if they are in the same location. Several companies like Amazon, Google, etc., use the cloud for storing their data. Thus the load sharing must be done in an optimum way of enabling a better service by the company.

Many research works have been carried out in cloud environments, very specifically in the load balancing. Based on those studies, we can understand the major roles of the algorithms for load-balancing. Only few researches and reviews are fully completed based on these algorithms. Initially, few recent reviews on load-balancing algorithms with some of its mechanisms were mentioned.

To help the future researchers to design novel algorithms in load balancing and some of its mechanisms, we analyze the mechanisms and surveyed the literature in a better manner. The objective of the work are described as follows:

- Reviewing the mechanisms of load balancing methodologies which already exists
- Enabling advanced taxonomy for load balancing mechanisms
- Explicating merits and demerits in each class of the load-balancing algorithms
- Outlining the key areas for the improvement of the load-balancing algorithms

Milani and Navimipour (2016) have analyzed the existing load balancing techniques. According to some different parameters analyzed, they presented the existing load balancing algorithms. The authors compared many familiar load-balancing algorithms and also well addressed many challenges of these algorithms and many issues are mentioned. But still, there exist some issues in the techniques for task scheduling in the HadoopMapReduce.

Rahmani and Mesbahi (2016) have reviewed the technique of load balancing. They discussed the major requirements required for enabling best fitting load balancing algorithms in heterogeneous cloud architecture. Also by means of some suitable metrics, they presented some load balancing techniques and discussed their merits and demerits. The recently trending load balancing algorithms were found, which focus only on saving the energy. But still, the lack of Simulators was an issue. However, they did not explain anything related to the open issues and future enhancements.

Kanakala et al.(2015) researched the execution of LB methodology in cloud computing. They reviewed various algorithms on load balancing mechanisms and compared with their speed, complexity, throughput etc. Finally, they reviewed all load balancing algorithms results not performs well in all environments. However, they did not explain anything related to the open issues and future enhancements.

Radivilova and Ivanisenko (2015) examines the LB methodologies importance on cloud systems. Thus, they provided different algorithms for load balancing after analyzing based on the metrics such as response time, throughput, migration time etc. They described the merits, features and also demerits of load-balancing algorithms. In spite of that, an exploration of open issues, challenges, and future trends are not discussed.

The main aim of this chapter is to analyze the present techniques, report their metrics, and elucidate their advantages and disadvantages. The main aims are discussed below:

- Analysing the load balancing mechanisms which already exists.
- Presenting a modern mechanism of load-balancing
- Resolving the merits and demerits in each class of load-balancing algorithms
- An effective way for the future researchers to improvise the load balancing mechanisms

In this paper, Section 2 provides a description of the Heterogeneous Cloud Environment. Section 3 describes various load balancing models along with its factors in literature. The literature also holds the various challenges of load balancing in cloud. The section 4, a review of existing load balancing techniques and providing new classifications. Section 5 covers the existing load balancing mechanism surveys. Section 6 outlined the open issues. Finally, section 7 having the conclusion of our survey and providing future works.

HETEROGENEOUS CLOUD ENVIRONMENT

Data Centres and computational Centres are often bounded by their density of power, efficiency and computing density. To improve the power efficiency of general-purpose microprocessor and server manufacturers are working. By using these metrics Heterogeneous processing resources can provide an order of magnitude or more improvement. There are various examples of problems well suited to specific architectures. Examples of such architectures include graphical processing units (GPUs, also known as GPGPUs, digital signal processors, symmetrical multiprocessors (SMPs), network packet processors, and conventional CPUs.

At present, the cloud infrastructure, with a few externally visible exceptions generally emphasis on hardware, with no control over any target architectures aside from choosing a fixed number of memory sizes. If cloud users are able to take advantage of the performance and efficiency advantages of heterogeneous computing, the cloud infrastructure software should recognize and handle this heterogeneity. In the year before, for large-scale computation, batch scheduling and grid computing have been used commonly. Cloud computing presents a distinct resource allocation paradigm that either grids or batch schedulers. In particular, Amazon EC2 is equipped to handle much smaller compute resource allocations, rather than a few, large requests as is normally the case with grid computing. The introduction of heterogeneity allows clouds to be competitive with traditional distributed computing systems, which often consist of various types of architectures as well. When combined with economies of scale, dynamic provisioning and comparatively lower capital expenditures, the benefits of heterogeneous clouds are infinite. Cloud computing allows individual users to have administrative access to a dedicated virtual machine instance. Compared to a scheduling approach, superior ability in separating users, where it is common to share a single operating system for multiple jobs. The merits of this are apparent from the perspectives of security as well as flexibility for users, offering a variety of operating systems.

THE LOAD BALANCING MECHANISM IN LITERATURE

As shown in the figure 1 (Gupta et al., 2014) load balancing model runs the load balancing algorithm, in which the load balancer receives the requests of users and to allocate the various requests between the Virtual Machines (VMs). VM will be selected and assigned to the next request after the load balancer decides. The task manager will be taken over the controller in the respective data center. VM manager takes control of all the Virtual Machines (VM). Virtualization, is the leading technology in cloud computing has aimed to share hardware which is more expensive among VMs. The software implementation in which the operating systems and applications were operates are entirely handled by the VM.

VMs process the users' requests which were submitted randomly. The task assignment is a remarkable issue in cloud computing since, for the process of processing, VMs handles the requests. If some VMs are overloaded, then automatically there exists a decrease in QoS. As a result of this issue, there exist users then need to leave the system and there is no possibility of return. Virtual Machine Monitor is available for managing and creating the Virtual Machines. It is available with the provision to perform the following four operations which are very essential for load balancing: storage capacity, multiplexing, facility & live migration Hwang et al (2013).

Figure 1. Load balancing model

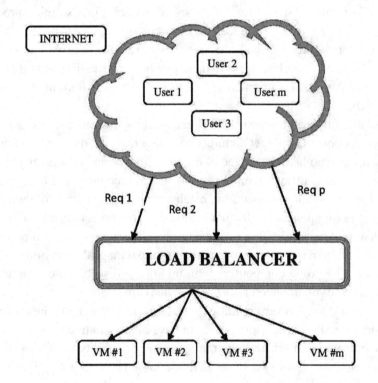

Load Balancing Metrics

In this chapter, load balancing cloud computing metrics were reviewed. As explained above there are various load balancing algorithms have been proposed by the researchers. In literature load balancing proposed metrics which are applied in load balancing algorithms are summarized as follows:

1. **Throughput:** To estimate the number of processes completed in per unit of time.
2. **Scalability:** Performing uniform load balancing, even when there is an increase in the number of nodes in the system.
3. **Response Time:** Time is taken to serve a submitted task.
4. **Fault Tolerance:** Capability of load balancing on the event of nodes or links failures.
5. **Performance:** System efficiency on load-balancing algorithm after implementation.
6. **Makespan:** Calculating maximum time completion of Resource Allocation.
7. **Migration Time:** Time required transferring a task to an under-loaded one from an overloaded node.
8. **Energy Consumption:** Energy consumed by all nodes.
9. **A Degree of Imbalance:** Imbalance among Virtual Machines.
10. **Carbon Emission:** Amount of carbon produced by all resources.

Taxonomy of LB Methodology

Prevailing classification of LB methodology were focused. In some analysis (Bhatia et al., 2012; Rastogi, (2015) Mishra et al (2015) the classification of load balancing are done based on two aspects: system state and initiating person of the process. This algorithms is generally based on system state such as static and dynamic. The static algorithms are Min-Min, Max-Min Algorithms, Round robin, Opportunistic Load Balancing (OLB). Dynamic algorithms are Ant Colony Optimization, Honey Bee Foraging, and Throttled. All the dynamic algorithms based on the below four steps;

1. **Load Monitoring**: Monitoring the load and the resources.
2. **Synchronization:** Exchange of state and load information.
3. **Criteria for Rebalancing:** Meant for Distribution of new works and to make load making decisions.
4. **Task Migration:** Occurrence of actual movement of data.

There are two approaches in Dynamic algorithms such as:

1. Distributed Approach
2. Non-Distributed Approach

Distributed approach execute every node dynamically with the load balancing algorithm and loads were balanced among them (Rastogi et al., 2015). The interaction takes place in either cooperative or non-cooperative forms. As in cooperative form, to achieve a common objective, the nodes work together. It decreases the responding time of all tasks. According to the non-cooperative term, every individual node works freely for achieving local goal. Nearly to reduce local task's responding time.

There are two classes in the Non-distributed algorithms such as:

1. Centralized Form
2. Semi-distributed Form

According to the centralized forms, the central node takes the execution of load-balancing algorithms by interacts with other nodes. As in semi-distributed approach, the nodes are separated as various clusters. All clusters ate in centralized form. In this, the central node performs load balancing of the systems.

According to Neeraj et al., 2014 there are two forms of static algorithms known as optimal, and sub-optimal. In the optimal algorithm, all details about the resources and tasks were determined by the controller in the data center. Optimal allocation within the reasonable time is done by the load balancer. At any cause the decision is not estimated, the sub-optimal allocation is estimated for an approximate mechanism. The LB approaches left out only if a perfect solution is attained. Then the by means of objective function these solutions were calculated. In an experimental method, The LB approaches execute sensible assumptions about the tasks as well as resources. On this way these kind of methodologies take more adaptive decisions which cannot restrict by the assumptions. Fig. 2 explains the classification schema in a better way;

As described, the system's current state uses dynamic load-balancing algorithms. In order to this, it applies some policies Daraghmi (2015); Kumar and Rana, (2015); Kanakala (2014); Yahaya (2011); Mukhopadhyay (2010); Alakeel (2010) Babul (2013). These policies are shown below:

*   **Transfer Policy:** It describes the circumstance on which the node is transferred from one another.
*   **Selection Policy:** It performs transferring task.
*   **Information Policy:** Collection of information's the system nodes and the other decision-making policies.
*   **Location Policy**: This policy transfers the task to the underloaded nodes.

CLOUD-BASED LOAD BALANCINGCHALLENGES

We have discussed the concept of LB and this section determines the various challenges of typical load balancing approaches in future. Many works describes the cloud-based load balancing challenges Sidhu and Kinger, (2013); Palta and Jee (2014); Nuaimiet al., (2012); Khiyaita (2012) Kanakala and Reddy, (2015) Ray and Sarkar, (2012), including:

*   Migration of Virtual Machine with respect to time and security
*   Distribution of nodes in a cloud spatially
*   Computational complexity if methodology
*   Cloud computing the evolution of small data centers

A SURVEY ON EXISTING LOAD BALANCING MECHANISMS

We surveyed prevailed load balancing mechanisms based on the cloudarchitecture. A deep analysis of various journals and conference results in an advanced classification of them. Below describes a classification of existing mechanisms.

Figure 2. Classification of Load Balancing Algorithms

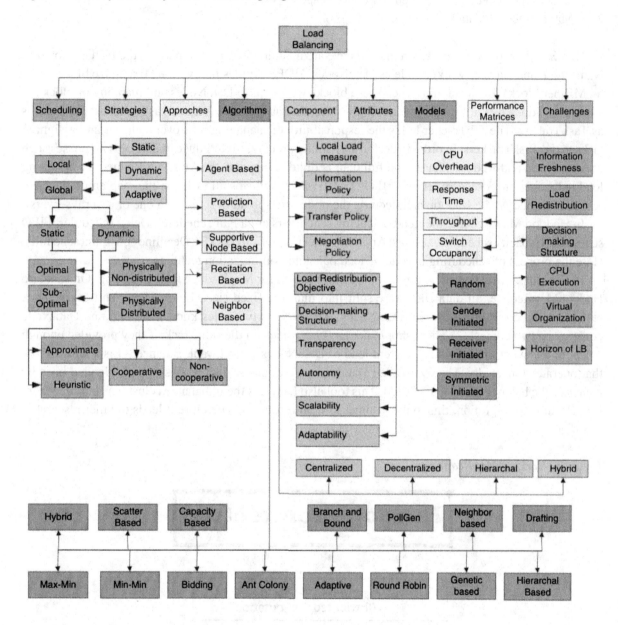

An Introduction to HadoopMapReduce

To form big data, a huge volume of data were collected from various sources like Facebook, Telegram, Twitter, and WEB on daily basis.

The most popular big data open source framework for processing on clusters is Hadoop (Dsouza et al., 2015; Hefny et al., 2014; Chethana et al., 2016). The Hadoop architecture is shown in Fig.3. Generally Hadoophas two core mechanisms such as

1. Hadoop Distributed File System for data storage
2. MapReduce for data processing.

HDFS and MapReduce based on master/slave architecture. The master node in the HDFS known as NameNode and slave or worker node as DataNodes. HDFS divides into various fixed-size blocks (i.e., 64 MB per block) for storing purpose. These blocks were sent to DataNodes and mapping of blocks to workers are done by the NameNode. In MapReduce, the master node is known as JobTracker and slaves as TaskTrakers. The JobTracker holds the responsibility of managing jobs over a cluster and assigning tasks to the TaskTrackers. In order to perform a parallel process, MapReduce undergoes two phases such as Map Phase and Reduce Phase. The full data is divided between the Map and Reduce for operating load balancing purposes (Sui et al., 2011). TaskTracker performs all tasks on the map and reduces in respective slots. At the Hadoop architecture, the nodes are spread over racks in one or several servers.

In Hadoop Map Reduce, the Load balancing schedulers are a Fair scheduler, Delay scheduler, FIFO scheduler, Capacity scheduler, Longest Approximate Time to End (LATE), Deadline constraint scheduler. Here the process of scheduling is done by load balancing optimization technique.

In this chapter, we consider some proposed algorithms for MapReduce load balancing. On standard HadoopMapReduce, all data files were split into multiple fixed-sized blocks. Each and every block resembles three on three different DataNodes. All contains two rules known as (1) Same DataNode contains no two copies, (2) There should not any two copies on the same rack, if they provided enough racks. In the event of duplication current load of DataNodes is irrelevant. Balancer, it is a built-in tool that operates repeatedly. The overloaded DataNodesare transfers data blocks to under-loaded ones by means of the balancer (Lin et al., 2015). This tool also balances the imbalanced cluster as possible from scratch. In load migration, this tool consumes system resources. Therefore it leads to other researches

Figure 3. Hadoop MapReduce

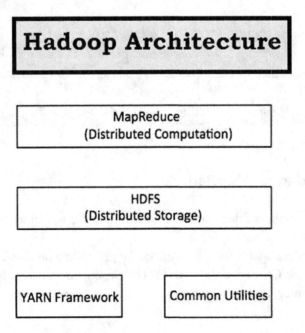

on gaining a effective load balancing mechanism in the Hadoop environment. We analyzed some works and reviewed here.

- Valvåg (2011,2009) Designed a unified engine known as Cogset especially for static load balancing. In order to overcome the performance issues of MapReduce in heterogeneous clusters, Ahmad(2012) proposed Tarazu. It's proven that heterogeneous clusters applying traditionalHadoopMapReducehave to get improved on using Tarazu
- Kolb et al. (2011) designed BlockSplit, a LB methodology which is ablock-based designedfor reducing the search space of Entity Resolution (ER).
- Hsueh et al. (2014) proposed a scalable and efficient LB methodology which is a block-based designedfor Entity Resolution using multiple keys in MapReduce.
- A dynamic LB methodology for Hadoop Map Reduce was framed by Hou et al. (2014). Here the workload are balances at the rack as previous algorithms were balanced between DataNodes.
- For improving the MapReduce performanceVernica et al. (2012) proposed adaptive techniques. They implemented Distributed Meta Data Store (DMDS) for sharing situation information between mappers.
- Chen and Yang (2015) framed the adaptive task allocation scheduler to optimize the MapReduce performance in heterogeneous clouds. In this work they implemented an effective scheduling scheme known as Adaptive Task Allocation Scheduler (ATAS).
- Bok et al. (2016) concentrate on minimizing the missing of jobs while processing large multimedia data like image and video in MapReduce frameworks.
- Ghoneem and Kulkarni (2016)in order to increase the performance efficiency of the MapReduce schedulerthey designed an effective adaptive scheduling technique. The result obtained is appreciable for heterogeneous clusters and workloads

Some approaches to load balancing in MapReduce are selected on various matrices, let's analyze them.

Natural Phenomena-Based Load Balancing Category

This section covers the survey of our various load balancing strategies and inspired by natural phenomena or biological behaviors like Ant-Colony, Honey-Bee, and Genetic algorithms

- Yakhchi et al. (2015) proposed Cuckoo Optimization Algorithm (COA). It is an energy saving LB method in cloud computing simulates the life of cuckoos birds family.
- Dasgupta et al. (2013) introduce a genetic algorithm (GA) based novel load-balancing strategy for balancing the load in the cloud infrastructure. Its main aim is reducing the execution time of a given task set.
- Nishant et al. (2012) proposed Ant Colony Optimization (ACO) in the LB algorithm which demonstrates ant colonies that perform together based on a foraging behavior.
- Babu et al. (2013) designed HBB-LB known as honeybee-based load balancing technique based on honeybee foraging behavior. It priorities the tasks to reduce the tasks waiting time in the queue

Figure 4. Natural Phenomena-Based Load Balancing Category

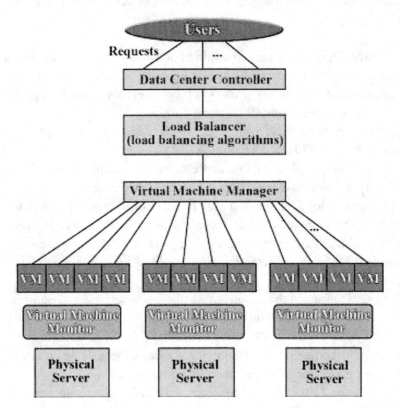

Agent-Based LB Techniques

In this section, we analysis the proposed agent-based techniques for load balancing cloud nodes. In which agent is like a software that operates automatically and frequently based on the needs in succeeding the design objectives.

- A multi-agent system interacts with each other by compromising other agents. To obtain success agent need to collaborate, organize and negotiate with each other Singha (2015) Sim (2011).
- A2LB a novel autonomous agent-based load-balancing algorithm for cloud environments is proposed by Singh et al. (2015). In which the three agents such as load agent, channel agent, and migration agent were applied to balance the load on VMs.
- Gutierrez-Garcia and Ramirez-Nafarrate (2015) developed a collaborative agent-based problem-solving technique. It is efficient in balancing workloads across commodity as well as heterogeneous servers by making use of VM live migration.
- Faghih and Keshvadi (2016) designed a multi-agent load balancing system applicable for IaaS cloud environment. It reduces the waiting time and assured in the Service Level Agreement (SLA). In this algorithm both sender-initiated and receiver-initiated approach to balance the IaaS load.
- Tasquier (2015) frames a perfect agent-based load balancer for multi-cloud environments. The algorithm is based on the combination multi cloud, application-aware and load-balancer based mechanism on a mobile agent paradigm.

Figure 5. Agent-Based Load Balancing Techniques

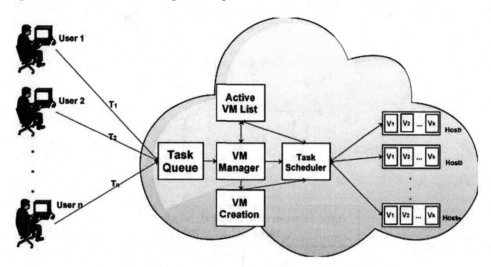

GENERAL LOAD BALANCING TECHNIQUES

This part holds the overviewed literature on general load balancing techniques. This category has various algorithms like Min- Min, Max-Min, First-In-First-Out (FIFO), Throttled and Equally Spread Current Execution Load (ESCEL).

Muthuswamy and Komarasamy (2016) introduced dynamic load balancing for the cloud environment. It is the combination of effective Bin Packing and VM Reconfiguration (DLBPR). In which DLBPR maps jobs into VMs according to the job's processing speed.

Reddy and Domanal (2015) proposed the combination of Throttled algorithms and Divide-and-Conquer referred to as DCBT. That is known to be a hybrid scheduling algorithm for load balancing in a distributed environment.

A novel LB algorithm for service time estimation is built by Chien et al. (2016).

This algorithm took the size of assigned jobs and VMs actual instant processing power. The end time estimation in VMs based on two aspects one is the selected VM as possible. The second is estimating all incoming jobs and queue the jobs to do on VM as per the request. The VM distribute the jobs correspondingly where earliest one will be chosen. The obtained simulation results prove the proposed algorithm is prominent in processing time and time to respond.

Kulkarni and BA (2015) determine a novel VM load-balancing algorithm for uniform assignment of requests to VMs delivering faster response times to users.

Application Based LB Techniques

- Wei et al. (2013) explain HLMCM known as Hybrid Local Mobile Cloud Model. This model consists of mobile devices and cloudlet. Cloudlet is a central broker and also along with neighbor mobile device plays the role of service provider. Here application scheduling is mainly used to maximize the lifetime of HLMCM as well as the profit.

Figure 6. General load balancing techniques

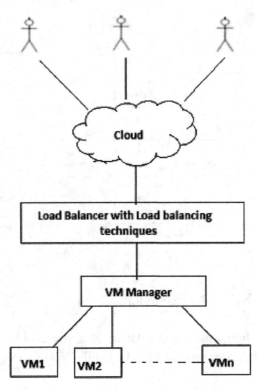

- Wei et al. (2015) implemented MAX-MIN ant system which is an application scheduling in mobile cloud computing. Initially, he first deployed local mobile cloud model with a structure of detail application scheduling. Then worked out MAX-MIN Ant System (MMAS) based scheduling algorithm for the mobile cloud model. The results prove a greater performance of the mobile cloud.
- Sarood et al. (2012) worked out with some relevant techniques and minimize the performance gap between supercomputers and application on the cloud. Here the tightly coupled parallel applications are operated on the virtualized environments to achieve load balances.
- Deye et al. (2013) developed a mechanism towards achieving better QoS of multi-instance applications in the cloud. It restricts the incoming user request at a given period. The load balancer effectively processes the request with a queue. The simulation result shows effective performance on the overall system.

Network-Aware Task Scheduling and Load Balancing

This section covers analysis of network-aware task scheduling and load balancing techniques.

Figure 7. Application oriented load balancing techniques

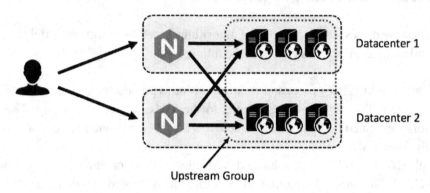

- For MapReduce schedulingShen et al. (2016) framed a network-aware task placement. It reduces the data transmission cost, delays and execution time. In addition, it also was shown effective in resource utilization.
- Scharf et al. (2015) developed an additional methodology of OpenStack scheduler. It makes the instances of network-aware placement by considering the bandwidth constraints to and from nodes. It mainly introduced for avoiding congestion of network resources.
- Shen et al. (2016) for specifying job deadline presented enhanced cloud job scheduler. It designed for cloud with elastic bandwidth reservation which reserves jobs bandwidth by leveraging the elastic feature for increasing the total job rewards. It enables overall successful execution completion by deadlines.
- For cloud computing applications Kliazovich et al. (2016) designed CA-DAG, It takes a variety of communication resources for its approach. In this method for each resource allocation separate decision making is done. This enables efficient processing of handling network resources and execution along with successful information transmissions.

Figure 8. Network-Aware task scheduling and load balancing

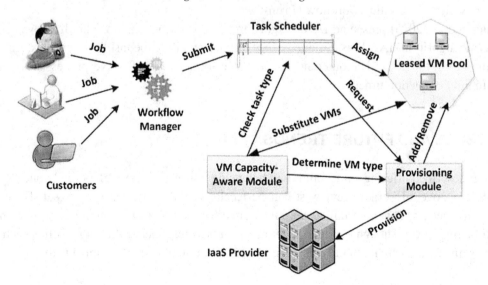

Workflow Specific Scheduling Algorithms

Here in this section we discussed the scheduling algorithms based on workflow articles in the aspect of tasks bag, dependent task, priority based task scheduling.

- Banerjee and Ghosh (2016) proposed their algorithm with additional features and applied it to cloud computing. The request was allocated to the VMs as per the priority. The request with higher priority executed first and other request was balanced by switching queue those are moved temporarily from VM.
- Jaikar et al. (2014) modeled an enhanced VM allocation algorithm based load balancer for a federated cloud. This method is examined in a scientific federated cloud and gained result proves minimal energy consumptions and increased resources utilization.
- Karatzaa and Moschakisa (2015) proposed thermodynamic simulated annealing. A multi-criteria scheduling algorithm of a dynamic multi-cloud system. It is mainly for processing heterogeneous performance serving Bag-of-Tasks (BoT) applications. By this implementation the simulation result shows, there is a good cost-performance trade-off and effective impact on overall performances.
- Cai et al. (2017) proposed a scheduling algorithm with a dynamic cloud resource provisionsfor cloud architecture. DDS A delay-based dynamic scheduling algorithm is mainly developed with goal of minimizing the resource renting cost. It functioning on bag-based deadline division and bag-based delay scheduling strategies to minimize the total renting cost. Compared to the existing algorithms the result obtained is better in reducing the renting cost meeting workflow deadlines.
- Cinque et al. (2016) designed GAMESH, entirely a distributed efficient management for data monitoring and troubleshooting job executions whenever a failure occursIt is a Grid Architecture for scalable Monitoring and Enhanced dependable job ScHeduling (GAMESH). Based on the throughput in both intra/inter-domain environments there is fair result is achieved from the processed jobs.
- Kianpisheh et al. (2016) handled the various issues in workflow scheduling by means of POV (probability of violation) of constraints. It is based on budget and deadline mainly for the robustness as well as scheduling workflow at run-time.
- Zhang and Li (2015) presented IAHA algorithm for task prioritization. This Improved Adaptive heuristic algorithm (IAHA) is designed especially for handling the task in a complex graph based on the graph topology. The outcome of the application proves effective process has done with minimum completion time.

OPEN ISSUES AND FUTURE TRENDS

This section described offering some valid load balancing concerns are not elaborately and deeply addressed. With our overall literature review, still no perfect load balancing algorithm that satisfies complete load balancing metrics. That is certain techniques were effective in time responding, resource optimization and time migration. Though the other techniques ignore these metrics and solve other metrics. We have found some metrics are mutually exclusive like the increase of response time due to relying on VM

Figure 9. Workflow Specific Scheduling Algorithms

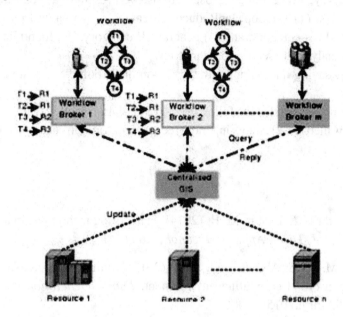

migration. In some articles, the service cost was not considered. It is possible to propose an enhanced technique for improving maximum metrics and it's very desirable.

In our study, we have highlighted that energy consumption and carbon emission are the major drawbacks. Since only a few articles were discussed about these two drawbacks in general. In that energy consumption were consider as economic efficiency factor and carbon emission as health-related. These two issues were critically important for load balancing mechanisms in a cloud environment to achieve effective performance.

Recently, huge data volume is collected from the e-commerce, e-shopping, e-pay, banking records, social media's, medical database, etc. on daily basis. This massive collection forms big data and required proper distributions for fast servicing. This concept is studied in very few articles in the recent years. In the future research it is most important about HadoopMapReduce optimization, it's also a necessary and promising concept for processing big data

Nowadays along with popular cloud providers like Amazon, Microsoft Google and other providers were also emerging too. It will happen on some aspect the sharing of a workload from one cloud provider to another mainly for load balancing process. In future using more than one cloud provider for load balancing will leads to critical requirement. We found that few articles addressed this issues in recent years. The data lock-in and cross-cloud servicing problems are also the most paid attention for future research.

CONCLUSION AND FUTURE WORKS

The workload balancing techniques among the cloud nodes were considered as the major obstacle in the cloud environment. In this paper, we analyzed the literature works on load balancing as the major key. It is clear that there were several metrics involves in load balancing techniques. These should be handled effectively in future mechanisms defined for load balancing

By means of the surveyed research and observations, we presented a modern classification methodology in LB techniques: (1) HadoopMapReduce LB category, (2) natural phenomenon- based LB category, (3) agent-based LB category, and (4) general LB category. We found that all categories with some techniques were analyzed based on some metrics.

Recently, the energy saving and reducing the emission of carbon dioxide are the two most focused critical metrics.

For future work, we recommended the followings: 1) Simulation toolkit evaluation of each technique and comparing with new metrics. 2) Analysing more recent techniques in each of our proposed categories.

REFERENCES

Abdolhamid, M., Shafi'i, M., & Bashir, M. B. (2014). Scheduling techniques in an on-demand grid as a service cloud: A review. *J. Theor. Appl.Inf. Technol.*, *63*(1), 10–19.

Abdullahi, M., Ngadi, M. A., & Abdulhamid, S. M. (2015). Symbiotic organism search optimization based task scheduling in cloud computing environment. *Future Generation Computer Systems*, *56*, 640–650. doi:10.1016/j.future.2015.08.006

Aditya, A., Chatterjee, U., & Gobata, S. (2015). A comparative study of different static and dynamic load-balancing algorithm in cloud computing with special emphasis on time factor. *Int. J. Curr. Eng. Technol.*, *3*(5).

Ahmad, F., Chakradhar, S. T., Raghunathan, A., & Vijaykumar, T. N. 2012. Tarazu: optimizing mapreduce on het-erogeneous clusters. *International Conference on Architectural Support for Programming Languages and Operating Systems (ASPLOS)*, *40*(1), 61-74.

Ahmad, R. W., Gani, A., Hamid, S. H. A., Shiraz, M., Yousafzai, A., & Xia, F. (2015). A survey on virtual machine migration and server consolidation frameworks for cloud data centers. *Journal of Network and Computer Applications*, *52*, 11–25. doi:10.1016/j.jnca.2015.02.002

Alakeel, A. M. (2010). A guide to dynamic load balancing in distributed computer systems. *Int. J. Comput. Sci. Netw. Secur.*, *10*(6), 153–160.

Apostu, A., Puican, F., Ularu, G., George Suciu, G., & Todoran, G. (2013). Study on advantages and disadvantages of cloud computing – the advantages of telemetry applications in the cloud. Recent Adv. Appl. Comput. Sci. Digit. Serv.

Babu, L. D. D., & Krishna, P. V. (2013). Honey bee behavior inspired load balancing of tasks in cloud computing environments. *Applied Soft Computing*, *13*(5), 2292–2303. doi:10.1016/j.asoc.2013.01.025

Bellavista, P., Cinque, M., Corradi, A., Foschini, L., Frattini, F., & Molina, J. P. (2016). GAMESH: A grid architecture for scalable monitoring and enhanced dependable job scheduling. *Future Generation Computer Systems*.

Benifa, J.V.B., & Dejey. (2017). Performance improvement of MapReduce for heterogeneous clusters based on efficient locality and Replica aware scheduling (ELRAS) strategy. *Wireless Personal Communications*, 1–25.

Bhatia, J., Patel, T., Trivedi, H., & Majmudar, V. (2012). HTV Dynamic Load-balancing algorithm for Virtual Machine Instances in Cloud. *International Symposium on Cloud and Services Computing*, 15–20. 10.1109/ISCOS.2012.25

Bok, K., Hwang, J., Jongtae Lim, J., Kim, Y., & Yoo, J. (2016). An efficient MapReduce scheduling scheme for processing large multimedia data. *Multimed. Tools Appl.*, 1–24.

Cai, Z., Li, X., Ruizc, R., & Lia, Q. (2017). A delay-based dynamic scheduling algorithm for bag-of-task workflows with stochastic task execution times in clouds. *J. Future Gener. Comput. Syst.*, *71*, 57–72. doi:10.1016/j.future.2017.01.020

Chethana, R., Neelakantappa, B.B., & Ramesh, B. (2016). Survey on adaptive task assignment in heterogeneous Hadoop cluster. *IEAE Int. J. Eng.*, *1*(1).

Chien, N. K., & Son, N. H. (2016). Load-balancing algorithm Based on Estimating Finish Time of Services in Cloud Computing. *International Conference on Advanced Commutation Technology (ICACT)*, 228-233.

Cinque, M., Corradi, A., Luca Foschini, L., Frattini, F., & Mol, J. P. (2016). Scalable Monitoring and Dependable Job Scheduling Support for Multi-domain Grid Infrastructures. *Proceedings of the 31st Annual ACM Symposium on Applied Computing*. 10.1145/2851613.2851762

Dagli, M. K., & Mehta, B. B. (2014). Big data and Hadoop: A review. *Int. J. Appl. Res. Eng. Sci.*, *2*(2), 192.

Daraghmi, E. Y., & Yuan, S. M. (2015). A small world based overlay network for improving dynamic load-balancing. *Journal of Systems and Software*, *107*, 187–203. doi:10.1016/j.jss.2015.06.001

Dasgupta, K., Mandalb, B., Duttac, P., Mondald, J. K., & Dame, S. (2013). A Genetic Algorithm (GA) based Load-balancing strategy for Cloud Computing. *International Conference on Computational Intelligence: Modeling Techniques and Applications (CIMTA)*, *10*, 340-347. 10.1016/j.protcy.2013.12.369

Destanoğlu, O., & Sevilgen, F. E. (2008). Randomized Hydrodynamic Load Balancing Approach. *IEEE International Conference on Parallel Processing*, *1*, 196-203.

Deye, M. M., & Slimani, Y. (2013). Load Balancing approach for QoS management of multi-instance applications in Clouds. *Proceeding on International Conference on Cloud Computing and Big Data*, 119–126. 10.1109/CLOUDCOM-ASIA.2013.69

Domanal, S. G., & Reddy, G. R. M. (2015). Load Balancing in Cloud Environment using a Novel Hybrid Scheduling Algorithm. *IEEE International Conference on Cloud Computing in Emerging Markets*, 37-42. 10.1109/CCEM.2015.31

Doulkeridis, C., & Nørvåg, K. (2013). A survey of large-scale analytical query processing in MapReduce. *The VLDB Journal*, 1–26.

Dsouza, M.B. (2015). A survey of HadoopMapReduce scheduling algorithms. *Int. J. Innov. Res. Comput. Commun. Eng.*, *3*(7).

Fadika, Z., Dede, E., & Govidaraju, M. (2011). Benchmarking MapReduce Implementations for Application Usage Scenarios. *2011 IEEE/ACM Proceedings of the 12th International Conference on Grid Computing*, 90–97. 10.1109/Grid.2011.21

Farrag, A. A. S., & Mahmoud, S. A. (2015). Intelligent Cloud Algorithms for Load Balancing problems: A Survey. *Proceedings of the Seventh International Conference on Intelligent Computing and Information Systems (ICICIS 'J 5)*, 210-216. 10.1109/IntelCIS.2015.7397223

Gautam, J. V., Prajapati, H. B., Dabhi, V. K., & Chaudhary, S. (2015). A Survey on Job Scheduling Algorithms in Big Data Processing. *IEEE International Conference on Electrical, Computer and Communication Technologies (ICECCT'15)*, 1-11. 10.1109/ICECCT.2015.7226035

Ghoneem, M., & Kulkarni, L. (2016). An Adaptive MapReduce Scheduler for Scalable Heterogeneous Systems. *Proceeding of the International Conference on Data Engineering and Communication Technology*, 603–6011.

Ghosh, S., & Banerjee, C. (2016). Priority Based Modified Throttled Algorithm in Cloud Computing. *International Conference on Inventive Computation Technology*.

Goyal, S., & Verma, M. K. (2016). Load balancing techniques in cloud computing environment: a review. *Int. J. Adv. Res. Comput. Sci. Softw. Eng., 6*(4). doi:10.1109/INVENTIVE.2016.7830175

Gupta, H., & Sahu, K. (2014). Honey bee behavior based load balancing of tasks in cloud computing. *Int. J. Sci. Res., 3*(6).

Gutierrez-Garcia, J. O., & Ramirez-Nafarrate, A. (2015). Agent-based load balancing in Cloud data centers. *Cluster Computing, 18*(3), 1041–1062. doi:10.100710586-015-0460-x

Hefny, H. A., Khafagy, M. H., & Ahmed, M. W. (2014). Comparative study load balance algorithms for MapReduce environment. *Int. Appl. Inf. Syst., 106*(18), 41.

Hou, X., Kumar, A., & Varadharajan, V. (2014). Dynamic Workload Balancing for HadoopMapReduce. *Proceeding of International Conference on Big data and Cloud Computing*, 56-62.

Hsueh, S.C., Lin, M.Y., & Chiu, Y.C. (2014). A load-balanced MapReduce algorithm for blocking-based entity-resolution with multiple keys. *Parallel Distrib. Comput. (AusPDC), 3*.

Hwang, K., Dongarra, J., & Fox, G.C. (2013). *Distributed and Cloud Computing: from Parallel Processing to the Internet of Things*. Academic Press.

Ivanisenko, I. N., & Radivilova, T. A. (2015). Survey of Major Load-balancing algorithms in Distributed System. *Information Technologies in Innovation Business Conference (ITIB)*. 10.1109/ITIB.2015.7355061

Jadeja, Y., & Modi, K. (2012). Cloud Computing - Concepts, *Architecture and Challenges. International Conference on Computing, Electronics and Electrical Technologies*.

Jaikar, A., Dada, H., Kim, G. R., & Noh, S. Y. (2014). Priority-based Virtual Machine Load Balancing in a Scientific Federated Cloud. *Proceedings of the 3rd International Conference on Cloud Computing*. 10.1109/CloudNet.2014.6969000

Kabir, M.S., Kabir, K.M., & Islam, R. (2015). Process of load balancing in cloud computing using genetic algorithm. *Electr. Comput. Eng.: Int. J., 4*(2).

Kanakala, V. R. T., & Reddy, V. K. (2015). Performance analysis of load balancing techniques in cloud computing environment. *TELKOMNIKA Indones. J. Electr. Eng., 13*(3), 568–573.

Kansal, N. J., & Inderveer Chana, I. (2012). Cloud load balancing techniques: A step towards green computing. *Int. J. Comput. Sci. Issues, 9*(1), 238–246.

Kaur, R., & Luthra, P. (2014). Load Balancing in Cloud Computing, International Conference on Recent Trends in Information. *Telecommunication and Computing*, 1–8.

Kc, K., & Anyanwu, K. (2010). Scheduling Hadoop Jobs to Meet Deadlines. *Proceedings of the 2nd IEEE International Conference on Cloud Computing Technology and Science (CloudCom)*, 388–392.

Keshvadi, S., & Faghih, B. (2016). A multi-agent based load balancing system in IaaS cloud environment. *Int. Robot. Autom. J., 1*(1).

Khalil, S., Salem, S. A., Nassar, S., & Saad, E. M. (2013). Mapreduce performance in heterogeneous environments: A review. *Int. J. Sci. Eng. Res., 4*(4), 410–416.

Khiyaita, A., Zbakh, M., Bakkali, H.E.I., & Kettani, D.E.I. (2012). Load balancing cloud computing: state of art. *Netw. Secur. Syst. (JNS2)*, 106–109.

Kianpisheh, S., Charkari, N. M., & Kargahi, M. (2016). Ant colony based constrained workflow scheduling for heterogeneous computing systems. *Cluster Computing, 19*(3), 1053–1070. doi:10.100710586-016-0575-8

Kliazovich, D., Pecero, J. E., Tchernykh, A., Bouvry, P., Khan, S. U., & Zomaya, A. Y. (2016). CA-DAG: Modeling communication-aware applications for scheduling in cloud computing. *Journal of Grid Computing*, 1–17.

Kolb, L., Thor, A., & Rahm, E. (2011). Block-based Load Balancing for Entity Resolution with MapReduce. *International Conference on Information and Knowledge Management (CIKM)*, 2397–2400. 10.1145/2063576.2063976

Kolb, L., Thor, A., & Rahm, E. (2012). Load Balancing for MapReduce-based Entity Resolution. *Proceedings of the 28th International Conference on Data Engineering*, 618-629.

Komarasamy, D., & Muthuswamy, V. (2016). A novel approach for dynamic load balancing with effective Bin packing and VM reconfiguration in cloud. *Indian Journal of Science and Technology, 9*(11), 1–6. doi:10.17485/ijst/2016/v9i11/89290

Koomey, J. G. (2008). Worldwide electricity used in datacenters. *Environmental Research Letters, 3*(3), 034008. doi:10.1088/1748-9326/3/3/034008

Kulkarni, A. K. (2015). Load-balancing strategy for Optimal Peak Hour Performance in Cloud Datacenters. *Proceedings of theIEEE International Conference on Signal Processing, Informatics, Communication and Energy Systems (SPICES)*.

Kumar, S., & Rana, D. H. (2015). Various dynamic load-balancing algorithms in cloud environment: A survey. *International Journal of Computers and Applications, 129*(6).

Lee, K. H., Choi, H., & Moon, B. (2011). Parallel data processing with MapReduce: A survey. *SIGMOD Record, 40*(4), 11–20. doi:10.1145/2094114.2094118

Li, R., Hu, H., Li, H., Wu, Y., & Yang, J. (2015). MapReduce parallel programming model: A state-of-the-art survey. *International Journal of Parallel Programming*, 1–35.

Lin, C. Y., & Lin, Y. C. (2015). A Load-Balancing Algorithm for Hadoop Distributed File System. *International Conference on Network-Based Information Systems*. 10.1109/NBiS.2015.30

Lua, Y., Xie, Q., Klito, G., Geller, A., Larus, J. R., & Greenberg, A. (2011). Join-Idle-Queue: A novel load-balancing algorithm for dynamically scalable web services. *Int. J. Perform. Eval., 68*(11), 1056–1071. doi:10.1016/j.peva.2011.07.015

Malladi, R. R. (2015). An approach to load balancing In cloud computing. *Int. J. Innov. Res. Sci. Eng. Technol., 4*(5), 3769–3777.

Manjaly, J.S. (2013). Relative study on task schedulers in HadoopMapReduce. *Int. J. Adv. Res. Comput. Sci. Softw. Eng., 3*(5).

Mesbahi, M., & Rahmani, A. M. (2016). Load balancing in cloud computing: A state of the art survey. *Int. J. Mod. Educ. Comput. Sci., 8*(3), 64–78. doi:10.5815/ijmecs.2016.03.08

Milani, A. S., & Navimipour, N. J. (2016). Load balancing mechanisms and techniques in the cloud environments: Systematic literature review and future trends. *Journal of Network and Computer Applications, 71*, 86–98. doi:10.1016/j.jnca.2016.06.003

Mishra, N.K., & Misha, N. (2015). Load balancing techniques: need, objectives and major challenges in cloud computing: a systematic review. *Int. J. Comput., 131*(18).

Moschakisa, I. A., & Karatzaa, H. D. (2015). Multi-criteria scheduling of Bag-of-Tasks applications on heterogeneous interlinked clouds with simulated annealing. *J. Softw. Syst., 101*, 1–14. doi:10.1016/j.jss.2014.11.014

Mukhopadhyay, R., Ghosh, D., & Mukherjee, N. (2010). A Study on the application of existing load-balancing algorithms for large, dynamic, and heterogeneous distributed systems ACM, A Study on the Application of Existing Load-balancing algorithms for Large, Dynamic, and Heterogeneous Distributed System. *Proceedings of 9th International Conference on Software Engineering, Parallel and Distributed Systems*, 238–243.

Neeraj, R., & Chana, I. (2014). Load balancing and job migration techniques in grid: A survey of recent trends. *Wireless Personal Communications, 79*(3), 2089–2125. doi:10.100711277-014-1975-9

Nishant, K., Sharma, P., Krishna, V., Gupta, C., Singh, K. P., Nitin, N., & Rastogi, R. (2012). Load Balancing of Nodes in Cloud Using Ant Colony Optimization. *Proceedings of the 14th International Conference on Modelling and Simulation*, 3-8. 10.1109/UKSim.2012.11

Nuaimi, K., Mohamed, N., Mariam Al-Nuaimi, M., & Al-Jaroodi, J. (2012). A Survey of Load Balancing in Cloud Computing: Challenges and Algorithms. *Proceedings of the Second Symposium on Network Cloud Computing and Applications*. 10.1109/NCCA.2012.29

Palta, R., & Jeet, R. (2014). Load balancing in the cloud computing using virtual machine migration: A review. *Int. J. Appl. Innov. Eng. Manag.*, *3*(5), 437–441.

Patel, H.M. (2015). A comparative analysis of MapReduce scheduling algorithms for Hadoop. *Int. J. Innov. Emerg. Res. Eng.*, *2*(2).

Polato, I., Re, R., Goldman, A., & Kon, F. (2014). A comprehensive view of Hadoop research – a systematic literature review. *Journal of Network and Computer Applications*, *46*, 1–25. doi:10.1016/j.jnca.2014.07.022

Rajabioun, R. (2011). Cuckoo optimization algorithm. *Applied Soft Computing*, *11*, 5508–5518.

Randles, M., Lamb, D., & Tareb-Bendia, A. (2010). A Comparative Study into Distributed Load-balancing algorithms for Cloud Computing. *Proceedings of the 24th International Conference on Advanced Information Networking and Applications Workshops*, 551–556.

Rao, B. T., & Reddy, L. S. S. (2011). Survey on improved scheduling in HadoopMapReduce in cloud environments. *International Journal of Computers and Applications*, *34*(9).

Rastogi, G., & Sushil, R. (2015). Analytical Literature Survey on Existing Load Balancing Schemes in Cloud Computing. *International Conference on Green Computing and Internet of Things (ICGCIoT)*. 10.1109/ICGCIoT.2015.7380705

Rathore, N., & Chana, I. (2013). A Sender Initiate Based Hierarchical Load Balancing Technique for Grid Using Variable Threshold Value. *Signal Processing, Computing and Control (ISPCC), IEEE International Conference*. 10.1109/ISPCC.2013.6663440

Rathore, N., & Channa, I. (2011). A Cognitive Analysis of Load Balancing and job migration Technique. *Grid World Congress on Information and Communication Technologies Congr. Inf. Commun. Technol. (WICT)*, 77–82.

Ray, S., & Sarkar, A.D. (2012). Execution analysis of load-balancing algorithms in cloud computing environment. *Int. J. Cloud Comput.: Serv. Archit. (IJCCSA)*, *2*(5).

Sarood, O., Gupta, A., & Kale, L. V. (2012). Cloud Friendly Load Balancing for HPC Applications: *Preliminary Work. International Conference on Parallel Processing Workshops*, 200–205.

Scharf, M., Stein, M., Voith, T., & Hilt, V. (2015). Network-aware Instance Scheduling in OpenStack. *International Conference on Computer Communication and Network (ICCCN)*, 1-6.

Selvi, R. T., & Aruna, R. (2016). Longest approximate time to end scheduling algorithm in Hadoop environment. *Int. J. Adv. Res. Manag. Archit. Technol. Eng.*, *2*(6).

Shadkam, E., & Bijari, M. (2014). Evaluation the efficiency of cuckoo optimization algorithm. *Int. J. Comput. Sci. Appl.*, *4*(2), 39–47.

Shaikh, B., Shinde, K., & Borde, S. (2017). Challenges of big data processing and scheduling of processes using various Hadoop Schedulers: A survey. *Int. Multifaceted Multiling. Stud.*, *3*, 12.

Shen, H., Sarker, A., Yuy, L., & Deng, F. (2016). Probabilistic Network-Aware Task Placement for MapReduce Scheduling. *Proceedings of the IEEE International Conference on Cluster Computing.* 10.1109/CLUSTER.2016.48

Shen, H., Yu, L., Chen, L., & Li, Z. (2016). Goodbye to Fixed Bandwidth Reservation: Job Scheduling with Elastic Bandwidth Reservation in Clouds. *Proceedings of the International Conference on Cloud Computing Technology and Science.* 10.1109/CloudCom.2016.0017

Sidhu, A. K., & Kinger, S. (2013). Analysis of load balancing techniques in cloud computing. *International Journal of Computers and Technology*, *4*(2).

Sim, K. M. (2011). Agent-based cloud computing. *IEEE Transactions on Services Computing*, *5*(4), 564–577.

Singh, P., Baaga, P., & Gupta, S. (2016). Assorted load-balancing algorithms in cloud computing: A survey. *International Journal of Computers and Applications*, *143*(7).

Singha, A., Juneja, D., & Malhotra, M. (2015). Autonomous Agent Based Load-balancing algorithm in Cloud Computing. *International Conference on Advanced Computing Technologies and Applications (ICACTA)*, *45*, 832–841. 10.1016/j.procs.2015.03.168

Sui, Z., & Pallickara, S. (2011). A survey of load balancing techniques forData intensive computing. In B. Furht & A. Escalante (Eds.), *Handbook of Data Intensive Computing* (pp. 157–168). New York: Springer. doi:10.1007/978-1-4614-1415-5_6

Tasquier, L. (2015). Agent based load-balancer for multi-cloud environments. *Columbia Int. Publ. J. Cloud Comput. Res.*, *1*(1), 35–49.

Vaidya, M. (2012). Parallel processing of cluster by Map Reduce. *Int. J. Distrib. Parallel Syst.*, *3*(1).

Valvåg, S. V. (2011). Cogset: A High-Performance MapReduce Engine. Faculty of Science and Technology Department of Computer Science, University of Tromsö.

Valvåg, S. V., & Johansen, D. (2009). Cogset: A unified engine for reliable storage and parallel processing. *Proceedings of the Sixth IFIP International Conference on Network and Parallel Computing*, 174–181. 10.1109/NPC.2009.23

Vasic, N., & Barisits, M. (2009). Making Cluster Applications Energy-Aware. *Proceedings of the 1st Workshop on Automated Control for Datacenters and Clouds*, 37–42.

Vernica, R., Balmin, A., Beyer, K. S., & Ercegovac, V. (2012). Adaptive MapReduce using situation-aware mappers. *International Conference on Extending Database Technology (EDBT)*, 420–431. 10.1145/2247596.2247646

Wei, X., Fan, J., Lu, Z., & Ding, K. (2013). Application scheduling in mobile cloud computing with load balancing. *Journal of Applied Mathematics*, 1–13.

Wei, X., Fan, J., Wang, T., & Wang, Q. (2015). Efficient application scheduling in mobile cloud computing based on MAX–MIN ant system. *Soft Computing*, 1–15.

Xia, Y., Wang, L., Zhao, Q., & Zhang, G. (2011). Research on job scheduling algorithm in Hadoop. *Journal of Computer Information Systems*, 7, 5769–5775.

Yahaya, B., Latip, R., Othman, M., & Abdullah, A. (2011). Dynamic load balancing policy with communication and computation elements in grid computing with multi-agent system integration. *Int. J. New Comput. Archit. Appl.*, 1(3), 757–765.

Yakhchi, M., Ghafari, S. M., Yakhchi, S., Fazeliy, M., & Patooghi, A. (2015). Proposing a Load Balancing Method Based on Cuckoo Optimization Algorithm for Energy Management in Cloud Computing Infrastructures. *Proceedings of the 6th International Conference on Modeling, Simulation, and Applied Optimization (ICMSAO)*. 10.1109/ICMSAO.2015.7152209

Yang, S. J., & Chen, Y. R. (2015). Design adaptive task allocation scheduler to improve MapReduce performance in heterogeneous clouds. *Journal of Network and Computer Applications*, 57, 61–70. doi:10.1016/j.jnca.2015.07.012

Zaharia, M. (2009). *Job Scheduling with the Fair and Capacity Schedulers 9*. Berkley University.

Zaharia, M., Borthakur, D., & Sarma, J. S. (2010). Delay Scheduling: A Simple Technique for Achieving Locality and Fairness in Cluster Scheduling. *Proceedings of the European conference on Computer systems (EuroSys'10)*, 265–278. 10.1145/1755913.1755940

Zaharia, M., Konwinski, A., Joseph, A. D., Katz, R., & Stoica, I. (2008). Improving MapReduce Performance in Heterogeneous Environments. *Proceedings of the 8th conference on Symposium on Opearting Systems Design and Implementation*, 29–42.

Zhang, Y., & Li, Y. (2015). An improved Adaptive workflow scheduling Algorithm in cloud environments. *Proceedings of the Third International Conference on Advanced Cloud and Big Data*, 112-116. 10.1109/CBD.2015.27

Chapter 11
Resource Management Techniques to Manage the Load Balancing in Cloud Computing

Pradeep Kumar Tiwari
Manipal University Jaipur, India

Sandeep Joshi
Manipal University Jaipur, India

ABSTRACT

Load balancing is one of the vital issues in cloud computing that needs to be achieved using proper techniques as it is directly related to higher resource utilization ratio and user satisfaction. By evenly distributing the dynamic local workload across all the nodes in the whole cloud, load balancing makes sure that no single node is overwhelmed, and some other nodes are kept idle. Hence, the technique helps to improve the overall performance resource utility of the system which will lead to high user satisfaction and resource utilization ratio. It also ensures the fair and effective distribution of each and every computing resource in the distributed system. Furthermore, the various load balancing techniques prevent the possible bottlenecks of the system created by the load imbalance. Maximization of the throughput, minimization of the response time, and avoidance of the overload are the other major advantages of the load balancing. Above all, by keeping resource consumption at the minimum, the load balancing techniques help to reduce costs.

INTRODUCTION

In order to attain high performance computing (HPC) and utilization of computing resources, the elementary concept of the distributed system is utilized to perform cluster, grid and cloud computing. The distributed application determines the distributed paradigms. Virtual machines (VMs) can comprise of separately functioning operating systems and applications. Virtualization is the core concept of resource pool and management. Hypervisor assists in attaining hardware virtualization and is segregated into Type 1 and Type 2. The Type 1 hypervisor is the bare-metal hypervisor that is installed directly on

DOI: 10.4018/978-1-5225-9023-1.ch011

the x86-based hardware and renders direct access to the hardware resources . The Type 2 hypervisor is the hosted hypervisor that is installed and run as an application on an operating system. The operating system and the applications of a VM function autonomously without any mutual interference. VM is migrated without downtime and VM failure does not affect the distribution of resources among VMs. The service level agreement (SLA) and the quality of service (QoS) must be managed by the load balance (LB) policy. The main causes of SLA violation are scattered data among heterogeneous servers, hot spot, load imbalance, and weak resource management (Zhang & Zhang, 2010). The occurrence of the load imbalance is when the demands in the heterogeneous environments are frequently changing. Load imbalance can be managed through LB between high load and low load machines. The management of LB is difficult on high resource demands that change frequently. The factors that help in the management of LB are information policies, location to migrate VM, selection of VM, and transfer of load.

Load Balancing

The management of demanded resources is known as load balancing mechanism in which the workload is distributed among the VMs. The mechanism of load balancing is a vital component of the hypervisor, which dynamically or statically manage the load imbalance in a distributed manner on the available VMs. The CPU, memory and network components are virtualized to maximize the utilization of resources. In computing, the distribution of workloads across multiple computing resources, such as disk drives, CPUs, network links, computer clusters, or computers, is enhanced by load balancing (Sreenivas et al., 2014). Figure 1 shows the load imbalance scenario in distributed computing. The figure shows that load imbalance is a cause of system inefficiency. The aims of load balancing are to avoid the overload situation in nodes, minimize the migration and response time, maximize throughput, and optimize the resource utilization. Availability and reliability may be increased through redundancy by utilizing multiple (and not single) components with load balancing. Dedicated software or hardware, such as a domain name system server process or a multilayer switch, is generally involved in load balancing.

In distributed computing, Load Balancing is vital for capable operations in appropriated circumstances. As Cloud computing is increasing and consumers are asking for more organizations and better results, load altering for the Cloud has transformed into an especially captivating and basic examining range. Load altering enables all processors in the structure or each of the center points in the framework

Figure 1. Load Imbalance scenarios

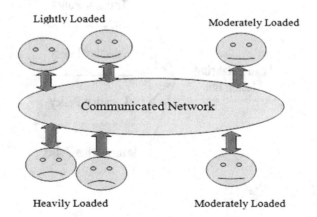

to generally do the proportionate measure of work at any given point of time. It is utilized for attaining a better resource utilization ratio and service provisioning, thereby enhancing the systems' general performance. Incoming tasks from different locations are received by the load balancer and then distributed to the data center, for a proper load distribution. Our research objective maximizes the CPU utilization of VMs with efficient results in load balancing metrics (Alakeel, A. M., 2010) Figure 2 shows the role of load balance manager.

Load Balancing Mechanism

Load balancing mechanism not only manages the load distribution among the available VMs, but also controls the load imbalance with a fault tolerance. The response time is minimized and the throughput is maximized by effective load balancing. Figure shows the load balancing policies, which play a vital role in distributing the fair load among the VMs.

Figure 2. Load balancing

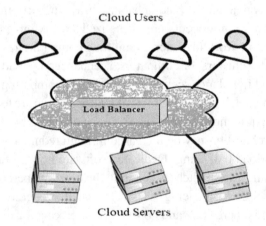

Figure 3. Load balancing policies

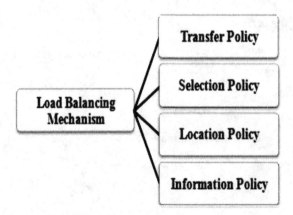

Transfer Policy

Transfer policy is based on the CPU's threshold state. It can be gauged from a high threshold that jobs needs migration, since none of them are being executed by the CPU. On the contrary, it can be gauged from a low threshold that the current CPU is capable of executing more loads and is anticipating the load from a high loaded VM.

Selection Policy

Selection policy selects high- and low-loaded VMs. The selection policy may be either static or dynamic, which will select the best fit low-load VM to migrate the jobs of high load VMs.

Location Policy

Location policy identifies the location of a high load VM to migrate the jobs to a low load VM. This mechanism is based on the timeout of CPU. Less timeout indicates that CPU is free to take more jobs from long timeout CPU.

Information Policy

Information policy has the resource information of the available VMs. It has the data centers (DCs) and the information on available VMs, which helps in mapping the VMs' resources to DCs. The manager separates the high and low loaded VMs to find the sender and receiver VMs. The information policy refreshes the dashboard information after every completed migration of jobs (Rathore & Chana, 2014).

These load balancing policies are interrelated to each other for managing the user base (UB) request on the available VMs and transferring the job from a high-loaded VM to a low-loaded VM (Xiao et al., 2015).

The Cloud system is rendered ineffective by the load imbalance, which is also caused due to poor availability of resources, reliability, scalability, and throughput. In order to enhance the reaction time of the employment and to compel the asset utilization, the total work load is reassigned to individual hubs on the framework. Such a process is termed as load balancing, which nullifies the situations in which the hubs are either under-stacked or over-stacked (Liao, 2012). Hence, load adjusting is generally a system that encourages systems and assets by giving a maximum throughput at the least reaction time by partitioning the movement between servers. Load adjusting calculations can be fundamentally classified into static, dynamic or symmetrically managed load balancing (Sammy et al., (2012); Vinothina et al., 2012).

Resource Management Strategies

The semantic association between resource distribution and resource availability is termed as resource management. The primary elements of a resource are storing, computing and networking. The SLA agreement and the availability of resources is considered in the resource management and are accordingly rendered to the consumers. The resource management includes modeling, estimation, brokering, discovery, adaptation, requirement mapping, provisioning, and allocation. The primary objectives of resource distribution are flexible administration, resource utilization, and performance isolation (Figure 4).

Figure 4. Goals of resource management

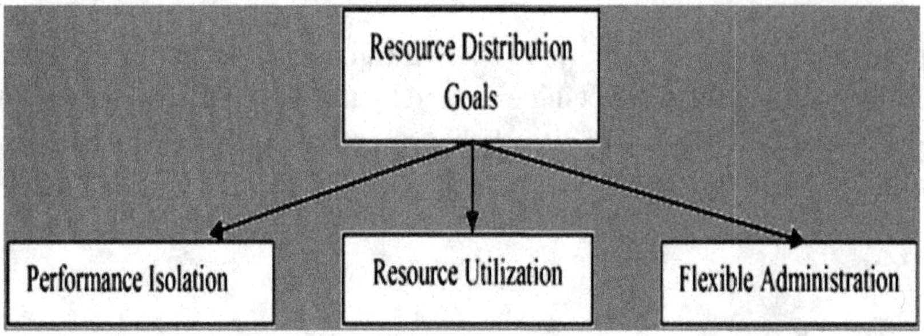

Performance Isolation

VMs do not interfere with the capacity of other VMs, as they are isolated from each other. The load and the performance are not affected by the VM's failure, because the load is migrated to other VMs. The facility of rapid migration is rendered by Hyper-V and the facility of live migration is rendered by VMware. Owing to the VM's failure and/or occurrences of high resource demands, the load must be migrated from one VM to another VM, and the load must eventually be migrated to a physical server (Lu & Lau, 1995; Rotithor, 1994).

Utilization of Resources

Resource utilization is affected by dynamic resource allocation management, which renders the resources from PM. Without any downtime, a minimum consumption of the available resources determines the resource utilization. The energy consumption is minimized and the resource availability is maximized by the efficient resource managers. Based on the requirements of demand resources, the resource managers must pay heed to and consider the SLA. The load of individual hosts and VMs is mapped and measured by the load manager.

Flexible Administration

High load resource demands must be managed well and utilized by resource administrators in a synchronized manner. In order to manage VMs' migration and VMs' capacity (resource limits, priorities and reservations), a distributed resource scheduler (DRS) is utilized by VMware. In order to attain energy efficient resource management, the power-on or power-off of utilized and non-utilized VMs is managed by the distributed power management (DPM) and VMware (Buyya, 2010). In order to manage virtual machine manager 2008 R2, the system center virtual machine manager (SCVMM) support system is used by Microsoft Hyper-V. The migration management of VMs is increased among the hosts by SCVMM. Additionally, the flexibility in storage management is increased by SCVMM.

CHALLENGES OF LOAD BALANCING

Since a centralized authority is absent for assigning the workload among various processors, several problems can be identified in the distributed systems' load balancing mechanism. Some of the mechanism's issues are stated below.

Overhead Associated

The quantum of overhead that is involved during the execution of a load balancing system is determined by overhead associated. The inter-process communication and the movement of tasks cause the overhead. In order to enhance the performance of a load balancing algorithm, overhead must be decreased.

Performance

For a load balancing system to be effective, the performance must be optimal. The utilization of resources is tested and improved by performance, which can be therefore defined as the system's efficiency.

Scalability

The quality of service is denoted by scalability. It must not change or get affected by the increase in number of users and nodes.

Response Time

The reaction time of a load balancing algorithm in a distributed system can be defined as the response time. The response time must be decreased for attaining a better performance (Gupta et al., 2006).

Fault Tolerance

A system's ability to execute uniform load balancing, despite the failure of node, is termed as fault tolerance. Load balancing must be an effective fault-tolerant method (Nathan, Kulkarni & Bellur, 2013).

Point of Failure

The designing of a point of failure is such that the provisioning of services is not affected by it. The entire system fails if one central node fails, and this phenomenon is similar to a centralized system. Therefore, this problem must be overcome by the design of the load balancing system (VMware.com, 2015).

LOAD BALANCING METRICS IN CLOUD

The metrics for load balancing mapping are discussed below.

Throughput

The quantum of tasks performed within a particular time is defined by throughput. In order to enhance the system's performance, the throughput must be high, as it denotes the system's implementation capacity.

Fault Tolerance

Despite the arbitrary node or link failure, the ability of an algorithm to perform uniform load balancing is referred to as fault tolerance, which is also the capability of recovering from failure. Reliability and availability execute the mapping of fault tolerance and the load balancing must ideally be an efficient fault tolerant method.

Scalability

The ability of mapping resources that are available in finite quantity of VMs is termed as scalability.

Migration Time

The process time consumed by a load manager to migrate a job from high-load VMs to low-load VMs is termed as migration time (Lin et al., 2011)

Response Time

The time consumed by a specific load balancing algorithm in responding to a system task is referred to as response time. In order to enhance the systems' performance the parameter of response time must be minimal (Calheiros et al., 2011).

PROBLEM FORMULATION

An efficient load balancing algorithm is proposed for efficient resource utilization and it also avoids over-loading and under-loading conditions. This load balancer is linked to the data center and all of the users. All VMs are managed by the datacenter controller. Load balancer computes the priorities of VMs by parsing its table, based on their speed, memory and power consumption. Load balancer then passes the load to the highest priority VM. The objective of the present research is to enable excellent rate of performance of cloud virtual resources through efficient and uniform workload scheduling and distribution. Two principles, namely, meta-heuristic algorithms and Push-Pull algorithms are used as the basis of the present work. These principles are executed for load balancing and scheduling in a cloud in such a way that the virtual resource is identified as either under-loaded or over-loaded. The chief aim of the present study is to formulate and create an effective load balancing algorithm within a heterogeneous and distributed environment termed as Cloud. The physical servers that are known as DCs having their own identity, multiple VMs, processing power, bandwidth, memory, and number of CPUs, are unavailable. In order to avoid a single failure point and bottlenecks, the suggested algorithm is decentralized.

This chapter is conducting a depth review of the studies regarding the existing load balancing techniques in cloud networking and attempt to find shortcomings exist in those proposals as a mean to come up with a novel proposal which can overcome these shortcomings. The review also targets the studies which deal with the factors such as, parameters for identifying hotspots, an algorithm that can evaluate how balanced a system is, a prediction algorithm for estimating the workload after a migration has occurred and an algorithm to determine how costly a migration will be.

ANALYSIS OF LOAD BALANCING MECHANISM IN CLOUD

Load balancing problems in cloud networks can be defined in two ways: (1) task allocation based load balancing, which involves the random distribution of a finite number of tasks into different physical machines (PMs) and further these tasks are allocated to different VMs of respective PM, and (2) VM migration, which involves the movement of a VM from one PM to another PM in order to improve the resource utilization of the data center for which the PM is overloaded (Kim & Kameda,1992). The following sections will provide the in depth review of the studies pertained to these load balancing mechanisms.

Task Allocation Based Load Balancing Techniques

The load balancing techniques using task allocation can be broadly divided into static and dynamic techniques. Several static and dynamic approaches, such as Min-Min, Max-Min, receiver initiative, sender initiative, token routing, round robin, heuristic honey bee, genetic, agent, and ants, are suggested by researchers for managing the load balance. The following section will discuss the studies pertained to various static and dynamic load balancing algorithms.

Static Load Balancing Scheme

A static algorithm manages the traffic by evenly dividing the tasks among the servers. The dedicated and pre-reserved allocation of resources is defined by static load balancing scheme in accordance with the end users' requirement. This type of algorithms uses the prior knowledge of system resources, since the decision of shifting of the load does not depend on the current state of the system. The shifting is not performed until all demands are changing and the PM's total capacity forms the basis of the resource allocation of VMs. Static scheduling comprises of optimal and sub-optimal scheduling. The data about resources and job is possessed by optimal scheduling. Decisions about resource allocation and job scheduling can be taken on a viable timeframe (Figure 5. Sub-optimal management can be utilized if any problem is encountered during the viable job scheduling (Sharma, Singh, & Sharma, 2008).

In static approach the functioning of the processors is ascertained in the initial stages of execution. The master processor distributes the workload according to the performance. The allocated work is calculated by the slave processors and the results are submitted to the master. The static load balancing techniques are non-pre-emptive and a task is invariably accomplished on the processor to which it is allocated. Minimization of communication delays and reduction of the overall execution time of a concurrent program forms the objective of the static load balancing technique (Sharma, Singh, & Sharma, 2008; LD & Krishna, 2013).

Figure 5. Static load balancing

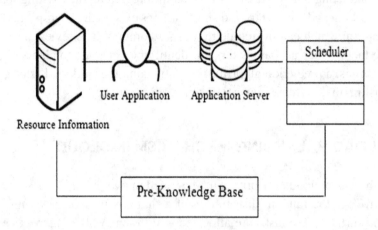

This section will review the studies pertained to the different static algorithm approach adopted by multifarious researchers.

Round Robin

The round robin scheduling executed in the process scheduling resembles the round robin algorithm in cloud computing. The random selection of VMs forms the basis of the performance of this algorithm. The service calls are cyclically allotted by the data center controller (DCC) to a pool of VMs. The round robin scheduling work situation is depicted in Figure 6. The requests are allotted by the DCC in a round manner after a VM is randomly chosen for the assignment of the initial request of client. The bottom of the VMs' pool receives the VM after its allocation (Mahalle, Kaveri & Chavan, 2013).

Sotomayor et al. (2009) proposed an algorithm, namely, round robin algorithm to balance the load in static environment. The algorithm followed first-cum-first-serve to fulfill the task. The resource which contains the node with the least number of connections is allocated to the task. However, the major

Figure 6. Round robin scheduling

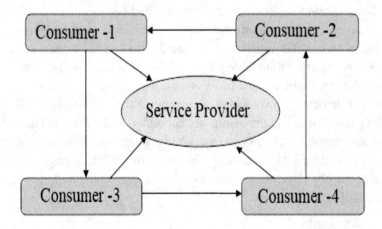

drawback of this algorithm was that the advanced load balancing requisites, such as the processing time and the response time for each individual service request, are not favored by this type of allocation tasks.

Radojevic and Zagar (2011) proposed an alternative version of Round Robin algorithm called central load balancing decision model (CLBDM). The proposed algorithm used the root principle of round robin, meanwhile it also measured the connectivity duration between server and client by calculating overall execution time of task on giving cloud resource. The findings indicate that the new algorithm integrates information from end user experience and virtualized computer environments and proactively influences load balancing decisions or reactively change decision in handling critical situations. However, the proposed algorithm introduced new elements that can compromise stability of the whole computer system even though the proposed model solves many issues that can happen with today's available models. The, introduction of CLBDM as a central management module influences both the load balancing decisions, and virtual server resources which can in turn lead to the possible single point of failure. Furthermore, in the absence of proper design and engineering in the factors, such as reliability, resilience and robustness, CLBDM can lead to severe performance issues or even the unavailability of the whole system. Another issue that made CLBDM become unreliable is that it always tends to enter into the unforeseen loops and start to flap its decision between nodes, resulting in poor performance and end-user experience.

Pasha, Agarwal and Rastogi (2014) proposed a Round Robin VM load balancing algorithm and adopted Java language for implementing the proposed VM scheduling algorithm in CloudSim toolkit. The study assumed the entire application is deployed in one data centers with virtual machine having 2048 MB of memory and running on physical processor capable of creating a speed of 1000 MIPS. The experimental findings indicated that Round Robin VM Load Balancing method improves the load balancing performance by consuming less time for scheduling virtual machine. However, the drawbacks, such as inability to measure the output metrics like response time and processing time, limits its usage.

Shah and Farik (2015) proposed a hybrid static algorithm by conjoining the weighted round robin algorithm and the max-min load balancing algorithm. This study calculated the capacity of the server's resources by using the weight assignment feature of the weighted round robin algorithm, before load assignment is done. Further, this is combined with features of the max-min algorithm where the minimum and maximum execution times are calculated. Thus calculated maximum time value is used to schedule tasks to the corresponding machines. This method can use the maximum time for task completion and scheduling the heavier tasks since it is known before scheduling of tasks is done. Furthermore, the technique also beats the starvation as all tasks will be circulated in a round robin fashion. However, a major drawback of this algorithm was its non-compatibility with complex infrastructures and changing user requirements.

Throttled Algorithm

In throttled algorithm the available or busy status is depicted on the VMs' index table and this status is governed by the load balancer. When a load balancer receives a request from a client, then the favorable VM is assigned through the throttled algorithm. All VMs are set to available mode in the initial stage. When a new request is received by the data center controller, the balancer is consulted for the subsequent VM allocation. Until an applicable match of VM is identified, the table is thoroughly checked by the balancer. The identity of a specific VM is returned to the data center controller by the balancer, if a favorable VM is identified. The VM found by that specific identity receives a request from the data center controller at that juncture. Later, in order to facilitate the update of the table, the balance of new allocation is notified by the data center controller.

The request is queued by the data center and a value of -1 is returned by the balancer, if a VM is not found. As soon as the assigned request is processed by the virtual machine, a response cloudlet is received by the data center controller and the VM de-allocation is notified to the balancer (James, & Verma, 2012; Dave et al., 2014)

Nayak and Patel (2015) conducted an analytical study regarding the existing throttled algorithms and their performance in the cloud networking so as a mean for balancing the load. The study proposed a modified throttled algorithm for balancing the load. The findings revealed that the proposed modified throttle algorithm worked well despite the difference in the underlying capacity of each VMs. This improved proposed algorithm used more parameters such as expected response time and loading condition while taking the decision of VM selection. The study calculated expected response time using CPU utilization of VM. The analysis revealed that the usage of improved throttled load balancing algorithm with less overhead, yielded an increased number of user request handling and better VM allocation, which in turn will reduce the denial in the number of requests arrived at the data center of the cloud. The findings revealed that the implementation of the proposed throttle algorithm reduces response time, datacenter request servicing time as well as cost. However, the comparative and analytical study of existing and proposed throttle algorithm revealed that in order to check the availability of VM for precise decision more load balancing parameters should be included. Furthermore, the implementation of the proposed algorithm in a different hardware configuration also needs to be checked.

Atul Raj (2015) proposed an algorithm which was the combination of Throttled and Active Monitoring Load Balancing Algorithms. The findings are compared with the results of Throttled Load Balancing Algorithm to measure the efficiency of the proposed algorithm. The findings indicated that the proposed algorithm yielded better overall response time and datacenter processing time compared with a Throttled load balancing algorithm.

Patel and Jha (2016) designed a local throttling load balancing approach for the distribution of incoming jobs uniformly among the virtual machines. The performance of the proposed algorithm was analyzed using Cloudanalyst simulator and result was compared with existing Throttled algorithms. The output parameters, such as response time and the data center serving time were measured to analyses the performance of the algorithms. The findings indicated that the proposed algorithm showed better performance than the existing one. However, the lack of flexibility and the inability to measure the other parameters, such as scalability, throughput, resource availability etc., limits the usage of this algorithm.

Aswathy, Nisha and Mahesh (2016) proposed a new algorithm which uses throughput of the host machine in order to enhance the throttled algorithm. The throughput of every host machine with respect to its virtual machine was being calculated and the result was stored in the hash table along with the details maintained in the load balancer. After that, based on this throughput, the algorithm performs a descending sort on the hash table. Based on this sorted hash table the task will be allocated to the available virtual machine. The findings revealed that the proposed algorithm outperformed the existing ones. According to the findings, the proposed algorithm minimized the overall response by transmitting the load to more efficient virtual machine. However, lack of compatibility with the output metrics, such as scalability, throughput, reliability, etc., functions as the major drawback of this algorithm. Furthermore, its usage was limited to simple homogenous systems only.

Min-Min and Max-Min

The primary idea behind the Min-Min calculation is to dispatch each assignment to virtual machines as assets, which can finish the errand in the briefest conceivable time (Chen, Chen & Kuo, 2017). The Min-Min calculation will execute short employments in parallel and the long occupations are executed after the short employments. The deficiency of this calculation is that the short employments are booked until the point that the machines are relaxed to plan and execute long occupations. Min-Min can cause both the entire group employments' executed time to get a longer and unequal load. Indeed, even long employments cannot be executed. When compared with the conventional Min-Min calculation, the enhanced calculation includes the three imperatives' (nature of the administration, the dynamic need display and the cost of administration) methodology, which can change this condition. The test consequences of enhanced Min-Min calculation demonstrate that asset usage rate can be built, long undertakings can be executed at a sensible time, and the clients' prerequisites can be met.

Kokilavani and Amalarathinem (2011) proposed a new task scheduling algorithm to balance load in distributed computing systems. The performance of the proposed algorithm was organized in two-phases. One of the prime advantages of the algorithm is that it uses the advantages of Max-Min and Min-Min algorithms and covers their disadvantages. The findings of the performance analysis of the algorithm indicated the fact that it outperforms the existing scheduling algorithms. However, the prime limitation of the study was that it was concerned with the number of the resources and task execution time, whereas compatibility with low and high machine heterogeneity and task heterogeneity were left out. Furthermore, the study was conducted in a limited environment. Hence, the implementation of the proposed algorithm on the actual grid environment is yet to be materialized. Above all, the comparatively higher cost also caused a considerable decline in its popularity.

Chen et al. (2017) presented an improved load balancing algorithm based on Min-Min algorithm in order to reduce the makespan and increase the resource utilization. The simulation results show that the proposed algorithm yielded significant performance gain and attained over 20% improvement on both resource utilization ratio and VIP user satisfaction. However, the major drawback of this algorithm is that the algorithm only considered the makespan, load balancing and user-priority for task scheduling, whereas the other parameters, such as throughput, scalability, etc. are left out. Furthermore, the study also did not consider deadline of each task, the geography location of tasks and resources, the high heterogeneity of interconnection and many other cases, which in turn limits its usage. Above all, the study considered the tasks which are independent, but in real life situation they may have some precedence relations which also needed to be considered.

Gopinath and Vasudevan (2015) proposed the implementation of the two load balancing algorithms, namely Max-Min and Min-Min. The result indicated in terms of makes span that the Max-Min performs better than Min-Min. However, both algorithms show their own pros and cons, with respect to the cloud environment. Max–Min performs well in terms of resource utilization and makespan if the number of lighter tasks outnumbers the heavier tasks. If there is large number of heavier tasks, then Min-Min performs better than Max-Min. So the study entered into the conclusion that the performance of load balancing in the cloud does not depend upon any algorithm, but it is purely based on the cloud environment chosen by the study.

Patel, Mehta and Bhoi (2015) studied about the existing task scheduling algorithms and proposed a unique modification of low balanced Min-Min algorithm for static meta scheduling. The proposed algorithm functions in two steps; in the first step Min-Min strategy is applied, which selects the tasks with minimum completion time and assigns it to suitable resource, the second step involves the rescheduling of the tasks to use the unutilized resources effectively so as a mean to increase the make span. The proposed algorithm was compared with existing Min-Min algorithm using the output parameter namely makes span. The findings revealed that the proposed enhanced algorithm provided better make span compared to the existing one.

Equally Spread Current Execution

Domanlal and Reddy (2014) proposed a local optimized load balancing approach named equally spread current execution (ESCE) algorithm for distributing of incoming jobs uniformly among the servers or virtual machines. The algorithm needs a load balancer, which can track the feasible jobs. Placing the tasks in the job pool and assigning them to discrete VMs is the primary function of the load balancer. The new tasks are assigned to discrete VMs after they are frequently monitored by the balancer in the job queue. The free VMs that need allocation to new tasks are checked by the load balancer due to its handling of the list of tasks being assigned to virtual servers. The study analyzed the performance of the algorithm using Cloudanalyst simulator and compared with existing Round Robin and Throttled algorithms. Simulation results demonstrated that the proposed algorithm distributed the load uniformly among virtual machines.

Nikita (2014) developed a novel algorithm called ESCE algorithm to enhance the load balancing in cloud networks. The proposed static load balancing algorithm will keep each node in the cloud busy so that it does not need to consider the current load on each node. It dispatched the selected job to a randomly selected available VM. The simulation result indicates are deduction of around 50%-60%in cost and time. These advance the business performance and results in total customer satisfaction. However, OLB does not consider the execution time of the task in that node. This may cause the task to be processed in a slower manner, increasing the makespan and will cause some bottlenecks since requests might be pending waiting for nodes to be free.

Figure 7. Equally spread current execution

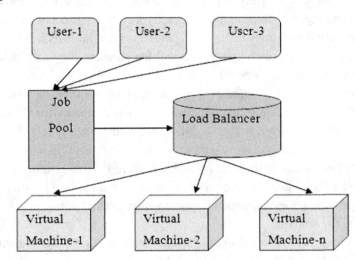

Map Reduce Algorithm

Gunaratne et al. (2011) proposed a novel MapReduce runtime algorithm called Azure MapReduce, using the Microsoft Azure cloud infrastructure services. The findings indicated that the proposed algorithm influenced the scalability, latency, and consistency of the output. These features help the proposed algorithm to provide an efficient, on demand alternative to traditional MapReduce clusters. Further the study also evaluated performance and the use of MapReduce frameworks, like Azure MapReduce, in cloud environments for scientific applications

Junjie et al. (2011) proposed a load balancing algorithm for the private Cloud using virtual machines to physical machine mapping. Central scheduling controller and a resource monitor are the two major components in the architecture of the proposed algorithm. The calculation for the determination of the apt resource to take the task and assignment of the task based on the calculation is the prime work of the scheduling controller. Meanwhile, the resource monitor does gather the details regarding the resource availability. Four main phases involve in the process of mapping tasks, which are: accepting the virtual machine request, getting the resources details using the resource monitor, the calculation of the resource ability to handle tasks by the controller and the reception of the task by the resource that gets the highest score.

Kolb, Thor and Rahm (2012) proposed two load balancing approaches, BlockSplit and PairRange, using MapReduce framework. Both approaches deal with skewed data distributions and distribute the workload among all reduce tasks. The evaluation of the study demonstrated that both approaches are robust against data skew. However, the multipass blocking that assigns multiple blocks per entity is not considered in this study. Furthermore, the study also keeps silence on the adaptation of the algorithm for other data intensive tasks, such as join processing or data mining.

Other Novel Algorithms

Penmatsa and Chronopoulos (2011)proposed two load balancing schemes for distributed systems. The study proposed the CCOOP algorithm that provides objectivity to all the jobs in a single-class job distributed system, using cooperative game theory. Further, using non-cooperative game theory study proposed another algorithm called NCOOPC distributed algorithm that delivers fairness to all users in a multi-user job distributed system. The study validated the derivation of CCOOP and NCOOPC using Game Theory results and simulations was used to evaluate their performance. The comparison of the scheme was performed by simulating the algorithms on a variety of system configurations. The findings indicated that both CCOOP and NCOOPC produced a performance near the system optimal schemes OPTIM and GOS respectively, and also provided fairness to the users and their jobs. However, the major drawback of the algorithm was that it was implemented in the homogenous systems and the efficiency of this algorithm in heterogeneous systems is questionable.

Sharma and Banga (2013) proposed a novel enhanced and efficient scheduling algorithm to balance the load in cloud networks and using CloudSim with the help of the Java language. The study analyzed response time, data center processing time and processing cost to analyze the efficiency of the proposed algorithm. From the graphs and tables it can be inferred that the data center processing time and overall response time is bettered and cost is reduced in comparison to the existing scheduling parameters. However, the problem of deadlocks and server overflow remains as the major drawbacks of the algorithm.

Dynamic Load Balancing Scheme

The difference between the static algorithms and the dynamic load balancing scheme is that the workload distribution is executed at runtime among the processors. The new information collected from the basis of assignment of new processes to the slaves by the master. Unlike static algorithms, under-loaded processors are dynamically allocated by the dynamic algorithms. Rather, they are dynamically allocated according to the remote hosts' requests and are buffered on the main host's queue. Conventional distributed systems' literature has deliberated the problem of load balancing for more than twenty years. Several policies, strategies and algorithms have been suggested, executed and classified (Fang, Wang & Ge, 2010).

The following concepts were visualized after a comparison with static schemes:

- Decisions are real time.
- Fewer complexes than static scheme.
- Overhead depends on real-time assignment.

Hence, based on the above comparisons between the static and dynamic schemes, and with the help of the following two main issues, the research focuses on the dynamic scheme.

- The present state of system forms the basis of load balancing decisions.
- Prior knowledge is not required.

The upcoming section will provide an extensive review of the studies pertained to the different dynamic algorithm approach adopted by multifarious researchers.

Agent Based Approach

Meera and Swamynathan (2013).proposed an agent based resource monitoring system aimed to balance the CPU and memory utilization. The proposed algorithm collects the information regarding the virtual machine resource usages and shows it in a dashboard. This display on the dashboard includes the key performance metrics such as CPU and memory utilization. The statistical report of the dashboard provides the key information to cloud administrator regarding the resource optimization. The findings of the evaluation revealed promising performance outcome regarding the CPU and memory utilization.

Singh et al. (2015) suggested an autonomous agent based load balancing (A2LB) algorithm, which rendered dynamic load balancing for cloud environments. A satisfactory outcome is provided by the suggested mechanism, which is already enforced. The performance of two different applications with two different approaches of conveyance forms the basis of the proposed mechanism. The load among machines can be consequently adjusted by few applications, as demonstrated by the experimental outcomes. Consequently, a superior functioning with a distribution approach can be anticipated in large scale simulations.

Load Balancing Algorithm Based on Ant Colony Optimization

Seeking an optimal way between the ant colony and the food source is the ant colony optimization's objective, which is attained by using the ants' behavior as the basis. The work load is effectively distributed among the nodes through this method. The movement is initiated by an ant from the head node to the food source after a request is received. In cloud computing service provider (CCSP), a regional load balancing node (RLBN) is selected as a head node. A record of each of the visited nodes is maintained by the ants as a future reference. The next node is selected by ants through the pheromones deposited by an ant. Several elements, such as quality of food, distance of food, etc., determine the pheromones' intensity. The successful completion of a job is followed by the updating of pheromones. A set of outcomes built by the ants is eventually utilized to formulate a comprehensive solution. Instead of updating their own outcome set, the ants update a single outcome set ceaselessly. The solution set is endlessly updated by the trials of the ant pheromones (Hua, Zheng, & Hu 2010).

Li et al.(2011)proposed a cloud task scheduling algorithm for balancing the load on the basis of Ant Colony Optimization (LBACO) algorithm. The study targeted the balancing of the entire system load and the minimization of the makespan of a given set of task. The study used the CloudSim toolkit to simulate the proposed scheduling strategy. The findings revealed the fact that the proposed LBACO algorithm outperformed FCFS and the basic ACO Ant Colony Optimization algorithms. However, the major draw is that the study left out the possibility of precedence constraint between tasks and also the study assumed the tasks are computationally intensive, which is not realistic for cloud systems. Above all, in order to accommodate the heterogeneous processing of the tasks, the availability vector should be extended to incorporate information about task requirements.

Song, Gao and Wang (2011) proposed a job scheduling algorithm based on ant colony algorithm so as to smoothen the balancing of load among the nodes. The findings indicated that the proposed one is a promising Ant Colony Optimization algorithm for job scheduling in a cloud computing environment.

Tawfeek et al. (2013) proposed a dynamic algorithm based on ant colony optimization for achieving cloud computing tasks scheduling. At first, the study experimentally determined the best values of parameters for ACO algorithm. Then, the evaluation of ACO algorithm in applications with the number of tasks, varying from 100 to 1000, is performed. The findings demonstrated that ACO algorithm outperforms FCFS and RR algorithms.

Xin (2016) presented an ant colony resource allocation algorithm for large-scale, sharing and dynamic characteristics of the cloud environment, and for the user's job search and allocate computing resources. The findings indicated that the proposed algorithm is performed effectively in searching and allocating resources in the cloud computing environment.

Guo (2017) proposed an ant colony algorithm to minimize the makespan and the total cost of the tasks, while balancing the system. Furthermore, the study also used the heuristic function, initialization of the pheromone, and the pheromone update method. The study used the CloudSim platform to carry out the simulation. The findings were compared with algorithms of ACO and Min-Min. The results indicated that the proposed algorithm outperformed the other two algorithms in system load balancing, makespan and costs. However, the study did not consider the dependency between tasks, increase the number of tasks in the experiment and customer satisfaction.

Decentralized Content Aware

Mehta, Kanungoand and Chandwani (2011) proposed a new decentralized workload and client aware scheduling algorithm named as workload and client aware policy (WCAP). In order to specify the special and particular assets of the computing nodes and requests, a parameter called USP is used by a new content aware load balancing policy known as workload and client aware policy. The appropriate node for processing the requests is determined by the scheduler, which is facilitated by USP. This method is executed with low overhead and in a decentralized manner. The system's overall performance is improved due to the narrowing of search enabled by the information on content. Additionally, the utilization of computing nodes is enhanced due to their idle time being reduced by the content information.

Casalicchio and Colajanni (2001) proposed an early version of decentralized content aware scheduling algorithm called client-aware policy (CAP). The proposed algorithm categorizes the client requests with respect to their anticipated impact on main server components. The classification of the web sites includes web commerce which provides the generated information using secure protocols like HTTPS or SSL, web publishing which contains the web pages with simple database access query, web transaction which contains the web pages with the complex database access query, and web multimedia which deliver audio, video streaming. The study compared the proposed CAP algorithm with round robin and LARD strategy. The findings of the simulation revealed that the proposed algorithm improved web cache hit rate and yielded better results for both static and dynamic web sites. However, the major drawback is that this strategy is analyzed and implemented only for web server cluster.

The study by Xu et al. (2007) proposed a scalable and decentralized content aware dispatching policy for web cluster. The proposed algorithm used distributed hash based dispatching mechanism. The findings indicated that the proposed algorithm resolved the scalability problem of centralized algorithm and the communication overhead problem existing in the decentralized strategies like locality and load balancing (L2S). However, the major drawback of this algorithm is that it incurs high overhead for the load communication between the servers.

Carton

Stanojevic and Shorten (2009) proposed a novel algorithm called *Carton*. The proposed algorithm combines the use of distributed rate limiting (DRL) and load balancing (LB). The study used LB for equally distributing the jobs to different servers, in order to minimize the associated costs and DRL is used assure the fair resource allocation. This algorithm is simple and easy to implement with very low computation and communication overhead.

Al-Rayisand Kurdi (2013) proposed the cloud is managed by a mechanism known as CARTON. The tasks are distributed by LB to unique servers for minimizing the related costs; and, in order to sustain a fair allocation of resources, the DRL is used. The CARTON algorithm is easy to execute and also with a low communication overhead and computation.

Event-Driven

Chen et al. (2005) proposed an early version of latterly developed event driven algorithm, based on a static partitioning of the game world. The algorithm attempted to obtain an adequately fine load balancing by using a high number of small zones. The algorithm also maps adjacent zones on topologically nearby nodes in order to reduce the communication overhead. However, the assumption of the method that the network load represents the bottleneck when provisioning games is the major drawback since the processor requirements are most critical in the fast-paced games.

Lu, Parkin and Morgan (2006) presented a load balancing algorithm which is similar to the latterly introduced event driven algorithm. This algorithm was specifically designed for massively multiplayer online games (MMOG) servers and hence involves the management of an arbitrary subset of the clients. The algorithm achieves load balancing by adjusting the number of clients assigned to each server. However, the complexity involved in the client management makes this approach unsuited for fast-paced FPS game.

Nae et al. (2010) proposed Real-time massively multiplayer online games (MMOG) comprise of an event-driven load balancing set of rules, which receive information on activities and capacity. The sport consultation load balancing actions are consequently generated by the algorithm as the components are examined in accordance with the resources and the worldwide sport consultation. A game session on multiple sources that are consistent with the variable person load can be scaled up and down by the algorithm. Nevertheless, breaches in QoS have been reported from time to time.

Adaptive Load Balancing Algorithms

Dinitto et al. (2007) proposed a self-aggregation algorithm based on simple local rules in order to determine certain global properties to the entire system without any centralized control or scaling issues. The study used a distributed simulator to analyze the performance of the proposed algorithm. The findings indicated that the fast and the adaptive algorithms favor high speed the fast algorithm with a passive protocol helps to reduce the number of messages. Furthermore, the study also found out that the adaptive algorithms are good choice if optimality is the critical factor. In conclusion, the adaptive algorithm, due to its "adaptive" nature, performs well in most common situations, except in extreme situations.

Tchernykh et al. (2014) presented a new adaptive load balancing algorithm for cloud networking. In this algorithm the system's present state and historical information is used by the scheduling strategy on load balancing of virtual machine resources. A generic set of rules is used by this technique for reducing the dynamic migration and attaining excellent load balancing. Further, higher useful resource utilization is attained due to the excessive migration cost being reduced and the difficulty of load imbalance being resolved by the strategy.

Lau, Lu and Leung (2006) proposed a class of adaptive LB algorithms, namely GR algorithms for heterogeneous distributed systems. The proposed algorithm has the distinguished characteristics, such as the dynamic sender–receiver negotiation on batch size and use of batch assignments. The GR algorithms consist of GR protocol for negotiation on batch size, symmetrically initiated location policy for pairing up senders and receivers and TBC scheme for composing the actual task batch. The proposed GR algorithm considers the processing speed of the task senders and receivers and their current workload while negotiating a task batch size. The GR protocol allows a natural preference in assigning tasks to the nodes with higher processing speeds. Furthermore, the proposed algorithm eliminates the possibility for processor thrashing and state waggling. The task batch composition (TBC) scheme which is independent of other algorithm components, has the capability of formulating themselves with respect to the different performance objectives. The simulation results indicated the performance advantages provided by GR algorithms over a number of well-known LD algorithms. Above all, the flexibility in formulating TBC schemes makes GR algorithms applicable in real-time systems and in systems subject to burst task arrivals. However, the effectiveness of GR algorithms in such areas is to be further investigated.

Table 1. Analysis of the load balancing mechanism

Author(s)	Technique	Strength	Scheme	Focus Area
Zhang et al.	Dynamically CP and Heuristic allocation of cloud data center's resources	Maximize the resource utilization from) first-fit and best-fit	Performance Based	Refining the model to account for the energy consumption for providing data center services
Lau et al.	Guarantee Reservation(GR) protocol and Task batch composition (TBC) scheme	Maximize the processing speed of sender and receiver	Demand Based Load Balanced	Performance on Real Time system
Ferreto et al.	LP formulation and heuristic	Server consolidation with migration control	Energy Efficient	Migration control without downtime
Forsman et al.	Push and Pull Strategy	Rebalance the load when VMs added and removed	Load Management	Downtime can be Less.
Li et al.	Dynamic VM Placement	Minimizing the total completion time	Performance Based	Hybrid scheme of integrating off-line Placement into online scenario.
Andreolini et al.	Dynamic load management of virtual machines	Robust and selective reallocations	Performance Based	Heterogeneous infrastructures and platforms
Beloglazov et al.	Dynamic consolidation of virtual machines	SLA based load management	Energy Efficient	Researchers can focus on multi-core CPU architectures
Joseph et al.	Genetic Approach	SLA based Resource Management, Maximize the Hardware resource Utilization with performance	Resource management	Modify the algorithm to decrease the calculation time in terms of prediction process to improve the Genetic algorithm convergence speed

CONCLUSION

This chapter conducted a set of research-literature reviews to decide what kind of infrastructure the system will use and to identify the appropriate algorithms and parameters. The reviews targeted various load balancing algorithms and approaches that can either be modified with minimal effort or can fit the study objectives directly. The study also conducted an in depth review of the research papers which are

Table 2. Review analysis on load balancing mechanism, strength, focuses area and used tools

Author(s)	Approach	Focus Area	Used Tools	Future Recommendation(s)
Singh et al.	Dynamic Load Balancing	Maximum resource utilization, maximum throughput, minimum response time	CloudSim	User can use Heuristic approach
Cao et al.	Performance-driven task scheduler	Resource Utilization	PACE resource tool	Use of another grid tool e.g. Globus MDS and NWS
Ferreto et al.	Server consolidation with migration control	Energy Efficient	Zimpl language using for LP formulation and Python using for Heuristic approach performed with Inter Core 2 Deo with 2.4 Ghz and 4 GB primary memory.	Migration control without downtime
Forsman et al.	Rebalance the load when VMs added and removed	Load Management	OMNeT++	Downtime can be Less
Bitam	Minimization the execution time on process resources	NP- Complete problem	Real Environment	Implement with Genetic approach
Lin	VMs resource management by computing application	Resources Utilization	CloudSim	Try with other approaches
Kabalan et al.	Never Queue Policy	Heteroge-neous Computing System	Simulate the operation of the modified SED, NQ and GT policies in a heterogeneous network	Use of Real Environment with some modification
Kopaneli et al.	Multi-criteria decision making (MCDM)	Information gathering and distribution of load	Unified cloud modeling language CloudML@artist	Adaptation and testing of advanced multi-criteria decision making algorithms
Kruekaew	Reduce the makespan of DC processing time	Longest Job first	CloudSim	Heterogeneous tasks can be used
Joseph CT et al.	Minimization of VM	Energy efficient	CloudSim	LP approach

Table 3. Authors' technique and description

Author(s)	Technique	Description
Singh et al.	Autonomous Agent Based	Agent based approach maximize the throughput; minimize the response time and migration time
Cao et al.	Agent-based grid management	Researchers uses the PACE resource management tool to maximize the resource utilization
Ferreto et al.	LP formulation and heuristic	Uses the heuristic approach to maximize the utilization of resources by automatic live migration of VMs
Forsman et al.	Push and Pull Strategy	Maximizes the utilization of physical machines by using bidding policy
Bitam	Honey Bee	Job Scheduling mechanism considered the NP- Complete formulation for proper distribution of load among the all available nodes
Lin	Threshold based Dynamic Approach	Resource allocation at the application level rather than physical management of resources
Kabalan et al.	Adaptive Load Sharing	Manages the heterogeneous computing system by never queue policy
Kopaneli et al.	Adaptive Cloud Target Selection CTS) tool methodology	Adaptive target selection mechanism approach and utilization of resources in near to real environment
Kruekaew	Honey Bee	Reduces the time of data processing
Joseph et al.	Genetic	Minimizes the energy consumption by reduction of VM migrations

closely related to the interest of the present study. Considering these factors, the present study conducted a comprehensive review of the studies pertained to a various task allocation based load balancing algorithms (static and dynamic) and the load balancing algorithms which uses virtual machine migration (non-live and live). The review analyzed the efficiency in term of their performance metrics such as scalability, throughput, reliability, response time, and migration time, etc.

REFERENCES

Al-Rayis, E., & Kurdi, H. (2013, November). Performance Analysis of load balancing Architectures in Cloud computing. In *Proceedings of the Modelling Symposium (EMS), 2013 European* (pp. 520-524). IEEE.

Alakeel, A. M. (2010). A guide to dynamic load balancing in distributed computer systems. *International Journal of Computer Science and Information Security*, *10*(6), 153–160.

Andreolini, M., Casolari, S., Colajanni, M., & Messori, M. (2009, October). Dynamic load management of virtual machines in cloud architectures. In *Proceedings of the International Conference on Cloud Computing* (pp. 201-214). Springer.

Aswathi, Sharma, & Mahesh. (2016). An Enhancement of Throttled Load Balancing Algorithm in Cloud using Throughput. *IJCTA*, *9*(15), 7603–7611.

Beloglazov, A., & Buyya, R. (2015). OpenStack Neat: A framework for dynamic and energy efficient consolidation of virtual machines in OpenStack clouds. *Concurrency and Computation*, *27*(5), 1310–1333. doi:10.1002/cpe.3314

Bitam, S. (2012 Feb). Bees life algorithm for job scheduling in cloud computing. *Proceedings of the Third International Conference on Communications and Information Technology*, 186-191.

Buyya, R., Ranjan, R., & Calheiros, R. N. (2010, May). Intercloud: Utility-oriented federation of cloud computing environments for scaling of application services. In *Proceeding of International Conference on Algorithms and Architectures for Parallel Processing* (pp. 13-31). Springer. 10.1007/978-3-642-13119-6_2

Calheiros, R. N., Ranjan, R., Beloglazov, A., De Rose, C. A., & Buyya, R. (2011). CloudSim: A toolkit for modeling and simulation of cloud computing environments and evaluation of resource provisioning algorithms. *Software, Practice & Experience*, *41*(1), 23–50. doi:10.1002pe.995

Casalicchio, E., & Colajanni, M. (2001). A client-aware dispatching algorithm for web clusters providing multiple services. *Proceedings of the 10th International World Wide Web Conference*, 535-544. 10.1145/371920.372155

Chen, H., Wang, F., Helian, N., & Akanmu, G. (2013, February). User-priority guided Min-Min scheduling algorithm for load balancing in cloud computing. In *Proceeding of Parallel computing technologies (PARCOMPTECH), 2013 national conference on* (pp. 1-8). IEEE.

Chen, J., Wu, B., Delap, M., Knutsson, B., Lu, H., & Amza, C. (2005, June). Locality aware dynamic load management for massively multiplayer games. In *Proceedings of the tenth ACM SIGPLAN symposium on Principles and practice of parallel programming* (pp. 289-300). ACM. 10.1145/1065944.1065982

Chen, S. L., Chen, Y. Y., & Kuo, S. H. (2017). CLB: A novel load balancing architecture and algorithm for cloud services. *Computers & Electrical Engineering, 58*, 154–160. doi:10.1016/j.compeleceng.2016.01.029

Dave, Y. P., Shelat, A. S., Patel, D. S., & Jhaveri, R. H. (2014, February). Various job scheduling algorithms in cloud computing: A survey. In *Proceedings of Information Communication and Embedded Systems (ICICES), 2014 International Conference on* (pp. 1-5). IEEE.

Di Nitto, E., Dubois, D. J., & Mirandola, R. (2007, December). Self-aggregation algorithms for autonomic systems. In Bio-Inspired Models of Network, Information and Computing Systems, 2007. Bionetics 2007 (pp. 120-128). IEEE.

Domanal, S. G., & Reddy, G. R. M. (2014, January). Optimal load balancing in cloud computing by efficient utilization of virtual machines. In *Proceeding of Communication Systems and Networks (COMSNETS), 2014 Sixth International Conference on* (pp. 1-4). IEEE.

Fang, Y., Wang, F., & Ge, J. (2010). A task scheduling algorithm based on load balancing in cloud computing. *Web Information Systems and Mining*, 271-277.

Ferreto, T. C., Netto, M. A., Calheiros, R. N., & De Rose, C. A. (2011). Server consolidation with migration control for virtualized data centers. *Future Generation Computer Systems, 27*(8), 1027–1034. doi:10.1016/j.future.2011.04.016

Forsman, M., Glad, A., Lundberg, L., & Ilie, D. (2015). Algorithms for automated live migration of virtual machines. *Journal of Systems and Software, 101*, 110–126. doi:10.1016/j.jss.2014.11.044

Gopinath, P. G., & Vasudevan, S. K. (2015). An in-depth analysis and study of Load balancing techniques in the cloud computing environment. *Procedia Computer Science, 50*, 427–432. doi:10.1016/j.procs.2015.04.009

Gunarathne, T., Qiu, J., & Fox, G. (2011). *Iterative mapreduce for azure cloud. CCA11 Cloud Computing and Its Applications*. Chicago: Academic Press.

Guo, Q. (2017, April). Task scheduling based on ant colony optimization in cloud environment. In *Proceedings of AIP Conference* (Vol. 1834, No. 1, p. 040039). AIP Publishing. 10.1063/1.4981635

Gupta, D., Cherkasova, L., Gardner, R., & Vahdat, A. (2015). (2006, November). Enforcing performance isolation across virtual machines in Xen. In *Proceedings of the ACM/IFIP/USENIX 2006 International Conference on Middleware* (pp. 342–362). Springer-Verlag New York, Inc. Retrieved from https://pubs.vmware.com/vsphere50/index.jsp#com.vmware.vsphere.vm_admin.doc_50/GUID-E19DA34B-B227-44EE-B1AB-46B826459442.html

Hua, X. Y., Zheng, J., & Hu, W. X. (2010). Ant colony optimization algorithm for computing resource allocation based on cloud computing environment. *Journal of East China Normal University, 1*(1), 127–134.

James, J., & Verma, B. (2012). Efficient VM load balancing algorithm for a cloud computing environment. *International Journal on Computer Science and Engineering, 4*(9), 1658.

Joseph, C. T., Chandrasekaran, K., & Cyriac, R. (2015). A novel family genetic approach for virtual machine allocation. *Procedia Computer Science, 46*, 558–565. doi:10.1016/j.procs.2015.02.090

Kabalan, K. Y., Smari, W. W., & Hakimian, J. Y. (2002). Adaptive load sharing in heterogeneous systems: Policies, modifications, and simulation. *International Journal of Simulation, Systems, Science and Technology, 3*(1-2), 89–100.

Kim, C., & Kameda, H. (1992). An algorithm for optimal static load balancing in distributed computer systems. *IEEE Transactions on Computers, 41*(3), 381–384. doi:10.1109/12.127455

Kokilavani, T., & Amalarethinam, D. G. (2011). Load balanced min-min algorithm for static meta-task scheduling in grid computing. *International Journal of Computers and Applications, 20*(2), 43–49.

Kolb, L., Thor, A., & Rahm, E. (2012, April). Load balancing for mapreduce-based entity resolution. In *Proceeding of Data Engineering (ICDE), 2012 IEEE 28th International Conference on* (pp. 618-629). IEEE.

Kopaneli, A., Kousiouris, G., Velez, G. E., Evangelinou, A., & Varvarigou, T. (2015). A model driven approach for supporting the Cloud target selection process. *Procedia Computer Science, 68*, 89–102. doi:10.1016/j.procs.2015.09.226

Kruekaew, B., & Kimpan, W. (2014). Virtual machine scheduling management on cloud computing using artificial bee colony. In *Proceedings of the International Multi-Conference of engineers and computer scientists* (*Vol. 1*, pp. 12-14). Academic Press.

Lau, S. M., Lu, Q., & Leung, K. S. (2006). Adaptive load distribution algorithms for heterogeneous distributed systems with multiple task classes. *Journal of Parallel and Distributed Computing, 66*(2), 163–180. doi:10.1016/j.jpdc.2004.01.007

LD, D. B., & Krishna, P. V. (2013). Honey bee behavior inspired load balancing of tasks in cloud computing environments. *Applied Soft Computing, 13*(5), 2292–2303. doi:10.1016/j.asoc.2013.01.025

Li, K., Xu, G., Zhao, G., Dong, Y., & Wang, D. (2011, August). Cloud task scheduling based on load balancing ant colony optimization. In *Proceeding of Chinagrid Conference (ChinaGrid), 2011 Sixth Annual* (pp. 3-9). IEEE.

Liao, J. S., Chang, C. C., Hsu, Y. L., Zhang, X. W., Lai, K. C., & Hsu, C. H. (2012, September). Energy-efficient resource provisioning with SLA consideration on cloud computing. In *Proceeding of Parallel Processing Workshops (ICPPW), 2012 41st International Conference on* (pp. 206-211). IEEE.

Lin, W., Wang, J. Z., Liang, C., & Qi, D. (2011). A threshold-based dynamic resource allocation scheme for cloud computing. *Procedia Engineering, 23*, 695–703. doi:10.1016/j.proeng.2011.11.2568

Lu, C., & Lau, S. M. (1995). An adaptive algorithm for resolving processor thrashing in load distribution. *Concurrency and Computation, 7*(7), 653–670. doi:10.1002/cpe.4330070706

Lu, F., Parkin, S., & Morgan, G. (2006, October). Load balancing for massively multiplayer online games. In *Proceedings of 5th ACM SIGCOMM workshop on Network and system support for games* (p. 1). ACM. 10.1145/1230040.1230064

Mahalle, H. S., Kaveri, P. R., & Chavan, V. (2013). Load balancing on cloud data centres. *International Journal of Advanced Research in Computer Science and Software Engineering, 3*(1).

Meera, A., & Swamynathan, S. (2013). Agent based resource monitoring system in IaaS cloud environment. *Proceeding of International Conference On Computational Intelligence: Modeling Techniques and Applications.* 10.1016/j.protcy.2013.12.353

Mehta, H., Kanungo, P., & Chandwani, M. (2011, February). Decentralized content aware load balancing algorithm for distributed computing environments. In *Proceedings of the International Conference & Workshop on Emerging Trends in Technology* (pp. 370-375). ACM. 10.1145/1980022.1980102

Nae, V., Prodan, R., & Fahringer, T. (2010, October). Cost-efficient hosting and load balancing of massively multiplayer online games. In *Proceedings of the Grid Computing (GRID), 2010 11th IEEE/ACM International Conference on* (pp. 9-16). IEEE.

Nathan, S., Kulkarni, P., & Bellur, U. (2013, April). Resource availability based performance benchmarking of virtual machine migrations. In *Proceedings of the 4th ACM/SPEC International Conference on Performance Engineering* (pp. 387-398). ACM. 10.1145/2479871.2479932

Nayak, S., & Patel. (2015). A Survey on Load Balancing Algorithms in Cloud Computing and Proposed a model with Improved Throttled Algorithm. *International Journal for Scientific Research & Development, 3*(1).

Ni, J., Huang, Y., Luan, Z., Zhang, J., & Qian, D. (2011, December). Virtual machine mapping policy based on load balancing in private cloud environment. In *Proceeding of Cloud and Service Computing (CSC), 2011 International Conference on* (pp. 292-295). IEEE.

Nikita. (2014). Comparative Analysis of Load Balancing Algorithms in Cloud Computing. *International Journal of Science and Engineering.*

Pasha, N., Agarwal, A., & Rastogi, R. (2014, May). Round Robin Approach for VM Load Balancing Algorithm in Cloud Computing Environment. *International Journal of Advanced Research in Computer Science and Software Engineering, 4*(5).

Patel, G., Mehta, R., & Bhoi, U. (2015). Enhanced load balanced min-min algorithm for static meta task scheduling in cloud computing. *Procedia Computer Science, 57*, 545–553. doi:10.1016/j.procs.2015.07.385

Patel, N. H., & Shah, J. (2016). Improved Throttling Load Balancing Algorithm With Respect To Computing Cost and Throughput For Cloud Based Requests. *IJARIIE, 2*(3), 2192-2198.

Penmatsa, S., & Chronopoulos, T. (2011, April). Game-theoretic static load balancing for distributed systems. *Journal of Parallel and Distributed Computing, 71*(4), 537–555. doi:10.1016/j.jpdc.2010.11.016

Radojevic, B., & Zagar, M. (2011). Analysis of issues with load balancing algorithms in hosted (cloud) environments. In *Proceedings of 34th International Convention on MIPRO.* IEEE.

Raj, A. (2015). A New Static Load Balancing Algorithm in Cloud Computing. *International Journal of Computers and Applications, 132*(2).

Rathore, N., & Chana, I. (2014). Load balancing and job migration techniques in grid: A survey of recent trends. *Wireless Personal Communications, 79*(3), 2089–2125. doi:10.100711277-014-1975-9

Rotithor, H. G. (1994). Taxonomy of dynamic task scheduling schemes in distributed computing systems. *Proceeding of IEEE -Computers and Digital Techniques, 141*(1), 1-10.

Sammy, K., Shengbing, R., & Wilson, C. (2012). Energy efficient security preserving vm live migration in data centers for cloud computing. *IJCSI International Journal of Computer Science Issues, 9*(2), 1694–0814.

Shah, N., & Farik, M. (2015). Static load balancing algorithms in cloud computing: Challenges & solutions. *International Journal Of Scientific & Technology Research, 4*(10), 365–367.

Sharma, E., Singh, S., & Sharma, M. (2008). M.: Performance Analysis of Load Balancing Algorithms. *In Proceeding of 38th. World Academy of Science, Engineering and Technology*.

Sharma, T., & Banga, V. K. (2013). Efficient and enhanced algorithm in cloud computing. *International Journal of Soft Computing and Engineering*.

Singh, A., Juneja, D., & Malhotra, M. (2015). Autonomous agent based load balancing algorithm in cloud computing. *Procedia Computer Science, 45*, 832–841. doi:10.1016/j.procs.2015.03.168

Song, X., Gao, L., & Wang, J. (2011). Job scheduling based on ant colony optimization in cloud computing. In *Proceeding of Computer Science and Service System (CSSS), International Conference on*. IEEE.

Sotomayor, B., Montero, R. S., Llorente, I. M., & Foster, I. (2009). Virtual infrastructure management in private and hybrid clouds. *IEEE Internet Computing, 13*(5), 14–22. doi:10.1109/MIC.2009.119

Sreenivas, V., Prathap, M., & Kemal, M. (2014, February). Load balancing techniques: Major challenge in Cloud Computing-a systematic review. In *Proceeding of Electronics and Communication Systems (ICECS), 2014 International Conference on* (pp. 1-6). IEEE.

Tawfeek, M. A., El-Sisi, A., Keshk, A. E., & Torkey, F. A. (2013, November). Cloud task scheduling based on ant colony optimization. In *Proceeding of Computer Engineering & Systems (ICCES), 8th International Conference on* (pp. 64-69). IEEE.

Tchernykh, A., Cortés-Mendoza, J. M., Pecero, J. E., Bouvry, P., & Kliazovich, D. (2014, October). Adaptive energy efficient distributed VoIP load balancing in federated cloud infrastructure. In *Proceedings of the Cloud Networking (CloudNet), 2014 IEEE 3rd International Conference on* (pp. 27-32). IEEE.

Vinothina, V., Sridaran, R., & Ganapathi, P. (2012). A survey on resource allocation strategies in cloud computing. *International Journal of Advanced Computer Science and Applications, 3*(6), 97–104. doi:10.14569/IJACSA.2012.030616

Xiao, Z., Jiang, J., Zhu, Y., Ming, Z., Zhong, S., & Cai, S. (2015). A solution of dynamic VMs placement problem for energy consumption optimization based on evolutionary game theory. *Journal of Systems and Software, 101*, 260–272. doi:10.1016/j.jss.2014.12.030

Xin, G. (2016). Ant Colony Optimization Computing Resource Allocation Algorithm Based on Cloud Computing Environment. *Proceeding of International Conference on Education, Management, Computer and Society (EMCS 2016)*, 1, 2.

Xu, Z., Han, J., & Bhuyan, L. (2007, April). Scalable and Decentralized Content-Aware Dispatching in Web Clusters. In *Proceedings of the Performance, Computing, and Communications Conference, 2007. IPCCC 2007. IEEE International* (pp. 202-209). IEEE.

Zhang, Z., & Zhang, X. (2010, May). A load balancing mechanism based on ant colony and complex network theory in open cloud computing federation. In *Proceeding of Industrial Mechatronics and Automation (ICIMA), 2010 2nd International Conference on* (Vol. 2, pp. 240-243). IEEE.

Chapter 12
Load Balancing and Prudential Hypervisor in Cloud Computing

G. Soniya Priyatharsini
Vel Tech Rangarajan Dr. Sagunthala R&D Institute of Science and Technology, India

N. Malarvizhi
Vel Tech Rangarajan Dr. Sagunthala R&D Institute of Science and Technology, India

ABSTRACT

Cloud computing is a service model in internet that provides virtualized resources to its clients. These types of servicing give a lot of benefits to the cloud users where they can pay as per their use. Even though they have benefits, they also face some problems like receiving computing resources, which is guaranteed on time. This time delay may affect the service time and the makespan. Thus, to reduce such problems, it is necessary to schedule the resources and then allocate it to using an optimized hypervisor. Here, the proposed method is used to do the above-mentioned problem. First, the available resources are clustered with respect to their characteristics. Then the resources are scheduled using this method. Finally, with respect to that of the clients request the resources, the resources are allocated. Here, the cost is the fitness of the allocation.

ELUCIDATING THE CLOUDIFICATION PROCESS

The mesmerizing cloud paradigm has become the mainstream concept in IT today and its primary and ancillary technologies are flourishing. The cloudification movement has blossomed these days and most of the IT infrastructures and platforms along with business applications are being remedied to be cloud-ready in order to reap all the originally envisaged benefits of the cloud idea.

The virtualization technique has put in a firm and fabulous foundation for the runaway success of cloud computing. Especially server machines are being logically partitioned to carve out a few highly insulated virtual machines (VMs). Then there are a number of standards-compliant and industry-strength automation tools for resource provisioning, configuration, orchestration, monitoring, and management, software deployment and delivery. A 360-degree view of IT infrastructural components through an integrated dashboard is the new normal. Thus powerful tools play out a very interesting and inspiring role

DOI: 10.4018/978-1-5225-9023-1.ch012

in making cloud pervasive, persuasive and penetrative. Most of the manual activities associated with the establishment of IT infrastructures, software installation, IT administration and operation, IT services management and maintenance are being automated through a variety of technologies. The concept of DevOps is very enticing these days in order to ensure the incredible requirements of IT agility, adaptivity, and affordability. Automation through templates, patterns, and tools is becoming a common affair in IT lately and to substantially reduce human errors. The productivity of IT systems is being remarkably increased through various ways and means. The processes are synchronized to be lean yet efficient. Domain-specific languages (DSLs) are being brought in to bring the required automation. Platforms are being readied to accelerate IT management, governance, and enhancement. There are standards such as OpenStack and their optimal implementations in order to enforce resource portability, interoperability, accessibility, scalability, live-in migration, etc. That is, the distributed deployment of compute instances and storage appliances under the centralized management is the key differentiator for the prodigious success of cloud computing.

Technology Choice Is Critical

There are several competent yet contrasting technologies in the IT space today and hence the selection of implementation technologies has to be strategically planned and carefully played out. Not only the technologies but also the methodologies need to be smartly carried out. In other words, the technology embarkation and usage have to be done with all seriousness and sagacity otherwise, even if the technologies chosen might be sound yet projects would not see the originally emphasized success. Further on, the history clearly says that many technologies emerged and disappeared from the scene without contributing anything substantial due to the lack of inherent strengths and sagacity. Very few technologies could survive and contribute copiously for a long time. Primarily the intrinsic complexity towards technologies' all-around utilization and the lack of revered innovations are being touted as the chief reasons for their abject and abysmal failure and the subsequent banishment into the thin air. Thus, the factors such as the fitment/suitability, adaptability, sustainability, simplicity, and extensibility of technologies ought to be taken into serious consideration while deciding technologies and tools for enterprise-scale, transformational and mission-critical projects. The cloud technology is being positioned as the best-in-class technology in the engrossing IT domain with all the necessary wherewithal, power, and potential for handsomely and hurriedly contributing for the business disruption, innovation and transformation needs. Precisely speaking, the cloud idea is the aggregation of several proven techniques and tools for realizing the most efficient, elegant and elastic IT infrastructure for the ensuing knowledge era.

The IT Commoditization and Compartmentalization

The arrival of cloud concepts has brought in remarkable changes in the IT landscape that in turn lead in realizing big transitions in the delivery of business applications and services and in the solid enhancement of business flexibility, productivity, and sustainability. Formally cloud infrastructures are centralized, virtualized, automated, and shared IT infrastructures. The utilization rate of cloud infrastructures has gone up significantly. Still, there are dependencies curtailing the full usage of expensive IT resources. Employing the decoupling technique among various modules to decimate all kinds of constricting dependencies, more intensive and insightful process automation through orchestration and policy-based configuration, operation, management, delivery, and maintenance, attaching external knowledge bases are widely prescribed to achieve still more IT utilization to cut costs remarkably. Lately, the aroma of commoditization and compartmentalization is picking up. These two are the most important ingredients of cloudification. Let us begin with the commoditization technique.

- **The Commoditization of Compute Machines**: The tried and time-tested abstraction aspect is being recommended for fulfilling the commoditization need. There is a technological maturity as far as physical / bare metal machines getting commoditized through partitioning. The server commoditization has reached a state of semblance and stability. Servers are virtualized, containerized, shared across many clients, publicly discovered and leveraged over any network, delivered as a service, billed for the appropriate usage, automatically provisioned, composed towards large-scale clusters, monitored, measured, and managed through tools, performance tuned, made policy-aware, automatically scaled up and out based on brewing user, data and processing needs, etc. In short, cloud servers are being made workloads-aware. However, that is not the case with networking and storage portions.

- **The Commoditization of Networking Solutions**: On the networking front, the propriety and expensive network switches and routers and other networking solutions in any IT data centers and server farms are consciously commoditized through a kind of separation. That is, the control plane gets abstracted out and hence, the routers and switches have only the data forwarding plane. That means, there is less intelligence into these systems thereby the goal of commoditization of network elements is technologically enabled. The controlling intelligence embedded inside various networking solutions are adroitly segregated and is being separately developed and presented as a software controller. This transition makes routers and switches dumb as they lose out their costly intelligence. Also, this strategically sound segregation comes handy in interchanging one with another one from a different manufacturer. The vendor lock-in problem simply vanishes with the application of the widely dissected and deliberated abstraction concept. Now with the controlling stake is in pure software form, incorporating any kind of patching in addition to configuration and policy changes in the controlling module can be done quickly in a risk-free and rapid manner. With such a neat and nice abstraction procedure, routers and switches are becoming commoditized entities. There is fresh business and technical advantages as the inflexible networking in present-day IT environments is steadily inching towards to gain the venerable and wholesome benefits of the commoditized networking.

- **The Commoditization of Storage Appliances**: Similar to the commoditization of networking components, all kinds of storage solutions are being commoditized. There are a number of important advantages with such transitions. In the subsequent sections, readers can find more intuitive and informative details on this crucial trait. Currently, commoditization is being realized through the proven abstraction technique.

Thus, commoditization plays a very vital role in shaping up the cloud idea. For enhanced utilization of IT resources in an affordable fashion and for realizing software-defined cloud environments, the commoditization techniques are being given more thrusts these days.

The compartmentalization is being realized through the virtualization and containerization technologies. There are several comprehensive books on Docker-enabled containerization in the market and hence we skip the details of containerization, which is incidentally being touted as the next best thing in the cloud era.

As indicated above, virtualization is one of the prime compartmentalization techniques. As widely accepted and articulated, virtualization has been in the forefront in realizing highly optimized, programmable, managed and autonomic cloud environments. Virtualization leads to the accumulation of virtualized and software-defined IT resources, which are discoverable, network-accessible, critically assessable, interoperable, composable, elastic, easily manageable, individually maintainable, centrally monitored, and expertly leveraged. The IT capabilities are being given as a service and hence we often come across the word "IT as a Service". There is a movement towards the enigma of granting every single IT resource as a service. With the continued availability of path-breaking technologies, resource provisioning is getting automated and this will result in a new concept of "resource as a service (RaaS)".

Bringing in the much-discoursed modularity in order to enable programmable IT infrastructures, extracting and centralizing all the embedded intelligence via robust and resilient software, distributed deployment, centralized management, and federation are being touted as the viable and venerable course of actions for attaining the originally envisaged success. That is, creating a dynamic pool of virtualized resources, allocating them on demand to accomplish their fullest utilization, charging them for the exact usage, putting unutilized resources back to the pool, monitoring, measuring and managing resource performance, etc. are the hallmarks of next-generation IT infrastructures. Precisely speaking, IT infrastructures are being software-defined to bring in much-needed accessibility, consumability, malleability, elasticity, and extensibility.

On-demand IT has been the perpetual goal. All kinds of IT resources need to have the inherent capability of pre-emptively knowing of users' as well as applications' IT resource requirements and accordingly fulfil them without any instruction, interpretation, and involvement of human resources. IT resources need to be scaled up and down based on the changing needs so that the cost can be under control. That is, perfect provisioning of resources is the mandate. Overprovisioning raises up the pricing whereas under-provisioning is a cause for performance degradation worries. The cloud paradigm transparently leverages a number of software solutions and specialized tools in order to provide scalability of applications through resource elasticity. The expected dynamism in resource provisioning and de-provisioning has to become a core and concrete capability of clouds.

That is, providing right-sized IT resources (compute, storage and networking) for all kinds of business software solutions is the need of the hour. Users increasingly expect their service providers' infrastructures to deliver these resources elastically in response to their changing needs. There is no cloud services infrastructure available today capable of simultaneously delivering scalability, flexibility and high operational efficiency. The methodical virtualization of every component of a cloud center ultimately leads to software-defined environments.

Cloud Resource Management Methods

Cloud computing serves a virtualization environment for the cloud user with the resources available. Using this technique, the users are able to store their data in internet. They also are able to use those data whenever they need through internet. This facility is commonly available in cloud as the user can user it by pay per use. The biggest advantage in this design is that the user need not install the software or any other hardware. There is no need for the cloud customers (Himthani et al, 2017) to find any huge geographical locations for the servers. Cloud service provider (CSP) provides all these to the customers as pay per use.

There are mainly three types of the services these CSPs are providing. They are Infrastructure as a service (IaaS), Platform as a Service (PaaS), and Software as a Service (SaaS). This work concentrates on IaaS for the resource allocation and scheduling process. (Patel et al, 2017) There are some hurdles in the resource management methods. Those are Resource fragmentation, Resource overlapping, Resource scarcity, Resource overprovisioning and Resource underprovisioning.

1. **Resource Fragmentation:** It is the situation of deadlock position where the resources are available but cannot be allocated to that instance.
2. **Resource Overlapping:** It is the situation of two instances tries to occupy the same resource.
3. **Resource Scarcity:** Here this situation occurs when there is not sufficient amount of the resources as per the cloud user's request.
4. **Resource Over Provisioning:** When a cloud user gets excess amount of the resources than he/she needs it leads to this situation.
5. **Resource Under Provisioning:** This situation is opposite to the overprovisioning state. That is, it occurs when the customer lacks the resources.

The resource scheduling process can be categorized by three types. It is shown in Figure 1.

Scheduling methods can be hugely clustered as resource scheduling, task scheduling and workflow scheduling. In this work the resource scheduling and its allocation is focused. Table 1 explains the various resource allocation methods with parameters.

To satisfy the customers throughout the internet world, the cloud providers are competing with various techniques. The major work of them is to provide the resources with 100% satisfaction to the customers. There are various techniques available for the resource provisioning. Some of them are,

- Cost benefit algorithm
- Resource rental planning
- Genetic algorithms
- Virtualization
- Dynamic scaling technique
- Reconfiguration algorithms

Figure 1. Types of scheduling methods

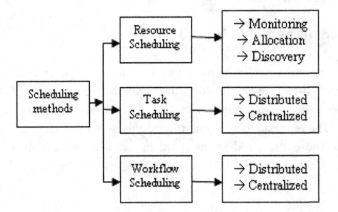

Table 1. Resource allocation methods

Methods	Description
Even	Evenly allocate residual resources to tasks.
First come Most	The task that starts the earliest is given residual resources.
Shortest time left most	The task that will complete the soonest is given residual resources (on a per-node basis).
Longest time left most	The task that will complete the latest is given residual resources (on a per-node basis).
Speculative-Tasks-Most	Speculative tasks are given residual resources.
Laggard-Tasks-Most	Straggler tasks are given residual resources.

This work concentrates on the cost benefit algorithm. Even though resource allocation plays a vital role in the cloud service providers, it also gives rigidity to the CSPs. Some of the challenges are given in Figure 2.

To overcome the above mentioned problems it is necessary to design an algorithm or a method which reduces the resource management problems. Here thus proposed method by identifying and consolidating the physical servers. The proposed work gives the solution for the above mentioned problems. The remaining sections explain the existing work, proposed method, results and conclusions of the work.

LITERATURE SURVEY

Several algorithms and various types of methods lead to the energy efficient in cloud computing (Priyatharsini et al, 2018). Gema (2018) in her paper explains the load balancing technique in cloud computing. This paper uses the throttle algorithm; the algorithm deploys the VM status in the available PMs. When the user requests the resource for the service provider checks the availability using load balancer. By using this algorithm, the VM is allocated. Thus in the implementation side they do not have much complexity.

In paper (Mistra et al, 2012) Mayank Mishra et al. describes about the cloud computing usage. He also highlights the advantages of the services of the cloud such as pay per use etc. Thus there is no need for the cloud consumer to create a big environment for the cloud infrastructure. The maintenance of the data center can also be taken care of the cloud service provider (CSP). Thus as a service model the cloud is good in maintaining the resources.

Figure 2. Threatening in Cloud resource management

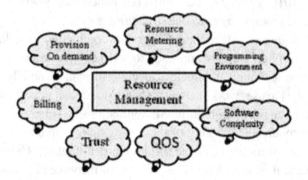

Jose et al (Lucas-Simarro et al, 2012) proposed an algorithm where the cloud manager periodically collects the information about the cost and the instance in the database. Here the CSP have to update the latest cost details to the cloud user. These types of the details can be useful for the dynamic data uploading. The scheduler in the CSP is fully taken care of the migration details of the VMs.

Hongbo et al (Liu et al, 2012) proposed a scheduling algorithm in workflow applications. A distributed security constraint for the data environments is contributed for the scheduling. Here this paper presents a variable for particle swarm for the neighborhood where it compares the algorithm with the genetic algorithm which is multi start.

In (Lee et al, 2012) the reconciliation of these conflicting objectives by scheduling service requests with the dynamic creation of service instances is addressed. Specifically, the scheduling algorithms attempt to maximize profit within the satisfactory level of service quality specified by the service consumer.

Haizea et al. (Nathani et al, 2012) proposed an abstraction method and implement those along with the VMs. This paper also listed 4 types of the allocation policies of resources. They are advanced reservation, best effort, and deadline sensitive. This concentrates on reducing the total number of the leases. This dynamic based scheduling allows new leases and allocates the schedule whenever the new request occurs. The result shown maximizes the resource utilization with respect to that of the existing algorithms.

Zhang et al. (Huaa et al, 2011) in his paper proposed a cloud database algorithm for the scheduling problem. It combines the genetic algorithm and ant colony algorithm. The initial value for the input of the ant colony is having the optimal solution. To control the two algorithms' fusion process, it sets up the genetic controller. It also proposes a database effectively and rapidly which also reduces the load balancing dynamically. It tries to prove that it is energy efficient.

Baomin et al (Xu et al, 2011) proposed a mechanism with an algorithm which provides the quality of service in the resource allocation and the scheduling policies. According to this paper the basic three principles of the algorithm is explained. Firstly, the task's general expectation is classified in the allocation of the resource. Next, to run the task the better resources of the virtual machines are selected. Finally based on the resource allocation's results, the fairness justice function is calculated. They mainly focus on the execution time, performance and QoS, while this paper focusses on load balancing and the makespan in cloud data center.

There are some scheduling methods in cloud which is described in Table 2.

Gihun et al. (Jung et al, 2011) proposed a customer resource allocation to the data center which is based on the consumer's geographical place and also the data center workload in the cloud environment. The method of the test bed method is used to test this method. While comparing the resource allocation, the proposed algorithm gives a better response time for allocation rather than the other resource allocation models.

Gopalakrishna et. al. (2016) explains an adaptive resonance theory which identifies and solves the pattern of incoming request problem by auto classifications and organizes pre-allocation strategies in a predictive way. This technique can reduce the cost per task completion in a cloud environment.

Nilolas et. al. (2016) introduces a new approach to self adaptive resource allocation in virtualized environments. It is based on an online architecture level performance models. Such models are used to predict the effects of changes in user workloads. It also used to predict the effects of the reconfigurations respectively. It also used in the prevention of the SLA violations and also the unwanted resource usage.

Xavier et. al. (2015) explains the working of the automatic resource allocation techniques for reinforcement learning to perform resource allocation in cloud computing. One of the main problems in cloud is resource allocation. It is listed here. The problem of resource allocation in cloud computing is

Table 2. Scheduling methods in cloud computing environment

Scheduling	Method	Parameters
Benefit Driven, Power Best Fit, Load Balancing	Energy Consumption, Cost, Load balancing	Cost and the power consumption is reduced
Cost Based Multi QoS Based DLT scheduling	Load balancing, Makespan, QoS, Performance, Cost	DLT based optimization model is designed for getting better overall performance
DENS	Traffic load balancing, Congestion, Energy consumption	Communication load is considered and job consolidation is done to save energy
Energy efficient method using DVFS	Energy Consumption, Makespan, Execution time	Energy saving as per load in the system producing better makespan
First Come first Serve	Arrival time	Simple in implementation
Genetic Algorithm	Makespan, Efficiency, Performance, Optimization	Better performance and efficiency in terms of makespan
Job Scheduling based on Horizontal Load Balancing	Load balancing, Response time, Resource utilization, cost	Probabilistic assignment based on cost.
K-percent Best	Makespan, Performance	Selects the best machine for scheduling
Minimum Execution Time Algorithm	Expected execution time	Selects the fastest machine for scheduling
Minimum Completion Time algorithm	Expected completion time, Load balancing	Load balancing is considered
Min-Min, Max-Min	Makespan, expected completion time	Better makespan compared to other algorithms
Opportunistic Load Balancing	Load balancing	Better resource utilization
Priority based Job Scheduling Algorithm	Priority of tasks, Expected completion time	Priority is considered for Scheduling. Designed based on multiple criteria decision making model
Round Robin	Arrival time, Time quantum	Less complexity and load is balanced more fairly
Switching Algorithm	Makespan, Load balancing, Performance	Schedules as per load of the system, better makespan
WLC based Scheduling	Load balancing, Efficiency, Processing Speed	Dynamic task assignment strategy proposed, task heterogeneity is considered

discussed which also deals with the problem in the framework of Q learning. The paper also presents the implementation of the workflow meant to bring reinforcement learning to real cloud computing infrastructures.

Saeed et. al. (2016) proposes a framework for the security aware approach in resource allocation in clouds. It allows the user for effective enforcement of defense in depth for cloud VMs. Modeling the customer's requirements and the cloud provider's constraints as a constraint satisfaction problem (csp), which can be solved by using satisfying ability module theories. solvers for reducing risk and improving manageability in cloud.

The remaining content of this paper explains the proposed method for energy efficiency in cloud computing. Then it compares with existing methods and the results and discussion is explained. Finally, the conclusion of the work is given.

PROPOSED WORK

There are many parameters which are used to weigh the resource scheduling. Some of the important factors are:

- Load Balancing
- Makespan
- Energy Consumption
- Cost
- Completion Time
- Performance
- Resource Utilization
- Efficiency

In this proposed method, the energy efficiency, completion time, load balancing and cost were considered. The resource monitoring steps for the proposed model is given in the Figure 3 and 4.

On the basis of the service level agreement, both the service provider and the cloud user have the rights to monitor the resources available. When it finds that the resources are over provision or crashed then the provider will stop or migrate the VM resourcing.

This monitoring process is done by the cloud service provider. Here the load balancing takes place when the resources are found to be underutilized. This process will give better resource utilization efficiently.

The common steps for resource monitoring are given in Figure 5.

Figure 3. Resource monitoring process at service and infrastructure

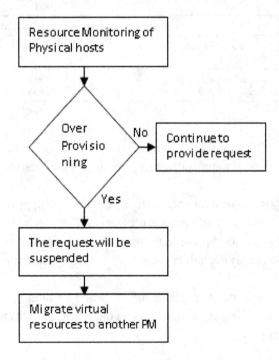

Figure 4. Monitoring resources with load balancing approach

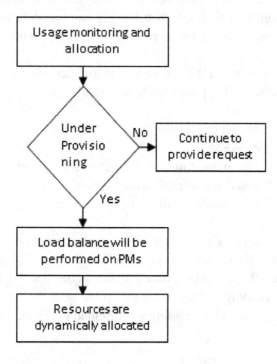

Figure 5. Resource monitoring steps

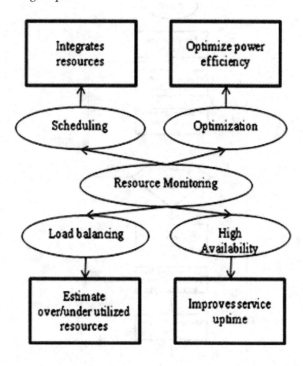

It is observed that for good resource management method, it should follow the four major steps. Optimizing, checking for high availability, load balancing and scheduling. In (Himthani et al, 2017) the availability of resource and the optimization process is detailed. Thus the scheduling process of the resources is shown here.

The goal of this work is to minimize the makespan and to distribute the loads efficiently to schedule the resources. To do this, the following points are to be considered:

- All the identified data to be deterministic.
- All the tasks must be independent
- The identified capacity of the request must be a positive real number.
- Every VM should be allocated to a sing physical machine.
- All the PMs should be readily available all the time.

The mentioned points are considered in this work for the betterment of the scheduling process. The workflow for the scheduling of the resources is given in Figure 6: For VM scheduling it is important to schedule the VM to the right PM. The appropriate PM should be allocated for the usage of the VM. If it is done, then the overprovisioning and the under provisioning of the resources can be avoided. This work describes the VM allocation and scheduling for the cloud user's request.

Figure 6. Workflow for proposed scheduling

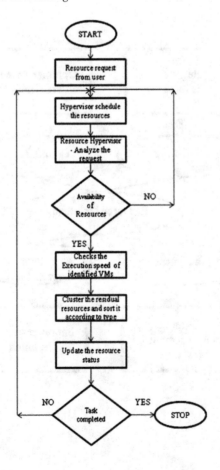

This work considering the n number of the requests, where the ith request is having the start time of s_i and finish time of f_i. Assuming the capacity required as c_i.

The resources considered here are the CPU, Memory and Network bandwidth. Zheng et al (Zheng et al, 2006) implements the indexing algorithm as below eq. 1.

$$I = a \times \frac{N1i \times Ci}{N1m \times Cm} + b \times \frac{N2i \times Mi}{N2m \times Mm} + c \times \frac{N3i \times Di}{N3m \times Dm} + d \times \frac{NETi}{NETm} \tag{1}$$

Here i, m are index and the id of the PM

N1,2,3 are parameters of CPU, Memory, Bandwidth

C, M, D is utilization of the CPU, Memory and transfer rate of HD. The goal here is to minimize the value of I which seeks to allocate request to PM. This work considers the parameters of PM resource, VM resource, Average CPU Utilization, Load efficiency, makespan, Imbalance level of CPU, skew of makespan.

PM resource can be mentioned by its index number i, storage capacity of CPU, Memory and Bandwidth as pCPU, pMemory, pBW. PM resource can be mentioned by its index number i, storage capacity of CPU, Memory and Bandwidth as vCPU, vMemory, vBW. T^{start}_j, T^{end}_j are the start time and end time of VM. The average CPU utilization of PM_i during the time slot 0 and T_n. It is considering as $pCPU^u_i$.

$$pCPU^u_i = \frac{\Sigma^n_k =_D pCPUui \times Ti}{\Sigma^n_k =_D Tk} \tag{2}$$

$$Avg_i = \frac{pCPUui + pMemui + pbw}{3} \tag{3}$$

Makespan is the same as the traditional definition and therefore the capacity makespan (Mathew et al, 2016) of all the PMs can be formulated as follows

$$Capacity_{makespan} = max_i(L_i) \tag{4}$$

Here $L_i = \sum_{j \in Avg(i)} cjtj$. cj and the tj gives total capacity request and length of the processing time request of VMj. Here the main objective is to minimize the total load.ie capacity makespan. Skew (Grahm, 2016) of the makespan is denoted by

$$skew_{makespan} = \frac{min \, i \, Li}{max \, i \, Li} \tag{5}$$

The result of this shows any degree of slanting.

The Load imbalance can be calculates using the formula

$$IL_{total} = IL_{cpu +} IL_{mem +} IL_{bw} \tag{6}$$

$$IL_{cpu} = \frac{\Sigma_k^n =_D (CPUui - pCPU\ avg)2}{n} \tag{7}$$

Higher the value of these gives the better degree of skewness.

With the help of the proposed model the skewness can be reduced so that the VM migrations can be done with the help of the proper scheduling technique.

```
private static void printCloudletList(List<Cloudlet> list) {
int size = list.size();
Cloudlet cloudlet;
String indent = "      ";
Log.printLine();
Log.printLine("=====OUTPUT ======");
Log.printLine("Cloudlet ID" + indent + "STATUS" + indent
+ "Data center ID" + indent + "VM ID" + indent + "Time" + indent + "Start
Time" + indent + "Finish Time");
DecimalFormat dft = new DecimalFormat("###.##");
for (int i = 0; i < size; i++) {
        cloudlet = list.get(i);
        Log.print(indent + cloudlet.getCloudletId() + indent + indent);
 if (cloudlet.getCloudletStatus() == Cloudlet.SUCCESS) { Log.print("SUCCESS");
Log.printLine(indent + indent + cloudlet.getResourceId() + indent + indent +
indent + cloudlet.getVmId()+ indent + indent + dft.format(cloudlet.getActual-
CPUTime()) + indent + indent + dft.format(cloudlet.getExecStartTime())+ indent
+ indent + dft.format(cloudlet.getFinishTime()));
        }}
```

This shows the complete allocated and scheduling process of the VMs. This continues until the user's request is completed. This can be proved while comparing with the existing methods. Blesson (2018) gives the future trends in the cloud computing along with the load balancing. . The results obtained are discussed in the next section.

RESULTS AND DISCUSSIONS

To justify and conclude the proposed method, the simulation is done by using the cloudsim 3.0 simulator on 32 bit windows 7 Operating System. The Physical and virtual machine set ups are given in tables 3 and 4. This paper uses the following VM configuration. It uses 3 types. The first PM uses the types of 1, 2 and 3. The second PM uses the types of 4, 5 and 6. Finally the type 3 is used by the third PM.

Table 3. VM types used

VM Type	Storage	Memory	CPU
1-1(1)	160 GB	1.7 GB	1 unit
1-2(2)	850 GB	7.5 GB	4 units
1-3(3)	1690 GB	15 GB	8 units
2-1(4)	420 GB	17.1 GB	6.5 units
2-2(5)	850 GB	34.2 GB	13 units
2-3(6)	1690 GB	68.4 GB	26 units
3-1(7)	350 GB	1.7 GB	5 units
3-2(8)	1690 GB	7 GB	20 units

The types of the VM mentioned in table 3 are explained briefly in table 4. Here the workload considered are 25, 50, 100,500 cloudlets for the cloud workflows.

Considering the VM requests as 200 and the duration time as varying the following results are obtained. The time duration considered here are 15, 30 and 60.

Figure 7, 8, 9 shows the comparison of the IL, makespan and skews with the various VM requests. Here the requests are considered as 200. It varies the maximum duration of VMs. The simulations of the three different simulations of the same inputs are given. By using the skew of the makespan, load balancing for the scheduling can be processed. It is the index for calculating load balancing.

Table 4. PM Types

Type	Storage	Memory	CPU
1	3380 GB	30 GB	16 units
2	3380 GB	136 GB	52 units
3	3380 GB	14 GB	40 units

Figure 7. Comparisons of load with varies VMs

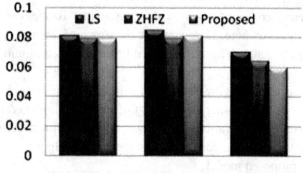

209

Figure 8. Comparisons of makespan with varies VMs

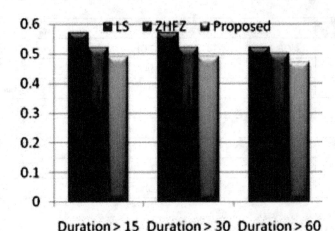

Figure 9. Comparisons of skews of makespan with varies VMs

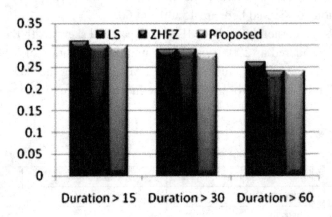

Figure 8 explains the comparison between the makespan with various virtual machines. Here the number of physical machine is fixed as 5. But PMs will vary between 5 and 20. As described in the code above, the characteristics, such as memory, Bandwidth, and CPU are considered here. It selects the PMs with the underneath integrated value as calculated in equ 6.

These results are given after 3 simulations with same inputs. To measure the load scheduling and the sharing skew is the key index here. Here assumes the usage of the homogeneous PMs. As per equ (3) it is proved that while allocating VM to the pooled PM with the minimum load balance creates the efficient scheduler.

In this paper the three formulations are tested for 15 times to retrieve the best, worst and the average values. So by comparing with the existing algorithms the proposed model is shown in tables 5, 6 and 7.

Table 5 and Figure 10 explain the various values, worst, best and the average test values for the various inputs. By comparing this it can be concluded that the existing algorithms can be overlapped by the values retrieved from the proposed model.

The comparisons of the skewness of the makespan with the various VMs are given in the Table 6 and Figure 11. It explains the various values, worst, best and the average test values for the given inputs. So

Table 5. Best, Worst and average results for the values of capacity makespan

Algorithm	Optimal	Worst	Average
LS	0.014858	0.0198452	0.0275211
ZHFZ	0.014321	0.0125425	0.0225841
Proposed	0.014210	0.0121314	0.0225841

Figure 10. Comparisons of the capacity makespan with various cases

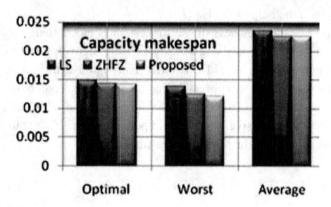

Table 6. Best, worst and average results for the values of load imbalance

Algorithm	Optimal	Worst	Average
LS	3.012547	2.9562147	2.9925631
ZHFZ	2.941257	2.6584121	2.9841253
Proposed	1.830146	136473010	1.8730142

Figure 11. Comparisons of skews of makespan with varies VMs

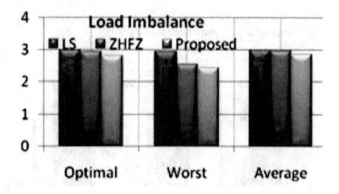

Table 7. Best, worst and average results for the values of skew makespan

Algorithm	Optimal	Worst	Average
LS	3.256847	2.5681201	3..4285296
ZHFZ	3.1254413	2.4125631	3.3052176
Proposed	3.0143302	2.2114512	3.2041061

by analyzing the obtained chart it can be concluded that the values of the model improve the quality of the scheduling process with the help of the Eq. 7.

By using the Equation 5, the skewness of the makespan is calculated. Table 7 and the Figure 12 illustrate the comparison of the proposed and already existing algorithm test values. By analyzing the values, and the chart obtained, it can be said to be effectively good as the existing algorithms.

From the simulated testing above it is observed that the total makespan of the existing and proposed model are ranging in some same minutes are some very few seconds difference. The results obtained are very close to capacity skewness. It also gives 0.2 to 1.3 percent more efficient in the scheduling process. Hence these simulations authorized the theoretical results.

CONCLUSION

The emerging technology cloud computing faces some problems in the resource allocation side. In this paper, the proposed method is used to allocate and schedule the resources. The resources like CPU, memory and Bandwidth are considered. The parameters like load imbalance, skew and capacity makespan are considered to find the result. From the result section it is concluded that by using this proposed method it is possible to schedule the resources and allocate it in a good manner. The simulation results shown works well for the given input. This method can be considered in the scheduling of the resources cost efficiently. This method combines the capacity and the skewness of the makespan which yields fair results. In future work, variation of the PMs and VMs, fixing the number of the PMs can be considered.

Figure 12. Comparisons of skews of makespan with varies VMs

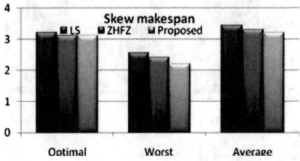

REFERENCES

Al-Haj, Al-Shaer, & Ramasamy. (2016). Security aware resource allocation in clouds. *IEEE 10th International Conference on Services Computing*. doi:10.1109/ SCC.2016.36

Dutreilhy, X., Kirgizov, S., Melekhova, O., Malenfant, J., Rivierrey, N., & Truckz, I. (2015). Using reinforcement learning for autonomic resource allocation in clouds: Towards a fully automated workflow. *ICAS 2015: The Seventh International Conference on Autonomic and Autonomous Systems*, 67 - 74.

Gopalakrishnan & Jayarekha. (2016). Pre allocation Strategies of computational resources in cloud computing using adaptive resonance theory 2. *International Journal on Cloud Computing Services and Architecture, 1*(2). doi:10.5121/ijccsa.2016.1203

Graham. (2016). Bounds on multiprocessing timing anomalies. *SIAM Application of Maths, 17*(2), 29-41.

Himthani, P. (2017). Efficient technique for allocation of processing elements to virtual machines in cloud environment. International Journal of Computer Science and Network Security, 16(8).

Huaa, Leia, & Zhia. (2011). Optimization of Cloud Database Route Scheduling Based on Combination of Genetic Algorithm and Ant Colony Algorithm. *Procedia Engineering, 15*, 3341 – 3345.

Huber, N., Brosig, F., & Kounev, S. (2016). *Model based self adaptive resource allocation in virtualized environments*. 6th International symposium on software engineering for Adaptive and Self Managing Systems, Honolulu, HI. doi: 10.1145/ 1988008.1988021

Jung, G., & Sim, K. M. (2017). Agent based adaptive resource allocation on the cloud computing environment. *40th International Conference on Parallel Processing Workshops*, 345-341. DOI 10.1117/ICPPW.2017.18

Lee, Y. C., Wang, C., Zomaya, A. Y., & Zhoua, B. B. (2012). Profit driven scheduling for cloud services with data access awareness. *J. Parallel Distrib. Comput., 72*, 591–602.

Liu, H., Abraham, A., Snanel, V., & McLoone, S. (2012). Swarm scheduling approaches for work-flow applications with security constraints in distributed data-intensive computing environments. *Information Sciences, 192*, 228–243. doi:10.1016/j.ins.2011.12.032

Lucas-Simarro, J. L., Vozmediano, R. M., Montero, R. S., & Llorente, I. M. (2012). *Scheduling strategies for optimal service deployment across multiple clouds*. Future Generation Computer Systems, SciVerse ScienceDirect.

Mathew, Sitaraman, & Shenoy. (2016). Energy aware load balancing in content level delivery networks. *Proceedings of IEEE INFOCOM*, 954-962.

Mistra, Das, Kulkarni, & Sahoo. (2012, September). Dynamic resource management using virtual machine migrations. *IEEE Communications Magazine*, 34-40.

Nathani, A., Chaudharya, S., & Somani, G. (2012). Policy based resource allocation in IaaS cloud. *Future Generation Computer Systems, 28*(1), 94–103. doi:10.1016/j.future.2011.05.016

Patel, J., & Prajapathi, J. (2017). A Survey scheduling algorithms and types of resources provisioning in cloud environment. *International Journal of Engineering and Computer Science, 4*(1), 10132-10134.

Priyatharsini & Malarvizhi. (2018). RHEA: resource hypervisor and efficient allocator in cloud. *International Journal of Engineering & Technology, 7*(1), 21-26.

Ramadhan, G., Purboyo, T. W., & Latuconsina, R. (2018). Experimental Model for Load Balancing in Cloud Computing Using Throttled Algorithm. *International Journal of Applied Engineering Research, 13*(2), 1139-1143.

Varghese, B., & Buyya, R. (2018). Next generation cloud computing: New trends and research Directions. *Future Generation Computer Systems, 79*, 849–886. doi:10.1016/j.future.2017.09.020

Xu, B., Zhao, C., Hua, E., & Hu, B. (2011). Job scheduling algorithm based on Berger model in cloud environment. *ScienceDirect, Advances in Engineering Software, 42*(7), 419–425. doi:10.1016/j.advengsoft.2011.03.007

Zheng, H., Zhou, L., & Wu, J. (2006). Design and implementation of load balancing in web server cluster system. *J Nanjing Univ Aeronaut, 38*(3).

Chapter 13
Cloud–Based Adaptable Energy–Efficient Medium–Access Control Protocol for Healthcare Analysis

M. J. Carmel Mary Belinda
Vel Tech Rangarajan Dr. Sagunthala R&D Institute of Science and Technology, India

E. Kannan
Vel Tech Rangarajan Dr. Sagunthala R&D Institute of Science and Technology, India

M. Hemanth Chakravarthy
Accenture Technology, India

ABSTRACT

A remote mechanism-based new technology called wireless body area network (WBAN) is provided to observe and collect patient health record data with the aid of some wearable sensors. It provides privacy for healthcare professionals and an excellent degree of system security and also plays a major task in storing and ensuring the patient's records. A novel focus for preventing resources of wireless sensor network is implemented to bring a convenient plat form for the healthcare professionals. The adaptable energy efficient MAC protocol is presented in this chapter for the preservations of energy, and its result is discussed for the healthcare analysis.

INTRODUCTION

WBAN is the technique for observing the health condition of the person through collecting the information from various embedded sensors. The main components of this network are sensor nodes and actuators. Sensors are designed based on the user needs and are embedded within the human body to observe the human body organ functionalities. Some instances are ECG sensor designed for monitoring heart activities, brain electrical activity and so on. WBAN nodes are suggested with taxonomy of IEEE

DOI: 10.4018/978-1-5225-9023-1.ch013

802.15.6 and these are embedded within the human body. WBAN gathers human body signals for health monitoring. Based on the enough reliability and equal balancing, the medium access protocols are more utilized in WBAN applications. This energy efficient MAC provides dynamic bandwidth allocation to meet all the sensors necessities and also avoids packet transfer delay.

Especially in several emergency medical things, there is increased need of data for the diagnosing and to create additional correct call. During information transfer, loss of some packets can offer threatening results that brings the human life panic. Therefore to enhance the dependability and potential of information transmission in WBAN, this approach works smart and offers strength and low energy consumption. This forms a final resolution for medical body area networks. This resolution is obtained by the collaboration of sensing element. This choice of IEEE 802.15.6 unit of MAC protocol provides the supply of quality of service (QoS), which is measured in terms of dependability, latency and energy potential.

In health care applications, MAC protocol based on the sensor network capable of adapting to the changes related to network like change of network size, sensor node density and network topology. This framework gives a stage to share therapeutic data, applications, and foundation in inescapable and completely mechanized way. Correspondence security and patient's information protection are the angles that would build the certainty of clients in such remote medicinal services frameworks. Also it increases the storage and the computing power of WBAN to maximum extent. The health care sensors will measure the Physiological Values (PVs) of the human body and transfer these values to the various servers very confidentially which are maintained under the cloud environment of hospital.

Based on the measured Physiological Values, medical personnel experts connected to the cloud can suggest the patient's treatment. The resources and data for all the registered users are created o within the hospital community cloud. Under this environment the secure communication of sensors and privacy of patients' knowledge are evaluated.

RELATED WORK

The term wireless network refers to Sensor Networks, Ad-hoc Networks, WBAN and WHAN. Wireless networks consist of a group of nodes with the wireless communication between the nodes. This network does not have any predefined infrastructure. Its begins from the home appliances to defense field communication applications. In an emergency, communication network for a rescue-team is one of the potential applications of a wireless network (Haas et al.,2006; Hamilton 2002).

Defining the WSN-based healthcare system is the difficult task. Under health care services; each component such as sensor is used in collecting the data from the health care receivers and establishes the hybrid wireless communication for establishing the network. Based on this idea, a simple WSN based heath care system is enhanced. In simple way, the definition for the WSN based Health care system is " A sensor network with set of sensing devices embed at home or at patient body with the proper communication links from the central data management system to attain the health care monitoring tasks". Among the many communication paradigms, structure of the logical service provider and communication interconnection infrastructure is paid more importance.

Mrinmoy Barua et al.(2011), proposed an secure data transmission design in WBAN for data integrity. This user-centric design shares the data among all the sensors with a secret key to minimize processing requirements and the additional memory requirement. The results obtained based on security analysis proves this scheme provides proper privacy and security. And also it reduces the waiting time of a real time traffic in WBAN.

Xigang Huang et al. (2011) examine the efficiency of energy in cooperative based wireless body area network. Single-relay cooperation, Direct transmission and multi-relay cooperation are three popular transmission schemes that are discussed in his paper. Optimal power allocation with targeted outage probability is analyzed to show its performance. Highly dynamic Destination-Sequenced Distance-Vector (DSDV) routing for mobile computers is discussed by Perkins et al.(1998).This method routes the mobile data to the group of mobile hosts without any involvement of any access point. Also this work proposes an innovative operation for ad-hoc networks.

Dynamic source routing protocol for mobile ad hoc networks is proposed by Johnson et al.(1998). This framework is designed particularly for multi-hop wireless ad hoc networks. Two important mechanism used under this frame work are route maintenance and route discovery. This two mechanism works together to maintain and to discover the routes to arbitrary destinations in the ad hoc network.

A novel algorithm named Ad hoc on demand distance vector (AODV) routing is proposed by Perkins et al. (1998) for the efficient operation of ad hoc networks. In this each mobile host works as a separate router and several routes are established between them on a requirement basis.

Haas et al. (2006) suggested a new hybrid routing protocol named ZRP - Zone Routing Protocol for mobile ad-hoc networks. This protocol is used to span large network and diverse mobility patterns. The routing zone maintains the route within a local region to improve the efficiency of a reactive routing mechanism.

Again Haas et al. (2002) proposed a routing protocol based on gossiping-based approach where each node forwards a message with some probability. This process is done to lessen the issues of the routing protocols.

Location-Aided Routing (LAR) is implemented by Ko et al.(2012),in which he improved the performance of the routing protocols for ad hoc networks. This protocol limits its searching up to the request zone by using the location information in the mobile ad hoc networks.

Basagni et al.(1998) introduced a 'DREAM'- Distance Routing Effect Algorithm for Mobility for ad hoc networks with two novel observations. The main one is the distance effect with the fact that 'if the distance between two nodes is greater than the movement between two nodes are slow with respect to each other.

A contention-based Medium Access Control protocol named T-MAC, an adaptive energy-efficient MAC protocol for wireless sensor networks is proposed by Dam et al.(2003).The reduction in the consumption of energy through the active or sleep duty cycle is the main objective of this protocol.

Wang et al.(2008) discussed the ideas for the health care applications, in which the ECG data taken for the analysis of human identification for the biometric recognition.In this analysis of the data an approach based on the auto correlation with Discrete Cosine Transform (DCT) is introduced for effective analysis of the ECG data for the health care analysis.

Agrafioti et al. (2009) also recognized the systematic analysis of the electrocardiogram (ECG) signal for application in human recognition. Here ECG biometric analysis in cardiac irregularity conditions is analyzed.

Biel et al. (2001) introduced a multivariate analysis for the identification task. This new approach performs ECG analysis by McDonagh et al.(2007) in human identification. A standard 12-lead electrocardiogram (ECG) is recorded during analysis. A person in the predetermined group is identified by the corresponding features extracted from the ECG data.

An study on verification of humans using the electrocardiogram data is applied by Wubbeler et al. (2007) This study is also based on the biomedical applications based on the realistic scenario for ECG biometrics is analyzed.

Stevan Marinkovic et al. (2011) implemented a nano power wake up radio based on the wireless networks for the low power consuming wireless applications. WSN based frame work for human health monitoring is proposed by Jananiet al. (2011) in which a radio is utilized to measure the robustness and power consumptions of the communications.

Srikkanth Govindaraajan et al. (2009) introduced an associate technology named Red tacton,this uses the physique for the transferring of the information .This methodology uses IEEE 802.3 common place to transmit the digital information .This methodology brings no damage to the physique while sending the signals.

Jae-Hoon Choi et al. (2011) planned a brand new Quadrature Amplitude-Position-Modulation (QAPM) for saving the ability. This methodology shows the real demo of however the WSN is applied for perceptive the patient's health. The main factors this methodology focuses square measure vary of power consumption and measurability.

Tommi Ttovinen et al. (2012) gift a unique UWB loop antenna with off-body link and on-body link to eliminate the harmful effects of physique tissues. Yao (2005) introduced a healthcare system that is wearable for home use and it has wireless standards and plug and-play features. The factors like power consumption, information storage, information transmission, and device synchronization and mobility are addressed by the IEEE 1073 standard.

Chevrollier et al, (2005) uses the wireless network technologies in health environments and conjointly it spotlight on the suitableness of wireless technologies in attention environments. Wireless Personal Area Network technologies like Bluetooth and therefore the low-rate specifications represented within the IEEE 802.15.4 standard is in

use here. Brunelli et al. (2006) introduced bio-feedback system. Communication protocols, power management policies and application-level management are tuned to optimize price, battery autonomy and period of time performance needed for this application. The sensor network is intended to be distributed on the user's body for balance observance and correction.

Lamprinos et al. (2005) established energy efficient MAC protocol for patient personal area networks. This includes a wireless infrastructure of medical sensors which is attached to the patient's body for laying a path for continuous and real-time monitoring. This infrastructure develops the context of remote healthcare services by supporting flexible acquisition of crucial vital signs.

REVIEW OF ROUTING IN MULTI SLOT MAC

Designing MAC Protocol is a complex research domain and widely focused with the area of Wireless Sensor Networks (WSN) Yew et al. (2006) and Heidemann (2003).In a research article proposed by Lamprinos et al.(2005) introduced a design for Patient Personal Area Networks based on MAC protocol in which master-slave architecture is employed. This scheme brings a limit on the duty cycles of slave node. Always the nodes with low duty cycle are preferred.

As a major project Yew et al.(2006) proposed a application based on the energy wastage in wireless sensor networks due to traffic fluxes and protocol overhead, listening, eavesdropping and are collisions are analyzed.

BACKGROUND STUDY

Communication Interconnection Structure

The logical structure of WSN-based healthcare system includes four Tier architecture .They are Patient Tier, Professional Tier, Relatives Tier and Back-communication-bone Tier, as shown in Figure 1.

Patient Tier includes the large collection of data stream flow within the network. The data collection about patient is done by BSN and HSN together. Some portion of data is send out of this tier through the gateway device.

Professional Tier with powerful computers play a vital role as data storage centre in determining the each movement of the patients in case of emergency issues. From the Patient tier, it receives the data and also sends the control data to the patient tier. With the help of Relatives Tier, the notification information to the patient's family members and other relatives are provided. The Relatives Tier act as information gathering platform composed of daily communication devices. Back communication bone Tier plays a vital role as a communication backbone in connecting with the other tiers.

Structure of Logical Service Provider

Service Oriented Approach (SOA) is followed in WSN-based healthcare system as shown in Figure 2. The body sensors provide the sensor data service to the BSN communication service client and HSN

Figure 1. Back communication bone tier

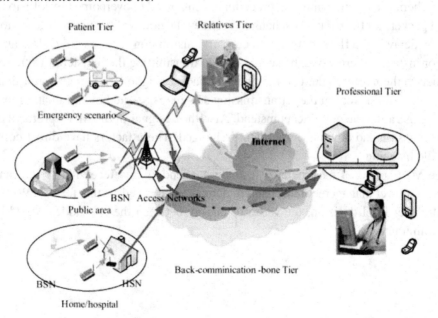

Figure 2. Service-oriented architecture for WSN-based healthcare system

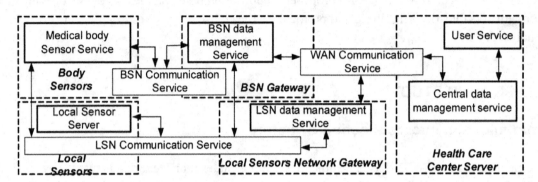

communication service Client through the HSN gateway and BSN Gateway. BSN communication service provider and HSN communication service provider helps in providing the service by requesting them through the BSN data management service. Hence, the healthcare centre server can also access the sensor data. Through this system the efficiency of healthcare personnel is improved and this is obvious in reducing the medical errors.

MAC SUBLAYER

MAC sub layer stands in the midst of the physical link layer and network layer to access the communication channel and manipulates the upcoming higher layer's payload of the communication stack. Design principle of the MAC protocol lies on most important factors like power consumption, throughput, quality of service (QoS) and transmission delay. Based on these factors, the MAC protocol designer design of the protocol by formulating the exact weight factors for each of them. The designer should design a MAC protocol for incorporating a avoidance of collision mechanism, correction of error algorithms with are transmission scheme. The retransmission procedure is enhanced to overcome the collision. The sending of recognized packets for the payload exchanged between the nodes of the network leads to issues which occurs variable delay in the flow of traffic. In certain transmission services only a less amount of delay is allowed. For instance, there would be small delay in transmitting the registered value from the medical sensor node to the master node. Until the current packet is ignored, the retransmission is permitted to a certain limit. For this reason the retransmission scheme is aborted by eliminating the current data packet and by generating the next packet instead. Also the designer of the MAC protocol deals the time taken for transmission and amount of the data exchanged. These factors have direct consistency with the issue of idle listening.

Lastly, the MAC protocol must be able to integrate sending and receiving power management. A geology specific power management mechanism demand is elevated by this feature. With dynamic and sophisticated power level decision, the waste of energy between the two nodes would be eliminated during the communication.

IMPLEMENTATION OF AEE- MAC PROTOCOL

AEE –MAC Protocol Design

For designing the MAC protocol, the prototype setup for the wireless network using different sensors of medical and a supervising node is established. To carry out the functions of physical link layer, the transceiver 'nRF2401' is constructed by Nordic. With the help of microcontroller, the resulted power and the frequency of the operating channel is programmed. The data rates supported by these operations are 250kbps and 1Mbps with certain meters of the distance covered. 2.4- 2.5 GHz ISM band single-chip radio transceiver is designed. Low power microcontroller is used for controlling the transceiver.

Mac Protocol Features

Eliminating the energy wastage, collision manipulation, channel overhearing and transmitting power level issues as handled by MAC protocol design. At the same time, it also ensures the reliability in data exchange, frame integrity check. Based on the master-slave architecture view, the slaves acts as the medical sensor nodes and the master nodes are administrating node and permits data transmission to the slave nodes. Data exchange is initiated by the application software of the master node. Each sensor is assigned a unique global address. Depending on the 'Request to send' system the information is transmitted from the slaves to master. Data loss is given by Forward Error Control (FEC). To avoid the issues, four types of timeslots is utilized . They are RX Slot (Receive Slot), TX Slot(Transmit Slot), RXS Slot (Receive to Synchronize Slot) and SB Slot (Stand By Slot).Receiving data is done during the RX Slot or RXS Slot and is implemented in the slave nodes. Master and slave nodes transceiver are switched off during the stand by slot.

MAC Sub Layer Functionality

Control packets and the data packets are the two important types of packets utilized by the communication layer. Also these packets are responsible for the request grant for the communication channel utilization, connection establishment between the slave and master node and right choice of selecting the slave by master node. CRC-16 is the cyclic redundancy check word and is calculated by making use of the normal generator polynomial. The generated CRC word is related to the received CRC field in same procedure. Hamming code is applied detect and correct up to 5 bit burst error comprises within each 16-bit block.

Each transmitted 26-bit block consists of 10-bit check word which is evaluated during several to CRC method. No data loss is assured by the error detection and correction process. In favor to reduce the recurrence of transmission rules we introduce a mechanism of piggy backing the acknowledgment of a received packet into the next packet to be transmitted.

Nodes Synchronization - Overhearing Avoidance

The coordination between the ace and the slaves of the system assumes a noteworthy part in the execution of a power sparing focused MAC convention, gave that it supplies in the avoidance of sit out of gear listening periods. In the first place, the slave hub replaces between SB Slot and RXS Slot. The beginning minimization in obligation cycle by 33% and an ensuing 33% lessening in utilization of vitality are portrayed in the technique of timeslot adjustment comes about. In these cases, the time amid which the handset capacities in rest mode in a RX opening can offer up to 99.97% of the timeslot length. The modification of timeslot plot does not bring about genuine deterioration of transmission postpone that ought to likewise be expressed.

Collision Avoidance

The second issue that the planned MAC convention that objectives is to determine is crash of bundles whose transportation meets one another. The procedure interest for retransmission that decays the throughput of the framework and augmentation the transmission postpone which inadequately influences the general proficiency of a MAC convention.

Power Management

As a conclusion we can accomplish a topology specific optimization of power consumption advancing in the more energy-efficiency. Exploits only the data of retransmissions number to determine the output power level that is built up by power management mechanism now.

ADAPTABLE ENERGY EFFICIENT MAC (AEE-MAC) FOR HEALTH CARE ANALYSIS

Timeliness and proficient vitality administration are the key target to the accomplishment of WSNs for well being applications. In AEE-MAC a dynamic obligation cycle highlight is actualized in Simple MAC with a specific end goal to accomplish the objective of diminishing the idleness for postpone touchy applications.

The fundamental favorable position of the dynamic obligation cycle modification subject is that it winds up in bring down idleness and higher quantifiability than S-MAC, though conveying a ton of sparing force utilization per parcel. All hubs begin with a similar obligation cycle at first. It duplicates its obligation cycle by shortening its rest period length, without changing its listening period. Patients admitted to social insurance foundations for the most part have infections or wounds of different severi-

Figure 3. Timeslot alteration and data exchange between master and slave nodes

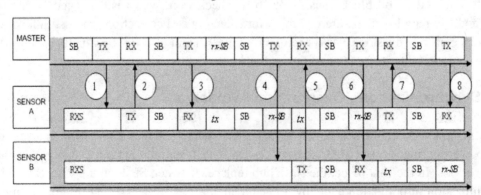

ties. In this way, the route inside which movement is portrayed for medicinal updates from patient to specialist should gather extraordinary idea. The Dynamic Sensor Adaptable vitality productive Medium Access Control (AEE-MAC) convention that records for the different movement sorts by contextualizing them as customary (routine information by Class 2), cautioning (high need by Class 1), and crisis activity (most elevated need by Class 0). This grants AEE-MAC convention to empower the organized channel provisioning for separated administration upheld the class.

To calculation to acknowledge class-based channel get to, AEE-MAC convention expands the IEEE 802.15.6 QoS MAC convention by using a preemptive administration planning.

Figure 4 give the particulars of WSN-based social insurance framework. In this structure, essential or ordinary physiological information are gained from the patients through sensors types of gear for medicinal practices by the specialists or attendants with low layer support of remote correspondence advances.

System Requirements AEE-MAC Protocol

For human services observing applications, there is an expanding need to create adaptable, reconfigurable, and clever low power remote sensor arrange (WSN) framework. Both outline and improvement of such very incorporated framework are specialized progressions in miniaturized scale sensors, smaller scale electromechanical framework (MEMS) gadgets, low power hardware, and radio recurrence (RF) circuits and frameworks have empowered.

In this remote sensor organize system, this is isolated into control and information ways with various transmission frequencies. By 2.4 GHz band, the control way sends the power and capacity control summons from PC to every sensor hubs. There are four levels in the WSN framework. The information way transmits estimated information from sensor layer to sensor amass layer by 2.4 GHz, and transmits between sensor gathering, application and framework layers by 60 GHz.

This progressive engineering will make it conceivable to reconfigurable guide application to WSN. The precise pipeline control framework will propel the execution effectively, and the versatile low power control framework that will lessen heaps of intensity utilizations. Efficient Energy Medium Access Control calculations are required for hubs to accomplish high throughput to share a transmission medium. A Medium Access Control calculation plans bundle transmissions in order to that control the time which

Figure 4. WSN-based healthcare system components

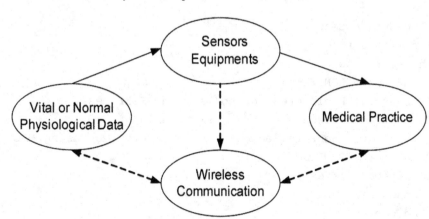

taken to send the parcels without impacts. When considering remote specially appointed and sensor organizes Medium Access Control calculation need to preserve vitality and also give great throughput.

Most of the previous MAC calculations for the remote systems are intended to figure well underneath less activity rates. Amid this outline, under nearly high movement rates a trade conveyed calculation Ad-ATMA for remote unforeseen and detecting component systems is anticipated. We show misuse reproductions that Ad-ATMA beats the least difficult existing calculations intended for higher activity rates as far as parcel conveyance greatness connection and inertness while overpowering for all intents and purposes indistinguishable vitality as them. There is decent enthusiasm for misuse rising remote innovations to help remote patient observing in an unnoticeable, solid and financially savvy way by giving customized property administrations to the patients. Potential to significantly enhance wellbeing arrangement, indicative checking, and illness following and related therapeutic methods in the Medical Body Area Networks (MBANs) that is one among the rising innovation.

MBANs need to provide highly reliable and low power communications for medical devices, that especially those implanted in the human body.

Obstruction can be caused by heritage frameworks that work in a similar recurrence groups or by different MBANs working at a similar recurrence and in a similar area. Impedance relief calculations and systems must be viably bolstered by developing conventions, the radio obstruction issues must be along these lines surely knew.

Algorithm for Proposed AEE-MAC Protocol

Algorithm 1 depicts the general procedure for the AEE-MAC protocol.

The sensor ID and sensor space are given in light of the fact that the info parameter. The ith enlisted sensor and Slots I (# demonstrates the quantityof assigned openings to it sensor). Consequently, the size of CFM is variable and its length relies upon the TDMA plan length that is up to 1600 bytes in our reenactments. Each sensor's offer inside the data gathering area is determined by (1)

Algorithm 1. The AEE-MAC Protocol

```
1.        Procedure AEEMAC
2.        SensorsCountRegistered← Empty
3.        While true do
4.        Send(create BCNFrame())
5.        SensorsCountRegistered.append(Receive REGFrames())
6.        Eliminatedepartedsensors(SensorsCountRegistered)
7.        LIST ←Listed Sensors(SensorsCountRegistered) by using MAC
8.        Send(create CFMFrame(LIST)
9.        ReceiveDataFrames()
10.        end While
11.        End procedure
```

$$\sigma_i = \left| \frac{\dfrac{d_i}{l_i}}{\displaystyle\sum_{j \in R} \dfrac{d_j}{l_j}} \eta_{slot} \right| \tag{1}$$

where σ_i, d_i, l_i, R, and n space individually indicate the quantity of distributed TDMA openings to sensor I, the rest of the measure of information in sensor to be transferred, the separation between sensor I and the finish of the dynamic zone in meters and the aggregate number of TDMA spaces. This condition infers that the sensors having a bigger measure of information to send and a shorter time to speak with the sensors will have a higher need. Subsequently, this strategy shares TDMA openings decently among the enlisted sensors. For this situation, the booking calculation gives the sensors more accumulated information to send, a higher need. The thought behind this reality is that we need to apportion openings just to the sensors that don't leave the dynamic region before the finish of the present time interim and the information gathering stage.

EXPERIMENTAL RESULTS AND DISCUSSIONS

Analysis of Duty Cycle MAC Protocols

Under this research the AEE MAC works fully considering the duty cycle for energy saving. AEE MAC protocols works sleep or wake cycle to recover energy by placing nodes to sleep in idle listening periods. Switch off the nodes when there is no use, this represents the nodes are not in duty phase and the same time it cut down the irrelevant power consumption by upto 70%.It also concentrate on latency for the energy efficient operation. Similar to MAC, our AEE MAC promises in saving the efficient energy in transferring nodes if the sensor to either idle or sleep. Figure 5 shows the normal power consumption of MICA2 sensor in different radio modes.

Figure 5. MICA2 sensor power consumption in normal mode

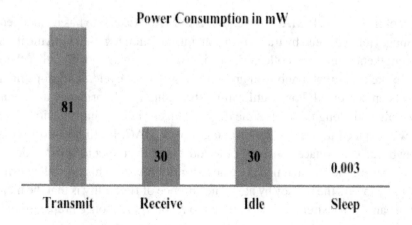

Power Consumption in mW

81 Transmit
30 Receive
30 Idle
0.003 Sleep

AEE- MAC protocol works each in synchronous and asynchronous modes. Because the property of the synchronous protocols, AEE MAC list the nodes to specify their wake and sleep up amount. Whereas, supported the asynchronous protocols property nodes are regular supported their receiver and transmitter initiation.

AEE MAC Protocols with Low Duty Cycle in Synchronous Mode

Every node has 2 modes, like wake and sleep. In wake cycle, nodes can hear the median for integrating requests and knowledge packets. Anywhere in sleep mode, nodes flip duty cycle off till consequent regular awaken time. Energy consumption begin by integration overhead will increase because the network grows in size. This can be as a result of nodes paying attention to the intermediate to induce management packets from several nodes. And any node with information able to be send can produce its way to the sink previous sending, that will increase the information delivery latency. Initial energy economical and most visited duty cycle MAC protocol is Sensor-MAC. Nodes additionally manage their sleep/listen cycles plan by making a plan table for each node to renew its acquaintance schedule. The result, neighbor nodes could have similar time slots for sending the data. Idle nodes can attend sleep throughout sending of different nodes. The receiving amount consists of SYNC and knowledge messages. SYNC may be a packet to integrate one node with its neighbours. Whereas information message is for information sending with the handshake ways of Request-To- Send (RTS)/ Clear-To-Send (CTS). AEE MAC uses a united rivalry theme and planning for conjection rejection.

In AEE MAC, lengthy messages are going to be split into little segments so as to be transmit as burst. This technique produces additional data to transmit, which needs longer connection to the medium.MAC was constructed in the main to cut energy consumption, however it neglects alternative vital performance factors, like fairness, throughput, bandwidth utilization, and latency. Legitimacy can weaken (MAC level perspective) as a few nodes with little information can got to wait MAC with reconciling listening, messages move two hop in every duty cycle. Therefore, latency gets greater as additional messages are remaining to be sent.

AEE MAC was characterized to redesign the execution of MAC with the assistance of dynamic obligation cycle instead of a settled one. The idea is to send all message starting with one hub then onto the next in blasts of various length. It additionally gives the amount of variable load by controlling an ideal time.

AEE MAC Protocols with Asynchronous Low Duty Cycle

A nonconcurrent obligation cycle MAC convention is B-MAC. Each hub has its independent obligation cycle programming. Hub will send by transmitting an introduction together with the information packet, that should be lengthened than the collector's resting time, to make positive that the recipient are in wake up mode. In the event that a hub is in an exceedingly wake cycle, it sections the median only an introduction has been perceived. Power utilization, throughput and dormancy are updated in B-MAC, in any case, catching and along these lines the disadvantages are long introduction.

AEE AMC was planned to beat the disadvantages of B-MAC. It utilizes short preface to elude the overhearing drawback. The preface consists of the address of the target to assist nodes which are untargeted to sleep and permit the targeted node to transmit initial ACK. This not solely evades overhearing however additionally lowers the latency by half. The absence of flexibility is that the major disadvantage of this protocol because it is extremely concentrated to reconfigure it once preparation. Other drawback with this process is that it declines to catch the traffic generated by the preamble transmissions under consideration. The power efficiency is impact once the traffic designed up, because the wireless medium is going to be engaged by the preamble transmissions.

The genuine issue is to advance the system inertness without giving the vitality. In traditional WSNs, a few parameters, e.g., mobility of hubs and density of the system, aggravate the convention opportuneness .However, versatility of hubs and high system thickness don't proceed in static LWSNs arrangements. Thus, issues identified with these parameters, similar to impacts, can be essentially disregard while charming conventions for LWSNs.

All of the obligation cycle MAC conventions considered here are developed without seeing the contact of the system layer all in all framework execution. End-to-end postpone can be overhauled at AEE MAC layers when utilizing the neighbor synchronization and occasional detecting, yet this is exorbitant as far as utilization of energy. Requirements of the applications can adjust the exchange off between the assets of system and entire execution of system. Utilizing two impossible to miss hubs capacity alongside the significant correspondence and division techniques can influenced these issues. Along these lines, our proposed work characterizes another transmission convention to accord with time basic applications without offering the effectiveness of the power. As per our survey, we distinguished that offbeat AEE MAC conventions are more extensible than synchronous AEE MAC conventions. Normal re-synchronization issues in higher utilization of vitality.

Experimental Observations

To lower consumption of power and usage of channel, measurements are organized and transmitted in huge packets. Three time intervals are treated between transmission of data: 5, 10 and 30 seconds. This tends to packet sizes of respectively 50, 75 and 150 bytes for the key three sensors, and of respectively 100, 150 and 300 for the fourth sensor. The measurement of latency is the time elapsed between the moment the AEE MAC receives the packet from the application and when it receives an acknowledgment from the destination device. WiseMAC engages by turns the radio into inactive mode for most of the time. Each year but serially all node wakes up and vote the channel. The channel will be considered as sleep mode when it is free or idle. The node will collecting frame whenever the channel is busy. a node transmits a so called lengthy wake-up preamble for transmission whose duration or turn is as long as the periodic active interval.

This wake-up prelude contains repeat of the information or the message to transmit. Accepting nodes can quickly find that the sending isn't routed to them and go back to rest while the goal hub expands tuning in till the complete of the preamble. As a matter of fact, it perceives the message and teaches the source hub of the time staying before its next active mode or wake up mode. This concedes the source hub to incredibly bring down the wake-up preface whenever that this connection is worn. AEE MAC wakeup interim effect control utilization, dormancy and throughput. It is in this manner important to choose its esteem suitably.

The parameters for AEE MAC are customary: for instance, the utilization of intensity appraises in Rx and Tx are taken from a model developed with parts of discrete. A bound together arrangement would overwhelm more like 8 mW in gathering and 4 mW in transmission. The parameters of the TI CC1100 radio were methodical on a framework helpful in remote sensor organize applications.

SIMULATIONS RESULTS AND DISCUSSIONS

The reproductions keep running with four estimations of the AEE MAC wake-up interim: 50, 100, 250 and 500 ms. Each sensor is creating evaluations once every second. The data is gathered into bigger parcels sent each TP =5, 10 or 30 seconds. The entire reproductions require Omnet++ and the Framework of versatility. The reenactment portrayal utilizes a correct radio state machine for utilization of intensity and appraisals of timing and a probabilistic flag to obstruction in addition to commotion (SINR) impedance portrayal. Check float is recreated in the MAC layer, with an exactness of 30 ppm.

Packet Delivery Success Rate

Changing the physical layer has no impact on reliability when ignoring interference from other systems. Figure 6 show the packet success rate varying with WiseMAC wakeup interval, for packet emission rates of 1 per 5, 10 and 30seconds. With little wake-up interferences, the accomplishment rate is high. For the bigger wake-up interims of 250 and 500 ms, the rate of mistake winds up imperative and propelled each time that the channel is discovered occupied when endeavoring to relate the goal hub, where the Wise MAC occasional wake-up gives the goal hub reachable just at one point in time each wake-up interim, along these lines synchronizing the source hubs and causes crashes.

By choice, a reconstruct of the backoff mechanism could take into consideration the wake-up interval when evaluating the size of the backoff window.

Figure 6. Packet delivery success rate

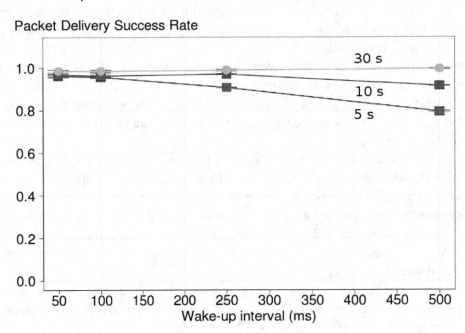

Latency

Figures 7 and seven show the packet latency average (in seconds) as a objective of Wise mac periodic wake-up interval (in ms). On each figures, the latency will increase with the wake-up interval.

Power Consumption

Figures 9 and 10 demonstrate the utilization of intensity for the sensors and for the sink, again as a goal of WiseMAC wake-up interim. For both the sink and the sensor, the FM-UWB handset uses greatly bring down vitality than the TI CC1100. This is a result of its less utilization of intensity, both in gathering and in transmission: individually 15 against 49.2 mW and 5.5 against 51 mW. The contact of changes in parameter is the comparative for the two radios. As traditional, utilization of intensity for the most part diminishes when the time utilized in rest mode between two wakeups makes strides. At the point when the rate of bundle turns out to be vast identified with the accessibility of goal i.e one parcel for each sensor at regular intervals and two wake-ups every second, the power utilization of goal enhances much. This is a result of the interruption at the goal hub, not sufficiently high to confine it from coordinating on the arriving parcel however not sufficiently less to give it a chance to get the packet correctly. Because of the required retransmissions, in that sythesis the sensors additionally have a somewhat more noteworthy utilization of intensity than anticipated.

It was built up to bring down fairly the transmission rate of bundle and to progress to loss of parcels and enhanced utilization of intensity in a specific case. This could be given by agreeing the particulars observing the backoff calculation to the chose wake-up interim. Extra arrangement is to transmit less however bigger bundles when the application stipends it. In this way, FM-UWB can endeavor ultra low power execution when coordinated to WiseMAC, while offering better strength than impedance when

Figure 7. Latency of the narrow band solution

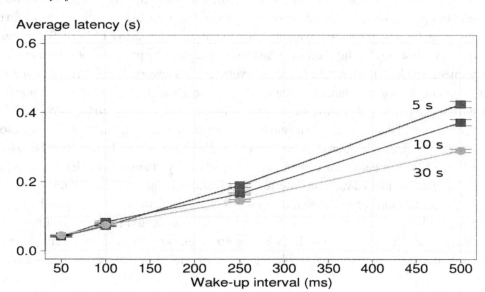

Figure 8. Latency of the AEE MAC solution.

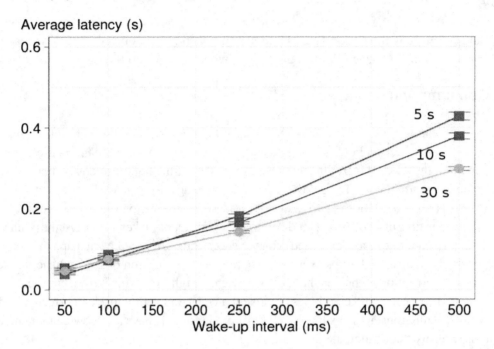

identified with tight band radios. This is a requesting segment for body region systems, as they are profoundly versatile and can work in questionable conditions.

Future work will moreover process the conceivable outcomes given by the blend of UWB-IR with the submitted ultra low power tradition WideMac. Enhancement to WideMac and WiseMAC to enable them to work over various channels, and to transform between two interoperable techniques for assignments, unimportant power usage mode and a high throughput and low latency mode, as given in WiseMAC-HA, are moreover considered.

This determined two remote answers for further medicinal body territory systems. The two answers utilize the ultra low power WiseMAC tradition at first planned for remote sensor frameworks. In the chief case it was facilitated to a tight band radio handset and in the second case to a FM-UWB transceiver. The execution to the extent steady quality, control usage and dormancy was processed with numerical Monte-Carlo reenactments made in the Omnet++discrete event test framework. It was built up that AEE MAC stipends to scope utilization of intensity underneath 1 mW even with relatively various transmissions. While considering FM-UWB, this utilization of intensity was even underneath 0.5 mW. AEE MAC occasional rest component, that awards it to achieve such low utilization of intensity levels, was sorted out to bring down to some degree the transmission rate of bundle and to prompt loss of parcels and enhanced utilization of intensity in a particular case. It would be given by changing the details keeping up the backoff calculation to the picked wake-up interim. Extra arrangement is to transmit less however bigger parcels when the application permits it. Remote systems give a medium of versatility and adaptability in this manner expanding proficiency in every day life action. It has brought forth a great deal of innovations with different application and guidelines giving arrangement from worldwide correspondence to individual correspondence to individual wellbeing and in of late circumstances, utilization of solution.

Figure 9. Average sensor power consumption

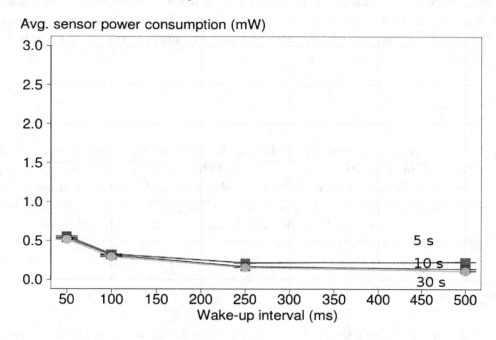

Figure 10. Power Consumption FM-UWB, sensor (above) and sink (below)

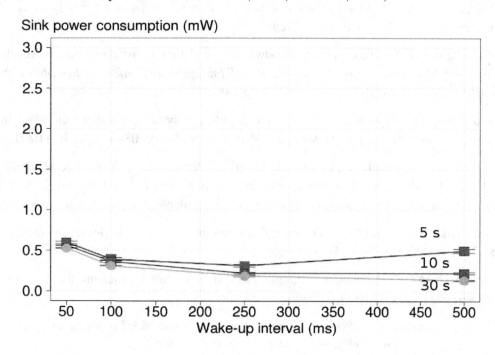

Developed purposely for medical applications although not limited for only medical application, body area network have shown a positive sign of reducing deficit in patient doctor and nurse ratio. BAN provides hope for life saving situation and hence will have an immerse contribution towards the provision of total health.

CONCLUSION

BAN standardization provides a baseline for technology takeoff in the implementation on mobile health (MobiHealth) as explained in section of this thesis. The technology is very refined and robust, providing various forms of techniques in MAC frame processing and comprehensive summary of the IEEE 802.15.6 physical layer specification and application of BAN respectively. BAN applications in medical health and other areas are unlimited. Its market shows huge potential and integrating BAN into health delivery will increase wellness and total health.

REFERENCES

Agrafioti, F., & Hatzinakos, D. (2009). ECG biometric analysis in cardiac irregularity conditions. *Signal, Image and Video Processing*, *3*(4), 329–343. doi:10.100711760-008-0073-4

Alam, Liang, & Xuemin. (2011). An efficient secure data transmission scheme in WBAN. *IEEE Wireless Communications and Networking Conference*.

Basagni, S., Chlamtac, I., Syrotiuk, V. R., & Woodward, B. A. (1998). A distance routing effect algorithm for mobility (DREAM). *Proc. Fourth Annual ACM/IEEE International Conference in Mobile Computing and Networking (MobiCom)*, 76-84. 10.1145/288235.288254

Biel, L., Pettersson, O., Philipson, L., & Wide, P. (2001). ECG analysis: A new approach in human identification. *IEEE Transactions on Instrumentation and Measurement*, *50*(3), 808–812. doi:10.1109/19.930458

Brunelli, D., Farella, E., Rocchi, L., Dozza, M., Chiari, L., & Benini, L. (2006). Bio-feedback system for rehabilitation based on a wireless human area network. In *Proc. 4th Ann. IEEE Int. Conf. Pervasive Comput. Communications Workshops*. Bluetooth SIG Inc. Available: http: //www.bluetooth.org/

Chevrollier, N., & Golmie, N. (2005). On the use of wireless network technologies in healthcare environments. *Proc. 5th IEEE ASWN*, 147–152.

Choi & Ryu. (2011). A QAPM(Quadrature Amplitude Position Modulation) scheme for improving power efficiency. *Wireless and Pervasive Computing*.

Dam, T. V., & Langendoen, K. (2003). An adaptive energy efficient MAC protocol for wireless sensor networks. *Proc. 1st Int. Conf. Embedded Netw. Sens. Syst*, 171–180.

Govindaraajan & Sivasankaran. (2009). Mr.Tacton (Mbedded Red Tacton). *IEEE Power Electronics and Intelligent Transportation System*, 374-377.

Haas, Z. J., & Halpern, J. Y. (2006). Gossip based ad hoc routing. *IEEE T. Netw.*, *14*(3), 497–491.

Haas, Halpern, & Li. (2002). Gossip based Ad Hoc Routing. *IEEE INFOCOM*.

Hamilton, P. (2002). Open source ECG analysis. *Proceeding of the IEEE Conference on Computer and Cardiology*, 101-104. 10.1109/CIC.2002.1166717

Heidemann, W. Y. J. (2003). *Medium access control in wireless sensor networks*. Univ. Southern Calif., Inf. Sci. Inst., USC/ICI Tech.Rep.ISI-TR580.

Johnson, D., Maltz, D., & Broch, J. (1998). *The dynamic source routing protocol for mobile ad hoc networks*. Internet Draft.

Lamprinos, I.E., Prentza, A., Sakka, E., & Koutsouris, D. (2005). Energy efficient MAC protocol for patient personal area networks. *IEEE Eng. Med. Biology Soc.*, 3799–3802.

Marinkovic & Popovici. (2011). Nano power Wake Up Radio mainly intended for Wireless Body Area Networks (WBANs). *IEEE Radio and Wireless*.

Perkins, C., & Royer, E. (1998). *Ad hoc on demand distance vector (AODV) routing*. Internet Draft. Retrieved from: http://www.cs.cornell.edu/people/egs/615/aodv.pdf

Wubbeler, G., Stavridis, D., Kreiseler, R., Bousseljot, R., & Elster, C. (2007). Verification of humans using the electrocardiogram. *Pattern Recognition Letters*, *28*(10), 1172–1175. doi:10.1016/j.patrec.2007.01.014

Yao, J., Schmitz, R., & Warren, S. (2005). A wearable point of- Care system for home use that incorporates plugand- Play and wireless standards. *IEEE Transactions on Information Technology in Biomedicine*, *9*(3), 363–371. doi:10.1109/TITB.2005.854507 PMID:16167690

Ye, W., Silva, F., & Heidemann, J. (2006). Ultra-low duty cycle mac with scheduled channel polling. In *Proceedings of the 4th International Conference on Embedded Networked Sensor Systems; SenSys '06*. New York: ACM.

Chapter 14
A Hybrid Routing Protocol Towards Secure and Smart Military Applications in Cloud Environments

M. Hemanth Chakravarthy
Vel Tech Rangarajan Dr. Sagunthala R&D Institute of Science and Technology, India

E. Kannan
Vel Tech Rangarajan Dr. Sagunthala R&D Institute of Science and Technology, India

M. J. Carmel Mary Belinda
Vel Tech Rangarajan Dr. Sagunthala R&D Institute of Science and Technology, India

ABSTRACT

Having understood the strategic significance of the flourishing cloud idea, enterprises across the globe are keenly strategizing and executing to embark on the cloud journey with all the clarity and confidence. There are product vendors bringing forth additional capabilities to easily and quickly setup and sustain competent cloud environments, which are being positioned as the one-stop IT solution for worldwide business organizations. The business domains such as governments, retail stores, healthcare providers, telecommunication service providers, supply chain and logistics, utilities, homeland security, etc. are keenly embracing the cloud idea to be ahead of their competitors in their operations, outputs, and offerings. However, there are some critical challenges and concerns being associated with the cloud paradigm. The widely quoted non-functional requirements (NFRs) and the quality of service (QoS) attributes such as security, performance, reliability, modifiability, and availability have to be fulfilled by cloud software, platform and infrastructures in order to boost the confidence level of business executives and institutions.

DOI: 10.4018/978-1-5225-9023-1.ch014

There are mission-critical and emergency services, which are finding their residence in cloud environments (private, public, and hybrid). Their requirements are quite unique and hence researchers across the globe are striving hard and stretching further to bring forth innovative, disruptive, and transformation technology solutions to fulfill the various needs. This chapter proposes a cloud-based network architecture that contributes a consistent and ubiquitous internet connection. The mesh topology is recommended here to ensure that the connectivity is available all the time without any fail and slowdown. The security of data when it gets transmitted over channels, persisted in data stores, and used by applications, has to be ensured in order to boost the confidence of data owners and users. Hence, this chapter proposes a secure cloud-based heterogeneous network using a novel routing protocol.

INTRODUCTION

The IoT era is upon us. Enterprises, governments, institutions and organizations are keen to embrace this paradigm in order to be right and relevant to their constituents, clients, consumers and customers. The newness of the various offerings being produced and supplied by business houses is being accomplished through the smart leverage of the various advancements happening in the IoT space. Product vendors, independent software vendors (ISVs), information technology (IT) companies, enterprising businesses, research labs, academic institutions, individuals and innovators are constantly pumping their contributions in order to boost the confidence of people in using this paradigm, which is sweeping the entire world. Not only businesses but also people are being directly and decisively impacted by the power of this new idea. This chapter is specially prepared and presented in order to tell all about the improvisations and innovations in the IT landscape. The figure below clearly articulates some of the key problems in various industries such as banking insurance, public sector and healthcare.

The IoT Data Analytics Use Cases

Having realized the significance of the IoT paradigm in solving some of the crucial issues, there are renewed focuses on IoT. Thereby, IoT data, these days, gets consciously collected, cleansed and crunched in order to solve some of the real-world industry problems as articulated below.

- **Medical Fraud:** Discovers fraud during provider, beneficiary and internal employee profiling using IBM's Fraud Asset Management System (FAMS)
- **Insurance Claim Fraud:** Enables insurers to detect suspicious activity for claims submitted by vendors, brokers and individuals using IBM's Loss Analysis and Warning System (LAWS)
- **Public Tax Fraud:** Empowers governments to address tax gaps by uncovering tax evasion activities and filing inaccuracies using IBM's Tax and Audit Compliance System (TACS)
- **Occupational Fraud:** Helps organizations discover fraud for accounts payable, travel and expense claims, and other fraud committed by employees

Thus, several industry verticals are keenly adopting path-breaking technologies in order to be in the limelight. The next section throws some light on the role and responsibility of the IoT idea in surmounting the major challenges of establishing and experiencing smarter cities.

Figure 1.

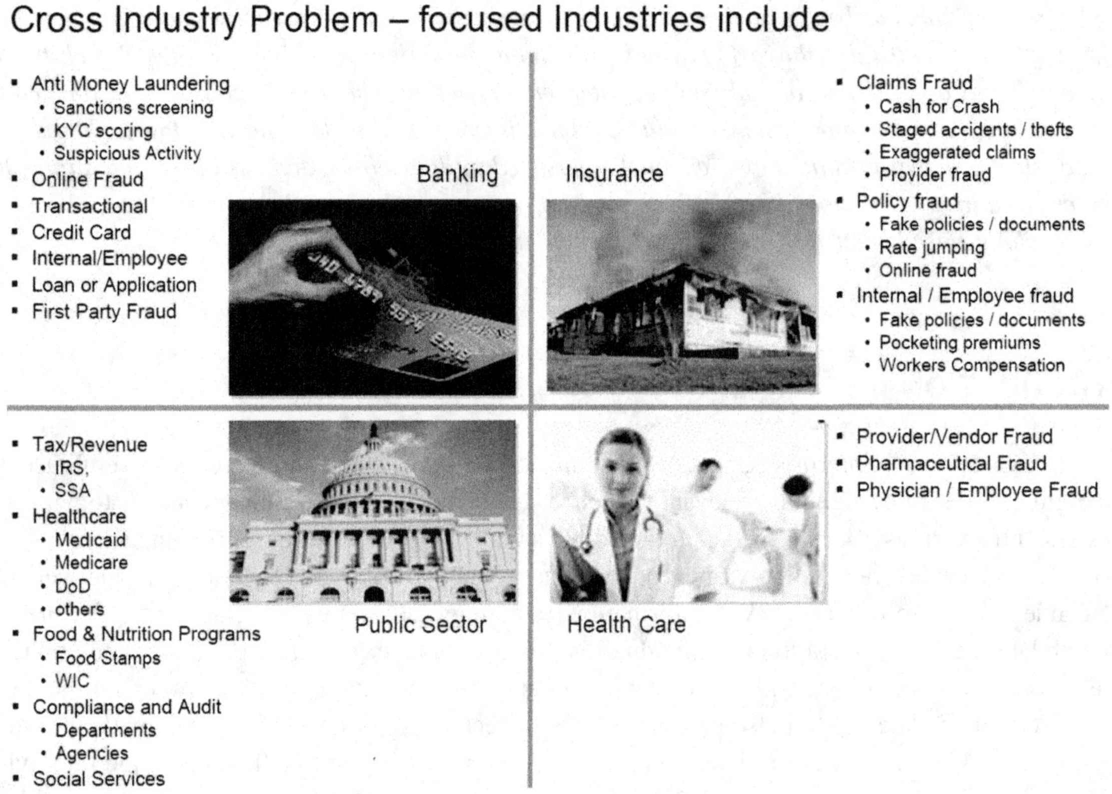

Cross Industry Problem – focused Industries include

A Pragmatic Framework for Enabling the Realization and Sustenance of Smarter Cities

Cities across the world have been providing its unique services to its constituents with all the alacrity and astuteness through multiple yet interconnected agencies. There will be a paradigm shift in the geography of the world that the forthcoming smarter world will be a dynamic collection of cities in the years ahead. Considering the brewing trends and transitions, there will be beneficial cooperation among cities rather than the nations in near future. Cities are bound to play a sparkling role in significantly shaping up everyone's life in this planet. However the heterogeneity and the multiplicity-induced complexities of worldwide cities come in the way of meeting the evolving aspirations of city residents. There are several city-centric challenges getting widely articulated in the media. Therefore there is a clarion call for refurbishing and remedying cities across the globe for deftly tackling city's internally as well as externally imposed constrictions. There are ways and means being bandied about for resolutely resolving the sickening and sagging city problems. At different layers and levels, competent strategies, approaches, frameworks and solutions are being prescribed and promoted by luminaries and visionaries to elegantly eradicate all kinds of bottlenecks and barriers to smoothen and brighten the city life.

Powerful information, sensing, vision, communication, perception, knowledge engineering, and actuation technologies, tools, platforms, and infrastructures are being highly recommended to enable cities to be right and relevant for their citizens. There are a few promising and pioneering technologi-

Figure 2.

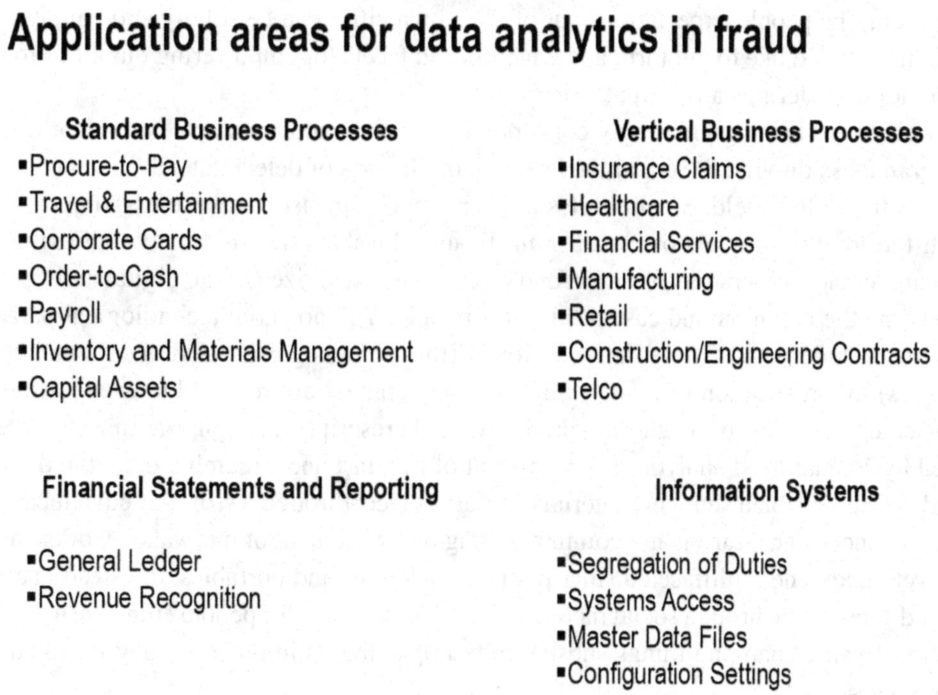

Application areas for data analytics in fraud
Standard Business Processes
▪Procure-to-Pay
▪Travel & Entertainment
▪Corporate Cards
▪Order-to-Cash
▪Payroll
▪Inventory and Materials Management
▪Capital Assets
Vertical Business Processes
▪Insurance Claims
▪Healthcare
▪Financial Services
▪Manufacturing
▪Retail
▪Construction/Engineering Contracts
▪Telco
Financial Statements and Reporting
▪General Ledger
▪Revenue Recognition
Information Systems
▪Segregation of Duties
▪Systems Access
▪Master Data Files
▪Configuration Settings

Figure 3.

Fraud analytics - Use Cases
Compliance & Audit
Insurance
Healthcare
Tax /Revenue
Claims
Credit Card
Retail
Fraudulent claims
Policy claims
Inflated Bills
Credit card transaction checks
Fraud analytics

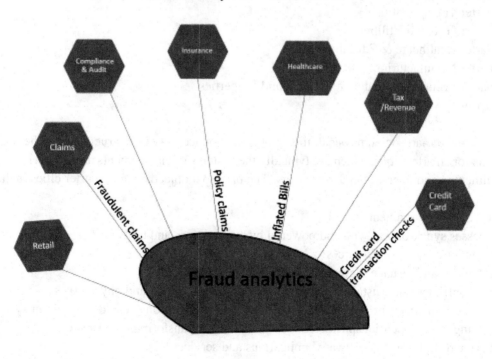

cal innovations and inventions in the happening and hot ICT domain and it is expected that by smartly leveraging them, the people expectations out of their own cities can be solidly and simply met. In this short write-up, I would like to put forth a few factors and facets for empowering our cities to be smarter in their operations, offerings and outputs.

Smarter cities are being increasingly conceptualized and concretized across the world with all the deserving grandness through the cognitive leverage of all sorts of delectable advancements being duly accomplished in the ICT field. Smarter cites are very much futuristic and professionals are at work to accomplish the long-term goals of establishing livable, lovable, and sustainable cities for providing enhanced care, choice, comradery, comfort and convenience to citizens. The digital and connected living will become the common and casual thing for people. The potential technological paradigms and developments include the software-defined clouds (the technologically optimized and organized IT infrastructures), the realization of real-world, real-time, context-aware, and knowledge-filled services through the extensive usage of diagnostic, predictive and prescriptive insights getting extracted through and emitted by standardized analytics platforms out of big, fast and streaming data, the digitized, connected, and service-enabled sentient materials / smart objects through a string of edge technologies for precisely and concisely capturing and communicating every moment of our walks, works and wanders, the trendy yet handy and multifaceted smartphones, wearables and portables, the steady accumulation of people and social data through social media and networking sites for people empowerment, etc. There are a variety of game-changing things substantially impacting us in our everyday personal as well as professional lives.

Typically, smarter cities are the grand accumulation of several modules such as

- Smarter Homes and Buildings
- Smarter Drainage, Wastage & Garbage Management
- Smarter Transportation
- Smarter Grid and Utilities
- Smarter Healthcare & Education
- Smarter Manufacturing
- Smarter Security and Safety for People and Properties
- Smarter Government

The state-of-the-art social, physical, life, cyber, and connectivity infrastructures are the mainstream ingredients for smarter cities, which are typically the systems of engagements and comprising multiple yet instrumented and intertwined departments. The principal objectives for smarter cities include

1. People and environment friendly,
2. Processes synchronized with and powered by technologies and tools
3. Optimal utilization of resources
4. Strategized and managed leveraging data-driven insights
5. Elastic, efficient and sustainable Infrastructures (Social, cyber, and physical)
6. Service-oriented, event-driven, accountable, sensitive & responsive and transparent systems
7. Enabling entrepreneurial spirit, creative mind-set, and transformative ideas, etc.
8. Smart and sophisticated software applications and services

A smarter cities transformational strategy is as follows.

- Leverage Data Assets Insightfully
- Optimize Infrastructure Technologically
- Innovate Processes Consistently
- Assimilate Architectures Appropriately
- Choose Technologies & Tools Carefully
- Ensure Accessibility, Elasticity, Simplicity & Consumability Cognitively

The cutting-edge technologies for establishing smarter cities are

- **Micro Services Architecture (MSA)** (service-based anything-to-anything integration and orchestration (sensor, device, service, application, data, infrastructure, digitalized objects, etc.) for Containerized Workloads
- **Software-defined Clouds** (IT infrastructure optimization)
- **Enterprise Mobility** (All kinds of web, enterprise, and cloud applications are mobile-enabled to access them on the move)
- **Big, Real-time, & Streaming Data Analytics**(Data to information and to knowledge transition)
- **The Internet of Things (IoT) / Machine-to-Machine (M2M) Connectivity** for Context-awareness & Cognitive Computing

A well-defined ICT framework for smarter cities is therefore involving the following.

1. **City Infrastructures**
   a. Physical, Social and Life Infrastructures
   b. Virtual / Digital and Connectivity Infrastructures
2. **City IT-enablement Platforms, Middleware and Databases**
   a. Unified City Planning, Enhancement, and Management Platforms
   b. Service Integration, Orchestration, and Delivery Platforms
3. **City and Citizen-specific Data, Services and Applications Repositories**

A sample list of services for smarter cities is given below.

- **Smart Homes:** Energy management, ambient assisted living (AAL), Remote monitoring and management, etc.
- **Smarter Buildings:** Security and Safety enablement,
- **Smart Parking:** Monitoring of parking spaces availability in the city.
- **Structural Health:** Monitoring of vibrations and material conditions in buildings, bridges and historical monuments.
- **Noise Urban Maps:** Sound monitoring in bar areas and centric zones in real time.
- **Smartphone Detection:** Detect smart phones and in general any device which works with Wi-Fi or Bluetooth interfaces.
- **Electromagnetic Field Levels:** Measurement of the energy radiated by cell stations and Wi-Fi routers.

- **Traffic Congestion:** Monitoring of vehicles and pedestrian levels to optimize driving and walking routes.
- **Smart Lighting:** Intelligent and weather adaptive lighting in street lights.
- **Waste Management:** Detection of rubbish levels in containers to optimize the trash collection routes.
- **Smart Roads -** Intelligent Highways with warning messages and diversions according to climate conditions and unexpected events like accidents or traffic jams.
- **Image and Video Analytics:** Traffic management, security and surveillance, homeland security, smarter healthcare, etc.
- **Context-Aware and Physical Services**

On concluding, our cities need to be subjected to a bevy of technologies-sponsored disruptions and transformations in order to excite residents, travelers, investors, professionals, etc. The role of the ICT capabilities and competencies in devising and delivering highly sophisticated and sustainable cities is on the consistently climb. This document has thrown some light here about the challenges and how they can be adequately addressed through the delicate usage of the fully matured and stabilized technologies and tools.

As articulated above, there are several business-critical and emergency services, which are being taken to cloud environments. Cloud infrastructures are the most optimized and organized IT infrastructures, which are centralized, consolidated, virtualized and increasingly containerized. The cloud-enablement aspect is capable of bringing forth a number of unique innovations for institutions, individuals and innovators. In the recent past, due to the faster maturity and stability of cloud centers, the well-known emergency services such as homeland security (military services), mainland and inland security (police services), healthcare providers (hospitals and clinics), fire service, etc. are being hosted and managed in cloud environments. The secondary emergency service providers include aviation, border security, etc. These services are becoming indispensable for our daily lives.

The IoT Contributions for the Military Field

The technologies and tools used by military services had been developed long time back and hence are not considered as modern and modular applications. The macro-level military application architecture is given below. The military networks are highly complicated and confused.

- **Maximum Obtainability:** Unlike the currently available telecommunication (wired as well as wireless) networks, the military networks ought to be highly available. The availability, reliability and resiliency of military networks have to be guaranteed at any cost. They have to be highly fault-tolerant.
- **Dependability:** The information has to reach the desired end-points without any hitch and hurdle.
- **Amenities:** The military networks have to be flexible enough to be integrated with other network such as Intranets and the Internet

From the above-mentioned requirements, it is clearly understood that the most important obligations of military services may be registered as 1) connectivity and obtainability of all communication mechanisms in all circumstances even after war occurrences 2) accessibility to internet and intranet facilities 3)

Figure 4. A sample representation of military networks

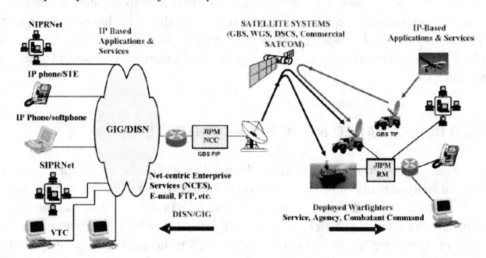

dependable and appropriate transmission. The rest are certain investigating ventures which are presently carried out in order to make the subsequent group of the Internet, on account of the Global Environment for Network (GENI), which is supported financially by the U.S. National Science Foundation (NSF).

The foremost objective of these projects is to establish a connection between the satellites and the internet, in order to obtain utility by satisfying past experiments. This paperwork determined this issue, and established the network architecture which could encompass every key mechanisms of networks with the network connection, known as anywhere and anytime network (to accomplish the physical / hardware requirements), a protocol called smart for improved dependable transmission (to accomplish the software requirements).

Figure 5. Heterogeneous network using mesh routers as gateways

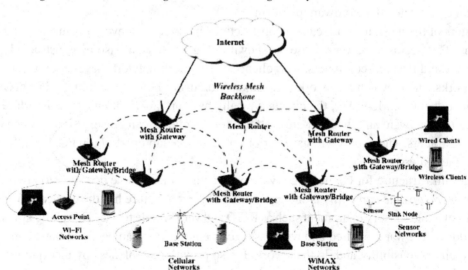

In section II, the paper explains the cloud based heterogeneous network architecture that contains of all the foremost communication devices and its interoperability with internet. In section III, the paper suggested protocol for dependable transmission to create the proposed heterogeneous network. In section IV& V, the paperwork defines the structure model, implementation as well as the result and performance analysis.

PROPOSED CLOUD BASED NETWORK ARCHITECTURE

In the past, the network structure was not built in the way that it could be used with a wide flexibility. But our proposed varied network construction deals with the integration of various network, called cloud computing. In cloud computing, many nodes which may be wired or wireless can integrate without compromising any characteristics. Fast expansion in this technology will also enlarge stern protection concern, since protection has an invariable concern, but this technology has several benefits such as lowering the cost, sufficient to maintain a wide service capture. The Network Interface Card (NIC) plays a key role here since it can outfit the systems such as the laptop, desktop computers, Mobile phone etc. Due to this outfit we can connect straight with the wireless mesh routers, which serve as the pathway for heterogeneous network.

It is attaining a noteworthy contemplation as a probable pathway for the Internet service providers (ISP), and the remaining to compress tough and consistent broadband service contact in a path which require low up-front reserves. The self-organization and self-configuration capacity of the cloud arranges each and every node at a particular instance as required. The more the nodes implemented, the consistency for the client will be increased. The conservative wireless router is used as the routing capability for the gateway working. Mesh router which could consist of some extra routing works can also be used which serves best for mesh networks.

In addition to increasing the suppleness of mesh-networks, a mesh router is typically outfitted among various cellular borders constructed on similar or dissimilar cellular contact equipment. Arbitrarily, MAC protocol in a mesh router is improved and has a good adaptability in a multiple hops mesh environment. These are all constructed in a hardware platform.

The routers of the mesh network can be constructed depending on devoted computers, e.g., embedded systems. This seems to be very dense, as shown in Fig.2. This can also be constructed depending on the laptops and desktop computers. The clients of the mesh network have essential functionality for the networks, and they can also work as a router. Moreover, the nodes could not be survived in the gateway functionalities. Moreover, the clients typically have an individual wireless interface. The end result is that the hardware and the software platform for the clients can be very simple when compared with the mesh routers. The clients will have various devices like laptop, desktop PC, PDA, RFID reader than that of the routers.

A typical infrastructure for connecting a variety of communication devices and to provide *always-on-line anywhere anytime capability* is shown in fig 2. This architecture has the capacity to bond wired, wireless, cellular and sensory equipment such as RFID and very simple to use. This could also survive for long since during the war the wired and wireless equipment may get damaged but these sensory equipment hold their responsibility and do their work. It also provides suppleness by incorporating through gateways and also connects the network through traditional equipment.

Organizing a WMN is very easy since every necessary component are by now obtainable in the form certain protocols like ad hoc network routing, IEEE 802.11 MAC, wired equivalent privacy (WEP) security, etc. Many investigation labs (BWN, n.d.; Aguayo et al, n.d.) have understood about impending these expertise and proffer mesh networking solution. Home Mesh (Ting et al, 2008), In-Home IPTV (Shihab et al, 2008) are certain WMN dependent relevancies. Moreover, to connect with the internet hard work of some researchers are required. For instance, the accessible MAC and routing protocols used in WMN do not have essential flexibility and the output falls when the nodes count is increased (Najah et al, 2008).

PROPOSED SECURED CLOUD BASED HETEROGENEOUS NETWORKS

Ant Colony Based Mobile Agent

This particular procedure is very essential and affordable too. This particular algorithm has the finest solution by developing the simulated ants. Naturally the ant's action is based on searching for food and moves to places and discovers new paths. Whereas these simulated ants look for the solution space. The motion of these ants depends on the cologne which is deposited and the ants follow that way. Once the cologne gets vanished the system does not remember the old information and negotiate the rapid junction to trifling solution. This certain number of paths permit us to search for a huge number of solutions. This algorithm is very successful to various optimization techniques namely traveling salesman problem (Subramanian et al, 1997), routing (Subramanian et al, 1997; Sim et al, 2003). Certain proof for this pathway of Ant Colony optimization technique is established at (Blum et al, 2010). In our paper, we used ant-like mobile agent for the gathering of data. The ant representatives budge in the network at random positions and scrutinize huge amount of nodes. Moreover, this will also gather some information regarding the network and contribute to its nodes. This process can be useful to speed up the optimization process by providing plenty of up to date information.

The routing table can be built by the formula given below: the neighbor j is selected by the destination D and node i and it is

$$prob(D,i,j) = \begin{cases} Fun(TD,i,j,\eta)----if, j \in N \\ \overline{\sum Fun(TD,i,j,\eta)---if, j \notin N} \end{cases} \tag{1}$$

Here TD denotes the cologne value which corresponds to acquaintance j at node i and $0 < TD < 1$ is the local empirical value of node j. $0 < \eta < 1$, represents the acquaintance's certain information like energy which remains, power required, delay process etc. Fun(TD, i, j, η) is a function in TD and η (when TD and η are maximum this value is maximum). N denotes the set of all possible acquaintances node demarcated by the ant's information as well as the direction-finding restrictions. The cologne value of every entrance in the table can be adjusted to equivalent terms which provides not biased hunt for the finest path. If certain information regarding the finest route is accessible then the cologne terms of the entrance could be fixed to the nearest value which fastens this algorithm.

Figure 6. Second level performance diagram of ant colony based data collection

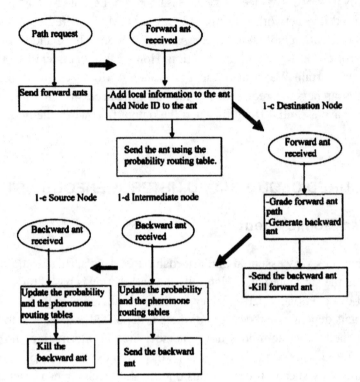

HECC Based Cloud Security

The proposed HECC is shown below:

- In the field of ECC, the prime case is denoted as 'p' and the binary case is denoted by 'm' and 'f' pair. The constants 'a' and 'b' are said as the elliptic curve in the equation.
- For current cryptographic purposes, the points of the plane curve over a known field should convince the below equation (2)

$$y^2 = x^3 + ax + b \qquad (2)$$

and also with a illustrious point at infinity.

- The cyclic subgroup is termed by its generator G. Many discrete logarithmic based protocol has been tailored to elliptic curves which reinstates the cluster $(Z_p)^x$ with an elliptic curve and this can be any of the five methods given below:
  - The elliptic curve Diffie–Hellman (ECDH) key agreement scheme depends on the Diffie–Hellman scheme,
  - The Elliptic Curve Integrated Encryption Scheme (ECIES)can also be said as Elliptic Curve Augmented Encryption Scheme,

    ◦   The Elliptic Curve Digital Signature Algorithm (ECDSA) depends on the Digital Signature Algorithm,

    ◦   The ECMQV key agreement scheme is based on the MQV key agreement scheme,

    ◦   the ECQV inherent the certificate scheme.

- For cryptographic purpose the order of G which is a small positive number n where nG is equal to infinity, is usually prime. As n denotes amount of a subcategory of $E(F_p)$, this depends on the Lagrange's theorem where the h is said to be an integer. The h is uttered in equation (3)

$$h = \frac{|E(F_p)|}{n} \tag{3}$$

where, h should be minimum (h≤4) and if possible, h is equal to one. Let's sum up: in the prime case the domain parameters are (p, a, b, G, n, h) and in the binary case they are (m, f, a, b, G, n, h). curvature and implement a universal point-counting algorithm, for example, Schoof's algorithm, choose an arbitrary curve from a folk that permit effortless reckoning the amount of points. This could provide disparity among the finite-field cryptography (e.g., DSA) that needs 3072-bit public keys and 256-bit private keys, and integer factorization cryptography (e.g., RSA) that needs 3072-bit amount of n, from that the private key must be huge but the public key may be small to lodge well-organized encryption, particularly in the place where slighter processors are disturbed. HECC method is productively been worn in (Chakravarthy et al, 2014).This method affords the most favorable refuge and the best among the accessible systems (Chakravarthy et al, 2015).

RESULT AND PERFORMANCE ANALYSIS

The proposed cloud based secured military architecture is the arrangement of various networks together with the amount of unit worn. In our design, these values are RTT values from TCP communications, average packet loss and average response time of probable route. Hence, it is simulated using network simulator. The table 2 and table 3 showing the throughput and response time of existing and proposed military systems. The figure 7 represents the packet loss of existing military systems and proposed cloud based military systems.

CONCLUSION

From the results inscribed above, it is observed that there is no packet loss even at 100 nodes are transferring data at the time as the proposed military system has cloud resources. And the packet loss on above 100 nodes is also less than 25% of existing military systems. Similarly, the response time of proposed military system is faster than the existing military systems. The data receiving capability of the proposed and existing system are recorded in terms of throughput. The throughput of the proposed military system is always higher than the existing military systems. Hence, it is concluded that the proposed cloud-based secured and smart military system is more optimal than the existing military systems.

Table 1. Simulation parameters

Simulation Parameters	Values Obtained
Simulated-area	200 × 200 m2
Propagation	Two ray ground
MAC-type	802.11
Antenna	Omni-Antenna
Queue	Drop Tail/Priority
Queue-Limit	50
Amount of node	10 to 500
Packet-Type	CBR
Packet-size	220 Bits

Table 2. Throughput of existing and proposed systems

Throughput in KB		
No of Nodes	Existing System	Proposed System
10	6	6
25	7	7
50	8	9
100	9	10
200	11	12
500	14	15

Table 3. Response time of existing and proposed systems

Response Time in ms		
No of Nodes	Existing System	Proposed System
10	110	102
25	107	92
50	104	82
100	102	78
200	112	99
500	128	111

Figure 7. Packet Loss of existing and proposed military systems

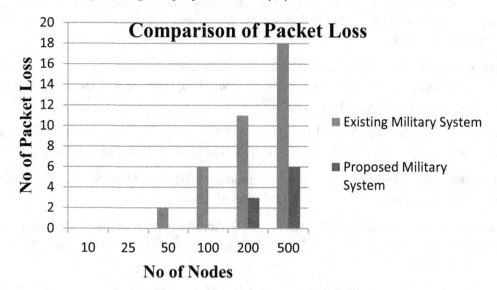

This work lays a stimulating foundation for cloud security researchers to unearth advanced security solutions and approaches for ensuring unbreakable and impenetrable security for essential and mission-critical services, which are increasingly deployed and delivered through cloud centers, which are coming up across the globe to meet up the growing needs of governments, business enterprises and commoners.

REFERENCES

Abu Ali, Taha, Hassanein, & Mouftah. (2008, January). IEEE 802.16 Mesh Schedulers: Issues and Design Challenges. *IEEE Transaction on Network*.

Aguayo, Bicket, Biswas, De Couto, & Morris. (n.d.). *MIT Roofnet Implementation*. Available from: http://pdos.lcs.mit.edu /roofnet /design /

BWN lab wireless mesh networks research project. (n.d.). Available from: http://www.ece.gatech.edu /research /labs /bwn /mesh /

Secured Cloud. (n.d.). *International Journal of Applied Engineering Research, 9*(24), 29329-29337.

Duan & Yu. (2007). Hybrid Ant Colony Optimization Using Memetic Algorithm for Traveling Salesman Problem. *Proceedings of the IEEE Symposium on Approximate Dynamic Programming and Reinforcement Learning*, 92-95.

He, T., Chan, S.-H. G., & Wong, C.-F. (2008, December). HomeMesh: A Low-Cost Indoor Wireless Mesh for Home Networking. *IEEE Communications Magazine, 46*(12), 79–85. doi:10.1109/MCOM.2008.4689211

Hemanth Chakravarthy, M., & Kannan, E. (2014). A review on secured cloud computing environment. *Journal of Computational Science, 11*(8), 1224–1228.

Hemanth Chakravarthy, M., & Kannan, E. (2015). Ant colony-based authentication system for cloud computing. *Research Journal of Applied Sciences, Engineering and Technology, 11*(2), 144–149. doi:10.19026/rjaset.11.1700

Hemanth Chakravarthy, M., & Kannan, E. (2015). Hybrid elliptic curve cryptography using ant colony-based authentication system for cloud computing. *Journal of Engineering and Applied Sciences (Asian Research Publishing Network), 10*(16), 7273–7279.

Lopez-Ibanez, M., & Blum, C. (2010). Beam ACO for the traveling sales man problem with time windows. *Computers & Operations Research, 37*(9), 1570–1583. doi:10.1016/j.cor.2009.11.015

Riggio, R. (2008, June). Hardware and Software Solutions for Wireless Mesh Network Test beds. *IEEE Communications Magazine.* doi:10.1109/MCOM.2008.4539480

Schoonderwoerd, R., Holland, O., & Bruten, J. (1997). Ant like agents for load balancing in telecommunication networks. In *Proceedings of the first int. conf. on autonomous agents* (pp. 209-216). New York: ACM Press. 10.1145/267658.267718

Shihab, Cai, Wan, & Gulliver. (2008, January). Wireless Mesh Networks for In-Home IPTV Distribution. *IEEE Transaction on Network.*

Sim, K. M., & Weng, H. S. (2003). Ant Colony Optimization for Routing and Load-Balancing: Survey and New Directions. *IEEE Transactions on Systems, Man, and Cybernetics, VOL., 33*(5), 560–572. doi:10.1109/TSMCA.2003.817391

Subramanian, D., Druschel, P., & Chen, J. (1997). Ants and reinforcement learning: A case study in routing in dynamic networks. In *Proceedings of the 15th int. joint conf. on artificial intelligence* (pp. 823-838). San Francisco: Morgan Kaufmann.

Chapter 15
A Study on Capabilities and Challenges of Fog Computing

R. Priyadarshini
Vel Tech Rangarajan Dr. Sagunthala R&D Institute of Science and Technology, India

N. Malarvizhi
Vel Tech Rangarajan Dr. Sagunthala R&D Institute of Science and Technology, India

E. A. Neeba
Rajagiri School of Engineering and Technology, India

ABSTRACT

Fog computing is a new paradigm believed to be an extension of cloud computing and services to the sting of the network. Similarly, like Cloud, Fog provides computing, data, storage, and various application services to the connected end-users. Fog computing uses one or a lot of combined end users or nearby end users edge devices to perform the configuration, communication, storage, control activity, and management functions over the infrastructure supported. This new paradigm solves the latency and information measure limitation issues encountered from the cloud computing. Primarily, the architecture of the fog computing is discussed and analyzed during this work and then indicates the connected potential security and trust problems. Then, however such problems are tackled within the existing literature is systematically reportable. Finally, the open challenges, analysis, trends, and future topics of security and trust in fog computing are mentioned.

INTRODUCTION

The faster maturity and stability of edge technologies (Ghahramani et al, 2017) has blossomed into a big factor in realizing scores of digitized elements / smart objects/sentient materials out of common, cheap and casual items in our midst. These empowered entities are data-generating and capturing, buffering, transmitting, etc. That is, tangible things are peppered with and prepared for the future. These are mostly resource-constrained and this phenomenon is called the Internet of Things (IoT). Further on, a wider variety of gadgets and gizmos in our working, walking and wandering locations are futuristically

DOI: 10.4018/978-1-5225-9023-1.ch015

instrumented to be spontaneously interconnected and exceptionally intelligent in their behaviours. Thus, we hear, read and even feel connected and cognitive devices and machines in our everyday life. Once upon of a time, all our personal computers were connected via networks (LAN and WAN) and nowadays our personal and professional devices (fixed, portables, mobiles, wearables, implantables, handhelds, phablets, etc.) are increasingly interconnected (BAN, PAN, CAN, LAN. MAN, and WAN) to exhibit a kind of intelligent behavior. This extreme connectivity and service-enablement of our everyday devices go to the level of getting seamlessly integrated with off-premise, online, and on-demand cloud-based applications, services, data sources, and content. This cloud-enablement is capable of making ordinary devices into extraordinary ones. However, most of the well-known and widely used embedded devices individually do not have sufficient computation power, battery, storage and I/O bandwidth to host and manage IoT applications and services. Hence performing data analytics on individual devices is a bit difficult.

As we all know, smart sensors and actuators are being randomly deployed in any significant environments such as homes, hospitals, hotels, etc. in order to minutely monitor, precisely measure, and insightfully manage the various parameters of the environments. Further on, powerful sensors are embedded and etched on different physical, mechanical, electrical and electronics systems in our everyday environments in order to empower them to join in the mainstream computing. Thus, not only environments but also all tangible things in those environments are also smartly sensor-enabled with a tactic as well as the strategic goal of making them distinctly sensitive and responsive in their operations, offerings, and outputs. Sensors are sweetly turning out to be the inseparable eyes and ears of any important thing in near future. This systematic sensor-enablement of ordinary things not only make them extraordinary but also lay out a stimulating and sparkling foundation for generating a lot of usable and time-critical data. Typically sensors and sensors-attached assets capture or generate and transmit all kinds of data to the faraway cloud environments (public, private and hybrid) through a host of standards-compliant sensor gateway devices. Precisely speaking, clouds represent the dynamic combination of several powerful server machines, storage appliances, and network solutions and are capable of processing tremendous amounts of multi-structured data to spit out actionable insights.

However, there is another side to this remote integration and data processing. For certain requirements, the local or proximate processing of data is mandated. That is, instead of capturing sensor and device data and transmitting them to the faraway cloud environments is not going to be beneficial for time-critical applications. Thereby the concept of edge or fog computing has emerged and is evolving fast these days with the concerted efforts of academic as well as corporate people. The reasonably powerful devices such as smartphones, sensor and IoT gateways, consumer electronics, set-top boxes, smart TVs, Web-enabled refrigerators, Wi-Fi routers, etc. are classified as fog or edge devices to form edge or fog clouds to do the much-needed local processing quickly and easily to arrive and articulate any hidden knowledge. Thus, fog or edge computing is termed and tuned as the serious subject of study and research for producing people-centric and real-time applications and services.

BRIEFING FOG / EDGE COMPUTING

Traditional networks, which feed data from devices or transactions to a central storage hub (data warehouses and data marts) can't keep up with the data volume and velocity created by IoT devices. Nor can the data warehouse model meet the low latency response times that users demand. The Hadoop platform in the cloud was supposed to be an answer. But sending the data to the cloud for analysis also poses a risk of data bottlenecks as well as security concerns. New business models, however, need data analytics in a minute or less. The problem of data congestion will only get worse as IoT applications and devices continue to proliferate.

There are certain interesting use cases such as rich connectivity and interactions among vehicles (V2V) and infrastructures (V2I). This emerging domain of IoT requires services like entertainment, education, and information, public safety, real-time traffic analysis and information, support for high mobility, context awareness and so forth. Such things see the light only if the infotainment systems within vehicles have to identify and interact with one another dynamically and also with wireless communication (Mukherjee et al, 2018) infrastructures made available on the road, with remote traffic servers and FM stations, etc. The infotainment system is emerging as the highly synchronized gateway for vehicles on the road. Local devices need to interact themselves to collect data from vehicles and roads/expressways/tunnels/bridges to process them instantaneously to spit out useful intelligence. This is the salivating and sparkling foundation for fog/edge computing.

The value of the data decreases as the time goes. That is, the timeliness and the trustworthiness of data are very important for extracting actionable insights. The moment the data gets generated and captured, it has to be subjected to processing. That is, it is all about real-time capture. Also, it is all about gaining real-time insights through rule / policy-based data filtering, enrichment, pattern searching, aggregation, knowledge discovery, etc. to take a real-time decision and to build real-time applications. The picture below clearly articulates how the delay in capturing and analyzing data costs a lot in terms of business, technical and user values.

The latest trend of computing paradigm is to push the storage, networking, and computation to edge/fog devices for availing certain critical services. As devices are interconnected and integrated with the Internet, their computational capabilities and competencies are uniquely being leveraged in order to lessen the increasing load on cloud infrastructures. Edge devices are adequately instrumented at the de-

Figure 1.

sign stage itself to interconnect with nearby devices automatically so that multiple devices dynamically can be found, bound, and composed for creating powerful and special-purpose edge clouds. Thus, the concept of fog or edge computing is blooming and booming these days.

The essence and gist of fog computing (Xia et al, 2015; Bonomi et al, 2012; Bonomi et al, 2011) are to keep data and computation close to end-users at the edge of the network and this arrangement has the added tendency of producing a new class of applications and services to end-users with low latency, high bandwidth, and context-awareness. Fog is invariably closer to humans rather than clouds and hence the name 'fog computing' is overwhelmingly accepted across. As indicated and illustrated above, fog devices are typically resource-intensive edge devices. Fog computing is usually touted as the supplement and complement to the popular cloud computing. Students, scholars, and scientists are keen towards unearthing a number of convincing and sellable business and technical cases for fog computing. Being closer to people, the revitalized fog or edge computing is to be extremely fruitful and fabulous in conceptualizing and concretizing a litany of people-centric software applications. Finally, in the era of big, fast, streaming and IoT data, fog/edge computing can facilitate edge analytics. Edge devices can filter out redundant, repetitive and routine data to reduce the precious network bandwidth and the data loads on clouds. Figure 2 vividly illustrates the fast-emerging three-tier architecture for futuristic computing.

The digitized objects (sensors, beacons, etc.) at the lowest level are generating and capturing poly-structured data in big quantities. The fog devices (gateways, controllers, etc.) at the second level are reasonably blessed with computational, communication and storage power in order to mix, mingle and merge with other fog devices in the environment to ingest and accomplish the local or proximate data processing to emit viable and value-adding insights in time. The third and final level is the faraway cloud centres. This introduction of fog devices in between clouds and digitized elements is the new twist

Figure 2. The end-to-end fog – cloud integration architecture

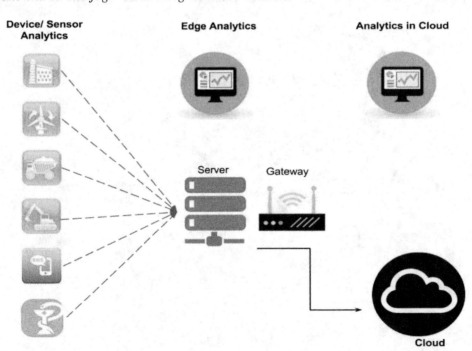

brought in towards the ensuing era of knowledge-filled services. Fog devices act as intelligent intermediaries between cloud-based cyber/virtual applications and sensor/actuator (Verma et al, 2016; Liu et al, 2017; Peralta et al, 2017) data at the ground level. Here is another representation of fog computing as articulated in figure 3.

Cloud computing has modified the data Technology Sector, by providing major edges there to users, like eliminating direct IT investment, proportional prices, measurability, then on (Ghahramani et al, 2017; Xia et al, 2015). However, several devices are unit connected; Latency-sensitive applications actively face the matter of enormous latency. Additionally, the Cloud has become too clumsy to accommodate the necessities of quality support and placement awareness. To beat these issues, a replacement paradigm referred to as Fog computing was planned in the year 2012, introduced by Cisco (Bonomi et al, 2012; Bonomi et al, 2011).

In Fog computing, administrations will be expedited at the edge devise, for instance, set-top-boxes or mobiles. By considering the new circulated computing which allows applications to stay running as such, as conceivable to detected vital and massive data, deed people, procedures and issue. Such Fog problem solving plan i.e., extremely a Cloud computing close to the 'ground', makes computerized reaction that drives the esteem. Each Cloud and Fog gives computation, information, storage and application services to end-users. However, Fog will be distinguished from Cloud by its contiguousness to end-users, the condensed geographical distribution and its support for quality (Bonomi et al, 2012). Fog has a tendency to adopt a straightforward 3 level hierarchy as in Figure 2.

Figure 3. The fog as the intermediary between the physical and the cyber worlds

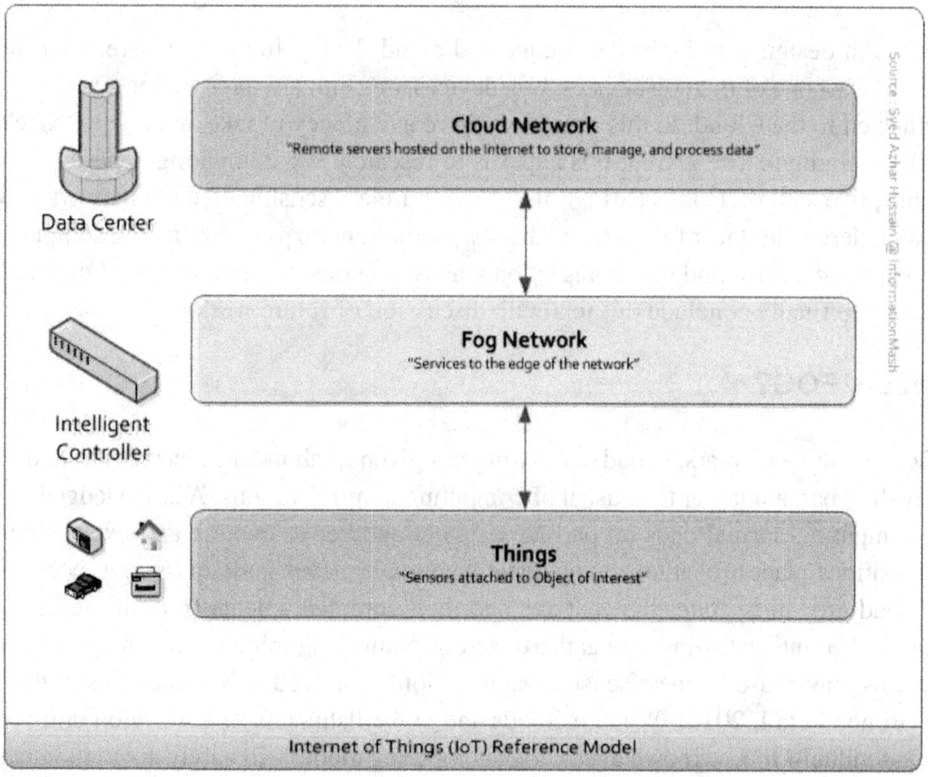

Figure 4. Three level fog computing hierarchy

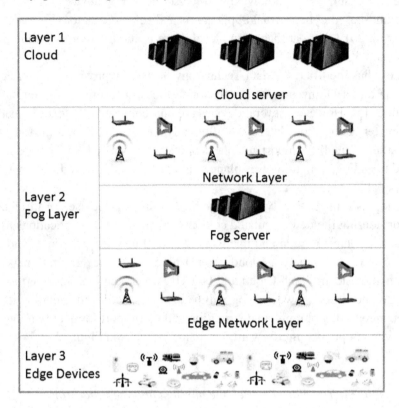

Fog layer is in designed to be between edge and cloud. In fog framework, every sensible issue is hooked up to at least one of the Fog devices. Fog devices area unit are inter- connected and every one of them is connected to the Cloud. In this article, we have a tendency to take an in depth check up on the fog computing paradigm. The goal of this paper is to research Fog computing benefits for services in many domains, like web of Things (IoT), Smart Grid, wireless sensing element networks. We have an inclination to undergo the state of-the-art and disclose some general problems in Fog computing together with security, privacy, trust, and repair migration among Fog devices and between Fog and Cloud. We have a tendency to finally conclude this text with discussion of future work.

What Attracts FOG?

In the proficient couple of years, Cloud computing has given in abundance chances to undertakings by philanthropy their bargain larger than usual of computing administrations. Acknowledged "pay-as-you-go" Cloud computing normal ends up partner efficient another to owning and overseeing concealed edited compositions places for trade antagonistic web applications and amassing process (Bonomi et al, 2011). Cloud growth liberates the ventures and their complete clients from the specification of in abundance points of interest, similar to gatherer assets, computing impediment and plan proposal cost. In any case, this may cause idleness sensitive applications that need hubs inside to suit their intermission needs (Bonomi eta l, 2012). When methods and embellishments of IoT region unit acknowledge progress in individuals' life, acknowledged Cloud computing model will barely divert their requirements of headway bolster, space colleague and low idleness. Fog gradual addition is needed for dwelling place overtop botheration (Bonomi et al, 2011). As Fog computing is upheld at the twist of the system, it gives low inactivity, area mindfulness, and enhances quality of service for a live and total time applications. Common precedents programmed computerization, transportation, and systems of sensors and actuators. In addition, this new storm cellar underpins unfavorable as Fog extras cowl end-client gadgets, confirmation focus, twist switches and switches. The Fog demonstrate is solid situated for outright time for colossal modified works investigation, bolsters thickly communicated digests gathering focuses, and gives benefits in diversion, publicizing, individualized computing and applications.

Fog Characteristics

Basically, fog processing is relating expansion of the cloud anyway closer to the things active with IoT data. As appeared in Figure 3, fog computing goes about as partner treated between the cloud and complete gadgets that brings procedure, stockpiling and systems administration benefits closer to the tip gadgets themselves. These gadgets region unit alluded to as fog hubs. They will be sent wherever with a system affiliation. Any gadget with computing, stockpiling and system property will be a fog hub, as mechanical controllers, switches, switches, implanted servers and video police examination cameras (verma et al, 2016).

Fog computing is considered to be the building squares of the cloud in venture with Ai et al (2017). The qualities of fog computing will be abridged as pursues:

Figure 5. Fog computing - cloud extension closer to end devices

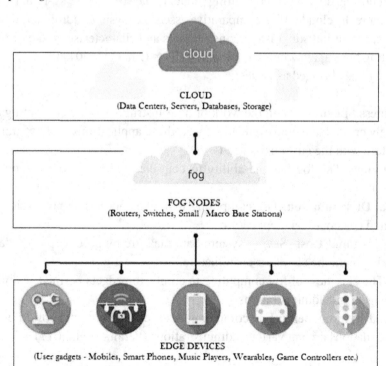

- **Reduced Latency and Location Awareness:** Fog processing underpins area mindfulness inside which fog hubs will be conveyed in various areas. Also, in light of the fact that the fog is closer to complete gadgets, it brings down dormancy of processed information of complete gadgets.
- **Geographical Dispersion:** In refinement of the brought together cloud, the administrations and applications given by the fog region unit circulated may be conveyed wherever.
- **Scalability:** There is a unit vast scale detecting component arranges that screen the encompassing setting. The fog gives appropriated computing and capacity assets which may work with such substantial scale complete gadgets.
- **Quality Support**: one in all the crucial parts of fog applications is that the capacity to join on to cell phones and in this manner change portability ways, similar to locate ID partition convention (LISP) that requires a circulated catalog framework.
- **Time Period Associations:** Fog computing applications gives day and age connections between fog hubs rather than the guidance execution used inside the cloud.
- **Heterogeneity:** Fog hubs or complete gadgets region unit structured by absolutely dissimilar creators are accessible in various structures and need to be conveyed in ventures with their stages. The fog has the ability to figure out totally unique stages.
- **Interoperability:** Fog parts will interoperate and work absolutely in varying areas and crosswise over various administration providers.
- **Cloud Associations:** The fog is put between the cloud and complete gadgets to assume a critical job inside the retention and procedure of the data close to complete gadgets.

Fog Computing Benefits

Fog computing extends the distributed computing model to the sting of the system. Despite the fact that the fog and furthermore the cloud utilize comparative assets like systems administration, processing and capacity, and offer a few of indistinguishable instruments and characteristics like virtualization, multitenure, fog computing brings a few benefits for IoT gadgets (Liu et al, 2017).

These benefits will be abridged as issues:

- **Larger Business Spryness:** With the work of their instruments, fog computing applications will be immediately created and conveyed. Moreover, these applications will program the machine to figure in venture with the customer's needs.
- **Reduced Latency:** The fog has the ability to help day and age administrations (e.g., gaming, video gushing)
- **Geographical Dissemination:** Fog computing will give appropriate processing and capacity assets to huge and cosmopolitan applications
- **Reduced Operational Cost:** Saving system data measure by process picked data locally as opposed to making them the cloud for examination.
- **Scalability:** The closeness of fog computing to complete gadgets permits scaling the measure of associated gadgets and administrations
- **Flexibility and Heterogeneity:** Fog computing licenses the joint effort of different physical situations and foundations among various administrations (Peralta et al, 2017)

Fog Computing Architecture

Fog computing is related with number of centers for tasks. It gives controlled computing, putting away and organizing administrations in an extremely conveyed way between complete gadgets and furthermore the exemplary distributed computing data focuses. The primary target of fog computing is to supply low and predictable dormancy for time-delicate IoT applications (Peralta et al, 2017). As per Muntjir et al. (Muntjir et al, 2017), the architecture of fog computing consists of six layers-physical and virtualization, monitoring, pre-processing, temporary storage, security and transport layer as shown in Figure 6.

Fog computing is a related approach that takes a portion of an information center the physical and virtualization layer incorporates changing sorts of centers like physical centers, virtual centers and virtual distinguishing segment frameworks. This center points zone unit supervised and kept up in endeavor with their sorts and fix demands. Differing sorts of sensors domain unit appropriated topographically to distinguish the nature of the accumulated information and send the same to higher layers by methods for entrances for any technique undertakings to the sting of the framework. The fog gives restricted computing, securing and sorting out organizations to a great degree passed on route between total devices and moreover the incredible conveyed computing information centers. The fundamental focus of fog computing is to supply low and unsurprising inertness for time-tricky IoT applications (Peralta et al, 2017). As demonstrated by Muntjir et al. (Muntjir et al, 2017), the building of fog computing includes six layers-physical and virtualization, checking, pre-liminary readinesss, brief accumulating, security and transport layer as showed up in Fig-3 (Liu et al, 2017). In spite of the fact that at the acknowledgment layer, resource utilization, the supply of sensors and fog center points and framework sections an area unit checked. All endeavors performed by center point's locale unit checked in the midst of this

Figure 6. Architecture of fog computing consists of six layers

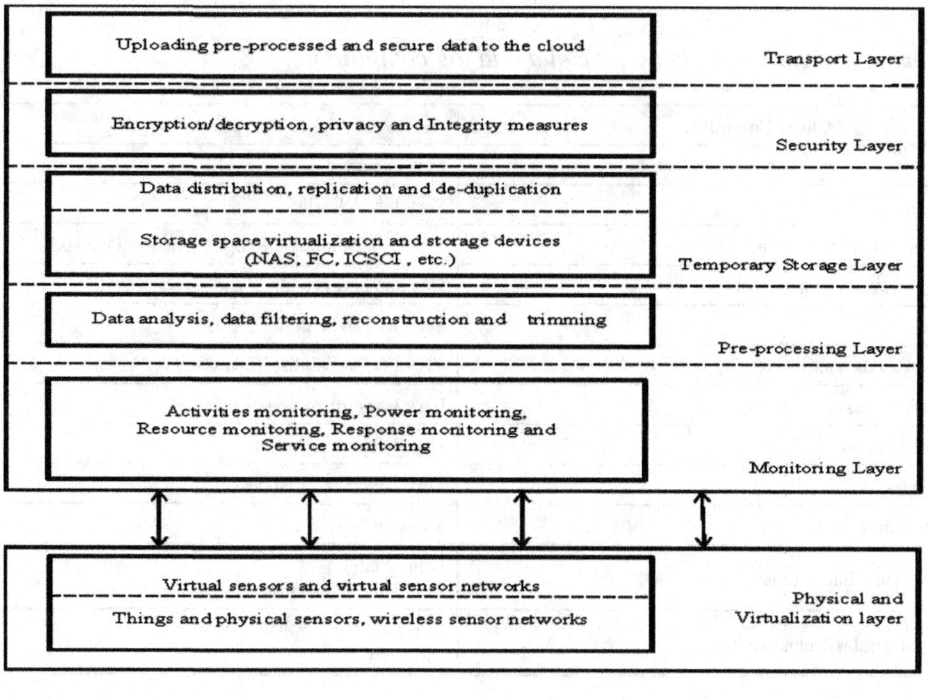

layer, acknowledgment that center is acting what errand, at what time and what will be required from it next. The execution and staying everything considered and benefits are passed on the structure of an area unit checked (Mukherjee et al, 2018). Likewise, the essentiality use of fog center points is watched; since fog computing uses a couple of devices with absolutely unprecedented dimensions of force use, imperativeness organization measures will be ideal and incredible.

The pre-dealing with layer performs information organization errands. Accumulated information region unit researched and information filtering and trimming zone unit guided in the midst of this layer to isolate conscious data. The pre-taken care of information zone unit by then holds tight quickly inside the temporary storing layer. At the point when the information region unit is transmitted to the cloud, they should not be held tight regionally and will be off from the fleeting accumulating media. For efficient control utility, sole designate of assembled information is exchanged to the cloud. In other words, the entranceway device partner the IoT to the cloud frames the information already making them the cloud. This kind of entranceway is named a sensible entranceway. Information assembled from recognizing part frameworks and IoT devices zone unit traded through sensible portals to the cloud. The data gotten by the cloud is then holding tight and wont to make organizations for customers (Vishwanath et al, 2016). For supported restricted resources of the fog, a correspondence tradition for fog computing must be efficient, light-weight and customizable. Thus picking up the correspondence tradition depends on the mechanical assembly condition of the fog.

Fog Computing With IoT

The present centralized cloud computing configuration is confronting serious difficulties for IoT applications. For instance, it cannot bolster IoT time-touchy applications like video spilling, play and expanded reality. Moreover, it needs area mindfulness since it might be a brought together model. Fog computing is in a situation to deal with these difficulties. Fog computing functions as an extension between capacity

Table 1. summarizes variations between cloud and fog computing

Cloud Computing	Fog Computing
High latency	Low latency
High delay jitter	Very low delay jitter
Service location Within the Internet	Service location at the edge of the local network
Multiple hops between client and server	One hop between client and server
Undefined security	Security can be defined
High probability of data attack	Very low probability of data attack
No Location awareness	Easy Location awareness
Centralized distribution	Distributed distribution
Few Server Nodes	Very large Server Nodes
Limited Support for Mobility	Supports Mobility
Supported Real Time Interactions	Supported Real Time Interactions
Leased Line and wireless connectivity	Wireless connectivity

administrations and IoT gadgets with huge distributed computing. In venture with Cisco ("Fog Computing", 2016), fog computing might be a piece of the distributed computing worldview that takes the cloud closer to the sting of the system. It gives amazingly virtualized model of calculation, stockpiling and systems administration assets between complete gadgets and established cloud servers. To expand the efficiency of IoT applications, the majority of the information created by these IoT objects/gadgets ought to be handled and broken down in day and age. Fog computing can bring cloud systems administration, computing and capacity abilities the distance down to the sting of the system, which can address the day and age Issue of IoT gadgets and supply efficient and secure IoT applications (Agarwal et al, 2012).

Fog computing delivers totally extraordinary administrations and applications with cosmopolitan arrangements. The fog has the ability to supply efficient day and age correspondence between totally unique IoT applications, as associated vehicles, through the intermediary and passageways situated in venture with long expressways and tracks. Fog computing is considered to be the best choice for applications with low dormancy needs like video spilling, gaming, expanded reality, and so forth (Agarwal et al, 2012).

The blend of fog computing with the IoT can convey a few benefits to various IoT applications. The fog supports era cooperation between IoT gadgets to downsize inertness, especially for time-touchy IoT applications. Moreover, one fact in all the crucial alternatives of fog computing is that the capacity to help vast scale detecting component arranges, that might be a tremendous drawback with the consistently developing assortment of IoT gadgets, which can a little while later be tallied in billions. Fog computing will give a few benefits to various IoT applications, as seen in Fig-4.

Fog computing will give effective ways that beat several existing computing architectures limitations that bank solely on computing within the cloud and on end-user devices that are associated with IoT devices.

Figure 7. Fog computing supports numerous IOT applications

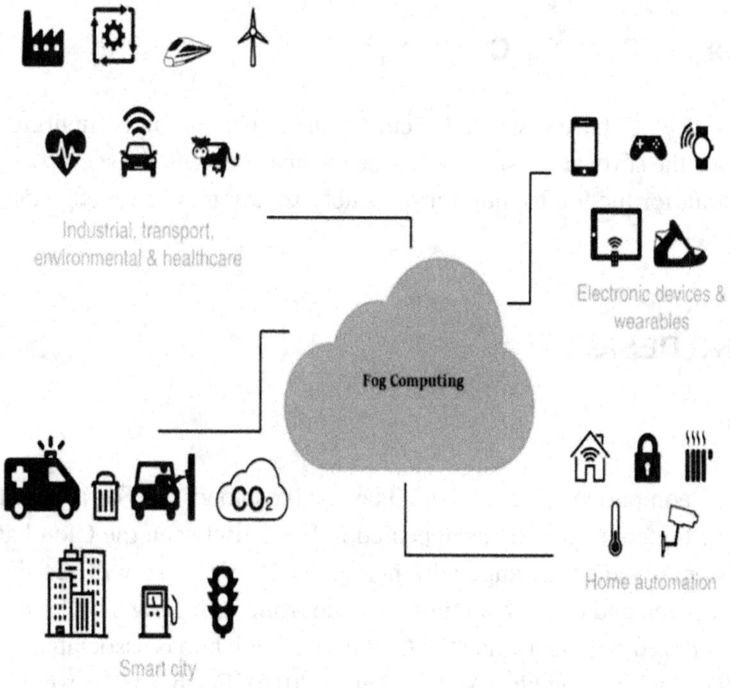

FOG COMPUTING CAN SOLVE IOT CHALLENGE

Constraints Over Latency

The fog plays out all calculation activity like overseeing and breaking down data and distinctive time-touchy activities close to complete clients that will be the perfect response to satisfy dormancy requirements of various IoT applications.

Constraints Over Network Data Measure

Fog computing permits the class-conscious handling of the cloud to IoT gadgets. This empowers handling to be controlled retribution on application requests out there in systems administration and computing assets. This, thus, lessens the quantity of data that should have been transferred to the cloud, which can spare system data measure.

Constraints Over Resource Gadgets

Fog computing will be wont to perform activities that require huge assets for the benefit of asset obliged gadgets when such tasks cannot be transferred to the cloud. Consequently, this empowers diminishing gadgets quality, lifecycle costs and power utilization.

Constraints Over Administrations

Fog computing will run severally to affirm persistent administrations even, once its sporadic system property is of the cloud.

Constraints Over IoT Security Challenges

Resource-constrained devices have restricted security functions; so, fog computing acts as a proxy for these devices to update the software system. Because of those devices the security credentials are to be monitored. It is difficult for the fog to monitor the safety standing of close edge devices present in the network.

FOG COMPUTING DESIGN

General Design

In view of the in vogue computing structure with 3 layers: the Cloud, the Fog and furthermore the Edge, we offer an exhaustive fog configuration as appeared in Fig-5, Between the Cloud and furthermore the Fog lies a center system to supply arrange administrations. From it we will see that the Cloud lies at the higher center dimension and is much unapproachable from edge gadgets. The Fog lies at the middle dimension and is closer to edge gadgets than the Cloud. Each Fog hub is associated with the Cloud. Each edge gadget is associated with a Fog hub (Mahmud et al, 2016). Furthermore, we will see that Fog hubs

Figure 8. A comprehensive fog design

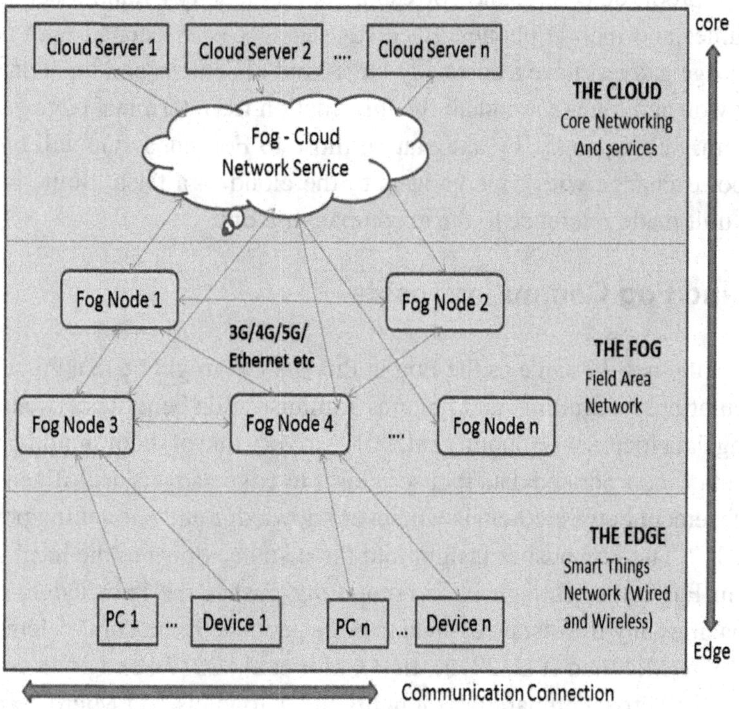

will be associated with each unique gadget. Interchanges between Fog-Fog, Fog-Cloud, and Fog-Edge computing, all are bi-directional.

- **The Cloud:** It incorporates predominant servers and capacity gadgets for broadcasting, data reposition and expansive data investigation (Mahmud et al, 2016). It is the remote and administration focus that may store large amount of data, and strategy to a great degree progressed anyway as a rule non-critical assignments. The data is dispersed to the Cloud through rapid remote or wired correspondences. The Cloud gives last and world inclusion. As a vault, it gives data stockpiling to satisfy clients' longstanding needs and astute data examination.

- **The Fog:** It comprises of a system of interconnected Fog hubs. It gives geo-conveyed, low inactivity and basic calculation besides area mindfulness. Each Fog hub might be an asset community for transient stockpiling. Its capacities grasp organize rebuild, data arrangement, interchanges, data exchange, data stockpiling, calculation and administration. In contrast to sting gadgets, Fog hubs have extra memory or capacity for computing, that makes it potential to process a major amount of data from edge gadgets. On the other hand, once requiring an extra progressed and old calculation, the calculation work should be sent to the Cloud by Fog hubs through changed out there interchanges advances, e.g., 3G/4G/5G cell systems and remote neighborhood. Fog hubs territory unit connects among Cloud and edge gadgets. Fog hubs territory is unit independent and may be interconnected for joint effort. Administration and agreeable methods zone is unit connected with Fog hubs to execute administration and administration. The cooperation among Fog hubs will be dead by means of remote or local correspondences among them.

- **The Edge:** It comprises of numerous physical gadgets (edge gadgets) empowered with their present recognizable proof, detecting, and correspondence capacity (Mahmud et al, 2016), similar to vehicles, machines and mobile phones. Each edge gadget is associated with no less than one of the Fog hubs. Edge gadgets have a curiously large kind of sensors and local data. It is awfully beyond all doubt won and longs to send all the information from terminal edge gadgets to the Cloud through a system. Subsequently, by associating those to Fog hubs, one will battle with the basic data anyway not exchange with edge gadgets to the cloud in a flash. Some basically misjudged thoughts zone unit made reference to the accompanying ones.

Between Edge and Fog Computing Inside

Edge computing is totally not the same as the Fog in this the last might be to a great degree virtualized stage that gives calculation, stockpiling, and systems administration benefits between complete gadgets and Cloud computing data focusses (Bonomi et al, 2012). Every one of them should push knowledge and process capacities out of incorporated data focuses closer to edge gadgets, as IoT sensors, transfers, and engines. The key refinement between them is wherever knowledge and computing power region unit set (Mukherjee et al, 2017). The Fog pushes insight into the distance down to the local space arrangement level, process data in Fog hubs. Though Edge computing pushes the knowledge, process power and correspondence capacities any the distance down to edge gadgets. Extra subtle elements between them are made reference to in (Mahmud et al, 2016). In (Okafor et al,, 2017), end point computing is viewed as Edge computing. Distinctive comparative thoughts like Cloudlets and Micro-server farms territory unit specified in (Okafor et al, 2017).

Between Wireless Sensing Element Networks and Fog Computing

WSNs region unit is intended to work at frightfully low capacity to build battery life or utilize vitality to collect home to continue them. A large portion of them confront the issues of little memory bits, low process control, and by and large problematic sensors. The Fog might be a fitting stage to help WSNs (Bonomi et al, 2012). Moreover, it separates the choices among Mobile Edge computing, Mobile Cloud computing, Fog and Cloud computing from Figure 2 and furthermore the over investigation, we tend to uncover the resulting security and trust issues for the Fog: Since the Fog is implied upon old systems administration parts, it is greatly at risk to security assaults. It is burdensome to affirm reported access to administrations and support of protection in an extremely monster Fog (Mahmud et al, 2016). We will conjointly observe that the dispersed and open nature of its information structure makes it subject to security dangers. Old security and trust issues, such as wiretapping, altering, loss of information, and Trojan steeds, still exist.

The new ones caused by Fog qualities unit recorded as pursues: For a grasp gadget, it will get the opportunity to change the relationship to its nearby Fog hub once blames occur. This should fabricate a substitution affiliation and exchange data from the past Fog hub to the enhanced one, which can prompt extra probability for fresh out of the plastic new security once such affiliation comes up short. It conjointly faces the emergency of re-finding a trade Fog hub for correspondences if it is associated Fog hub glitches once fabricating a substitution relationship from a Fog hub to the Cloud.

Cautious Design Style

In view of the plan in Fig. 5, the topological structures interchanges among Fog hubs and grasp net-like and transport as appeared in (Mahmud et al, 2016) severally. The past is extra exceptional and will cause extra correspondence overhead, security and trust hazard. The weaknesses of transport grasp data crash, limited correspondences separate and confined shift. It is conjointly hard to determine and disconnect deficiencies to have it. From the correspondence relationship among the Fog hubs, we tend to uncover the ensuing security and trust issues:

- Every Fog hub is not exclusively independent, anyway can likewise be helpful with various ones through message passing. On the off chance that Fog hubs neglect to be incorporated into the system and work along to shape intentional administrations, trust issues that could occur.
- Once a substitution Fog hub comes or partners past one cannot give its administration and requirements to stop, the contrary Fog hubs most likely got to adjust their topology and assemble their correspondence structure in this way on change and interchanges among them. This may instigate new security issues caused by such a topology remaking technique.
- Once Fog hubs team up with various hubs, on the off chance that one hub is assaulted by malignant clients and is tainted, the contaminated one could assault or taint diverse hubs. This incites security or trust emergency among all the agreeable hubs.
- Fog hubs will impart by means of a system. The correspondence overhead among them is likewise enormous. For inertness delicate applications, it will be an overwhelming drawback. It lowers the framework dependablity at that point, cause trust emergency for clients once their errand due dates zone unit become tremendous. Consequently, the best approach to diminish the correspondence overhead to an appropriate dimension might be an imperative issue.

Structure Execution

A three-layer Fog configuration is expert as appeared in Figure 7. Its IoT administrations, coordination layer and disseminated message transport, and deliberation layer. IoT administrations: The Fog stage has a gathering of various administration applications, as sensible town. Relate IoT benefit is seen as the route for clients to get to their required usefulness (Fortino eta 1, 2017). Organization layer and circulated message transport: Orchestration is that technique through which the Fog frameworks affirm anyway the virtualized assets zone unit distributed and worked between.

It is fundamental that coordination is receptive to the quick condition of the Fog arrangement, and responds rapidly to any adjustments in its setup, load, or standing. The center issues, difficulties, and future investigation headings in fog-empowered organization for IoT administrations is outlined in (Fortino et al, 2017). Because of its administrations and foundation territory unit distribution, the Fog should give vital implies for dispersed approach based arrangement, which winds up inside the versatile administration of individual subsystems and furthermore in the general administrations. The organization common sense is appropriated over the Fog preparing while dispersed administration gives higher flexibility, higher quantifiability, and speedier arrangement for topographically disseminated organizations than concentrated administration. The electronic informing transport is utilized for interchanges. The layer gives arrangement based and dynamic life cycle administration for Fog administrations. There exists in fog unit four components inside the existence cycle: requesting, analyzing, planning, and executing.

Abstraction layer: It gives consistency in an exceptionally heterogeneous foundation setting over changed access, administration and administration of assets through customized Application Programming Interfaces (APIs) and User Interfaces. Nonexclusive variety APIs concern security, detachment and protection to various inhabitants. In Fig. 6, from the Fog hubs themselves, we tend to watch the resulting security and trust issues. New security and trust issues territory unit rose on account of administration organization. It must determine that be as it may administrations need to be enchained before conveyance. Amazingly dependable administrations should be executed over the entire administration. At the deliberation layer, security is said with seclusion and protection in multi-tenure. Because of an entranceway there will be a Fog hub inside the Fog that is totally not the same as the entranceway in applications.

A five-layer plan of the Fog entranceway as a Fog hub is appeared in Fig-7. Beneath the 5 layers the base unit consists of a few things, sensors and WSNs in an exceptionally physical and virtualization setting. The consequent 5 layers zone unit on the most astounding of nature:

1. **Monitoring Layer:** It screens exercises, power, reactions, and administrations once acting errands. Compelling estimates zone unit taken in time.
2. **Preprocessing Layer:** It investigates channels, reproduces and trims data.
3. **Temporary Capacity Layer**: It bolsters data dispersion, replication and organizer space virtualization. It stores preprocessed data in Fog hubs and passes them to the Cloud.
4. **Security Layer:** Some close to home data is likewise created by means of IoT gadgets and WSNs, similar to show human services data. Location based information is large and delicate once security and protection issues zone unit are included.
5. **Transport Layer:** It transfers the prepared to-send data to the Cloud. Once being transferred, the information is off from Fog hubs.

We find the ensuing security and trust issues:

- **Storage is Required Inside the Fog:** Identifying with the capacity, a few issues are additionally confronted. For example, when a hold gadget sends data to its associated Fog hub,
- What data is inside the Fog hub and inside the Cloud?
- In the event that the basic data is goliath and not admissible to exchange to the Cloud, anyway will we tend to utilize the Fog hub's coordination to comprehend security and high conservative storing?
- A crossover storing approach for IoT in PaaS cloud league is arranged. The issues with respect to anchor data stockpiling and look for mechanical IoT by integration Fog Computing and Cloud Computing region unit examined.
- However will we tend to comprehend cost-viability and high versatility against disappointments in significant applications (Okofor et al, 2017)
- If a larger than average occupation is required to be handled at the preprocessing layer and is on the far side the calculation capacity of the associated Fog hub, anyway should it do? A few estimates should be taken for it.
- Gateways filling in as Fog hubs is likewise traded off or supplanted by artificial ones. From the over examination of the fog computing plan, we will see a few trust and security issues to act naturally tended to. The associated work is made reference to straightaway.

Figure 9. Five-layer design of the Fog

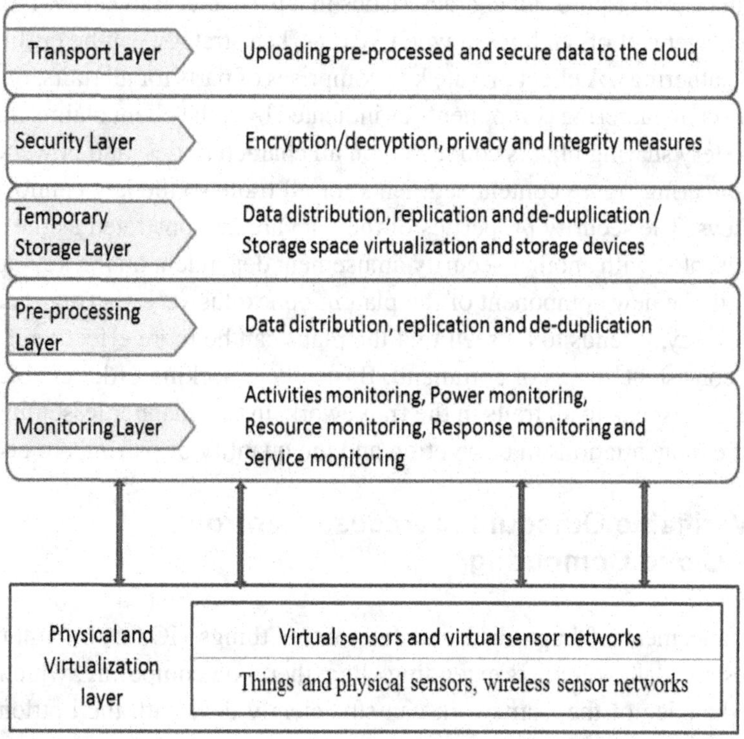

LITERATURE SURVEY

An Attribute-Based Encryption Scheme to Secure Fog Communications (Jiang et al, 2017)

With the end goal to accomplish the security prerequisites of the correspondences between fog hubs and the cloud, an encoded key trade convention dependent on CP-ABE has been proposed. All the more extraordinarily, we plan a convention to such an extent that each fog hub is related to an arrangement of properties, and dole out each figure content with an expressive access structure that is characterized over these traits. This component authorizes the decoding strategy dependent on the fog hub's characteristics. Each figure content conveys an entrance structure to such an extent that the fog can unscramble the figure message and get the common key just on the off chance that it has the predetermined qualities in the entrance structure. The convention depends on the mix of CP-ABE and computerized signature systems.

Cipher Text-Policy ABE Against Key-Delegation Abuse in Fog Computing (Jiang et al, 2017)

In this paper, figure content approach trait based encryption plot is proposed in which clients cannot wrongfully produce new private keys of a subset of the clients' unique arrangements of qualities. The entrance structure utilized in CP-ABE is developed by an AND-entryway, which is a subset of the entrance structures utilized. In our plan, a figure content with the entrance structure A, which comprises of a solitary AND-door that requires all characteristics in a particular trait set W, must be decoded by a private key of an arrangement of qualities ω when W C ω. The strategy can be outlined as usage of the property of bilinear gatherings. A client private key comprises of parts for all traits, of which each is built dependent on either set of gathering components as indicated by if the client claims this quality or not. In this manner, the mystery sharing plan is connected on all characteristics, and powers the bilinear guide of key parts and comparing figure content segments for all traits so the key cannot be part nor joined with other private keys. The security properties of the plan are demonstrated as the standard particular model. Likewise presented with another security amusement dependent on the key-appointment misuse issue and demonstrate the new component of the plan in nonexclusive gathering model.

Regarding proficiency, it tends to be seen that the plans can be more effective if characteristics are masterminded into consistent chains of command. Basically, a pecking order enables us to utilize less gathering components to speak to all traits in the framework, in this manner lessening the figure content size, the quantity of exponentiations in encryption and the quantity of pairings in decoding.

A Secure and Verifiable Outsourced Access Control Scheme in Fog-Cloud Computing

With the quick enhancement of huge data and Internet of things (IOT), the amount of frameworks organization devices and data volume is extending altogether. Fog computing, which extends appropriated computing to the edge of the framework can sufficiently deal with the bottleneck issues of data transmission and data accumulating. In any case, security and insurance challenges are in like manner rising in the fog conveyed computing condition. Figure content methodology property based encryption (CP-ABE) can be grasped to recognize data get the chance to control in fog conveyed computing systems. In this paper, we propose a verifiable re-appropriated multi-expert get the chance to control plot, named VO-MAACS. In our advancement, most encryption and unraveling estimations are redistributed to fog devices and the figuring results can be checked by using our affirmation system. Meanwhile, to address the repudiation issue, we plan a capable customer and trademark refusal strategy for it. Finally, examination and generation results exhibit that our arrangement is both secure and exceedingly capable.

CCA-Secure ABE With Outsourced Decryption for Fog Computing

OD-ABE fathoms the fine-grained get the opportunity to control the encoded data for resource basic devices in disseminated computing incredible. In any case, the fog computing has changed the fundamental establishment. In particular, the data is physically secured significantly closer to the customers and has various copies in many fog contraptions. This new system empowers the enemy to dispatch more mind boggling ambushes than whenever in ongoing memory. Of course, it is eminent that the picked figure content security is all around considered as the most imperative security thought for a cryptosystem and it can restrict the dark present day strikes to the unstable data in fog computing. Regardless, none of the present OD-ABE designs achieve CCA security. The standard CCA security of open key encryption guarantees that any figure content can't be flexible. Everything considered, the figure content change is ordinary as a standard value in OD-ABE, which makes the significance of CCA security unstable. In this paper, to fill the gap between the security need of fog computing and the security of OD-ABE, we will propose the CCA security for OD-ABE by following the spirit of the regular CCA security as close as would be prudent.

Security in Fog Computing Through Encryption

Data Encryption standard (DES) was once most broadly utilized encryption standard, which utilizes symmetric key calculation for encryption of information. A portion of the assaults that could break the key quicker than the Brute power are Differential Crypt-investigation, Linear Crypt-examination and Improved Davies Attack. The antecedent of the DES calculation is 3DES which is named as Triple Data Encryption Standard. Where 3 occasions of DES are fell. Indeed, even in Triple DES is powerless against security assaults compromise assault. As DES calculation was intended for equipment usage, it is not solid in equipment similarly Triple DES does not work appropriately in programming applications. To defeat this Advanced Encryption Standard (AES) is utilized as it is considered more compelling, which is viewed as the most progressive and anchored standard for encryption of electronic information. AES is viewed as successor of the DES which utilizes standard symmetric key encryption for a significant number of the US government associations. AES acknowledges the key size of 128, 192, 256 bits of size. While 128 is now viewed as unbreakable and there were many open rivalry held by numerous association to break the key yet it was never done. On looking at all the accessible encryption calculations, AES would be the better and the most anchored sort of calculation that is executed in the fog, applying of AES calculation for security of the information in fog computing through an edge gadget of versatile.

OPEN ANALYSIS PROBLEMS

Offering high security and trust is very important to the Fog customers. Many open analysis problems stay.

Trustworthy Environment Setting

Devices within the Fog area unit usually deployed while not under strict observance and protection, thereby facing all types of security threats. The way to increase the trust within the Fog is the primary challenge. Public key infrastructure (PKI) primarily based technique might part solve this downside. Trustworthy execution setting (TEE) technique could have its potential within the Fog. The open network setting of the Fog makes a malicious procedure simply unfold to intelligent devices and produces serious threat to user information (Bonomi et al, 2012). The way to management and avoidance of such unfolding of a malicious procedure is incredibly vital in trustworthy execution setting.

Trust and Security Throughout Fog Adaptation

Accomplishing between nodal secure joint effort and dependable asset provisioning is an essential issue (Dsouza et al, 2014). Fog hubs zone unit circulated virtualized and shared. Fog coordination should be enhanced for a multi-occupant demonstrates. Finish detachment should be kept up among occupants through a virtualization framework to maintain a strategic distance from cross-divulgence and protection trade off of utilization particular data. Upheld strategy driven security administration for the Fog, the work (Dsouza et al, 2014) ponders on asset administration expanding the present Fog stage to help secure coordinated effort and capacity among totally unique client asked for assets inside the Fog. Nonetheless, staggered cooperation winds up in monster security and trust issues, principally together with personality administration, confirmation, get to administration, information sharing and QoS, for example, when a Fog hub encounters a disappointment, close Fog hubs on indistinguishable or nearby layers should venture in to hold the heap that is in any investigations.

Access Administration

It is burdensome anyway essential to upgrade secrecy in getting to generally circulated Fog. Secrecy inside the Fog must be adaptable and efficient to address asset compelled Fog gadgets. Old ways need strength for the Fog. Light-weight coding calculations should be helpful for Fog hubs and edge gadgets. In the Fog, we will conjointly raise questions like the best approach to style new access administration ways traversing client Fog-Cloud, to beat the limitations of edge gadgets at totally extraordinary dimensions (Dsouza et al, 2014). The Fog is pictured as an ideal possibility to allow get to tokens to affirmed parties. A brought together structure is additionally wont to approve access and transfer data between endorsed gatherings and edge gadgets (IoT gadgets) (Okafor et al, 2017) Be that as it may, in an extremely dispersed Fog setting, a brought together structure could come up short and end in conflicting information. Thus, new systems giving reliable assurance should structure.

Attack During Collision

Arrangement aggressors are likewise masked. New advancements should be produced to shield the framework protection once confronting a potential agreement attack (Wang et al, 2017). In the fog have 2 styles of agreement assault:

- Brokers contrive with administration providers: Malicious specialists and suppliers could unfurl the artificial or copy occasions to the Fog arrange. Also, the last will spill guide.
- Brokers plan with clients: Malicious representatives and clients could deny conceding any match achieving or using data and administrations from lawful providers.

In any case, the present work has not thought of the assault from providers plotting with clients. Malignant providers could spill advice to clients for a couple of adventure as last mentioned. Conspiring clients could deny conceding getting any guidance from the past. Subsequently, the best approach to fabricate high-security and shoddy intrigue assault location measure is one in all the key issues inside the Fog. New ways, similar to helpful discovery, is additionally wont to watch and notice this kind of troublesome assaults.

Security Over Data-Reliance and Context-Awareness

In the Fog, to improve information subordinate security, reinforcement is required for vital data. Furthermore, the data over numerous end-client gadgets faces bigger assault hazard and extra difficulties (Wang et al, 2017). Because of partner resister will bargain data honesty by endeavoring to switch or crush genuine data, it's basic to plot a security system to supply data trustworthiness check of the transmitted data between the Fog hubs and furthermore the Cloud. The character of supporting for quality and vicinity to end-clients of the Fog suggests a substitution security approach for straightforwardly and adaptively overseeing setting changes, especially for verification, get to administration and trust degree in various setting mindful conditions.

Trust in Service Provided

In the Fog, a safe and reliable way for clients is required. Nonetheless, the Service Level Agreement (SLA) is normally tormented by a few elements like, benefit value, vitality utilization, application attributes, information stream, and system standing. Along these lines, given a chosen circumstance, it is very hard to determine an administration which believes the merits inside out in investigation. Trust examination systems inside the Cloud will be changed to broaden the security of Fog administrations (Xia et al, 2017). Upheld operational necessities and execution conditions, one needs to pick proper and dependable Fog hubs, their relating asset setup and spots of preparing inside the Fog. Current ways (Okaofr et al, 2017), need similarity and quantifiability to follow and confirm their trust esteems and screen them for the Fog. SLA (Mukherjee et al, 2017) that has picked up achievement in arranging a trust show in Cloud computing is likewise changed to use inside the Fog.

FUTURE WORK

In view of the present investigation results, we tend to propose the consequent issues to act naturally tended to inside what is to come:

Trusted Manageable Fog Models

A reliable outsider is embraced in the fog spaces. It will enhance the security. Be that as it may, the past work neglects to think about the district drawback. The strategy includes locale issues for the Fog, as appeared in Fig. 5. Nonetheless, the Fog hub appointive as an agent from an area Fog is likewise a noxious hub that makes the Fog confront a greater trust hazard. To determine the issue and enhance trusted responsibility, relate enhanced trust, administration demonstrates are required. One answer is likewise arranged as pursues:

- Employing a dependable outsider will diminish the trust administration and calculation overhead of the Fog through the cautious idea of the Fog scope. At that point exploitation the parcel thought relatively will diminish the administration and calculation overhead inside the Fog.
- Managing the between area trust esteems for Fog hubs by means of exploitation correspondence and chronicled data with each other inside the district Fog.
- Managing the area locale trust esteems for the district Fog by human action with the Cloud and exploitation authentic data inside the Cloud.
- Some techniques will be embraced in an extremely district fog, for example can actualize biometric components for fog hubs.

Identification of Trusted Fog Nodes

Fog clients with asset obliged gadgets will source their errands to their reliable Fog hubs. The best approach to decide such hubs is pivotal. Numerous strategies are additionally received:

- If fog immediate or circuitous trust assessments of the objective hubs, dependable hubs region unit picked in venture with their trust esteems.
- Otherwise, by utilizing a shot model bolstered chronicled conduct of the objective hubs, we will survey their trust esteems and assemble the choice therefore.
- Collusion double dealings are likewise directed by worked together clients or Fog hubs. It implies plot conduct introduced and directed each by clients or by malevolent Fog hubs. The sort of conspiracy conduct should be identified to spot dependable hubs in an extremely district Fog.
- As a consequence Fog hubs will in general be asset obliged, it is important to style light-weight arrangements. Consequently, the trust calculation recipe should be simple and involve limited memory exclusively. The Fog is of dynamic nature and brings new test for trust computing once confronting constrained assets and low inactivity needs. A light-weight technique for trust calculation bolstered a territory Fog is additionally intended for meeting bound constrained asset needs. On the off chance that the calculation assignment is gigantic, it will be dead inside the Cloud.

Secure Arrangement Adaption

Upgraded Fog organization is required to stay away from cross-exposure and security trade off of use particular data. Quality of Service (QoS) and Service level Agreements (SLA) territory unit required to affirm that every one application gets the base and enough dimensions of assets for orchestration (Mukherjee et al, 2017). 2 styles of organization be any investigation. Application organization: Large-scale IoT benefits inside the Fog frameworks, as sensible urban areas, medicinal services, and marine recognition territory unit made out of sensors, computing assets and gadgets. Arranging such applications will alter upkeep and framework responsibility. Nonetheless, the best approach is with proficiency screen and strategy,These applications' transient conduct and dynamic changes might be a vital test (Agarwal et al, 2012). Relate operator based trust calculation display is likewise utilized for coordination.

A multi-operator arrangement strategy is likewise received to watch the applications and facilitate them immovably progressively inside the Fog. Fog hubs' arrangement: The organization of Fog hubs will convey virtual administrations to Fog framework and encourage asset cooperation. When Fog hubs team up with others, one hub is additionally assaulted by malevolent clients or Fog hubs. On the off chance that it's contaminated, the tainted one could assault and contaminate distinctive hubs. This instigates security and trust chance spreading among Fog hubs even to a full locale Fog. A few techniques should be taken to diminish this kind of hazard, by coming up short the contaminated hub. On the off chance that a Fog hub is framed, disappointments remaining all through coordination, the contrary Fog hubs likely got to alteration their topology and fabricate their correspondence structure loyally. The data inside the coming up short hub should even be exchanged to various solid Fog hubs indicated the arrangement will go before. An approach based administration organization is additionally received.

CONCLUSION

The Fog might be a great degree virtualized environment but not a substitution of Cloud computing. It gives storing, computing and systems administrations among edge gadgets moreover as antiquated Cloud computing data focusses. It basically fathoms the issues of low inertness, quality help and situation mindfulness in a few digital physical frameworks. Be that as it may, it is dispersed and an open structure, makes it defenseless and feeble to security dangers. This work examines the designs of the Fog from a general to watchful ones. The associated security and trust examination results with respect to the Fog computing can be outlined, and furthermore the discourses with regard to open security and trust issues given, and future work made open. A dispersed and remotely worked Fog will cause new security and trust difficulties, that do not appear to be presented inside the brought together Cloud. We tend to fabricate some last comments for the Fog: New ways territory unit required. Because the Fog is to a great degree disseminated, usage of security systems for information driven uprightness will affect its QoS to a decent degree. Thus, we need to search out better approaches to upgrade the wellbeing and trust of the Fog. Low-inertness and a larger than average assortment of asset compelled gadgets inside the Fog rouse analysts and specialists to propose new ways indicated the Fog will extravagant high security and trust. So Fog hubs should move with totally extraordinary equipment in stages given by various sellers, new interfaces region unit required for Fog programming framework to affirm dependable computing. New conventions territory unit is required. A few conventions have just been structured. In any case, novel conventions territory unit lack mechanical security and trust bargains inside the Fog. Considering the restriction of the present investigations and research inclines, it is fundamental to create an altogether new style, a gathering to expand security and trust countermeasures. A few security and trust issues seem to remain open and have so pulled in rich consideration from scientists and specialists.

REFERENCES

Agarwal, S., Yadav, S., & Yadav, A. K. (2016). An Efficient Architecture and Algorithm for Resource Provisioning in Fog Computing. *Int. J. Inf. Eng. Electron. Bus.*, 8, 48–61.

Ai, Y., Peng, M., & Zhang, K. (2017). Edge cloud computing technologies for internet of things: A primer. *Digit. Commun. Netw.*

Bonomi, F. (2011). Connected vehicles, the internet of things, and fog computing. *The Eighth ACM International Workshop on Vehicular Inter-Networking (VANET).*

Bonomi, F., Milito, R., Zhu, J., & Addepalli, S. (2012). Fog computing and its role in the internet of things. *Proceedings of the First Edition of the MCC Workshop on Mobile Cloud Computing, ser. MCC'12*, 13–16. 10.1145/2342509.2342513

Bonomi, F., Milito, R., Zhu, J., & Addepalli, S. (2012). Fog computing and its role in the Internet of Things, *Proc. of MCC'12*, 13-15. 10.1145/2342509.2342513

Dsouza, C., Ahn, G. J., & Taguinod, M. (2014). Policy-driven security management for Fog computing: Preliminary framework and a case study. *Proc. of IEEE International Conference on Information Reuse & Integration*, 16-23. 10.1109/IRI.2014.7051866

Fan, K., Wang, J., Wang, X., Li, H., & Yang, Y. (2017). A Secure and Verifiable Outsourced Access Control Scheme in Fog-Cloud Computing. *Sensors (Basel)*, *17*(7), 1695. doi:10.339017071695 PMID:28737733

Fog Computing and the Internet of Things: Extend the Cloud to Where the Things Are. (2016). White Paper. Available online: http://www.cisco.com/c/dam/en_us/solutions/trends/iot/docs/computing-overview.pdf

Fortino, G., Russo, W., Savaglio, C., Viroli, M., & Zhou, M. (2017). Modeling Opportunistic IoT Services in Open IoT Ecosystems. *17th Workshop From Objects to Agents (WOA 2017)*, 90-95.

Ghahramani, Zhou, & Hon. (2017). Toward CloudComputing QoS Architecture: Analysis of Cloud Systems and Cloud Services. *IEEE/CAA Journal of Automatica Sinica, 4*(1), 5-17.

Jiang, Y., Susilo, W., Mu, Y., & Guo, F. (2017). Ciphertext-policy attribute-based encryption against key-delegation abuse in fog computing. *Future Generation Computer Systems*. doi:10.1016/j.future.2017.01.026

Liu, Y., Fieldsend, J. E., & Min, G. (2017). A Framework of Fog Computing: Architecture, Challenges and Optimization. *IEEE Access: Practical Innovations, Open Solutions*, *4*, 1–10.

Mahmud, R., & Buyyar, R. (2016). *Fog computing: A Taxonomy, Survey and Future Directions.* arXiv:1611.05539

Mukherjee, M., Matam, R., Shu, L., Maglaras, L., Ferrag, M. A., Choudhury, N., & Kumar, V. (2017). Security and Privacy in Fog computing: Challenges. *IEEE Access: Practical Innovations, Open Solutions*, *5*, 19293–19304. doi:10.1109/ACCESS.2017.2749422

Mukherjee, M., Shu, L., & Wang, D. (2018). Survey of Fog Computing: Fundamental, Network Applications, and Research Challenges. *IEEE Commun. Surv. Tutor.*

Muntjir, M., Rahul, M., & Alhumyani, H. A. (2017). An Analysis of Internet of Things (IoT): Novel Architectures, Modern Applications, Security Aspects and Future Scope with Latest Case Studies. *Int. J. Eng. Res. Technol.*, *6*, 422–447.

Okafor, K. C., Achumba, I. E., Chukwudebe, G. A., & Ononiwu, G. C. (2017). Leveraging Fog Computing for Scalable IoT Datacenter Using Spine-Leaf Network Topology. *Journal of Electrical and Computer Engineering*, *2017*, 1–11. doi:10.1155/2017/2363240

Peralta, G., Iglesias-Urkia, M., Barcelo, M., Gomez, R., Moran, A., & Bilbao, J. (2017). Fog computing based efficient IoT scheme for the Industry 4.0. *Proceedings of the 2017 IEEE International Workshop of Electronics, Control, Measurement, Signals and their application to Mechatronics*, 1–6. 10.1109/ECMSM.2017.7945879

Verma, M., Bhardwaj, N., & Yadav, A. K. (2016). Real Time Efficient Scheduling Algorithm for Load Balancing in Fog Computing Environment. *Int. J. Inf. Technol. Comput. Sci.*, *8*, 1–10.

Vishwanath, A., Peruri, R., & He, J. (2016). Security in Fog Computing through Encryption. *International Journal of Information Technology and Computer Science.*, *8*(5), 28–36. doi:10.5815/ijitcs.2016.05.03

Wang, Q., Chen, D., Zhang, N., Ding, Z., & Qin, Z. (2017). PCP: A Privacy-Preserving Content-Based Publish-Subscribe Scheme With Differential Privacy in Fog computing. *IEEE Access: Practical Innovations, Open Solutions*, *5*, 17962–17986. doi:10.1109/ACCESS.2017.2748956

Xia, Zhou, Luo, & Zhu. (2015). Stochastic Modeling and Quality Evaluation of Infrastructure-as-a-Service Clouds. *IEEE Trans. on Automation Science and Engineering, 12*(1), 160-172.

Xia, Y., Hong, H., Lin, G., & Sun, Z. (2017). A Secure and Efficient Cloud Resource Allocation Scheme with Trust Evaluation Mechanism Based on Combinatorial Double Auction, KSII. *Transactions on Internet and Information Systems (Seoul), 11*(9), 4197–4219.

Zuo, C. (2016). CCA-secure ABE with outsourced decryption for fog computing. *Future Generation Computer Systems*.

Chapter 16
Smart City Applications:
The Smart Leverage of the Internet of Things (IoT) Paradigm

B. Janet
National Institute of Technology, India

Pethuru Raj
Reliance Jio Infocomm Ltd. (RJIL), India

ABSTRACT

We have been writing about the significant contributions of several proven and promising technologies in ensuring the desired success of smart cities. However, the selection of technologies for establishing intelligent cites has to be made after a careful consideration of multiple factors. There are several technologies coming and going without contributing anything substantial for the originally visualized and articulated needs, and hence, the choice plays a vital role in shaping up and strengthening our cities for future challenges and changes. Another noteworthy point is that instead of going for a single technology, it is prudent and pertinent to embrace a cluster of technologies to reach the desired state comfortably. Technology clusters are becoming prominent these days. Especially considering the growing complexity of smart cities (being touted as the system of systems), the need for a collection of competent technologies is being felt across not only the technology-cluster choice but also the appropriate usage of it also is pivotal in achieving the target in a risk-free and relaxed manner. Thus, any smart city strategy has to clearly illuminate resilient technologies and methodologies together towards accelerating and attaining the varied goals of smart cities in this vast and vivacious planet. In this chapter, the authors discuss the immense potential and promise of the newly coined paradigm of the internet of things (IoT) in making next-generation cities that sharply elevate the features, facilities, and functionalities of our crumbling and clogging cities.

DOI: 10.4018/978-1-5225-9023-1.ch016

INTRODUCTION

The future Internet comprises not only the millions of compute machines, personal/professional electronic devices and distributed software services but also the billions of diminutive sensors, actuators, robots, etc. and finally the future Internet is to be blessed with trillions of sentient, smart or digitized objects. It is an overwhelmingly accepted statement that the fast-emerging and evolving IoT idea is definitely a strategic and highly impactful vision to be decisively realized and passionately sustained with the smart adaption and adoption of state-of-the-art technologies, composite and cognitive processes, optimal and versatile infrastructures, integrated platforms, enabling tools, pioneering patterns, and futuristic architectures. Industry professionals and academicians are constantly looking out for appropriate use of business and technical cases in order to confidently and cogently proclaim the transformational value and power of the IoT concept to the larger audience of worldwide executives, end-users, entrepreneurs, evangelists, and engineers.

A growing array of open and industry-strength standards are being formulated, framed and polished by domain experts, industry consortiums and standard bodies to make the IoT thought more visible, viable and valuable. National governments across the globe are setting up special groups in order to come out with pragmatic policies and procedures to take forward the solemn ideals of IoT and to realize the strategic significance of the envisioned IoT in conceiving and concretizing a bevy of citizen-centric services to ensure and enhance peoples' comfort, choice, care, and convenience. Research students, scholars and scientists are working collaboratively towards identifying the implementation challenges and overcoming them via different means and ways especially standard technological solutions.

In this chapter, we would like to give a broader perspective of what exactly is the idea of IoT, as well as trends setting the stimulating stage for the IoT realization and demonstration, why it has to be pursued with all seriousness and sincerity, what are the prickling and prime concerns, changes and challenges associated with it, where it will be applied extensively and expediently, what is the near and long-term future, the key benefits, nightmares, risks, etc. The dominant facet of this chapter is exposing the usefulness of IoT for shaking up the world cities to become smart and sustainable.

Envisioning the Internet of Things (IoT) Era

Due to digitization, distribution, and decentralization, there is a renewed focus on realizing a legion of digitized objects, which are termed and touted as sentient materials / smart objects that are being derived out of ordinary and everyday objects. That is, common and casual things are being empowered or modernized to possess some of the (Information Technology) IT capabilities such as computing, networking, communication, and sensing, actuation and display. That is, not only computers and electronic devices but also everyday articles and artifacts in our midst too join in the mainstream computing. In short, minimization, integration, federation, consolidation, virtualization, automation, orchestration technologies are fast maturing towards producing disappearing, disposable, affordable, connected, dependable, people- centric, context-aware devices. These are service-enabled to form high-quality smart device services. Actually, the Web journey has much to appreciate.

The initial web (web 1.0) was just for reading (simple web), then the web 2.0 has emerged for not only reading but also writing (social web), now it is the web 3.0 for reading, writing and for linking multiple web content, applications, services, and data (semantic web) and the future is definitely the web 4.0 for the envisioned era of knowledge (smart web). That is, every important thing in our environments is web-enabled to interact with cloud-based data, applications, services, content, etc. Further on, everything is connected with entities in the vicinity. Cloud infrastructures are being continuously enhanced to be a centralized and core platform for the smart web. The future Internet is therefore the Internet of Things (IoT).

IoT is all about enabling extreme connectivity among various objects across the industry domains. In this book, we would like to focus on the following themes and titles. We would like to write all about the key drivers for the IoT vision, the enabling technologies, infrastructures and platforms, prominent solutions, facilitating frameworks and tools, enabling architectures, business and use cases, concerns and challenges, etc.

As mentioned above, a string of promising and positive trends in the IT space have laid a strong and sustainable foundation for the out-of-the-box visualization of the future prospects of the raging IoT idea. In a nutshell, the prevailing trend is all about empowering all kinds of casual and cheap articles and artifacts in our everyday environments to be IT-enabled, networking them in an ad hoc manner using a variety of communication technologies on the basis of need to leverage their distinct capabilities individually as well as collectively in order to decisively and concisely understand the various needs of the people in that particular environment, and deciding, disseminating and delivering the identified services and information unobtrusively to right people at the right time and at the right place.

The Emerging IoT Trends

There are a few interesting and inspiring trends sweeping the IT industry. The IT industrialization being represented by the cloud paradigm whereas the IT consumerization through a host of mobile, wearable, assistive, hearable, implantable, and portable devices. The IT compartmentalization is being met through the realization of virtualization and containerization. There are a host of breakthrough technologies. Microservices architecture (MSA) is being personified and presented as the most optimized and organized architectural pattern.

Deeper Digitization Towards Smart Objects

Every tangible thing is getting digitized with the aim of attaching the much-needed sensing and communication capabilities so that each and everything in our midst is capable of participating and contributing for the mainstream computing. There are multiple ways for empowering ordinary objects to become useful, usable and extraordinary artifacts. The minuscule tags, stickers, chips, sensors, motes, smart dust, actuators, LED displays, etc. are the most common elements and entities for the speedy, simpler and copious realization of smart objects. For a prime example, we people are increasingly and intimately connected to the outside world for outward as well as inward communication through slim, sleek, handy and trendy smartphones. The ubiquity and utility of multifaceted phones are foretelling a lot of positives for humans in the days to unfold. In the same way, each and every commonly found item in our environment becomes connected and becomes smart in their operations, outlooks and outputs. The smartness derived via such internal as well as external enhancements enable them to be elegantly and eminently constructive, cognitive and contributive.

The maturity and stability of mesh network topology and technologies ensure these empowered and emboldened materials to find and bind with other similarly enabled articles (local as well as remote) to leverage their unique functionalities and features in order to fulfil the varying needs (information, transaction, and physical) of people. Such a longstanding empowerment goes a long way in unearthing a host of nimbler business and IT models and services, fresh possibilities and opportunities for businesses and people, scores of optimization methods for swiftly heading towards the vision of IT people, solid and sharp increment in user experience of diverse business and IT offerings, etc.

John Hagel and John Seely Brown in one of their articles write that big and marvelous shifts are happening in how things get made from the scratch and how the hitherto untapped value is being created and aggregated. And digital technologies aren't just impacting production and manufacturing; but they're changing the physical world altogether. Our physical world is now technology-enabled by the digitization of everything from books to movies to tools such as the flashlights, cameras, calculators, day planners, music players and bus schedules that now reside on our handhelds and smartphones. The internet communication infrastructure and the digital technologies are the most powerful and path-breaking combination to bring forth big transformations in our physical world.

Due to a growing litany of praiseworthy improvisations, we have achieved a lot in the virtual / cyber world. Now is the time to embark on the delayed modernization of the physical world. The principal transition for empowering our physical environments smart is to make ordinary things smart. The idea is to meticulously enable dumb things in our daily environments to join in and contribute to the mainstream computing.

Already with the maturity of cyber physical system (CPS) technologies, the effective utilization of physical assets and articles is going up steadily. The efficiency of physical machines may be achieved in a number of ways like improving the "up-time" for a costly machine that has become self-correcting or by renting out excess capacity to external parties to generate new revenue streams.

Digital technology can locate a car and deliver it to our feet when we need a ride. It matches a spare bed looking for income with an individual in need of a place to stay. It lets us find and modify a design rather than create one and then lets us use a manufacturing-grade tool to execute the design, with limited skill or invested time. The pavement we drive on becomes smarter with sensors that communicate traffic information; heavy earth-moving equipment becomes smarter when sensors monitor tyre wear to reduce the risk of down-time. Smart materials can collect and conduct information for the clothing a runner wears or the pipe that water flows through. All of these examples require a degree of human intervention to make them useful and the next step seems to be eliminating the human intervention.

Tech-enabled physical objects are starting to be able to adapt or take action automatically. Think of the anti-skid technology or collision-avoidance features in a car, a set of components communicating with each other and taking action as a result. That type of real-time adjustment and feedback that eliminates or reduces the need for human intervention has begun to extend into larger systems, like wind turbines and complex machinery interacting within a processing plant. Self-correction and automated load adjustment are bound to increase the efficiency. There will be far more value unlocked when that information can be fed back to humans for pattern analysis and systemic intervention.

The goal is to pull all of the data back into a human sphere where people can add value. Imagine a beverage company that faces fairly frequent stock-outs that cause customer dissatisfaction and lost sales. A year's worth of data shows that the stock-outs typically occur in conjunction with local and hyper-local events. Now the company has the opportunity not only to track and respond to stock-out situations faster, but to program the inventory-replenishment system to cross-check with event calendars, weather reports, and Twitter feeds to prepare. Companies' skills in tapping user data will determine the data's value, but the potential is greater than just cost efficiencies.

The Growing Device Ecosystem

The device space is fast evolving (implantable, wearable, mobile, portable, nomadic, fixed, etc.). The tough and rough passage from the mainframe and the pervasive PC cultures to trendy and handy portables, handhelds and wearables, disappearing implantable, invisible tags, stickers, labels, and chips, and versatile mobiles subtly and succinctly conveys the quiet and ubiquitous transition from the centralization to the decentralization mode. This positive and path-breaking trend however brings the difficult and dodging issues of heterogeneity, multiplicity and incompatibility. That is, all kinds of participating and contributing devices, machines, instruments, and electronics in our personal as well as professional environments need to be individually as well as collectively intelligent enough to discover one another, link, access, and use to be competent and distinctive to accomplish bigger and better things for humans. The end-result is that constructing and managing cross-institutional and functional applications in this sort of dynamic, disparate, decentralized and distributed environments is laced with a few unpredictable possibilities. That is, there are chances for risky interactions among varied services, sensors and systems resulting in severe complications and unwanted implications for the safety and security of the human society. Also it is envisioned that the future spaces will be highly digitized environments with a fabulous collection of digital devices and digitized artifacts, each is distinct in its face, feature and functionality.

This compendium of devices will be increasingly interlinked to local as well as the global network transparently. With this sophisticated yet complicated scenarios brewing silently and strongly, it is logical to think about the ways and means of ably and adaptively utilizing, managing and extracting their inherent capabilities (specific as well as generic) and capacities for arriving at a horde of people-centric, pioneering and premium services. As we are keenly waiting for the paradigm of "computing everywhere every time" to cherish and flourish, it is imperative to nourish and nudge any variety of participating devices to be extremely agile and adaptive and to empower them to proactively, pre-emptively and purposefully collaborate, correlate and corroborate to figure out the user(s)' contextual needs by dynamically connecting, complementing and sharing the dynamic resources with one another accordingly and unobtrusively. At the other end, there are a wider variety of input and output devices such as tablets and smartphones to assist people to finish their personal as well as professional assignments effectively and efficiently. That is, devices are becoming device ensembles and clusters through internal as well as external integration.

To summarize, there are a wider variety of machines, appliances, consumer electronics, instruments, smartphones, tablets, notebook computers, sophisticated specific as well as generic robots, personal yet compact and multipurpose gadgets & gizmos, kitchen utensils, etc. On the other side, there are resource-constrained, low-cost, low-power, yet multifaceted, smart and semantic elements and entities such as miniaturized yet multifunctional sensors, actuators, microcontrollers, stickers, tags, etc. The real beauty here is that all these are getting connected with one another in their vicinity as well as with the remote cloud platforms and infrastructures.

- **Machine-to-Machine (M2M) Integration:** The pervasiveness of ultra-high communication (wired as well as wireless) technologies facilitate the important and longstanding goal of enabling devices to seamlessly and spontaneously interact with one another to share their potentials. The communication field is going through a stream of praiseworthy transformations. There are new paradigms such as autonomic, unified, and ambient communication. With the maturity and stability of adaptive communication platforms and infrastructures, there arises a bunch of highly beneficial communication features and models. Even business processes are tightly coupled with communication capabilities so that more intimate and intensive processes are bound to erupt and evolve fast towards the fulfilment of peoples' aspirations.

This newly found ad hoc connectivity capability among a whole lot of devices ranging from invisible and infinitesimal tags, smart dust, stickers, and sparkles in our daily environments to highly sophisticated machines in the manufacturing floors and hospitals has resulted in a series of people-centric and premium applications and services. Several industrial domains are very optimistic and looking forward for this paradigm shift in conceptualizing and concretizing a growing array of creative and cognitive applications for their user community. Telecommunication service providers are the very vital partners for the unprecedented and inhibited success of (Device to Device) D2D integration. A bevy of next-generation applications are being conceived and constructed based on this grandeur transformation brought in by the D2D integration idea as pictorially illustrated in figure 1.

There are a number of noteworthy use and business cases escalating the gripping popularity of the idea of M2M communication. The prominent ones among them include home integration solutions (proprietary as well as standardized) that are in plenty these days in order to simplify and streamline the rough and tough tasks associated with home networking and automation. This has led to innumerable smart or intelligent homes at least in the advanced countries. Again smart metering of all the modules and devices of electricity grids results in scores of smart grids across the globe. The seamless communication among the various components of classic cars has resulted in connected or smart cars. This is endless. Fueled by such an abundant enthusiasm and optimism among product and platform vendors, telecom companies, IT service providers, system integrators (SIs), government departments, standard bodies, research labs in academic institutions and business organizations, the idea of deeper and extreme connectivity among all kinds of devices of varying sizes, scopes, and structures is to produce a multitude of robust and resilient services.

Figure 1. Multi-device Assistance for Humans

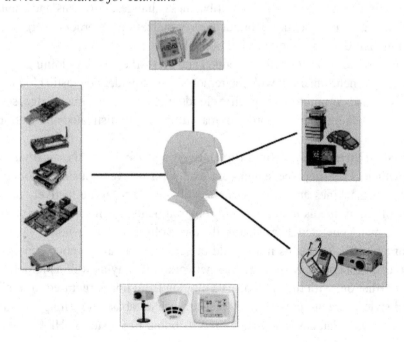

Software-Defined Cloud Infrastructures

- **Cloud-Enabled Embedded Applications**: As we all know, the much-dissected and discoursed cloud paradigm has laid a stimulating and sound foundation for compactly fulfilling the grand vision of IT infrastructure optimization through a seamless synchronization of several proven, enterprise-scale and mission-critical technologies such as virtualization, grid, on-demand, utility, and autonomic computing models, service orientation, multi-tenancy, etc. This ground-breaking evolution and elevation in the IT field has brought in innumerable and insightful impacts on business as well as IT domains these days. Clouds are being positioned and proclaimed as the highly consolidated, converged, virtualized, shared and automated IT environments for hosting and compactly delivering a galaxy of diverse IT solutions and business services. The cloud technology ensures anytime, anywhere and any device information and service access and leverage. That is, the much- anticipated ubiquitous service delivery is being fully facilitated with the arrival, articulation and adoption of the powerful cloud idea. That is, all kinds of services, applications, and data are now being modernized accordingly and adroitly migrated to cloud platforms and infrastructures in order to reap all the originally envisioned benefits (technical, user and business cases).

The cloud paradigm has become a versatile IT phenomenon and a fabulous fertile ground that have inspired many out in the world to come out with a number of newer cloud-centric services, products, and platforms that facilitate scores of people-centric, multifaceted and rich cloud applications to reach out many in this connected world. Besides, there have been a variety of generic as well as specific innovations in the form of pragmatic processes, patterns, best practices, key guidelines, metrics, etc. for moderating the rising IT complexity, for enhancing IT agility, autonomy and affordability and for heightened IT productivity. All the instinctive improvisations happening in the IT landscape with the smart adaption of the robust and resilient cloud model are directly helping out worldwide business enterprises to achieve the venerable mission of "more with less". Thus, cloud as the core, central, cheap, and cognitive infrastructure for implicitly taking care of all kinds of business changes, concerns and challenges portends and portrays a brighter and fulsome future for business organizations in order to surge ahead and to keep their edge earned in their offerings, outputs and outlooks.

With a legion of resource-constrained, embedded and networked devices joining in the IT landscape and with the seamless synchronization with the remote, on-demand, and elastic clouds (generic clouds such as public, private and community or specific clouds such as storage, knowledge, science, data, sensor, device, and mobile), there abounds hordes of real- time and sophisticated applications and services.

- **Cloud Infrastructures for Real-time Big Data Analytics**: Today the most visible and valuable trend is nonetheless the unprecedented data explosion in every business domain. As there are more number of machines and sensors pervasively deployed and effectively used and managed for a variety of requirements in our everyday environments, the machine- generated data is much larger than the man-generated data. That is, the data volume is exponentially growing with a number of remarkable advancements in the field of sensors, actuators, robots, connectivity, service-enablement, etc. Embedded systems getting networked locally as well as remotely are the newer attractions. Further on, with the data formats ranging from non-structured to semi-structured and to structured style, there are pressures to unearth fresh database modelling and management systems such as NoSQL databases and Hadoop distributed file systems (HDFS) in order to swiftly capture, store, search large-scale and multi-structured data and to extract actionable insights without much pain. Besides the volume and the variety, the data velocity is another critical factor to be considered very carefully in order to derive and deduce usable intelligence and to contemplate the next course of actions in time with all clarity and confidence. Precisely speaking, big data is all about the three data Vs: volume, variety and velocity. The traditional data management systems find it difficult to manage terabytes and petabytes of data and hence different NoSQL databases have become very popular to handle voluminous databases with ease.

Besides big data storage and management, big data analytics has acquired an important phenomenon that cannot be sidestepped at any cost as data across cloud, social, device, mobile, and enterprise spaces need to be comprehensively identified and aggregated, subjected to powerful data mining, processing and analysis tasks through well-defined policies dynamically and disseminated promptly in order to be highly beneficial for businesses, governments, financial institutions, and for firms involved in digital marketing, security and retail intelligence, high-performance science and healthcare research and quick customer on-boarding, etc. The widely used Hadoop implementations, commodity servers, specific data appliances, and so on are the prominent and dominant methods being effectively handpicked and handled in order to accommodate terabytes and even petabytes of incongruent data and to empower executives, entrepreneurs and engineers to take informed decisions in time and to plan pragmatic action plans with all alacrity. With the sustained eruption of inventive technologies, the data architecture for new-generation enterprises will go through a tectonic and meteoric shift. Leading market watchers predict that big data management and intelligence will become common and casual along with the already-established data management solutions.

There are high-performing and assuring cloud platforms and appliances by the leading infrastructure solution providers such as IBM, Amazon, HP, Google, and other niche providers (Oracle, SAP, etc.) in order to accomplish big data analytics. Thus clouds are stuffed with quite a lot of integrated platforms for analytics, a growing array of cloud-native software services for multifaceted devices, cloud-enabled enterprise applications, etc. signaling the onset of the Internet of Things (IoT) era. Cloud will be the marketplace and hosting of different repositories of services and data to be easily discovered and used for the ultimate empowerment of devices and people.

- **Cloud Infrastructures for Smartphone Services**: Every application is mobile-enabled to facilitate distributed applications that can be accessed and used at the vehicular speed. The mobile interfacing is being mandated widely. There are a number of mobile technologies and tools facilitating the leverage of all kinds of applications while on the move. With the explosion of smartphones and tablets, every kind of cloud and enterprise applications is being provided with mobile interfacing. There are several operating systems such as Android, iOS, Windows Phones, BlackBerry OS, etc. for powering up smartphones and mobile clouds (say, iCloud is the mobile cloud for iOS phones, tablets, etc.) They are being set up in order to host and store all kinds of smartphone services, multi-structured data, etc. That is, cloud-connectivity is essential for phones to be relevant for users. In short, an integrated network of disparate and distributed resources, assets, and articles is the principal need for the eulogized smart world.

- **Device-to-Cloud (D2C) Integration:** Different types of devices and digitized objects via multiple types of networks can communicate with a variety of locally as well as remotely deployed applications. The Internet is the global-scale open, public and cheap communication infrastructure. These applications may have multiple interfaces. Importantly a backhaul network, the communication backbone of the Internet infrastructure, is a very essential ingredient in enforcing and ensuring devices at the ground level to talk to different applications at Cloud-enabled Data Centers (CeDCs), the new kind of software-defined data centers.

The iDigi Device Cloud (http://www.idigi.com/) is an infrastructure service designed to empower different devices and their networks. The iDigi Device Cloud solves the challenges of massive scalability and service reliability while meeting the requirements for utmost security and privacy. It is also indicated that the iDigi Connector is the appropriate bridge for integrating client's applications with the iDigi Device Cloud. The cloud paradigm has grown enormously and its grip on several business domains is simply incredible. There are specific cloud infrastructures emerging. That is, we often hear about sensor cloud, device cloud, knowledge cloud, mobile cloud, science cloud, etc. The pervasiveness and popularity of the cloud technology is surging ahead with enhanced awareness about its strategic contributions for the whole humanity.

- **Cloud-to-Cloud (C2C) Integration:** There are several types of Cloud Service Providers (CSPs) leveraging diverse technologies delivering different business-centric services. Due to the enhanced complexity and heterogeneity, the goal of cloud interoperability has become a tough challenge for cloud services and application developers. Cloud brokers, procurers and auditors are therefore emerging and joining in the already complicated cloud ecosystem. Even cloud consumers are afraid of the vendor lock-in issue as there are manifold barriers being erected around cloud infrastructures and platforms. There are a couple of well-known trends gripping the cloud landscape. First, geographically distributed and differentiating clouds are being established and sustained.

Second, institutions, individuals and innovators are eyeing cloud software, platforms and infrastructures for reaping the originally postulated and pronounced benefits. That is, same services are being provided by multiple providers with different SLAs and OLAs. Incidentally business processes that span across several clouds and services of multiple clouds need to be found, bound, and aggregated to build composite data, services, processes and applications. All these clearly insist on the urgent need for competent federation techniques, standards, patterns, platforms and best practices for a global network of clouds.

Intra as well as inter-enterprise integration has to happen via cloud integration services and solutions. Service organizations and system integrators are embarking on a new fruitful journey as cloud brokerages in order to silken the rough edges therefore distinct and distributed clouds can be identified and integrated seamlessly and spontaneously to work collaboratively to achieve bigger and better things. Cloud service brokers (CSBs) are a kind of new software solution for cloud data, service, application and process integration.

- **Sensor-to-Cloud (S2C) Integration:** Sensors and actuators are found in many environments in plenty these days used for different purposes. A sensor network is a group of specialized transducers to monitor and record conditions at diverse locations. Commonly monitored parameters are temperature, humidity, pressure, wind direction and speed, illumination, vibration and sound intensities, power-line voltage, chemical concentrations, pollutant levels and vital body functions. Every sensor node is equipped with a transducer, microcomputer, transceiver and power source. The transducer generates electrical signals based on sensed physical effects and phenomena. The microcomputer processes and stores the sensor output. The transceiver, which can be hard-wired or wireless, receives commands from a central computer and transmits data to that computer. The power for each sensor node is derived from the electric utility or from a battery. Potential applications of sensor networks include: Industrial automation, automated and smart homes, video surveillance, traffic monitoring, medical device monitoring, monitoring of weather conditions, air traffic control, and robot control.

As indicated above, every empowered entity in our environments is further strengthened by getting integrated with local IT and remote cloud IT. As sensors are being prescribed as the ear and eye of futuristic digital world, sensor networking with nearby sensors as well as with far-off applications needs to be facilitated. There are frameworks and middleware platforms for enabling ad hoc networking of diverse sensors within themselves as well as with distant software components.

In the past few years, wireless sensor networks (WSNs) have been gaining significant traction because of their potential for enabling very intimate and interesting solutions in areas such as smart homes, industrial automation, environmental monitoring, transportation, health care and agriculture. The tremendous progress in WSN design fosters their increasingly widespread usage and leading to growth in both, number of nodes per deployment and infrastructure complexity. Nowadays, a city-scale WSN deployment is not a novelty anymore. This trendy phenomenon generates lots of data of different type which has to be synchronized, interpreted, adapted for specific needs, interconnected with other data and/or distinguished in service and application data. If we add a collection of sensor-derived data to various social networks or virtual communities, blogs, musings, etc., then there will be fabulous transitions in and around us. With the faster adoption of micro and nano technologies, everyday things are destined to become digitally empowered to be distinctive in their actions and reactions. Thus the impending goal is to seamlessly link digitized objects / sentient materials at our environments, other frequently used and handled devices such as consumer electronics, kitchen utensils & containers, household instruments and items, portable, nomadic, and mobile gadgets and gizmos, etc. with remote cloud-based applications via federated messaging middleware. That is, cyber systems are being inundated with streams of data and messages from different and distributed physical elements and entities. Such an extreme and deeper connectivity and collaboration is to pump up and sustain cool, classic and catalytic situation-aware applications.

Clouds have emerged as the centralized, compact and capable IT infrastructure to deliver people-centric and context-aware services to users with all the desired qualities embedded. This long-term vision demands that there has to be a comprehensive connectivity between clouds and the billions of minuscule sensing systems.

Big Data Analytics (BDA)

We have exclusively discussed about this field and its continued impact in the previous chapter. The gist of the matter is how easily and quickly you can transition your data heaps into information and then to knowledge which can put you in top. Any organization that has the innate capacity and capability to extract rightful and right insights is bound to grow and glow immensely. There are BDA platforms, processes, practices, patterns, and products in plenty to facilitate the hard task of knowledge engineering.

Thus, there are several positive and progressive indications in the hot field of IT erupting and evolving fast to spruce up the changing and challenging situations and needs of people. For the knowledge world, the role of BDA is immense and imminent to swiftly transform data into information and into usable knowledge.

Data Science

There are three major trends emerging and evolving fast with the conscious adoption of pioneering technologies and tools in the most happening IT space. It is forecast that there will be billions of connected devices (due to the surge in the consistently growing device ecosystem) and trillions of digitized objects (due to the widespread leverage of the digitization and edge technologies such as sensors, actuators, stickers, microchips and controllers, tags and codes, beacons, LEDs, speck). On the other side, with the arrival and articulation of scores of promising digital technologies, business transformation sees a tectonic shift. Specially, as microservices architecture (MSA) emerging as the most optimized and organized application architecture pattern, it is anticipated that there will be millions of polyglot microservices, which, when systematically and smartly composed, result in path-breaking, business-critical, process-aware, people-centric and composite services.

With these, physical and cyber/virtual entities are set to interact (locally and remotely) with one another in a purpose-specific manner, there will be massive amount of multi-structured data, which has to be cleanly captured, cleansed and crunched in order to extract actionable insights in time. The knowledge discovered through a host of data analytics platforms, machine and deep learning algorithms, and practices can be disseminated to software applications, devices, and IT systems. This process-driven knowledge-enablement empowers software applications, IT services, system, and network, connected devices, digitized elements, etc. in order to be adaptive in their decisions, deals and deeds. That means, every system is intrinsically enriched with appropriate intelligence in order to be self, surroundings and situation-aware. Every tangible entity, being stuffed with required insights in time exhibits, is able to be computational, communicative, sensitive, responsive, perceptive, decision-making, and active.

The data volume, variety, velocity, and viscosity are seeing a lot of strategically sound changes. The data size challenge is very humongous. And making sense and money out of exponentially growing data heaps poses a greater challenge. The new discipline of data science is all set to untangle hidden knowledge out of data. There are deterministic, diagnostic, predictive, prescriptive and personalized analytics procedures. Data mining and analytics approaches are fast maturing and stabilizing in order extricate usable insights. With the surging popularity of machine and deep learning algorithms, automated and self-analytics of tremendous amount of poly-structured data is seeing the reality. Thus, with the continued support of product and platform vendors, domain experts, data scientists, artificial intelligence (AI) and augmented reality (AR) research scientists, we can easily expect smarter hotels, homes, hospitals, etc., in the days ahead. This chapter is a hugely beneficial for faculty members and researchers to gain a deeper and decisive understanding of the futuristic technologies and tools in order to embark on a variety of investigations on collected and stocked data to bring forth actionable insights, which can be looped back to business workloads and IT services to demonstrate adroit behavior.

The IoT Reference Architecture

The raging IoT idea has been making waves these days. Every allied discipline is consciously contributing for the realization of the IoT vision. It is all about realizing smart objects, enabling them to talk to one another on need-basis to create value for humans in their daily chores. There are exceptional advancements in edge and embedded computing fields. Communication is becoming unified, ambient and autonomic. Lean communication protocols and stacks and other lightweight network components (switches, routers, modems, application delivery controllers (ADCs), load balancers, network gateways, etc.) are being readied and refined towards digitized objects to find and interact with one another smoothly.

In short, the shining and strategic IoT concept is making the Internet even more immersive and pervasive. By enabling ubiquitous access and interaction with a wider variety of devices such as home appliances, surveillance cameras, monitoring sensors, actuators, displays, terminals, vehicles, and so on, the IoT field is poised to foster the development and deployment of a number of hitherto unseen people-centric applications that implicitly make use of the potentially enormous amount of data. Every sector is bound to go through IoT-inspired disruptive and innovative transformations facilitating the goals of home and industrial automation, smart healthcare, intelligent energy management, traffic management, smart cars, etc.

The game-changing IoT domain is innately capable of bringing in a number of benefits in the management and optimization of public services such as transport and parking, lighting, surveillance and maintenance of public areas, preservation of cultural heritage, water and energy management, safety of people and public assets, garbage collection, salubrity of hospitals and schools. Furthermore, the ready availability of different types of data emitted by pervasive sensors and actuators and the real-time knowledge extraction capability go hand in hand in bringing in the much-required transparency in public administration, the greater responsibility amongst government officials, etc. Better and fool-proof service delivery systems can be in place, the co-creation of newer services and outside-in thinking will flourish and there will be a timely awareness of city facilities and events, etc. Therefore, the IoT paradigm is a huge booster to establish and sustain smart cities.

Building a general architecture for IoT is hence a very complex task, mainly because of the extremely large variety of devices, link layer technologies, and services that may be involved in such a system as described in the figure 2.

The architecture pictorially expressed above primarily comprises of the following components

- **Information Capture**: To have context-aware applications, it is prudent and profoundly true that all kinds of situation / scenario information have to be gleaned. As explained above, our everyday environment is being stuffed with scores of digitized entity, sensors and actuators, instrumented electronics, smart objects, connected devices, information appliances, cyber physical systems, network gateways, communication elements, etc. These elegantly contribute for information capture about their environments and happenings there. Sensors powerful enough to interconnect and interact with one another, are being used to continuously monitor human's physiological activities (Min Chen, 2013) and actions such as health status and motion patterns. Infinitesimal tags, codes,

Figure 2. The reference architecture for the IoT

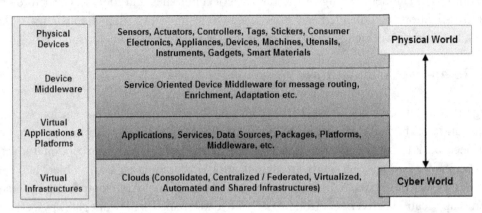

and specks are being overwhelmingly utilized for monitoring and collecting crucial information about various activities in a particular place and sending them to central systems for precise and decisive analysis towards engineering actionable insights.

- **Information Delivery**: Today we have a variety of communication technologies and network topologies to carry forward all sorts of collected information. There are sensor networks, body area networks, car area networks, home networks, campus area networks, etc. There are 3G and 4G communication technologies flourishing across the world. It is anticipated that by 2020, we will have full-fledged 5G technologies and their infrastructures in place in order to meet rising bandwidth requirements. Bandwidth on demand, video on demand, ambient communication, ad hoc networks are some of the often heard terms in securely delivering information to different destinations without any compromise.

- **Information Processing**: With the emergence of powerful and standards-complying data analytics platforms, frameworks and tools, the analytics domain is bound to grow substantially. In the case of big data, any Hadoop implementation could filter out routine data to bring forth value-added information. That is, transitioning multi-structured data into structured form so that the stabilised analytical systems such as data warehouses, cubes and marts can proceed towards fine-grained analytics is the gist of Hadoop technology. There are powerful, optimised, bundled and purpose-specific appliances for data analytics. Real-time and streaming analytics are also maturing fast to provide real-time analytics for certain use cases. There are pioneering algorithms towards predictive and prescriptive analytics. Further on, information visualization solutions are to disseminate any extracted and extrapolated knowledge to the respective users. Thus data crunching, information processing, and knowledge discovery are being simplified with noteworthy advancements in the hot IT field.

- **Smarter Applications**: Thus the transition from data to information and to knowledge is being facilitated through a plethora of automation and acceleration technologies. There are widespread improvements in effective data integration, virtualization, synchronization, and polishing towards knowledge engineering. Once knowledge gets created, corroborated, correlated and then conveyed to appropriate software applications to show the much-wanted smart behaviour.

That is, automated data capture and interpretation resulting in actionable intelligence that goes a long way in empowering software applications to be distinct in their operations, offerings and outputs.

The Advantages of the IoT Concept for Smart Cities

With the growing stability and maturity of IoT and M2M standards, reference architectures, toolsets, platforms, and infrastructures, inspired innovators, individuals and institutions could bring forth a number of unique use-cases for championing (Pawar, 2013) and sustaining the IoT technology campaign. In short, as with the continued emergence and evolution of fresh technologies, newer benefits arise continuously and city dwellers are getting newer enablement and empowerments (Zanella and Vangelista, 2014) in their everyday lives with the correct and cognitive usage of technologies. At a macro level, the following advancements are being expected out of the revolutionary and raging IoT idea.

1. **Optimized Systems**: Optimization has been the primary goal for any system to ensure enhanced efficacy. Powerful technologies enable an optimal sharing of various resources that are becoming scarce. That is, there will be a shared usage of city resources through a plethora of technology empowerments. The cities will see a climb in developing and deploying pioneering IoT applications that are to tell us when, where, what and how to use resources for their preservation and productivity. It is estimated that major cities waste up to 50% of water due to leaky pipes. Similarly, there are several other well-known and everyday scenarios. For example, irrigation systems run when it is raining, street lights remain on during day time also, etc. As explained above, sensor-attached devices are being increasingly hooked up with cloud services so that they can be locally as well as remotely monitored minutely and activated adeptly. Thus smart sensors enable all kinds of systems to be intelligent. Thereby a variety of automation, simplification, rationalization, and complexity-mitigation needs in peoples' lives are easily fulfilled through the incorporation of the IoT's advanced features and functionalities.

2. **Service-enabled & Connected Systems**: All kinds of devices including resource-constrained ones in our midst will undergo radical transformations with the smart leverage of the proven and potential IoT principles, patterns and platforms. Every single object is blessed with a service API and hence all other artifacts could find, match, and use their unique offerings. Thus connectivity and service-enablement are the two prime parameters for all kinds of dumb items to be active, articulative, adaptive, participative, and contributive.

For instance, public transportation could work better with the apt usage of IoT-provided features, a growing array of vehicle-centric cloud-based services and the very recent phenomenon of big data analytics. Transport operators and control centers can get a 360 degree view of the traffic movement, the whereabouts of vehicles and other related information in real time. Predictive analytics go a long way in establishing predictive maintenance of transports. Connected systems can supply all sorts of decision-enabling information such as the ticket sale, the peak hours or seasons, busy junctions, etc. in order to facilitate the introduction of user-centric and premium service offerings. With the pervasiveness and persuasiveness of smartphones, bus users can save time by having the visuals of the exact location of their buses, the speed and the bus occupancy on their mobile phones. Bus operators can generate newer revenues through location-based advertising and services.

3. **Self, Surroundings and Situation-Aware Systems:** Every digitally empowered device is capable of knowing its identity and neighbours explicitly. That is, when a system on its own or in synchronization with others is context-aware, then people can easily get context-sensitive services.

4. **People-Centric Systems – The IoT-inspired capabilities for Enhanced Care, Comfort, Choice and Convenience:** We have written about these factors and facets extensively in other chapters. Ambient assisted living (AAL) is one prominent use case. Air conditioners (ACs) adjust as per the users' requirements, washing machines set up the washing level as per the dresses' states and needs, etc. Citizens can monitor the pollution concentration in each street of the city or they can get an automatic alarm when the radiation-level rises above the threshold in an emergency environment.

The Co-Creation of IoT-Enabled Services for Smarter Cities

In Vicini et al. (2012), the authors have clearly elucidated about the needs and the ways of co-creating technology-stimulated services that are people-aware and centric. Especially as the IoT idea is transitioning from the conceptual stage to the realization state, the quality and quantity of next-generation services are to be great. For example, with the surging popularity of smartphones, there come thousands of fresh and fascinating services being developed by developers across the globe, deposited, and delivered through a variety of mobile cloud environments. Similarly with the emergence of specific and generic devices and instruments for smart cities, it is precisely expected that there will be a plethora of city-specific services.

We already had discussed the IoT idea and its huge and untapped potentials for automating, accelerating and augmenting peoples' tasks both trivial and complex. The idea of IoT is to improve the value chain between users, devices, applications and environments considerably and therefore the synergy is to lay a scintillating and stimulating foundation for innovators for deriving and delivering sophisticated and smart services that have the greatest impact on people life. Providing adaptive, innovation-filled, supple, and personalized services based on meaningful data collected via scores of interconnected digital objects, networked electronics and cloud-based applications facilitates our cities to be intelligent in their offerings, operations and outlooks.

The Role of Advanced Sensing in Smart Cities

As urban areas consume the vast majority of resources that are quickly becoming scarce due to the over-exploitation by teeming population, it is vital to make cities optimized and organized to sustain them for the future generations. IT is the foremost domain to bring in the necessary transformation in our cities. Process orchestration, advanced ambient systems, infrastructure optimization, architecture assimilation, etc. are the major contributions for the dreamt smart cities across the world. From the smart design of buildings, which capture rain water for later use, to intelligent control systems, which can monitor infrastructures autonomously, the possible improvements enabled by sensing, perception and actuation technologies are enormous. The paper Hancke et al. (2013) has illustrated several sensing applications in smart cities, sensing platforms and technical challenges associated with these technologies. Infrastructures are very critical for formulating and firming up different services for city dwellers as illustrated in the figure 3 below.

Figure 3. Smart city is a system of systems

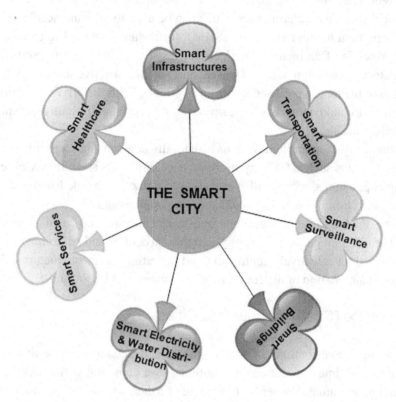

Sensing is being insisted for infrastructures to be smart. That is, the need for autonomy capability is being mandated for public infrastructures now. We would have extensively read, heard and even felt self-configuring, diagnosing, healing, defending, governing, and organizing compute infrastructures. It is all about having self-managing infrastructural components towards autonomic computing. Here too, smart physical infrastructures such as bridges, buildings, homes, roads, etc. are the ones that can monitor themselves and act on their own intelligently. Clusters of smart sensors are the main components for deriving smart infrastructures in our daily living.

Using sensors to monitor public infrastructures provides awareness that enables a more efficient use of resources, based on the data collected by these sensors. Real-time monitoring eliminates the need for regular scheduled inspections, therefore reducing operational costs. Measuring energy consumption in households allows for accurate load forecasting and sensors deployed in roads for traffic monitoring collect data which is necessary for the implementation of intelligent transportation systems (ITS). For these approaches to be effective, sensors have to be deployed in very large numbers, and they have to be interconnected so that the collected data can be sent to a central information system, where intelligent decisions based on this data can be made.

Sensors Everywhere and in Everything

In a nutshell, the emergence of smart sensors is a good omen for self-managing infrastructures. For example, there are sensors for determining gas, electricity, and water consumption. Further on, in a smart home, there are light, pressure, gas, temperature, fire, humidity, and presence sensors in plenty. More sophisticated sensors include accelerometers which can be used to measure acceleration and vibration. In the context of structural health monitoring (SHM), for instance, sensors like corrosion rate sensors (working on the principle of an increase in electrical resistivity due to corrosion), acoustic emission sensors (used to detect propagation of sound waves) and magnetostrictive sensors (detects the change in magnetic induction in the material caused by strain or stress). With the arrival of miniaturization technologies such as MEMS and nanotechnology, sensors are becoming diminutive, disposable, randomly deployable and indispensable.

The surging popularity of smartphones opens up a totally new sensing scenario. Smartphones are fitted with a variety of sensors such as GPS, gyroscopes, accelerometers and compasses, enabling a variety of crowd sourcing applications, which will eventually be augmented by the IoT paradigm. In particular, collaborative data collection is a popular crowd sourcing application.

On summarizing, the usage of heterogeneous sensors and actuators is growing rapidly for monitoring and measurement of different parameters in physical infrastructures and environments and the resulting knowledge is leveraged for effectively controlling and operating the infrastructures. Sensors explicitly ensure the functional automation of different elements and entities in our midst.

Sensing as a Service (SaaS) for Futuristic Cities

Considering the unique contributions of smart sensors and actuators in facilitating people-centric, situation-aware, and real-time applications, the authors have come out with a new sensor deployment and delivery model to accentuate the sensor technology further. The sensing as a service model (Perera et al., 2014) consists of four conceptual layers: 1) sensors service providers, 2) sensor service publishers (SSPs), 3) extended service providers (ESPs) and 4) sensor service consumers. This is definitely a stimulating trend towards the vision of everything as a service. Sensors producers and consumers are at the extreme ends. In between, we have sensor service publishers and sensor service integrators. In this model, users do view sensors as sensing services. The main responsibility of a sensor service publisher (SSP) is to aggregate all kinds of sensor services and publish them in a cloud-based service registry & repository for public discovery and consumption. Sensor producers and owners have to register their sensors and their services with one or more SSPs so that sensor service consumers can easily find, bind and leverage those sensor services to compose real-world applications. ESPs are a kind of system integrators and service brokers. Sensor service consumers connect with ESPs with all their requirements and ESPs work with them to fulfil their expectations by sensor service connectivity, aggregation, monitoring & measurement, management, arbitration, data dissemination, etc.

Xively is a public cloud for the IoT that simplifies and accelerates the creation, deployment, and management of sensors in scalable manner. Further on, it allows sharing sensor data with each other. The OpenIoT project focuses on providing an open source middleware framework enabling the dynamic formulation of self-managed cloud environments for IoT applications. Global Sensor Networks (GSN) is a middleware which supports sensor deployments and offers a flexible, zero-programming deployment and integration infrastructure for IoT. These developments strengthen the vision towards sensing as a service. Here are a couple of nice use cases for this new service model.

Waste management is one of the toughest challenges that modern cities have to deal with every day. A deeper penetration of ICT solutions however, may result in significant savings and economical and ecological advantages. For instance, the use of intelligent waste containers that detect the level of load and allow for an optimization of the collector trucks' route can reduce the cost of wastage collection and improve the quality of recycling. To realize such a smart waste management service, the IoT shall connect the end devices, i.e., intelligent waste containers, to a control center where an optimization application processes the data and determines the optimal management of the collector truck fleet.

Waste management consists of different processes such as collection, transport, processing, disposal, managing, and monitoring of waste materials. In the figure 5, this use case is illustrated on how the sensing as a service model works in the waste management domain. In a modern smart city, there are several parties who are interested in waste management (e.g. city council, recycling companies, manufacturing plants, and authorities related to health and safety). Instead of deploying sensors and collecting information independently, the sensing as a service model allows all the interest groups to share the infrastructure and bear the related costs collectively. The most important aspect of such a collaboration is the cost reduction that individual groups need to spend otherwise. All the interested parties can retrieve and process sensor data in real time in order to achieve their own objective.

Smart Homes

A futuristic scenario explains the interactions in sensing as a service model. The scenario illustrated in figure 5is based on smart home domain which also plays a significant role in the Smart Cities.

Smart Agriculture

This sensing as a service model can be elegantly extended towards many real-world application scenarios. Currently, the authors are actively involved in designing and developing open platforms for sensor data collection, processing and sharing in the domain of agriculture. Agriculture is an important part

Figure 4. The reference architecture for sensing as a service

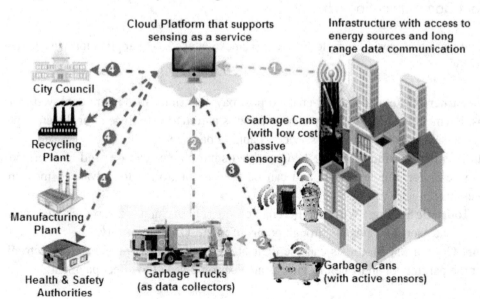

Figure 5. The control and data flow in a smart home use case

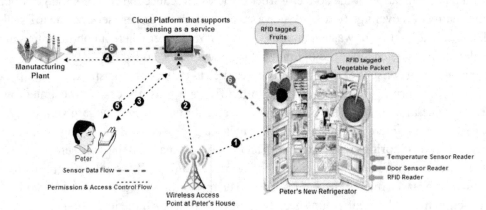

of smart cities as it contributes to the food supply-chain that facilitates a large number of communities concentrated into cities.

Environment Management

Environment monitoring and management is a bigger domain wherein multiple kinds of sensors are being leveraged. Most of the sensors used for environment monitoring are commonly found in other domains such as climate, wild fire detection, and structure-health monitoring. Using the sensing as a service model, interest groups can acquire relevant sensor data without spending for sensors. Further, environment management is a large domain where a single organization cannot deal with (e.g. wild fire) comprehensively. Therefore a model like sensing as a service comes handy to stimulate a bevy of innovative solutions that use the same data but produce different results using different processing and analysing techniques (e.g. prediction, visualization, and simulation).

Near Field Communication (NFC)

The following are real-world examples of NFC (Hancke et al., 2013) application within the context of the smart city

- **Smart Energy Metering:** NFC-enabled post-pay electricity meters are deployed in various nations. Payment for the electricity consumption is automatically done after the encrypted reading has been sent over-the-air to the service's banking back-end.
- **Data Acquisition and Control:** NFC enabled smartphones can be used to interface with control systems for remote control and can be used as platforms for advanced measurement and processing.
- **City Touristic Surfing:** With an NFC enabled smart phone and smart posters disseminated along the city, the user can navigate through points of interest within the city.
- **Smart Car Parks:** Motorists can use their NFC enabled smart phone as an electronic ticket to enter the parking lot and when leaving as an electronic wallet to affect payment.

With the addition of NFC to smartphones and the widespread of smartphones, NFC is envisaged as a key enabling technology in smart cities.

The Popular IoT /M2M Applications

As enunciated elsewhere, the IoT domain is surging due to the five intriguing trends in the IT field. Therefore, the IoT conundrum has a captivating and cognitive impact on every human in this increasingly connected world.

1. Digitization
2. Distribution
3. Industrialization
4. Commoditization
5. Consumerization

You can find a few well-known and widely articulated applications that gain immensely through the modernizations mentioned above. It is a foregone conclusion that fresh technologies would bring fresh perspectives and bring forth provisions for overcoming complexities and foretasting original applications that are really transformative, innovative and disruptive. In this section and the ones that are to come, we have enlisted a plethora of existing services that are getting transitioned to be smart as well as altogether newer applications from the ground up. We could discuss the technologies in this and previous chapters and hereafter you will read more city-specific applications.

A Typical IoT Application

In an extended enterprise scenario, all kinds of functional divisions are interconnected with one another via the cloud-hosted middleware suite. Clearly cloud occupies the prime spot in any integrated environment. All the common services are getting deployed in network-accessible cloud platforms. Only specific functionalities are being maintained at the edges. The cloud service broker (CSB), which is explained in detail below, plays a stellar role in streamlining and simplifying the complex integration hurdles and hitches as the figure 6 shows below.

Figure 6. Cloud is the central environment for next-generation connected applications

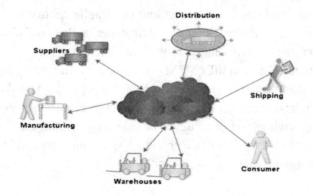

There are cloud integration appliances and solutions in plenty in order to effortlessly integrate data across clouds (private, public, and hybrid clouds). In short, CSBs are very relevant for distributed computing. There are federation approaches for realizing the vision of the Intercloud. Standards are being formulated to establish run-time linkage between geographically distributed clouds in order to attend some specific scenarios. There are cloud orchestration platforms for uniting clouds. Cloud interoperability is vehemently insisted as clouds are very vital for the success of the IoT concept. Both generic and specific clouds need to be integrated in order to fulfil the unique demands of any IoT applications and hence cloud integration, orchestration and automation are very essential for the projected success. At different levels and layers, the much-needed linkage is being tackled. There are integration appliances, middleware, service repository, and scores of tools for enabling cloud connectivity and interactions. Like system integrators, we will hear more about cloud integrators / brokers in the days to emerge for providing next-generation connected applications to people.

Structural Health of Buildings

The proper maintenance of the historical and cultural buildings of a city requires the continuous monitoring and measurement of the actual health parameters of each building and the identification of the areas that are vulnerable for any easy prey. The urban IoT may setup a distributed database for capturing and storing the sensor readings of buildings. In the recent past, there are building-specific sensors such as vibration and deformation sensors to monitor the building stress, atmospheric agent sensors in the surrounding areas to monitor pollution levels, and temperature and humidity sensors to have a complete characterization of the environmental conditions.

This database is to reduce the need for expensive periodic structural testing by human operators and will allow targeted and proactive maintenance and restoration actions. Finally, it will be possible to combine vibration and seismic readings in order to better study and understand the impact of light earthquakes on city buildings. This database can be made publicly accessible in order to make the citizens aware of the care taken in preserving the city historical heritage. The practical realization of this service requires the installation and maintenance of specific sensors in the buildings and surrounding areas. These sensors have to collectively collect, corroborate, and correlate to extract the right insights in time in synchronization with a cloud-based cyber application.

Smart Energy

Energy has become a scarce commodity and hence its preservation is very much obligatory. Also, more energy consumption means more heat dissipation into our fragile environment. That is, with efficient usage of precious power energy, the much-feared environmental degradation and global warming can be grossly minimized to achieve environmental sustainability.

Smart metering solutions (this is an IoT / M2M solution connecting every energy-gobbling device in a network with the centralized smart meter) are very much accepted and used in advanced countries in order to accurately understand the usage. In other words, smart electricity meters help energy consumers to decode how energy-savings can be achieved based on the readings and alerts being rendered by smart meters. The Advanced Metering Infrastructure (AMI) is an active and ongoing research area to generate solutions for energy efficiency.

Smart Healthcare

Healthcare is turning out to be a huge industry in the years to unfold. There are a number of specific devices for measuring and managing a number of health parameters of humans. IoT solutions are capable of reminding the patient and their family members as well as the doctor in case of any emergency arising out of any abnormality in any of the health readings.

Smart Home Security

Sophisticated home networking, integration, automation, security, and control mechanisms are hitting the market very frequently. M2M solutions for home security are merging with energy management to provide remote alarm controls as well as remote HVAC controls for homes and businesses through mobile phones.

Smart Cargo Handling

IoT solutions are being manufactured into a variety of storage/handling containers including cargo containers, money & document bags, and nuclear waste drums. The real-time location of the container, whether it has been opened or closed, how containers are being handled through motion sensors, can be easily obtained to prevent any possible security and theft risks and to increase recovery capability of stolen or lost material.

Smart Traffic Management

M2M solutions are able to provide real-time road traffic information to vehicles' drivers via automobile GPS devices to enable them to contemplate better alternatives.

Smart Inventory and Replenishment Management

IoT solutions can be integrated into the sensors measuring the amount of bulk product in a storage bin. This information can be made available to both the supplier and the user so proactive reorders can be initiated when inventories reach a predetermined level. This is very beneficial for manufacturing process that do not consume a consistent and predictable amount of product or the transport time of the bulk product results in product run-out.

Smart Cash Payment

M2M / IoT solutions allow mobile credit/debit card readers to provide secure and encrypted data transmissions at the transaction and ticketing counters in hyper malls, hotels, movie theaters, food joints, etc. Retailing becomes a smooth affair without standing on the queue for cash payment. The seamless connectivity between tags, tag readers, cash cards, merchant banks, retailers, etc. goes a long way in considerably enhancing the customer experience.

Smart Tracking

IoT / M2M solutions allow parents to track their children very precisely sitting from the office and empower caregivers to remotely track those with disabilities as well as independently living, disease-stricken, debilitated and bed-ridden people. Managers can monitor their employees performing duties in rough and tough places. Especially those who are working in oil wells, fighting forest fire, helping out in disaster-struck places, battling in war zones, hiking in mountains, etc to immensely get benefited through such kinds of technological innovations.

The items inside vending machines can connect with their suppliers and provide all the relevant information about the number of bins and bottles inside and how many more are needed to fill up the vending machine. This is definitely a sharp improvement over the current practice.

Smart Displays

All kinds of machines such as ATMs, vending machines, television sets, security video cameras, sign posts, dash boards, etc. can be intertwined together at strategic locations. With such intimate integration through a competent M2M solution, customized video as well as static images can be dispatched to these machines to flash time-sensitive and preferred details and displays. A hungry person could order his pizzas on his mobile phone yet see the pizza details and pictures in the larger screen of any one of these machines or with connected projectors showing the images in a white wall to give a clear vision.

Smart Asset Management

Every industry has its own set of specific assets. For example, hospitals should have a number of scanning machines, diagnostic equipment, healthcare monitors, robots, and other instruments. That is, there are a variety of devices both small and large. The real challenge lies in their effective location identification in case of any emergency, upkeep, management, monitoring, inventory, security, etc. There are several unique benefits of an IoT / M2M solution in this complicated scenario. An advanced M2M solution sharply reduces the time consumed by employees to pinpoint the assets' exact location, considerably increments their utilization, and provides the ability to share high-value assets between departments and facilities. With every asset in a hospital environment is integrated with one another and with the remote web / cloud platforms via the M2M product, remote monitoring, repairing, and management is being lavishly facilitated. Through the connectivity established with cloud-hosted healthcare applications, every machine could update and upload its data to the centralized and cyber applications thereby a number of activities get automated fully by avoiding manual intervention, interpretation and instruction.

Air Quality

It is well-known that nations across the world have set in appropriate mechanisms in place to arrest the threatening climate-change. There are attempts through a host of ways to cut down greenhouse gas emission into our fragile environment, to enforce energy preservation, and subsequently to decrement heat dissipation so that the global objective of sustainability can be realised sooner than later. To such an extent, an urban IoT can provide means to monitor the quality of the air in all kinds of crowded areas and joints such as open air stadiums, parks and play grounds, etc. In addition, communication facilities can be provided to let health applications on joggers' devices to capture and transmit data to remotely held applications and data sources. In this way, people can always find the healthiest path for outdoor activities and can be continuously connected to their preferred personal training application or trainer. The realization of such a service requires that air quality and pollution sensors be deployed across the city and the sensor data has to be made publicly available to citizens.

Noise Monitoring

Noise can be seen as a form of acoustic pollution as much as carbon Monooxide (CO) is for air. An urban IoT can offer a noise-monitoring service to measure the amount of noise produced at any given hour in particular areas. Besides building a space-time map of the noise pollution in the area, this service can also be extended to enforce the safety of people and public properties by means of sound-detection algorithms that can recognize, for instance, the noise of glass crashes or brawls. This service can remarkably improve both the quietness of the nights in the city and the confidence of public establishment owners. However the installation of sound detectors or environmental microphones is bound to face a strong opposition as it is being portrayed that these sensors and devices are penetrating too much into the privacy of people.

Traffic Congestion

This is an important service for future cities. An urban IoT has the innate capability to closely monitor city traffic and if there is any congestion or complication on the roads, it could be immediately captured and conveyed to the concerned. At this point of time, camera-based traffic monitoring systems are doing a yeomen service. However minute sensors can do a better job. Next-generation traffic monitoring may be realized by using widely deployed sensors, road infrastructures, and GPS installed on modern vehicles in synchronization with acoustic sensors. This information is of great importance for city authorities to discipline traffic and to send officers where needed and it helps people to plan in advance the route to reach the office or to better schedule a shopping trip to the city centre.

Smart Parking

This facility is being given based on road sensors and intelligent displays that direct motorists along the best path for parking in the city. The benefits are many. It helps drivers to find a parking slot quickly thereby there is a less CO emission from the car and subdued traffic snarl. The smart parking service can be directly integrated in the urban IoT infrastructure to get proper visibility through widespread advertisements. Further on, through short-range communication technologies, it is possible to remotely verify whether vehicles are getting parked properly and in the right slots allocated for them. Disabled people can get priority too.

Professionals and experts are exploring, experimenting and expounding an increasing array of value-added business and use cases for a variety of industry segments to keep the momentum on the IoT / M2M space intact. There is another trend fast picking up these days with the active participation of academicians and industry veterans. Cyber physical systems (CPSs) are the new powerful entities in this complicated landscape. That is, all kinds of physical systems at the ground level are being empowered with scores of generic as well as specific cyber applications, services and data. That is, not only connectivity but also software-inspired empowerment is being ticked as the next-generation evolution in the machine space. There is no doubt that there will be more IT-automation for all kinds of dumb and dormant systems.

Cyber Physical System (CPS) for Smart City Needs

Cyber physical systems (CPSs) (Gelenbe and JingWu, 2013) use wireless communication, sensing, perception and actuation technologies, and distributed decisions overwhelmingly with immensely potential benefits in very diverse areas of human activity such as the personal as well as professional environments, homeland security, transport systems, emergency management, discovery of bombs, mines and unexploded ordnances, leisure and tourism. There are fresh possibilities and opportunities in waiting to be eloquently fulfilled with the smart leverage of the distinct concepts and capabilities of the fast-flourishing CPS domain.

CPS for Emergency Response

There are a plenty of review articles that have detailed the research activities on sensor-aided CPSs that enable intelligent and fast response to emergencies such as fires, earthquakes or terrorist attacks. Real-time monitoring and quick response are the two inherent requirements for emergency response.

During a fire, different types of sensors can cooperate and interact with the evacuees and the environment to bring down the intensity of fire and the material loss. Temperature and gas sensors can help monitor the spread of hazards. Rotatable cameras track the spread of the fire and the movement of civilians. Ultrasonic sensors can calculate the distance to obstacles in the environment and monitor dynamic changes of maps due to sudden changes in some built structures through destruction and debris. Smart evacuation schemes can help evacuees using the cooperation between first-aid decision nodes, sensors and civilians with mobile devices. Evacuees with mobiles and wearables can follow personalised navigation paths with distributed decisions that mitigate congestion. Those without smartphones may follow audio or visible LED directions. Integrated applications in clouds can gather sensing information and dynamically predict the movement of evacuees and hazards to make the best decisions regarding resource allocation and response. A search may also be conducted with the help of robotic devices despite their limited autonomy. For emergency response, there are a few challenges as described below.

Communication Issues

Many-to-many information flow and opportunistic connection are inevitable in emergency situations. Considering a fire emergency, to find safe paths, sensing information need to be aggregated from many live sensors and conveyed to many evacuees on the move in real time. Communication channels are liable to failure and hence it is a serious issue. In addition, query-and-reply communications may also proceed between different groups of people, e.g., first responders, evacuees, members of the press and robots. In these cases, the typical communication protocols, such as broadcast, unicast, and multicast, may be not able to deal with these diverse communication requirements.

- **Information Acquirement and Dissemination**: Cross-domain sensing and heterogeneous information flow are inherent features in an emergency response system. To guarantee the safety of people, information in different domains must be acquired. Moreover, sensors are not the only information contributors, but also all the interactions amongst sensors, actuators, people, smart objects and events. All the captured information has to be subjected to a series of real-time investigations to extract insights that need to be taken to the concerned.
- **Knowledge Discovery**: Data are everywhere in plenty, in different format, speed, scope, etc. However generating pragmatic knowledge is the most crucial thing in any emergent situations to tide over the crisis effectively. Partial information and dynamic changes are inherent in an emergency. In the recent past, whatever may be the volume of data getting generated, the data analytics platforms are capable of squeezing intelligence to rely upon and to work on.
- **Resource Allocation and Management:** Limited resources make timely response more difficult. Unlike other sensor-aided applications, the needs of intelligent actuation, scheduling and efficient resource allocation will increase in emergency response systems. Intelligent scheduling is needed to select the best course of action, while scarce resources must be allocated efficiently to perform actions.
- **Heterogeneous System Integration and Asynchronous Control**: Multifaceted technologies will be accurately chosen and used to enhance the capability and diversity of emergency response. Furthermore, functionally separated tasks such as sensing, storage, computation and decision-making, need to be accomplished by independent functional units so as to facilitate the integrated asynchronous control of multiple technologies.

As reported before, the maturity and stability of CPS technologies, newer application domains will emerge in the smart city space.

Smart City Platforms and Frameworks

There are smart city solutions in the forms of integrated platforms and enabling frameworks by product vendors. IBM, Oracle, Hitachi, etc. are the leading IT solutions providers to facilitate the faster and simpler realization of smart cities across the globe. There are many software infrastructure solutions being developed and deployed along with supporting toolkits and tips to provide end-to-end smart city functionalities. Considering the growing market for smart city solutions, IT product vendors are in fast track in order to bring forth highly competent solutions to keep the edge earned. In this section, we are to discuss a smart city communication platform and a framework for sensor-cloud integration, which is occupying a major chunk in building and enhancing intelligent cities.

A Communication Platform for Smart Cities

M2M communication platforms (Elmangoush et al., 2013) will take the role of insightful controlling of the communication between all connected machines to ensure the intended tasks. All kinds of devices are nowadays instrumented to have the innate communication capability. The communication infrastructures (cellular as well as radio) too are becoming pervasive. Thus enabling devices to connect with one another in the vicinity as well as to the remote cyber systems dawns a variety of hitherto unforeseen applications for individuals and institutions. The software development community is at the forefront in designing, developing, debugging and deploying a variety of device-centric services. That is, all kinds of existing and emerging devices are being shown to be service-providing, requesting and brokering systems. That means, the Internet of Services (IoS) paradigm is to power on the world on many ways. The IoS leads to streams of highly sophisticated cloud, enterprise, embedded, social and analytical applications being constructed very quickly through integrated platforms, powerful tools and pioneering techniques such as service integration, orchestration and choreography. The seamless and spontaneous connectivity results in intelligent devices to exhibit distinct behaviours as per the varying scenarios and needs. The point is that M2M communication is to lead to a growing array of original smart city applications.

Smart city IT has to have the following four main points: i) smart infrastructures to connect physical objects and sensors through heterogeneous communication networks realizing the interconnection between human and machines (H2M) and between machines (M2M) ii) smart operations for improving the citizens' quality of life by offering innovative services in every sector by integrating systems and information and the core elements for supporting urban operation and management iii) smart ecosystem, where the analysis of the interconnected information should yield new insights for driving decisions and actions that lead to process innovations and other noteworthy outcomes of pioneering systems, organizations, and industry value chains iv) smart governance: the interconnection of urban components with integrated application systems need to be governed through policy establishment and enforcements. Thus any smart city platform has to have the functionality, feature and facility to provision the above four requirements. The authors of this platform also have listed the research challenges as follows.

- **Scalability:** Considering the rapid increase in the number of smart devices coupled with the sickening heterogeneity in sensor networks, scalability is a main technical challenge for enabling ubiquitous information and service access. How, naming and addressing of all the participants and constituents, networking and communication, data management, service provisioning and delivery, are to be accomplished are some of the research challenges.
- **Governance:** Smart city services involve many different stakeholders such as service developers, integrators and brokers, communication and cloud service providers, device manufacturers, administrators, policy makers and end-users etc. In order to be able to manage the overall system consistently, flexible and generic solutions are needed for optimized sharing and governance.
- **Lack of Test Beds**: In order to perform reliable large-scale experimentations for the verification and validation of research results, the need of a city-scale test bed is being insisted.
- **Security and Privacy**: To ensure seamless delivery of service, the security of the M2M communication and accommodating invasion into the privacy of an individual must also be included.

A Smart City M2M Platform

Having understood the limitations of the existing platforms, the authors have built a flexible and futuristic platform for smart cities. You can find the main functionalities of the platform in their research paper. The platform could overcome the above-mentioned limitations to a major extent. With the accumulation of connected machines, the direct fallout is the huge data growth and heaps. Thus communication networks and infrastructures need to have the inherent capability of comfortably carrying data to target systems to initiate the process of knowledge extraction, engineering and exposition. RESTful services APIs are pervasive and distinctively popular in the cloud, analytics, mobile and IoT era due to its extreme simplicity. That is, data traffic is regulated, tracked and tackled with the standard interfaces. Devices send out data as well as event messages to be unambiguously understood and acted by devices on the other side. Data compression, de-duplication, analysis, and processing algorithms are very critical for the success of this platform and hence there are validated and refined data processing techniques and methods embedded in this platform. There are other capabilities such as impenetrable security and privacy, ease of participatory development, simplified use and operation of the platform.

A Framework of Sensor-Cloud Integration

In this section, a robust and resilient framework to enable this exploration by integrating sensor networks to clouds (Hassan et al., 2009) is explained. There are many challenges to realize this framework. The authors of this framework have proposed a pub-sub based model, which simplifies the integration of sensor networks with cloud-based and community-centric applications. Also there is a need for inter-networking cloud providers in case of any violations of service level agreements (SLAs) with users.

Use Cases

A virtual community consisting of a team of researchers who come together to solve a complex problem and they need huge data storage, compute capability, security, etc. For example, this team is working on the outbreak of a new virus strain sweeping through a population. They have deployed bio-sensors on a patient body to monitor his / her condition continuously and to use this data for large and multi-dimensional simulations to track the origin and spread of infection as well as the virus mutation and possible cures. This might require large computational resources and a versatile platform for sharing data and results that are not immediately available for the insights into the problem. So the sensor data obtained needs to be aggregated, processed and disseminated based on the subscriptions.

On the other hand, as sensor data require huge team.Here, researchers need to register their interest to get various patients' state (blood pressure, temperature, pulse rate etc.) from the bio-sensors for large-scale parallel analysis and to share this information with each other to find actionable computational power and storage, one cloud provider may not be able to handle this requirement. This insists for a dynamic collaboration with other cloud providers. Thus the formation of a virtual organization (VO) with cloud integration methods is gaining importance.

In the healthcare domain, doctors need real-time and historical data to thoroughly diagnose and analyse the health condition of patients and to prescribe the correct course of medication with right dosage. There are specialized sensors to continuously monitor, measure, and dispatch a variety of healthcare parameters to centralised control centers and care-givers. Further on, due to the unprecedented improvisations in ad hoc networking, there are body area networks (BANs) and smart sensor networks (SSNs) to clinically capture and cognitively collaborate with cloud-based applications to corroborate and correlate the accuracy and recency of the data obtained. Then competent data analytics platforms emit actionable insights that in turn gets visualised and disseminated to doctors, specialists, surgeons and care-givers as well as other actuation systems.

Roads have sensors that can communicate with the vehicles passing over them to determine useful traffic patterns, find more sustainable ways to route cars, and perhaps even generate data to be sold to insurance companies or other businesses seeking to tap transportation and logistics information.

Traditional high-performance computing (HPC) approach like the Sensor-Grid model can be used in this particular case, but setting up the appropriate infrastructure to deploy and scale it quickly is not easy in this environment. However, the cloud paradigm is an admirable and awesome move. Current cloud providers unfortunately did not address this issue of integrating sensor networks with the cloud applications. To integrate sensor networks to the cloud, the authors have proposed a content-based pub-sub model. A pub-sub system encapsulates and transitions sensor data into events and provides the services of event publication and subscription for asynchronous data exchange among system entities. MQTT-S is an open, topic-based and pub-sub protocol that hides the topology of sensor network and allows data to be delivered based on interest rather than the individual device addresses. It allows a transparent data exchange between WSNs and traditional networks and even between different WSNs.

In this framework, like MQTT-S, all of the system's complexities reside on the broker's side but differs from MQTT-S in one aspect. That is, this uses a content-based pub-sub broker rather than the topic-based method. When an event is published, it gets transmitted from a publisher to one or more subscribers without the publisher having to do anything to take up the message to any specific subscriber. Matching is done by the pub-sub broker outside of the WSN environment. In content-based pub-sub system, sensor data has to be augmented with meta-data to identify different data fields. For example, a meta-data of a sensor value (also event) can be body temperature, blood pressure etc.

To deliver published sensor data (events) to subscribers, an efficient and scalable event matching algorithm is required by the pub-sub broker. This event matching algorithm targets a range of predicate cases suitable to application scenarios and has to be highly efficient and scalable when the number of predicates increases sharply. In this framework, sensor data are coming through gateways to a pub/sub broker that is required to deliver information to the consumers of SaaS applications as the entire network is very dynamic. On the WSN side, sensor or actuator (SA) devices may change their network addresses at any time. Wireless links are quite likely to fail. Furthermore, SA nodes could also fail at any time and instead of being repaired, it is expected that they will be replaced by new ones. Besides, different SaaS applications can be hosted and run on any machines anywhere on the cloud. In such situations, the conventional approach of using network address as communication means between the SA devices and the applications may be very problematic because of their dynamic and temporal nature.

Several SaaS applications may have an interest in the same sensor data but for different purposes. In this case, the SA nodes would need to manage and maintain communication means with multiple applications in parallel. This might exceed the limited capabilities of the simple and low-cost SA devices. So, a pub-sub broker is needed and is located on the cloud side because of its higher performance in terms of bandwidth and capabilities.

On concluding, to deliver published sensor data or events to appropriate users of cloud applications, an efficient and scalable event-matching algorithm called Statistical Group Index Matching (SGIM) is leveraged. The authors have also evaluated the algorithm's performance and compared it with the existing algorithms in a cloud-based ubiquitous healthcare application scenario. The authors have clearly described that this algorithm in sync up with the foundational and fruitful framework enables sensor-cloud connectivity to utilize the ever-expanding sensor data for various community-centric sensing and responsive applications on the cloud. It can be seen that the computational tools needed to launch this exploration is more appropriately built from the data center "cloud" computing model than the traditional HPC approaches or Grid approaches. Based on this creative work, it is bound for many to visualize new-generation cloud-sensor platforms and applications. Finally, a very important ingredient in the smarter planet is the pervasiveness of adaptive middleware solutions for seamlessly and spontaneously integrating devices in the physical world with the business and IT applications and packages in the virtual / cyber world over all kinds of networks.

Figure 7. The framework architecture of sensor - cloud integration

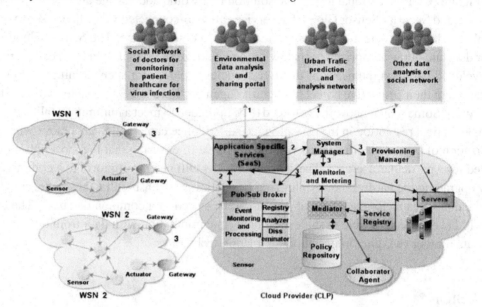

The final outcome of these delectable and desirable trends and technologies is the internet of devices and services that in turn lead to smarter and sophisticated applications for humans. That is, with self-, surroundings- and situation-aware devices along with cloud infrastructures and the Internet as the communication infrastructure, people-centric services and applications can be precisely and perfectly decided, developed and delivered to humans in real-time.

Homeland Security and the Sensor Cloud

The Sensor Cloud takes the cloud concepts and applies it to sensor networks (The Sensor Cloud the Homeland Security, 2019). That is, intelligent wired or wireless sensors store their data in the cloud, subscribers are allowed to view and analyze the data, and administrators carry out remote management of the sensors. The concept of the sensor cloud has caught on because of the ubiquity of sensors consequent on support for a variety of sensors on a standard smartphone platform (accelerometer, cameras, microphone, GPS, compass, proximity, ambient light, etc.). Specialized sensors are embedded in most electronic and electrical equipment.

Companies are now building clouds to store the data captured by such sensors. There are several surveillance sensor networks in place throughout the world. Each state government is responsible for setting up and running its surveillance sensor network and different state agencies run their own networks (city surveillance, traffic management, VIP security, critical infrastructure, coastal surveillance, border control, etc.). In addition, other Homeland Security-impacting agencies have their own networks: Railways, airports, critical infrastructure, etc. Each network of sensors (video surveillance cameras in most cases) has its own infrastructure for video/content management (DVRs/NVRs/VMS Servers) and storage.

The problem with the current decentralized architecture is that many of the agencies do not have the required resources for managing the infrastructure. Older sensor data is not properly archived or is misplaced. Further on, silos of surveillance sensor networks prevent the emergence of a Common Operational Picture (COP) at a global level. One solution that would address the above issues would be to build a Homeland Security Sensor Cloud that services all web-connected surveillance sensor networks: video, audio, radar, trace detectors, access control, motion detectors, etc. The Sensor Cloud will store the sensor data and allow authorized users to view and analyze the same. Agency-specific applications can be developed based on the needs of the user-agencies. In order for such an initiative to get off the ground states and their respective homeland security agencies have to be agreeable to having their data stored in clouds. Some sensor networks will need to be upgraded to meet a minimum quality-of-data level (for example, optical resolution in the case of video surveillance cameras). Such a move will also allow homogenization of sensor specifications with the objective of ensuring that the most optimum sensors are selected for a particular use-case. The sensor networks will need to conform to a common standard (either by upgrading the hardware or by plugging in a gateway) to ensure that they connect to the cloud and that the data streams for each type of sensor can be stored in a common database. The owners of the data will have to be agreeable to share their data (in combination with data from other owners) for analysis, data mining and other information- extraction techniques.

CONCLUSION

In the last decade, the Internet of Things (IoT) paradigm has slowly but steadily conquered the minds of researchers and engineers to the point of becoming one of the most exciting, innovative, transformative and disruptive domains. In this chapter, we have explained the radical contributions of the raging IoT concept in setting up and sustaining next-generation cities, the incredible IoT technologies, the noteworthy transformations that are bound to flourish in the days ahead, the network architectures that are to shape up the forthcoming applications for simplifying and streamlining city processes, etc. We have described the industry-strength of IoT frameworks emerging in order to build city-specific applications and services. There are data analytics platforms to create reliable and usable insights and feed them to respective applications to be exceptionally resilient, versatile and adroit.

REFERENCES

An Information Technology (IT) Portal. (2019). Retrieved from http://www.peterindia.net

Chen, M. (2013). Towards smart city: M2M communications with software agent intelligence. *Multimedia Tools and Applications*, *67*(1), 167–178. doi:10.100711042-012-1013-4

Elmangoush, A., Coskun, H., Wahle, S., & Magedanz, T. (2013). Design Aspects for a Reference M2M Communication Platform for Smart Cities. *9th International Conference on Innovations in Information Technology*. 10.1109/Innovations.2013.6544419

Gelenbe & Wu. (2013). *Future Research on Cyber-Physical Emergency Management Systems*. Future Internet.

Hancke, & de Carvalho e Silva & Hancke Jr. (2013). The Role of Advanced Sensing in Smart Cities. *Sensors (Basel)*. PMID:23271603

Hassan, M. M., Song, B., & Huh, E.-N. (2009). *A Framework of Sensor-Cloud Integration Opportunities and Challenges*. ICUIMC. doi:10.1145/1516241.1516350

Jin, J., Gubbi, J., Luo, T., & Palaniswami, M. (2012). Network Architecture and QoS Issues in the Internet of Things for a Smart City. *International Symposium on Communications and Information Technologies (ISCIT)*. 10.1109/ISCIT.2012.6381043

Pawar, S. P. (2013). *Smart City with Internet of Things (Sensor networks) and Big Data. Institute of Business Management & Research (IBMR)*.

Perera, C., Zaslavsky, A., Christen, P., & Georgakopoulos, D. (2014). Sensing as a Service Model for Smart Cities Supported by Internet of Things. *Transactions on Emerging Telecommunications Technologies*, 25(1), 81–93. doi:10.1002/ett.2704

Raj, P. (2012). Cloud Enterprise Architecture. CRC Press.

The Sensor Cloud the Homeland Security. (2011). Retrieved from http://www.mistralsolutions.com/hs-downloads/tech-briefs/nov11-article3.html

Vicini, S., Bellini, S., & Sanna, A. (2012). How to Co-Create Internet of Things-enabled Services for Smarter Cities. *SMART 2012: The First International Conference on Smart Systems, Devices and Technologies*.

Zanella, A., & Vangelista, L. (2014). Internet of Things for Smart Cities. IEEE Internet of Things Journal, 1(1).

Chapter 17
Leveraging the Internet of Things (IoT) Paradigm Towards Smarter Applications

E. A. Neeba
Rajagiri School of Engineering and Technology, India

J. Aswini
Jawahar Engineering College, India

R. Priyadarshini
Siddharth Institute of Science and Technology, India

ABSTRACT

Intelligent processing with smart devices and informative communications in everyday tasks brings an effective platform for the internet of things (IOT). Internet of things is seeking its own way to be the universal solution for all the real-life scenarios. Even though many theoretical studies pave the basic requirement for the internet of things, still the evidence-based learning (EBL) is lacking to deal with the application of the internet of things. As a contribution of this chapter, the basic requirements to study about internet of things with its deployment architecture for mostly enhanced applications are analyzed. This shows researchers how to initiate their research focus with the utilization of internet of things.

INTRODUCTION

The future Internet comprises not only the millions of compute machines, personal/ professional electronic devices and distributed software services but also the billions of diminutive sensors, actuators, robots, etc. and finally the trillions of sentient or digitized objects. It is an overwhelmingly accepted statement that the fast-emerging and evolving IoT idea is definitely a strategic and highly impactful vision to be decisively realized and passionately sustained with the smart adaption and adoption of state-of-the-art technologies, composite and cognitive processes, optimal and versatile infrastructures, integrated platforms, enabling tools, pioneering patterns, and futuristic architectures. Industry professionals and

DOI: 10.4018/978-1-5225-9023-1.ch017

academicians are constantly looking out for appropriate use, business and technical cases in order to confidently and cogently proclaim the transformational value and power of the IoT concept to the larger audience of worldwide executives, end-users, entrepreneurs, evangelists, and engineers.

A growing array of open and industry-strength standards are being formulated, framed and polished by domain experts, industry consortiums and standard bodies to make the IoT thought more visible, viable and valuable. National governments across the globe are setting up special groups in order to come out with pragmatic policies and procedures to take forward the solemn ideals of IoT and to realize the strategic significance of the envisioned IoT in conceiving, concretizing and providing a bevy of next-generation citizen-centricservices to ensure and enhance peoples' comfort, choice, care, and convenience. Research students, scholars and scientists are working collaboratively towards identifying the implementation challenges and overcoming them via different means and ways especially standard technological solutions.

In this chapter, we would like to give a broader perspective of what exactly is the idea of IoT, as well as trends setting the stimulating stage for the IoT realization and demonstration, why it has to be pursued with all seriousness and sincerity, what are the prickling and prime concerns, changes and challenges associated with it, where it will be applied extensively and expediently, what is the near and long-term future, the key benefits, nightmares, risks, etc.

A Reflection on the IoT Paradigm

Information technology (IT) has been in the forefront in precisely and perfectly automating and accelerating a variety of business tasks in order to immensely empower businesses, partners and consumers to accrue the widely circulated and IT-enabled business benefits. IT is being positioned as the best business enabler in totality. IT is constantly evolving to do better and bigger things. These days, IT, besides the greatest enabler of simple as well as complicated business operations, is penetrating powerfully into every tangible industry segment in order to proactively ensure newer and nimbler customer-centric business offerings. In short, IT is able to simplify and amplify business outputs and outlooks significantly. It is absolutely clear that the strategically sound association and alignment between business and IT is on the consistent climb to create and sustain real-time, adaptive, composable, and instant-on enterprises. Having comprehensively understood the outstanding contributions of IT in keeping up the business expectations in the cut-throat competitive marketplace, business executives and entrepreneurs are striving hard and stretching further to put in more money to conceive, concretize and deliver next-generation IT-enabled business services and solutions to worldwide clients and consumers, to devise workable mechanisms and methods to understand peoples' needs and deliver them with all the quality of service (QoS) attributes embedded through the smart adaption of all kinds of exquisite advancements in the hot and happening IT field. Decision-makers and other stakeholders are constantly looking out for fresh avenues for enhanced revenues.

With businesses are achieving the desired successes in different fronts, there is a tectonic shift in IT being leveraged for empowering people in their daily activities. That is, the movement towards consumer centric IT is on the fast track with the emergence of innovative, transformative and disruptive technologies.

The Era of Smart Computing

How human life will be in this planet in and around the year 2025? What kind of lasting impacts, cultural changes, and perceptible shifts will be achieved in the human society due to the constant and consistent innovations, evolutions, and inventions in information, communication, sensing, vision, perception, knowledge engineering, dissemination, and actuation technologies? Today this has become a dominating and lingering question among leading researchers, luminaries, and scientists? Many vouch for a complete and comprehensive turnaround in our social, personal, and professional lives due to a dazzling array of technological sophistications, creativities and novelties. Presumably

computing, communication, perception and actuation will be everywhere all the time. The days of Ambient Intelligence (AmI) is not far away with the speed and sagacity with which scores of implementation technologies are being unearthed and sustained.

It is also presumed and proclaimed that the ensuing era will be fully knowledge-backed. It is going to be the knowledge-driven society. Databases will pave the way for knowledge bases and there will be specialized engines for producing and persisting with self-managing systems. Knowledge systems and networks are readied for autonomic communication. Cognition-enabled machines and expert systems will become our casual and compact companions. A growing array of smarter systems will surround, support and sustain us in our class rooms, homes, offices, motels, coffee houses, airport lounges, gyms, and other vital junctions, eating joints, and meeting points in big numbers. They will seamlessly connect, collaborate, corroborate and correlate to understand our mental, social and physical needs and deliver them in a highly unobtrusive, secure and relaxed fashion. That is, right information and rightful services will be conceived, constructed and delivered to the right person, at the right time at the right place. Extensively smart furniture, sensors, and artifacts will become the major contributors for this tectonic and tranquil modernization and migration.

Smart Environments

Our living, relaxing, and working environment is envisioned to be filled up with a variety of electronics including environment monitoring sensors, actuators, monitors, controllers, processors, tags, labels, stickers, dots, motes, stickers, projectors, displays, cameras, computers, communicators, appliances, gateways, high- definition IP TVs, etc. Apart from these, all the physical and concrete items, articles, furniture, and packages will become empowered with computation and communication-enabled components by attaching specially made electronics onto them. Whenever we walk into such kinds of empowered and augmented environments lightened up with a legion of digitized objects, the devices we carry and even our e-clothes will enter into calm yet logical collaboration mode and form wireless ad hoc networks with the inhabitants in that environment. For example, if someone wants to print a document in his smartphone or tablet, and if he enters into a room, where a printer is situated, then the smartphone will begin a conversation with the printer automatically and sends the document to be printed.

Thus, in that era, our everyday spots will be made informative, interactive, intuitive, and inspiring by embedding and imbedding intelligence and autonomy into their constituents (audio / video systems, cameras, information and web appliances, consumer and household electronics, and other electronic gadgets besides digitally augmented walls, floors, windows, doors, ceilings, and any other physical objects and artifacts etc.). The disappearing computers, communicators, sensors and robots will be instructing, instigating, alerting, and facilitating decision-making in a smart way, apart from accomplishing all kinds of everyday needs proactively for human beings. Humanized robots will be extensively used in order to fulfil our daily physical chores. That is, computers in different sizes, looks, capabilities, interfaces and prizes will be fitted, glued, implanted, and inserted everywhere to be coordinative, calculative and coherent yet invisible for discerning human minds. On summary, the IoT technologies in sync up with cloud infrastructures are to result in people- centric smarter environments.

The Brewing and Blossoming Trends in the IT Space

The Key Drivers for the IoT Discipline

Worldwide enterprises yearn for remarkable and resilient transformations on two major aspects: business operation model and business information leverage. Another vital point not to be lightly taken is to sharply enhance the user experience of business offerings. It is an overwhelmingly accepted truth that the desired enterprise transformation happens through the following four things.

1. Infrastructure Optimization
2. Process Excellence
3. Architecture Assimilation
4. Technology Adaption and Adoption

It is a fact that there are a number of noteworthy transitions and trends happening in the IT field. At the fundamental and foundation level, a variety of nimbler technologies, techniques and tips are emerging and evolving in order to bring in desirable and delectable transformations in data capture, representation, transmission, enrichment, storage, processing, analysis, mining, visualization, and virtualization tasks. Other prevailing and promising trends include

*   The device ecosystem is embracing a bevy of miniaturization technologies to be slim and sleek, yet smart in their operations, outlooks and outputs.
*   **Digitization and distribution** are gaining a lot of ground nowadays thereby all kinds of tangible items in our home, social and office environments are getting transfigured to be sensing, communication-enabled, display-attached, actuation, etc. That is, ordinary articles become extraordinary, common, casual and cheap objects in our working, walking and wandering places become connected and cognitive to seamlessly and spontaneously join in the mainstream computing process. In short everything gets emboldened to be smart, every device becomes smarter, and every human being is the smartest in their actions, reactions and decision-making portions of his earthly living with the pervasive, unceasing and unobtrusive assistance of service-oriented, sustainability-insisted, and smartness-ingrained devices, systems, applications and networks.
*   **Extreme and deeper connectivity** is another well-known phenomenon in order to establish and sustain ad-hoc connectivity among different and distributed devices at the ground level and with remote, off-premise, on-demand and online applications.

Data becomes big data with the data being produced, gathered and processed in multiple structures (structured, semi-structured and non-structured). The machine- generated data is far larger than man-generated data. The data volume, velocity and variety are seeing a remarkable climb. With innumerable devices, tags, stickers, sensors, appliances, machines, instruments, gadgets, etc. getting fervently deployed indistributed and decentralized fashion in an increasingly important locations such as homes, hospitals, hotels, etc., the tasks such as data collection, classification, fusion, transition to information and knowledge, and dissemination have to be accomplished in real time using a series of greatly sophisticated and dependable technologies.

- **Real-time analysis** results in a nice and neat realization towards producing actionable insights in time with the emergence and escalation of converged, centralized, automated, shared, optimized, virtualized, and even federated cloud infrastructures.
- A family of futuristic and **flexible architectural paradigms**, patterns and principles such as service-oriented architecture (SOA), event driven architecture (EDA), model driven architecture (MDA), etc.

According to IT experts, there will be a seamless and spontaneous merger of everyday technologies to create a kind of technology cluster to fulfil our personal as well as professional requirements instantly and instinctively. That is, there comes the possibility of transparent merging of our minds with machines. Learning will be everywhere and every time affair because we will have intimate and real-time access to the world's information assets and knowledgebase using any of our accompanying electronic gizmos and on the reverse side, we will have a unfailing backup of our brains on massive-scale digital storages. Massive research endeavors and efforts are concertedly put into these seemingly magical and leading-edge technology themes, which will let to connect our nervous systems to computers beneficially.

Disruptive and transformative technologies with the smart synchronization of a galaxy of information and communication technologies will emerge to realize revolutionary applications and to accomplish hitherto unheard social networking and digital knowledge societies. Auto- identification tags carrying our personal profile and preferences digitally, will map, mix, merge and mingle with others in realization of novel human aspirations. Our daily tools and products can be converted into smart products by attaching ultra-small computers. For example, our coffee cups, dinner plates, tablets, and clothes will be empowered to act smart in their operations and interactions with other products in the vicinity or even with the human beings. Finally all the tangible and worthy things, objects, materials, and articles will be transitioned into smart and sentient digital artifacts. This will result in the Internet of things in the decades to come. It is hence no doubt that future generations will experience and realize complete and compact digital and technology-driven, -enabled, -sponsored, and - flourished living. The impact of IT in our life becomes bigger, deeper, yet calmer as days go by.

The Shift Towards People IT

Having contributed to the unprecedented uplift of business-operation productivity and for composable businesses, IT is turning towards the people productivity. There are several noteworthy advancements in the IT landscape as listed below. Therefore, the shift towards people empowerment is on the right track. That is, not only business services and applications, but also there will be conceptualization, best-of-breed implementations and maintenance ofpeople-centric information, transaction, decision-enabling, knowledge, and context-aware physical services. There are best practices, patterns, platforms, processes, and products being unearthed and built to silken the route towards the envisioned people centric IT. There are a series of delectable and desired developments in the IT landscape. Below you can find them in an orderly manner.

- **The Technology Space**: There is a cornucopia of disruptive, transformative and innovative technologies such as Connectivity, Miniaturization & Instrumentation, Sensing, Fusion, Perception, & Actuation, Real-time Analyses that results in actionable Insights, Knowledge Engineering, Dissemination & Interfacing, etc.)
- **The Process Space**: With new kinds of sophisticated technologies, services and applications, big data, converged, elastic and instant-on infrastructures and trendy devices joining into the mainstream IT, fresh process consolidation and orchestration, process innovation, control, and reengineering, process governance and management mechanisms are emerging and evolving.
- **Infrastructure Space**: The emerging infrastructure consolidation, convergence, centralization, federation, automation and sharing methods clearly indicate that the much- maligned infrastructure landscape is bound to reach greater and greener heights in the days to unfold. Compute, communication, storage, analysis and presentation infrastructures are trekking towards a bevy of exemplary transitions. Physical infrastructures are turned and tuned to be network discoverable and accessible, loosely coupled yet cohesive, programmable and remotely manageable virtual infrastructures.
  - ○ **System Infrastructure:** Hardware infrastructures (servers, storage, network solutions, specific appliances, etc.)
  - ○ **Application and Data Infrastructure**: Development, Deployment, Execution containers and consoles, Databases and Warehouses
  - ○ **Middleware and Management Infrastructure**: There are Integration Buses, Backbones, & Fabrics, Messaging Brokers and Containers. With the intensifying complexity of IT space due to uninhibited complicity and heterogeneity of technologies, products, programming languages, design approaches, protocols, data formats, etc., the importance of introspective middleware goes up considerably.

Infrastructures are becoming lean, mean and green. Further on, with IT agility is getting operationalized as IT infrastructures become dynamically programmable, autonomic, auto- provisioning, on-demand and online, the goal of business agility is steadily seeing the neat and nice reality. These are possible due to integration brokers, execution containers, and messaging middleware, event capturing and processing engines, development, deployment and delivery platforms, analytical software, management solutions, etc.

- **Architecture Space:** Service oriented architecture (SOA), event-driven architecture (EDA), model-driven architecture (MDA), service component architecture (SCA), resource-oriented architecture (ROA), and so on are the leading architectural patterns simplifying and streamlining the enterprise, mobile, embedded, and cloud IT. With the unparalleled and surging popularity of the service-orientation paradigm, everything is being presented and prescribed as a service. That means everything is given its functional interface so that other systems and services can find, bind, and leverage the distinct capabilities and competencies of one another.

The veritable trend is that with the stability and maturity of the service paradigm, everything is being presented as a service providing, brokering, and consumer entity. Data, applications, platforms, and even infrastructures are being consciously codified and co-mingled as publicly discoverable, remotely accessible, autonomous, highly available, usable, reusable, and composable services. The vision of "Everything is a service" is seeing a neat and nice reality. The service-enablement delicately hides the implementation and operational complexities of all kinds of IT resources and only exposes the functionality and capability of those resources in the form of public interfaces in order to be dynamically found and bound.

Describing the IoT Architecture

Internet of things is the representation of interconnecting several smart devices and its services. Currently billions of things (objects) are interconnected to internet to reveal the name fact of internet of things. Also IoT provides the seven layered architecture for deploying the application model based on their domain knowledge (Li, Xu, & Zhao, 2014).

As stated by the past survey, more than 25 billion devices will be connected to the internet by 2020 to make the intelligent decision making. Based on the report provided by US National Intelligence Council (NIC), IoT act as service providing sector for the several smart livings such as smart city, smart health, smart transport, smart business, smart agriculture, smart assisted living and other applications (Gubbia et al., 2013; Miorandi, Sicari & Chlamtac, 2012; Giusto et al., 2010).

Generally, the IOT can be defined as "A global infrastructure for the information society enabling advanced services by interconnecting (physical and virtual) things based on, existing and evolving, interoperable information and communication technologies" (ICTP workshop, 2015). Alternatively, IOT can defined as "3A concept: anytime, anywhere and any media, resulting into sustained ratio between radio and man around 1:1" (Srivastava, 2006). Based on the principles of Networked Enterprise & RFID with Micro & Nano systems, IOT is defined as Things having identities and virtual personalities operating in smart spaces using intelligent interfaces to connect and communicate within social, environmental, and user contexts" (Srivastava, 2006).

The following sections deals with IOT architecture, IOT functional blocks, IoT issues and about the review of significant works on IoT on many smart applications under the following perspectives such as smart building, smart irrigation and smart and analyzed the major research findings. The discussion for the future scope based on the evidence-based learning is provided for the further research enhancements.

Semantically, IOT is phrased as a world-wide network of interconnected objects uniquely addressable, based on standard communication protocols. Based on the definition provided, it is clear there is no standard architecture of all the applications. Based on the issues occurring during the deployment of IoT based applications it also no doubt a specific IOT architecture is designed by connecting the required physical components like sensors, actuators, cloud services, specific IoT protocols, communication layers and the application layer (Atzori, Iera & Morabito, 2010). Based on this idea the definition of IoT is again redefined as a dynamic global network infrastructure with self-configuring capabilities based on standard and interoperable communication protocols where physical and virtual things have identities, physical attributes, and virtual personalities and use intelligent interfaces, and are seamlessly integrated into the information network. In general, a well-defined IoT architecture is designed with seven layers is shown in figure 1.

Figure 1. Seven layered architecture of IOT

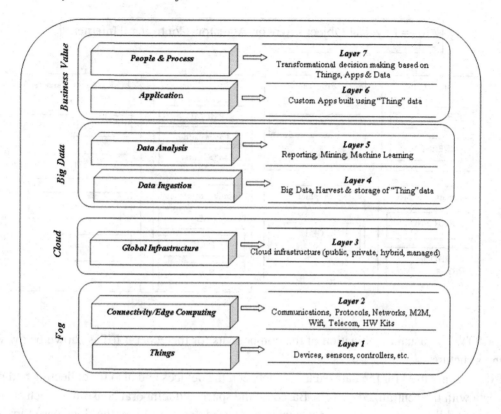

These seven layers are grouped under the four main paradigms such as Fog Computing, Cloud Computing, Big Data Analytics, and Business Value. Layer 1 includes all the IOT components which would like to share its services are specified. some of the components are sensors, controllers and all computing devices. Layer 2 includes the network infrastructure, communication protocols, Wi-Fi, telecom, and Machine to Machine communications. Layer 1 and Layer 2 are grouped under the Fog computing. Cloud computing brings the global infrastructure and behaves like the Layer 3 of IOT architecture. Under this cloud paradigm all types of cloud such as private, public and hybrid clouds are maintained and managed. The effective data handling and the processing is done under the Big Data paradigm which includes the Layer 4 and Layer 5.

Layer 4 deals with handling of big data with its storage provision. Layer 5 applies all the machine learning tools, data mining algorithms and reports the data to the users of the model. Finally the business value group focuses on the applications developed under Layer 6 and the people and process under the Layer 7 for the decision making based on data transformation using the IOT components and its data. The overall architecture of IOT is shown in the figure 1.

Functional Blocks of IOT

In order to facilitate various utilities of IOT system, the number of functional blocks such as sensors for sensing, device identification, actuation, communication establishment and management is employed (McEwan & Cassimally, 2013; Sebastian & Ray, 2015). Figure 2 shows the description for the functional

Figure 2. Device Components of IOT

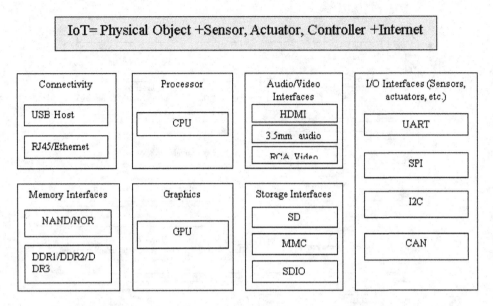

blocks of IOT. The usual combination of the components for the general IoT is shown below with the following structure.

IOT devices are used for the data exchange between the devices and also for collecting and processing the data with the centralized servers. Based on the space and temporal constraints such as memory, processing capabilities, communication latencies, and speeds, and deadlines the cloud based applications are used as back end for processing the data. To make the wired and wireless communications several interfaces are used. Some of the interfaces are audio/ video interfaces, memory and storage interfaces, interfaces for Internet connectivity and I/ O interfaces for sensors. All the IOT devices generate its own from of data which are analyzed by the data analytic tools or algorithms to generate the processed data. For the communication of the IOT, the communication protocols in data link layer, network layer, transport layer, and application layer is performed.IOT system provides various services for device modeling, device control, data publishing, data analytics, and device discovery. The duty of the management block is to manage all the actions of the IOT system. Application layer is the user dependent layer which acts as the medium to visualize, and analyze the system status at present stage of action, sometimes prediction of innovative próspects.

Technologies of IOT

The various technologies supporting the IOT enhancement is listed below in Table 1 with the complete description for the employment of the IOT based applications.

Issues of IOT

It includes various threads under the IOT layers (Wu, 2010) which are shown in Figure 3

Table 1. Technologies of IOT

Technology	Description
Radio Frequency IDentification (RFID)	RFID makes the unique identification of the objects. Due to it miniatures and economical cost it is highly utilized and embedded in any object (Paul et al., 2013; Sarkar, Maiti & Sarkar, 2010). Depends on the type of application this is used as transceiver microchip and is activated under passive or active tags. Under the active tag the presence of the battery always keeps its active to emit the data signals continuously. But the passive tags are activated when they are triggered. This technology is applied to emit the identification location and the data signals are transmitted to the readers using radio frequencies which are then passed onto the processors to analyze the data.
Bar Code	A technology similar to RFID is Bar code which acts same like the RFID. A difference between the RFID and Barcode is RFID is the radio technology where as barcode is the optical technology which works with the aid of reader. Another special feature of RFID is it can act as trigger but the barcode fails in this feature.
Wireless Sensor Network (WSN)	WSN is network of sensors connected in a multi-hop fashion in which each sensor works independently to collect data. Each sensor is a transceiver having an antenna, a micro-controller and an interfacing circuit. Wireless Sensors Network technology and RFID technology both combined together in many smart devices. For instance, Wireless Identification Sensing Platform (WISP) is a passive wireless sensor network with built-in light, temperature and many other sensors.
Cloud Computing	Cloud provides the environment of storing and analyzing the data efficiently. By 2020, more than millions of deices are expected to integrated under the cloud computing environment. It is an intelligent computing technology in which number of servers is converged on one cloud platform to allow sharing of resources between each other which can be accessed at any time and any place. Cloud computing integrated with IOT brings many open challenges to the researchers to bring large scale development under IOT.
Networking Technologies	In order to have a fast and effective network, the familiar technologies like Bluetooth, WiFi and so on is utilized.
Nano Technologies	Internet of Nano-Things is the network made up of group of nano devices. This technology enables the development of nano devices in nano meters scale.
Micro-Electro-Mechanical Systems (MEMS) Technologies	A combination of electrical and mechanical devices brings the term MEMS which is widely applied in transducers and accelerometers. In many cases MEMS combines with nano technologies to perform the effective task under the IOT.
Optical Technologies	Some of the optical technologies are Cisco's BiDi optical technology and Li-Fi. Bi-Directional (BiDi) technology gives a 40G ethernet for a big data from multifarious devices of IoT. Li-Fi, an epoch-making Visible Light Communication (VLC) technology, will provide a great connectivity on a higher bandwidth for the objects interconnected on the concept of IoT.

Figure 3. IOT threads

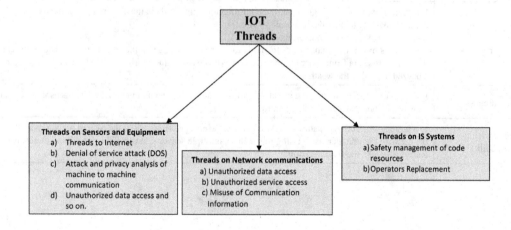

Another challenge is the privacy of the users under the IOT environment. Some of the privacy issues addressed here below includes

1. **Device Privacy:** It includes device location, Non- identifiability of device nature, device theft and Resilience to side channel attacks.
2. **Communication Privacy:** It includes encryption during the communication.
3. **Storage Privacy:** It deals with the information stored and it is retrieved on the basis of requirement.
4. **Processing Privacy:** The data processing is done with the knowledge of data owner.

Efficacy of IoT

The efficiency of IOT is revealed by the following factors for any real time applications. This is well understood from the Table 2.

Table 2.

Characteristics	Utility
Dynamic and self-adapting	Capable of dynamically adapting with the changing contexts and taking self actions based on their operating conditions, user's context, or sensed environment. **Application: surveillance system** The surveillance cameras can adapt their modes to either normal or infra-red night modes based on whether it is day or night. Cameras could switch from lower resolution to higher resolution modes when any motion is detected and alert nearby cameras to do the same. In this example, the surveillance system is adapting itself based on the context and changing (e.g., dynamic) conditions.
Self-configuring	Allows a large number of devices to work together to provide certain functionality **Application: Weather Monitoring** These devices have the ability to configure themselves in association with IoT infrastructure, setup the networking, and fetch latest software upgrades with minimal manual or user intervention.
Interoperable communication protocols	Support a number of interoperable communication protocols and can communicate with other devices and also with the infrastructure.
Unique identity	Unique identity and unique identifier refers the IP address which brings the communicating with users. IoT device interfaces allow users to query the devices, monitor their status, and control them remotely, in association with the control, configuration and management infrastructure.
Integrated into information network	IoT devices are usually integrated into the information network that allows them to communicate and exchange data with other devices and systems. **Application: Weather Monitoring** Describe its monitoring capabilities to another connected node so that they can communicate and exchange data. Thus, the data from a large number of concerned weather monitoring IoT nodes can be aggregated and analyzed to predict the weather.
Context-awareness	Based on the sensed information about the physical and environmental parameters, the sensor nodes gain knowledge about the surrounding context.
Intelligent decision-making capability	In a large area, multi-hop nature of IOT enhances the energy efficiency of the overall network, and hence, the network lifetime increases. Using this feature, multiple sensor nodes collaborate among themselves, and collectively take the final decision.

Application Domains of IoT Cloud Platforms

IoT cloud solutions pave the facilities like real time data capture, visualization, data analytics, decision making, and device management related tasks through remote cloud servers while implying "pay-as-you-go" notion. Various cloud service providers are gradually becoming popular in the several application domains such as agriculture and so on (Nandurkar, Thool & Thool, 2014). Following sub section describes how IoT clouds may be placed appropriately according to their applicability in several domains of importance with the aid of the figure 4.

EVIDENCE BASED LEARNING ON SEVERAL IOT APPLICATIONS

Smart Waste Collection System Based on Location Intelligence (Jose M. Gutierreza, Michael Jensenb, Morten Heniusa and Tahir Riazc, 2015)

Realistic Scenario

Cities around the world become smarter by proper maintaining and service providing. In this work the contribution of IOT for city management with smart waste collection system based on location intelligence is studied and analyzed. This work integrates the IOT with Geographic Information Systems (GIS), combinatorial optimization, data access networks and electronic engineering (Gutierreza et al., 2015).

Figure 4. Application domains of IoT cloud platforms

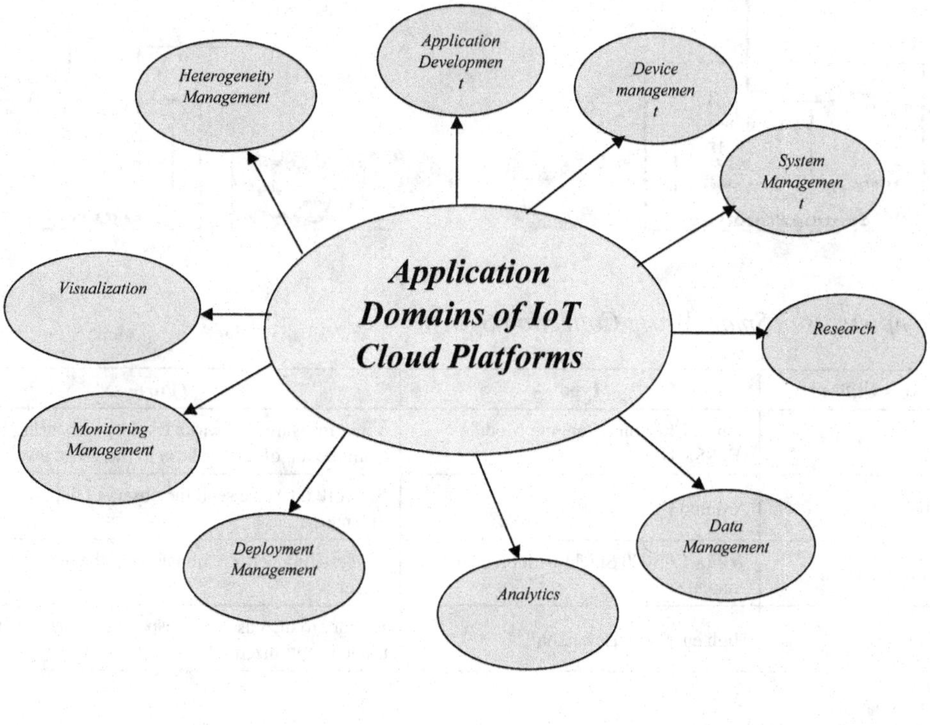

Open Data from the city of Copenhagen is taken as realistic scenario to highlights the opportunities for the IOT to develop Smart city solutions (Gaura et al., 2015).

System Design Based on Chore of IOT

Building a smart city using an intelligent waste collection cyber physical system is focused in this paper. With the help of Internet of Things senses the waste level of trashcans and sends the observed data to the server through the internet for the processing. This model acts as an optimized model by routing the workers with optimal path for the waste collection.

This model with the help of sensors senses the data with the IOT prototype. Then the sensed data is read and transmitted over the internet. Finally, those data are processed by graph theory optimization algorithms to efficiently manage waste collection process. The general architecture for this model is provided in figure 5.

In addition, the MYSQL is employed for the data processing and optimization algorithms based on artificial intelligence is utilized to learn the waste levels. In order to avoid traffic congestion, route optimization algorithm is applied to calculate the best route. Navigation systems such as tablets or mobile phones are utilized for the data access and those are send to the users in readable format (Wen, 2010).

Figure 5. Smart waste collection system

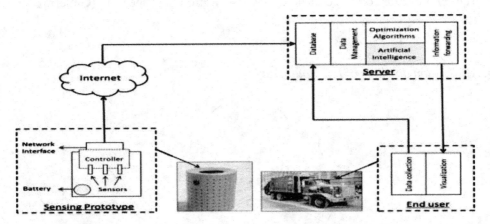

Table 3. Components of Smart Waste Collection System

Components Utilized	Type	Purpose
Sensors	Sonar- Ultrasonic Ranging Module (HC-SR04)	Sonar measures the waste level by measuring the distance from the top of the trashcan to the waste level.
Microcontroller	Arduino Uno - ATMega328	Network interface send the observed data of the sensors to the internet.
Access Network Interface	WiFi - CC3000 Shield with on board Antenna	wireless link helps in transferring the data to the network server.
Battery	High energy consumption	In order to increase the lifespan of the devices the battery usage is optimized.

Major Contributions and Findings

- Simulation results ensure that the experiment is carried out in the Geographic Information Systems simulation environment (GIS) with the help of graph optimization algorithms on open data about the city of Copenhagen, Denmark.
- This provides the intelligent solutions for the other city services which are common to all.
- Economic feasiablity and efficiency shows this model is superior than other similar models.

Smart City Architecture and its Applications Based on IoT (Aditya Gaura, Bryan Scotneya, Gerard Parra, Sally McCleana,2015)

Realistic Scenario

Currently Wireless Sensor Network (WSN) has been acted as backbone for the many realistic scenarios such as smart transport, smart health, smart irrigation, smart farming and so on. Similarly, under this research a smart city based on the multi level architecture is suggested with the aid of the Dempster-Shafer uncertainty theory and semantic web technologies.

System Design Based on Chore of IOT

The general diagram for the smart city architecture is provided below in figure 6.

As multi layer architecture, the smart city deployed here generates the heterogeneous information by the sensor nodes with communication services. The sources like navigation devices, satellite network for GPS devices, internet services and GSM/3G/4G for smart phone cellular services are widely used.The processing and analyzing of data is done by semantic web technologies and Dempster-Shafer combination rules.The main focus of this study is to build an architecture for the cloud platform for software as a service (SaaS).

Major Contributions and Findings

- Provides as smart city for the urban peoples with the flexible and intelligent support.
- Provides high-level context-aware customized real time services.
- Provides smart living environments (Zeng et al., 2012) for the real life scenarios like guiding a driver to take diversion in case of road congestion, alerting heart patients when increase of the heart beat occurs and warning the conditions of food items stored in the refrigerators.

VIRTUALIZATION OF FOOD SUPPLY CHAINS WITH THE INTERNET OF THINGS

Realistic Scenario

Food supply chains virtualization with the internet of things is discussed as the dynamic realistic scenario in this paper. This model is used to find the stringent food safety and sustainability requirements, perishable products and unpredictable supply variations. This provides the continuous monitoring the

Figure 6. Smart city architecture

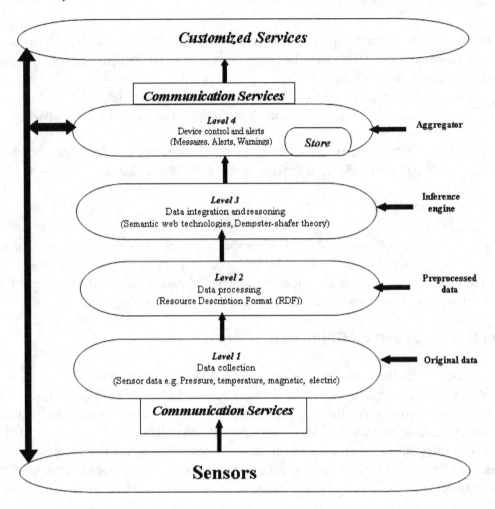

business process with the help of internet. This virtual model is applied for the fish supply chain which acts as a self-adaptive system with many internets of things acting autonomously (C.N. Verdouw, J. Wolfert, A.J.M. Beulens, A. Rialland, 2016)

System Design Based on Chore of IoT

This system works under the cloud environment in combination with Internet of Things (IoT). Under this all the objects are virtually connected and remotely controlled to provide the operations for the food supply chain virtualizations. The overall system view is shown in the figure 7.

Major Contributions and Findings

- Provides high level of granularity through virtual supply chain monitoring and event management.
- Finally, food supply chains act as autonomous, self-adaptive systems and works without the remote intervention by humans.

Figure 7. Virtualization of food supply chains

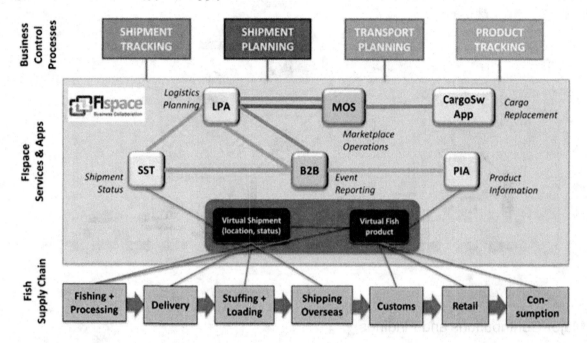

IoT-RFID Test Bed for Supporting Traffic Light Control

Realistic Scenario

A perfect control system for the traffic light to assist the police officers are discussed in the real life scenario. This system helps in pointing out the traffic congestion level at each road junction with the complete support of RFID technology. Sequencing and timing of traffic lights are properly completed with the help of this proposed model. Also as the intention of this work is to used to find illegal vehicles involved in the crimes. The test bed prototype has been built successfully as a proof-of-the concept of IoT (Choosri et al., 2015).

System Design Based on Chore of IoT

The system architecture IOT based Traffic light control system is shown below in figure 8.

The set up environment mimics a typical intersection and the RFID Readers are mounted to the imaginary traffic lights, such as Traffic light 1 and Traffic light 2. Under this set up, one Reader is installed to capture the traffic information of one uni-lane at one intersection. The specification of RFID readers using in this testbed system is a reader operated at passive Ultra Height Frequency (UHF), which means tags used in this system require no-battery. Tags have been measured for their maximum reading distance, and the result shows that they can support the reading distance of approximately 9 metres.

Figure 8. IOT system for traffic light control

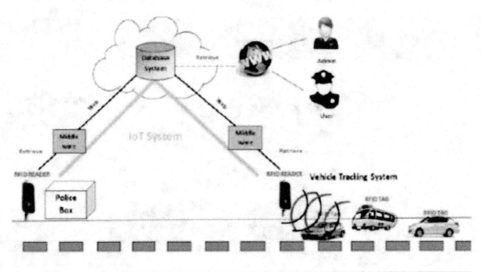

Major Contributions and Findings

- Opens up a new research opportunity for all and investigates the issues involving decentralized or even centralized traffic control using RFID technologies.
- The practical problem for smart traffic management system is defined, the solution is proposed under this research.
- Solutions for the many issues are addressed and the solution can be tested and applied to real-life problems dealing with heterogeneity of devices, concurrency of the services, responding times, data volume, human factors, and intelligence

OBSERVATIONS AND DISCUSSIONS

In this article, we reviewed the main contributions of IoT research in a set of well-known real life applications. The main issue that emerge as common problems in the all the applications to predict the accurate manner of framing the architecture. As a need of this issue, the familiar realistic scenarios are taken and its architecture is well analyzed with the IoT components under this study. In all these works, the working function of each IoT components are focused and their role of importance is well determined. Also among the various IoT components, the most essential component based on their role has been identified by the readers of this article for their future research enhancement. As a result of this step, the design complexity and computational complexity is also reduced to a significant amount.

CONCLUSION

An efficient effort has been focused during the last three years in the proposal of several IoT based applications. The proposal of unified architecture for the promising realistic scenarios is well realized. A wealth of IoT based applications has been designed by researchers in realistic scenarios is well discussed. Based on the suggestions of this research direction, as a future development of such techniques, an IoT combined architecture for the smart agriculture for vast ground will be proposed as future research. This design promotes the cultivation with proper monitoring of the agriculture oriented parameters to increase the yield of the production. Undoubtedly this article acts as other interesting opportunities for many IoT based applications in near future.

REFERENCES

Atzori, L., Iera, A., & Morabito, G. (2010). The Internet of Things: A survey. *J. Computer Networks*, *54*(15), 2787–2805. doi:10.1016/j.comnet.2010.05.010

Choosri, N., Park, Y., Grudpan, S., Chuarjedton, S. & Ongvisesphaiboon, A. (2015). IoT-RFID Test bed for Supporting Traffic Light Control. *International Journal of Information and Electronics Engineering, 5*(2).

Gaura, A., Scotneya, B., Parra, G., & McCleana, S. (2015). Smart City Architecture and its Applications based on IoT. *Procedia Computer Science*, *52*(1), 1089–1109. doi:10.1016/j.procs.2015.05.122

Giusto, D., Iera, A., Morabito, G., & Atzori, L. (Eds.). (2010). *The Internet of Things*. Springer. doi:10.1007/978-1-4419-1674-7

Gubbia, J., Buyya, R., Marusica, B. S., & Palaniswamia, M. (2013). Internet of things (IoT): A vision, architectural elements, and future directions. *Future Generation Computer Systems*, *29*(7), 1645–1660. doi:10.1016/j.future.2013.01.010

Gutierreza, J. M., Jensenb, M., Heniusa, M., & Riazc, T. (2015). Smart Waste Collection System Based on Location Intelligence. *Procedia Computer Science*, *61*(1), 120–127. doi:10.1016/j.procs.2015.09.170

ICTP Workshop, . (2015) ITU work on Internet of things. *ICTP Workshop*.

Li, S., Xu, L. D., & Zhao, S. (2014). The internet of things: A survey. *Information Systems Frontiers*.

McEwen, A., & Cassimally, H. (2013). *Designing the Internet of Things*. John Wiley & Sons.

Miorandi, D., Sicari, S., & Chlamtac, I. (2012). Internet of things: Vision, applications and research challenges. *Ad Hoc Networks*, *10*(7), 1497–1516. doi:10.1016/j.adhoc.2012.02.016

Nandurkar, S. R., Thool, V. R., & Thool, R. C. (2014). Design and Development of Precision Agriculture System Using Wireless Sensor Network. *IEEE International Conference on Automation, Control, Energy and Systems (ACES)*. 10.1109/ACES.2014.6808017

Paul, J. (2013). *RFID based vehicular networks for smart cities*. Presented at *2013 IEEE 29th International Conference on Data Engineering Workshops (ICDEW)*. 10.1109/ICDEW.2013.6547439

Sarkar, S., Pal, S., Maiti, S., & Sarkar, S. K. (2010). Development of a statistical algorithm for cost efficient RFID tag and reader connectivity. *Proc. the International Conference and Workshop on Emerging Trends in Technology 2010*, 1009-1009. 10.1145/1741906.1742181

Sebastian, S., & Ray, P. P. (2015). Development of IoT invasive architecture for complying with health of home. Proceedings of I3CS, 79–83.

Srivastava, L. (2006). Pervasive, ambient, ubiquitous: the magic of radio. *Proceedings of European Commission Conference From RFID to the Internet of Things*.

Verdouw, C. N., Wolfert, J., Beulens, A. J. M., & Rialland, A. (2016). Virtualization of food supply chains with the internet of things. *Journal of Food Engineering*, 1–9.

Wen, W. (2010). An intelligent traffic management expert system with RFID technology. *Expert Systems with Applications*, *37*(4), 3024–3035. doi:10.1016/j.eswa.2009.09.030

Wu, T. (2010). The Security Problem of the Internet of Things is Analyzed. *J. Network Security Technology & Application*, *1*, 7–8.

Zeng, W., Huang, C., Duan, B., & Gong, F. (2012). *Research on internet of things of environment monitoring based on cloud computing*. IET.

Chapter 18
Big Data Analytics in Cloud Computing:
Effective Deployment of Data Analytics Tools

Rajganesh Nagarajan
A. V. C. College of Engineering, India

Ramkumar Thirunavukarasu
VIT University, India

ABSTRACT

In this chapter, the authors consider different categories of data, which are processed by the big data analytics tools. The challenges with respect to the big data processing are identified and a solution with the help of cloud computing is highlighted. Since the emergence of cloud computing is highly advocated because of its pay-per-use concept, the data processing tools can be effectively deployed within cloud computing and certainly reduce the investment cost. In addition, this chapter talks about the big data platforms, tools, and applications with data visualization concept. Finally, the applications of data analytics are discussed for future research.

INTRODUCTION

Big data is an evolving term that describes huge amount of structured, semi-structured and unstructured data. In addition, big data (Kolomvatsos et al., 2015) refers to the use of predictive analytics, behavior analytics, or advanced data analytics for extracting the real inside values from different kind of data (Boyd et al., 2012). The basic characteristics of big data includes volume, variety and velocity (Hilbert & Martin, 2016). Volume represents the quantity of generated and stored data. The size of the data is the key factor to determine the value and its potential insight for considering the whether it is big data or not. Variety includes the data type and its nature such as structured, semi-structured and unstructured data. Velocity represents the speed of the data in which generated and processed to meet the demands and challenges.

DOI: 10.4018/978-1-5225-9023-1.ch018

Big data environments require clusters of computing servers to support the tools that process the structured, semi-structured and unstructured data. Though big data offers various kinds of analysis such as descriptive modeling, predictive modeling, and prescriptive modeling, it is crucial to analyze and synthesize interesting pattern from diversified data sources. This makes cloud based data analytics, a viable research field and open new research avenues in modeling and analyzing complex data. Furthermore, cloud services enable infrastructures to be scaled up and down rapidly, adapting the system to the actual demand. Hence, this chapter addresses the importance of cloud computing in order to support the big data analytics. In such circumstances, the primary features of cloud computing such as on-demand provisioning, pay-per-usage provides significant improvement in the process of data analytics. The important challenges of big data are discussed and further research directions with the aid of cloud computing is presented.

CATEGORIES OF BIGDATA AND CHALLENGES ASSOCIATED

With the advent of internet and smart devices, the manipulation of data increases rapidly. In addition, there is no such common mechanism followed for the representation of data. In such scenario, it is important to process different kinds of data (Agresti & Kateri, 2011) before formulating the information. With respect to the existing data processing mechanisms, it is essential to invent a new data processing methodology with less capital investment. Accordingly, cloud computing has been highly recommended to incorporate the data processing activities by running the new data analytics tools. Hence, this section highlights the various categories of big data and its processing tool. Finally, the incorporation of cloud computing enhances the data analytics process in an effective manner.

Categories of Data

1. **Structured Data**: Refers to any kind of data that has a proper format and resides in a record or file. Structured data (Chang et al., 2008) are easy to input, query, store, and analyse. Examples of structured data include numbers, words, and dates.
2. **Semi-Structured Data:** The data that are not following the conventional or relational data base system are called as semi-structured data (Sagiroglu & Sinanc, 2013). The data are not organized in table format. In order to analyse the semi-structured data, the complex rules must be used.
3. **Unstructured Data:** The text messages, location information, videos, and social media information (Feldman & Sanger, 2007) are data that do not follow any prescribed format. Always the size of this data is increasing because of the use of new technological devices such as smartphones. Therefore, the understanding of such data become a more challenging one.

Challenges in Big Data

The challenges in big data require more attention to avoid the failure of technology with some unpleasant results. Some of the identified challenges (Labrinidis et al., 2012; Chen et al., 2014) are given here to understand the common issues.

Data Storage

The volume, velocity and variety of big data leads to storage challenges. Storage of data on traditional device such as Hard Disk Drives (HDD) is very tedious and the data protection mechanisms are inefficient (Robinson, 2012). In addition, the traditional storage systems failed to scale up for the effective handling of big data. However, cloud computing provides the facility such as Amazon S3, Elastic Block Store to address big data storage challenges.

Processing of Reliable Data

Because of diversified nature, the processing of data becomes inefficient and affects the quality of data. Hence, the feature selection methods has to be considered for processing the data.

Accessing of Data

The inadequate platform and the programming language complicates the data access among the various resources. As a result, the effectiveness of data access have not achieved.

Processing of Complex Data

The analysis of data such as image, video, and the representation of the physical as well as the living world is very complex. It is necessary to reinvent the big data tools with programming architectures to capture, store and analyze the data in an effective manner.

Data Visualization

Data visualization discovers unknown correlations to improve decision-making (Nasser & Tariq, 2015) process. Though the big data is heterogeneous in structure and semantics, the visualization is critical to make sense of big data (Chen et al., 2014). Similarly, the real time visualization and interaction is always difficult (Sun et al., 2012; Nasser & Tariq, 2015).

Privacy and Security

A more sensitive issue of the big data is the privacy and security. The inner details of the data are shared and used by many user. Therefore, it is important to ensure the security of the personal's information while processing the data for any commercial purpose.

Data Quality

The complex and heterogeneity (Lohr, 2012) nature of big data makes data accuracy and completeness is a difficult one. The quality of the data includes the features such as, accuracy, completeness, redundancy and consistency (Chen et al., 2014). With respect to the case of social media, the data are highly skewed in space with different time and demographic details. Therefore, controlling of data redundancy in the collection point is needed. Similarly, data consistency and integrity becomes a challenging one (Khan et al., 2014).

EMERGENCE OF CLOUD COMPUTING

According to National Institute of Standards and Technology (NIST), the cloud computing is defined as, 'a model for enabling convenient, on-demand network access to a shared pool of configurable computing resources that can be rapidly provisioned and released with minimal management effort or service provider interaction'. In short, cloud computing involves deploying groups of remote servers and software networks that allow centralized data storage and online access to computer services or resources. The implementation of cloud computing has been realized with 3 service models, 4 deployment models, and 5 characteristics (Zhang et al., 2010; Rajganesh & Ramkumar, 2016) is shown in Figure 1.

Deployment Model

As per the nature of consumption, the type of cloud are labelled as public, private and hybrid (Hu et al., 2011). In public cloud, the services are offered as open access for all the public. In private cloud, the services are offered for the exclusive use of single person or an organization which comprising many business units. Hybrid cloud contains a combination of both public and private type clouds (Sabahi, 2011).

Figure 1. Cloud computing architecture

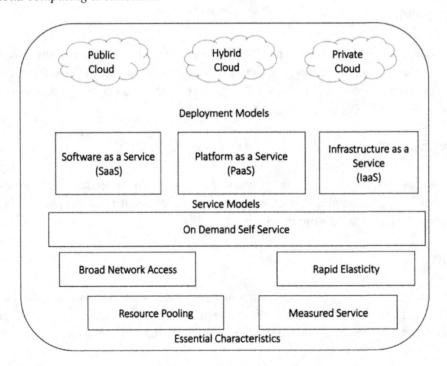

Public Cloud

Theoretically, there may be no difference between public and private clouds. However, the security consideration may be significantly different for services like storage, applications, and networks. Some of the public cloud service providers are Amazon Web Services (AWS), Oracle, Microsoft and Google. Generally, these providers own and operate the infrastructure at their data centre and provide access to cloud user via the Internet.

Private Cloud

A cloud infrastructure resources provided to a single organization and solely utilized by the authorized team in order to ensure the resource security is called private cloud. With this cloud type, the organization is expected to re-evaluate the decisions about existing resources. It can improve business, but every step in the project raises security issues that must be addressed to prevent serious vulnerabilities.

Hybrid Cloud

A composition of two or more clouds for offering the benefits of multiple deployment models is achieved with the hybrid type of cloud. Hybrid cloud is composed of public, private, and community cloud services from various service providers. Hence, it allows the cloud user to extend either the capacity or the capability of a cloud service, by aggregation, integration or customization with another cloud service. Hybrid cloud depend upon the factors such as data security and control, amenability requirements, and the applications an organization uses.

Service Models

The service models provides Software, Platform, and Infrastructure services to the cloud user and the layered architecture is shown in Figure 2.

Figure 2. Layered architecture of service models

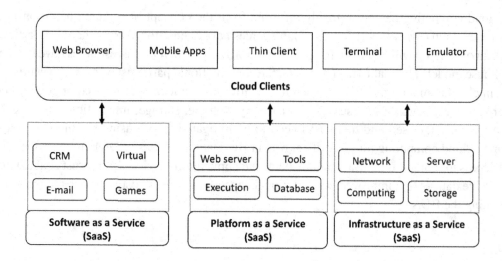

The *Software as a Service (SaaS)* model allows the consumers to avail the predefined compound functionalities from the cloud service provider. The objective is to deliver the application services as per user requirements. Hence, the end users need not worry about the issues such as installation and future maintenance overheads.

The second service called *Platform as a Service (PaaS)* is an implausible model for offering the computing platform that includes operating systems, program-developing environment, web servers and database systems to the cloud user. From this model, the user can share the platform resources.

The third service namely, *Infrastructure as a Service (IaaS)* meant for delivering the cloud computing infrastructure such as physical computers, storage, network and related resources for the deployment of user operating system, application software. Through this, the users can own the peripherals and configure as per their wish. In short, the major offering (Rimal et al., 2009) of the cloud is classified as computational services, storage and other services such as scheduling and management of tasks, provision of user access interface, web APIs, framework for programming.

Characteristics of Cloud Computing

Cloud computing exhibits five important characteristics namely, on demand self-service, broad network access, resource pooling, rapid elasticity, and measured service.

On-demand self-service. A cloud user are provisioned the computing capabilities (server, network storage) as per their need without requiring human interaction.

Broad network access. The utilization of resources over the network through the standard mechanisms that helps the user to avail the services from their terminal.

Resource pooling. The effective allocation of resources among the requested service user can be obtained with this characteristic. Hence, the provider's computing resources are pooled to serve multiple consumers with different physical and virtual resources. These resources can be dynamically assigned and reassigned according to user's need.

Rapid elasticity. The resource capabilities can be elastically provisioned to meet out the dynamic need of cloud user.

Measured service. Every cloud systems control and optimize the resource through the metering capability. Resource usage can be monitored, controlled, and reported immediately for assisting the cloud provider and user.

The cloud computing has been greatly differing from the concept of big data based on following reasons: (i) In cloud computing (Mell, 2011), resources have been utilized from the third-party vendors and the data ownership will be on the hand of service provider, whereas the resources have been utilized in an in-house model at big data. (ii) In big data, the computational part must be moved towards the data, whereas in cloud computing, data have been moved towards the location of the computing processors. However, several research issues such as data variety, volume, storage, integration, and visualization of data are to be addressed and their risks need to be mitigated before using the big data with cloud computing. Cloud computing plays a critical role in Big Data Analytics (BDA) process as it offers on-demand access for computing infrastructure, data, and application services (Armbrust et al., 2010). Due to the massive dataset, the improved computational capacity with less cost becomes more attention for implementing the BDA.

BIG DATA ANALYTICS IN CLOUD ENVIRONMENT

The 3 V's of big data represents the semantic meaning of data. Whereas, big data analytics represents pragmatic meaning of big data (Wu et al., 2016), is shown in Figure 3.

Big Data Analytics

The process of examining different data to uncover hidden patterns, unknown correlations, market trends, customer preferences, and other useful information is termed as big data analytics. Most of the companies implement Big Data Analytics to make more informed business decisions. Big data analytics gives analytics professionals, such as data scientists and predictive modelers, the ability to analyze big data from multiple and varied sources, including transactional data and other structured data.

The processing requirements of Big data may also make traditional data warehousing a poor fit. As a result, newer, bigger data analytics environments and technologies have emerged, including Hadoop, MapReduce and NoSQL databases. These technologies can use the cloud computing platforms to serve better for the user needs and reduces the installation cost of these tools from the customer point.

Data Analytics in Cloud Computing

The effectiveness of data analytics through the cloud computing is mostly preferred by the data owners. The nature of cloud computing will always simplify the work with respect to the cost and time. Also, the demand for the analytics tools have been fulfilled in cloud computing with its service categories such as Infrastructure as a Service (IaaS), Platform as a Service (PaaS) and Software as a Service (SaaS).

Figure 3. Pragmatic meaning of big data

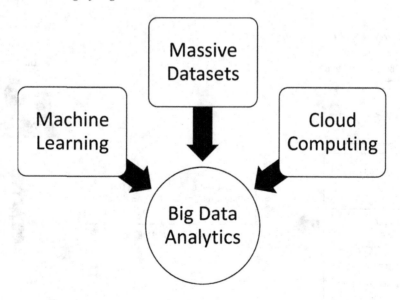

Processing the big data with cloud computing improves the performance with less investment. Figure 4 shows the integration of the big data with the cloud computing architecture. The various big data sources have been processed with in the cloud computing and reduces the computation and storage cost. Normally, the existing data processing methodologies are having the limitation in order to process the big data sources. By using the various services of cloud computing, it is better to improve the effectiveness of the data with respect to the customer's need.

BIG DATA PLATFORMS: TOOLS AND APPLICATIONS

Nowadays, there are thousands of big data tools available to process the data. All of them promising to save the time, money and help the user to understand the data in a simple way (Dhar, 2013).

Cloud Based Big Data Analytics Tools

Data analytics tools (Witten et al., 2016; Vukotic & Gardner, 2016) automatically collect, clean, and analyze data for making decision. Table 1 elaborates the usage of tools with its pros and cons. In addition, the most important open source tools, which are commonly used to process the data is given.

Hadoop

The Apache distributed data processing software is so pervasive that often the terms 'Hadoop' and 'big data' are used synonymously (Strang & Sun, 2017). The Apache foundation extend the capabilities of Hadoop by adding additional projects. In addition, many vendors offer supported versions of Hadoop and related technologies in Windows and Linux platforms. The Hadoop project provides the basic services

Figure 4. Data analytics in cloud computing

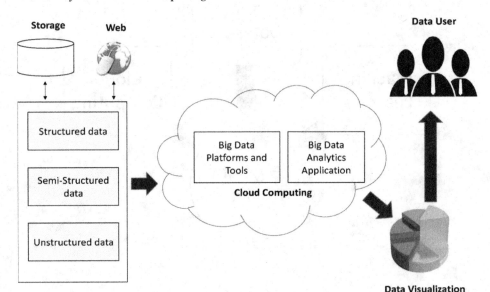

for building a cloud computing environment with hardware and software to support the user tasks. The two fundamental pieces of Hadoop are the MapReduce framework and the Hadoop Distributed File System (HDFS).

MapReduce

MapReduce is a programming model (Wang et al., 2017) developed by Google for writing applications that rapidly process huge amounts of data. The independent nature MapReduce allows other computing platforms to work together. The following Figure 5 shows the MapReduce architecture with mapper and reducer classes.

MapReduce includes two major functions, called 'Map' and 'Reduce'. The Map function is applied in parallel to every input (*key, value*) pair, and produces new set of intermediate (key, value) pairs. With the help of MapReduce library, all the produced intermediate (*key, value*) pairs are sorted and grouped based on the '*key*' part. Finally, the Reduce function is applied in parallel to each group producing the collection of values as output.

Hadoop Distributed File System (HDFS)

HDFS is a file system that is designed for use with MapReduce jobs that read large chunks of input, process it, and write potentially large chunks of output. In HDFS the file data is simply mirrored to multiple storage nodes. With this replication of data nodes, the availability of data is achieved.

Figure 5. MapReduce framework

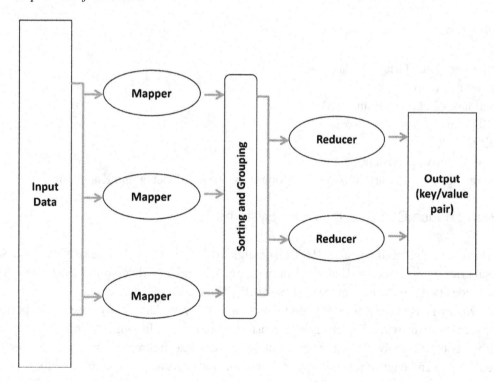

HDFS contains two nodes called Name node and Data node. Name node handles management of the file system metadata, and provides management and control services. Data node provides block storage and retrieval services. HDFS is designed for specific type of applications. Hence, it is not a general-purpose file system; it does not need all the requirements of a general distributed file system.

GridGain

GridGrain is supported in Windows, Linux and OS X platforms. It is an alternative to Hadoop's MapReduce (Belcastro, 2017) and is compatible with the Hadoop Distributed File System (HDFS). GridGain includes an in-memory data grid, database, streaming analytics in a single platform. Through this, user can create modern, scalable, real-time applications for digital transformation. In addition, GridGain can scale horizontally by adding the cluster node for automatic rebalancing of workload.

GridGain can integrates with the with the existing database technologies such as RDBMS, NoSQL and Hadoop. The presence of API's in GridGain allows it to work with other programming paradigms also. GridGain integrates with many common management and data processing operations and can run on premises of public cloud such as, AWS, Mirosoft Azure, Google Cloud Platform.

Key Benefits

- In-memory computing platform
- Scalable to petabytes of in-memory data
- Easy integration with other databases
- Less complexity
- Low cost - built on open source software

Key Features

- In-memory Data Grid and Database
- Streaming Analytics
- Continuous Learning Framework
- ACID transactions
- Unified API
- Optional native persistence
- Native support for Spark, Cassandra, MongoDB, YARN, Docker and Kubernetes

High Performance Computing Cluster Systems

High Performance Computing Cluster (HPCC) (Zong, 2017) is developed by LexisNexis Risk Solutions to offer superior performance to Hadoop. Linux supports it and a paid version is available. The HPCC system includes two processing environments namely, Data refinery and Roxie.

Data refinery is used for processing the huge volumes of raw data of any type. Also, performs the operations such as data extraction, cleansing, transformation, record linking and entity resolution, large-scale ad-hoc complex analytics, and creation of keyed data and indexes to support high-performance structured queries and data warehouse applications. The data refinery is also referred to as *Thor*.

The second part, *Roxie* is designed as an online high-performance structured query and analysis platform and functions as a rapid data delivery engine. Roxie utilizes a distributed indexed file system to provide parallel processing of queries using an optimized execution environment. The functionalities of a Roxie cluster is similar to Hadoop and provides real time predictable query latencies. Both Thor and Roxie clusters utilize the ECL programming language for implementing applications, increasing continuity and programmer productivity.

Application Areas

- *Computer aided engineering (CAE)*. Automotive design and testing, transportation, structural, mechanical design.
- *Chemical engineering*. Process and molecular design.
- *Digital content creation (DCC) and distribution*. Computer aided graphics in film and Media.
- *Economics/financial*. Portfolio management and automated trading.
- *Electronic design and automation (EDA)*. Electronic component design and verification.
- *Geosciences and geo-engineering*. Oil and gas exploration and reservoir modelling.
- *Mechanical design and drafting*. 2D and 3D design and verification, mechanical Modelling.
- *Defense and energy*. Nuclear stewardship, basic and applied research.
- *Government labs/University/academic*. Basic and applied research.
- *Weather forecasting*. Near term and climate/earth modelling.

Storm

Storm offers distributed real-time computation capabilities and often described as the 'Hadoop of Real-time'. Storm is simple, highly scalable, robust, fault tolerant and works with nearly all programming languages. Storm has the use cases such as real time analytics, online machine learning, continuous computation, and distributed RPC. It is owned by Twitter and its platform is Linux.

The Apache Storm cluster comprises following critical components:

- **Nodes:** There are two types of nodes, i.e., Master Node and Worker Node. The Master Node executes a daemon Nimbus that assigns tasks to machines and monitors their performances. On the other hand, the Worker Node runs the daemon called Supervisor, which assigns the tasks to other worker node and operates them as per the need.
- **Components:** Storm has three critical components namely Topology, Stream, and Spout. Topology is a network made of Stream and Spout. Stream is an unbounded pipeline of tuples and Spout is the source of the data streams, which converts the data into the tuple of streams and sends to the bolts to be processed.

Data Visualization

An important step in data analytics is the data visualization process. The goal is to communicate the information very clearly and effectively to the users. According to Friedman (1998), the goal of data visualization is "to communicate information clearly and effectively through graphical means". It doesn't

Table 1. Data analytics tools: An overview

S. No	Name of the Tool	Definition	Uses	Limitations
1	Tableau Public	Communicates insights through data visualization	Publish interactive data visualizations in to the web. No programming skills required. Shared through email or social media.	Data is public. Limited data size. Cannot connect with R.
2	OpenRefine (Google Refine)	A data cleaning software that helps to get everything ready for analysis. It is based on relational database tables.	Messy data cleaning. Transformation of data. Parsing of data from websites.	Not suitable for large datasets. It does not work very well with big data.
3	Knime	A tool to manipulate, analyze, and modeling data in an intuitive way via visual programming.	Drop and Drag based method. Supports programming languages.	Poor data visualization.
4	RapidMiner	Provides machine learning procedures and data mining including data visualization, processing, statistical modeling, deployment, evaluation, and predictive analytics.	Performs business analytics, predictive analysis, text mining, data mining, and machine learning. Used for application development, rapid prototyping, training, education, and research.	Size constraints problem with respect to the increase of rows. More hardware resources are needed.
5	Google Fusion Tables	A free and incredible tool for data analysis, mapping, and large dataset visualization.	Easy filtering and summarizing of row data. Allows table merging for better visualization.	Limitation in rows processing. The size is limited to 1MB only.
6	NodeXL	A free open source visualization and analysis software for providing the exact calculations.	Data Import. Graph visualization and Graph Analysis. Data Representation. Elements of a graph structure like nodes and edges.	Multiple seeding terms. Data extractions in different time interval.
7	Wolfram Alpha	It is a computational knowledge engine allows getting answers for factual queries directly.	Provides detailed responses to technical searches. Providing information charts and graphs.	It can only deal with number and facts, not with viewpoints. Limited Computation Time for Each query.
8	Google Search Operators	Instantly filters Google results to get most relevant and useful information.	Fast in filtering of data. Help to discover new information or market research.	-
9	DataIKU DSS	A collaborative data science software platform that helps team build, prototype, explore, and deliver their own data products more efficiently.	Provides an interactive visual interface. Faster in data preparation.	Limited visualization capabilities. Difficult to compile entire code into a single document. Need to integrate with SPARK.

mean that data visualization (Langseth et al., 2017) needs to look boring to be functional or extremely sophisticated to look beautiful.

Terminology in Data Visualization

Data visualization (Nolan & Perrett, 2016) involves specific terminology such as;

- **Categorical:** Text labels describing the nature of the data, such as 'Name' or 'Age'. This term also covers qualitative (non-numerical) data.
- **Quantitative:** Numerical measures, such as '25' to represent the age in years.

Two primary types of information displays are tables and graphs.

- A *table* contains quantitative data organized into rows and columns with categorical labels.
- A *graph* is used to show relationship among data and portrays values as *visual objects* (e.g., lines, bars, or points). Numerical values are displayed within an area delineated by one or more *axes*. These axes provide *scales* (quantitative and categorical) used to label and assign values to the visual objects. The following Figure 6 shows the decision tree generated with the help of R Studio for the input values of cloud infrastructure services (Nagarajan & Thirunavukarasu, 2018). The input values are given in the form of *.csv* file. The selection of services are considering either the storage capacity or the computational speed with a small change in the price value.

Figure 6. Data visualization through R studio

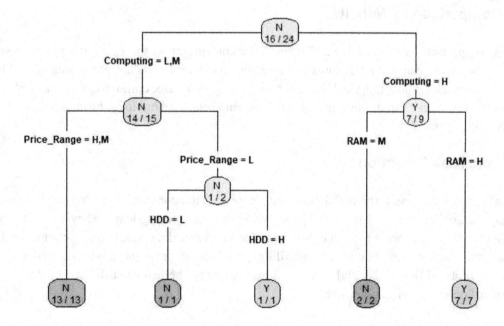

APPLICATIONS OF DATA ANALYTICS

Big data management strategies and best practices (Gunasekaran et al., 2016) are still evolving, but joining the big data, movement has become an imperative for companies across a wide variety of industries. Here, some of the application area is highlighted which are mostly benefited from the big data.

Internet Search

All the search engines are make use of data science algorithms to deliver the best result for the user query. By considering the popular search engine such as Google, it processes more than 20 petabytes of data every day. It is possible because of the data analytics only.

Recommender Systems

Based on the user needs, right prediction of services or products is a challenging one. Internet giants like Amazon, Twitter, Google Play, Netflix, Linkedin uses this system to improve user experience. The recommendation have been made based on the previous search results of a user.

Speech Recognition

Some of the best example of speech recognition products are Google Voice, Siri, Cortana etc. The usage of speech recognition feature really uses the data analytics for the easy understanding and its action sequences.

Price Comparison in Websites

Products comparison based on price and feature is a challenging in the existing data processing applications. Now, the data analytics tools are emerged to enhance the data processing. PriceGrabber, PriceRunner, Junglee, Shopzilla, DealTime are some examples of price comparison websites. Nowadays, price comparison can be found in almost every domain such as technology, hospitality, automobiles, durables, apparels etc.

Fraud and Risk Detection

In a marketing environment, the bad debts causes a loss for the companies every year. However, they had many data, collected during the initial paper work while sanctioning loans. They decided to bring in data science practices in order to rescue them out of losses. Over the years, banking companies learned to divide and conquer data via customer profiling, past expenditures, and other essential variables to analyze the probabilities of risk and default. Moreover, it also helped to push their banking products based on customer's purchasing power.

CONCLUSION

At present, the big data analytics through cloud computing has been established as one of the hot topics. The different categories of data and their processing with the data analytics tools are briefly explained in this overview. Besides, the overall challenges in the processing of big data is addressed. The effectiveness of data analytics through the cloud computing is mostly preferred by the data owners, since the nature of cloud computing simplifies the work with respect to the cost and time. The chapter outlines the cloud-based open source tools, which are commonly used to process the data towards to communicate the information very clearly and effectively to the users. Followed that, the need for the data visualization is justified with few terminologies. Finally, the important applications of the data analytics are pointed out for further work.

REFERENCES

Agresti, A., & Kateri, M. (2011). *Categorical data analysis*. Springer Berlin Heidelberg.

Armbrust, M., Fox, A., Griffith, R., Joseph, A. D., Katz, R., Konwinski, A., & Zaharia, M. (2010). A view of cloud computing. *Communications of the ACM*, *53*(4), 50–58. doi:10.1145/1721654.1721672

Belcastro, L., Marozzo, F., Talia, D., & Trunfio, P. (2017). Big Data Analysis on Clouds. In *Handbook of Big Data Technologies* (pp. 101–142). Springer International Publishing. doi:10.1007/978-3-319-49340-4_4

Boyd, D., & Crawford, K. (2012). Critical questions for big data: Provocations for a cultural, technological, and scholarly phenomenon. *Information Communication and Society*, *15*(5), 662–679.

Chang, F., Dean, J., Ghemawat, S., Hsieh, W. C., Wallach, D. A., Burrows, M., & Gruber, R. E. (2008). Bigtable: A distributed storage system for structured data. *ACM Transactions on Computer Systems*, *26*(2), 4.

Chen & Zhang. (2014). Data-intensive applications, challenges, techniques and technologies: A survey on Big Data. *Information Sciences*, *275*, 314–347.

Chen, Z. K., Yang, S. Q., Tan, S., Zhao, H., He, L., Zhang, G., & Yang, H. Y. (2014). The Data Allocation Strategy Based on Load in NoSQL Database. *Applied Mechanics and Materials*, *513–517*, 1464–1469.

Dhar, V. (2013). Data science and prediction. *Communications of the ACM*, *56*(12), 64–73.

Feldman, R., & Sanger, J. (2007). *The text mining handbook: advanced approaches in analyzing unstructured data*. Cambridge University Press.

Friedman, J. H. (1998). Data mining and statistics: What's the connection? *Computing Science and Statistics*, *29*(1), 3–9.

Gunasekaran, A., Kumar Tiwari, M., Dubey, R., & Fosso Wamba, S. (2016). Big data and predictive analytics applications in supply chain management. *Computers & Industrial Engineering*, *101*(C), 525–527.

Hilbert & Martin. (2016). Big data for development: A review of promises and challenges. *Development Policy Review*, *34*(1), 135–174.

Hu, F., Qiu, M., Li, J., Grant, T., Taylor, D., McCaleb, S., & Hamner, R. (2011). A review on cloud computing: Design challenges in architecture and security. *CIT. Journal of Computing and Information Technology*, *19*(1), 25–55. doi:10.2498/cit.1001864

Khan, N., Yaqoob, I., Hashem, I. A. T., Inayat, Z., Mahmoud Ali, W. K., Alam, M., ... Gani, A. (2014). Big Data: Survey, Technologies, Opportunities, and Challenges. *The Scientific World Journal*, 1–18. PMID:25136682

Kolomvatsos, K., Anagnostopoulos, C., & Hadjiefthymiades, S. (2015). An efficient time optimized scheme for progressive analytics in big data. *Big Data Research*, *2*(4), 155–165. doi:10.1016/j.bdr.2015.02.001

Labrinidis, A., & Jagadish, H. V. (2012). Challenges and opportunities with big data. *Proceedings of the VLDB Endowment International Conference on Very Large Data Bases*, *5*(12), 2032–2033. doi:10.14778/2367502.2367572

Langseth, J., Aref, F., Alarcon, J., & Lindner, W., III. (2017). *U.S. Patent No. 9,612,742*. Washington, DC: U.S. Patent and Trademark Office.

Lohr, S. (2012). The age of big data. *New York Times*, p. 11.

Mell, P., & Grance, T. (2011). *The NIST definition of cloud computing*. Gaithersburg, MD: Computer Security Division, Information Technology Laboratory, National Institute of Standards and Technology, United States Department of Commerce. doi:10.6028/NIST.SP.800-145

Nagarajan, R., & Thirunavukarasu, R. (2018). A fuzzy-based decision-making broker for effective identification and selection of cloud infrastructure services. *Soft Computing*. doi:10.100700500-018-3534-x

Nasser, T., & Tariq, R. S. (2015). Big Data Challenges. *Journal of Computer Engineering & Information Technology*, *4*(3), 1–10.

Nolan, D., & Perrett, J. (2016). Teaching and learning data visualization: Ideas and assignments. *The American Statistician*, *70*(3), 260–269. doi:10.1080/00031305.2015.1123651

Rajganesh, N., & Ramkumar, T. (2016). A review on broker based cloud service model. *CIT. Journal of Computing and Information Technology*, *24*(3), 283–292. doi:10.20532/cit.2016.1002778

Rimal, B. P., Choi, E., & Lumb, I. (2009). *A taxonomy and survey of cloud computing systems*. INC, IMS and IDC. doi:10.1109/NCM.2009.218

Robinson, S. (2012). *The Storage and Transfer Challenges of Big Data*. Retrieved from http://sloanreview. mit.edu/article/the-storage-and-transfer-challenges-of-big-data/

Sabahi, F. (2011). Cloud computing security threats and responses. *IEEE 3rd International Conference on Communication Software and Networks (ICCSN)*, 245-249. 10.1109/ICCSN.2011.6014715

Sagiroglu, S., & Sinanc, D. (2013). Big data: A review. *IEEE International Conference on Collaboration Technologies and Systems (CTS)*, 42-47. 10.1109/CTS.2013.6567202

Strang, K. D., & Sun, Z. (2017). Analyzing relationships in terrorism big data using Hadoop and statistics. *Journal of Computer Information Systems*, *57*(1), 67–75. doi:10.1080/08874417.2016.1181497

Sun, M., Li, J., Yang, C., Schmidt, G. A., Bambacus, M., Cahalan, R., ... Li, Z. (2012). A Web-Based Geovisual Analytical System for Climate Studies. *Future Internet*, *4*(4), 1069–1085. doi:10.3390/fi4041069

Vukotic, I., & Gardner, R. (2016). *Big Data Analytics Tools as Applied to ATLAS Event Data* (No. ATL-SOFT-SLIDE-2016-649). ATL-COM-SOFT-2016-079.

Wang, C. S., Lin, S. L., & Chang, J. Y. (2017). MapReduce-Based Frequent Pattern Mining Framework with Multiple Item Support. In *Asian Conference on Intelligent Information and Database Systems*. Springer. 10.1007/978-3-319-54430-4_7

Witten, I. H., Frank, E., Hall, M. A., & Pal, C. J. (2016). *Data Mining: Practical machine learning tools and techniques*. Morgan Kaufmann.

Wu, C., Buyya, R., & Ramamohanarao, K. (2016). *Big Data Analytics= Machine Learning+ Cloud Computing*. arXiv preprint arXiv:1601.03115

Zhang, Q., Cheng, L., & Boutaba, R. (2010). Cloud computing: State-of-the-art and research challenges. *Journal of Internet Services and Applications*, *1*(1), 7–18. doi:10.100713174-010-0007-6

Zong, Z., Ge, R., & Gu, Q. (2017). *Marcher: A Heterogeneous System Supporting Energy-Aware High-Performance Computing and Big Data Analytics*. Big Data Research.

Compilation of References

Abdolhamid, M., Shafi'i, M., & Bashir, M. B. (2014). Scheduling techniques in an on-demand grid as a service cloud: A review. *J. Theor. Appl.Inf. Technol.*, *63*(1), 10–19.

Abdullahi, M., Ngadi, M. A., & Abdulhamid, S. M. (2015). Symbiotic organism search optimization based task scheduling in cloud computing environment. *Future Generation Computer Systems*, *56*, 640–650. doi:10.1016/j.future.2015.08.006

Abu Ali, Taha, Hassanein, & Mouftah. (2008, January). IEEE 802.16 Mesh Schedulers: Issues and Design Challenges. *IEEE Transaction on Network*.

Aditya, A., Chatterjee, U., & Gobata, S. (2015). A comparative study of different static and dynamic load-balancing algorithm in cloud computing with special emphasis on time factor. *Int. J. Curr. Eng. Technol.*, *3*(5).

Agarwal, S., Yadav, S., & Yadav, A. K. (2016). An Efficient Architecture and Algorithm for Resource Provisioning in Fog Computing. *Int. J. Inf. Eng. Electron. Bus.*, *8*, 48–61.

Agrafioti, F., & Hatzinakos, D. (2009). ECG biometric analysis in cardiac irregularity conditions. *Signal, Image and Video Processing*, *3*(4), 329–343. doi:10.100711760-008-0073-4

Agresti, A., & Kateri, M. (2011). *Categorical data analysis*. Springer Berlin Heidelberg.

Aguayo, Bicket, Biswas, De Couto, & Morris. (n.d.). *MIT Roofnet Implementation*. Available from: http: //pdos.lcs.mit.edu /roofnet /design /

Ahmad, F., Chakradhar, S. T., Raghunathan, A., & Vijaykumar, T. N. 2012. Tarazu: optimizing mapreduce on heterogeneous clusters. *International Conference on Architectural Support for Programming Languages and Operating Systems (ASPLOS)*, *40*(1), 61-74.

Ahmad, R. W., Gani, A., Hamid, S. H. A., Shiraz, M., Yousafzai, A., & Xia, F. (2015). A survey on virtual machine migration and server consolidation frameworks for cloud data centers. *Journal of Network and Computer Applications*, *52*, 11–25. doi:10.1016/j.jnca.2015.02.002

Ai, Y., Peng, M., & Zhang, K. (2017). Edge cloud computing technologies for internet of things: A primer. *Digit. Commun. Netw.*

Ai, Y., Peng, M., & Zhang, K. (2018). Edge computing technologies for Internet of Things: A primer. *Digital Communications and Networks*, *4*(2), 77–86. doi:10.1016/j.dcan.2017.07.001

Ajuntament de Barcelona. (2016). *Statistical yearbook of Barcelona 2016*. Retrieved from www.bcn.cat/estadistica/angles/dades/anuari/index.htm

Alakeel, A. M. (2010). A guide to dynamic load balancing in distributed computer systems. *Int. J. Comput. Sci. Netw. Secur.*, *10*(6), 153–160.

Alakeel, A. M. (2010). A guide to dynamic load balancing in distributed computer systems. *International Journal of Computer Science and Information Security, 10*(6), 153–160.

Alam, Liang, & Xuemin. (2011). An efficient secure data transmission scheme in WBAN. *IEEE Wireless Communications and Networking Conference.*

Alexandre, D., Tomasik, J., Cohen, J., & Dufoulon, F. (2017). Load prediction for energy-aware scheduling for Cloud computing platforms. *IEEE 37th International Conference on Distributed Computing System.*

Al-Haj, Al-Shaer, & Ramasamy. (2016). Security aware resource allocation in clouds. *IEEE 10th International Conference on Services Computing.* doi:10.1109/ SCC.2016.36

Ali, S., & Smith, K. A. (2016). On Learning Algorithm Selection for Classification. *Journal on Applied Soft Computing, 6*(2), 119–138. doi:10.1016/j.asoc.2004.12.002

Al-Qudah, Z., Alzoubi, H. A., Allman, M., Rabinovich, M., & Liberatore, V. (2009). Efficient application placement in a dynamic hosting platform. *'09 Proceedings of the 18th ACM International Conference on World Wide Web*, 281-290. 10.1145/1526709.1526748

Al-Rayis, E., & Kurdi, H. (2013, November). Performance Analysis of load balancing Architectures in Cloud computing. In *Proceedings of the Modelling Symposium (EMS), 2013 European* (pp. 520-524). IEEE.

An Information Technology (IT) Portal. (2019). Retrieved from http://www.peterindia.net

Andreolini, M., Casolari, S., Colajanni, M., & Messori, M. (2009, October). Dynamic load management of virtual machines in cloud architectures. In *Proceedings of the International Conference on Cloud Computing* (pp. 201-214). Springer.

Anguelovski, I. (2016). From toxic sites to parks as (green) LULUs? New challenges of inequity, privilege, gentrification, and exclusion for urban environmental justice. *CPL Bibliography, 31*(1), 23-36.

Apostu, A., Puican, F., Ularu, G., George Suciu, G., & Todoran, G. (2013). Study on advantages and disadvantages of cloud computing – the advantages of telemetry applications in the cloud. Recent Adv. Appl. Comput. Sci. Digit. Serv.

Armbrust, M., Fox, A., Griffith, R., Joseph, A. D., Katz, R., Konwinski, A., & Zaharia, M. (2010). A view of cloud computing. *Communications of the ACM, 53*(4), 50–58. doi:10.1145/1721654.1721672

Ashton, K. (2009). That 'Internet of Things' thing: In the real world, things matter more than ideas. *RFID Journal.* Retrieved from http://www.rfidjournal.com/articles/view?4986

Aslam & Shah. (2015). Load Balancing Algorithms in Cloud Computing A Survey of Modern Techniques. In *National Software Engineering Conference (NSEC 2015).* IEEE Xplore.

Aswathi, Sharma, & Mahesh. (2016). An Enhancement of Throttled Load Balancing Algorithm in Cloud using Throughput. *IJCTA, 9*(15), 7603–7611.

Atzori, L., Iera, A., & Morabito, G. (2010). The Internet of Things: A survey. *J. Computer Networks, 54*(15), 2787–2805. doi:10.1016/j.comnet.2010.05.010

Babu, L. D. D., & Krishna, P. V. (2013). Honey bee behavior inspired load balancing of tasks in cloud computing environments. *Applied Soft Computing, 13*(5), 2292–2303. doi:10.1016/j.asoc.2013.01.025

Balan, R., Flinn, J., Satyanarayanan, M., Sinnamohideen, S., & Hen-I., Y. (2002). The case for cyber foraging. *Proceedings of the 10th workshop on ACM SIGOPS European workshop*, 87-92. 10.1145/1133373.1133390

Basagni, S., Chlamtac, I., Syrotiuk, V. R., & Woodward, B. A. (1998). A distance routing effect algorithm for mobility (DREAM). *Proc. Fourth Annual ACM/IEEE International Conference in Mobile Computing and Networking (MobiCom)*, 76-84. 10.1145/288235.288254

Beck, M. T., Werner, M., Feld, S., & Schimper, S. (2014). Mobile edge computing: A taxonomy. *Proc. of the Sixth International Conference on Advances in Future Internet*, 48-55.

Belcastro, L., Marozzo, F., Talia, D., & Trunfio, P. (2017). Big Data Analysis on Clouds. In *Handbook of Big Data Technologies* (pp. 101–142). Springer International Publishing. doi:10.1007/978-3-319-49340-4_4

Bellavista, P., Cinque, M., Corradi, A., Foschini, L., Frattini, F., & Molina, J. P. (2016). GAMESH: A grid architecture for scalable monitoring and enhanced dependable job scheduling. *Future Generation Computer Systems*.

Beloglazov, A., & Buyya, R. (2015). OpenStack Neat: A framework for dynamic and energy efficient consolidation of virtual machines in OpenStack clouds. *Concurrency and Computation*, 27(5), 1310–1333. doi:10.1002/cpe.3314

Benifa, J.V.B., & Dejey. (2017). Performance improvement of MapReduce for heterogeneous clusters based on efficient locality and Replica aware scheduling (ELRAS) strategy. *Wireless Personal Communications*, 1–25.

Bhatia, J., Patel, T., Trivedi, H., & Majmudar, V. (2012). HTV Dynamic Load-balancing algorithm for Virtual Machine Instances in Cloud. *International Symposium on Cloud and Services Computing*, 15–20. 10.1109/ISCOS.2012.25

Biel, L., Pettersson, O., Philipson, L., & Wide, P. (2001). ECG analysis: A new approach in human identification. *IEEE Transactions on Instrumentation and Measurement*, 50(3), 808–812. doi:10.1109/19.930458

Bilal, K., Khalid, O., Erbad, A., & Khan, S. U. (2018). Potentials, trends, and prospects in edge technologies: Fog, cloudlet, mobile edge, and micro data centers. *Computer Networks*, 130, 94–120. doi:10.1016/j.comnet.2017.10.002

Bitam, S. (2012 Feb). Bees life algorithm for job scheduling in cloud computing. *Proceedings of the Third International Conference on Communications and Information Technology*, 186-191.

Bok, K., Hwang, J., Jongtae Lim, J., Kim, Y., & Yoo, J. (2016). An efficient MapReduce scheduling scheme for processing large multimedia data. *Multimed. Tools Appl.*, 1–24.

Bond, J. (2015). *How the Internet of Things is Transforming Manufacturing Today - Supply Chain 24/7*. Available at: http://www.supplychain247.com/article/how_the_internet_of_things_is_transforming_manufacturing_today

Bonomi, F. (2011). Connected vehicles, the internet of things, and fog computing. *The Eighth ACM International Workshop on Vehicular Inter-Networking (VANET)*.

Bonomi, F., Milito, R., Zhu, J., & Addepalli, S. (2012). *Fog Computing and its Role in the Internet of Things*. MCC Work. Mob. Cloud Comput.

Bonomi, F., Milito, R., Zhu, J., & Addepalli, S. (2012). Fog computing and its role in the internet of things. *Proceedings of the First Edition of the MCC Workshop on Mobile Cloud Computing, ser. MCC'12*, 13–16. 10.1145/2342509.2342513

Boschrexroth.com. (2017). *Industry 4.0: Smart Manufacturing - Bosch Rexroth AG*. Available at: https://www.boschrexroth.com/en/xc/trends-and-topics/industry-4-0/internet-ofthings/internet-of-things-1#

Boyd, D., & Crawford, K. (2012). Critical questions for big data: Provocations for a cultural, technological, and scholarly phenomenon. *Information Communication and Society*, 15(5), 662–679.

Brunelli, D., Farella, E., Rocchi, L., Dozza, M., Chiari, L., & Benini, L. (2006). Bio-feedback system for rehabilitation based on a wireless human area network. In *Proc. 4th Ann. IEEE Int. Conf. Pervasive Comput. Communications Workshops*. Bluetooth SIG Inc. Available: http: //www.bluetooth.org/

Budde. (2015). *Smart Grid Australia Provided the Vision for the Smart Grid/Smart City Project.* Smart Grid Australia.

Buntz, B. (2016). *The 20 Most Important IoT Firms according to You.* Available at: http://www.ioti.com/iot-trends-and-analysis/20-most-important-iot-firmsaccording-you

Buyya, R., Yeo, C. S., & Venugopal, S. (2008). Market-Oriented Cloud Computing: Vision, Hype, and Reality for Delivering IT Services as Computing Utilities. *High Performance Computing and Communications, 2008. HPCC '08. 10th IEEE International Conference.*

Buyya, R., Ranjan, R., & Calheiros, R. N. (2010, May). Intercloud: Utility-oriented federation of cloud computing environments for scaling of application services. In *Proceeding of International Conference on Algorithms and Architectures for Parallel Processing* (pp. 13-31). Springer. 10.1007/978-3-642-13119-6_2

BWN lab wireless mesh networks research project. (n.d.). Available from: http://www.ece.gatech.edu /research /labs / bwn /mesh /

Cai, Z., Li, X., Ruizc, R., & Lia, Q. (2017). A delay-based dynamic scheduling algorithm for bag-of-task workflows with stochastic task execution times in clouds. *J. Future Gener. Comput. Syst., 71*, 57–72. doi:10.1016/j.future.2017.01.020

Calheiros, R. N., Ranjan, R., De Rose, C. A. F., & Buyya, R. (2009). *CloudSim: A novel framework for modeling and simulation of cloud computing infrastructure and services.* Technical Report GRIDS-TR-2009-1, Grid Computing and Distributed Systems Laboratory.

Calheiros, R. N., Ranjan, R., Beloglazov, A., De Rose, C. A., & Buyya, R. (2011). CloudSim: A toolkit for modeling and simulation of cloud computing environments and evaluation of resource provisioning algorithms. *Software, Practice & Experience, 41*(1), 23–50. doi:10.1002pe.995

Cao, Q. (2010). Present research on IOT. *Software Guide, 59*, 6–7.

Casalicchio, E., & Colajanni, M. (2001). A client-aware dispatching algorithm for web clusters providing multiple services. *Proceedings of the 10th International World Wide Web Conference*, 535-544. 10.1145/371920.372155

Chang, H., Hari, A., Mukherjee, S., & Lakshman, T. V. (2014). Bringing the cloud to the edge. *Computer Communications Workshops (INFOCOM WKSHPS), 2014 IEEE Conference*, 346-351.

Chang, F., Dean, J., Ghemawat, S., Hsieh, W. C., Wallach, D. A., Burrows, M., & Gruber, R. E. (2008). Bigtable: A distributed storage system for structured data. *ACM Transactions on Computer Systems, 26*(2), 4.

Chase, J. S., Anderson, D. C., Thakar, P. N., Vahdat, A. M., & Doyle, R. P. (2001, October). Managing energy and server resources in hosting centers. *Operating Systems Review, 35*(5), 103–116. doi:10.1145/502059.502045

Chen & Zhang. (2014). Data-intensive applications, challenges, techniques and technologies: A survey on Big Data. *Information Sciences, 275*, 314–347.

Chen, H., Wang, F., Helian, N., & Akanmu, G. (2013, February). User-priority guided Min-Min scheduling algorithm for load balancing in cloud computing. In *Proceeding of Parallel computing technologies (PARCOMPTECH), 2013 national conference on* (pp. 1-8). IEEE.

Chen, C.-H. (2018). MapReduce Scheduling for Deadline-Constrained Jobs in Heterogeneous Cloud Computing Systems. *IEEE Transaction on Cloud Computing.*

Chen, J., Wu, B., Delap, M., Knutsson, B., Lu, H., & Amza, C. (2005, June). Locality aware dynamic load management for massively multiplayer games. In *Proceedings of the tenth ACM SIGPLAN symposium on Principles and practice of parallel programming* (pp. 289-300). ACM. 10.1145/1065944.1065982

Chen, M. (2013). Towards smart city: M2M communications with software agent intelligence. *Multimedia Tools and Applications*, *67*(1), 167–178. doi:10.100711042-012-1013-4

Chen, S. L., Chen, Y. Y., & Kuo, S. H. (2017). CLB: A novel load balancing architecture and algorithm for cloud services. *Computers & Electrical Engineering*, *58*, 154–160. doi:10.1016/j.compeleceng.2016.01.029

Chen, Z. K., Yang, S. Q., Tan, S., Zhao, H., He, L., Zhang, G., & Yang, H. Y. (2014). The Data Allocation Strategy Based on Load in NoSQL Database. *Applied Mechanics and Materials*, *513–517*, 1464–1469.

Chesa, M. J. (2016). *Stormwaer management in Barcelona. Evolving approaches*. Paper presented at the Baltic Flows Conference, Barcelona, Spain.

Chethana, R., Neelakantappa, B.B., & Ramesh, B. (2016). Survey on adaptive task assignment in heterogeneous Hadoop cluster. *IEAE Int. J. Eng., 1*(1).

Chevrollier, N., & Golmie, N. (2005). On the use of wireless network technologies in healthcare environments. *Proc. 5th IEEE ASWN*, 147–152.

Chien, N. K., & Son, N. H. (2016). Load-balancing algorithm Based on Estimating Finish Time of Services in Cloud Computing. *International Conference on Advanced Commutation Technology (ICACT)*, 228-233.

Choi & Ryu. (2011). A QAPM(Quadrature Amplitude Position Modulation) scheme for improving power efficiency. *Wireless and Pervasive Computing*.

Choosri, N., Park, Y., Grudpan, S., Chuarjedton, S. & Ongvisesphaiboon, A. (2015). IoT-RFID Test bed for Supporting Traffic Light Control. *International Journal of Information and Electronics Engineering, 5*(2).

Christensen, C. M., Raynor, M. E., & McDonald, R. (2015). Disruptive innovation. *Harvard Business Review*, *93*(12), 44–53. PMID:17183796

Chun, B.-G., Ihm, S., Maniatis, P., Naik, M., & Patti, A. (2011). Clonecloud: elastic execution between mobile device and cloud. *Proceedings of the sixth conference on Computer systems*, 301-314. 10.1145/1966445.1966473

Ciena. (2018). Retrieved from https://www.ciena.com/insights/what-is/What-is-Edge-Cloud.html

Cinque, M., Corradi, A., Luca Foschini, L., Frattini, F., & Mol, J. P. (2016). Scalable Monitoring and Dependable Job Scheduling Support for Multi-domain Grid Infrastructures. *Proceedings of the 31st Annual ACM Symposium on Applied Computing*. 10.1145/2851613.2851762

Cisco G. C. I. Forecast and Methodology 2016–2021. (2018). Retrieved from https://www.cisco.com/c/en/us/solutions/collateral/service-provider/global-cloud-index-gci/white-paper-c11-738085.html

Cisco. (2015). *The IoT threat environment*. Available at: http://theinternetofthings.report/Resources/Whitepapers/4c7c4eca-6167-45c3-aac8bff6031cadc9_IoT%20Threat%20Environment.pdf

Columbus, L. (2017). How IoT, big data analytics and cloud continue to be high priorities for developers. *Cloud Tech News*. Available at: https://www.cloudcomputingnews.net/news/2016/jun/27/internet-of-things-machine-learning-robotics-are-high-prioritiesfor-developers-in-2016/

Cousins, J. J. (2016). Volume control: Stormwater and the politics of urban metabolism. *Geoforum*. doi:10.1016/j.geoforum.2016.09.02021016

Dagli, M. K., & Mehta, B. B. (2014). Big data and Hadoop: A review. *Int. J. Appl. Res. Eng. Sci.*, *2*(2), 192.

Dam, T. V., & Langendoen, K. (2003). An adaptive energy efficient MAC protocol for wireless sensor networks. *Proc. 1st Int. Conf. Embedded Netw. Sens. Syst*, 171–180.

Daraghmi, E. Y., & Yuan, S. M. (2015). A small world based overlay network for improving dynamic load-balancing. *Journal of Systems and Software*, *107*, 187–203. doi:10.1016/j.jss.2015.06.001

Dasgupta, K., Mandalb, B., Duttac, P., Mondald, J. K., & Dame, S. (2013). A Genetic Algorithm (GA) based Load-balancing strategy for Cloud Computing. *International Conference on Computational Intelligence: Modeling Techniques and Applications (CIMTA)*, *10*, 340-347. 10.1016/j.protcy.2013.12.369

Dastjerdi, Gupta, Calheiros, Ghosh, & Buyya. (2016). Fog computing: Principles, architectures, and applications. *Internet of Things*, 61-75.

Dastjerdi, A. V., & Buyya, R. (2016). Fog computing: Helping the Internet of Things realize its potential. *IEEE Computer Society*, *49*(8), 112–116. doi:10.1109/MC.2016.245

Data never sleeps 6.0. (2018). Retrieved from https://www.domo.com/assets/downloads/18_domo_data-never-sleeps-6+verticals.pdf

Dave, Y. P., Shelat, A. S., Patel, D. S., & Jhaveri, R. H. (2014, February). Various job scheduling algorithms in cloud computing: A survey. In *Proceedings of Information Communication and Embedded Systems (ICICES), 2014 International Conference on* (pp. 1-5). IEEE.

Davidson, M. (2015). *Smart Grid Australia: An Overview. Technical Report*. Wessex Consult.

Davis, R. (2015). *Industry 4.0: Digitalisation for productivity and growth*. European Parliamentary Research Service.

Deakin, S., Sausman, C., Sones, B., & Twigg, C. (2015). *The Internet of Things: Shaping Our Future*. Cambridge, UK: Cambridge Public Policy.

Destanoğlu, O., & Sevilgen, F. E. (2008). Randomized Hydrodynamic Load Balancing Approach. *IEEE International Conference on Parallel Processing*, *1*, 196-203.

Devi, C., & Uthariaraj, R. (2016). *Load balancing in cloud computing environment using improved weighted Round Robin Algorithm for non-preemptive dependent tasks*. Hindawi Publishing Corporation. doi:10.1155/2016/3896065

Deye, M. M., & Slimani, Y. (2013). Load Balancing approach for QoS management of multi-instance applications in Clouds. *Proceeding on International Conference on Cloud Computing and Big Data*, 119–126. 10.1109/CLOUDCOM-ASIA.2013.69

Dhar, V. (2013). Data science and prediction. *Communications of the ACM*, *56*(12), 64–73.

Di Nitto, E., Dubois, D. J., & Mirandola, R. (2007, December). Self-aggregation algorithms for autonomic systems. In Bio-Inspired Models of Network, Information and Computing Systems, 2007. Bionetics 2007 (pp. 120-128). IEEE.

Domanal, S. G., & Reddy, G. R. M. (2014, January). Optimal load balancing in cloud computing by efficient utilization of virtual machines. In *Proceeding of Communication Systems and Networks (COMSNETS), 2014 Sixth International Conference on* (pp. 1-4). IEEE.

Domanal, S. G., & Reddy, G. R. M. (2015). Load Balancing in Cloud Environment using a Novel Hybrid Scheduling Algorithm. *IEEE International Conference on Cloud Computing in Emerging Markets*, 37-42. 10.1109/CCEM.2015.31

Doulkeridis, C., & Nørvåg, K. (2013). A survey of large-scale analytical query processing in MapReduce. *The VLDB Journal*, 1–26.

Doyle, B., & Lopes, C. V. (2005). Survey of technologies for Web application development. *ACM Journal, 2*(3), 1–43.

Dsouza, M.B. (2015). A survey of HadoopMapReduce scheduling algorithms. *Int. J. Innov. Res. Comput. Commun. Eng., 3*(7).

Dsouza, C., Ahn, G. J., & Taguinod, M. (2014). Policy-driven security management for Fog computing: Preliminary framework and a case study. *Proc. of IEEE International Conference on Information Reuse & Integration*, 16-23. 10.1109/IRI.2014.7051866

Duan & Yu. (2007). Hybrid Ant Colony Optimization Using Memetic Algorithm for Traveling Salesman Problem. *Proceedings of the IEEE Symposium on Approximate Dynamic Programming and Reinforcement Learning*, 92-95.

Duggan, J., Cetintemel, U., Papaemmanouil, O., & Upfal, E. (2011). Performance prediction for concurrent database workloads. *SIGMOD '11, 978*(1), 337-348. 10.1145/1989323.1989359

Dutreilhy, X., Kirgizov, S., Melekhova, O., Malenfant, J., Rivierrey, N., & Truckz, I. (2015). Using reinforcement learning for autonomic resource allocation in clouds: Towards a fully automated workflow. *ICAS 2015: The Seventh International Conference on Autonomic and Autonomous Systems*, 67 - 74.

Edge computing and IoT 2018 – when intelligence moves to the edge. (2018). Retrieved from https://www.i-scoop.eu/internet-of-things-guide/edge-computing-iot

Edge computing consortium. (2017). Retrieved from https://www.iotaustralia.org.au/wp-content/uploads/2017/01/White-Paper-of-Edge-Computing-Consortium.pdf

Edge Computing Driving New Outcomes from Intelligent Industrial Machines. (2018). Retrieved from https://www.ge.com/digital/sites/default/files/download_assets/Edge-Computing-Driving-New-Outcomes.pdf

EdgeA. (2018). Retrieved from https://docs.apigee.com/api-platform/get-started/what-apigee-edge#make-avail-web

EdgeC. R. A. 2.0. (2017). Retrieved from http://en.ecconsortium.net/Uploads/file/20180328/1522232376480704.pdf

El Periódico. (2016, November 17). *Barcelona beberá agua reciclada en la depuradora de El Prat*. Author.

Elmangoush, A., Coskun, H., Wahle, S., & Magedanz, T. (2013). Design Aspects for a Reference M2M Communication Platform for Smart Cities. *9th International Conference on Innovations in Information Technology*. 10.1109/Innovations.2013.6544419

El-Sayed, H., Sankar, S., Prasad, M., Puthal, D., Gupta, A., Mohanty, M., & Lin, C.-T. (2018). Edge of things: The big picture on the integration of edge, IoT and the cloud in a distributed computing environment. *IEEE Access: Practical Innovations, Open Solutions, 6*, 1706–1717. doi:10.1109/ACCESS.2017.2780087

Fadika, Z., Dede, E., & Govidaraju, M. (2011). Benchmarking MapReduce Implementations for Application Usage Scenarios. *2011 IEEE/ACM Proceedings of the 12th International Conference on Grid Computing*, 90–97. 10.1109/Grid.2011.21

Fang, Y., Wang, F., & Ge, J. (2010). A task scheduling algorithm based on load balancing in cloud computing. *Web Information Systems and Mining*, 271-277.

Fan, K., Wang, J., Wang, X., Li, H., & Yang, Y. (2017). A Secure and Verifiable Outsourced Access Control Scheme in Fog-Cloud Computing. *Sensors (Basel), 17*(7), 1695. doi:10.339017071695 PMID:28737733

Farrag, A. A. S., & Mahmoud, S. A. (2015). Intelligent Cloud Algorithms for Load Balancing problems: A Survey. *Proceedings of the Seventh International Conference on Intelligent Computing and Information Systems (ICICIS 'J 5)*, 210-216. 10.1109/IntelCIS.2015.7397223

Fastly. (2018). Retrieved from https://www.fastly.com/press/press-releases/fastly-builds-content-delivery-network-heritage-unveils-edge-cloud-platform

Fastly. (2018a). Retrieved from https://www.fastly.com/edge-cloud-platform

Fastly. (2018b). Retrieved from https://en.wikipedia.org/wiki/Fastly

Fei, L., Scherson, I. D., & Fuentes, J. (2017). *Dynamic Creation of Virtual Machines in Cloud Computing Systems*. Las Vegas, NV: IEEE.

Feldman, R., & Sanger, J. (2007). *The text mining handbook: advanced approaches in analyzing unstructured data*. Cambridge University Press.

Ferreto, T. C., Netto, M. A., Calheiros, R. N., & De Rose, C. A. (2011). Server consolidation with migration control for virtualized data centers. *Future Generation Computer Systems*, *27*(8), 1027–1034. doi:10.1016/j.future.2011.04.016

Fog Computing and the Internet of Things: Extend the Cloud to Where the Things Are. (2016). White Paper. Available online: http://www.cisco.com/c/dam/en_us/solutions/trends/iot/docs/computing-overview. pdf

Forsman, M., Glad, A., Lundberg, L., & Ilie, D. (2015). Algorithms for automated live migration of virtual machines. *Journal of Systems and Software*, *101*, 110–126. doi:10.1016/j.jss.2014.11.044

Fortino, G., Russo, W., Savaglio, C., Viroli, M., & Zhou, M. (2017). Modeling Opportunistic IoT Services in Open IoT Ecosystems. *17th Workshop From Objects to Agents (WOA 2017)*, 90-95.

Friedman, J. H. (1998). Data mining and statistics: What's the connection? *Computing Science and Statistics*, *29*(1), 3–9.

Furlong, C., Gan, K., & De Silva, S. (2016). Governance of integrated urban water management in Melbourne, Australia. *Utilities Policy*, *43*, 48–58. doi:10.1016/j.jup.2016.04.008

Gabrielli, L., Pizzichini, M., & Spinsante, S. (2014). Smart water grids for smart cities: A sustainable prototype demonstrator. *Proceedings of the 2014 European Conference on Networks and Communications (EuCNC)*, 1–5. 10.1109/EuCNC.2014.6882685

Gamal, M., Rizk, R., Mahdi, H., & Elhady, B. (2017). Bio-inspired load balancing algorithm in cloud computing. *Proceedings of the International Conference on Advanced Intelligent Systems and Informatics*, 579-589.

Gaura, A., Scotneya, B., Parra, G., & McCleana, S. (2015). Smart City Architecture and its Applications based on IoT. *Procedia Computer Science*, *52*(1), 1089–1109. doi:10.1016/j.procs.2015.05.122

Gautam, J. V., Prajapati, H. B., Dabhi, V. K., & Chaudhary, S. (2015). A Survey on Job Scheduling Algorithms in Big Data Processing. *IEEE International Conference on Electrical, Computer and Communication Technologies (ICECCT'15)*, 1-11. 10.1109/ICECCT.2015.7226035

Gavalas, D., Venetis, I. E., & Konstantopoulos, C. (2016). Energy-efficient multiple itinerary planning for mobile agents-based data aggregation in WSNs. *Telecommunication Systems*, 1–15.

Gelenbe & Wu. (2013). *Future Research on Cyber-Physical Emergency Management Systems*. Future Internet.

Ghahramani, Zhou, & Hon. (2017). Toward CloudComputing QoS Architecture: Analysis of Cloud Systems and Cloud Services. *IEEE/CAA Journal of Automatica Sinica*, *4*(1), 5-17.

Ghoneem, M., & Kulkarni, L. (2016). An Adaptive MapReduce Scheduler for Scalable Heterogeneous Systems. *Proceeding of the International Conference on Data Engineering and Communication Technology*, 603–6011.

Ghosh, S., & Banerjee, C. (2016). Priority Based Modified Throttled Algorithm in Cloud Computing. *International Conference on Inventive Computation Technology*.

Gilchrist, A. 2016. Industrial Internet of Things. In Industry 4.0 (pp. 153-160). Apress.

Giusto, D., Iera, A., Morabito, G., & Atzori, L. (Eds.). (2010). *The Internet of Things*. Springer. doi:10.1007/978-1-4419-1674-7

Gopalakrishnan & Jayarekha. (2016). Pre allocation Strategies of computational resources in cloud computing using adaptive resonance theory 2. *International Journal on Cloud Computing Services and Architecture, 1*(2). doi:10.5121/ijccsa.2016.1203

Gopinath, P. G., & Vasudevan, S. K. (2015). An in-depth analysis and study of Load balancing techniques in the cloud computing environment. *Procedia Computer Science, 50*, 427–432. doi:10.1016/j.procs.2015.04.009

Govindaraajan & Sivasankaran. (2009). Mr.Tacton (Mbedded Red Tacton). *IEEE Power Electronics and Intelligent Transportation System*, 374-377.

Goyal, S., & Verma, M. K. (2016). Load balancing techniques in cloud computing environment: a review. *Int. J. Adv. Res. Comput. Sci. Softw. Eng., 6*(4). doi:10.1109/INVENTIVE.2016.7830175

Graham. (2016). Bounds on multiprocessing timing anomalies. *SIAM Application of Maths, 17*(2), 29-41.

Grid Intelligent Grid. (n.d.). Technical Report. Retrieved from http://www.igrid.net.au/

Guang, Guining, Jing, Zhaohui, & He. (2011). Security threats and measures for the Internet of Things. *Qinghua Daxue Xuebao/Journal of Tsinghua University, 51*(10), 1335-1340.

Gubbia, J., Buyya, R., Marusica, B. S., & Palaniswamia, M. (2013). Internet of things (IoT): A vision, architectural elements, and future directions. *Future Generation Computer Systems, 29*(7), 1645–1660. doi:10.1016/j.future.2013.01.010

Gunarathne, T., Qiu, J., & Fox, G. (2011). *Iterative mapreduce for azure cloud. CCA11 Cloud Computing and Its Applications*. Chicago: Academic Press.

Gunasekaran, A., Kumar Tiwari, M., Dubey, R., & Fosso Wamba, S. (2016). Big data and predictive analytics applications in supply chain management. *Computers & Industrial Engineering, 101*(C), 525–527.

Guo, Q. (2013). Task Scheduling Based on Ant Colony Optimization in Cloud Environment. *8th International Conference on Computer Engineering and Systems (ICCES)*.

Guo, Q. (2017, April). Task scheduling based on ant colony optimization in cloud environment. In *Proceedings of AIP Conference* (Vol. 1834, No. 1, p. 040039). AIP Publishing. 10.1063/1.4981635

Gupta, H., & Sahu, K. (2014). Honey bee behavior based load balancing of tasks in cloud computing. *Int. J. Sci. Res., 3*(6).

Gupta, D., Cherkasova, L., Gardner, R., & Vahdat, A. (2015). (2006, November). Enforcing performance isolation across virtual machines in Xen. In *Proceedings of the ACM/IFIP/USENIX 2006 International Conference on Middleware* (pp. 342–362). Springer-Verlag New York, Inc. Retrieved from https://pubs.vmware.com/vsphere50/index.jsp#com.vmware.vsphere.vm_admin.doc_50/GUID-E19DA34B-B227-44EE-B1AB-46B826459442.html

Gutierreza, J. M., Jensenb, M., Heniusa, M., & Riazc, T. (2015). Smart Waste Collection System Based on Location Intelligence. *Procedia Computer Science, 61*(1), 120–127. doi:10.1016/j.procs.2015.09.170

Gutierrez-Garcia, J. O., & Ramirez-Nafarrate, A. (2015). Agent-based load balancing in Cloud data centers. *Cluster Computing, 18*(3), 1041–1062. doi:10.100710586-015-0460-x

Haas, Halpern, & Li. (2002). Gossip based Ad Hoc Routing. *IEEE INFOCOM*.

Haas, Z. J., & Halpern, J. Y. (2006). Gossip based ad hoc routing. *IEEE T. Netw.*, *14*(3), 497–491.

Haight, J., & Park, H. (2015). *IoT Analytics in Practice*. Available at: https://www.sas.com/content/dam/SAS/en_us/doc/research2/iot-analytics-in-practice107941.pdf

Ha, K., Chen, Z., Hu, W., Richter, W., Pillai, P., & Satyanarayanan, M. (2014). Towards wearable cognitive assistance. *Proceedings of the 12th annual international conference on Mobile systems, applications, and services*, 68-81.

Hamilton, P. (2002). Open source ECG analysis. *Proceeding of the IEEE Conference on Computer and Cardiology*, 101-104. 10.1109/CIC.2002.1166717

Hancke, & de Carvalho e Silva & Hancke Jr. (2013). The Role of Advanced Sensing in Smart Cities. *Sensors (Basel).* PMID:23271603

Hashem, W., & Nashaat, H., & Rizk. (2017). Honey bee based load balancing in cloud computing. *Transactions on Internet and Information Systems (Seoul)*, *11*(12).

Hassan, M. M., Song, B., & Huh, E.-N. (2009). *A Framework of Sensor-Cloud Integration Opportunities and Challenges*. ICUIMC. doi:10.1145/1516241.1516350

Hefny, H. A., Khafagy, M. H., & Ahmed, M. W. (2014). Comparative study load balance algorithms for MapReduce environment. *Int. Appl. Inf. Syst.*, *106*(18), 41.

Heidemann, W. Y. J. (2003). *Medium access control in wireless sensor networks*. Univ. Southern Calif., Inf. Sci. Inst., USC/ICI Tech.Rep.ISI-TR580.

Hemanth Chakravarthy, M., & Kannan, E. (2014). A review on secured cloud computing environment. *Journal of Computational Science*, *11*(8), 1224–1228.

Hemanth Chakravarthy, M., & Kannan, E. (2015). Ant colony-based authentication system for cloud computing. *Research Journal of Applied Sciences, Engineering and Technology*, *11*(2), 144–149. doi:10.19026/rjaset.11.1700

Hemanth Chakravarthy, M., & Kannan, E. (2015). Hybrid elliptic curve cryptography using ant colony-based authentication system for cloud computing. *Journal of Engineering and Applied Sciences (Asian Research Publishing Network)*, *10*(16), 7273–7279.

He, T., Chan, S.-H. G., & Wong, C.-F. (2008, December). HomeMesh: A Low-Cost Indoor Wireless Mesh for Home Networking. *IEEE Communications Magazine*, *46*(12), 79–85. doi:10.1109/MCOM.2008.4689211

Hilbert & Martin. (2016). Big data for development: A review of promises and challenges. *Development Policy Review*, *34*(1), 135–174.

Himthani, P. (2017). Efficient technique for allocation of processing elements to virtual machines in cloud environment. International Journal of Computer Science and Network Security, 16(8).

Hou, X., Kumar, A., & Varadharajan, V. (2014). Dynamic Workload Balancing for HadoopMapReduce. *Proceeding of International Conference on Big data and Cloud Computing*, 56-62.

Hsueh, S.C., Lin, M.Y., & Chiu, Y.C. (2014). A load-balanced MapReduce algorithm for blocking-based entity-resolution with multiple keys. *Parallel Distrib. Comput. (AusPDC)*, 3.

Hu, Y. C., Patel, M., Sabella, D., Sprecher, N., & Young, V. (2015). Mobile edge computing—A key technology towards 5G. *ETSI White Paper, 11*, 1-16.

Huaa, Leia, & Zhia. (2011). Optimization of Cloud Database Route Scheduling Based on Combination of Genetic Algorithm and Ant Colony Algorithm. *Procedia Engineering, 15*, 3341 – 3345.

Hua, X. Y., Zheng, J., & Hu, W. X. (2010). Ant colony optimization algorithm for computing resource allocation based on cloud computing environment. *Journal of East China Normal University, 1*(1), 127–134.

Huber, N., Brosig, F., & Kounev, S. (2016). *Model based self adaptive resource allocation in virtualized environments.* 6th International symposium on software engineering for Adaptive and Self Managing Systems, Honolulu, HI. doi: 10.1145/ 1988008.1988021

Hu, F., Qiu, M., Li, J., Grant, T., Taylor, D., McCaleb, S., & Hamner, R. (2011). A review on cloud computing: Design challenges in architecture and security. *CIT. Journal of Computing and Information Technology, 19*(1), 25–55. doi:10.2498/cit.1001864

Hwang, K., Dongarra, J., & Fox, G.C. (2013). *Distributed and Cloud Computing: from Parallel Processing to the Internet of Things.* Academic Press.

IBM Internet of Things (Software Group). (2016). *Journey to Industry 4.0 and beyond with Cognitive Manufacturing.* Available at: https://www.slideshare.net/IBMIoT/journey-toindustry-40-and-beyond-with-cognitivemanufacturing?cm_mc_uid=11464795721414860817594&cm_mc_sid_50200000=1498031505&cm_mc_sid_52640000=1498031505

ICTP Workshop, . (2015) ITU work on Internet of things. *ICTP Workshop.*

Infradata. (2018). Retrieved from https://www.infradata.com/resources/what-is-edge-cloud

Issawi, S. F., Halees, A. A., & Radi, M. (2015). An efficient adaptive load-balancing algorithm for cloud computing under bursty workloads. Engineering, Technology, &. *Applied Scientific Research, 5*(3), 795–800.

ITU. (2017). *ICT Facts and Figures, s.l.* International Telecommunication Union.

Ivanisenko, I. N., & Radivilova, T. A. (2015). Survey of Major Load-balancing algorithms in Distributed System. *Information Technologies in Innovation Business Conference (ITIB).* 10.1109/ITIB.2015.7355061

Jadeja, Y., & Modi, K. (2012). Cloud Computing - Concepts, *Architecture and Challenges. International Conference on Computing, Electronics and Electrical Technologies.*

Jaikar, A., Dada, H., Kim, G. R., & Noh, S. Y. (2014). Priority-based Virtual Machine Load Balancing in a Scientific Federated Cloud. *Proceedings of the 3rd International Conference on Cloud Computing.* 10.1109/CloudNet.2014.6969000

James, J., & Verma, B. (2012). Efficient VM load balancing algorithm for a cloud computing environment. *International Journal on Computer Science and Engineering, 4*(9), 1658.

Jena, S. R., & Ahmad, Z. (2013). Response time minimization of different load balancing algorithms in cloud computing environment. *International Journal of Computers and Applications, 69*(17), 22–27.

Jeschke, S., Brecher, C., Song, H., & Rawat, D. (2017). *Industrial Internet of Things* (1st ed.). Cham: Springer International Publishing. doi:10.1007/978-3-319-42559-7

Jiang, Y., Susilo, W., Mu, Y., & Guo, F. (2017). Ciphertext-policy attribute-based encryption against key-delegation abuse in fog computing. *Future Generation Computer Systems.* doi:10.1016/j.future.2017.01.026

Jin, J., Gubbi, J., Luo, T., & Palaniswami, M. (2012). Network Architecture and QoS Issues in the Internet of Things for a Smart City. *International Symposium on Communications and Information Technologies (ISCIT).* 10.1109/ISCIT.2012.6381043

Johnson, D., Maltz, D., & Broch, J. (1998). *The dynamic source routing protocol for mobile ad hoc networks*. Internet Draft.

Jones, J. (2017). How the Internet of Things is Driving Sustainability Strategy. *Conscious Connection Magazine*. Available at: https://www.consciousconnectionmagazine.com/2017/02/internet-of-things-sustainabilitystrategy/

Joseph, C. T., Chandrasekaran, K., & Cyriac, R. (2015). A novel family genetic approach for virtual machine allocation. *Procedia Computer Science*, *46*, 558–565. doi:10.1016/j.procs.2015.02.090

Jung, G., & Sim, K. M. (2017). Agent based adaptive resource allocation on the cloud computing environment. *40th International Conference on Parallel Processing Workshops*, 345-341. DOI 10.1117/ICPPW.2017.18

Kabalan, K. Y., Smari, W. W., & Hakimian, J. Y. (2002). Adaptive load sharing in heterogeneous systems: Policies, modifications, and simulation. *International Journal of Simulation, Systems, Science and Technology*, *3*(1-2), 89–100.

Kabir, M.S., Kabir, K.M., & Islam, R. (2015). Process of load balancing in cloud computing using genetic algorithm. *Electr. Comput. Eng.: Int. J., 4*(2).

Kanakala, V. R. T., & Reddy, V. K. (2015). Performance analysis of load balancing techniques in cloud computing environment. *TELKOMNIKA Indones. J. Electr. Eng.*, *13*(3), 568–573.

Kansal, N. J., & Inderveer Chana, I. (2012). Cloud load balancing techniques: A step towards green computing. *Int. J. Comput. Sci. Issues*, *9*(1), 238–246.

Katrina, L., Mogul, J.C., Balakrishnan, H., & Turner, Y. (2014). *Cicada: Predictive Guarantees for Cloud Network Bandwidth*. Cambridge, MA: MIT.

Kaur & Kaur. (2015). Energy Efficient Resource Allocation for Heterogeneous Cloud Workloads. In *2nd International Conference on Computing for Sustainable Global Development (INDIA COM)*. IEEE Xplore.

Kaur, R., & Luthra, P. (2014). Load Balancing in Cloud Computing, International Conference on Recent Trends in Information. *Telecommunication and Computing*, 1–8.

Kc, K., & Anyanwu, K. (2010). Scheduling Hadoop Jobs to Meet Deadlines. *Proceedings of the 2nd IEEE International Conference on Cloud Computing Technology and Science (CloudCom)*, 388–392.

Kedia. (2015). *Water Quality Monitoring for Rural Areas - A Sensor Cloud Based Economical Project*. 1st International Conference on Next Generation Computing Technologies (NGCT - 2015), Dehradun, India.

Keshvadi, S., & Faghih, B. (2016). A multi-agent based load balancing system in IaaS cloud environment. *Int. Robot. Autom. J., 1*(1).

Khalil, S., Salem, S. A., Nassar, S., & Saad, E. M. (2013). Mapreduce performance in heterogeneous environments: A review. *Int. J. Sci. Eng. Res.*, *4*(4), 410–416.

Khan, N., Yaqoob, I., Hashem, I. A. T., Inayat, Z., Mahmoud Ali, W. K., Alam, M., ... Gani, A. (2014). Big Data: Survey, Technologies, Opportunities, and Challenges. *The Scientific World Journal*, 1–18. PMID:25136682

Khiyaita, A., Zbakh, M., Bakkali, H.E.I., & Kettani, D.E.I. (2012). Load balancing cloud computing: state of art. *Netw. Secur. Syst. (JNS2)*, 106–109.

Kianpisheh, S., Charkari, N. M., & Kargahi, M. (2016). Ant colony based constrained workflow scheduling for heterogeneous computing systems. *Cluster Computing*, *19*(3), 1053–1070. doi:10.100710586-016-0575-8

Kim, C., & Kameda, H. (1992). An algorithm for optimal static load balancing in distributed computer systems. *IEEE Transactions on Computers*, *41*(3), 381–384. doi:10.1109/12.127455

Kliazovich, D., Pecero, J. E., Tchernykh, A., Bouvry, P., Khan, S. U., & Zomaya, A. Y. (2016). CA-DAG: Modeling communication-aware applications for scheduling in cloud computing. *Journal of Grid Computing*, 1–17.

Klimova, A., Rondeau, E., Andersson, K., Porras, J., Rybin, A., & Zaslavsky, A. (2016). An international master's program in green ict as a contribution to sustainable development. *Journal of Cleaner Production*, *135*, 223–239. doi:10.1016/j.jclepro.2016.06.032

Klonoff, D. C. (2017). Fog computing and edge computing architectures for processing data from diabetes devices connected to the medical Internet of things. *Journal of Diabetes Science and Technology*, *11*(4), 647–652. doi:10.1177/1932296817717007 PMID:28745086

Kokilavani, T., & Amalarethinam, D. G. (2011). Load balanced min-min algorithm for static meta-task scheduling in grid computing. *International Journal of Computers and Applications*, *20*(2), 43–49.

Kolb, L., Thor, A., & Rahm, E. (2012, April). Load balancing for mapreduce-based entity resolution. In *Proceeding of Data Engineering (ICDE), 2012 IEEE 28th International Conference on* (pp. 618-629). IEEE.

Kolb, L., Thor, A., & Rahm, E. (2011). Block-based Load Balancing for Entity Resolution with MapReduce. *International Conference on Information and Knowledge Management (CIKM)*, 2397–2400. 10.1145/2063576.2063976

Kolb, L., Thor, A., & Rahm, E. (2012). Load Balancing for MapReduce-based Entity Resolution. *Proceedings of the 28th International Conference on Data Engineering*, 618-629.

Kolomvatsos, K., Anagnostopoulos, C., & Hadjiefthymiades, S. (2015). An efficient time optimized scheme for progressive analytics in big data. *Big Data Research*, *2*(4), 155–165. doi:10.1016/j.bdr.2015.02.001

Komarasamy, D., & Muthuswamy, V. (2016). A novel approach for dynamic load balancing with effective Bin packing and VM reconfiguration in cloud. *Indian Journal of Science and Technology*, *9*(11), 1–6. doi:10.17485/ijst/2016/v9i11/89290

Koomey, J. G. (2008). Worldwide electricity used in datacenters. *Environmental Research Letters*, *3*(3), 034008. doi:10.1088/1748-9326/3/3/034008

Kopaneli, A., Kousiouris, G., Velez, G. E., Evangelinou, A., & Varvarigou, T. (2015). A model driven approach for supporting the Cloud target selection process. *Procedia Computer Science*, *68*, 89–102. doi:10.1016/j.procs.2015.09.226

Krauss, Do, & Huck. (2017). Deep neural networks, gradientboosted trees, random forests: Statistical arbitrage on the S&P 500. *European Journal of Operational Research*.

Kruekaew, B., & Kimpan, W. (2014). Virtual machine scheduling management on cloud computing using artificial bee colony. In *Proceedings of the International Multi-Conference of engineers and computer scientists* (Vol. 1, pp. 12-14). Academic Press.

Kulkarni, A. K. (2015). Load-balancing strategy for Optimal Peak Hour Performance in Cloud Datacenters. *Proceedings of the IEEE International Conference on Signal Processing, Informatics, Communication and Energy Systems (SPICES)*.

Kumar, S., & Rana, D. H. (2015). Various dynamic load-balancing algorithms in cloud environment: A survey. *International Journal of Computers and Applications*, *129*(6).

Labrinidis, A., & Jagadish, H. V. (2012). Challenges and opportunities with big data. *Proceedings of the VLDB Endowment International Conference on Very Large Data Bases*, *5*(12), 2032–2033. doi:10.14778/2367502.2367572

LaCurts, K. L. (2014). *Application workload prediction and placement in cloud computing systems* (Unpublished doctoral dissertation). Massachusetts Institute of Technology, Cambridge, MA.

LaCurts, K. L. (2014, June). *Application workload prediction and placement in cloud computing systems* (Unpublished doctoral dissertation). Massachusetts Institute of Technology, Cambridge, MA.

Lamprinos, I.E., Prentza, A., Sakka, E., & Koutsouris, D. (2005). Energy efficient MAC protocol for patient personal area networks. *IEEE Eng. Med. Biology Soc.*, 3799–3802.

Langseth, J., Aref, F., Alarcon, J., & Lindner, W., III. (2017). *U.S. Patent No. 9,612,742*. Washington, DC: U.S. Patent and Trademark Office.

Lau, S. M., Lu, Q., & Leung, K. S. (2006). Adaptive load distribution algorithms for heterogeneous distributed systems with multiple task classes. *Journal of Parallel and Distributed Computing, 66*(2), 163–180. doi:10.1016/j.jpdc.2004.01.007

Lee, J., Bagheri, B., & Kao, H. (2015). A Cyber-Physical Systems architecture for Industry 4.0-based manufacturing systems. *Manufacturing Letters, 3*, 18–23. doi:10.1016/j.mfglet.2014.12.001

Lee, K. H., Choi, H., & Moon, B. (2011). Parallel data processing with MapReduce: A survey. *SIGMOD Record, 40*(4), 11–20. doi:10.1145/2094114.2094118

Lee, R., & Jeng, B. (2011). Load-balancing tactics in cloud. *Proceedings of the International Conference on Cyber-Enabled Distributed Computing and Knowledge CyberC Discovery*, 447-454.

Lee, Y. C., Wang, C., Zomaya, A. Y., & Zhoua, B. B. (2012). Profit driven scheduling for cloud services with data access awareness. *J. Parallel Distrib. Comput., 72*, 591–602.

Lewis, D. (2016). Will the internet of things sacrifice or save the environment? *The Guardian*. Available at: https://www.theguardian.com/sustainable-business/2016/dec/12/willthe-internet-of-things-sacrifice-or-save-the-environment

Li, K., Xu, G., Zhao, G., Dong, Y., & Wang, D. (2011, August). Cloud task scheduling based on load balancing ant colony optimization. In *Proceeding of Chinagrid Conference (ChinaGrid), 2011 Sixth Annual* (pp. 3-9). IEEE.

Liao, J. S., Chang, C. C., Hsu, Y. L., Zhang, X. W., Lai, K. C., & Hsu, C. H. (2012, September). Energy-efficient resource provisioning with SLA consideration on cloud computing. In *Proceeding of Parallel Processing Workshops (ICPPW), 2012 41st International Conference on* (pp. 206-211). IEEE.

Limelight. (2018). Retrieved from https://www.limelight.com/resources/data-sheet/edge-analytics

Lin, C. Y., & Lin, Y. C. (2015). A Load-Balancing Algorithm for Hadoop Distributed File System. *International Conference on Network-Based Information Systems*. 10.1109/NBiS.2015.30

Lin, W., Wang, J. Z., Liang, C., & Qi, D. (2011). A threshold-based dynamic resource allocation scheme for cloud computing. *Procedia Engineering, 23*, 695–703. doi:10.1016/j.proeng.2011.11.2568

Li, R., Hu, H., Li, H., Wu, Y., & Yang, J. (2015). MapReduce parallel programming model: A state-of-the-art survey. *International Journal of Parallel Programming*, 1–35.

Li, S., Xu, L. D., & Zhao, S. (2014). The internet of things: A survey. *Information Systems Frontiers*.

Liu, H., Abraham, A., Snanel, V., & McLoone, S. (2012). Swarm scheduling approaches for work-flow applications with security constraints in distributed data-intensive computing environments. *Information Sciences, 192*, 228–243. doi:10.1016/j.ins.2011.12.032

Liu, Y., Fieldsend, J. E., & Min, G. (2017). A Framework of Fog Computing: Architecture, Challenges and Optimization. *IEEE Access: Practical Innovations, Open Solutions, 4*, 1–10.

Lohr, S. (2012). The age of big data. *New York Times*, p. 11.

Lopez, G., Pedro, A. M., Epema, D., Datta, A., Higashino, T., Iamnitchi, A., ... Riviere, E. (2015). Edge-centric computing: Vision and challenges. *Computer Communication Review, 45*(5), 37–42. doi:10.1145/2831347.2831354

Lopez-Ibanez, M., & Blum, C. (2010). Beam ACO for the traveling sales man problem with time windows. *Computers & Operations Research, 37*(9), 1570–1583. doi:10.1016/j.cor.2009.11.015

Lua, Y., Xie, Q., Klito, G., Geller, A., Larus, J. R., & Greenberg, A. (2011). Join-Idle-Queue: A novel load-balancing algorithm for dynamically scalable web services. *Int. J. Perform. Eval., 68*(11), 1056–1071. doi:10.1016/j.peva.2011.07.015

Lu, C., & Lau, S. M. (1995). An adaptive algorithm for resolving processor thrashing in load distribution. *Concurrency and Computation, 7*(7), 653–670. doi:10.1002/cpe.4330070706

Lucas-Simarro, J. L., Vozmediano, R. M., Montero, R. S., & Llorente, I. M. (2012). *Scheduling strategies for optimal service deployment across multiple clouds.* Future Generation Computer Systems, SciVerse ScienceDirect.

Lu, F., Parkin, S., & Morgan, G. (2006, October). Load balancing for massively multiplayer online games. In *Proceedings of 5th ACM SIGCOMM workshop on Network and system support for games* (p. 1). ACM. 10.1145/1230040.1230064

Mahalle, H. S., Kaveri, P. R., & Chavan, V. (2013). Load balancing on cloud data centres. *International Journal of Advanced Research in Computer Science and Software Engineering, 3*(1).

Mahmood, Z. (2011). Cloud computing: characteristics and deployment approaches. *11th IEEE International Conference on Computer and Information Technology,* 121-126. 10.1109/CIT.2011.75

Mahmud, R., & Buyyar, R. (2016). *Fog computing: A Taxonomy, Survey and Future Directions.* arXiv:1611.05539

Mahmud, R., Kotagiri, R., & Buyya, R. (2018). Fog computing: A taxonomy, survey and future directions. In *Internet of everything.* Springer.

Malladi, R. R. (2015). An approach to load balancing In cloud computing. *Int. J. Innov. Res. Sci. Eng. Technol., 4*(5), 3769–3777.

Manjaly, J.S. (2013). Relative study on task schedulers in HadoopMapReduce. *Int. J. Adv. Res. Comput. Sci. Softw. Eng., 3*(5).

Marinkovic & Popovici. (2011). Nano power Wake Up Radio mainly intended for Wireless Body Area Networks (WBANs). *IEEE Radio and Wireless.*

Mathew, Sitaraman, & Shenoy. (2016). Energy aware load balancing in content level delivery networks. *Proceedings of IEEE INFOCOM,* 954-962.

Mathur, S., Larji, A. A., & Goyal, A. (2017). Static load balancing using SA Max-Min algorithm. *International Journal for Research in Applied Science and Engineering Technology, 5*(4), 1886–1893.

Matthias, S., Klink, M., Tomforde, S., & Hahner, J. (2016). *Predictive Load Balancing in Cloud Computing Environments based on Ensemble Forecasting* (4th ed.; Vol. 11). Augsburg: IEEE.

McEwen, A., & Cassimally, H. (2013). *Designing the Internet of Things.* John Wiley & Sons.

Medvedev, A., Fedchenkov, P., Zaslavsky, A., Anagnostopoulos, T., & Khoruzhnikov, S. (2015). Waste management as an IoT-enabled service in smart cities. In *Conference on Smart Spaces.* Springer International Publishing.

Meera, A., & Swamynathan, S. (2013). Agent based resource monitoring system in IaaS cloud environment. *Proceeding of International Conference On Computational Intelligence: Modeling Techniques and Applications.* 10.1016/j.protcy.2013.12.353

Mehta, Prasad., & Bhavsar. (2017). Efficient Resource Scheduling in Cloud Computing. *International Journal of Advanced Research in Computer Science, 18.*

Mehta, H., Kanungo, P., & Chandwani, M. (2011, February). Decentralized content aware load balancing algorithm for distributed computing environments. In *Proceedings of the International Conference & Workshop on Emerging Trends in Technology* (pp. 370-375). ACM. 10.1145/1980022.1980102

Mei, F. (2009). Smart planet and sensing china—analysis on development of IOT. *Agricultural Network Information, 12,* 5–7.

Mell, P., & Grance, T. (2011). *The NIST definition of cloud computing.* Gaithersburg, MD: Computer Security Division, Information Technology Laboratory, National Institute of Standards and Technology, United States Department of Commerce. doi:10.6028/NIST.SP.800-145

Mesbahi, M., & Rahmani, A. M. (2016). Load balancing in cloud computing: A state of the art survey. *Int. J. Mod. Educ. Comput. Sci., 8*(3), 64–78. doi:10.5815/ijmecs.2016.03.08

Microsoft Azure IoT Reference Architecture. (2018). Retrieved from http://download.microsoft.com/download/A/4/D/A4DAD253-BC21-41D3-B9D9-87D2AE6F0719/Microsoft_Azure_IoT_Reference_Architecture.pdf

Milani, A. S., & Navimipour, N. J. (2016). Load balancing mechanisms and techniques in the cloud environments: Systematic literature review and future trends. *Journal of Network and Computer Applications, 71,* 86–98. doi:10.1016/j.jnca.2016.06.003

Miorandi, D., Sicari, S., & Chlamtac, I. (2012). Internet of things: Vision, applications and research challenges. *Ad Hoc Networks, 10*(7), 1497–1516. doi:10.1016/j.adhoc.2012.02.016

Mishra, N.K., & Misha, N. (2015). Load balancing techniques: need, objectives and major challenges in cloud computing: a systematic review. *Int. J. Comput., 131*(18).

Mistra, Das, Kulkarni, & Sahoo. (2012, September). Dynamic resource management using virtual machine migrations. *IEEE Communications Magazine,* 34-40.

Monika, K. A., Rao, N., Prapulla, S. B., & Shobha, G. (2016). *Smart Dustbin-An Efficient Garbage Monitoring System. International Journal of Engineering Science and Computing, 6,* 7113–7116.

Moschakisa, I. A., & Karatzaa, H. D. (2015). Multi-criteria scheduling of Bag-of-Tasks applications on heterogeneous interlinked clouds with simulated annealing. *J. Softw. Syst., 101,* 1–14. doi:10.1016/j.jss.2014.11.014

Moss, T. (2016). Conserving water and preserving infrastructures between dictatorship and democracy in Berlin. *Water Alternatives, 9*(2), 250–271.

Mukherjee, M., Shu, L., & Wang, D. (2018). Survey of Fog Computing: Fundamental, Network Applications, and Research Challenges. *IEEE Commun. Surv. Tutor.*

Mukherjee, M., Matam, R., Shu, L., Maglaras, L., Ferrag, M. A., Choudhury, N., & Kumar, V. (2017). Security and Privacy in Fog computing: Challenges. *IEEE Access: Practical Innovations, Open Solutions, 5,* 19293–19304. doi:10.1109/ACCESS.2017.2749422

Mukhopadhyay, R., Ghosh, D., & Mukherjee, N. (2010). A Study on the application of existing load-balancing algorithms for large, dynamic, and heterogeneous distributed systems ACM, A Study on the Application of Existing Load-balancing algorithms for Large, Dynamic, and Heterogeneous Distributed System. *Proceedings of 9th International Conference on Software Engineering, Parallel and Distributed Systems,* 238–243.

Muntjir, M., Rahul, M., & Alhumyani, H. A. (2017). An Analysis of Internet of Things (IoT): Novel Architectures, Modern Applications, Security Aspects and Future Scope with Latest Case Studies. *Int. J. Eng. Res. Technol., 6*, 422–447.

Nae, V., Prodan, R., & Fahringer, T. (2010, October). Cost-efficient hosting and load balancing of massively multiplayer online games. In *Proceedings of the Grid Computing (GRID), 2010 11th IEEE/ACM International Conference on* (pp. 9-16). IEEE.

Nagarajan, R., & Thirunavukarasu, R. (2018). A fuzzy-based decision-making broker for effective identification and selection of cloud infrastructure services. *Soft Computing.* doi:10.100700500-018-3534-x

Nandurkar, S. R., Thool, V. R., & Thool, R. C. (2014). Design and Development of Precision Agriculture System Using Wireless Sensor Network. *IEEE International Conference on Automation, Control, Energy and Systems (ACES).* 10.1109/ACES.2014.6808017

Nasser, T., & Tariq, R. S. (2015). Big Data Challenges. *Journal of Computer Engineering & Information Technology, 4*(3), 1–10.

Natesan & Chokkalingam. (2018). *Task scheduling in heterogeneous cloud environment using mean grey wolf optimization algorithm.* The Korean Institute of Communications and Information Sciences (KICS), publishing services by Elsevier.

Nathani, A., Chaudharya, S., & Somani, G. (2012). Policy based resource allocation in IaaS cloud. *Future Generation Computer Systems, 28*(1), 94–103. doi:10.1016/j.future.2011.05.016

Nathan, S., Kulkarni, P., & Bellur, U. (2013, April). Resource availability based performance benchmarking of virtual machine migrations. In *Proceedings of the 4th ACM/SPEC International Conference on Performance Engineering* (pp. 387-398). ACM. 10.1145/2479871.2479932

Navghane, S. S., Killedar, M. S., & Rohokale, D. V. (2016). *IoT Based Smart Garbage and Waste Collection Bin. International Journal of Advanced Research in Electronics and Communication Engineering, 5*, 1576–1578.

Nayak, S., & Patel. (2015). A Survey on Load Balancing Algorithms in Cloud Computing and Proposed a model with Improved Throttled Algorithm. *International Journal for Scientific Research & Development, 3*(1).

Neeraj, R., & Chana, I. (2014). Load balancing and job migration techniques in grid: A survey of recent trends. *Wireless Personal Communications, 79*(3), 2089–2125. doi:10.100711277-014-1975-9

Nema, R., & Edwin, S. T. (2016). A new efficient virtual machine load balancing algorithm for a cloud computing environment. *International Journal of Latest Research in Engineering and Technology, 2*(2), 69–75.

Ni, J., Huang, Y., Luan, Z., Zhang, J., & Qian, D. (2011, December). Virtual machine mapping policy based on load balancing in private cloud environment. In *Proceeding of Cloud and Service Computing (CSC), 2011 International Conference on* (pp. 292-295). IEEE.

Nikita. (2014). Comparative Analysis of Load Balancing Algorithms in Cloud Computing. *International Journal of Science and Engineering.*

Nishant, K., Sharma, P., Krishna, V., Gupta, C., Singh, K. P., Nitin, N., & Rastogi, R. (2012). Load Balancing of Nodes in Cloud Using Ant Colony Optimization. *Proceedings of the 14th International Conference on Modelling and Simulation*, 3-8. 10.1109/UKSim.2012.11

Nokia launches industry-first Edge Cloud data center solution for the 5G era, supporting industry automation and consumer applications. (2018). Retrieved from https://www.nokia.com/about-us/news/releases/2018/04/25/nokia-launches-industry-first-edge-cloud-data-center-solution-for-the-5g-era-supporting-industry-automation-and-consumer-applications

Nokia Solutions and Networks, Increasing Mobile Operators' Value Proposition with Edge Computing. (2013). Retrieved from http://nsn.com/portfolio/liquid-net/intelligent-broadband-management/liquid-applications

Nokia. (2018). *The edge cloud: an agile foundation to support advanced new services.* Nokia White paper. Retrieved from https://onestore.nokia.com/asset/202184

Nolan, D., & Perrett, J. (2016). Teaching and learning data visualization: Ideas and assignments. *The American Statistician, 70*(3), 260–269. doi:10.1080/00031305.2015.1123651

Nuaimi, K., Mohamed, N., Mariam Al-Nuaimi, M., & Al-Jaroodi, J. (2012). A Survey of Load Balancing in Cloud Computing: Challenges and Algorithms. *Proceedings of the Second Symposium on Network Cloud Computing and Applications.* 10.1109/NCCA.2012.29

Okafor, K. C., Achumba, I. E., Chukwudebe, G. A., & Ononiwu, G. C. (2017). Leveraging Fog Computing for Scalable IoT Datacenter Using Spine-Leaf Network Topology. *Journal of Electrical and Computer Engineering, 2017*, 1–11. doi:10.1155/2017/2363240

Palta, R., & Jeet, R. (2014). Load balancing in the cloud computing using virtual machine migration: A review. *Int. J. Appl. Innov. Eng. Manag., 3*(5), 437–441.

Panachakel, J. T., & Finitha, K. C. (2016). Energy Efficient Compression of Shock Data Using Compressed Sensing. Intelligent Systems Technologies and Applications, 273-281.

Panda, Gupta, & Prasanta.(2015). Allocation Aware Task Scheduling for Heterogeneous Multi Cloud Systems. *2nd International Symposium on Big Data and Cloud Computing Procedia Computer Science, 50.*

Panwar & Mallick. (2016). Load Balancing in Cloud Computing Using Dynamic Load Management Algorithm. In *International Conference on Green Computing and Internet of Things (ICGCIoT). IEEE Xplore.*

Pasha, N., Agarwal, A., & Rastogi, R. (2014, May). Round Robin Approach for VM Load Balancing Algorithm in Cloud Computing Environment. *International Journal of Advanced Research in Computer Science and Software Engineering, 4*(5).

Patel, H.M. (2015). A comparative analysis of MapReduce scheduling algorithms for Hadoop. *Int. J. Innov. Emerg. Res. Eng., 2*(2).

Patel, J., & Prajapathi, J. (2017). A Survey scheduling algorithms and types of resources provisioning in cloud environment. *International Journal of Engineering and Computer Science, 4*(1), 10132-10134.

Patel, N. H., & Shah, J. (2016). Improved Throttling Load Balancing Algorithm With Respect To Computing Cost and Throughput For Cloud Based Requests. *IJARIIE, 2*(3), 2192-2198.

Patel, G., Mehta, R., & Bhoi, U. (2015). Enhanced load balanced min-min algorithm for static meta task scheduling in cloud computing. *Procedia Computer Science, 57*, 545–553. doi:10.1016/j.procs.2015.07.385

Paul, J. (2013). *RFID based vehicular networks for smart cities.* Presented at *2013 IEEE 29th International Conference on Data Engineering Workshops (ICDEW).* 10.1109/ICDEW.2013.6547439

Pawar, S. P. (2013). *Smart City with Internet of Things (Sensor networks) and Big Data. Institute of Business Management & Research (IBMR).*

Penmatsa, S., & Chronopoulos, T. (2011, April). Game-theoretic static load balancing for distributed systems. *Journal of Parallel and Distributed Computing, 71*(4), 537–555. doi:10.1016/j.jpdc.2010.11.016

Peralta, G., Iglesias-Urkia, M., Barcelo, M., Gomez, R., Moran, A., & Bilbao, J. (2017). Fog computing based efficient IoT scheme for the Industry 4.0. *Proceedings of the 2017 IEEE International Workshop of Electronics, Control, Measurement, Signals and their application to Mechatronics*, 1–6. 10.1109/ECMSM.2017.7945879

Perera, C., Zaslavsky, A., Christen, P., & Georgakopoulos, D. (2014). Sensing as a Service Model for Smart Cities Supported by Internet of Things. *Transactions on Emerging Telecommunications Technologies*, 25(1), 81–93. doi:10.1002/ett.2704

Perkins, C., & Royer, E. (1998). *Ad hoc on demand distance vector (AODV) routing*. Internet Draft. Retrieved from: http://www.cs.cornell.edu/people/egs/615/aodv.pdf

Phi, Tin, Nguyen, & Hung. (2018). Proposed Load Balancing Algorithm to Reduce response time and processing time on cloud computing. *International Journal of Computer Networks and Communications, 10*.

Polato, I., Re, R., Goldman, A., & Kon, F. (2014). A comprehensive view of Hadoop research – a systematic literature review. *Journal of Network and Computer Applications*, 46, 1–25. doi:10.1016/j.jnca.2014.07.022

Praveen, P., Rao, K. T., & Janakiramaiah, B. (2018). Effective Allocation of Resources and Task Scheduling in Cloud Environment using Social Group Optimization. *Arabian Journal for Science and Engineering*, 43(8), 4265–4272. doi:10.100713369-017-2926-z

Predix Edge – GE Digital. (2018). Retrieved from https://www.ge.com/digital/asset/predix-edge-ge-digital

Premsankar, G., Di Francesco, M., & Taleb, T. (2018). Edge computing for the Internet of Things: A case study. *IEEE Internet of Things Journal*, 5(2), 1275–1284. doi:10.1109/JIOT.2018.2805263

Priyatharsini & Malarvizhi. (2018). RHEA: resource hypervisor and efficient allocator in cloud. *International Journal of Engineering & Technology, 7*(1), 21-26.

Radojevic, B., & Zagar, M. (2011). Analysis of issues with load balancing algorithms in hosted (cloud) environments. In *Proceedings of 34th International Convention on MIPRO*. IEEE.

Raj, P. (2012). Cloud Enterprise Architecture. CRC Press.

Raj, A. (2015). A New Static Load Balancing Algorithm in Cloud Computing. *International Journal of Computers and Applications, 132*(2).

Rajabioun, R. (2011). Cuckoo optimization algorithm. *Applied Soft Computing*, 11, 5508–5518.

Rajganesh, N., & Ramkumar, T. (2016). A review on broker based cloud service model. *CIT. Journal of Computing and Information Technology*, 24(3), 283–292. doi:10.20532/cit.2016.1002778

Ramadhan, G., Purboyo, T. W., & Latuconsina, R. (2018). Experimental Model for Load Balancing in Cloud Computing Using Throttled Algorithm. *International Journal of Applied Engineering Research, 13*(2), 1139-1143.

Randles, M., Lamb, D., & Tareb-Bendia, A. (2010). A Comparative Study into Distributed Load-balancing algorithms for Cloud Computing. *Proceedings of the 24th International Conference on Advanced Information Networking and Applications Workshops*, 551–556.

Rao, B. T., & Reddy, L. S. S. (2011). Survey on improved scheduling in HadoopMapReduce in cloud environments. *International Journal of Computers and Applications, 34*(9).

Rastogi, G., & Sushil, R. (2015). Analytical Literature Survey on Existing Load Balancing Schemes in Cloud Computing. *International Conference on Green Computing and Internet of Things (ICGCIoT)*. 10.1109/ICGCIoT.2015.7380705

Rathore, N., & Chana, I. (2013). A Sender Initiate Based Hierarchical Load Balancing Technique for Grid Using Variable Threshold Value. *Signal Processing, Computing and Control (ISPCC), IEEE International Conference.* 10.1109/ISPCC.2013.6663440

Rathore, N., & Channa, I. (2011). A Cognitive Analysis of Load Balancing and job migration Technique. *Grid World Congress on Information and Communication Technologies Congr. Inf. Commun. Technol. (WICT)*, 77–82.

Ray, S., & Sarkar, A.D. (2012). Execution analysis of load-balancing algorithms in cloud computing environment. *Int. J. Cloud Comput.: Serv. Archit. (IJCCSA), 2*(5).

Riggio, R. (2008, June). Hardware and Software Solutions for Wireless Mesh Network Test beds. *IEEE Communications Magazine.* doi:10.1109/MCOM.2008.4539480

Rimal, B. P., Choi, E., & Lumb, I. (2009). *A taxonomy and survey of cloud computing systems.* INC, IMS and IDC. doi:10.1109/NCM.2009.218

Robinson, S. (2012). *The Storage and Transfer Challenges of Big Data.* Retrieved from http://sloanreview. mit.edu/article/the-storage-and-transfer-challenges-of-big-data/

Rolim, Koch, Westphall, Werner, Fracalossi, & Salvador. (2010). *A Cloud Computing Solution for Patient's Data Collection in Health Care Institutions.* IEEE Xplore.

Rotithor, H. G. (1994). Taxonomy of dynamic task scheduling schemes in distributed computing systems. *Proceeding of IEEE -Computers and Digital Techniques, 141*(1), 1-10.

Ryden, M., Oh, K., Chandra, A., & Weissman, J. (2014). Nebula: Distributed edge cloud for data-intensive computing. *IEEE 2014 International Conference on "In Collaboration Technologies and Systems (CTS)"*, 491-492.

Sabahi, F. (2011). Cloud computing security threats and responses. *IEEE 3rd International Conference on Communication Software and Networks (ICCSN)*, 245-249. 10.1109/ICCSN.2011.6014715

Sagiroglu, S., & Sinanc, D. (2013). Big data: A review. *IEEE International Conference on Collaboration Technologies and Systems (CTS)*, 42-47. 10.1109/CTS.2013.6567202

Saha, D., & Mukherjee, A. (2003). Pervasive computing: A paradigm for the 21st century. *IEEE Perspectives, 36*(3), 25–31.

Sammy, K., Shengbing, R., & Wilson, C. (2012). Energy efficient security preserving vm live migration in data centers for cloud computing. *IJCSI International Journal of Computer Science Issues, 9*(2), 1694–0814.

Sarkar, S., Pal, S., Maiti, S., & Sarkar, S. K. (2010). Development of a statistical algorithm for cost efficient RFID tag and reader connectivity. *Proc. the International Conference and Workshop on Emerging Trends in Technology 2010*, 1009-1009. 10.1145/1741906.1742181

Sarood, O., Gupta, A., & Kale, L. V. (2012). Cloud Friendly Load Balancing for HPC Applications: *Preliminary Work. International Conference on Parallel Processing Workshops*, 200–205.

Satyanarayanan, M. (2017). The emergence of edge computing. *Computers & Society, 50*(1), 30–39. doi:10.1109/MC.2017.9

Satyanarayanan, M., Lewis, G., Morris, E., Simanta, S., Boleng, J., & Ha, K. (2013). The role of cloudlets in hostile environments. *IEEE Pervasive Computing, 12*(4), 40–49. doi:10.1109/MPRV.2013.77

Satyanarayanan, M., Schuster, R., Ebling, M., Fettweis, G., Flinck, H., Joshi, K., & Sabnani, K. (2015a). An open ecosystem for mobile-cloud convergence. *IEEE Communications Magazine, 53*(3), 63–70. doi:10.1109/MCOM.2015.7060484

Satyanarayanan, M., Simoens, P., Xiao, Y., Pillai, P., Chen, Z., Ha, K., ... Amos, B. (2015b). Edge analytics in the internet of things. *IEEE Pervasive Computing, 2*(2), 24–31. doi:10.1109/MPRV.2015.32

Scharf, M., Stein, M., Voith, T., & Hilt, V. (2015). Network-aware Instance Scheduling in OpenStack. *International Conference on Computer Communication and Network (ICCCN)*, 1-6.

Schoonderwoerd, R., Holland, O., & Bruten, J. (1997). Ant like agents for load balancing in telecommunication networks. In *Proceedings of the first int. conf. on autonomous agents* (pp. 209-216). New York: ACM Press. 10.1145/267658.267718

Sebastian, S., & Ray, P. P. (2015). Development of IoT invasive architecture for complying with health of home. Proceedings of I3CS, 79–83.

Secured Cloud. (n.d.). *International Journal of Applied Engineering Research, 9*(24), 29329-29337.

Selvi, R. T., & Aruna, R. (2016). Longest approximate time to end scheduling algorithm in Hadoop environment. *Int. J. Adv. Res. Manag. Archit. Technol. Eng., 2*(6).

Shadkam, E., & Bijari, M. (2014). Evaluation the efficiency of cuckoo optimization algorithm. *Int. J. Comput. Sci. Appl., 4*(2), 39–47.

Shafiullah, Oo, Jarvis, Ali, & Wolfs. (2016). Prospects of Renewable Energy—A Feasibility Study in the Australian Context. *Journal of Renewable Energy, 39*(1).

Shah, N., & Farik, M. (2015). Static load balancing algorithms in cloud computing: Challenges & solutions. *International Journal Of Scientific & Technology Research, 4*(10), 365–367.

Shaikh, B., Shinde, K., & Borde, S. (2017). Challenges of big data processing and scheduling of processes using various Hadoop Schedulers: A survey. *Int. Multifaceted Multiling. Stud., 3*, 12.

Sharma, T., & Banga, V. K. (2013). Efficient and enhanced algorithm in cloud computing. *International Journal of Soft Computing and Engineering*.

Sharma, E., Singh, S., & Sharma, M. (2008). M.: Performance Analysis of Load Balancing Algorithms. *In Proceeding of 38th. World Academy of Science, Engineering and Technology*.

Sheng, Q. Z., Qiao, X., Vasilakos, A. V., Szabo, C., Bourne, S., & Xu, X. (2014). Web services composition: A decade's overview. *Information Sciences, 280*, 218–238. doi:10.1016/j.ins.2014.04.054

Shen, H., Sarker, A., Yuy, L., & Deng, F. (2016). Probabilistic Network-Aware Task Placement for MapReduce Scheduling. *Proceedings of the IEEE International Conference on Cluster Computing*. 10.1109/CLUSTER.2016.48

Shen, H., Yu, L., Chen, L., & Li, Z. (2016). Goodbye to Fixed Bandwidth Reservation: Job Scheduling with Elastic Bandwidth Reservation in Clouds. *Proceedings of the International Conference on Cloud Computing Technology and Science*. 10.1109/CloudCom.2016.0017

Shihab, Cai, Wan, & Gulliver. (2008, January). Wireless Mesh Networks for In-Home IPTV Distribution. *IEEE Transaction on Network*.

Shi, W., Cao, J., Zhang, Q., Li, Y., & Xu, L. (2016). Edge computing: Vision and challenges. *IEEE Internet of Things Journal, 3*(5), 637–646. doi:10.1109/JIOT.2016.2579198

Sidana & Tiwari. (2017). NBST Algorithm: A load balancing algorithm in Cloud computing. In *International Conference on Computing, Communication and Automation (ICCCA2016)*. IEEE Xplore.

Sidhu, A. K., & Kinger, S. (2013). Analysis of load balancing techniques in cloud computing. *International Journal of Computers and Technology, 4*(2).

Sim, K. M. (2011). Agent-based cloud computing. *IEEE Transactions on Services Computing, 5*(4), 564–577.

Sim, K. M., & Weng, H. S. (2003). Ant Colony Optimization for Routing and Load-Balancing: Survey and New Directions. *IEEE Transactions on Systems, Man, and Cybernetics, VOL., 33*(5), 560–572. doi:10.1109/TSMCA.2003.817391

Singha, A., Juneja, D., & Malhotra, M. (2015). Autonomous Agent Based Load-balancing algorithm in Cloud Computing. *International Conference on Advanced Computing Technologies and Applications (ICACTA), 45*, 832–841. 10.1016/j.procs.2015.03.168

Singh, P., Baaga, P., & Gupta, S. (2016). Assorted load-balancing algorithms in cloud computing: A survey. *International Journal of Computers and Applications, 143*(7).

Singh, S., & Chana, I. (2016). A Survey on Resource Scheduling in Cloud Computing Issues and Challenges. *Journal of Grid Computing, 14*(2), 217–264. doi:10.100710723-015-9359-2

Song, X., Gao, L., & Wang, J. (2011). Job scheduling based on ant colony optimization in cloud computing. In *Proceeding of Computer Science and Service System (CSSS), International Conference on*. IEEE.

Sotomayor, B., Montero, R. S., Llorente, I. M., & Foster, I. (2009). Virtual infrastructure management in private and hybrid clouds. *IEEE Internet Computing, 13*(5), 14–22. doi:10.1109/MIC.2009.119

Sreenivas, V., Prathap, M., & Kemal, M. (2014, February). Load balancing techniques: Major challenge in Cloud Computing-a systematic review. In *Proceeding of Electronics and Communication Systems (ICECS), 2014 International Conference on* (pp. 1-6). IEEE.

Srivastava, L. (2006). Pervasive, ambient, ubiquitous: the magic of radio. *Proceedings of European Commission Conference From RFID to the Internet of Things*.

Strang, K. D., & Sun, Z. (2017). Analyzing relationships in terrorism big data using Hadoop and statistics. *Journal of Computer Information Systems, 57*(1), 67–75. doi:10.1080/08874417.2016.1181497

StreetSmart. (2018). Retrieved from http://help.streetsmart.schwab.com/edge/printablemanuals/EdgeManual.pdf

Subramanian, D., Druschel, P., & Chen, J. (1997). Ants and reinforcement learning: A case study in routing in dynamic networks. In *Proceedings of the 15th int. joint conf. on artificial intelligence* (pp. 823-838). San Francisco: Morgan Kaufmann.

Sui, Z., & Pallickara, S. (2011). A survey of load balancing techniques forData intensive computing. In B. Furht & A. Escalante (Eds.), *Handbook of Data Intensive Computing* (pp. 157–168). New York: Springer. doi:10.1007/978-1-4614-1415-5_6

Sun, M., Li, J., Yang, C., Schmidt, G. A., Bambacus, M., Cahalan, R., ... Li, Z. (2012). A Web-Based Geovisual Analytical System for Climate Studies. *Future Internet, 4*(4), 1069–1085. doi:10.3390/fi4041069

Suresh, A. & Varatharajan, R. (2018). Recognition of pivotal instances from uneven set boundary during classification. *Multimed Tools Appl.*

Taleb, T., Mada, B., Corici, M.-I., Nakao, A., & Flinck, H. (2017b). PERMIT: Network slicing for personalized 5G mobile telecommunications. *IEEE Communications Magazine, 55*(5), 88–93. doi:10.1109/MCOM.2017.1600947

Taleb, T., Samdanis, K., Mada, B., Flinck, H., Dutta, S., & Sabella, D. (2017a). On multi-access edge computing: A survey of the emerging 5G network edge cloud architecture and orchestration. *IEEE Communications Surveys and Tutorials*, *19*(3), 1657–1681. doi:10.1109/COMST.2017.2705720

Tasquier, L. (2015). Agent based load-balancer for multi-cloud environments. *Columbia Int. Publ. J. Cloud Comput. Res.*, *1*(1), 35–49.

Tawfeek, M. A., El-Sisi, A., Keshk, A. E., & Torkey, F. A. (2013, November). Cloud task scheduling based on ant colony optimization. In *Proceeding of Computer Engineering & Systems (ICCES), 8th International Conference on* (pp. 64-69). IEEE.

Tchernykh, A., Cortés-Mendoza, J. M., Pecero, J. E., Bouvry, P., & Kliazovich, D. (2014, October). Adaptive energy efficient distributed VoIP load balancing in federated cloud infrastructure. In *Proceedings of the Cloud Networking (CloudNet), 2014 IEEE 3rd International Conference on* (pp. 27-32). IEEE.

The lifeline for a data driven world. (2018). Retrieved from https://www.happiestminds.com/Insights/internet-of-things

The Sensor Cloud the Homeland Security. (2011). Retrieved from http://www.mistralsolutions.com/hs- downloads/tech-briefs/nov11-article3.html

The Smart Grid: An Introduction. (2018). Technical report by US Department of Energy.

Tian, W., Xu, M., Chen, A., Li, G., Wang, X., & Chen, Y. (2015). Open-source simulators for Cloud computing: Comparative study and challenging issues. *Simulation Modelling Practice and Theory*, *58*, 239–254. doi:10.1016/j.simpat.2015.06.002

Townsville Solar City. (n.d.). *Ergon Energy, Queensland*. Retrieved from http://www.townsvillesolarcity.com.au/Home/tabid/36/Default.aspx

Udendhran, R. (2017). A hybrid approach to enhance data security in cloud storage. *Proceeding ICC '17 Proceedings of the Second International Conference on Internet of things, Data and Cloud Computing*. 10.1145/3018896.3025138

Vaidya, M. (2012). Parallel processing of cluster by Map Reduce. *Int. J. Distrib. Parallel Syst.*, *3*(1).

Valvåg, S. V. (2011). Cogset: A High-Performance MapReduce Engine. Faculty of Science and Technology Department of Computer Science, University of Tromsö.

Valvåg, S. V., & Johansen, D. (2009). Cogset: A unified engine for reliable storage and parallel processing. *Proceedings of the Sixth IFIP International Conference on Network and Parallel Computing*, 174–181. 10.1109/NPC.2009.23

Varghese, B., & Buyya, R. (2018). Next generation cloud computing: New trends and research Directions. *Future Generation Computer Systems*, *79*, 849–886. doi:10.1016/j.future.2017.09.020

Vasic, N., & Barisits, M. (2009). Making Cluster Applications Energy-Aware. *Proceedings of the 1st Workshop on Automated Control for Datacenters and Clouds*, 37–42.

Verdouw, C. N., Wolfert, J., Beulens, A. J. M., & Rialland, A. (2016). Virtualization of food supply chains with the internet of things. *Journal of Food Engineering*, 1–9.

Verma, M., Bhardwaj, N., & Yadav, A. K. (2016). Real Time Efficient Scheduling Algorithm for Load Balancing in Fog Computing Environment. *Int. J. Inf. Technol. Comput. Sci.*, *8*, 1–10.

Vernica, R., Balmin, A., Beyer, K. S., & Ercegovac, V. (2012). Adaptive MapReduce using situation-aware mappers. *International Conference on Extending Database Technology (EDBT)*, 420–431. 10.1145/2247596.2247646

Vicini, S., Bellini, S., & Sanna, A. (2012). How to Co-Create Internet of Things-enabled Services for Smarter Cities. *SMART 2012: The First International Conference on Smart Systems, Devices and Technologies.*

Vinothina, V., Sridaran, R., & Ganapathi, P. (2012). A survey on resource allocation strategies in cloud computing. *International Journal of Advanced Computer Science and Applications, 3*(6), 97–104. doi:10.14569/IJACSA.2012.030616

Vishwanath, A., Peruri, R., & He, J. (2016). Security in Fog Computing through Encryption. *International Journal of Information Technology and Computer Science., 8*(5), 28–36. doi:10.5815/ijitcs.2016.05.03

Vukotic, I., & Gardner, R. (2016). *Big Data Analytics Tools as Applied to ATLAS Event Data* (No. ATL-SOFT-SLIDE-2016-649). ATL-COM-SOFT-2016-079.

Wahab, M. N., Mexiani, S. N., & Atyabi, A. (2015). A comprehensive review of swarm optimization algorithms. *PLoS One, 10*(5), 1–36. doi:10.1371/journal.pone.0122827 PMID:25992655

Wang, C. S., Lin, S. L., & Chang, J. Y. (2017). MapReduce-Based Frequent Pattern Mining Framework with Multiple Item Support. In *Asian Conference on Intelligent Information and Database Systems.* Springer. 10.1007/978-3-319-54430-4_7

Wang, Q., Chen, D., Zhang, N., Ding, Z., & Qin, Z. (2017). PCP: A Privacy-Preserving Content-Based Publish-Subscribe Scheme With Differential Privacy in Fog computing. *IEEE Access: Practical Innovations, Open Solutions, 5*, 17962–17986. doi:10.1109/ACCESS.2017.2748956

Wang, W., Liang, B., & Li, B. (2015). Multi-Resource Fair Allocation in Heterogeneous Cloud Computing Systems. *IEEE Transactions on Parallel and Distributed Systems, 26*(10), 2822–2835. doi:10.1109/TPDS.2014.2362139

Weedall. (2016). *BPA Smart Grid Overview*. Energy and Communications, Washington House Technology.

Wei, X., Fan, J., Lu, Z., & Ding, K. (2013). Application scheduling in mobile cloud computing with load balancing. *Journal of Applied Mathematics*, 1–13.

Wei, X., Fan, J., Wang, T., & Wang, Q. (2015). Efficient application scheduling in mobile cloud computing based on MAX–MIN ant system. *Soft Computing*, 1–15.

Wen, W. (2010). An intelligent traffic management expert system with RFID technology. *Expert Systems with Applications, 37*(4), 3024–3035. doi:10.1016/j.eswa.2009.09.030

What Edge Computing Means for Infrastructure and Operations Leaders. (2018). Retrieved from https://www.gartner.com/smarterwithgartner/what-edge-computing-means-for-infrastructure-and-operations-leaders

Witten, I. H., Frank, E., Hall, M. A., & Pal, C. J. (2016). *Data Mining: Practical machine learning tools and techniques*. Morgan Kaufmann.

Wolke, A., Bichler, M., & Setzer, T. (2015). *Planning vs. dynamic control: Resource allocation in corporate clouds.* Academic Press.

Wu, C., Buyya, R., & Ramamohanarao, K. (2016). *Big Data Analytics= Machine Learning+ Cloud Computing*. arXiv preprint arXiv:1601.03115

Wubbeler, G., Stavridis, D., Kreiseler, R., Bousseljot, R., & Elster, C. (2007). Verification of humans using the electro-cardiogram. *Pattern Recognition Letters, 28*(10), 1172–1175. doi:10.1016/j.patrec.2007.01.014

Wu, T. (2010). The Security Problem of the Internet of Things is Analyzed. *J. Network Security Technology & Application, 1*, 7–8.

Xia, Zhou, Luo, & Zhu. (2015). Stochastic Modeling and Quality Evaluation of Infrastructure-as-a-Service Clouds. *IEEE Trans. on Automation Science and Engineering, 12*(1), 160-172.

Xiao, Z., Jiang, J., Zhu, Y., Ming, Z., Zhong, S., & Cai, S. (2015). A solution of dynamic VMs placement problem for energy consumption optimization based on evolutionary game theory. *Journal of Systems and Software, 101*, 260–272. doi:10.1016/j.jss.2014.12.030

Xia, Y., Hong, H., Lin, G., & Sun, Z. (2017). A Secure and Efficient Cloud Resource Allocation Scheme with Trust Evaluation Mechanism Based on Combinatorial Double Auction, KSII. *Transactions on Internet and Information Systems (Seoul), 11*(9), 4197–4219.

Xia, Y., Wang, L., Zhao, Q., & Zhang, G. (2011). Research on job scheduling algorithm in Hadoop. *Journal of Computer Information Systems, 7,* 5769–5775.

Xin, G. (2016). Ant Colony Optimization Computing Resource Allocation Algorithm Based on Cloud Computing Environment. *Proceeding of International Conference on Education, Management, Computer and Society (EMCS 2016), 1,* 2.

Xu, Z., Han, J., & Bhuyan, L. (2007, April). Scalable and Decentralized Content-Aware Dispatching in Web Clusters. In *Proceedings of the Performance, Computing, and Communications Conference, 2007. IPCCC 2007. IEEE International* (pp. 202-209). IEEE.

Xu, B., Zhao, C., Hua, E., & Hu, B. (2011). Job scheduling algorithm based on Berger model in cloud environment. *ScienceDirect, Advances in Engineering Software, 42*(7), 419–425. doi:10.1016/j.advengsoft.2011.03.007

Yahaya, B., Latip, R., Othman, M., & Abdullah, A. (2011). Dynamic load balancing policy with communication and computation elements in grid computing with multi-agent system integration. *Int. J. New Comput. Archit. Appl., 1*(3), 757–765.

Yakhchi, M., Ghafari, S. M., Yakhchi, S., Fazeliy, M., & Patooghi, A. (2015). Proposing a Load Balancing Method Based on Cuckoo Optimization Algorithm for Energy Management in Cloud Computing Infrastructures. *Proceedings of the 6th International Conference on Modeling, Simulation, and Applied Optimization (ICMSAO).* 10.1109/ICMSAO.2015.7152209

Yang, S. J., & Chen, Y. R. (2015). Design adaptive task allocation scheduler to improve MapReduce performance in heterogeneous clouds. *Journal of Network and Computer Applications, 57,* 61–70. doi:10.1016/j.jnca.2015.07.012

Yao, J., Schmitz, R., & Warren, S. (2005). A wearable point of- Care system for home use that incorporates plugand-Play and wireless standards. *IEEE Transactions on Information Technology in Biomedicine, 9*(3), 363–371. doi:10.1109/TITB.2005.854507 PMID:16167690

Ye, W., Silva, F., & Heidemann, J. (2006). Ultra-low duty cycle mac with scheduled channel polling. In *Proceedings of the 4th International Conference on Embedded Networked Sensor Systems; SenSys '06.* New York: ACM.

Yu, Jiang, & Yang. (2014). Foundation and development strategy for wise water affair management. *China Water Resources, 2014*(20), 14-17.

Zaharia, M. (2009). *Job Scheduling with the Fair and Capacity Schedulers 9.* Berkley University.

Zaharia, M., Borthakur, D., & Sarma, J. S. (2010). Delay Scheduling: A Simple Technique for Achieving Locality and Fairness in Cluster Scheduling. *Proceedings of the European conference on Computer systems (EuroSys'10),* 265–278. 10.1145/1755913.1755940

Zaharia, M., Konwinski, A., Joseph, A. D., Katz, R., & Stoica, I. (2008). Improving MapReduce Performance in Heterogeneous Environments. *Proceedings of the 8th conference on Symposium on Opearting Systems Design and Implementation,* 29–42.

Zahedi, A. (2011). Developing a System Model for Future SmartGrid. *Proceedings in 2011 IEEE PES Innovative SmartGrid Technologies Conference*, 1-5.

Zanella, A., & Vangelista, L. (2014). Internet of Things for Smart Cities. IEEE Internet of Things Journal, 1(1).

Zeng, W., Huang, C., Duan, B., & Gong, F. (2012). *Research on internet of things of environment monitoring based on cloud computing*. IET.

Zhang, Liu, & Chen.(2017). An Advanced Load Balancing Strategy for cloud Environment. *17th International Conference on Parallel and Distributed Computing, Applications and Technologies*.

Zhang, Z., & Zhang, X. (2010, May). A load balancing mechanism based on ant colony and complex network theory in open cloud computing federation. In *Proceeding of Industrial Mechatronics and Automation (ICIMA), 2010 2nd International Conference on* (Vol. 2, pp. 240-243). IEEE.

Zhang, Q., Cheng, L., & Boutaba, R. (2010). Cloud computing: State-of-the-art and research challenges. *Journal of Internet Services and Applications*, 1(1), 7–18. doi:10.100713174-010-0007-6

Zhang, Y., & Li, Y. (2015). An improved Adaptive workflow scheduling Algorithm in cloud environments. *Proceedings of the Third International Conference on Advanced Cloud and Big Data*, 112-116. 10.1109/CBD.2015.27

Zheng, H., Zhou, L., & Wu, J. (2006). Design and implementation of load balancing in web server cluster system. *J Nanjing Univ Aeronaut, 38*(3).

Zhou, X., Lin, F., Yang, L., Nie, J., Tan, Q., Zeng, W., & Zhang, N. (2016). Load balancing method of cloud storage based on analytical hierarchy process and hybrid hierarchical genetic algorithm. *SpringerPlus, 5*(1), 1–23. doi:10.118640064-016-3619-x PMID:26759740

Zong, Z., Ge, R., & Gu, Q. (2017). *Marcher: A Heterogeneous System Supporting Energy-Aware High-Performance Computing and Big Data Analytics*. Big Data Research.

Zuo, C. (2016). CCA-secure ABE with outsourced decryption for fog computing. *Future Generation Computer Systems*.

About the Contributors

Pethuru Raj has been working as the chief architect and vice president in the Site Reliability Engineering (SRE) Center of Excellence, Reliance Infocomm Ltd. (RIL), Bangalore. He previously worked as a cloud infrastructure architect in the IBM Global Cloud Center of Excellence (CoE), IBM India Bangalore for four years. Prior to that, He had a long stint as TOGAF-certified enterprise architecture (EA) consultant in Wipro Consulting Services (WCS) Division. He also worked as a lead architect in the corporate research (CR) division of Robert Bosch, Bangalore. In total, He have gained more than 17 years of IT industry experience and 8 years of research experience. He obtained his PhD through CSIR-sponsored PhD degree in Anna University, Chennai and continued the UGC-sponsored postdoctoral research in the department of Computer Science and Automation, Indian Institute of Science, Bangalore. Thereafter, He was granted a couple of international research fellowships (JSPS and JST) to work as a research scientist for 3.5 years in two leading Japanese universities. Regarding the publications, He have published more than 30 research papers in peer-reviewed journals such as IEEE, ACM, Springer-Verlag, Inderscience, etc. He has authored 7 books thus far and He focus on some of the emerging technologies such as IoT, Cognitive Analytics, Blockchain, Digital Twin, Docker-enabled Containerization, Data Science, Microservices Architecture, etc. He has contributed 25 book chapters thus far for various technology books edited by highly acclaimed and accomplished professors and professionals. The CRC Press, USA had also released his first book titled as "Cloud Enterprise Architecture" in the year 2012 and you can find the book details in the page http://www.crcpress.com/product/isbn/9781466502321 He has edited and authored a book on the title" Cloud Infrastructures for Big Data Analytics" published by IGI International USA in March 2014. A new book on the title" Smarter Cities: the Enabling Technologies and Tools" by CRC Press, USA, is to hit the market in the month of June 2015. He has collaborating with a few authors to publish a book on the title "High-Performance Big Data Analytics" to be published by Springer-Verlag in the year 2015.

S. Koteeswaran, currently working as an Associate Professor in the Department of Computer Science and Engineering & Dean (Research Studies) at Vel Tech Rangarajan Dr. Sagunthala R&D Institute of Science and Technology, Chennai-62, Tamilnadu, India. He has authored and co-authored several papers in various reputed journals and conference proceedings. He is a reviewer for more than a dozens of journals. His research interests include Theory of Computation, Software Engineering, Data Mining, Big Data and Cloud Computing. He is a Member of ACM, Member of IET, Senior Member of IEEE and Life Member of ISTE.

* * *

T. Lucia Agnes Beena is working as a Assistant Professor and Head in the department of Information Technology, St. Joseph's College, Tiruchirappalli, Tamil Nadu, India. She has 16 years of teaching experience and 4 years of research experience. She has published number of research articles in Scopus indexed Journals. She received her Ph.D degree in the year 2017 and has cleared National Eligibility Test and State Level Eligibility Test. Her areas of interest are Cloud Computing and Psychology of Computer Programming.

Suresh Annamalai, B.E., M.Tech., Ph.D, works as the Professor & Head, Department of the Computer Science and Engineering in Nehru Institute of Engineering & Technology, Coimbatore, Tamil Nadu, India. He has been nearly two decades of experience in teaching and his areas of specializations are Data Mining, Artificial Intelligence, Image Processing, Multimedia and System Software. He has published 75 papers in International journals. He has published more than 40 papers in National and International Conferences. He has served as a reviewer for Springer, Elsevier, and Inderscience journals. He is a member of ISTE, IACSIT, IAENG, MCSTA, MCSI, and Global Member of Internet Society (ISOC). He has organized several National Workshop, Conferences and Technical Events. He is regularly invited to deliver lectures in various programmes for imparting skills in research methodology to students and research scholars. He has published three books, in the name of Data structures & Algorithms, Computer Programming and Problem Solving and Python Programming in DD Publications, Excel Publications and Sri Maruthi Publisher, Chennai, respectively.

M.J Carmel Mary Belinda, currently working as an Associate professor in the Department of Computer Science and Engineering at Vel Tech Rangarajan DrSagunthala R&D Institute of science and Technology,Avadi, Chennai, Tamilnadu, India. She completed her B.E. in Computer Science and Engineering from Mepco Schelenk Engineering College, Madurai Kamaraj University, in the year 1993 and obtained M. E. degree in Computer Science and Engineering from Manonmanium Sundaranar University in the year 2007. She is having more than 25 years of teaching experience. She is a member of IEEE and CSI. Her area of interest include Network Security, Wireless Sensor Network and Big Data Analytics.

M. Hemanth Chakravarthy, currently working as an Application Development Lead in Accenture Services. He obtained his M.E (Software Engineering) from GIET, Rajahmundry (JNTU, Kakinada). He Completed his Ph.D in the Department of Computer Science and Engineering at Vel Tech Rangarajan Dr. Sagunthala R&D Institute of Science and Technology, Chennai-62, Tamilnadu, India. He has been in Software Industry for the past 10 years and has expertise in Salesforce, Software Testing and Java. He has primarily worked in Sales, Services and Marketing Clouds and has expertise in Roles, Profiles, Hierarchies, Workflows, Rules and Validations along with Chatter and Triggers. He has also Extensively worked on integration systems with legacy applications to SFDC. His area of research is Cloud Computing. He has published 5 research articles in International Journals and 2 papers presented in international Conferences. He has attended various Training Programmes, Workshops and FDPs related to his area of interest.

Sandeep Joshi was born in Rajasthan, India. He received the Ph.D. degree from Banasthali University, Banasthali, Rajasthan, India. He is currently an associate professor at Manipal University Jaipur (MUJ), Jaipur, India. He was an associate professor at Sobhasaria Engineering College, Sikar, Rajasthan, India.

He has 18 years of teaching and industrial experience. He has 25 papers in journals and conferences of international repute. His research interest covers optical network, MANET and Network security.

Gokulakrishnan Kandaswamy completed his B.E Degree in ECE in the year 2001 at M.K.University and M.E Degree in Optical Communication at Anna University in the year 2005. He completed his doctoral program in the year 2015 at Anna University. He is working as an Assistant Professor in the Department of Electronics and Communication Engineering at Anna University Regional Campus-Tirunelveli since 2009. He has published more than 10 Papers in SCI indexed journals. He is having more than 14 years of experience both in teaching and industry. His field of interest Optical Communication, Soft Computing, Data Analytics and Electromagnetics.

N. Malarvizhi, currently working as Professor & Head in the Department of Computer Science and Engineering at Vel Tech Rangarajan Dr. Sagunthala R&D Institute of Science and Technology, Chennai-62, Tamilnadu, India. She is having more than 15 years of teaching experience. She has written a book titled "Computer Architecture and Organization", Eswar Press, The Science and Technology Book Publisher, Chennai. She serves as a reviewer for many reputed journals. She has published numerous papers in International Conferences and Journals. Her area of interest includes Parallel and Distributed Computing, Grid Computing, Cloud Computing, Big Data Analytics, Internet of Things, Computer Architecture and Operating Systems. She is a life member of Computer Society of India (CSI), Indian Society for Technical Education (ISTE), IARCS and IAENG. She is a Senior Member of IEEE and IEEE Women in Engineering (WIE). She is a Member of Association for Computing Machinery (ACM).

Udendhran Mudaliyar has completed M.Tech in computer science and engineering. He worked as a data scientist and presented research work in international conferences held in University of Cambridge and published many research papers. His research work focuses on deep learning and cryptography.

Rajganesh Nagarajan is working as an Assistant Professor [SL] in the Department of Information Technology, A.V.C. College of Engineering, Mayiladuthurai, Tamilnadu, India. He has completed his Ph.D in Information and Communication Engineering under Anna University (2018). His research interest includes SOA, Cloud Computing, Big Data Analytics, and Machine Learning.

E. A. Neeba, currently working as an Assistant Professor in the Department of Information Technology at Rajagiri School of Engineering & Technology, Kochi, Kerala, which is affiliated to the A.P.J Abdul Kalam Technological University, Kerala. She received her doctoral degree from Vel Tech Rangarajan Dr. Sagunthala R&D Institute of Science and Technology, Chennai, Tamil Nadu. She completed her Masters in Computer Science & Engineering from SRM Institute of Science and Technology, Chennai. Her research interests include Analysis of data, Data Mining and Big Data, knowledge representation, and ontology. Having a rich industrial experience of around 10 years prior to joining academia, and also she has publications in around 10 SCI/ SCIE/Scopus indexed international journals and a few national journals. She is entrusted with leadership positions such as the Accreditation coordinator for the college, and Head of the Quality Cell, besides organizing various national and international events.

J. Jesu Vedha Nayahi completed her B.E., Computer Science and Engineering in 2001 and M.E., Computer Science and Engineering in 2004 and secured University rank. She completed her Ph.D. in Information and Communication Engineering under Anna University in 2016. She is working as an Assistant Professor in the Department of Computer Science and Engineering, Anna University Regional Campus, Tirunelveli. She has more than 11 years of experience in teaching. She has published many papers in international journals and conferences. Her research interest includes data privacy and security, data mining, and automata theory. Her ORCID Id is 0000-0002-5445-0301.

G. Soniya Priyatharsini, is pursuing research in the Department of Computer Science and Engineering, Vel Tech Rangarajan Dr.Sagunthala R&D Institute of Science and Technology, Chennai, Tamil Nadu, India. She obtained her B.Tech degree in Information Technology from C.S.I Institute of Technology, Anna University, Chennai, Tamil Nadu, India, and M.E degree in Computer Science & Engineering from Manonmaniyam Sundaranar University, Thirunelveli, Tamil Nadu, India. She is a member of AWS. Her research interests include Cloud resourcing techniques, Allocation algorithms, and server sprawl techniques.

Nirmalan R. works as an Assistant Professor in the Department of Computer Science and Engineering since 2nd July 2014 to Till date at Sri Vidya College of Engineering & Technology, Virudhunagar. Pursuing Ph.D. (Information and Communication Engineering), Anna University, Chennai since January 2017 to till date. Completed M.E (Computer Science & Engineering) from Sri Vidya College of Engineering & Technology, Virudhunagar in the year 2014.Completed B.Tech (Computer Science & Engineering) from Kalasalingam University, Krishnankoil in the year 2012.My Research Area in Big Data - Hadoop & Heterogeneous Clusters.

Priyadarshini R, is pursuing research in the Department of Computer Science and Engineering, Vel Tech Rangarajan Dr.Sagunthala R&D Institute of Science and Technology, Chennai, Tamil Nadu, India. She is currently working as an Assistant professor in the Department of Computer Science and Engineering at Siddharth Institute of Engineering and Technology, Andhra Pradesh, India. She is having more than 10 years of teaching experience. She has guided more than 20 projects in the under graduate level. Her research interests include Cloud Computing, Fog Computing, and Internet of Things.

Jothimani S., Faculty of Computer Science and Engineering Department, Nehru Institute of Engineering and Technology, Anna University, Chennai. Received her Master Degree in Mainframe Technology in 2013 and Bachelor of Engineering in Computer Science and Engineering in 2009. She is the Member of Professional Societies IRED, IAENG and IAE. Research Interest Includes Internet Of Things, Networking and Grid and Cloud Computing. She published book chapters in Computer Programming and Problem Solving and Python Programming.

Vimal S. is currently working as an Assistant professor (Senior Grade) in Department of Information Technology, National Engineering College, Kovilpatti, Tamilnadu, India. He has around Twelve years of teaching experience, EMC certified Data science Associate and CCNA certified professional too. He is a member in various professional bodies and organized varied funded workshops and seminars. He has wide publications in the highly impact journals in the area of networking and security issues. His areas of interest include Game Modelling, Cognitive radio networks, network security and Big data Analytics.

Ramkumar Thirunavukarasu is working as an Associate Professor in School of Information Technology & Engineering, VIT University, Vellore, Tamilnadu, India. He has received his Ph.D degree in Computer Science, Anna University, Chennai, India. His area of specialization includes knowledge discovery from multiple databases and big data analytics with machine learning. He has contributed numerous top notching publications in various SCI journals. Presently he is guiding three research scholars in the area of cloud brokerage, secondary structure proteins, health informatics and e-learning.

Pradeep Kumar Tiwari is an Assistant Professor in Computer & Communication Engineering Department at Manipal University Jaipur, India. He has received his Ph.D degree in Faculty of Engineering from Manipal University Jaipur, India, M.Phil in Computer Science from Mahatma Gandhi Chitrakoot Gramodaya Vishwavidyalaya, M.P., India. The M.C.A degree in Computer Application from the Rajiv Gandhi Proudyogiki Vishwavidyalaya, M.P., India, in 2008. He has held Asst. Professor Positions at The Vindhya Institute of Technology, and the Aditya College of Technology, Satna, M.P, India. His research interests cover the Distributed Computing, Cloud Computing, Virtualization, Grid Computing, Cluster Computing and Network Security. He has published 6 articles in refereed international journal and 10 publications in international conferences (i.e. IEEE, Springer). He is the reviewer of 5 international conferences and at present. He is reviewer and editorial member of 4 journals.

Index

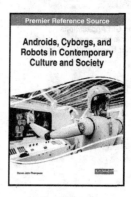

Ensure Quality Research is Introduced to the Academic Community

Become an IGI Global Reviewer for Authored Book Projects

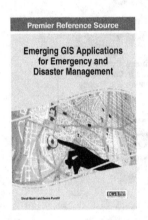

Premier Reference Source

Emerging GIS Applications for Emergency and Disaster Management

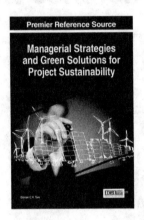

Premier Reference Source

Managerial Strategies and Green Solutions for Project Sustainability

Premier Reference Source

Comparative Approaches to Using R and Python for Statistical Data Analysis

Premier Reference Source

Solutions for High-Touch Communications in a High-Tech World

The overall success of an authored book project is dependent on quality and timely reviews.

In this competitive age of scholarly publishing, constructive and timely feedback significantly expedites the turnaround time of manuscripts from submission to acceptance, allowing the publication and discovery of forward-thinking research at a much more expeditious rate. Several IGI Global authored book projects are currently seeking highly qualified experts in the field to fill vacancies on their respective editorial review boards:

Applications may be sent to:
development@igi-global.com

Applicants must have a doctorate (or an equivalent degree) as well as publishing and reviewing experience. Reviewers are asked to write reviews in a timely, collegial, and constructive manner. All reviewers will begin their role on an ad-hoc basis for a period of one year, and upon successful completion of this term can be considered for full editorial review board status, with the potential for a subsequent promotion to Associate Editor.

If you have a colleague that may be interested in this opportunity, we encourage you to share this information with them.

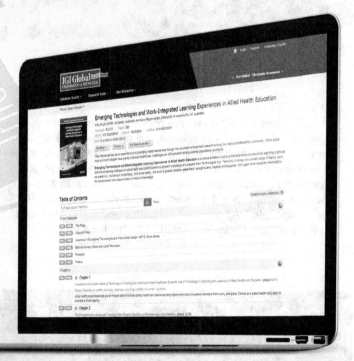

Are You Ready to Publish Your Research?

IGI Global offers book authorship and editorship opportunities across 11 subject areas, including business, healthcare, computer science, engineering, and more!

Benefits of Publishing with IGI Global:

- Free one-to-one editorial and promotional support.

- Expedited publishing timelines that can take your book from start to finish in less than one (1) year.

- Choose from a variety of formats including: Edited and Authored References, Handbooks of Research, Encyclopedias, and Research Insights.

- Utilize IGI Global's eEditorial Discovery® submission system in support of conducting the submission and blind-review process.

- IGI Global maintains a strict adherence to ethical practices due in part to our full membership to the Committee on Publication Ethics (COPE).

- Indexing potential in prestigious indices such as Scopus®, Web of Science™, PsycINFO®, and ERIC – Education Resources Information Center.

- Ability to connect your ORCID iD to your IGI Global publications.

- Earn royalties on your publication as well as receive complimentary copies and exclusive discounts.

Get Started Today by Contacting the Acquisitions Department at:

acquisition@igi-global.com